3-16-76

How can we confront the inevitability of death with fortitude and faith?

*A Treasury of Comfort* provides wisdom and inspiration in the face of this universal problem for people of all creeds and backgrounds.

This expanded and revised edition of *A Treasury of Comfort* is designed to further meet the needs of those who find themselves in "the valley of the shadow." It will prove a trustworthy companion, offering the consolation and guidance of psalmist and prophet, poet and philosopher, sage and scientist—and even of humble folk whose claim to a hearing is their own heroic encounter with grief.

The best time to develop a mature attitude toward death is *before* it strikes. It is important to develop an intelligent understanding of death and a triumphant faith by which to live in dignity.

This volume brings together a vast collection of sources which have been chosen for their power to inspire and to instruct all who seek meaning and strength in a difficult hour.

# A Treasury
## of
## Comfort

Consolation, hope, and guidance
for the bereaved

*edited by Dr. Sidney Greenberg*

Expanded and revised edition

**HARTMORE HOUSE**
New York & Bridgeport

The Editor wishes to make acknowledgment to the following for permission to quote the designated items (number before hyphen indicates page, after hyphen, position on page):

Abingdon-Cokesbury, 75-2, from *Sunset to Dawn* by Leslie R. Smith, copyright 1944 by Whitmore and Stone; 78-1, *The Glory of God* by Georgia Harkness, copyright 1943 by Whitmore and Stone; Abingdon-Cokesbury Press and The Pilgrim Press, 257-2; Rabbi Morris Adler, Detroit, Mich., 44-3, 133-2, 202-3; Brandt and Brandt, 35-2, from *Collected Poems* pub. by Oxford Univ. Press, copyright 1916 by Conrad Aiken; The American Ethical Union, 248-2; Association Press, 215-2; Atlantic Monthly, 14-5, 39-1; Reuben Avinoam, 82-1; Francis H. Bangs, 4-3; Behrman's Jewish Book House, 156-1, from *Anthology of Modern Jewish Poetry;* Rabbi Louis Beinstock, Temple Sholom, Chicago, Ill., 127-2, 133-1, 126-1; Ernest Benn, Ltd., 244-3; Bloch Pub. Co., 25-1, from *A Book of Jewish Thoughts;* Bobbs Merrill, 166-1, 247-2; Rabbi Ben Zion Bokser, Forest Hills, N. Y., 185-2; Margaret E. Bruner and Kaleidograph Press, 72-3, 72-4, 9-3, 23-1; Margaret E. Bruner and Indianapolis Sunday Star, 10-4, 14-3; Central Conference of American Rabbis, 100-3, 209-4, 238-3; Chicago Sun-Times, 152-2, from *God Called Him* by James J. Metcalfe; Thomas Curtis Clark, 261-4, 271-2; Rabbi Beryl D. Cohon, Brookline, Mass., 13-2, 227-3, 229-1; Bob Considine, 232-1; Thomas Y. Crowell Co., 192-1; Dept. for the Commemoration of the Fallen, Ministry of Defense, Israel, 30-3, 170-2, 230-1; Detroit News, 62-1, from Verses I Like by Winnie Lynch Rockett; Doubleday & Co., 42-4, from *We Bereaved* by Helen Keller, 80-2, 125-2, 161-1, 162-1, 207-1, 255-1, from *When Sorrow Comes* by Grace Perkins Oursler and April Armstrong, 130-2, 136-1, 142-1, 201-2, from *Modern Parables* by Fulton Oursler; E. P. Dutton & Co., 113-1, from *The Wall of Weeping* by Edmund Fleg, 9-1, 172-2, from *The Light of the World* by Phillips Brooks, 23-3, from *Harp of My Heart* by Hugh Robert Orr, 29-2, from *Death and General Putnam* by Arthur Guiterman, 112-1, 175-4, from *The Best-Loved Poems of the American People* by Hazel Felleman, 98-1, from *An Airman's Letter to His Mother;* Evangelical Pub., 101-3; Farrar, Strauss & Young, 145-1 from *Victory in My Hands* by Harold Russell; Forward Movement Pub., 63-2, 107-2; Free Thought Press Assoc., 157-1; Funk & Wagnalls Co., 172-1, from *Inspiration and Ideals* by Grenville Kleiser; Rabbi R. B. Gittlesohn, Temple Israel, Boston, Mass., 233-1; Harcourt, Brace & Co., 250-2, from *Basic Judaism* by Milton Steinberg, copyright 1950; Harper & Bros., 208-2, from *The Secret of Victorious Living* by H. E. Fosdick, 71-3, 150-1, 181-1, from *Death Be Not Proud* by John Gunther, 54-1, 62-3, 189-1, 249-2, from *Masterpieces of Religious Verse* by J. D. Morrison, 105-4, from *The Funeral Encyclopedia* by Charles L. Wallis, 160-1; Sarah Henderson Hay, 260-3; Houghton, Mifflin & Co., 254-3; Jewish Agency for Palestine, 194-3; The Jewish Publication Society, 47-5, from *The Spirit Returneth* by Selma Stern, 115-2, from *Mesillat Yesharim* by Moses Luzatto, 94-5, from *Kiddush Ha-Shem* by Sholem

Asch; Rabbi Leo Jung, The Jewish Center, N. Y. C., 226-2; Alfred A. Knopf, 5-2, 17-1, 72-1, 122-1, from *The Green Leaf* by Robert Nathan, copyright 1950 by Robert Nathan; Dr. Francis Litz, 251-2; Longmans, Green, 92-3, from *Survival and Immortality* by Dean Inge; Macfadden Publications, 140-2, 163-1; The Macmillan Co., 11-2, from *You Can Master Life* by James Gordon Gilkey, 128-4, 137-1, 199-1, 205-1, 210-2, 257-1, 265-1, from *In Time of Sorrow* by Charles Lewis Slattery, 242-2, from *Live for Tomorrow* by Ralph W. Sockman, 245-3, from *Assurances of Immortality* by H. E. Fosdick, 206-3, from *If They Don't Come Back* by Henry Adye Pritchard; Rabbi Julius Mark, Temple Emmanuel, N. Y. C., 104-1; Virgil Markham, 197-1, 265-3; M. C. A. Management, Ltd., 26-2, 44-1, 46-2, 64-4, 105-3, 129-2, 154-4, 177-2, from Coronet, copyright March, 1953 by Esquire, Inc.; McCalls and Kate Holliday, 56-2, 57-2, from *How Does It Feel to Die;* Message of Israel, 16-2, 58-3, 59-2, 170-1, 181-4, 225-1; Julian Messner, Inc., 176-2, from *The Complete Life* by John Erskine; N. Y. Sun, Inc., 271-1; Rabbi Louis I. Newman, 143-3, 229-2, from *Sermons and Addresses*, Bloch; W. W. Norton & Co., 176-4, from *A Free Man's Worship* by Bertrand Russell; Pennsylvania Co., 34-1; Daniel A. Poling, 222-1; G. P. Putnam & Sons, 114-1, from *The Adventure of Death* by Robert W. MacKenna; The Presbyterian Tribune, 171-1; Proprietors of Punch, 227-1; Rabbinical Assembly of America for Prayer, 231-2; Howard Whitman, The Christian Advocate and Reader's Digest, 145-2; Reilly & Lee, 96-3; Religion and Health, 102-4; Fleming H. Revell, 179-4, from *Letters to Bill on Faith and Prayer* by John Gardner; Round Table Press, 8-3, from *Beatitudes for the Family* by Leland Foster Wood; Rabbi Jacob Philip Rudin, Great Neck, N. Y., 28-3, 183-2; Margaret E. Sangster, 21-3, 109-3, 110-1; Leo W. Schwartz, 66-4, from *Golden Treasury of Jewish Literature*, pub. by Farrar & Rhinehart; Sci-Art Publishers, 106-3, from *The Golden Peacock* by Joseph Leftwich; Charles Scribner's Sons, 225-2, from *A Sheaf* by John Galsworthy; Simon and Schuster, 3-4, 54-3, 86-2, 123-1, 141-1, 184-3, 224-2, 260-1, from *Peace of Mind* by Joshua Loth Liebman, copyright 1946; Society of Authors and Mrs. Cicely Binyon, 212-4, from *Collected Poems of Lawrence Binyon*, pub. by Macmillan; St. Martin's Press, 167-1, from *Aphorisms and Reflections* by Thomas H. Huxley; Edith Steinberg, 272-1, from *A Believing Jew* by Milton Steinberg; This Week and Joseph Auslander, 29-1, copyright United Newspapers Magazine Corp.; Dorothy Thompson, 61-2, from N. Y. Herald Tribune; Viking Press, 93-2, 144-1, from *Jeremiah* by Stefan Zweig; Milton Waldman, 26-3, from *Ardours and Endurance* by Robert Nichols; Rabbi Joseph I. Weiss, Neponsit, L. I., 81-3, 93-3, 226-1; Eliezer Whartman, 30-2, 35-1, 126-3, 186-2; William Allen White, Jr. & Emporia Gazette, 88-2, from *Condolence Letters;* Yale Univ. Press, 263-2, from *Freedom of Man* by Arthur H. Compton; Your Life, 138-1, from *Lord Help Me to Forget* by Ross L. Holman.

LIBRARY OF CONGRESS CATALOGING IN PUBLICATION DATA

Greenberg, Sidney, 1917–      ed.
    A treasury of comfort.

    1. Consolation—Collected works.
I. Title.
BV4900.G68  1975      242'.4      74–32508
ISBN 0–87677–022–7

To

Hilda

and our three daughters

Shira Beth, Reena Keren

and Adena Joy


## IN APPRECIATION

The publication of this revised and expanded edition affords an opportunity to express appreciation to those publishers, authors and individuals whose generosity made this book possible, and who placed me deeply in their debt. I am intensely grateful to my dear wife and helpmate upon whose counsel and sympathetic understanding I depended heavily and often. Her gracious assumption of the added duties, domestic and communal, occasioned by my preoccupation with this work in the midst of an already crowded rabbinate, made it possible for me to devote the necessary energies to the completion of this work.

Dr. Simon Greenberg, Vice Chancellor of the Jewish Theological Seminary of America, and the late Rabbi Morris Adler of Detroit, Michigan, were exceedingly kind to read the manuscript of the original edition and made many valuable suggestions.

My very good friend, Mr. Marty Josephs, cannot be thanked too warmly. It was his persistent urging which encouraged me to undertake the work and kept me from abandoning it in moments when my own enthusiasm waned. His enormous experience in the field of publishing was unselfishly placed at my disposal.

Compiling a book of this size involves a staggering amount of typing and mechanical work. Most of the work in this instance was done voluntarily by Mrs. Albert Wanicur, whose kindness was matched only by her competence. This expression of warmest appreciation is meager recompense for countless hours of cheerful labor.

Mrs. Herman Leff, the uncommonly efficient secretary of our congregation, was helpful in many ways—big and small. Her availability at all times for discussion and suggestions lightened my task considerably. My gratitude is also extended to Mrs. William Eisenberg who was ever willing to contribute her effort to the book. Mr. Zev Shanken provided helpful assistance in the final stages of the revised edition.

Lastly, I pay affectionate tribute to the good men and women of Temple Sinai whose grief spurred me on in this venture in the fervent hope that I could create some literary medium which would soften the shock of bereavement and offer the courage and the faith to carry on.

# CONTENTS

# INTRODUCTION

THE twentieth century enjoys many significant claims to distinction. Among these, none is more noteworthy than the impressive gains scored in the direction of lengthening the human life-span. Spectacular scientific discoveries in preventive as well as curative medicine, improved living conditions, the shortening of the working day and week—these are some of the more important factors which have added decades to the life expectancy of our generation. Optimistic forecasts for the future anticipate an even longer life-span for our children.

Notwithstanding these dramatic forward strides, death will not be denied. It will only be deferred. Each of us has an appointment with sorrow, "a rendezvous with death." None can hope for exemption from death's inexorable laws nor from the poignant sadness of parting from loved ones.

Despite its inevitability, the death of a dear one is often a deeply disturbing emotional experience. We are rarely, if ever, quite prepared for it. We read daily of the death of strangers, from time to time we hear of the passing of acquaintances. Our passion for life, however, is so strong that we cannot truly assimilate the thought that those we love are also heir to the common fate which awaits all with severe impartiality.

This is especially true when death comes to a child or to a young parent. The impact of such tragedy always finds us in a state of total emotional unpreparedness. The shock is compounded by its maddening untimeliness, by the bitter realization that there were so many unlived years of love and laughter, adventure and hope. We who live during these turbulent days of international strife must reckon seriously with the grievous prospect of countless young lives prematurely cut down by "man's inhumanity to man."

To be sure, sorrow does not strike all with equal intensity. The impact will vary according to the circumstances surrounding the death, the age of the departed, the intimacy of the relationship that prevailed and the inner resources of the survivor.

As a rabbi who is called upon quite regularly to minister to people in their bereavement, I have long felt the need for a volume which can bring strength and solace to the mourners. Well-meaning friends help by their very presence during the initial days of mourning but beyond that they usually are able to contribute little. Most believe that avoiding the subject of the grief is the healthiest procedure. Actually, the very reverse is true. Where sorrow is concerned, not repression but expression is the wholesome discipline. The emotional catharsis afforded by an opportunity to speak of the departed should be welcomed not shunned, yet one rarely hears any real therapeutic conversation in a home touched by sorrow. After the first few days immediately following the death, the flow of friends to the mourner's home usually subsides and soon stops altogether. The members of the family who were brought together by sorrow return to their respective homes. Now the full impact of the loneliness and the loss begins to be felt. How genuine is the need for help at this time! How numerous are the parasitic weeds that may now begin to flourish in the soil of sorrow!

This volume is designed primarily to meet the needs of those who find themselves in the valley of the shadow. It should prove a trustworthy companion which offers the consolation and guidance of psalmist and prophet, poet and philosopher, sage and scientist, and even the humble folk whose only claim to a hearing is their own heroic encounter with grief. It brings together the distilled wisdom of the Jewish heritage as it speaks through its texts and representatives. Because the influence of Judaism has been diffused throughout western culture and thought, its basic attitudes and teachings have found expression in the lives of writings of non-Jews as well. The editor has therefore not hesitated to include selections of non-Jewish authors where he felt that the views were in harmony with Jewish insight and doctrine. All selections have been chosen with a view to their power to inspire and instruct. It is the sincere hope of the editor that this volume may serve as a tunnel dug through the mountain of grief which opens into the green fields of revived hope and renewed faith in life's creative possibilities.

While the book is aimed especially at the mourner, its value is not restricted to the hour of bereavement. Realistically speaking, we are all potential mourners. The time to develop a mature philosophy toward death is before, not after, it strikes, just as one should learn to swim before one gets shipwrecked, not after. The analogy suffers in only one respect. Most of us will never be shipwrecked but the need for a sustaining outlook upon death and a reasonable knowledge of how to handle our grief is one which we shall all almost certainly experience. Moreover, we are frequently involved in the sorrows of others, and our own spiritual resources and insights can be of distinct service. It is therefore of crucial significance that we develop a mature understanding of death, a courageous acceptance of life, a triumphant faith by which to live with dignity and die without fear. If this book contributes however slightly to the achievement of such an outlook, the labors that went into its creation will have been very amply rewarded.

SIDNEY GREENBERG

Temple Sinai                                        August, 1954; Elul 5714
Philadelphia, Pa.

## PREFACE TO THE EXPANDED EDITION

TWENTY years have passed since the publication of the first edition of *A Treasury of Comfort*. Much has changed in these years—but not the reality which this book seeks to confront.

The warm reception accorded to the eight printings of *A Treasury of Comfort* during the past two decades encouraged the editor to prepare this expanded edition. Several new passages have been introduced at key points in the original text and a new chapter now appears at the conclusion of the book.

The appearance of this new edition provides an opportunity to reiterate the hope that it will provide strength, wisdom, and insight to all who read these pages.

SIDNEY GREENBERG
February, 1975

Pain is hard to bear. . . .
But with patience, day by day
Even this shall pass away.

—Theodore Tilton

# TIME—THE GENTLE HEALER

*In the hour of bereavement we feel most acutely what Swift called "the sting of perishable things." At the moment of deep hurt it appears indeed that there is no balm for our gaping wounds. We tend to despair of ever regaining our emotional equilibrium.*

*At such a time we are scarcely amenable to solace. Words of comfort ring hollow in the dark night of sorrow. That is why an ancient sage counseled wisely: "Do not comfort thy friend when his deceased is still lying before him." Premature comfort can often be more harmful than no comfort because it seems to mock the hurt, to make light of our torment.*

*It is never too soon, however, to accept the reassuring thought that pain, no less than pleasure, is transient. A simple farmer was asked by a visitor from the city during a severe rainstorm whether he thought it would stop raining. He answered drily: "It usually does."*

*Nature rushes benevolently to our assistance when we have been hurt, whether in body or in spirit. If we do not despair, the healing process does restore us as it has healed other mourners from the beginning of time. To be sure, the scar may very well continue to throb sensitively when we experience emotional bad weather. The sense of loss may always remain with us; but the sharp pain subsides and we discover the way to a healthy readjustment to our new circumstances. The Psalmist wisely spoke of walking "through the valley of the shadow." No road of life can detour around the valley. By the same token, however, the valley is open on both sides. Having entered into it, we need not make of it our permanent dwelling place. After we have lingered there for a while, we can walk through it and out. With the Psalmist we can then affirm*

1

*gratefully out of the depths of our own experience: "Though weeping tarries in the night, joy comes in the morning."*

---

## ISAIAH

Thy sun shall no more go down,
Neither shall thy moon withdraw itself;
For the Lord shall be thine everlasting light,
And the days of thy mourning shall be ended.

## ANGEL OF PATIENCE

*John Greenleaf Whittier*

To weary hearts, to mourning homes,
God's meekest Angel gently comes:
No power has he to banish pain,
Or give us back our lost again;
And yet in tenderest love, our dear
And Heavenly Father sends him here.

There's quiet in that Angel's glance,
There's rest in his still countenance!
He mocks no grief with idle cheer,
Nor wounds with words the mourner's ear,
But ills and woes he may not cure
He kindly trains us to endure.

Angel of Patience! sent to calm
Our feverish brows with cooling palm;
To lay the storms of hope and fear,
And reconcile life's smile and tear;
The throbs of wounded pride to still,
And make our own our Father's will!

O thou who mournest on thy way,
With longings for the close of day;
He walks with thee, that Angel kind,

And gently whispers, "Be resigned;
Bear up, bear on, the end shall tell
The dear Lord ordereth all things well!"


## IN THE NIGHT GOD SPEAKS

*Moses Ibn Ezra (Translated by Emma Lazarus)*

He speaks: "My son, yea, I will send thee aid,
Bend thou thy steps to me, be not afraid.
No nearer friend than I am, hast thou made,
Possess thy soul in patience one more night."


## A PEAR TREE

*Rachel (Translated from the Hebrew by the editor)*

This is the conspiracy of Spring. . . .
A man awakens from sleep
and sees a pear tree flowering before his window.
Suddenly, the mountain of sorrow that lay upon
his heart
is shattered and is gone.

You understand: he could not persist
in grieving for his one blossom withered by
angry autumn's blast—
Since smiling Spring was bringing for his solace
a giant garland of flowers
To his very window.


*William Makepeace Thackeray*
To endure is greater than to dare.


## WE SHOULD LEARN NOT TO GROW IMPATIENT

*Joshua Loth Liebman*

We should learn not to grow impatient with the slow healing
process of time. We should discipline ourselves to recognize that

there are many steps to be taken along the highway leading from sorrow to renewed serenity and that it is folly to attempt prematurely to telescope and compress these successive stages of recuperation into a miraculous cure. We should not demand of ourselves more than nature herself will permit. We should anticipate these stages in our emotional convalescence: unbearable pain, poignant grief, empty days, resistance to consolation, disinterestedness in life, gradually giving way under the healing sunlight of love, friendship, social challenge, to the new weaving of a pattern of action and the acceptance of the irresistible challenge of life.

## PSALMS

Resign thyself unto the Lord, and wait patiently for Him. . . .

## PATIENCE
### *Emma Lazarus*

The passion of despair is quelled at last;
The cruel sense of undeserved wrong,
The wild self-pity, these are also past;
She knows not what may come, but she is strong;
She feels she hath not aught to lose nor gain,
Her patience is the essence of all pain. . . .

There is a deeper pathos in the mild
And settled sorrow of the quiet eyes.
Than in the tumults of the anguish wild,
That made her curse all things beneath the skies;
No question, no reproaches, no complaint,
Hers is the holy calm of some meek saint.

## I NEVER KNEW A NIGHT SO BLACK
### *John Kendrick Bangs*

I never knew a night so black
Light failed to follow on its track.
I never knew a storm so gray
It failed to have its clearing day.

I never knew such bleak despair
That there was not a rift, somewhere.
I never knew an hour so drear
Love could not fill it full of cheer!


## ACCEPT THE JUDGMENT
*Rachel (Translated from the Hebrew by the editor)*

Accept the judgment, O humbled heart,
Accept the judgment this time, too,
Without struggle, without wrath.

High in the north, snow-covered fields
Conceal the grain ripening
Secretly, silently.

O humbled heart, bear your wintry fate
And be like those seeds
That wait for summer.


## FROM "AUTUMN SONNETS #4"
*Robert Nathan*

It would be wiser, since we live in fear,
To use our sorrows to correct our ways.
If winter be the color of our days,
Then learn of winter to be still and clear.
The greener spring, the new and happy year
Is not for us but for the birds to praise;
It is the snow that over autumn lays
Its quiet hand that is our teacher here.
For see, it has its lesson for the soul:
Look how the tree with piety keeps fast
The bud and blossom hidden in the bole.
So bear the winter with its frosty blast,
And seek, beneath the season of our grief,
The spring unending and the waiting leaf.

## SERVIUS SUPLICIUS

There is no grief which time does not lessen.

### *Elizabeth Barrett Browning*

Thank God, bless God, all ye who suffer not
More grief than ye can weep for; . . . those tears will run
Soon in long rivers down the lifted face,
And leave the vision clear for stars and sun.

## PSALMS

Who healeth the broken in heart,
And bindeth up their wounds.

### *Jeremiah*

I will change their grief to gladness
I will console and cheer them after their sorrow.

## FROM "TRANSIENCE"

### *Sarojini Naidu*

Nay, do not grieve tho' life be full of sadness,
Dawn will not veil her splendor for your grief,
Nor spring deny their bright, appointed beauty
To lotus blossom and ashoka leaf.

Nay, do not pine, tho' life be dark with trouble,
Time will not pause or tarry on his way;
Today that seems so long, so strange, so bitter,
Will soon be some forgotten yesterday.

Nay, do not weep; new hopes, new dreams, new faces,
The unspent joy of all the unborn years,
Will prove your heart a traitor to its sorrow,
And make your eyes unfaithful to their tears.

*Talmud*

God says to man: "With thy very wounds I will heal thee."

## PLINY THE YOUNGER

As a fresh wound shrinks from the hand of the surgeon, then gradually submits to and even calls for it; so a mind under the first impression of a misfortune shuns and rejects all comfort, but at length, if touched with tenderness, calmly and willingly resigns itself.

## *John Henry Newman*

There are wounds of the spirit which never close, and are intended in God's mercy to bring us nearer to Him, and to prevent us leaving Him, by their very perpetuity. Such wounds, then, may almost be taken as a pledge, or at least as a ground for the humble trust, that God will give us the great gift of perseverance to the end. . . . This is how I comfort myself in my own great bereavements.

## ENDURANCE
### *Elizabeth Akers Allen*

How much the heart may bear and yet not break!
How much the flesh may suffer and not die!
I question much if any pain or ache
Of soul or body brings our end more nigh:
Death chooses his own time; till that is sworn,
All evil may be borne.
    Behold, we live through all things—famine, thirst,
Bereavement, pain, all grief and misery,
All woe and sorrow; life inflicts its worst,
On soul and body—but we cannot die,
Though we be sick, and tired, and worn—
Lo, all things can be borne!

*Job*

It is good that a man should quietly wait, till my relief should come.

*Forbes Robinson*

God knows how much you can bear, and He will not, if you will only persevere, allow you to be utterly confounded.

## SORROW SHALL PASS

*Leland Foster Wood*

Times of sorrow come in all families, yet there is always hope of better things. After cold and barrenness come seasons of life and fruitfulness.

> An old, old voice
> Deeper than sorrow and pain
> Speaks in the inner ear
> Like the rhythmic beat of rain.
>
> As the rain wets the trees
> And feeds the roots of the grass
> And refreshes the waiting world,
> So also sorrow shall pass;
>
> Shall pass like a drifting cloud
> That moves across the sky;
> For every cloud moves on,
> And the sun comes out by and by.
>
> And as fresh flowers come
> Where the earth was bare and cold
> So the seeds of joy shall grow
> Though long they lie in the mold.

## GRIEF MUST SEE THE END
### *Phillips Brooks*

I beg you, if God sends you grief, to take it largely by letting it first of all show you how short life is, and then prophesy eternity. Such is the grief of which the poet sings so nobly:

> Grief should be
> Like joy, majestic, equable, sedate;
> Confirming, cleansing, raising, making free,
> Strong to consume small troubles, to command
> Great thoughts, grave thoughts, thoughts lasting
> to the end.

But grief, to be all that, must see the end; must bring and forever keep with its pain such a sense of the shortness of life that the pain shall seem but a temporary accident, and all that is to stay forever after the pain has ceased, the exaltation, the unselfishness, the mystery, the nearness of God, shall seem to be the substance of the sorrow.

### *Job*

Behold, happy is the man whom God correcteth; therefore despise not thou the chastening of the Almighty. For He maketh sore and bindeth up; He woundeth, and His hands make whole.

## TIME'S HEALING SNOWS
### *Margaret E. Bruner*

> I would not dwell too long upon my grief,
> But let it lie much like the fallen leaf;
> Then hallowed by time's many healing snows,
> Its residue may blossom in a rose.

## ISAIAH

And in that day thou shalt say: I will give thanks unto Thee, O Lord;

For though Thou wast angry with me
Thine anger is turned away and Thou comfortedst
    me.
Behold, God is my salvation;
I will trust and not be afraid
For God the Lord is my strength and song
And He has become my salvation.

*Cicero*

No grief is so acute but time ameliorates it.

## PSALMS

They that sow in tears
Shall reap in joy.

*Ralph Waldo Emerson*

Patience and fortitude conquer all things.

## FOR ONE LATELY BEREFT
*Margaret E. Bruner*

Though now you are bereft and ways seem black,
    With emptiness and gloom on every hand;
Some day Time's healing touch will lead you back,
    And gradually your heart will understand
That what you bore must come to one and all,
    And Peace, the clean white flower born of pain,
Will slowly, surely, rise from sorrow's pall,
    And happiness will come to you again.

## ISAIAH

For a small moment have I forsaken thee;
But with great compassion will I gather thee.

In a little wrath I hid My face from thee for a moment;
But with everlasting kindness will I have compassion on thee,
Saith the Lord thy Redeemer.


## LAMENTATIONS

For the Lord will not cast off forever: but though He cause grief, yet will He have compassion according to the multitude of His mercies. For He doth not afflict willingly nor grieve the children of men.


## THE HEALING POWER OF NATURE

### *James Gordon Gilkey*

Some years ago one of the giant Sequoia trees in California was cut down, and scientists were given the opportunity to make a detailed examination of it. They counted the rings in the wood, determined the age and the history of the tree, and then published this interesting statement: "This Sequoia was a seedling in 271 B.C. Five hundred and sixteen years later, it was severely damaged by a forest fire. But Nature immediately set to work to repair the damage, and began to fold successive layers of living tissue over the gigantic scar left by the flames. This effort continued for more than a century, and by the year 350, the wounds had been completely healed. In later centuries two other fires damaged the tree badly. But when the tree was finally cut down, the scar left by the first of these fires had been completely obliterated, and the scar left by the second was in process of being covered. That last scar was a gigantic wound eighteen feet wide and thirty feet high, but had Nature been given a chance even that wound would have been entirely healed."

You and I are not living in a world which injures us, and then does nothing to aid us. Ours is a world which brings pain and hardship, suffering and disaster, but then sets in motion ingenious agencies which quietly but steadily repair the damage. "The healing power of Nature"—how familiar and how beneficent it is! What help it brings, to men as well as to trees!

## AND THOU SHALT CHOOSE LIFE

*An Associated Press story carrying the date-line June 19, 1954, conveyed a reassuring lesson to those who have been pulled to the abyss of despair by the heavy hand of grief.*

*The incident unfolded when a Mr. Donald Robertson in Herkimer, N.Y., received an unsigned letter of appreciation from a woman whom he had met briefly nine years previous aboard an eastbound train from California. He was returning from the Pacific theatre where he had flown 69 missions in his B-25. She was a young widow of a serviceman killed in action. When they met in the vestibule of the car he did not even remotely suspect that he had interrupted her attempt to commit suicide by jumping off the speeding train. Her letter made all that quite plain now.*

February 1, 1945, that was the date nine years ago. The Battle of the Bulge had ended and the telegrams were being delivered. Mine came in the morning. "The War Department regrets to inform you that your husband—." Those words will be engraved in my mind forever.

February 1, 1945, that night I was on the train speeding on a journey that seemed endless. You were on the train, too, speeding to the wife you hadn't seen since the war began. I doubt if you remember me now. The girl in the black dress, sad and lonely, sitting across the aisle.

If you hadn't come into the vestibule when you did, I'd have opened the door and jumped out. Did I thank you for that, and for all the kind things you did for me . . . ?

Two years later I married again. I have a fine husband, two wonderful children and a lovely home. To think that I am so happy now and owe it all to a stranger on the train who helped me through my darkest hours. . . .

Tonight I think I'll look at the moon—I'll say, "Hi, Mr. Robertson. Thanks for saving my life." I'm truly grateful.

The letter was signed only, "Sincerely . . ."

*Our anonymous widow was on the verge of a desperate irrevocable act because she had seen no possibility of ever finding happiness or even meaning in life. But after the grim, dark hours had passed, the dawn of revived hope broke, and with it came new opportunities for creative, zestful living. Such is the reward of those who hold on tenaciously and do not surrender, those who*

*respond heroically to the challenging Biblical summons: "And thou
shalt choose life."*

## GOD'S PLEDGE TO YOU

### *Anonymous*

Not cloudless days;
Not rose-strewn ways;
Not care-free years,
Devoid of sorrow's tears—
But—strength to bear
Your load of human care,
And grace to live aright
And keep your raiment white,
And love to see you through;
That is God's pledge to you.

## THE HIDDEN AND THE REVEALED

### *Beryl D. Cohon*

Some of us . . . do not give nature a chance to rebuild its landscape
within our own minds and hearts. . . .

We know that God in His wisdom has given us the power to
regain vision after whatever blow strikes us. The power to regain
vision and regain balance, to muster our energies anew, is a capacity
that goes with the healthy personality.

In front of our Temple is a bush. I hope you noticed it this
morning as you passed by it. It is straightening itself out; it is
showing signs of green. Soon it will be a glorious bush—thriving,
bursting with color. But last January it was crushed to earth.
I feared it would never come up again. Snow drifts burdened it
to the ground. Snow slides from the roof of the Temple buried it
all the more. On top of that, the snow plow heaped added burdens
of snow on it. It was completely buried. But now, a glorious miracle!

Nature rebuilds its landscape. It will rebuild the landscapes of
our lives if we give it a chance. . . .

*Hosea*

For He hath torn, and He will heal us,
He hath smitten, and He will bind us up.

*Job*

Thou shalt forget thy misery, and remember it as waters that pass
away.

## TIME'S HAND IS KIND

*Margaret E. Bruner*

For those who place their blooms on new-made graves
And feel that life holds nought but emptiness,
Know that time's hand in kindness ever saves
The heart from too much sorrow and distress.
Yet all deep wounds heal slowly, it would seem,
But gradually the yearning pain will cease . . .
Thus will your grief become a hallowed dream
And, in its stead, will come a strange new peace.

## TIME GILDS WITH GOLD

*Ella Wheeler Wilcox*

*From "This, Too, Shall Pass Away"*

Has some misfortune fallen to your lot?
This, too, will pass away; absorb the thought,
And wait—your waiting will not be in vain,
Time gilds with gold the iron links of pain.
The dark today leads into light tomorrow;
There is no endless joy, no endless sorrow.

## ANTIDOTES FOR ADVERSITY

*M. Beatrice Blankenship*

A few years ago I was facing one of the most difficult complications
of a never-too-simple existence. Every path I tried seemed to be un-

mistakably marked "No Exit." Driving home from the city late one afternoon with my small children, I was wearily pondering my problems once more, going over and over what could be done. Suicide had more than once occurred to me, but I could not reconcile it with my responsibility toward the children. Suddenly it flashed in my mind that I could take them, too, thereby saving them the weariness and futility of which life seemed to be composed.

Just ahead of us lay a curve in the road where four people had recently been killed. I only needed to step a little harder on the accelerator and keep my hand steady on the wheel, and before any of us had time to be afraid, we should all have escaped from living. There was a black flash before my eyes, I stepped on the brake instead of the accelerator, and came around the curve at my usual cautious speed. . . .

In less than three months the complications had resolved themselves and were succeeded by two of the happiest years of my life. Though things have a way of turning difficult every once in a while, and though I have not as much strength to encounter them as I used to have, I have not again considered suicide as a way out. . . .

I think I was held back, first, by consideration for my family, coupled with a doubt whether, no matter what my own feelings about life, I had the right to deprive the children of theirs although I had given it to them. As a secondary but still powerful consideration, there was even then reluctance to acknowledge once and for all that I was defeated. And while I was confusedly thinking these things, we rounded the curve and came out facing the somber beauty of the afterglow over a purple winter sea.

I have always especially loved the time when the sky burns dark orange on the horizon, the ocean shades from ice-green to darkest purple and the little waves near the shore are for the moment as rigid as if carved out of lapis lazuli, but the utter beauty and peace of that evening sea brought tears to my eyes. I realized then, and at intervals I have ever since, that no matter what life does to you, there is still a refuge from which you cannot be torn. The "sweet things" are still free, and there is no one of us, no matter how lonely and poor, who cannot have his share by just looking around him. . . .

If there is one merciful thing about life, it is that things do change. If joy goes and sorrow comes, why, sorrow goes and peace comes, if we will let it—and peace is a sweeter thing than joy, and more lasting. If we will only give ourselves time, and if we will live each hour, each moment, as it comes,—not trying to face in one instant's comprehension the entire future stripped of all we may have cherished, or of everything that to us makes life worth living, and before we know it months have rolled by, and the particular burden which made our life intolerable is softened on the horizon of memory, or else has changed and modified so that, even if it still exists, we can almost forget it.

### Bret Harte

Never a tear bedims the eye
That time and patience will not dry.

## HOLD ON! HOLD FAST!
### David Polish

A survivor of a concentration camp tells of one ghastly night when he thought that no one in the camp could endure any longer. After a day of satanic torture, all the inmates were routed out in the dead of night and compelled to go through fiendishly conceived drills and exercises. In the numbing cold, men fell and were shot or beaten. Toward dawn, they were all lined up, the stronger ones holding up the dying and the maimed. There they stood at rigid and grotesque attention, freezing and bleeding. From somewhere, no one knows where, a single word ran like an electric current down the lines: *"Aushalten—hold on, hold fast!"* They clung to each other, but unseen hands supported them. That hour of endurance was fraught with cosmic meaning. And for us, too, a call goes out to stand and to endure, for God and for the ages.

"Weeping may tarry for the night, but joy will surely come in the morning."

## FROM "THE HARDEST TIME OF ALL"
### Sarah Doudney

There are days of silent sorrow
In the seasons of our life,
There are wild, despairing moments,
There are hours of mental strife;

There are times of stony anguish,
  When the tears refuse to fall;
But the waiting time, my brothers,
  Is the hardest time of all.

But at last we learn the lesson
  That God knoweth what is best;
For with wisdom cometh patience,
  And with patience cometh rest.
Yea, a golden thread a-shining
  Through the tangled woof of fate;
And our hearts shall thank Him meekly,
  That He taught us how to wait.

## LAST YEAR'S GRIEF

*Robert Nathan*

Here's last year's grief
In the green leaf
And all he knows is
That Time will take
All heartbreak,
And turn it to roses.

*Shakespeare*

How poor are they who have not patience!
What wound did ever heal, but by degrees?

*Leigh Hunt*

It is a part of the benignity of Nature that pain does not survive like pleasure, at any time, much less where the cause of it is an innocent one. The smile will remain reflected by memory, as the moon reflects the light upon us when the sun has gone into heaven. . . .

## LEARN TO WAIT

*Author unknown*

Learn to wait—life's hardest lesson
Conned, perchance, through blinding tears;
While the heart throbs sadly echo
To the tread of passing years.
Learn to wait—hope's slow fruition;
Faint not, though the way seems long;
There is joy in each condition;
Hearts through suffering may grow strong.
Thus a soul untouched by sorrow
Aims not at a higher state;
Joy seeks not a brighter morrow;
Only sad hearts learn to wait.

## FOUR THINGS

*Author unknown*

These things are beautiful beyond belief:
The pleasant weakness that comes after pain,
The radiant greenness that comes after rain,
The deepened faith that follows after grief,
And the awakening to love again.

## SORROW—A SOLEMN INITIATION

*George Eliot*

For the first sharp pangs there is no comfort; whatever goodness
may surround us, darkness and silence still hang about our pain.
But slowly, the clinging companionship with the dead is linked with
our living affections and duties, and we begin to feel our sorrow as
a solemn initiation, preparing us for that sense of loving, pitying
fellowship with the fullest human lot, which I must think, no one
who has tasted it will deny to be the chief blessedness of our life.

To live in hearts we leave behind
Is not to die.

—Thomas Campbell

# MEMORY—LIFE'S AFTERGLOW

*In Maeterlinck's beautiful play* The Blue Bird, *the children Tyltyl and Mytil are about to set out in search of the fabled blue bird of happiness. The Fairy tells them that on their journey they will come to the land of memory where upon turning the magic diamond in Tyltyl's hat they will see all their departed loved ones—their grandparents, brothers and sisters. "But how can we see them when they are dead?" asks Tyltyl in amazement. To which the Fairy answers gently: "How can they be dead, when they live in your memory?"*

*This power of memory to confer immortality upon those we love has been gratefully acknowledged by mourners of all times. Death cannot rob us of our past. The days and years we shared, the common adventures and hopes, the "little nameless, unremembered acts of kindness and of love"—all these are part of the ineradicable human record. Death has no dominion where memory rules. This thought received eloquent affirmation by Whittier who prayerfully asked: "Grant but memory to us and we can lose nothing by death." Centuries before him a Talmudic sage declared: "The righteous are considered alive even in death."*

*Strangely, these very memories which ultimately help us to cheat death are likely to be quite painful while the anguish of parting is still fresh.*

*A husband of my acquaintance whose wife died after a brief illness refused to return from the funeral to the home they had shared. For some time he also sought to avoid meeting any persons they had known or visiting any places which would tend to evoke reminiscences of the past. He was thus expressing in a rather extreme way a feeling many mourners experience. "The leaves of memory" do seem "to make a mournful rustling in the dark" when the darkness has just fallen.*

19

*Time, however, that most faithful ally of the mourner serves him loyally here, too. With its benign alchemy it gradually draws the sting out of memory and converts it into a source of comfort and often, if the departed has lived well, inspiration. Those who have witnessed a western sunset know that the most enchanting time of day is often around evening. After the hot summer sun sets, while nature breathlessly waits for the light to be rolled away before the darkness, the sky is suddenly clad in the spectacular brilliance of multicolored light. These indescribably gorgeous colors are the day's afterglow.*

*Wordsworth said that infants who come into the world come "trailing clouds of glory." It is equally true to observe that many depart from the world trailed by "clouds of glory." Memory perpetuates these and does not let them die. "God gave us memory so that we might have roses in December."*

---

## MEMORY

### Percy Bysshe Shelley

Music, when soft voices die,
Vibrates in the memory—
Odors, when sweet violets sicken,
Live within the sense they quicken.

Rose leaves, when the rose is dead,
Are heaped for the beloved's bed;
And so thy thoughts, when thou art gone,
Love itself shall slumber on.

## IMMORTALITY

### Edwin Hatch

For me—to have made one soul
The better for my birth;
To have added but one flower
To the garden of the earth;
To have struck one blow for truth

In the daily fight with lies;
To have done one deed of right
In the face of calumnies;
To have sown in the souls of men
One thought that will not die—
To have been a link in the chain of life
Shall be immortality.

## FROM "THE EXCURSION"
### *William Wordsworth*

And, when the stream
Which overflowed the soul was passed away,
A consciousness remained that it had left,
Deposited upon the silent shore
Of memory, images and precious thoughts
That shall not die, and cannot be destroyed.

## BLESSING HANDS OVER OUR LIVES
### *Hans Zinsser*

At times the dead are closer to us than the living, and the wisdom and affection of the past stretch blessing hands over our lives, projecting a guardian care out of the shadows and helping us over hard places. For there are certain kinds of love that few but the very wise fully understand until they have become memories.

## THEY NEVER QUITE LEAVE US
### *Margaret E. Sangster*

They never quite leave us, our friends who have passed
Through the shadows of death to the sunlight above;
A thousand sweet memories are holding them fast
To the places they blessed with their presence and love.
The work which they left and the books which they read
Speak mutely, though still with an eloquence rare,
And the songs that they sang, the words that they said,
Yet linger and sigh on the desolate air.

And oft when alone, and oft in the throng,
  Or when evil allures us, or sin draweth nigh,
A whisper comes gently, "Nay, do not the wrong,"
  And we feel that our weakness is pitied on high.


*Jerusalem Talmud*

Monuments need not be erected for the righteous; their deeds are their memorials.


*Maccabees*

And thus this man died, leaving his death for an example of a noble courage, and a memorial of virtue, not only unto young men, but unto all his nation.


## LOVE WHICH SURVIVES THE TOMB
### *Washington Irving*

The sorrow for the dead is the only sorrow from which we refuse to be divorced. Every other wound we seek to heal—every other affliction to forget; but this wound we consider it a duty to keep open—this affliction we cherish and brood over in solitude. Where is the mother who would willingly forget the infant that perished like a blossom from her arms, though every recollection is a pang? Where is the child that would willingly forget the most tender of parents, though to remember be but to lament? Who, even in the hour of agony, would forget the friend over whom he mourns? Who, even when the tomb is closing upon the remains of her he most loved; when he feels his heart, as it were, crushed in the closing of its portal, would accept of consolation that must be bought by forgetfulness?

No, the love which survives the tomb is one of the noblest attributes of the soul. If it has its woes, it has likewise its delights; and when the overwhelming burst of grief is calmed into the gentle tear of recollection; when the sudden anguish and the convulsive agony over the present ruins of all that we most loved is softened away into pensive meditation on all that it was in the days of its loveliness—who would root out such a sorrow from the heart? Though it may sometimes throw a passing cloud over the bright hour of gaiety, or spread a deeper sadness over the hour of gloom, yet who would exchange it, even for the song of pleasure or the burst of revelry? No, there is a voice from the tomb sweeter than song. There is a remembrance of the dead to which we turn even from the charms of the living.

## REMEMBERING

### Margaret E. Bruner

Once when a silence fell upon the heart,
The world at hand grew dim—almost unreal;
And wrapped in thought it seemed that I could feel
Your presence near, though we were far apart;
There was no need of any conjurer's art—
I saw your face in questioning appeal,
As if some message you would thus reveal,
Trusting I, too, would turn to memory's chart.

And in this mood the years were brushed aside—
We walked together down a woodsy hill;
We stood upon the ledge and viewed the wide
Fields where the river glided by, until
There was no other world . . . our spirits met
Briefly to say that neither would forget.

## DEATH CANNOT KILL WHAT NEVER DIES

### William Penn

They that love beyond the world cannot be separated. Death cannot kill what never dies. Nor can Spirits ever be divided that love and live in the same Divine Principle; the Root and Record of their Friendship. Death is but crossing the world, as Friends do the Seas; they live in one another still.

## FROM "THEY SOFTLY WALK"

### Hugh Robert Orr

They are not dead who live
In hearts they leave behind.

In those whom they have blessed
They live a life again,
And shall live through the years
Eternal life, and grow
Each day more beautiful
As time declares their good,
Forgets the rest, and proves
Their immortality.

## FROM "JOYCE LIEBERMAN, A TRIBUTE OF FAREWELL"

### Milton Steinberg

Not often in my lifetime have I come upon a spirit so loving and lovable, so gentle, sensitive and truly innocent as Joyce Lieberman. . . . as long as I knew Joyce—and it was for well over half of her brief life span—she was first a very sick child, then an invalided and foredoomed young woman. Yet in her presence, even at her bedside, one was rarely, if ever, aware of illness, so gay, so eager, so vital and alive in spirit was she. . . .

She did no one ill because she wished no one ill. She practiced no guile because she was incapable of it. . . . Under the extremest of provocations she remained altogether sweet, gentle, kindly, a wisher-well to all the world.

Indeed, in her case illness seems to have been, as it were, a crucible, in which her spirit was progressively refined and purified until nothing base or ignoble was left in it.

Always affectionate, she became ever more affectionate as her numbered days slipped by, steadily more devoted to her friends, among whom I was and am proud to be counted; ever more loving to her so much-loved mother, father and brother.

From earliest childhood she was responsive and poetic, wide awake to beauty in nature, to goodness in men, to grace in art and literature, to nobility in religion and moral aspiration. This sensitivity, too, broadened and deepened with time. At the end it included almost everything good and lovely—from trees budding in the spring, to Beethoven Quartets, the Jewish tradition and the American democratic dream. Some of this sensitivity found an outlet in the poetry she composed. But most of it went into the ardor with which she appreciated life, her wide-eyed, breathless wonder and love of it. . . .

This, it seems to me, is the crowning paradox of her being—that she who had so slight reason to love life loved it so well; that she who had so little ground for happiness was a fundamentally happy person. . . .

And so, Joyce, the loving and lovable, the gentle, sensitive, innocent child, is gone from us. And yet not altogether and entirely.

Long, long ago, a wise man said that he who touches pitch must be defiled with it. But if that be so, then it is also true that he who touches what is warm and luminous must carry away with him something of warmth and light.

On the hearts and minds of all who knew and loved Joyce, something of her soft, quiet sweetness will remain forever. All of us are, I am sure, somehow better, gentler, truer people for having had the privilege of her companionship, so brief yet so lovely.

## KINDLING THE SABBATH LIGHT
### Philip M. Raskin

From memory's spring flows a vision tonight,
My mother is kindling and blessing the light;

The light of Queen Sabbath, the heavenly flame,
That one day in seven quells hunger and shame.

My mother is playing and screening her face,
Too bashful to gaze at the Sabbath light's grace.

She murmurs devoutly, "Almighty, be blessed,
For sending Thy angel of joy and of rest.

"And may as the candles of Sabbath divine
The eyes of my son in Thy Law ever shine."

Of childhood, fair childhood, the years are long fled:
Youth's candles are quenched, and my mother is dead.

And yet ev'ry Friday, when twilight arrives,
The face of my mother within me revives;

A prayer on her lips, "O Almighty, be blessed,
For sending us Sabbath, the angel of rest."

And some hidden feeling I cannot control
A Sabbath light kindles deep, deep in my soul.


*Talmud*

The righteous are called living even when they are dead, and the wicked are called dead even when they are living.


## REMEMBERING ADDS RICHNESS
### *Zelda Popkin*

In the spiritual gifts of a marriage, the giving and receiving of life, lie the strengths from which many a new life is built. One lives with all of one's past. Nothing and no one ever completely dies. It is not necessary or desirable to forget. Remembering adds richness to all our remaining days.

Years of being together have left their impact, a heritage intangible yet rich, made out of gestures and words, experiences shared, the casual warmths of daily contacts. There lies man's true immortality. He lives on in every person whose life touched his.

Going on means opening the little passageways, sealed off in the first weeks of grief because they held memories too poignant, opening the doors, letting the richness of shared experiences come through, saying, "I'd like to go there—I remember what fun we had in that place," not, "I can't bear to go. Our happy times there are over now."


## OUR DEAD
### *Robert Nichols*

#### *From "Ardours and Endurance"*

They have not gone from us. O no! they are
The inmost essence of each thing that is
Perfect for us; they flame in every star;
The trees are emerald with their presences.
They are not gone from us; they do not roam
The flaw and turmoil of the lower deep,
But have now made the whole wide world their home,
And in its loveliness themselves they steep.

They fail not ever; theirs is the diurn
Splendour of sunny hill and forest grave;
In every rainbow's glittering drop they burn;
They dazzle in the massed clouds' architrave;
They chant on every wind, and they return
In the long roll of any deep blue wave.

## MOTHER WILL HUSH YOU AND HEAL YOU

*A condolence letter to a friend upon the death of his aged mother after a period of illness.*

Dear Bill: I was truly saddened to learn of the passing of your mother and I am writing to add my expression of sympathy to the outpouring of condolences which must be reaching you from countless friends.

Mother's death was neither shocking nor tragic. Perhaps as you contrasted her fading powers with the vigorous personality you had drawn upon so heavily, her end might even have brought with it a measure of relief. Yet the coming of nightfall is always accompanied by poignant sorrow even when the day has been long, the sun bright and the twilight difficult.

At a time like this, we usually find a real measure of comfort in contemplating the imperishable role our departed have played in our lives. The pulsating memories, the sustaining influence, the invisible roots entwined around the very essence of our being—all these we know cannot be erased by the hand of death from the blackboard of our lives.

In your own case I strongly feel that your solace must have another dimension. You can derive comfort not only from the thought of what your mother meant to you, but also from the realization of what you meant to her. Your extraordinary success as a human being and as a friend to so many was a profound source of joy to her. How she basked in your reflected glory! In addition, the extreme kindness and thoughtfulness you and Rose always showed her were her favorite topic of discussion. Directly and indirectly you discharged well your filial duties.

In one of her poems, Sara Teasdale says: "Places I know come back to me like music—Hush me and heal me when I am very tired." In the time to come, I know, your mother will come back to hush you and heal you.

Sincerely,
Sidney Greenberg

## SORROWS HUMANIZE OUR RACE

### *Jean Ingelow*

Sorrows humanize our race;
Tears are the showers that fertilize this world
And memory of things precious keepeth warm
The heart that once did hold them.

They are poor that have lost nothing: they are poorer far
Who losing, have forgotten: they most poor
Of all, who lose and wish they might forget;
For life is one, and in its warp and woof
There runs a thread of gold that glitters fair,
And sometimes in the pattern shows more sweet
Where there are sombre colors. It is true
That we have wept. But O, this thread of gold,
We would not have it tarnish; let us turn
Oft and look back upon the wondrous web,
That memory is possession.

### *William Wordsworth*

The thought of our past years in me doth breed Perpetual benediction.

## LIFE WATERED BY STREAMS OF MEMORY

### *Jacob P. Rudin*

The exact circumstances surrounding the death of the poet Ibn Gabirol are unknown. According to one legend, however, a certain Mohammedan, jealous of Ibn Gabirol's genius, killed him and buried his body beneath a tree. Some time after, people began to notice that a fig tree in the garden of the Mohammedan was bearing a particularly large and luscious fruit, like none that grew elsewhere. Curiosity was aroused, and the tree was dug up in order to discover the secret of its remarkable fertility. Then it was discovered that Ibn Gabirol was buried there.

All life grows riper and fuller when rooted in the lives of upright men and women; when its soil is enriched by deeds of loving kind-

ness and mercy. All life becomes lovelier when it is watered by
streams of memory and fed by the cool springs of recollection and
remembrance.

## IN MEMORIAM

*Joseph Auslander*

They are not dead, our sons who fell in glory,
Who gave their lives for Freedom and for Truth.
We shall grow old, but never their great story,
Never their gallant youth.
In a perpetual springtime set apart,
Their memory forever green shall grow,
In some bright secret meadow of the heart
Where never falls the snow.

## FOR ALL WHO MOURN

*Arthur Guiterman*

That he was dear to you so many a year
　　But darkens your distress.
Would you he were less worthy and less dear
　　That you might grieve the less?

He was a golden font that freely poured
　　What goldenly endures,
And though that font be gone, its bounty, stored
　　And treasured, still is yours.

The Past is deathless. Souls are wells too deep
　　To spend their purest gains.
All that he gave to you is yours to keep
　　While memory remains.

Who never had and lost, forlorn are they
　　Far more than you and I
Who had and have. Grudge not the price we pay
　　For love that cannot die.

*Psalms*

The righteous shall be had in everlasting remembrance.


# FOR YOU I SHALL CONTINUE TO LIVE

### Avraham Kreizman
### (Translated from the Hebrew by Eliezer Whartman)

*One of the most poignant letters to come to light was that written by Chicago-born Avraham Kreizman, who came to Palestine as a child in 1921. Avraham fell in the War of Independence, alone, hurling hand grenades to protect the withdrawal of his friends. He left a wife and two young daughters. Here, three days before the end, he writes to his wife:*

I know: When I die, for you I shall continue to live. No one will take me from your faithful and tender heart. But if you meet a comrade who will understand your sorrow, and you love him a bit and your love brings forth a new life and a son is born to you—give him and let him carry my name and let him be my continuation.

And if it comes to pass that he does not understand—leave him without pain and let the child be our son alone. . . .

And when it comes to pass that a new settlement is built here, come and plant poppies in this place: they grow so beautifully here and thrive so well! And let this be the place of my grave. . . .

And perhaps you will err and your flowers will not be planted on my grave but on that of one of my comrades nearby. Well . . . another wife will think of her husband as she plants flowers on mine.

No one will be overlooked. Because we lay close to each other in this spot and there is no space here to divide a man and his friends. . . .


# WHEN THE DAY COMES

### Avraham Kreizman (Translated from the Hebrew by the editor)

And if I will not be with you
When the day comes
To hold you and support you,
To look into your eyes

And whisper silently: Be strong!
Please, dear,
Remember the last glance
In the night of parting. . . .

And if I will not be with you
When they bring him for the first time,
To feed him, warm him, fondle him
And whisper words of love to him,
Please, dear,
Remember the rock, the ocean
And the whisper of the waves. . . .

And if I will not be with you
The first to kiss you and him
And to call you "Mother" and him
"My child, my precious child" . . .
Please, dear,
Remember a moonlit night
And a bridge by the side of the road. . . .

And if I will not be with you
I, your husband,
Whom you chose for a companion
To believe, to love,
To be a father to your child,
And to bring
Two flowers to your bed,
Please, dear,
Remember the field of flowers
And we picking in it. . . .

And if I will not be with you
When you return to the nest,
When you see my reflection in his eyes
Or when his mouth will remind you of mine,
And for a moment you will forget
That I am no longer,
Please, dear,
Remember that I am with you,
With you always, always. . . .

# TRANSFIGURATION

*Louisa May Alcott*

Mysterious death! who in a single hou
    Life's gold can so refine,
    And by thy art divine
Change mortal weakness to immortal power!
How can we mourn like those who are bereft,
    When every pang of grief
    Finds balm for its relief
In counting up the treasures she has left?
Faith that withstood the shocks of toil and time;
    Hope that defied despair;
    Patience that conquered care;
And loyalty whose courage was sublime;
The great deep heart that was a home for all,
    Just, eloquent and strong
    In protest against wrong;
Wise charity, that knew no sin, no fall;
The Spartan spirit that made life so grand,
    Mating poor daily needs
    With high, heroic deeds
That wrested happiness from Fate's hard hand.
We thought to weep, but sing for joy instead,
    Full of the grateful peace
    That follows her release;
For nothing but the weary dust lies dead.
Oh, noble woman! never more a queen
    Than in the laying down
    Of scepter and of crown
To win a greater kingdom, yet unseen.
Teaching us how to seek the highest goal,
    To earn the true success—
    To live, to love, to bless—
And make death proud to take a royal soul.

## FROM "SNOW-BOUND"

### John Greenleaf Whittier

And yet, dear heart! remembering thee,
Am I not richer than of old?
Safe in thy immortality,
What change can reach the wealth I hold?
What chance can mar the pearl and gold
Thy love hath left in trust for me?
And while in life's long afternoon,
Where cool and long the shadows grow,
I walk to meet the night that soon
Shall shape and shadow overflow,
I cannot feel that thou art far,
Since near at need the angels are;
And when the sunset gates unbar,
Shall I not see thee waiting stand,
And, white against the evening star,
The welcome of thy beckoning hand?


## NO FUNERAL GLOOM

### William Allingham

No funeral gloom, my dears, when I am gone,
Corpse-gazings, tears, black raiment, graveyard grimness;
Think of me as withdrawn into the dimness,
Yours still, you mine; remember all the best
Of our past moments, and forget the rest;
And so, to where I wait, come gently on.


## MADE DEARER BY MEMORIES

### Morris Joseph

The balm, according to the Rabbinical idea, is created before the wound . . . with the sorrow, comes the remedy for it; for it is enfolded in the sorrow. We are taught by our trouble, uplifted by it, consoled by it. . . . We take the ruins of the old happiness and build upon them a fairer and more durable edifice. We let our beloved

go, but we receive him back, made dearer, more living, by sanctified
and inspiring memories. . . .

## IMMORTAL

### *Florence Earle Coates*

How living are the dead!
Enshrined, but not apart,
How safe within the heart
We hold them still—our dead,
Whatever else be fled!

Our constancy is deep
Toward those who lie asleep
Forgetful of the strain and mortal strife
That are so large a part of this, our earthly life.
They are our very own—
From them—from them alone
Nothing can us estrange,
Nor blight autumnal, no, nor wintry change.

The midnight moments keep a place for them,
And though we wake to weep
They are beside us still in joy, in pain,
In every crucial hour, they come again
Angelic from above—
Bearing the gifts of blessing and of love
Until the shadowy path they lonely trod
Becomes for us a bridge,
That upwards leads to God.

### *Hannah Senesh*

There are stars whose light reaches the earth only after they themselves have disintegrated and are no more. And there are men whose
scintillating memory lights the world after they have passed from
it. These lights which shine in the darkest night are those which
illumine for us the path. . . .

# EVEN NOW NOAM STANDS BEFORE ME
## (*Translated from the Hebrew by the editor*)

*Noam Grossman was killed in Israel's War of Independence at the age of twenty-one.*

To my esteemed friends, the Grossmans:

I know that it would be futile to try to comfort you. Ordinary words and customary phrases cannot help carry the burden—so sacred and heavy a burden. If only I could help you ever so slightly. . . .

Noam was very dear to us. He was strong and good and brave and the possessor of rare beauty of soul. How we loved him! We admired the serenity that flowed from his eyes and his modesty.

High school, guard duty, university, Haganah—stages along the road. We were friends. And today, when so many of our friends fall en route to our goal, those with whom we learned, dreamed, fought and sweated, comrades in jest and in deadly earnest, they come back to us. Among them the noble figure of our Noam stands out. His winning smile floats in upon us like the gentle evening breeze. And it is possible . . . that those we love, who dwell deep in our hearts, these do not die for us. They will visit us often, they will stand by us at all times. In difficult moments they will sustain us with counsel, with vision and with a smile. For us they live and nothing is taken away from them, nothing. . . .

Even now Noam stands before me. . . . He assures all of us that the ideals for which he died remain firm and abide and that we shall be privileged to witness their fulfilment—and he shall be with us. . . !

> Respectfully yours,
> Baruch Amon

## FROM "DISCORDANTS"
### *Conrad Aiken*

Music I heard with you was more than music,
And bread I broke with you was more than bread.
Now that I am without you, all is desolate,
All that was once so beautiful is dead.

Your hands once touched this table and this silver,
And I have seen your fingers hold this glass.
These things do not remember you, beloved:
And yet your touch upon them will not pass.

For it was in my heart you moved among them,
And blessed them with your hands and with your eyes.
And in my heart they will remember always:
They knew you once, O! Beautiful and wise!

## REQUIEM

### Lucia Trent

When I have died
Let there be no recalling
Of the procession of broken days;
Autumn must come,
And in her wake the falling
Of tired leaves on old and hardened ways.

When I have died
Let there be but rejoicing
For all the sunlit beauties I have known;
Remembrance of friendship,
And the voicing
Of each new joy in radiant overtone!

Let there be but the memory
Of my dreaming,
Of star-domed vistas down the unborn years;
The memory of a faith
I have kept gleaming,
The broken benediction of my tears!

## FROM "VOICES OF THE PAST"

### Adelaide Ann Procter

O there are Voices of the Past
Links of a broken chain,
Wings that can bear me back to Times

Which cannot come again;
Yet God forbid that I should lose
The echoes that remain!

## THE DEAD

*Mathilde Blind*

The dead abide with us. Though stark and cold,
Earth seems to grip them, they are with us still:
They have forged our chains of being for good or ill,
And their invisible hands these hands yet hold.

## THE KADDISH

*L. Kompert*

Its origin is mysterious; angels are said to have brought it down
from heaven and taught it to men. About this prayer the tenderest
threads of filial feeling and human recollection are entwined; for it
is the prayer of the orphans! When the father or mother dies, the
surviving sons are to recite it thrice daily, morning and evening,
throughout the year of mourning, and then also on each recurring
anniversary of the death—on the Yahrzeit.

It possesses wonderful power. Truly, if there is any bond strong
and indissoluble enough to chain heaven to earth, it is this prayer.
It keeps the living together, and forms the bridge to the mysterious
realm of the dead. One might almost say that this prayer is the
watchman and the guardian of the people by whom alone it is
uttered; therein lies the warrant of its continuance. Can a people
disappear and be annihilated so long as a child remembers its
parents? It may sound strange: in the midst of the wildest dissipa-
tion has this prayer recalled to his better self a dissolute character,
so that he has bethought himself and for a time at least purified
himself by honoring the memory of his parents.

Because this prayer is a resurrection in the spirit of the perishable in man, because it does not acknowledge death, because it
permits the blossom, which, withered, has fallen from the tree of
mankind, to flower and develop again in the human heart, therefore it possesses sanctifying power. To know that when thou diest,
the earth falling on thy head will not cover thee entirely; to know
that there remain behind, those who, wherever they may be on

this wide earth, whether they may be poor or rich, will send this prayer after thee; to know that thou leavest them no house, no estate, no field by which they must remember thee, and that yet they will cherish thy memory as their dearest inheritance—what more satisfying knowledge canst thou ever hope for? And such is the knowledge bequeathed to us all by the Kaddish.

### Cicero

The life of the dead is placed in the memory of the living.

## MY HEREAFTER

### Juniata De Long

Do not come when I am dead
To sit beside a low green mound,
Or bring the first gay daffodils
Because I love them so,
For I shall not be there.
You cannot find me there.

I will look up at you from the eyes
Of little children;
I will bend to meet you in the swaying boughs
Of bud-thrilled trees,
And caress you with the passionate sweep
Of storm-filled winds;
I will give you strength in your upward tread
Of everlasting hills;
I will cool your tired body in the flow
Of the limpid river;
I will warm your work-glorified hands through the glow
Of the winter fire;
I will soothe you into forgetfulness to the drop, drop
Of the rain on the roof;
I will speak to you out of the rhymes
Of the Masters;
I will dance with you in the lilt
Of the violin,
And make your heart leap with the bursting cadence

Of the organ;
I will flood your soul with the flaming radiance
Of the sunrise,
And bring you peace in the tender rose and gold
Of the after-sunset.

All these have made me happy:
They are a part of me;
I shall become a part of them.

## TESTAMENT

### Anne Morrow Lindbergh

But how can I live without you?—she cried.
I left all world to you when I died:
Beauty of earth and air and sea;
Leap of a swallow or a tree;
Kiss of rain and wind's embrace;
Passion of storm and winter's face;
Touch of feather, flower and stone;
Chiseled line of branch or bone;
Flight of stars, night's caravan;
Song of crickets—and of man—
All these I put in my testament,
All these I bequeathed you when I went.

*But how can I see them without your eyes*
*Or touch them without your hand?*
*How can I hear them without your ear,*
*Without your heart, understand?*

These, too, these, too
I leave to you!

# "IN MY EYES ALL ARE EQUAL"

*It was a period of profound crisis for Samaria, the capital of the
northern kingdom of ancient Israel. The King of Aram and his
armies had besieged the city and its inhabitants were being starved
to death. So intense had the hunger become, that mothers began
to devour their young. When this news reached the King of Israel,
the Bible tells us, "he rent his clothes . . . and the people looked
and behold he had sackcloth within upon his flesh."*

*What a shock that sight must have been to the people! Each
citizen knew of his personal troubles and tragedies. But how amazed
they all must have been to see that beneath his royal robe, even
the king was wearing sackcloth—the symbol of personal sorrow and
misfortune.*

*A deep truth speaks out to us from this incident—one that we
ought to keep steadily before us especially in time of grief. "Why
did this happen to me?" we frequently ask amidst sorrow, as though
we alone were singled out by a malicious destiny.*

*In the bitter mood of the Book of Lamentations we complain:
"Behold and see if there be any sorrow like unto my sorrow . . .
wherewith the Lord hath afflicted me in the day of fierce anger."
We rarely stop to realize that even kings wear sackcloth.*

*The better we get to know people, the more impressed do we
become with this one fact. Rare indeed is the individual without
a sackcloth. Some of us wear a sackcloth of a deep frustration—a
career to which we aspired but did not attain, a heart we sought
but failed to win. Some of us wear the sackcloth of a haunting
sense of inadequacy, or a deeply bruised conscience. Blasted hopes,*

40

unrealized dreams, anguish and grief—is any life unfamiliar with them? Has anyone ever been granted an exemption from sorrow or made a truce with death? Is not the sackcloth the common garment of all men?

If we would learn to wear life's sackcloths properly, we must cover them with the robe of understanding. We must realize that, as the Bible puts it, "Man is born to trouble." Trouble far from being a gate-crasher in life's arena actually has a reserved seat there. Human life is attended at its beginning by the piercing cries of the infant and at its end by the agonized wailing of the bereaved. In between, there are sadness, heartbreak, disease. For that reason, the great tragedians of literature have not wanted for themes. All they had to do was to observe life carefully and report it faithfully, and the tragedy spelled itself out. "Yet, though men bolt and bar their house from thee, To every door, O Pain, thou hast a key."

In our own hour of sorrow our human oneness is most poignantly underscored. We are indeed knit to one another in a common brotherhood of pain. This kinship should evoke our most compassionate regard for one another. In our hour of tribulation we can become more keenly attuned to "the still sad music of humanity," we can become more sensitive to the needs and hurts of others. Out of such moments there can be born, too, the firm resolve to unite with our fellowmen to delay death and to soften some of the ravages it leaves in its wake. Our common destiny can spur us on to uncommon achievement.

## VISION

### Elizabeth N. Hauer

There have been times when I have looked at life
From out the eyes of sorrow, and have felt
The utter loneliness of black night vigils.
There have been times when I have wept hot tears
And tasted of their salt
And drunk the dregs of sadness to the end.

There have been times—and then another's heartaches,
So deep and rending as to mock my own,

Has cut, flamelike, across my blurring vision,
Dwarfing my paltry tragedies to nought.

## FROM "RESIGNATION"
### Henry Wadsworth Longfellow

There is no flock, however watched and tended,
    But one dead lamb is there!
There is no fireside, howsoe'er defended,
    But has one vacant chair!

The air is full of farewells to the dying,
    And mournings for the dead;
The heart of Rachel for her children crying,
    Will not be comforted!

### George Crabbe

Grief is to man as certain as the grave:
Tempests and storms in life's whole progress rise,
And hope shines dimly through o'er-clouded skies;
Some drops of comfort on the favour'd fall,
But showers of sorrow are the lot of all.

### Metastasio

If inward griefs were written on the brow, how many would be
pitied who are now envied!

## THE BEREAVED—THE LARGEST COMPANY IN THE WORLD
### Helen Keller

We bereaved are not alone. We belong to the largest company
in all the world—the company of those who have known suffering.
When it seems that our sorrow is too great to be borne, let us think
of the great family of the heavy-hearted into which our grief has

given us entrance and, inevitably, we will feel about us their arms, their sympathy, their understanding.

Believe, when you are most unhappy, that there is something for you to do in the world. So long as you can sweeten another's pain, life is not in vain. . . .

Robbed of joy, of courage, of the very desire to live, the newly bereaved frequently avoids companionship, feeling himself so limp with misery and so empty of vitality that he is ill-suited for human contacts. And yet no one is so bereaved, so miserable, that he cannot find someone else to succor, someone who needs friendship, understanding, and courage more than he. The unselfish effort to bring cheer to others will be the beginning of a happier life for ourselves. . . .

Often when the heart is torn with sorrow, spiritually we wander like a traveler lost in a deep wood. We grow frightened, lose all sense of direction, batter ourselves against trees and rocks in our attempt to find a path. All the while there is a path—a path of Faith—that leads straight out of the dense tangle of our difficulties into the open road we are seeking. Let us not weep for those who have gone away when their lives were at full bloom and beauty. Who are we that we should mourn them and wish them back? Life at its every stage is good, but who shall say whether those who die in the splendor of their prime are not fortunate to have known no abatement, no dulling of the flame by ash, no slow fading of life's perfect flower?

### Wisdom of Ben Sira

Fear not the sentence of death;
Remember them that have been before thee, and that
    come after:
This is the sentence from the Lord over all flesh.

### Susan Coolidge

Men die, but sorrow never dies;
The crowding years divide in vain,
And the wide world is knit with ties
Of common brotherhood in pain.

## OUR KINSHIP WITH ALL HUMANITY
### *Zelda Popkin*

Many reach out for and feel for the first time their kinship with all humanity. "At first, when my husband died," a woman told me some time ago, "I felt it was a special punishment visited just upon me. My friends had their families. My world had collapsed. Then one day I read in the papers of a plane crash. It was carrying important people. All were lost.

"It hit me like a flash of revelation. I said to myself: 'The wives of those men are traveling the same road I am. All over the world there are women like me.' I stopped feeling sorry for myself. I felt sorry for them, instead."

### *Chateaubriand*

It is with sorrows, as with countries, each man has his own.

## THE UNIVERSAL HERITAGE
### *Morris Adler*

Sorrow is the obverse side of love. To ask for immunity from sorrow is to ask for more than a special dispensation granted no other. It is to ask that we love not, gain no friends or devotedly serve any cause. To enter into any relationship of deep meaning is to run the risk of sorrow. When we become parents, or link our life to another's, or find a friend who is closer than brother, we inevitably expose ourselves to the pangs of separation or the grief of injury or illness or death. But let us for a moment consider the alternative. One meets people whom life has wounded deeply. Fate dealt them a harsh blow. A dear one died, or a friend betrayed a trust. A hope failed of fulfillment or a kindness was repaid with ingratitude. They decide never again to give hostages to life. Life is not going to find an exposed flank in their case. They will not open their hearts in trust; they will not permit acquaintance to ripen into friendship; they are prepared to forego love, family, children. They are resolved that no human being will become so dear to them that his passing will bring grief. They protect themselves against sorrow. But they also shut out the possibilities of joy, companionship, the richest and most vital satisfactions of life. Charles Dickens' *Great Expectations* tells of a woman whose groom disappeared on their wedding day. She wears her wedding gown through the years and compels her life to stop still and deathlike at the hour of her great sorrow.

But such surrender does not necessarily indicate deepest feeling. There are people whose self-pity is greater than their grief and who in mourning replace the object of their sorrow with their own hurt.

We shall be helped in maintaining our balance during life's trials if we remember that sadness is the universal heritage of mankind. The contingency of pain is the only condition on which love, friendship and happiness are ever offered to us. This recognition is the hallmark of maturity.

### Daniel Webster

One may live as a conqueror, a king or a magistrate; but he must die as a man.

## DEPART SATISFIED

### Marcus Aurelius

Man, thou hast been a citizen in this great state (the world): what difference does it make to thee whether for five years (or three)? for that which is conformable to the laws is just for all. Where is the hardship then, if no tyrant nor yet an unjust judge sends thee away from the state, but nature who brought thee into it? the same as if a praetor who has employed an actor dismisses him from the stage. "But I have not finished the five acts, but only three of them."

—Thou sayest well, but in life the three acts are the whole drama; for what shall be a complete drama is determined by him who was once the cause of its composition, and now of its dissolution: but thou art the cause of neither. Depart then satisfied, for he also who releases thee is satisfied.

### Shakespeare

. . . all that live must die,
Passing through nature to eternity.

*John Gay*

The prince, who kept the world in awe,
The judge, whose dictate fix'd the law,
The rich, the poor, the great, the small,
Are level'd: death confounds 'em all.

## THE COMMON DATE WITH ADVERSITY
### *Morris Adler*

Who among men has not at one time or another known the sharp pain of grief, the poignant hurt of loss? Who has been able to insulate himself against the slings and arrows of outrageous fortune, or escape the disappointment and melancholy to which human flesh is heir? Is there anyone here to whom sadness is strange or anguish alien? Is there an individual from whom life has not wrung tears or whose lips have never uttered a sigh? Every mortal has a date with adversity, loss and death. . . .

If there is one experience that is common to all men, then, it is sorrow. An old and familiar story illustrates the universality of sadness. A patient came to a physician in the city of Naples. He complained of melancholia. He could not rid himself of a deep feeling of sadness. The physician said, "I advise you to visit the theatre where the incomparable Carlini is appearing. This great comedian daily convulses large crowds with laughter. By all means go to see Carlini. His amusing antics will drive away your melancholy."

At these words, the patient burst into tears and sobbed, "But, doctor, I am Carlini." . . . This awareness that sorrow is man's common lot will not restore a lost one, or heal an ailment. It should, however, save us from an outpouring of that self-pity to which we would succumb were we to feel that none has ever suffered as we.

*Job*

There the wicked cease from troubling;
And there the weary are at rest.
There the prisoners are at ease together;
They hear not the voice of the taskmaster.

The small and great are there alike;
And the servant is free from his master.

### First Chronicles

For we are strangers before Thee, and sojourners, as all our fathers
were: our days on the earth are as a shadow, and there is no abiding.

### Joseph Jefferson

*Inscription on Joseph Jefferson's monument at Sandwich, Cape
Cod, Mass.*

We are but tenants, and . . . shortly the great Landlord will give
us notice that our lease has expired.

### Psalms

What man is he that liveth and shall not see death, that shall
deliver his soul from the power of the grave?

### Horace

Pale death enters with impartial step the cottages of the poor and
the palaces of the rich.

## THE MOTHER OF THE GREAT KING

In *The Spirit Returneth,* by Selma Stern, Deborah asks her grandmother how she managed to recover after a family sorrow. Others
in the family, according to Grandmother, never got over it, their
hearts turning to stone within them.

"How did it come about, Grandmother, that you yourself grew
to be so different?" Deborah asked.

The old woman smiled. "It was a little song that caused me to
change."

"A little song?" Deborah asked wonderingly.

"Yes, it was a song which a minstrel sang many years ago in
our dance house. It is a sad song, but it is also a very consoling

song, and all who think that they have suffered more ill than any of their fellows ever have should hear it and take it to heart. For it tells how Alexander of Macedon consoled his own mother. When he knew that his death was near, he wrote her a letter. 'My mother, remember that all earthly things are transitory and that your son was not a small king but a great king. Wherefore you are not to bear yourself like the mother of a little king, but like the mother of a great king. And so after my death command a great hall to be built and command furthermore that on a given day all the princes of the empire shall come thither and be merry and be of good cheer. And cause it to be proclaimed that none is to come who has suffered any ill, for the joy at that feast shall be a pure and perfect joy and shall not be darkened by the thoughts of any concerning any sorrow that has come upon him.'

"When now the time had come that her son was dead, she acted exactly according to his will. She caused a magnificent hall to be built; she named the day on which the princes were to come to the feast. When the appointed day came, on which the feast was to take place, she was prepared for many, many people. And not a single soul came. She asked the people in her court: 'What is the meaning of this thing? Why do not the guests come to this great hall which I have caused to be built?' The answer she received was this: 'Dear Queen, you issued the command that none should come who has suffered any grief or any ill. But there is no such human being in the whole world, and therefore there is no guest who could come.' And this consoled the mother of the great king."

*Henry Wadsworth Longfellow*

Believe me, every man has his secret sorrows, which the world knows not; and oftentimes we call a man cold when he is only sad.

## HEARTBREAK ROAD

*Helen Gray Cone*

As I went up by Heartbreak Road
  Before the break of day,
The cold mist was all about,
  And the wet world was gray;
It seemed that never another soul
  Had walked that weary way.

But when I came to Heartbreak Hill,
   Silver touched the sea;
I knew that many and many a soul
   Was climbing close to me;
I knew I walked that weary way
   In a great company.

## TO LEARN HOW TO DIE

*Montaigne*

The profit of life consists not in the space, but rather in the use. Some man hath lived long, that hath a short life, Follow it whilst you have time. It consists not in number of years, but in your will, that you have lived long enough. Did you think you should never come to the place, where you were still going? There is no way but hath an end. And if company may solace you, doth not the whole world walk the same path?

*Thomas Southerne*

Sooner or later, all things pass away,
And are no more: The beggar and the king,
With equal steps, tread forward to their end.

## THE EMPEROR EXITS LIKE THE BEGGAR

*Richard C. Trench*

I remember an Eastern legend which I have always thought furnished a remarkable though unconscious commentary on the words of the Psalmist. Alexander the Great, we are there told, being upon his deathbed, commanded that when he was carried forth to the grave his hands should not be wrapped as was usual in the cere-cloths, but should be left outside the bier, so that all might see them, and might see that they were empty, that there was nothing in them; that he, born to one empire, and the conqueror of another, the possessor while he lived of two worlds—of the East and of the West—and of the treasures of both, yet now when he was dead could retain no smallest portion of these treasures; that in this matter the poorest beggar and he were at length upon equal terms.

### Joshua

And, behold, this day I am going the way of all the earth.

## THE RAINY DAY

### Henry Wadsworth Longfellow

The day is cold, and dark, and dreary;
It rains, and the wind is never weary;
The vine still clings to the mouldering wall,
But at every gust the dead leaves fall,
    And the day is dark and dreary.

My life is cold, and dark, and dreary;
It rains, and the wind is never weary;
My thoughts still cling to the mouldering past,
But the hopes of youth fall thick in the blast,
    And the days are dark and dreary.

Be still, sad heart! and cease repining;
Behind the clouds is the sun still shining;
Thy fate is the common fate of all,
Into each life some rain must fall
    Some days must be dark and dreary.

### Socrates

If all the misfortunes of mankind were cast into a public stock, in order to be equally distributed among the whole species, those who now think themselves the most unhappy would prefer the share they are already possessed of, before that which would fall to them by such a division.

## DEATH THE LEVELER

*James Shirley*

The glories of our blood and state
  Are shadows, not substantial things;
There is no armor against Fate;
  Death lays his icy hand on kings:
    Sceptre and Crown
    Must tumble down,
And in the dust be equal made
With the poor crooked scythe and spade.
Some men with swords may reap the field,
  And plant fresh laurels where they kill:
  But their strong nerves at last must yield;
  They tame but one another still:
    Early or late
    They stoop to fate,
And must give up their murmuring breath
When they, pale captives, creep to death.
The garlands wither on your brow;
  Then boast no more your mighty deeds!
Upon Death's purple altar now
See where the victor-victim bleeds.
    Your heads must come
    To the cold tomb:
Only the actions of the just
Smell sweet and blossom in their dust.

## CREATURE AND CREATOR

*Daniel Webster*

One may live as a conqueror, a king, or a magistrate; but he must die a man. The bed of death brings every human being to his pure individuality, to the intense contemplation of that deepest and most solemn of all relations—the relation between the creature and his Creator.

Death stands above me, whispering low
I know not what into my ear;
Of his strange language all I know
Is, there is not a word of fear.

—Walter Savage Landor

# FEAR NOT DEATH

*The emotion grief is actually a composite of many different feelings. Added to the pain of parting, there may be loneliness, remorse or even a harrowing sense of guilt. Not infrequently grief also contains a burdensome ingredient of fear—the fear of death.*

*However one looks upon death, it is certainly a venture into the unknown, and man usually experiences deep anxiety in the presence of the unfamiliar. Little wonder then that the thought of death has so often evoked dread. William Randolph Hearst had so powerful a fear of death that the very mention of the word in his presence was strictly prohibited. Even in his newspapers, the subject had to be handled with utmost delicacy.*

*Yet it is possible to face death without dread. Many have so faced it. When the father of Robert Browning lay on his deathbed his cheerfulness so surprised his physician that he asked the patient's daughter in a low voice: "Does the old gentleman know he is dying?" The patient overheard the question and answered: "Death is no enemy in my eyes."*

*In Jewish history there have been tens of thousands of men and women who in times of persecution deliberately chose death rather than live with dishonor. These acts of Kiddush Hashem, "sanctification of the Name of God," are a powerful tribute to the loyalty and the heroism of the martyrs. In a sense, they also reveal the equanimity with which these pious souls faced death.*

*Perhaps the most famous of Jewish martyrs in Talmudic times was Rabbi Akiba. As he was being put to death by the Romans for the capital offense of teaching Judaism, he said to his weeping*

52

disciples: "All my life I was disturbed over the verse 'And Thou shalt love the Lord thy God with all thy heart, with all thy soul and with all thy might.' The phrase 'with all thy soul' has been interpreted to mean that we must serve God even at the peril of our soul. And I was agitated over my inability to fulfil this verse. At last the opportunity has presented itself to me to love God 'with all my soul.' Now I am at peace."

Strangely, it is not the exceptional person who faces death serenely. While so many live with a fear of death, they actually seem to die in a spirit of calm acceptance. Such at least, is the overwhelming testimony of those who see people die.

Dr. Frank Adair is only one of many prominent physicians who bear witness to the courage and calm ninety-nine per cent of dying patients exhibit. Dr. Adair said: "The haunting fear which the average person carries all through life is dissipated by the approach of death."

If we can succeed in accepting the inexorable fact of our own death with equanimity, perhaps it will mitigate our sorrow over the death of our loved one. We can even learn to regard death not as an enemy but as a friend, who at the appointed hour leads us like Longfellow's little child at bedtime "half willing half reluctant to be led." Sancho Panza in "Don Quixote" spends a desperate night clinging to a window ledge, afraid of falling. When day breaks, he discovers that all the while his feet had been only an inch from the ground. Our fear of death may be as groundless as Sancho's fear of falling. Death may be but the threshhold over which we pass from time to eternity; from the realm of the perishable to the realm of the indestructible. And if we come to terms with death, who would dare to set a limit on what we could extract from life?

It is a real hour of triumph when a man can banish the fear of death from his heart and honestly say with the poet Sarah Williams "Though my Soul may set in darkness, it will rise in perfect light,

I have loved the stars too fondly to be fearful of the night."

to die. The ship goes down. What, then, am I to do? Whatever I can. I drown without fear, neither shrinking nor crying out against God, but recognizing that what is born must also perish. For I am part of the whole, as an hour is part of a day. I must come on as the hour, and like an hour, pass away. Regard yourself as but a single thread of all that go to make up the garment. Seek not that the things which happen to you should be as you wish, but wish the things that happen to you to be as they are, and you will find tranquillity.

*Author unknown*

Death is terrible, but still more terrible is the feeling that you might live forever and never die.

## A VISION WITH NO TERRORS

### *Dr. H. D. Van Fleet*

I have sat with dying men of every race and creed—Hindus, Shintoists, Catholics, Protestants, Jews, Mohammedans. They died in peace. And I have found that the sweetness of death is intensified in all men by a childlike faith in their own religion. Except for their own interpretation of religion, what men cling to is the same throughout the world.

Thus the occasional temporary apprehension about death stems, I believe, from the fact that an individual may not have prepared to meet it. His goals in life may have been too high; he isn't satisfied with what he has done; he may never have felt close to God. These anxieties can make the idea of dying untenable to him for the moment, until—consciously or unconsciously—he goes back to the religious beliefs that he learned as a child. . . .

As a doctor who has seen many people expire after a protracted illness, I know that it is often sweet to die. Frequently I have seen a change of expression as the moment of death approached, almost a smile, before the last breath was taken.

Science cannot explain this, as science cannot explain the dynamic power which controls life. What a man may see at the point of death will probably remain an eternal mystery. But it should remain, too, a vision with no terrors for any of us.

*Epictetus*

Not death or pain is to be feared, but the fear of death or pain. Well said the poet therefore: "Death has no terror; only a death of shame!"

## HE HAD NO FEAR

*Dr. Walter C. Alvarez*

. . . I have seen any number who were conscious and clear-headed up to the last few moments of life. They didn't seem to be too much concerned with what was happening to them. Others, of course, are told of their fate honestly.

I remember in particular a man with a hopeless cancer who listened to the results of my examination and then said: "Doctor, answer me this: If you had this thing and you had a brilliant boy in his junior year in medical school, would you expend your savings on an operation which might prolong your life for a few months or do nothing?"

"I'd leave the money for the boy," I answered.

"That's what I hoped you'd say," he replied. "That's what I'm going to do."

That man's wife told me that he had not the remotest idea what was the matter with him, that he'd kill himself if he learned the truth. Little did she know her husband. He knew perfectly well what was wrong with him before I told him. And his only thought was for his son.

That man's courage was typical of men and women I have seen with fatal illnesses. He not only was brave, he had no fear.

## REQUIEM

*Robert Louis Stevenson*

Under the wide and starry sky,
Dig the grave and let me die.
Glad did I live and gladly die,
    And I laid me down with a will.

This be the verse you grave for me:
Here he lies where he longed to be;
Home is the sailor, home from the sea,
And the hunter home from the hill.

### Robert Louis Stevenson

*Robert Louis Stevenson, on his death-bed wrote to a friend about an old woman who had frightened some primitive natives with her ventriloquism:*

All the old women in the world might talk with their mouths shut and not frighten you or me, but there are plenty of other things that frighten us badly. And if we only knew about them, perhaps we should find them no more worthy to be feared than an old woman talking with her mouth shut. And the names of some of these things are Death and Pain and Sorrow.

### Epictetus

Reflect that the chief source of all evils to man, and of baseness and cowardice, is not death, but the fear of death.

## SERENELY TO ACCEPT WHAT HAPPENS
### Joshua Loth Liebman

Judaism encourages us . . . to recognize that it (death) is as natural an aspect of human life as birth. When man has established a confidence in life and the God of life, he is prepared serenely to accept what happens after death even as he does not worry about what took place before birth. When we become morbidly and obsessively preoccupied with the thought of the end of life, we show that we have fallen in love with ourselves to such an extent that we cannot tolerate the idea of a possible final sleep. Yet the fear of death is a deceiver. We think that we are frightened of death, when actually beneath the surface we are frightened of many things that life has inflicted upon us—some forgotten rejection in childhood, some imprisonment in a dark and foreboding closet as a punishment for a childish prank or tantrum, some identification with an annihilationist mother or a punishing father. It should come as a liberation to recognize that it is not death that is to be feared, but many of the scares of life which are to be removed, understood, discarded.

As mature people we must learn not to love ourselves excessively nor to mistrust the universe morbidly. The truth is that we change and die every day a little. Yes, we die every day a little bit without fear. Our skins change. The cells in our hands and in our brains perish and are reborn. Our whole life is strewn with the bones of hopes discarded, dreams outgrown, loves broken, friendships embraced. We change and die every dawn and every sunset, yes, without fear. Let us recognize that we are part of nature, both in life and in death. The atoms composing us are arranged differently in the moment of our conception, at the time of birth as we grow and clothe our skeleton with the flesh and muscles, the tendons and the veins of maturity, and then when the curtain is drawn over our earthly frame, the atoms of our being are rearranged and enter once again the treasury of nature and we are at rest. The shock of corn has fallen upon the soil from which it sprang and we are once more in the bosom of the Divine.

### Marcus Aurelius

Think not disdainfully of death, but look on it with favor, for nature wills it like all else. . . . Look for the hour when the soul shall emerge from this its sheath, as now thou awaitest the moment when the child she carries shall come forth from the wife's womb.

# IF THE GENERATIONS DID NOT
# COME AND GO
### Joshua Loth Liebman

Judaism . . . teaches us to understand death as part of the Divine pattern of the universe. Actually we could not have our sensitivity without fragility. Mortality is the tax that we pay for the privilege of love, thought, creative work—the toll on the bridge of being from which clods of earth and snow-peaked mountain summits are exempt. Just because we are human, we are prisoners of the years, yet that very prison is the room of discipline in which we, driven by the urgency of time, create.

We can face death without dread when we learn that the Angel of Death plays a very vital role in life's economy. Actually there could be no growth, no progress, if generations did not come and go. There also would be very little meaning to existence if the years were not marked off in the calendar of time by childhood, adolescence, youth, and age. There is a time to run gaily with all the intense excitement of a boy with flushed cheeks racing on a summer's day towards the winding river of sport and adventure; there is also the time when that boy, transformed by the alchemy of the years into an old man, no longer seeks to run but is quite content to sit and browse even unto the twilight.

## THE VALIANT TASTE DEATH BUT ONCE

*Shakespeare*

Cowards die many times before their deaths;
The valiant never taste of death but once.
Of all the wonders that I yet have heard,
It seems to me most strange that men should fear;
Seeing that death, a necessary end,
Will come when it will come.

## NOTHING IN HIS LIFE

*Shakespeare*

Nothing in his life
Became him like the leaving it; he died
As one that had been studied in his death
To throw away the dearest thing he owed,
As 'twere a careless trifle.

## DO NOT DESPISE DEATH

*Marcus Aurelius*

Do not despise death, but be well content with it, since this, too, is one of those things which nature wills. For such as it is to be young and to grow old, and to increase and to reach maturity, and to have teeth and beard and gray hairs, and to beget, and to be pregnant, and to bring forth, and all the other natural operations which the seasons of thy life bring, such also is dissolution. This, then, is consistent with the character of a reflecting man, to be neither careless nor impatient nor contemptuous with respect to death, but to wait for it as one of the operations of nature.

## DEATH
### William Croswell Doane

We are too stupid about death. We will not learn
How it is wages paid to those who earn,
How it is the gift for which on earth we yearn,
To be set free from bondage to the flesh;
How it is turning seed-corn into grain,
How it is winning Heaven's eternal gain,
How it means freedom evermore from pain,
How it untangles every mortal mesh.

## ACCEPTING DEATH
### Dorothy Thompson

The mother of a friend of mine died the other day. My friend's eleven-year-old daughter was sent away until after the funeral. She must be spared a knowledge of death. Is this not characteristic of our society? We treat death as if it were an aberration. Age approaches but beauticians, masseur and gland specialists cooperate to keep alive the illusion that we are not really growing older. Anything that reminds us of the inescapable fact that we are to die seems morbid to us. Yet without the serene acceptance of death as inexorable we lose all the magic and wonder of life and live in constant unconscious fear. For only when one is no longer afraid to die is one no longer afraid at all. And only when we are no longer afraid do we begin to live in every experience, painful or joyous; to live in gratitude for every moment, to live abundantly.

## DEATH IS A FRIEND
### Montaigne

Nature herself gives us courage. . . . Death is not to be feared. It is a friend. No man dies before his hour. The time you leave behind was no more yours than that which was before your birth and concerneth you no more. Make room for others as others have done for you. Like a full-fed guest, depart to rest. . . . The profit of life consists not in the space, but in the use. Some man hath lived long that has had a short life. . . .

Depart then without fear out of this world even as you came into it. The same way you came from death to life, return from life to death. Yield your torch to others as in a race. Your death is but a piece of the world's order, but a parcel of the world's life.

## HIS TENDER HANDS

*Winnie Lynch Rockett*

His tender hands have fashioned tiny things:
The wee blue petals of forget-me-nots;
A drop of mist; an insect's tissue wings;
A poppy seed; a caterpillar's spots;
The sensitive antennae of a bee;
Each amber globule of the desert sands—
Then shall I fear, when He has said to me,
"Thy days, my little one, are in my hands?"

## THE FAITH OF THE POET

*Victor Hugo*

You say, "Where goest thou?" I cannot tell,
And still go on. If but the way be straight,
It cannot go amiss! Before me lies
Dawn and the Day; the Night behind me; that
Suffices me; I break the bonds; I see,
And nothing more; believe, and nothing less.
My future is not one of my concerns.

## MY SOUL AND I

*Charles Buxton Going*

As treading some long corridor,
My soul and I together go;

Each day unlocks another door
    To a new room we did not know.
And every night the darkness hides
    My soul from me awhile—but then
No fear nor loneliness abides:
    Hand clasped in hand, we wake again.
So when my soul and I at last
    Shall find but one dim portal more,
Shall we, remembering all the past,
    Yet fear to try that other door?

## APOLOGY OF SOCRATES

### *Plato*

Let us reflect in another way, and we shall see that there is great reason to hope that death is a good, for one of two things: either death is a state of nothingness and utter unconsciousness, or, as men say, there is a change and migration of the soul from this world to another. Now if you suppose that there is no consciousness, but a sleep like the sleep of him who is undisturbed even by the sight of dreams, death will be an unspeakable gain. For if a person were to select the night in which his sleep was undisturbed even by dreams, and were to compare with the other days and nights of his life, and then were to tell us how many days and nights he had passed in the course of his life better and more pleasantly than this one, I think that any man, I will not say a private man, but even the great king, will not find many such days or nights, when compared with the others. Now if death is like this, I say that to die, is gain: for eternity is then only a single night. But if death is the journey to another place, and there, as men say, all the dead are, what good, O my friends and judges, can be greater than this?

## DEATH IS NOT THE ENEMY OF LIFE

### *Anonymous*

### *From "Forward Movement"*

Much of our horror of death comes from the feeling (even though it may never be expressed) that it is the enemy of life. We love life; therefore it is natural to dread death. But death is no more the enemy of life than sleep is the enemy of work and play. Sleep makes it possible for us to work and play the next day. Death makes it possible for us to live on. It has therefore a real contribution to make to life in the large, being the gateway through which we slip from the lower life into the higher, from the briefer into that which is eternal.

## THE BIRTHDAY OF ETERNITY

### Seneca

As the mother's womb holds us for ten months, making us ready, not for the womb itself, but for life, just so, through our lives we are making ourselves ready for another birth. . . . Therefore look forward without fear to that appointed hour—the last hour of the body, but not of the soul. . . . That day, which you fear as being the end of all things, is the birthday of your eternity.

### Lucan

None but those shadowed by death's approach are suffered to know that death is a blessing; the gods conceal this from those who have life before them, in order that they may go on living.

### Henry Wadsworth Longfellow

Good-night! good-night! as we so oft have said,
Beneath this roof at midnight, in the days
That are no more, and shall no more return.
Thou hast but taken up thy lamp and gone to bed;
I stay a little longer, as one stays
To cover up the embers that still burn.

## DEATH IS AN AFFIRMATIVE EXPERIENCE

### Zelda Popkin

There is no human experience which man fears more and understands less, and this very dread largely prevents him from understanding it. He pushes it back in his mind, as though by refusing to acknowledge the possibility, he may avert it. Yet death is a major experience of life. It is an affirmative experience, since through it, the living grow in depth.

## DEATH IS NOT A THING TO BE FEARED
### *Cicero*

What a poor dotard must he be who has not learnt in the course of so long a life that death is not a thing to be feared? Death, that is either to be totally disregarded, if it entirely extinguishes the soul, or is even to be desired, if it brings him where he is to exist forever. A third alternative, at any rate, cannot possibly be discovered. Why then should I be afraid if I am destined either not to be miserable after death or even to be happy?

## TERMINATION OF ACTIVITY IS NO EVIL
### *Marcus Aurelius*

Termination of activity, cessation from movement and opinion, and in a sense their death, is no evil. Turn thy thoughts now to the consideration of thy life, thy life as a child, as a youth, thy manhood, thy old age, for in these also every change was a death. Is this anything to fear? Turn thy thoughts now to thy life under thy grandfather, then to thy life under thy mother, then to thy life under thy father; and as thou findest many other differences and changes and terminations, ask thyself, Is this anything to fear? In like manner, then, neither are the termination and cessation and change of thy whole life a thing to be afraid of.

## CONQUER THE FEAR OF DEATH
### *Leo Tolstoy*

Man is a being beyond time and beyond space who is conscious of himself in the conditions of space and time. One should conquer the fear of death; and when you cease to fear it, you cease to serve yourself, a mortal, and you will serve an immortal God, from whom you came and to whom you are going.

Not long ago I experienced a feeling, not exactly a reasoning, but a feeling, that everything that is material and I myself, with my own body, is only my own imagination, is the creation of my spirit, and that only my soul exists. It was a very joyous feeling.

### Mrs. *Thomas Henry Huxley*
#### *Lines on the gravestone of Thomas Henry Huxley*

And if there be not meeting past the grave,
If all is darkness, silence, yet 'tis rest.
Be not afraid, ye waiting hearts that weep,
For still he giveth His beloved sleep,
And if an endless sleep He wills, 'tis best.

## WE NEED NOT DIE WHILE WE ARE LIVING
### *Henry Ward Beecher*

What if the leaves were to fall a-weeping, and say, "It will be so painful for us to be pulled from our stalks when autumn comes?" The glory of death is upon the leaves; and the gentlest breeze that blows takes them softly and silently from the bough, and they float slowly down like fiery sparks upon the moss. It is hard to die when the time is not ripe. When it is, it will be easy. We need not die while we are living.

### *Isaiah*

Say to them that are of fearful heart, be strong, fear not.

## MEDITATIONS
### *Solomon Ibn Gabirol (Translated by Emma Lazarus)*

Forget thine anguish,
Vexed heart, again.
Why shouldst thou languish,
With earthly pain?
The husk shall slumber,
Bedded in clay
Silent and sombre,
Oblivion's prey!

But, Spirit immortal,
Thou at Death's portal,
Tremblest with fear.
If he caress thee,
Curse thee or bless thee,
Thou must draw near,
From him the worth of thy works to hear.

Why full of terror,
Compassed with error,
Trouble thy heart,
For thy mortal part?
The soul flies home—
The corpse is dumb.
Of all thou didst have,
Follows naught to the grave.
Thou fliest thy nest,
Swift as a bird to thy place of rest.


### *Wisdom of Ben Sira*

Make little weeping for the dead, for he is at rest.


## FROM "THE SLEEP"
### *Elizabeth Barrett Browning*

Of all the thoughts of God that are
Borne inward unto souls afar,
Along the Psalmist's music deep,
Now tell me if that any is,
For gift or grace, surpassing this—
"He giveth His beloved sleep"?

What would we give to our beloved?
The hero's heart, to be unmoved,
The poet's star-tuned harp, to sweep,
The patriot's voice, to teach and rouse,
The monarch's crown, to light the brows?
He giveth His beloved sleep.

What do we give to our beloved?
A little faith all undisproved,
A little dust to overweep,
And bitter memories to make
The whole earth blasted for our sake:
He giveth His beloved sleep.

"Sleep soft, beloved!" we sometimes say,
But have no tune to charm away
Sad dreams that through the eyelids creep.
But never doleful dream again
Shall break the happy slumber when
He giveth His beloved sleep.

And, friends, dear friends, when it shall be
That this low breath is gone from me,
And round my bier ye come to weep,
Let One, most loving of you all,
Say, "Not a tear must o'er her fall!
He giveth His beloved sleep."

## WHEN THOU PASSEST THROUGH THE WATERS

### Cecil

My first convictions on the subject of religion were confirmed by observing that really religious persons had some solid happiness among them, which I felt the vanities of the world could not give. I shall never forget standing by the bedside of my sick mother. "Are you not afraid to die?" I asked. "No." "No? Why does the uncertainty of another state give you no concern?" "Because God has said, 'Fear not; when thou passest through the waters, I will be with thee; and through the rivers, they shall not overflow thee.' Let me die the death of the righteous."

### Wisdom of Solomon

The souls of the righteous are in the hand of God,
And no torment shall touch them.
In the eyes of the foolish they seemed to have died:

And their departure was accounted to be their hurt,
And their journeying away from us to be their ruin:
But they are in peace.

## WHAT IS DEATH?

*Author unknown*

What is death? A little broadening of a ripple
Upon the eternal shore.
A little loosening of the bands that cripple—
This and nothing more.
What's death? A parting of the cloud above us
Which hides the sun,
A gold vision of the souls that love us
And labor done.
What's death? The opening of a perfect flower;
No watcher sees
The silent spirit, who at twilight hour
The bondman frees.
What's death? God's mercy strange
Uncomprehended;
The undiscovered goal;
The land of promise when the toil
Is ended—
The day-dawn of the soul.

## *Psalms*

The Lord is my shepherd; I shall not want.
He maketh me to lie down in green pastures;
He leadeth me beside the still waters.
He restoreth my soul;
He guideth me in straight paths for His name's sake.
Yea, though I walk through the valley of the shadow of death,
I will fear no evil,
For Thou art with me;
Thy rod and Thy staff, they comfort me.

### T. C. Williams

Death is an angel with two faces:
To us he turns
A face of terror, blighting all things fair;
The other burns
With glory of the stars, and love is there.

### Ella Wheeler Wilcox

I think of death as some delightful journey
That I shall take when all my tasks are done.

### Cato

He who fears death has already lost the life he covets.

## PROSPICE

### Robert Browning

Fear death?—to feel the fog in my throat,
    The mist in my face,
When the snows begin, and the blasts denote
    I am nearing the place,
The power of the night, the press of the storm,
    The post of the foe;
Where he stands, the Arch Fear in a visible form,
    Yet the strong man must go;
For the journey is done and the summit attained,
    And the barriers fall,
Though a battle's to fight ere the guerdon be gained,
    The reward of it all.
I was ever a fighter, so—one fight more,
    The best and the last!
I would hate that death bandaged my eyes, and forbore,
    And bade me creep past.
No! let me taste the whole of it, fare like my peers
    The heroes of old,

Bear the brunt, in a minute pay glad life's arrears
    Of pain, darkness, and cold.
For sudden the worst turns the best to the brave,
    The black minute's at end,
And the elements' rage, the fiend-voices that rave,
    Shall dwindle, shall blend,
Shall change, shall become first a peace out of pain,
    Then a light, then thy breast,
O thou soul of my soul! I shall clasp thee again,
    And with God be the rest!

### Wisdom of Ben Sira

Fear not the sentence of death; why dost thou refuse when it is the good pleasure of the Most High?

### Plutarch

What can they suffer that do not fear to die?

## FRIENDSHIP WITH DEATH AS WITH LIFE
### John Gunther

No fear of death or any hereafter. During our last summer at Madison, I would write in my diary when I couldn't sleep. "Look Death in the face. To look Death in the face, and not be afraid. To be friendly to Death as to Life. Death as a part of Life, like Birth. Not the final part. I have no sense of finality about Death. Only the final scene in a single act of a play that goes on forever. Look Death in the face: it's a friendly face, a kindly face, sad, reluctant, knowing it is not welcome but having to play its part when its cue is called, perhaps trying to say, "Come, it won't be too bad, don't be afraid, I understand how you feel, but come—there may be other miracles!" No fear of Death, no fight against Death, no enmity toward Death, friendship with Death as with Life.

## THE LANDSMAN

*Robert Nathan*

Oh, troubled heart, the fall with colder breath
Blows in the tassel as the farmers reap;
So in the autumn comes the landsman, death,
His step is quiet, and his house is sleep.

## Richard Baxter

Richard Baxter, when on his deathbed suffering great pain, was asked how he felt, and replied, "Almost well." At length the final hour arrived, and he became, in his own language, "Entirely well."

## SELFISHNESS

*Margaret E. Bruner*

Death takes our loved ones—
We are bowed in grief. For whom?
Are we not selfish?
A mourner weeps for himself,
The dead know not of sorrow.

## THERE IS NO SADNESS

*Margaret E. Bruner*

Oh, you who mourn that autumn's loveliness
Must pass—her gold and crimson glory fade—
Earth's music for a space must have an end,
These last high notes conclude her serenade.

For like the climax of a perfect song,
The singer's ardor dies and he must rest;
So must the shriveled leaf and withered flower
Sink to oblivion on earth's deep breast.

And pity not the trees whose boughs are bare,
They knew creation's pangs—its joy and grief;
They meet with eagerness the icy wind—
There is no sadness in the falling leaf.


### *Deuteronomy*

And the Lord, He it is that doth go before thee
He will be with thee, He will not fail thee,
Neither forsake thee: fear not, neither be dismayed.


### *David Weinberg*

He who fears death is really afraid of life.


## THE CARRIAGE IS DISMISSED
### *John Bigelow*

Sleep and death—they differ in duration rather than in quality. Perhaps both are sojourns in the spiritual, the real world. In one case our carriage waits nightly to take us back from the entrance of slumber, while in the other, having arrived at our destination and with no further use for the carriage, it is dismissed.


### *Rabbi Bunam*

When Rabbi Bunam was lying on his deathbed, he said to his wife who wept bitterly, "Why dost thou weep? All my life has been given to me merely that I might learn to die."


## A NURSE BOTH AFFECTIONATE AND STERN
### *From H. G. Wells*

On his seventieth birthday, H. G. Wells was honored by a group of English authors. When he arose to acknowledge their tributes, he said that he was reminded of his feelings as a child when his nurse would say to him: "Master Henry, it's your bedtime." He would protest, of course, as all children do at bedtime, even though he knew in his heart that sleep would bring him much welcome rest. "Death," continued Wells, "is a nurse both affectionate and stern; when the time comes, she says to us: 'Master Henry, it's your bedtime.' We protest a little, but we know quite well that the time for rest has come and that in our hearts we are longing for it."

### Jonathan Swift

It is impossible that anything so natural, so necessary, and so universal as death should ever have been designed as an evil to mankind.

### Samuel Coleridge

Death came with friendly care, the opening bud to heaven conveyed, and bade it blossom there.

### Francis Bacon

Men fear Death as children fear to go in the dark; and as that natural fear in children is increased with tales so is the other. . . . It is as natural to die as to be born; and to a little infant perhaps the one is as painful as the other.

### Henry Wadsworth Longfellow

And as she looked around, she saw how Death the consoler,
Laying his hand upon many a heart, had healed it forever.

## NATURE
### Henry Wadsworth Longfellow

As a fond mother, when the day is o'er,
    Leads by the hand her little child to bed,
    Half willing, half reluctant to be led,
    And leave his broken playthings on the floor,

Still gazing at them through the open door
Nor wholly reassured and comforted
By promises of others in their stead,
Which though more splendid, may not
     please him more;
So Nature deals with us, and takes away our
Playthings one by one, and by the hand
Leads us to rest so gently, that we go
Scarce knowing if we wish to go or stay,
Being too full of sleep to understand
How far the unknown transcends
     what we know.

## WHY SHOULD WE FEAR?

### Sir Philip Sidney

Since Nature's works be good, and death doth serve
As Nature's work, why should we fear to die?
Since fear is vain, but when it may preserve,
Why should we fear that which we cannot fly?

## THE LESSON OF THE STARS

### Leslie R. Smith

A small child who saw the stars for the first time was greatly impressed and intrigued by them. Childlike, she had many questions. Were they there all the time? Why couldn't you see them during the day? Couldn't you see them until it got dark? Her mother replied: "Yes, their beauty is hidden all through the day. You can see them only at night. Aren't they lovely?" And then she added: "Darkness is always beautiful, if we will only look up at the stars instead of into the corners."

How true! If we will just look up at the stars! They tell us that night is the most joyous part of the day. It is the time of homecoming after a hard day's work. We step out of the limited interest of business associates and friends into the boundless love of home and family. In this happy fellowship we relax after the strain of a busy day. Night is the time for rest and for sleep. So it is with death. It is life's night. It is a glorious homecoming. It is a reunion with those who have gone before. It is rest from labor. It is simply to lie back in the Everlastng Arms.

### William Wordsworth

But when the great and good depart,
What is it more than this—
That Man, who is from God sent forth,
Doth yet again to God return?—
Such ebb and flow must ever be,
Then wherefore should we mourn?

## NO ONE SHOULD FEAR DEATH
### Eddie Rickenbacker

No one should fear death. I know, because I have come face to face with death several times. It is really a pleasant experience. You seem to hear beautiful music and everything is mellow and sweet and serene—no struggle, no terror, just calmness and beauty. When death comes, you will find it to be one of the easiest and most blissful experiences you have ever had.

## GOD WILL NOT CAST US ASIDE
### Joshua Loth Liebman

We master fear through faith—faith in the worthwhileness of life and the trustworthiness of God; faith in the meaning of our pain and our striving, and confidence that God will not cast us aside but will use each one of us as a piece of priceless mosaic in the design of His universe.

### Lord Bolingbroke

God who placed me here will do what He pleases with me hereafter, and He knows best what to do.

I hold it true, whate'er befall;
I feel it when I sorrow most;
'Tis better to have loved and lost
Than never to have loved at all.

—Alfred Tennyson

# GRIEF SOFTENED BY GRATITUDE

*The* dreary clouds of grief which gather in the wake of death cast thick gloom over the lives of the bereaved. An aching void, an overpowering loneliness, a fear of facing the future alone, a gnawing pain over the unlived years—all these combine to throw deep darkness over our days. Yet there are small pin points of light that penetrate the overcast. Amidst our grief, if we pause to reflect, we can find, as others have, genuine cause for gratitude. This gratitude may not dispel the gloom but it can relieve it.

Even while we mourn the death of a loved one, there is room in our hearts for thankfulness for that life. We have lost what we have had. For those years of love and comradeship there is no adequate compensation. Impoverished as we are by the passing of our beloved, we should be poorer by far if we had never tasted the joy and richness of that union. Sadder than losing a loved one is never having had a loved one to lose. Helen Hayes expressed this thought most pointedly after the death of her highly gifted daughter. "Tragic that it should have ended," she said of Mary's life, "but how much better than if it had never been."

We can be grateful, too, that while death robs us of our loved ones, it cannot take from us the years that passed and their abiding impression. These have entered into our lives and become part of ourselves. With the poet Georgia Harkness we can say of the loved one we mourn:

77

*To know this life was good—*
*It left its mark on me.*
*Its work stands fast.*

*Sober reflection can also lead us to a more sympathetic appreciation of the vital role death plays in the economy of life. Life's significance and zest issue from our awareness of its transiency, its "fragile contingency." The urge to create, the passion to perfect, the will to heal and cure—all the noblest of human enterprises grow in the soil of human mortality. They would vanish if life on earth were an endless, unrelieved process.*

*To the person of religious faith there remains the profoundest source of gratitude amidst grief. His is the reassuring conviction that the soul is imperishable and "the grave is not its goal." The souls of our loved ones, like our own, come from the great Source of Life, Himself, and flow back into the eternal stream after the earthly pilgrimage is ended.*

*Thus the pain of parting is mitigated by faith in a divine providence which permits no life to be utterly destroyed. It was this faith which spoke out of Job in his hour of anguish and has since been repeated by countless bereaved believers: "The Lord hath given, The Lord hath taken back, praised be the name of the Lord."*

---

## TO MY FATHER

### Georgia Harkness

A giant pine, magnificent and old,
Stood staunch against the sky and all around
Shed beauty, grace, and power. Within its fold
Birds safely reared their young. The velvet ground
Beneath was gentle, and the cooling shade
Gave cheer to passers-by. Its towering arms
A landmark stood, erect and unafraid,
As if to say, "Fear naught from life's alarms."

It fell one day. Where it had dauntless stood
Was loneliness and void. But men who passed

Paid tribute—said, "To know this life was good,
It left its mark on me. Its work stands fast."
And so it lives. Such life no bonds can hold—
This giant pine, magnificent and old.


## IS IT REALLY THE END?

*Rachel (Translated from the Hebrew by the editor)*

Is it really the end? The path is still clear.
The mists of life still beckon from afar
The sky is still blue, the grass green;
Autumn is coming.

I shall accept the judgment. My heart harbors no complaint.
How red were my sunsets, how clear my dawns!
And flowers smiled along my path
As I passed.


## SHED NOT TOO MANY TEARS

*Author unknown*

Shed not too many tears when I shall leave;
  Be brave enough to smile.
It will not shorten, howsoe'er you grieve,
  Your loneliness the while.
I would not have you sorrowful and sad,
  But joyfully recall
The glorious companionship we've had,
  And thank God for it all.
Don't let your face grow tear-streaked,
    pale and wan:
  Have heart for mirth and song—
Rejoice, though for a little while I've gone,
  That I was here so long,
For if I thought your faith would fail you so,
  And leave you so distressed,
That sobbing to my body's grave you'd go,
  My spirit could not rest.

## SOMEHOW STRENGTH LASTED

*Author unknown*

Somehow strength lasted through the day,
Hope joined with courage in the way;
The feet still kept the uphill road,
The shoulders did not drop their load,
And unseen power sustained the heart
When flesh and will failed in their part,
    While God gave light
    By day and night,
And also grace to bear the smart.
For this give thanks.


## I THANK GOD SHE WAS MINE FOR
## THE WHILE I HAD HER

*Grace Perkins Oursler and April Armstrong*

So it is with love gone. You've had it. In your heart you know you wouldn't trade it for all the riches on earth.

Many people never know it. There are millions who never taste the cup of love, though it is brewed constantly about them, poured before their eyes, left steaming with enticing promises of dreams unfulfilled, and poured out on the ground before dogs. There are those who have never heard a child's call, or looked into eyes that trusted them with overwhelming confidence; men and women who have never been chosen and cherished, however briefly —people who do not know the meaning of friend.

"I've heard so many folks say they would never again have a dog or a bird," a famous statesman, who lost his small daughter, told his father one day, "because it broke their heart so when the pet died. I do not pretend to know why Susan was given to me and snatched away. But I thank God she was mine for the while I had her. I wouldn't have not had her whatever my heartbreak now. And I know that her going brought out whatever of greatness in me that I have. One has to surmount—or fall by the wayside."

*John Vance Cheney*

The soul would have no rainbow
Had the eyes no tears.

## FROM "AT EIGHTY-THREE"

### *Thomas Durley Landels*

Thank God for life, with all its endless store
Of great experiences, of hill and dale,
Of cloud and sunshine, tempest, snow and hail.
Thank God for straining sinews, panting breast,
No less for weary slumber, peaceful rest;
Thank God for home and parents, children, friends,
For sweet companionship that never ends:
Thank God for all the splendor of the earth,
For nature teeming with prolific birth:
Thank God for sea and sky, for changing hours,
For trees and singing birds and fragrant flowers.
And so in looking back at eighty-three,
My final word to you, my friends, shall be:
Thank God for life; and when the gift's withdrawn,
Thank God for twilight bell, and coming dawn.

## THE SPARK OF GRATEFULNESS

### *Joseph I. Weiss*

However short, however long the time given to those who are
near to us, strength will be fashioned through the gratitude of
our hearts for the blessing of life itself. When the days of life are
short, shall we curse the moments of beauty for their brevity, or
prize them that they came to us at all? When toll is taken in the
middle years, shall we be bitter for lack of more, or wall our tears
with thanksgiving for what has been? When the bridge of three-
score and ten has been crossed, shall we be torn with argument
for a longer term, or be grateful for the fullness of the granted
time?
Our sages said that all things might be lost save one: the spirit
of gratitude that is ever present in the heart of man. They further

said that as long as thanksgiving lasts, the world will endure. The waters of sadness are deep, but they will never extinguish the spark of gratefulness that is fed by man's inherent recognition of God's goodness toward him. Let us fan that spark into a flame that will guide us happily into the future.

## THEREFORE, WE THANK THEE GOD

### Reuben Avinoam (Translated by L. V. Snowman)

*The Hebrew poet Reuben Grossman was born in Chicago. His son Noam studied at the Hebrew University, became an officer of Haganah when the fighting started and fell in March, 1948, along with seventeen of his comrades. After the son's death, the poet changed his name to Avinoam which in Hebrew means "father of Noam."*

*This poem appeared in "Davar," the Hebrew publication, and the following translation is taken from "The Living Rampart," an anthology of stories and poems written in Israel during the war.*

At the end of a week of mourning for our son Noam.

Incline Thine ear, O God,
Consider a brief space
In this night hour of sombre rage
The word of parents bewildered by bereavement.
We approach Thee not with regret, nor complaint.
Nor do we come to litigate with Thee,
Only thanks pouring from the wound of our heart we offer
    Thee.
Accept it, O God.
For these three things thanksgiving be to Thee:

For pleasant years,
For one and twenty years
Wherein Thou didst honour us with him and lent him us,
For his steps walking humbly by our side on the little isle
    of life:
Years sown with the peace of his being,
When like a gliding swan he made his way erect with grace;
Years shining with smiles
Which like sunrays he spread around him,

With good-hearted whispers, pardons by concession and
  understanding,
Years shining with the light of his two eyes,
Where dreams yearned, mingled with the sorrow of fate,
Having a pure look and upright before God and man.
For this little gift.
For twenty-one full years of life Thou gavest him and us,
We thank Thee. . . .

And for a hero's death
Thou didst appoint him,
For all the limbs of his body were taut in strength,
And welded in pride
And on all his sinews was spread the essence of power,
The wine kept for the saints of Thy people who hallow its
  land.
Thou didst lead him among the evening-hills in the heights
  of Judah,
No voice being heard but the bidding of the Maccabees of old.
The echoes of their blood set his exultant heart tramping
  to victory,
No other lodestar but the light of his own soul,
A tongue of fire
Born of the flame of Bar Kochba which he kindled,
Marching serene, stepping with confidence
In the height of dread and solitude,
Girt with the armour of hope, encircled with the girdle of
  power,
To meet the beginning of freedom or the end of glory. . .
For death which was like a kiss
At the lips of Mattathias the Hasmonean
With which Thou didst favour him
When he ascended the holy ladder,
We thank Thee. . . .

And for the flowing tear
When Thou didst make Thy host of clouds and
Thy bands of cherubs weep—
When the news of the bereavement reached us—
And when Thou didst roll the sighs of the thunder of Thy
  heart
Among the terrible heights,

And us here on the gloomy earth,
When our soul was clothed with grief for our son!
For Thy tears shed and Thy sigh breathed
Together with those of a father and a mother
We thank Thee. . . .

## FROM "ODE: INTIMATION OF IMMORTALITY"

### *William Wordsworth*

What though the radiance which was so bright
Be now for ever taken from my sight,
Though nothing can bring back the hour
Of splendour in the grass, of glory in the flower;
We will grieve not, rather find
Strength in what remains behind;
In the primal sympathy
Which having been must ever be;
In the soothing thoughts that spring
Out of human suffering;
In the faith that looks through death,
In years that bring the philosophic mind.

## LIFE OWES ME NOTHING

### *Author unknown*

Life owes me nothing. Let the years
Bring clouds or azure, joy or tears,
Already a full cup I've quaffed;
Already wept and loved and laughed,
And seen, in ever endless days.

Life owes me naught. No pain that waits
Can steal the wealth from memory's gates;
No aftermath of anguish slow
Can quench the soul-fire's early glow.
I breathe, exulting, each new breath,
Embracing Life, ignoring Death.

Life owes me nothing. One clear morn
Is boon enough for being born;
And be it ninety years or ten,
No need for me to question when.
While Life is mine, I'll find it good,
And greet each hour with gratitude.

## LET US COUNT THE PAST AS GAIN

### *Morris Joseph*

It is not God's part to spare us suffering—for that is essential to his plan—but to help us to bear it. If the visitation we dread finds us—for it may be for our good that it should find us—then we do right to ask for the strength that will uphold us under the load, for the insight that reveals the wisdom of it, for the magic power that will transform it into blessing. And to that prayer there is always an answer. . . .

Something precious is taken from us, and we think of it as something we have lost, instead of something we have had. We remember only how empty our lives are now, we forget how full and rich they were before; we forget all the many days and years of happiness we lived while the beloved object was still with us. We praise God for our treasures while we have them; we cease to praise him for them when they are fled. But God never gives; He only lends. What is life itself but a loan? "Everything," cry the old sages, "is given in pledge" to be restored when the Master wills. . . . No. When God claims His own shall we rebel or repine? Instead of murmuring because He takes our precious things from us, let us be grateful to Him for having spared them to us so long. Let us count the past happy days not as loss, but as gain. We have had them; and, now that they are ended, let us turn the loss to glorious gain— the gain that comes with new courage, with nobler tasks, with a wider outlook on life and duty. . . .

## PRAYER IN SORROW

### *Sidney Greenberg*

Help me, loving Father, to bear bravely the burden of bereavement which weighs upon my heart. May the grief over the death of my loved one not suffocate the gratitude I owe for the years of life we shared together.

Thou hast created us with a wisdom which we can only partially understand. If it is Thy law that the brightness of noon is followed by the blackness of night and the joy of love by the pain of parting, teach me to accept my sorrow as the spiritual coin with which I pay in part for the blessings of love. Help me to understand, too, that just as the night which blots out the mid-day light fades in turn before the rising sun, so does the death of the body make way for the everlasting life of the soul.

Abide with me in the valley of the shadow. Keep aglow my candle of hope until I shall reach the open meadows of healing and sunshine that lie beyond. *Amen.*

## THE TWO SHIPS
### Midrash

Two ships were once seen near land. One of them was leaving the harbor, and the other was coming into it. Everyone was cheering the outgoing ship, giving it a hearty send-off. But the incoming ship was scarcely noticed.

A wise man standing nearby explained the people's reaction. "Rejoice not," he said, "over the ship that is setting out to sea, for you know not what destiny awaits it, what storms it may encounter, what dangers lurk before it. Rejoice rather over the ship that has reached port safely and brought back all its passengers in peace."

It is the way of the world, that when a human being is born, all rejoice; but when he dies, all sorrow. It should be the other way around. No one can tell what troubles await the developing child on its journey through life. But when a man has lived well and dies in peace, all should rejoice, for he has completed his journey successfully and he is departing from this world with the imperishable crown of a good name.

## DEATH MAKES LIFE MORE MEANINGFUL
### Joshua Loth Liebman

The presence of death makes more meaningful all of the values of life. . . . In our rebellious moments we feel, that if we had designed the universe, we would have given man an ever-renewable fountain of youth, so that death could never come and the end of life could never be felt. Yet when we analyze this feeling, we realize that this is the petulant, unreflective desire of a distraught child. . . .

. . . The joy of our striving and the zest of our aspirations, so precious because of their fragile contingency, would vanish if earthly immortality were our inescapable lot and destiny. . . .

. . . The more mature we grow, the more we recognize unsuspected wisdom in the way that nature arranges things. . . .

. . . Apparently, nature does not have the power to create such marvelously sensitive organisms as we human beings are, and at the same time arrange for the durability in us of stone or mountain. This is a universe where everything has a price, and we cannot expect to purchase the fragile beauty of love and consciousness without the suffering of transciency and decay. . . .

. . . The glory of life consists in our very ability to feel deeply and experience widely; it is the part of wisdom to taste of the cup of joy and sorrow without inner rebelliousness, to accept with equanimity the inevitable fact that we and all we possess are transient just because we are such sensitive creatures; that the marvel of our make-up, the superb intricacy of our chemical, physical, spiritual organization gives us our supreme blessings and makes our little day on earth infinitely more significant than all of the rocks and stones which last unchanged but also untouched by the winds of the centuries. . . .

## FROM "RUGBY CHAPEL"

*Matthew Arnold*

And through thee I believe
In the noble and great who are gone,
Pure souls honored and blest
By former ages who else—
Such, so soulless, so poor,
Is the race of men whom I see—
Seem'd but a dream of the heart,
Seem'd but a cry of desire
Yes, I believe that there lived
Others like thee in the past,
Not like the men of the crowd

Who all round me today
Bluster or cringe, and make life
Hideous and arid, and vile,
But souls tempered with fire,
Fervent, heroic, and good,
Helpers and friends of mankind.


*Marcus Aurelius*

Spend your brief moment according to nature's law, and serenely greet the journey's end as an olive falls when it is ripe, blessing the branch that bare it, and giving thanks to the tree that give it life.


## WE ARE FLOODED WITH JOYOUS MEMORIES
### *William Allen White*

*A letter written by William Allen White to the late Judge C. A. Leland of El Dorado, Kansas, at the time of Mary's death, and dated June 13, 1921. The letter was first published in the* El Dorado Times *in January, 1952.*

I am sure you will pardon my delay in answering your letter about Mary's death. Mrs. White and I appreciated it very much. It is a great comfort to know in sorrow that one's friends are standing by in spirit. Words count for little. Sympathy is not important. But that spiritual sustenance which comes from the thoughtful love of friends—I suppose the thing which some way makes for the answering of prayers—is the only thing that helps in grief, and your letter helped. We want to thank you for it most sincerely.

I wonder if you saw all of the article about Mary that I wrote the day after her funeral. I am taking a chance and enclosing it herewith. It may interest you to know that it has been more widely copied than any other article that ever appeared in the *Gazette*. From Boston to San Diego, in all the towns north, south, east and west, this little article appeared, and I have had literally hundreds of letters from men and women who have been touched by it.

Surely it has brought her life into the lives of others, and I hope for good; by good I mean I hope that she may be an influence to soften other lives and to inspire them with some impulse which will work out for the common good, for some little addition through

each heart to our larger social inheritance. These are large words
and large thoughts and maybe futile, but anyway they seem to make
me feel Mary has had this sure immortality, no matter what else
may come, and that helps, too.

Mrs. White and I are standing on our feet, realizing that the loss
is heavy and the blow is hard, but not beating our hands against
the bars and asking why. On our books Mary is a net gain. She was
worth so much more than she cost, and she left so much more behind than she took away that we are flooded with joyous memories
and cannot question either the goodness of God or the general
decency of man.

## LIFE'S LESSON

### *Anonymous*

> I learn, as the years roll onward
> And I leave the past behind,
> That much I had counted sorrow
> But proved that God is kind;
> That many a flower I'd longed for
> Had hidden a thorn of pain
> And many a rugged bypath
> Led to the fields of ripened grain.
> The clouds that cover the sunshine;
> They cannot banish the sun,
> And the earth shines out the brighter
> When the weary rain is done.
> We must stand in the deepest shadow
> To see the clearest light;
> And often through wrong's own darkness
> Comes the welcome strength of Right.

A man should discipline himself to say:
"Whatever God does, He does for the best."

—Talmud

# FAITH IN THE GOODNESS OF GOD

*Prince Albert upon his death bed is reported to have said: "I have had wealth, rank and power. But if this were all I had, how wretched I should be now." When we are confronted with the stark reality of death, life's true values become crystallized and our emphasis shifts from the tangibles we so ardently pursue to the intangibles we so persistently neglect. Faith in God may be an elective in our university of daily living. In the presence of death it assumes crucial significance.*

*For all its urgency, however, faith in God is not easily attained in the hour of grief. Indeed, even the believer finds it difficult to retain his faith in a good God when he is assaulted by the sharp pangs of bereavement and the resultant gnawing doubts fashioned out of his agony. It is undoubtedly for this very reason that Judaism placed such heavy emphasis upon the Kaddish. This prayer which the mourner recites daily for eleven months does not contain a single reference to the deceased. Rather does it embody a powerful affirmation of belief in God in spite of personal sorrow. "Magnified and sanctified be the great name of God throughout the world which He hath created according to His will." But is this a tenable faith? Can we discern any method in what appears like divine madness?*

*The unprecedented scientific progress of the last century has revealed whole vistas of information which had hitherto been beyond the human ken. At the same time, however, it has served to underscore by how much the unknown still exceeds the known. Our ignorance far outweighs our knowledge.*

*A very prosaic illustration of this truth is found where physical sight is concerned. Today the scientist informs us that there are en-*

90

tire ranges of wave-lengths which our eyes literally cannot see. The wave-lengths of the visible spectrum range from red at one end to violet at the other. These do not exhaust all the existing wave-lengths. Indeed, these are actually only a small portion of the many wave-lengths which exist. Invisible to our eyes, there are the infra-red beyond the red, and beyond the violet at the other end of the spectrum, there are the ultra-violet wave-lengths. Nor are these all. Beyond these there are many more wave-lengths no human eye has even seen because of its own physical limitations. It would appear then that even in the physical realm we are equipped to see only a fragment of reality, a small arc of the infinite circle.

If this is true in the physical world, is it not also true to a greater degree of the spiritual world? How infinitesimal is the area of our vision, how circumscribed is our spiritual color spectrum. Are we really in a position to comprehend fully the drama of which our present plight is only a fleeting scene?

A mine disaster in England some time ago claimed the lives of forty men. Their stunned and grief-stricken families gathered at the entrance to the mine. The spiritual leader of the community was asked by someone to address the bewildered mourners, to speak some word of comfort or guidance. These are the words he spoke to them: "We stand today in the face of mystery, but I want to tell you about something I have at home. It is a bookmark, embroidered in silk by my mother and given me many years ago. On one side the threads are crossed and recrossed in wild confusion, and looking at it you would think it had been done by someone with no idea of what he was doing. But when I turned it over I see the words beautifully worked in silken threads 'God is Love.' Now we are looking at this tragedy from one side and it does not make sense. Some day we shall be permitted to read its meaning from the other side. Meanwhile, let us wait and trust."

This is the point at which belief in a benign providence becomes so vital. Where knowledge retires, faith awakens. Faith does not dissolve our sorrow nor does it anesthetize us against pain. What it can do for us is to strengthen us for the fierce ordeal which we now regard as part of the divine purpose. Faith goes beyond our range of vision and affirms with Emerson, who himself experienced the tragedy of the death of his young son, "All I have seen teaches me to trust the Creator for all I have not seen." There is much we cannot see but the world we do see about us contains so much of love and beauty, goodness and truth. It attests to a Divine intelligence and points to a universe which has design and plan. A God who fash-

*ioned His marvelous universe in so majestic a form is a God who can be relied upon to care for our loved ones who have gone, to give courage to us who remain. It has been finely said: "We cannot go where God is not and where God is, all is well."*

---

## AS ONE WHOM HIS MOTHER COMFORTETH

### W. L. Alexander

Benighted on a lone and dreary wild,
Perplexed, exhausted, helpless, in despair,
I cast me down, and thought to perish there,
When through the gloom a face appeared and smiled;
And a sweet voice said: "Courage! rise, my child!
And I will guide thee safely on thy way."
As to night-watchers comes the morning ray,
So came that voice to me; and on that face
I seemed a loving tenderness to trace,
That soothed and cheered me as, forlorn, I lay;
I felt as feels the child whose throbbing grief
A mother's love assuages in its source;
And asking strength of Him who gave relief,
I straightway rose, and onward held my course.

### Proverbs

The wicked is thrust down in his misfortune;
But the righteous, even when he is brought to death, hath hope.

## FAITH CAN OVERCOME BEREAVEMENT

### Dean Inge

Bereavement is the deepest initiation into the mysteries of human life, an initiation more searching and profound than even happy love. Love remembered and consecrated by grief belongs, more clearly than the happy intercourse of friends, to the eternal world; it has proved itself stronger than death.

Bereavement is the sharpest challenge to our trust in God; if faith can overcome this, there is no mountain which it cannot remove. And faith can overcome it. It brings the eternal world nearer to us, and makes it seem more real.

### Isaiah

Fear thou not, for I am with thee,
Be not dismayed, for I am thy God;
I strengthen thee, yea, I help thee;

## SORROW BUT PROVES US

### Stefan Zweig

Have no fear, have no fear, that the Lord will forsake us!
Mistrust him not, brothers, in days that are dark!
For when he debases us, when he afflicts us,
The suffering he sends is but sign of his love.
Then bow ye, my brothers, bend necks to the yoke,
Accept gladly the lot by Jehovah decreed.
Know that sorrow but proves us, that trial uplifts us,
That affliction, though sore, brings us nearer to God.
Each pang that we feel is a step toward his kingdom,
Since the vanquished on earth are in heaven beloved.
Up, brothers, march onward, march onward to God.

## FAITH IS ABIDING STRENGTH

### Joseph I. Weiss

Our abiding strength is told in terms of faith. For life to have meaning we must believe that the universe represents the purposeful creation of God. We look into the sky and behold the worlds that are the heaven's jewels. We look upon the earth and stand in awe of nature's ordered realm. At every turn we witness the lawful process that bespeaks the accomplishment of an Intelligence far beyond our mental scope. The mind of man never stops in its search for the ultimate truth. What we have learned and what is yet to be known can only lead us to the truth that above and beyond is God, and that the universe is His domain.

### Samuel Longfellow

Discouraged in the work of life,
Disenheartened by its load,
Shamed by its failures or its fears,
I sink beside the road;
But let me only think of Thee,
And then new heart springs up in me.

### J. E. Saxby

Oh, ask not thou, How shall I bear
The burden of to-morrow?
Sufficient for today its care,
Its evil and its sorrow;
God Imparteth by the way
Strength sufficient for the day.

### Isaiah

He giveth power to the faint;
And to him that hath no might He increaseth strength.

## FROM "TO A WATER FOWL"
### William Cullen Bryant

There is a Power whose care
Teaches thy way along the pathless coast—
The desert and illimitable air—
Lone wandering, but not lost.
He who from zone to zone
Guides through the boundless sky thy certain flight,
In the long way that I must tread alone,
Will lead my steps aright.

## I SELL FAITH
### Sholom Asch

*The following incident forms the conclusion of Sholom Asch's*
Kiddush Ha-Shem. *The novel describes the frightful massacre of the*

*Jews in seventeenth-century Poland. Shlomo is one of the very few survivors of the decimated Jewish section of Lublin.*

In Lublin he came upon refugees from Tulchin, from Bar and from other towns, and he learned from some of the forced converts of the death of his father and mother, who had died for the sanctification of His Name together with the other Jews of Tulchin. But no one knew what had become of Deborah—of Deborah or of the Christian nurse.

But Shlomo knew. He knew that she had gone up to heaven in holiness and purity. In heaven she was, and waiting for him.

He did not mourn for her. Only a great longing for her took possession of him, and for the day when he would again be with her.

And he roamed about through the fair of Lublin among the refugees, among the husbands separated from their wives and the wives separated from their husbands, among the widows and the orphans. He heard the sighs and moans of his people which rose up over the fair. And he pondered deeply on the matter. He sought to understand the meaning of it all. For a minute the meaning escaped him—he could not understand, and he fell in a state of melancholy. And this caused him deep grief, for it is a matter of common knowledge that melancholy is only one degree removed from doubting.

And one day he walked in a narrow street in Lublin where the merchants' stalls were located. And he saw standing before an empty booth an old man who was calling buyers into his booth. And he marveled greatly, for the booth was empty, there was nothing in it to sell. And he walked into the booth and asked the old man: "What do you sell here? Your booth is void and empty, and there is no merchandise in it."

And the old man answered: "I sell faith."

And he looked intently at the old man, and the old man appeared to him familiar as though he had seen him before. . . .

## FROM "RESIGNATION"

*Henry Wadsworth Longfellow*

Let us be patient! These severe afflictions
  Not from the ground arise,
But oftentimes celestial benedictions
  Assume this dark disguise.

*II Chronicles*

The Lord is with you, while ye are with Him;
And if ye seek Him, He will be found of you.


*Edward Young*

Faith builds a bridge across the gulf of death.


## WHEN SORROW COMES
### *Edgar A. Guest*

When sorrow comes, as come it must,
In God a man must put his trust.
There is no power in mortal speech
The anguish of his soul to reach,
No voice, however sweet and low,
Can comfort him or ease the blow.

He cannot from his fellow men
Take strength that will sustain him then.
With all that kindly hands will do,
And all that love may offer, too,
He must believe throughout the test
That God has willed it for the best.

We who would be his friends are dumb;
Words from our lips but feebly come;
We feel, as we extend our hands,
That one Power only understands
And truly knows the reason why
So beautiful a soul must die.

We realize how helpless then
Are all the gifts of mortal men.
No words which we have power to say
Can take the sting of grief away—
That Power which marks the sparrow's fall
Must comfort and sustain us all.

When sorrow comes, as come it must,
In God a man must place his trust.
With all the wealth which he may own,
He cannot meet the test alone,
And only he may stand serene
Who has a faith on which to lean.

### Victor Hugo

Have courage for the great sorrows of life and patience for the small ones; and when you have laboriously accomplished your daily task, go to sleep in peace. God is awake.

## A PRAYER

### Thomas Moore

O Thou who dry'st the mourner's tear!
    How dark this world would be,
If, when deceived and wounded here,
    We could not fly to Thee.
The friends, who in our sunshine live,
    When winter comes are flown;
And he, who has but tears to give,
    Must weep those tears alone.
But Thou wilt heal that broken heart,
    Which, like the plants that throw
Their fragrance from the wounded part,
    Breathes sweetness out of woe.

When joy no longer soothes or cheers,
    And e'en the hope that threw
A moment's sparkle o'er our tears,
    Is dimmed and vanished too!
Oh! who could bear life's stormy doom,
    Did not Thy wing of love
Come brightly wafting through the gloom
    Our peace-branch from above?
Then sorrow, touched by Thee, grows bright
    With more than rapture's ray;
As darkness shows us worlds of light
    We never saw by day.

## HE KNOWS WHAT IS GOOD FOR US

*(From a British aviator's last letter to his mother)*

Dearest Mother: Though I feel no premonition at all, events are moving rapidly and I have instructed that this letter be forwarded to you should I fail to return from one of the raids which we shall shortly be called upon to undertake. You must hope on for a month, but at the end of that time you must accept the fact that I have handed my task over to the extremely capable hands of my comrades of the Royal Air Force, as so many splendid fellows have already done.

First, it will comfort you to know that my role in this war has been of the greatest importance. . . . Though it will be difficult for you, you will disappoint me if you do not at least try to accept the facts dispassionately, for I shall have done my duty to the utmost of my ability. No man can do more, and no one calling himself a man could do less.

I have always admired your amazing courage in the face of continual setbacks; in the way you have given me as good an education and background as anyone in the country; and always kept up appearances without ever losing faith in the future. My death would not mean that your struggle has been in vain. Far from it. It means that your sacrifice is as great as mine. . . .

You must not grieve for me, for if you really believe in religion and all that it entails that would be hypocrisy. I have no fear of death; only a queer elation. . . . I would have it no other way. The universe is so vast and so ageless that the life of one man can only be justified by the measure of his sacrifice. We are sent to this world to acquire a personality and a character to take with us that can never be taken from us. Those who just eat and sleep, prosper and procreate, are no better than animals if all their lives they are at peace.

I firmly and absolutely believe that evil things are sent into the world to try us; they are sent deliberately by our Creator to test our mettle because He knows what is good for us. The Bible is full of cases where the easy way out has been discarded for moral principles.

I count myself fortunate in that I have seen the whole country and known men of every calling. But with the final test of war I consider my character fully developed. Thus at my early age my mission is already fulfilled and I am prepared to die with just one regret, and one only—that I could not devote myself to making your declining years more happy by being with you; but you will live in peace and freedom, and I shall have directly contributed to that, so here again my life will not have been in vain.

## WHENCE SHALL MY HELP COME?

*Psalms*

I will lift up mine eyes unto the mountains;
From whence shall my help come?
My help cometh from the Lord,
Who made heaven and earth.

He will not suffer thy foot to be moved;
He that keepeth thee will not slumber.
Behold, He that keepeth Israel
Doth neither slumber nor sleep.

The Lord is thy keeper;
The Lord is thy shade upon thy right hand.
The sun shall not smite thee by day,
Nor the moon by night.

The Lord shall keep thee from all evil;
He shall keep thy soul.
The Lord shall guard thy going out and thy coming in,
From this time forth and for ever.

*Isaiah*

Though he walketh in darkness,
And hath no light,
Let him trust in the name of the Lord,
And stay upon his God.

## HE GIVETH POWER TO THE FAINT
### *Isaiah*

Why sayest thou, O Jacob,
And speaketh, O Israel:
"My way is hid from the lord,
And my right is passed over from my God?"
Hast thou not known? hast thou not heard
That the everlasting God, the lord,
The Creator of the ends of the earth,
Fainteth not, neither is weary?
His discernment is past searching out.
He giveth power to the faint;
And to him that hath no might He increaseth strength.
Even the youths shall faint and be weary,
And the young men shall utterly fall;
But they that wait for the Lord shall renew their strength;
They shall mount up with wings as eagles;
They shall run, and not be weary;
They shall walk, and not faint.

## FROM "RESIGNATION"
### *Henry Wadsworth Longfellow*

We see but dimly through the mists and vapors;
Amid these earthly damps
What seem to us but sad, funereal tapers
May be heaven's distant lamps.

## OUT OF THE DARK PASSAGES WE EMERGE INTO LIGHT
### *From "Blessings and Praise"*

When suffering comes upon us, as it comes to all, we often fret desparingly and repine. We cannot understand why we should be made the apparent sport of misfortune and calamity. We wonder why tender affection should be created, only to be rudely broken; why agonizing pain should wreck our nerves and consume our flesh;

In moments of great sorrow, the stricken heart is apt to exclaim: "Surely God does not care, or else why does He inflict upon me such cruel pain!" The presence of evil—how baffling it is to our finite understanding!

Yet it is through struggle and sorrow that we learn to know more of the love and faithfulness of God than in any other way! We know only too well that sorrow often breaks the crust of a superficial life, uncovers its deepest realities. Through the dark cloud that envelops us, there breaks forth a new vision of the aim and purpose of our earthly existence. Not always on the heights, sometimes from the depths do we best see God. And seeing Him, we come to realize that our life is not a haphazard occurrence of chance events and circumstances, that a Divine hand and purpose are discernible in all that befalls us. Out of the dark passages of life, we emerge into the light of faith, purified in spirit, more keenly alert and responsive to the soft whisperings of the still small voice ever striving to speak to our hearts.

*Mary Frances Butts*

Build a little fence of trust around to-day;
Fill the space with loving works, and therein stay;
Look not through the sheltering bars upon tomorrow,
God will help thee bear what comes, of joy and sorrow.

*Job*

Though He slay me, yet will I trust in Him.

## WHAT GOD HATH PROMISED
*Annie Johnson Flint*

God hath not promised
Skies always blue,
Flower-strewn pathways
All our lives through;
God hath not promised
Sun without rain,
Joy without sorrow,
Peace without pain.

But God hath promised
Strength for the day,
Rest for the labor,
Light for the way,
Grace for the trials,
Help from above,
Unfailing sympathy,
Undying love.

*J. G. Holland*

Faith draws the poison from every grief, takes the sting from every loss, and quenches the fire of every pain; and only faith can do it.

*Nahum*

The Lord is good,
A stronghold in the day of trouble;
And He knoweth them that take refuge in Him.

*Abraham J. Heschel*

Faith is like a flashlight beam thrown ahead of us into the darkness. Its beam is always more visible when grief clouds about us. In some such events, an experience of faith kindles an unquenchable light.

## A TREE

*Esther M. Campbell*

A tree spoke to me today.
Can you see it? A strange sight,
Gnarled and twisted by the fury of the winds and sea.
You say, "How can you find beauty in its jagged form?"
Ah! But to me its message is more appealing
Than the quiet symmetry of a perfect tree.
My tree stands on a rocky crag jutting out over the mighty ocean.

Its footing seems precarious
Yet its roots are twined in and about the rock
Enabling it to withstand the storms that come.
And come they do—fierce gales that bend the tree back toward the
    land.
Whipping off its branches on the seaward side.
Again and again the winds have done their worst.
Trying to uproot my tree,
Trying to tear it from its moorings.
Yes, it has had to bend its back but it has never broken;
Its green arms can always stretch out to land.
The ocean spray has spit upon it,
Laughing at the seeming bravery of a single tree.
The tree is like a life—yours or mine perhaps.
The gales sweep about us
Threatening to tear us from our footing.
Sometimes they are about us; sometimes within us.
And we become twisted and warped,
Not able to maintain the beauty God intended for us.
Yet as we send down our roots of faith
His love and mercy flows through us and heals our scars
And helps us to reach out to others arms of help and kindness,
Enabling His beauty to still be seen in us,
Imperfect though we are.
Help us, O God,
To be as brave and unswerving as my tree.

## FROM "TRUST"

*John Greenleaf Whittier*

The same old baffling questions! O my friend,
I cannot answer them. In vain I send
My soul into the dark, where never burn
The lamps of science, nor the natural light
Of Reason's sun and stars! I cannot learn
Their great and solemn meanings, nor discern
The awful secrets of the eyes which turn
Evermore on us through the day and night
With silent challenge and a dumb demand,
Proffering the riddles of the dread unknown,
Like the calm Sphinxes, with their eyes of stone

Questioning the centuries from their veils of sand!
I have no answer for myself or thee,
Save that I learned beside my mother's knee:
"All is of God that is, and is to be;
And God is good." Let this suffice us still.
Resting in childlike trust upon his will
Who moves to his great ends unthwarted by the ill.

## EVERYTHING BEAUTIFUL IN ITS TIME

*Julius Mark*

"God hath made everything beautiful in its time. . . ."

A time for death? Yes, even death can be beautiful in its time and even when death may appear senseless and tragic, men of faith will declare with Job: "The Lord hath given; the Lord hath taken away. Blessed be the Name of the Lord," and derive strength from this confidence in the ways of God.

The late Jacob H. Schiff, perhaps the most distinguished American Jew of his generation, was such a man of complete faith in God. When a brother-in-law of Mr. Schiff's passed away at a comparatively young age, he felt the loss most keenly, since he had been strongly attached to him. From a friend, he received a letter of sympathy in which the former wrote: "Such events create atheists and agnostics, and embitter thinking people against the 'inscrutable ways of Providence.'"

Mr. Schiff replied: "It is true, sometimes goodness and righteousness appear for a time to go for naught, but the ways of God are always right. The laws of nature cannot be changed for anybody, or chaos would result; and even if we pray to God that He may hear us and do this or that for us, we pray for our own benefit and to strengthen ourselves, and not for the benefit of the Almighty. Pardon me, if I should appear to write you a sermon, but such is far from my intention; I only give expression to my own feelings, which have given me strength and courage in many a difficult situation during life."

This is the conviction of a man who believed that "God hath made everything beautiful in its time."

### Isaiah

The mind stayed on Thee Thou keepest in perfect peace;
Because it trusteth in Thee.

### F. L. Holmes

Faith will turn any course, light any path, relieve any distress, bring joy out of sorrow, peace out of strife, friendship out of enmity, heaven out of hell. Faith is God at work.

## ACCEPTANCE OF THE UNANSWERABLE
### Zelda Pophin

"Why did it have to happen?" everyone asks. The answer to this is the test of the individual's religious conviction. If his faith is deep and sincere, he replies simply: "This is God's will. This is divine wisdom. There is a higher judgment." Such a man possesses the faith which comforts and heals.

In others, an important recognition must be made—that there are things to which we have no answers at all, and that it is possible to accept what has happened without knowing why. For them, in that acceptance of the unanswerable, is the beginning of wisdom.

## WITHOUT GOD WHAT SENSE DOES LIFE MAKE?
### Walter Russel Bowie

What sense can be made out of the existence if rocks and earth and water and the dust beneath our feet go on enduring and human souls, which seem to be the fruition toward which all the slow forces of evolution have been working, should blindly and stupidly be brought to naught? In the face of such a universe, a man might laugh with contempt before he went to his annihilation. But we cannot believe that contemptuous laughter is the ultimate verdict to be passed upon our world. There must be within it something that has caused our own ideals, something akin to our passion for continuing life, and something upon which eternally we can rely.

God must be in it, and God is life, and God is love. Even in the moments when our intellect is baffled, and even in those times when contradictions beset our faith, still we refuse to be put to permanent intellectual and spiritual confusion and still our deepest souls declare that beyond the shadows there is light, and in the depths of the utmost darkness life goes upon its undefeated way.

## FROM "THE ONE PRAYER"

### James Montgomery

One prayer I have—all prayers in one—
    When I am wholly Thine;
Thy will, my God, thy will be done,
    And let that will be mine.

All-wise, almighty, and all-good,
    In thee I firmly trust;
Thy ways, unknown or understood,
    Are merciful and just.

May I remember that to thee
    Whate'er I have I owe;
And back, in gratitude, from me
    May all thy bounties flow.

And though thy wisdom takes away,
    Shall I arraign thy will?
No, let me bless thy name, and say,
    "The Lord is gracious still."

### Talmud

Let us thank God for the evil as well as for the good—indeed even though He take from us all our strength and possessions, for it is written: "Thou shalt love the Lord thy God with all thy might."

## I LEAVE IT TO GOD

### Joseph Rolnick (Translated from the Yiddish by Joseph Leftwich)

I leave all to God! Let Him lead me
Whither He will and how He will.

In not a thing shall I resist Him,
But like a child will follow still.

On mountain tops, in gaping chasms,
With eyes wide open, and yet blind,
Into the dens of wild beast, even.
Father leads—child follows behind.


*Samuel T. Coleridge*

He prayeth well who loveth well
Both man and bird and beast;
He prayeth best who loveth best
All things both great and small;
For the dear God who loveth us,
He made and loveth all.


# THE BULWARK AGAINST FINAL DESPAIR

## *Chad Walsh*

If a loved one dies, do you feel equal to meeting the loss single-handed? . . . The truth is that we are not built to bear the burden of sorrow and fear and loss alone. In any time of trouble we instinctively turn to our friends, and by their love and sympathy they share their strength with us. But friends are human beings like ourselves, and their strength is limited. They have their own heavy burdens. And sometimes our friends prefer to fade quietly out of the picture and leave us to ourselves and our private griefs and fears.

Only God is strong enough to give us the strength to face—everything that must be faced. . . . He is beside us when death robs us of those dearest to us. No barbed wire and steel doors can keep Him out. This is not mere theorizing. There is testimony from unnumbered voices that the man who carries a real sense of God's presence with him onto the battlefield or into the internment camp finds his Companion more unmistakably with him than before. "Where is your God now?" asked a Nazi guard of a Rabbi in an internment camp. "He is here," answered the Rabbi, "even here."

There is nothing sloppy or sentimental about this discovery. We remain ordinary men and women; our nerves and our emotions are still raw to suffering. But thanks to God, we are not overcome. We are able to endure what must be endured, and to find God in the midst of the worst that can assail us. God is the bulwark against final despair, the one completely solid and trustworthy source of lasting hope.

## AT THE PLACE OF THE SEA

*Annie Johnson Flint*

Have you come to the Red Sea place in your life
    Where, in spite of all you can do,
There is no way out, there is no way back,
    There is no other way but through?
Then wait on the Lord, with a trust serene,
    Till the night of your fear is gone;
He will send the winds, He will heap the floods,
    When He says to your soul, "Go On!"

And His hand shall lead you through, clear through,
    Ere the watery walls roll down;
No wave can touch you, no foe can smite,
    No mightiest sea can drown.
The tossing billows may rear their crests,
    Their foam at your feet may break,
But over their bed you shall walk dry-shod
    In the path that your Lord shall make.

In the morning watch, 'neath the lifted cloud,
    You shall see but the Lord alone,
When He leads you forth from the place of the sea,
    To a land that you have not known;
And your fears shall pass as your foes have passed
    You shall no more be afraid;
You shall sing His praise in a better place,
    In a place that His hand hath made.

*Samuel Longfellow*

Now our wants and burdens leaving
    To his care who cares for all,
Cease we fearing, cease we grieving,
    At his touch our burdens fall.

### Psalms

The Lord is my light and my salvation; whom shall I fear?
The Lord is the stronghold of my life; of whom shall I be afraid?

### Psalms

He shall call upon Me, and I will answer him;
I will be with him in trouble;
I will rescue him, and bring him to honour.

### Margaret E. Sangster

Oh, face to face with trouble,
Friend, I have often stood,
To learn that pain hath sweetness,
To know that God is good.
Arise and meet the daylight,
Be strong and do your best,
With an honest heart and a childlike trust
That God will do the rest.

### Psalms

God is our refuge and strength, An ever present help in trouble.

### Psalms

The sacrifices of God are a broken spirit; a broken and a contrite
heart, O God, Thou wilt not despise.

### Marcus Aurelius

Nothing happens to any man which he is not formed by nature
to bear.

### Author unknown

My life is but the weaving
Between my God and me.

I only choose the colors
He weaveth steadily.
Sometimes he weaveth sorrow
And I in foolish pride
Forget he sees the upper
And I the under side.

## THE BLIND MAN

*Margaret E. Sangster*

I see a blind man every day
Go bravely down the street;
He walks as if the path were clear
Before his steady feet.
Save when he fumbles with his cane,
I almost feel he sees
The passers-by who smile at him,
The flowers and the trees.

He comes to corners where the crowd
Of traffic swirls about,
But when he hesitates, some hand
Will always help him out.
He crosses pavements fearlessly,
It is as if he knows
That there are unknown, watchful friends
Along the way he goes!

Sometimes we walk through unseen paths,
Sometimes the road ahead
Is shrouded in the mists of fear;
But we are being led
As surely as the blind man is. . . .
And, if we seem to sway,
A hand will find us in the dark
And guide us on our way.

## *Isaiah*

As one whom his mother comforteth,
So will I comfort you;

## THE SHEPHERD KNOWS BEST
### *H. W. Smith*

The Shepherd knows what pastures are best for his sheep, and they must not question nor doubt, but trustingly follow him. Perhaps He sees that the best pastures for some of us are to be found in the midst of opposition or of earthly trials. If He leads you there, you may be sure they are green for you, and you will grow and be made strong by feeding there. Perhaps He sees that the best waters for you to walk beside will be raging waters of trouble and sorrow. If this should be the case, He will make them still waters for you, and you must go and lie down beside them, and let them have all their blessed influences upon you.

## NOT WITHOUT DESIGN DOES GOD WRITE
### *John Ruskin*

Not without design does God write the music of our lives. Be it ours to learn the time, and not be discouraged at the rests. If we say sadly to ourselves, "There is no music in a rest," let us not forget "there is the making of music in it." The making of music is often a slow and painful process in this life. How patiently God works to teach us! How long He waits for us to learn the lesson!

### *Midrash*

God has compassion like a father and comforts like a mother.

## THE ETERNAL GOODNESS
### *John Greenleaf Whittier*

I dimly guess from blessings known
Of greater out of sight,
And, with the chastened Psalmist, own
His judgments, too, are right.

I long for household voices gone,
   For vanished smiles I long,
But God hath led my dear ones on,
   And he can do no wrong.

I know not what the future hath
   Of marvel or surprise,
Assured alone that life and death
   His mercy underlies.

And if my heart and flesh are weak
   To bear an untried pain,
The bruised reed he will not break,
   But strengthen and sustain.

No offering of my own I have,
   Nor works my faith to prove;
I can but give the gifts he gave,
   And plead his love for love.

And so beside the Silent Sea
   I wait the muffled oar;
On ocean or on shore
   No harm from him can come to me.

I know not where his islands lift
   Their fronded palms in air,
I only know I cannot drift
   Beyond his love and care.

## FROM "SOMETIME"

*May Riley Smith*

Sometime, when all life's lessons have been learned,
And suns and stars forevermore have set,
The things which our weak judgments here have spurned,
The things o'er which we grieved with lashes wet,
Will flash before us out of life's dark night,
As stars shine most in deeper tints of blue;
And we shall see how all God's plans were right,
And what most seemed reproof was love most true.

## FROM "THE END OF SORROW"
*Edmond Fleg (Translated by Humbert Wolfe)*

We of our sorrows build in the days to come
For the soul of man that tall and ultimate home.
But you that pass tomorrow, as you pass today,
Build you as true as we, and go your way.

And then the sleeper, rising, cried on God:
"Again the torture, and again the road."
And stepping out into the dawn of all
He heard the Jews still weeping by the Wall.

"Dark are thy ways! O who can find them?
O Lord of distance, and yet we see
The day spring a wisp of Thy glory behind them,
The nightfall a step on the path to Thee."

## RAISING DOWNCAST EYES
*Jay Kaufman*

Slowly, with the recitation of the Kaddish and its words of Divine praise, there pierces the shroud of grief the realization that it was God in his endless mercy who had vouchsafed unto us the lifetime of the departed one and thus bequeathed us countless precious hours of exquisite love and sublime companionship. Such treasured memories gleaned in the rich harvest of daily living are not destroyed by death but live on imperishably. Tenderly they minister to aching hearts, these reflections on a life well lived, healing with all the magic of Gilead's balm. Inspiringly, they animate the noblest impulses, these memories of a life which cherished lofty ideals.

In moments when one is cast down, the Kaddish may raise downcast eyes heavenward offering the surest consolation, reassuring the mourner that He who taketh away, giveth in even greater measure.

## DEATH SERVES LIFE
### Robert W. MacKenna

Practically all the progress that man has made is due to the fact that he is mortal. If man knew that his days on earth were to be endless, all incentive to bestir himself—except to seek food and clothing—would be lost. There would be no desire to make his mark in the world, no stimulating ambition to leave the world a little better than he found it, no hungry aspiration to be remembered after he is dead. If there were no death, life would become a thing stagnant, monotonous and unspeakably burdensome.

### Deuteronomy

And thou shalt consider in thy heart, that, as a man chasteneth his son, so the Lord thy God chasteneth thee. . . .

### Talmud

God prepares the cure before the hurt.

### Henry H. Barry

In "pastures green?" Not always; sometimes He
Who knoweth best, in kindness leadeth me
In weary ways, where heavy shadows be.

So, whether on the hill-tops high and fair
I dwell, or in the sunless valleys, where
The shadows lie, what matter? He is there.

### Wisdom of Solomon

For Thou lovest all the things that are, and abhorrest nothing which Thou hast made: for never wouldst Thou have made any thing, if Thou hadst hated it. But Thou sparest all: for they are Thine O Lord, Thou lover of Souls.

## MY THOUGHTS ARE NOT YOUR THOUGHTS
### *Isaiah*

For My thoughts are not your thoughts,
Neither are your ways My ways, saith the Lord.
For as the heavens are higher than the earth,
So are My ways higher than your ways,
And My thoughts than your thoughts.
For as the rain cometh down and the snow from heaven,
And returneth not thither,
Except it water the earth,
And make it bring forth and bud,
And give seed to the sower and bread to the eater;
So shall My word be that goeth forth out of My mouth:
It shall not return unto Me void,
Except it accomplish that which I please,
And make the thing whereto I sent it prosper.


## WHATEVER HEAVEN DOES IS FOR THE BEST

*Moses Chayyim Luzzato (Translated from the Hebrew by Mordecai M. Kaplan)*

One mode of reasoning is, "Whatever Heaven does is for the best." This means that even suffering and hardship are only apparently evil; in reality they are good. The surgeon amputates a muscle or a limb which has been injured in order to preserve the health of the rest of the body, and to save the person from death. Though this seems cruel, it is in reality an act of mercy, and meant for the good of the person upon whom it is performed. That patient does not love the surgeon any the less because of what he has done to him; on the contrary, he loves him all the more. In like manner, if a man were to realize that whatever the Holy One, blessed be He, does to him, whether it affects his body or his possessions, is intended for his benefit, neither suffering nor hardship would lessen his love for God in any way, though he may little understand how he is benefited. On the contrary, his love would even become more intense and fervent.

*Deuteronomy*

The eternal God is a dwelling place, and underneath are the everlasting arms.

## IF I WERE GOD
### Frank S. Mead

Nasr-ed-Din Hodja, in the heat of the day, sat under a walnut tree looking at his pumpkin vines. He said to himself, "How foolish God is! Here he puts a great heavy pumpkin on a tiny vine without strength to do anything but lie on the ground. And he puts tiny walnuts on a big tree whose branches could hold the weight of a man. If I were God, I could do better than that!"

Just then a breeze dislocated a walnut in the tree, and it fell on the head of the skeptical Nasr-ed-Din Hodja, who rubbed his head, a sadder and a wiser man. "Suppose," he mused, "there had been a pumpkin up there, instead of a walnut. Never again will I try to plan the world for God, but I shall thank God that He has done so well!"

*Isaiah*

I, even I, am He that comforteth you;

*Lamentations*

For He doth not afflict willingly,
Nor grieve the children of men.

## WHATEVER IS—IS BEST
### Ella Wheeler Wilcox

I know as my life grows older
And mine eyes have clearer sight—
That under each rank wrong, somewhere
There lies the root of Right!

That each sorrow has its purpose,
By the sorrowing oft unguessed;
But, as sure as the sun brings morning,
Whatever is—is best.

## FROM "IN MEMORIAM"
### Alfred Tennyson

Oh, yet we trust that somehow good
    Will be the final goal of ill,
    To pangs of nature, sins of will,
Defects of doubt and taints of blood;

That nothing walks with aimless feet;
    That not one life shall be destroyed,
    Or cast as rubbish to the void,
When God hath made the pile complete;

Behold, we know not anything;
    I can but trust that good shall fall
    At last—far off—at last, to all,
And every winter change to spring.

### Ralph Waldo Emerson

The powers of the soul are commensurate with its needs.

## THE LOOM OF TIME
### Anonymous

Man's life is laid in the loom of time
To a pattern he does not see,
While the weavers work and the shuttles fly
Till the dawn of eternity.

Some shuttles are filled with silver threads
And some with threads of gold,
While often but the darker hues
Are all that they may hold.

But the weaver watches with skillful eye
Each shuttle fly to and fro,
And sees the pattern so deftly wrought
As the loom moves sure and slow.

God surely planned the pattern,
Each thread, the dark and fair,
Is chosen by His master skill
And placed in the web with care.

He only knows its beauty,
And guides the shuttles which hold
The threads so unattractive,
As well as the threads of gold.

Not till each loom is silent
And the shuttles cease to fly,
Shall God reveal the pattern
And explain the reason why

The dark threads were as needful
In the weaver's skillful hand
As the threads of gold and silver
For the pattern which He planned.

## DAILY BLESSINGS

*Louis Zangwill*

In the "Blessings on Various Occasions" we find a very warm jubilation of life—a spontaneous lyric appreciation of earth; joy in the fruits of the tree, the vine and the field; enchantment in the fragrant odours of barks, plants, fruits and spices; exaltation at the sight of stars, mountain, desert, sea and rainbow. Beautiful trees and animals, spring-blossoms equally with scholars and sages—all evoke their grace of appreciation. For storm and evil tidings, too, have their graces—in fortitude! The Hebrew genius could find growth through sorrow; and for the Hebrew, good tidings have their grace, no less than fair sights and experience. Everywhere the infiltration of Earth by Heaven.

## FROM "THE MYSTERY OF PROVIDENCE"
### *William Cowper*

God moves in a mysterious way
    His wonders to perform;
He plants his footsteps in the sea,
    And rides upon the storm.

Judge not the Lord by feeble sense,
    But trust him for his grace;
Behind a frowning providence
    He hides a smiling face.

His purposes will ripen fast,
    Unfolding every hour;
The bud may have a bitter taste,
    But sweet will be the flower.

Blind unbelief is sure to err,
    And scan his work in vain;
God is his own interpreter,
    And he will make it plain.

## I HAVE HAD THE DAY
### *S. Weir Mitchell*

I know the night is near at hand,
The mists lie low on hill and bay,
The autumn sheaves are dewless, dry;
But I have had the day.

Yes, I have had, dear Lord, the day:
When at Thy call I have the night,
Brief be the twilight as I pass
From light to dark, from dark to light.

You cannot prevent the birds of sorrow from flying over your head, but you can prevent them from building nests in your hair.

—Chinese Proverb

# HOW TO FACE SORROW

*Sorrow tests us as no other experience. It kicks out from under us the social stilts on which we frequently stand and rubs off the veneer we habitually wear. It most accurately mirrors us as we truly are, because in the fearful encounter with it we are compelled to draw most heavily upon our own human resources. Kind friends and loved ones can be of real service, but the ultimate verdict, whether sorrow defeats us or we surmount it, is rendered by our own wisdom and courage. When Macbeth asks the doctor whether he can prescribe "some sweet oblivious antidote" to a sorrowing heart, he answers: "Therein the patient must minister to himself."*

*This is not to say, however, that there are no outside sources of strength and counsel available to us. Quite the reverse is true. Others before us have endured the agony of grief and from the experience they distilled a measure of wisdom which they have recorded. In more recent times the psychology of grief has been explored more scientifically and the findings, taken together, constitute a genuine strategy for meeting sorrow and subduing it.*

*The passages which follow in this section can be reduced to three basic principles. In the first place, we ought not to feel ashamed to √ express the genuine grief we feel. It is for such a time as this that our tear ducts were made. The poet in a romantic mood may speak of "the silent manliness of grief" but it is hardly evidence of manliness to remain silent in grief. Such silence, such repressed emotions may be most dangerous to the mourner when they erupt at some later day in a more violent and damaging form. Ovid stood on firm psychological grounds when he cautioned "Suppressed grief suffocates." Judaism encourages us to "weep for the dead."*

120

*The second principle to guide us in our sorrow is that we must avoid the temptation to overindulge our grief. Grief in moderation is beneficial and healing. Taken in excess, it can destroy our will to live and rob us of our initiative. If we do not retain a vigilant emotional watch, grief can easily degenerate into self-pity which Fulton Oursler correctly called "a passport to insanity."*

*To guard against this psychic pitfall, we resort to a third principle which urges us to accept bravely what we cannot change, to go out of ourselves to transmute sorrow into service, to pass from feeling sorry for ourselves, which paralyzes, to feeling concern for others, which heals. The therapeutic power of this strategy is attested to by a number of genuine experiences which are described in this section. It is also reflected in an old Oriental tale.*

*There is a legend of a sorrowing woman who came to a wise man with the heart-rending plea that he return to her her only son whom she had just lost. He told her that he could comply with her request on one condition. She would have to bring to him a mustard seed taken from a home entirely free from sorrow. The woman set out on her quest. Years elapsed and she did not return. One day the wise man chanced upon her, but he hardly recognized her, for now she looked so radiant. He greeted her and then asked her why she had never kept their appointment. "Oh," she said in a tone of voice indicating that she had completely forgotten about it, "well, this is what happened. In search of the mustard seed, I came into homes so burdened with sorrow and trouble that I just could not walk out. Who better than I could understand how heavy was the burden they bore? Who better than I could offer them the sympathy they needed? So I stayed on in each home as long as I could be of service. And," she added apologetically, "please do not be angry, but I never again thought about our appointment."*

*Here is a most profound truth to remember when grief darkens our lives. Trouble and sorrow naturally make us think only of ourselves. But after the first impact of the blow has worn off, our emotional recovery depends upon our ability to forget ourselves. And there is no better way of forgetting about ourselves than by thinking of and serving others. Human experience every day confirms the truth of the legend. He who can do no better after sorrow than engage in the futile search for the mustard seed, to restore the loss which is in fact irretrievable, is destined to spend years of avoidable heartache. But happy is he who can rise from his mourner's bench and so lose himself in the service of others that he finds him-*

*self unknowingly climbing the mountain of healing to which the
road of service inevitably leads.*

---

## FROM "AUTUMN SONNETS #23"
### *Robert Nathan*

Hast thou a grief? Go clasp it to thy breast;
Hast thou a poison? Drain it to the end.
Cry then, cry all thy heart out with its pain;
Hearts grow again, and eyes have better sight
After too many tears, as summer rain
Washes the air, and leaves it sweet and bright,
And birds step out on trees, whose happy song
Is often stilled, but never stilled for long.

### *Henry Seidel Canby*

Success, as Shakespeare and Sophocles understood it, is the persistence of man's potential nobility in the teeth of circumstance and up to tragedy and beyond it.

## CONVERTING SORROW INTO SERVICE
### *Sidney Greenberg*

A story both sad and inspiring is woven about Leland Stanford University near San Francisco. It is named after the only son of the former governor of California. While on a visit to Italy with his parents, Leland Stanford, Jr., age nine, became ill and died. The grief-stricken parents returned to California and resolved to become the benefactors of other children, to give them the opportunities they could no longer lavish upon their own son. Thus they erected and heavily endowed the university which bears the name of their son. Here boys and girls of every group in America enjoy the opportunity of a university education. This blessing to untold young people was born in the anguish of a personal sorrow which heroic parents converted into a public service.

# THE LAWS OF GRIEF

## *Joshua Loth Leibman*

One of the greatest illusions about human nature is that the expression of grief will lead to a breakdown. *Quite the reverse.* No one has ever broken down nervously through the legitimate expression of an emotional reaction. . . . How absurd is that notion current in modern society that men and women must be safeguarded, coddled, and shielded against emotional outbursts. It is not those outbursts which harm the human organism, but the complete avoidance of them, which scars and tears the fabric of the inner soul.

The first law, then, which should be followed in the time of the loss of a loved one is: express as much grief as you actually feel. Do not be ashamed of your emotions. . . . Instead of trying to distract attention from the loss—a procedure that should come much later in the healing process—friends should offer the opportunity and encouragement to the man who has lost a loved one, to talk about his loss, to dwell upon his sorrow, and to rehearse the beauty and the virtues of the departed one.

A second new truth about the grief situation is this: *we must learn how to extricate ourselves from the bondage of the physical existence and coexistence of the loved one.* . . . Too many people make the mistake, in hours of bereavement, of closing the door to the mines of their spirits and permitting no entrance to new friends and comrades who could bring up much precious ore. These grief-stricken lives become abandoned mines with all of the unused shafts covered wth the cobwebs of self-pity.

The melody that the loved one played upon the piano of our life will never be played quite that way again, but we must not close the keyboard and allow the instrument to gather dust. We must seek out other artists of the spirit, new friends who gradually will help us to find the road to life again, who will walk on that road with us. The establishment of new patterns of interaction with other people, beginning with the interaction of language and moving on to new avenues of creative expression, is the second law for the conquest of grief and the conquest of death.

A third law may be expressed as follows: when death destroys an important relationship, it is essential that someone be found partially capable of replacing that relationship. Equilibrium will be restored when the bereaved person discovers some situation demanding the same or similar patterns of conduct. For example, a mother who loses a young child has suffered one of the most tragic bereavements of all. . . . What can be done to bring into play this law of pattern replacement? A mother after the death of her own child should be encouraged, for example, to interest herself in daily work at a nursery school. She should be stimulated to transfer the conduct pattern which she had fashioned in her relationship with her own child into work with a group of children.

It would be unwise for this mother to adopt a baby immediately, because unconsciously she would feel disloyal to her own dead child in this speedy transference of love to a stranger. A very wise solution occurs if the bereaved mother dilutes her affection at first over a wide area in working with the nursery-school children. Then, when the first deep wound has partially healed, she either adopts a child or has one of her own and bestows upon it her mature and devoted affection.

## TEARS REFRESH

### Leigh Hunt

A Grecian philosopher being asked why he wept for the death of his son, since the sorrow was in vain, replied, "I weep on that account." And his answer became his wisdom. It is only for sophists to contend that we, whose eyes contain the fountains of tears, need never give way to them. It would be unwise not to do so on some occasions. Sorrow unlocks them in her balmy moods. The first bursts may be bitter and overwhelming; but the soil on which they pour would be worse without them. They refresh the fever of the soul. . . .

Where we feel that tears would relieve us, it is false philosophy to deny ourselves at least that first refreshment; and it is always false consolation to tell people that because they cannot help a thing, they are not to mind it. The true way is, to let them grapple with the unavoidable sorrow, and try to win it into gentleness by a reasonable yielding. There are griefs so gentle in their very nature that it would be worse than false heroism to refuse them a tear. . . . The end is an acquittal from the harsher bonds of affliction, from the tying down of the spirit to one melancholy idea.

It is the nature of tears of this kind, however strongly they may gush forth, to run into quiet waters at last. We cannot easily, for the whole course of our lives, think with pain of any good and kind person whom we have lost. It is the divine nature of their qualities to conquer pain and death itself; to turn the memory of them into pleasure; to survive with a placid aspect in our imaginations.

### William Cowper

Oh, then indulge thy grief, nor fear to tell
The gentle source from whence thy sorrows flow!
Nor think it weakness when we love to feel,
Nor think it weakness what we feel to show.

## TEARS BORDER ON THE SACRED

### Grace Perkins Oursler and April Armstrong

What is this taboo on tears? Men hate to see tears. They shy away from crying women, and frown on tears in their own sex. Tears disfigure and ravage, yes. But modern mankind's distress stems from the abuse of weeping. The tears of the morally weak, the infantile personality, the self-indulgent, and the spiritual thief who uses them to burglarize another's principles are so repelling and so degenerating as to give rise to general condemnation of weepers.

But God Almighty gave us tears. It is unlikely that they are meant merely to chap our cheeks when the wind stings our eyes. Or just to keep the eyeballs moist.

No one really denies their importance. We must breathe, eat, sweat, digest, expel—and weep. Tears border on the sacred; they are the only off-casting of our bodies that flows from spiritual and emotional wounds. They are the only channel to release dammed-up sensibilities, letting out the poisonous streams of anxiety that can infect our whole being. Even those we cause ourselves, due to temper, self-will, self-pity, pride, fear of punishment or terror are a safeguard against more disastrous behavior. . . .

We weep at separations that we would not change, but which cut deep at habits and comforts nonetheless. Beyond such weeping are emotions of faith and hope—and great selflessness. . . . The tears for another, the tears of grief, these are holy tears when shed from a pure heart. . . .

So why be ashamed or nonplused at grief, then, or cheat ourselves in denying its expression? Tears are a necessary adjunct to shock. . . .

In Oriental countries one can still find the delicate little tear vases used by the mourners in bereavement. Their philosophy did not discount the cleansing and draining purposes of crying. And they held that the most sacred tears we have are wept for those who have done with this world and are carried on to the mysteries of the next, leaving us to battle out the finish. Those tear bottles were kept and often were buried with the person mourned, where archaeologists now come across them.

## *Amiel*

It is dangerous to abandon one's self to the luxury of grief: it deprives one of courage, and even of the wish for recovery.

## *Herbert Spencer*

He oft finds medicine who his grief imparts.

## "DO NOT WEEP TOO MUCH"

*Hannah Avrech (Translated from the Hebrew by the editor)*

*A letter sent to parents of a casualty in Israel's War of Independence by his fiancee. She herself was killed in an airplane accident shortly after she wrote this letter.*

Warmest greetings, dear friends:

It is difficult for me to write, for the pain has not yet left my heart and my soul still weeps over the tragedy which befell us.

. . . It happened on the 15th of May, in the battle for Malchiya in Galilee. There were many killed and wounded in this engagement and fate selected us, too. I still do not know all the details. One thing I am certain of, however, is that Yehuda died a hero's death. He knew what he was fighting for and the goal to which he dedicated all his strength and energy. He was always prepared for anything that might happen and I am certain that his last wish was that we should be strong and know how to conquer everything.

. . . I have one request to make: Be brave and do not weep too much. He was one of many and the duty which he fulfilled compels us to carry on in his way. Be courageous and strong! This is the wish of your daughter whose fiancé fell in battle. It will be easier for me to carry on if I know that you have gained mastery over your feelings.

### Fulton Oursler

Sometimes it is hard, when life gets tough not to feel sorry for ourselves. Yet self-pity is deadly as arsenic to peace of the heart. If we can only keep our souls clean of that poison, we can generally find a way out of trouble.

## THE DANGERS OF SELF-PITY
### Louis Binstock

We must see the danger in sorrow when allowed to become a source of self-pity. Man, even as the lower animals, delights in licking and nursing his own wounds. It is not only the child that feels a peculiar pleasure in believing itself to be misunderstood and mistreated, but also the adult. One of the basic causes for self-inflicted injury, and sometimes suicide, is this human tendency to be sorry for oneself, and to make others also suffer the consequences of the sorrow. "You'll be sorry," cries the child. The adult does not use these words, yet his actions clearly express them. Many an adult becomes a child again when sorrow comes into his life. He cannot rest content until he has made all those around him share his sorrow and suffer with him.

Self-pity wastes time and weakens energy. Self-pity dilutes initiative and destroys venturesomeness. That is true of peoples and nations as well as individuals. Stefan Zweig has written a novel entitled *Beware of Pity,* in which he warns against the pitfalls of pity. Self-pity, however, holds hidden for us the deepest and most dangerous pitfalls of all. Let us understand that it is of no avail for peoples and nations any more than individuals to spend their days being sorry for themselves, bewailing their fate. Time and energy consumed in weeping over a sorrow may be put to much more intelligent and helpful use if conserved for meeting the grave problems that the sorrow has created. Self-pity never removes the sorrow. It only delays the solution of the difficulties and the danger out of which the sorrow grew. And it blinds us to larger and wider sorrows which we share in common with all humanity.

*Benjamin Disraeli*

Grief is the agony of an instant; the indulgence of grief, the blunder of a life.

*Shakespeare*

Moderate lamentation is the right of the dead;
Excessive grief the enemy to the living.

## THE THREE CHOICES
### Harry Lauder

When, during World War I, Sir Harry Lauder, the great Scot comedian, heard that his son had been killed in France, he said: "In a time like this there are three courses open to a man. He may give way to despair, sour upon the world, and become a grouch. He may endeavor to drown his sorrow in drink or by a life of waywardness and wickedness. Or he may turn to God."

## COMING THROUGH THE STORM
### Charles Lewis Slattery

A story is told of the artist Turner, that one day he invited Charles Kingsley into his studio to see a picture of a storm at sea. Kingsley was rapt in admiration. "How did you do it, Turner?" he exclaimed. Turner answered: "I wished to paint a storm at sea, so I went to the coast of Holland, and engaged a fisherman to take me out in his boat in the next storm. The storm was brewing, and I went down to his boat and bade him bind me to its mast. Then he drove the boat out into the teeth of the storm. The storm was so furious that I longed to lie down in the bottom of the boat and allow it to blow over me. But I could not: I was bound to the mast. Not only did I see that storm and feel it, but it blew itself into me, till I became part of the storm. And then I came back and painted that picture."

Turner's experience is a parable of life. Life is sometimes cloud and sometimes sunshine; sometimes pleasure, sometimes pain; sometimes defeat, sometimes victory. Life is a great mingling of happiness and tragic storm. He who comes out of it rich in living is he who dares to accept it all, to face it all, to let it blow its power and its mystery and its tragedy into the inmost recesses of his soul. The victory, so won in this life, will then be an eternal possession. A loving God allows us to be absorbed in one life at a time, quite ignorant of what is ahead, lest we lose the glory which He provides for our enriching as we pass through it.

## FROM "A PRAYER"

*Max Ehrmann*

Let me do my work each day;
And if the darkened hours of despair overcome me
May I not forget the strength that comforted me
In the desolation of other times.
May I still remember the bright hours that found me
Walking over the silent hills of my childhood,
Or dreaming on the margin of the quiet river,
When a light glowed within me,
And I promised my early God to have courage
Amid the tempests of the changing years.

## GREAT GOOD HAS COME FROM BEREAVEMENT

*Zelda Popkin*

Out of the human understanding which grows from bereavement great good has come. No single force in the modern world has been as constructive as the urge to perpetuate the memory of our beloved dead by service to humanity.

Once, men built pyramids and palaces of stone. Today they add to the goodness of life and to its progress, through the scholarship, the children's ward and the research fund. Each cancer laboratory and hospital is a memorial to some man or woman whose life was cut short.

Damon Runyon is immortalized as much by the Cancer Fund raised in his name as by the stories he wrote. The daughter of a great actress and a famous playwright died of polio at nineteen, but hundreds of children may live because the Mary MacArthur Memorial Fund provides iron lungs and nursing care for polio victims.

The daughter of the Spencer Trasks could not speak clearly when she gave their Saratoga estate its name, but "Yaddo," her childish rhyme for "shadow," has meant to a generation of creative workers a chance to write and paint in gracious, inspiring surroundings.

## MEETING SORROW UPRIGHT

### Joseph H. Hertz

According to ancient Jewish custom the ceremony of cutting our garments, when our nearest and dearest on earth is lying dead before us, is to be performed standing up. This teaches: meet all sorrow standing upright. The future may be dark, veiled from the eye of mortals—but not the manner in which we are to meet the future. To rail at life, to rebel against a destiny that has cast our lines in unpleasant places, is of little avail. We cannot lay down terms to life. Life must be accepted on its own terms. But hard as life's terms are, life (it has been finely said) never dictates unrighteousness, unholiness, dishonor.

## HELPING THE LIVING

### Fulton Oursler

This is the story of a miracle.

It was a miracle witnessed by a recording clerk in a cemetery. Every week, for several years, this mild little man had received a letter from a woman he did not know, enclosing a money order and directing him to put fresh flowers on the grave of her son. Then one day he met her face to face. A car drove up to the cemetery gates and a chauffeur hastened into the tiny administration building to speak to the birdlike little clerk whose hands fluttered over the papers on his desk.

"The lady outside is too ill to walk," he explained. "Would you mind coming with me?"

Waiting in the car was a frail elderly woman with a face whose imperious eyes could not hide some deep, long-lasting hurt. In her arms was a great heap of flowers.

"I am Mrs. Adams," she explained. "Every week for years I have been sending you a five-dollar money order—"

"For the flowers!" the clerk exclaimed.

"Yes—to be laid on the grave of my son."

"I have never failed to attend to it," chirped the little man.

"I came here today," Mrs. Adams confided softly, "because the doctors have let me know I have only a few weeks left. I shall not be sorry to go. There is nothing left to live for. But before I die I wanted to drive here for one last look and place the flowers myself."

The little clerk blinked up at her irresolutely. Then, with a wry smile, he made up his mind and spoke.

"You know, ma'am, I was always sorry you kept sending the money for the flowers."

"Sorry?"

"Yes—because the flowers last such a little while! And nobody ever could see them or smell them. It was a shame."

"Do you realize what you are saying?"

"Oh, please don't be angry. I belong to a visiting society. State hospitals. Insane asylums. People in places like that dearly love flowers, and they can see them and can smell them. Lady, there's living people in places like that. But there isn't anybody in that grave. Not really."

The woman did not answer, but sat for a brief while, silently repeating a prayer. When she left, without a word, the little clerk feared that his impulsive frankness might have overcome her, might even have hastened her end.

But some months later he was astonished to have another visit; doubly astonished, in fact, because there was no chauffeur this time; the woman sat at the wheel, driving her car alone.

"I take the flowers to the people myself," she confided with a friendly smile. "You were right; it does make them happy. And it makes me happy. The doctors don't know what is making me well— but I do! I have something to live for now!"

She had discovered what most of us know and forget—in helping others she had miraculously helped herself. It is still true that our chief need in life is somebody who shall make us do what we can. Nothing makes us so strong as a cry for help.

## HOW TO BEAR SORROW
*Charles Kingsley*

I believe that the wisest plan is sometimes not to try to bear sorrow—as long as one is not crippled for one's everyday duties—but to give way to it utterly and freely. Perhaps sorrow is sent that we may give way to it, and in drinking the cup to the dregs, find some medicine in it itself, which we should not find if we began doctoring ourselves or letting others doctor us. If we say simply, "I am wretched—I ought to be wretched," then we shall perhaps hear a voice: "Who made thee wretched but God? Then what can He mean but thy good?" And if the heart answers impatiently: "My good? I don't want it, I want my love," perhaps the voice may answer: "Then thou shalt love both in time."

*Miguel de Cervantes*

He who loses wealth loses much. He who loses a friend loses more. But he that loses his courage loses all.

*Proverbs*

If thou faint in the day of adversity, thy strength is small.

*Samuel Johnson*

Sorrow is the mere rust of the soul. Activity will cleanse and brighten it.

## INVICTUS
*William Ernest Henley*

Out of the night that covers me,
Black as the pit from pole to pole,
I thank whatever gods may be
For my unconquerable soul.

In the fell clutch of circumstance
I have not winced nor cried aloud.
Under the bludgeonings of chance
My head is bloody, but unbowed.

Beyond this place of wrath and tears
Looms but the horror of the shade,
And yet the menace of the years
Finds and shall find me unafraid.

It matters not how strait the gate,
How charged with punishments the scroll,
I am the master of my fate:
I am the captain of my soul.

## WE CAN CONQUER SORROW

### *Louis Binstock*

. . . He who has entered within the doors of another's sorrow stands on the threshold of the gates of heaven. He understands the wisdom contained in the old rabbinic teaching: "This also for good." He has caught something of the religious spirit implicit in the two divine truths basic to both Judaism and Christianity: the one fatherhood of God and the one brotherhood of man—"Thou shalt love the Lord thy God with all thy heart, and with all thy soul, and with all thy might, and thou shalt love thy neighbor as thyself." Love of God means, fundamentally, faith in His sorrow and His love for mankind. For sorrow is universal and inevitable —but we can control it, we can conquer it.

## WE DO NOT STAND ALONE

### *Morris Adler*

It is an early weekday morn. A quiet residential street of the dynamic city is still enveloped in a drowsy stillness. Soon life will awake in its silent and comfortable houses and noisy children, after a hasty breakfast, will leap through doors, schoolward bound. Men can be seen entering one of the houses. Their bearing is marked by reverence and solemnity. Sorrow has recently visited one of the homes on the street and friends are gathering for the mourning service. Within the residence, candles are lit, tefillin and talesim are quietly donned and the voice of prayer is heard in the hushed atmosphere.

Long ago a people developed this practice so rich in meaning that neither the passing of centuries nor the roaring life of a metropolitan center has been able to render it obsolete. The friends are no longer individuals come to express sympathy, each in his particular way, with the feeling that the degree of his own friendship with the mourners dictates. The individuals have merged into a "minyan," a congregation. They have coalesced into an "eidah," a community. Though this community is small in numbers, it represents in every religious detail the larger K'lal Yisroel of which each identified Jew is part. Thus does a community symbolically and actually share in the sorrow of one of its members. The grief of the individual re-echoes in the life of the group. No Jew stands alone in his bereavement, while his personal anguish serves as a wall between him and all those upon whose way in life the dark shadow has not fallen. A people closes ranks and encircles its stricken member with the warmth of brotherly sympathy.

The religious service of this little group, representing the larger community, takes place in the home. It is a tribute to the central position of the home. Where a family lives and loves and fashions the most intimate bonds to link persons one to the other—you have a sanctuary appropriate for worship. For the home is a sanctuary no less than the Synagogue. Its holiness is of no lesser kind than that with which the formal house of prayer of the entire community is invested. The poignancy and sanctity of grief are best expressed in the intimate sanctuary of the home. The sanctuary of the home can never be replaced by Synagogue or Temple, however large or magnificent.

The prayer is concluded. The imperatives of modern living compel the minyan to dissolve once again into its component individuals who hurry through streets, now filled with romping and laughing children and speeding automobiles, to offices, shops and plants. The mourners remain. They are, however, no longer completely alone. In the atmosphere of their home the prayers linger and bespeak the solace of a tradition and the brotherhood of a community.

### William James

Be willing to have it so. Acceptance of what has happened is the first step to overcoming the consequences of any misfortune.

*Leigh Hunt*

Whenever evil befalls us, we ought to ask ourselves, after the first suffering, how we can turn it into good. So shall we take occasion, from one bitter root, to raise perhaps many flowers.

*Chaim Nachman Bialik*

Afflictions are really not a good gift—neither they nor their consequences. However, if afflictions do come, it is well that we convert them into afflictions of love. Herein lies the power of man.

## TURNING GRIEF INTO THE GIVING OF SUCCOR

*John Bright*

I was in the depths of grief, I might almost say of despair, for the light and sunshine of my house had been extinguished. All that was left on earth of my young wife, except the memory of a sainted life and a too brief happiness, was lying still and cold in the chamber above us. Mr. Cobden called upon me, and addressed me, as you might suppose, with words of condolence. After a time he looked up and said, "There are thousands of houses in England at this moment where wives, mothers and children are dying of hunger. Now," he said, "when the first paroxysm of your grief is past, I would advise you to come with me, and we will never rest till the Corn Law is repealed."

I accepted his invitation. I knew that the description he had given of the homes of thousands was not an exaggerated description. I felt in my conscience that there was a work which somebody must do, and therefore I accepted his invitation, and from that time we never ceased to labor hard on behalf of the resolution which we had made.

*Ben Jonson*

To struggle when hope is banished!
To live when life's salt is gone!
To dwell in a dream that's vanished—
To endure, and go calmly on!

## THE WISDOM OF ACCEPTING THE INEVITABLE

*Fulton Oursler*

Much of our happiness and our misery spring entirely from our attitude toward events. It depends on how you look at a thing— how you change it, or else how you accept it. There's no use fighting the inevitable. The only way to argue with a cold wind is to put on your overcoat. And then there's that famous prayer: "God give me the courage to change the things I can change, and the serenity to accept the things I can't change, and the wisdom to know the difference."

Like the soldier who lost his arm. Or did he?

This soldier was wounded in one of the early battles of the Second World War. On the operating table in a field hospital he opened his eyes and saw a doctor bending over him.

"It's all right, kid," the surgeon was saying, "you're going to get well. But I'm afraid you've lost your arm."

The soldier grinned, and in a faint voice replied: "I didn't lose my arm—I gave it."

In great matters and small, what happens to us is not nearly so important as our attitude toward it. The future of that maimed soldier was full of hope because of his positive point of view. He did not yield to despair. Every misfortune in life is an opportunity for advancement in spiritual strength for which we should be truly grateful. It all depends on how we meet God's challenge to us.

*Madame Guyon*

Ah, if you knew what peace there is in an accepted sorrow!

*William Cowper*

Beware of desperate steps; the darkest day,
Lived till tomorrow, will have passed away.

## TO FACE LIFE WITH DARING
*Charles Lewis Slattery*

. . . Think of the people great and small who do not accept sorrow with poise and with strength. Think of the people who shelter their children from every peril, till their children, grown fat and useless, cumber the roadway of life. . . .

. . . Think of the people who, when sorrow smites them, go madly afield in gay revels, so hoping to drown their agony in forgetfulness. Think of the people who, having compassed every known device to avoid the inevitable sorrow to which all flesh is heir, and who, having it thrust upon them at the last, still protest against it, cursing God because He allows it and filling the air with their groans. Like children they are, who when sent to bed go because they must, but as they climb the stairs nastily kick each stair, by way of angry protest. One glance at these groups of people who refuse with any sort of grace to accept the sorrow of life, shows one the high relief in which those others stand who, though they know not why, take the sorrow in, and take it consciously in all its bitterness.

. . . Sorrow endures but for a season, and joy comes with the morning. But the joy comes because the sorrow has been felt and gracefully, nobly accepted. Then let us pray for a recklessness which is beyond the recklessness of war; a recklessness which faces life with equal daring whether it presents pleasure or pain, joy or sorrow, life or death.


## BEND WITH THE WIND

*Grandma Fontaine, one of the tart characters in Margaret Mitchell's* Gone With the Wind, *gave forth a bit of wisdom which is worth singling out for reflection right now when some people are finding it hard to sustain their courage.*

"We bow to the inevitable. We're not wheat, we're buckwheat! When a storm comes along, it flattens ripe wheat because it's dry and can't bend with the wind. But ripe buckwheat's got sap in it and it bends. And when the wind has passed, it springs up almost as straight and strong as before."

Bend with the wind—don't let life break your spirit. After your trials and disappointments and discouragements, spring back again like buckwheat! Don't let the things that can't be helped flatten you. Bide your time. Have patience. And after the storm straighten up and go forward.

## LORD, HELP ME TO FORGET

### Ross L. Holman

I realize, of course, how much easier it is to want to forget than it is to do it, but noted psychiatrists say it can be done not only by the substitution of pleasant memories for unpleasant ones, but by engaging in mind-diverting activities. A married couple lost an only child. The doctor had already told them they could never have another. It looked as though their rose-tinted world had collapsed beneath them. Ever since he was born they had been practically living for that kid.

For months after the child had been laid away, the couple spent much of their time at the grave, mourning their hearts out. The man's business affairs suffered.

Finally their pastor suggested that they could find release by interesting themselves in other people's children. They did. The man organized a basketball team among the boys in his community. In his spare time he led them on hikes and took them on camping trips. The wife found it great fun to invite smaller children in for a party, kiddy games, and refreshments. She directed recreational activities for older girls.

The youngsters of the community idolized this couple and the feeling was shared by their parents. Life took on a new meaning. Their many interests crowded out the aching memory of a tragic event.

W. E. Sangster says: "Conscious memory has a preference for the pleasant. She is always trying to stuff painful experiences down the hole of oblivion and to preserve only the things we are glad to recall. . . . One may not always be able to forget a tragic occurrence . . . the real danger in remembering the wrong things is that we remember them not as facts, but as convulsive experiences."

*Robert Louis Stevenson*

Quiet minds cannot be perplexed or frightened, but go on in fortune or misfortune at their own private pace, like a clock during a thunderstorm.

*Author unknown*

When you dig another out of his trouble, you find a place to bury your own.

*Midrash*

Said Rabbi Elazar ben Jacob: "When sufferings come upon him, man must utter thanks to God, for suffering draws man near unto the Holy One, blessed be He. As it saith: Whom the Lord loveth, He correcteth, even as a father correcteth the son in whom he delighteth. When griefs come upon a man, let him stand up and receive them, thus his reward will be beyond measure."

## AS YOU GO THROUGH LIFE

*Ella Wheeler Wilcox*

This world will never adjust itself
To suit your whims to the letter;
Some things must go wrong your whole life long
And the sooner you know it the better.
It is folly to fight with the Infinite,
And go under at last in the wrestle,
The wiser man shapes into God's plan
As the water shapes into a vessel.

## USING THE DARK THREADS

*Sidney Greenberg*

Oriental rugs which are found in many homes are all woven by hand. Usually, there will be a group of people weaving a single rug together under the directions of an artist who issues instructions to the rest. He determines the choice of colors and the nature of the pattern.

It often happens that one of the weavers inserts the wrong color thread. The artist may have called for blue and instead black was used. If you examine an oriental rug carefully, you may be able to detect such irregularities. What is significant about them is that they were not removed. The skillful artist just proceeded to weave them into the pattern.

Here is a wise procedure that we can follow in life. We should like the pattern of our lives to be woven exclusively of bright-colored threads. But every now and then a dark thread steals into the fabric. If we are true artists of life we can weave even this thread into the pattern and make it contribute its share to the beauty of the whole.

*Thomas Carlyle*

From the lowest depth there is a path to the loftiest height.

## COMFORT IN SERVICE
### *Helen Hayes*

I have found comfort in doing, in visiting those who have been struck down, the children and the parents, in thinking that through Mary's death perhaps she and I were destined to have a little part in the final victory. I have learned ineffable gratitude for the Scriptural commandment to love thy neighbor as thyself. Now at last I know the solace that comes from its meaning. Once I thought it old-fashioned, empty, but it now shines with a new radiance out of the depths of its truth and simplicity.

Before I had only loved myself. My aim was to make others love me. It wasn't selfish or mean, but I had never known what it was to love others as myself. I will not say that my world has been made whole again—it never can be—but there has been acceptance, even happiness, in giving and doing. "For," as Pearl S. Buck has so knowingly written, "there is an alchemy in sorrow. It can be transmuted into wisdom which, if it does not bring joy, can yet bring happiness."

## WE MUST NOT EXPECT MIRACULOUS HEALING

### *Joshua Loth Liebman*

We must face grief without any expectation of miraculous healing, but with the knowledge that if we are courageous and resolute we can live as our loved ones would wish us to live, not empty, morose, self-centered, and self-pitying, but as brave and undismayed servants of the greater life. Rabbinic wisdom teaches this approach to grief in the following passages: "When the second Temple in Jerusalem was destroyed, many Jews began to withdraw from life and sank into a state of depressed mourning for the sons and daughters of Israel that had perished and also for the Temple that had gone up in smoke. They refused to eat and to drink." Rabbi Joshua said to them: "My sons, I know that it is impossible not to mourn, but to mourn excessively is forbidden." Why? Because that great Jewish sage felt that we human beings must think not only of the past but of the future. We are commanded by our religion to be the servants of life as long as we live.


### *Martin F. Tupper*

Never give up! If adversity presses,
Providence wisely has mingled the cup,
And the best counsel, in all your distresses,
Is the stout watchword of "Never give up."


### *George Moore*

So long as one does not despair, so long as one doesn't look upon life bitterly, things work out fairly well in the end.


### *C. F. Deems*

To dare is great. To bear is greater. Bravery we share with brutes. Fortitude with saints.

*Helen Keller*

I thank God for my handicaps, for, through them, I have found myself, my work, and my God.

## THE JACKPOT OF COURAGE

*Fulton Oursler*

The law of recompense for unselfish heroism is seldom talked about. Yet here is a remarkable illustration of the potency of the law.

Take the strange case of Dr. McAlister, the weeping physician of the Eastern Shore, as he was known in Maryland. Dr. McAlister's beautiful wife, whom he loved devotedly, died while still young. The shock of her passing plunged him into a melancholy that was like a paralysis; he would not talk or eat, and he was obsessed with a desire for self-destruction. For years he was guarded by three nurses, on eight-hour duty. Grieving more and more, he became an emaciated shell of his former self; he had to be lifted from his chair to his bed and coaxed to eat. How he detested his three nurses!

In summer he was taken to the seashore, where he liked to sit in his wheel chair on a bluff overlooking the ocean. One afternoon he surprised his nurse by suggesting that she take a swim.

"You can watch me just as well from the water," he said cunningly.

When the nurse, who should have suspected what he was up to, did go in swimming, Dr. McAlister sat quietly watching her, waiting for the opportune moment to throw himself from the cliffs to the rocks below. Then came a scream; the nurse, seized with a cramp, was drowning.

It is a matter of historical record that Dr. McAlister stood up, walked without hesitation to a point on the headland jutting out over the water, and plunged down. Swimming to the help of the screaming nurse, he brought her in to the beach. And, with strength from fathomless sources, he worked over her until she was safely alive. That was the end of Dr. McAlister's melancholy. In restoring life to the nurse, whom he thoroughly disliked, he had lost all desire to die, and thereafter found a new pleasure in living.

Can it be true, what so many believe, that there is some deep therapeutic power in the sacrifice love offers up? A power affecting not only spirit, but body—removing and remedying physical ills?

## A NEW HORIZON

### *Myrtle Dean Clark*

Dead wood carried—heavy rot became;
Dead wood burned—a brilliant flame.
Misfortune carried—the very heart grew lame;
Misfortune used—a new horizon came.

### *Harriet Beecher Stowe*

When you get into a tight place and everything goes against you, till it seems as though you could not hold on a minute longer, never give up then, for that is just the place and time that the tide will turn.

## THE WEEPING FATHER

### *Louis I. Newman*

An ancient parable of the East tells of the father who daily went to weep at the tomb of his son. The son from his abode of happiness looked with compassion upon his father, and at length, assuming human form again, descended on earth, and throwing himself down near the tomb where his father lay, began to weep with violence. The father, approaching, said: "Young man, why are you weeping?" "I am weeping," replied the youth, "because I yearn for the sun and the moon to make a pair of wheels for my chariot." "Young man," said the father, "you must have lost your reason. We cannot make chariot-wheels out of the sun and the moon?" The youth answered: "You are weeping for a mortal whose transient life has passed away; but I weep for the sun and the moon which I continually have before me."

## LET US REJOICE AT OUR TRIALS
### Stefan Zweig

Our God, the God of our fathers, is a hidden God; and not until we are bathed in sorrow are we enabled to discern him. He chooses those only whom he has tried, and to none but the suffering does he give his love. Let us therefore rejoice at our trials, brothers, and let us love the suffering God sends. He has broken us with affliction, that he may sink the deeper into the freshly ploughed ground of our hearts, and that we may be ready for the scattering of his seed. He has weakened our bodies that we may strengthen our souls. Let us joyfully enter the smelting furnace of his will, that thereby we may be purified. Follow the example of your forefathers, and thankfully accept the scourgings of the Almighty!

## MAKING STEMS OUT OF SCRATCHES
### A Parable of the Dubner Maggid

A king once owned a large, beautiful, pure diamond of which he was justly proud, for it had no equal anywhere. One day, the diamond accidentally sustained a deep scratch. The king called in the most skilled diamond cutters and offered them a great reward if they could remove the imperfection from his treasured jewel. But none could repair the blemish. The king was sorely distressed.

After some time a gifted lapidary came to the king and promised to make the rare diamond even more beautiful than it had been before the mishap. The king was impressed by his confidence and entrusted his precious stone to his care. And the man kept his word.

With superb artistry he engraved a lovely rosebud around the imperfection and he used the scratch to make the stem.

We can emulate that craftsman. When life bruises us and wounds us, we can use even the scratches to etch a portrait of beauty and charm.

## IT IS WHAT YOU HAVE LEFT
## THAT COUNTS
### *Harold Russell*

There is no easy formula for a happy living. Anyone who says he has one is either joking or lying. Even if I could, I have no intention or desire of putting forth any patented, neatly packaged recipe of my own. But there is one simple thought I should like to pass on, if I may. It is no sure-fire prescription for happiness; it is not guaranteed to bring any bluebirds singing in your back yard. I offer it merely because I found it can help prevent much vain regret and self-defeat. It is not what you have lost, but what you have left that counts. Too many of us squander precious energy, time, and courage dreaming of things that were and never can be again, instead of dedicating ourselves to realities and the heavy tasks of today.

## HOW TO HELP SOMEONE IN SORROW
### *Howard Whitman*

Most of us want to be helpful when grief strikes a friend, but often we don't know how. We may end up doing nothing because we don't know the right—and helpful—things to say and do. Because that was my own experience recently, I resolved to gather pointers which might be useful to others as well as to myself.

Ministers, priests and rabbis deal with such situations every day. I went to scores of them, of all faiths, in all parts of the country.

Here are some specific suggestions they made:

1. *Don't try to "buck them up."* This surprised me when the Rev. Arthur E. Wilson of Providence, R. I., mentioned it. But the others concurred. It only makes your friend feel worse when you say, "Come now, buck up. Don't take it so hard."

A man who has lost his wife must take it hard (if he loved her). "Bucking him up" sounds as though you are minimizing his loss. But the honest attitude, "Yes, it's tough, and I sure know it is," makes your friend feel free to express grief and recover from it. The "don't take it so hard" approach deprives him of the natural emotion of grief, stops up the safety valve God has given him.

**2. Don't try to divert them.** Rabbi Martin B. Ryback of Norwalk, Conn., pointed out that many people making condolence calls purposely veer away from the subject. They make small talk about football, fishing, the weather—anything but the reason for their visit.

The rabbi calls this "trying to camouflage death." The task of the mourner, difficult as it is, is to face the fact of death, and go on from there. "It would be far better," Rabbi Ryback suggested, "to sit silently and say nothing than to make obvious attempts to distract. The sorrowing friend sees through the effort to divert him. When the visitor leaves, reality hits him all the harder."

**3. Don't be afraid to talk about the person who has passed away.** Well-intentioned friends often shy away from mentioning the deceased. The implication is that the whole thing is too terrible to mention.

"The helpful thing," advised Rabbi Henry E. Kagan of Mount Vernon, N. Y., "is to talk about the person as you knew him in the fullness of his life, to re-create a living picture to replace the picture of death."

Once Rabbi Kagan called on a woman who had lost her brother. "I didn't know your brother too well," he said. "Tell me about him." The woman started talking and they discussed her brother for an hour. Afterward she said, "I feel relieved now for the first time since he died."

**4. Don't be afraid of causing tears.** When a good friend of mine lost a child I said something which made his eyes fill up. "I put my foot in it," I said, in relating the incident to the Rev. D. Russell Hetsler of Brazil, Ind. "No, you didn't," he replied. "You helped your friend to express grief in a normal, healthy way. That is far better than to stifle grief when friends are present, only to have it descend more crushingly when one is all alone."

Fear of causing tears, probably more than anything else, makes people stiff and ineffective. Visiting a friend who has lost his wife, they may be about to mention a ride in the country when they remember the man's wife used to love rides in the country. They don't dare speak of peonies because they were her favorite flower. So they freeze up.

"They really are depriving their friend of probably the greatest help they could give him," Pastor Hetsler commented. "That is, to help him experience grief in a normal way and get over it." Medical and psychological studies back up the pastor's contention that *expressing* grief is good and *repressing* it is bad. "If a comment of yours brings tears," he concluded, "remember—they are healthy tears."

5. *Let them talk.* "Sorrowing people need to talk," explained the Rev. Vern Swartsfager of San Francisco. "Friends worry about their ability to *say* the right things. They ought to be worrying about their ability to *listen.*"

If the warmth of your presence can get your friend to start talking, keep quiet and listen—even though he repeats the same things a dozen times. He is not telling you news but expressing feelings that need repetition. Pastor Swartsfager suggested a measuring stick for the success of your visit: "If your friend has said a hundred words to your one, you've helped a lot."

6. *Reassure—don't argue.* "Everybody who loses a loved one has guilt feelings—they may not be justified but they're natural," Rabbi Joseph R. Narot of Miami pointed out. A husband feels he should have been more considerate of his wife; a parent feels he should have spent more time with his child; a wife feels she should have made fewer demands on her husband. The yearning, "If only I had not done this, or done that—if I only had a chance to do it now," a hallmark of grieving.

These feelings must work their way out. You can give reassurance. Your friend must slowly come to the realization that he or she was, in all probability, a pretty good husband, wife or parent.

7. *Communicate—don't isolate.* Too often a person who has lost a loved one is overwhelmed with visitors for a week or so; then the house is empty. Even good friends sometimes stay away, believing that people in sorrow "like to be alone."

"That's the 'silent treatment,'" remarked Father Thomas Bresnaham of Detroit. "There's nothing worse." Our friend has not only lost his loved one—he has lost us too.

It is in that after-period, when all the letters of sympathy have been read and acknowledged and people have swung back into daily routine, that friends are needed most.

Keep in touch, Father Bresnaham urges. See your friend more often than you did before. See him for any purpose—for lunch, for a drive in the country, for shopping, for an evening visit. He has suffered a deep loss. Your job is to show him, by implication, how much he still has left. Your being with him is a proof to him that he still has resources.

8. *Perform some concrete act.* The Rev. William B. Ayers, of Wollaston, Mass., told me of a sorrowing husband who lost all interest in food until a friend brought over his favorite dish and

simply left it there at suppertime. "That's a wonderful way to help, by a concrete deed which in itself may be small yet carries the immense implication that you care," Pastor Ayers declared.

We should make it our business, when a friend is in sorrow, to do at least one practical, tangible act of kindness. Here are some to choose from: run errands with your car, take the children to school, bring in a meal, do the dishes, make necessary phone calls, pick up mail at the office, help acknowledge condolence notes, shop for the groceries.

9. *Swing into action.* Action is the symbol of going on living.

By swinging into action with your friend, whether at his hobby or his work, you help build a bridge to the future. Perhaps it means painting the garage with him, or hoeing the garden. Or spending an afternoon with a woman friend mending the children's clothes, or browsing through antique shops.

In St. Paul, Minn., the Rev. J. T. Morrow told me of a man who had lost a son. The man's hobby had been refinishing furniture. When he called on him Pastor Morrow said, "Come on, let's go down to the basement." They sanded a table together. When Pastor Morrow left, the man said, "This is the first time I've felt I could go on living."

Sorrowing people, Pastor Morrow pointed out, tend to drop out of things. They're a little like the rider who has been thrown from a horse. If they are to ride again, better get them back on the horse quickly.

10. *"Get them out of themselves,"* advised Father James Keller, leader of the Christophers. Once you have your friend doing things for himself, his grief is nearly cured. Once you have him doing things for others, it *is* cured.

Grief runs a natural course. It will pass. But if there is only a vacuum behind it, self-pity will rush in to fill it. To help your friend along the normal course of recovery, guide him to a new interest.

Volunteer work for a charity, enrollment in a community group to help youngsters, committee work at church or temple are ways of getting people "out of themselves."

If you and I, when sorrow strikes our friends, follow even a few of these pointers, we will be helpful.

Rachel weeps for her children,
She refuses to be comforted.

—Jeremiah

# THE DEATH OF THE YOUNG

*The grief of a parent for a child is the most difficult of all to bear.
Bereaved parents feel keenly the burning anguish of King David's
lament: "O my son Absalom, my son, my son Absalom! Would I had
died for thee, O Absalom, my son, my son." Almost these very words
were found recently by explorers in an Egyptian tomb. Upon the
exquisitely carved sarcophagus of a little child there were inscribed
the parent's words: "O my life, my love, my little one, would God
I had died for thee!"*

*Jeremiah pictured mother Rachel weeping so bitterly for her
children who "are not" that "she refused to be comforted." Indeed
is there any comfort equal to the hurt, any solace adequate to the
loss?*

*Nevertheless, the voice of the Divine Comforter speaks softly to
the bereft mother: "Refrain thy voice from weeping and thine eyes
from tears . . . there is hope for thy future."*

*There are some genuine sources of hope and courage to tap at
such a time. The awareness that other parents have found the
strength to endure a similar affliction can be reassuring. Somehow,
from somewhere, there comes the endurance and the fortitude equal
to our desperate need. The Psalmist undoubtedly experienced this
in his own life for he praised God "who healeth the broken in
heart and bindeth up their wounds." A measure of comfort may
also be derived from the realization that there is a precious store of
memories which death cannot take away and which no mother
would surrender even if she could thereby be relieved immediately
of all her sorrow. In those memories, the ravages of time and decay
no longer hold sway. There the child "grows not older," it remains*

149

*eternally "fair and kind and young." And perhaps the greatest
comfort lies in the thought that all of life is but a loan to us and
when the Lender asks for the return of the jewel, He promises to
care for it better than we can.*

---

## HE IS STILL ALIVE

### John Gunther

*An acquaintance said of Johnny Gunther: "He had the most
brilliant promise of any child I have ever known." When he suc-
cumbed at the age of seventeen to a vicious brain tumor, his father
wrote a moving memoir entitled* Death Be Not Proud—*from which
the following is taken. Significantly, the very last words the dying
lad wrote on the inside back cover of his diary were: "Hebrew
Toast: Le-Hy-eem—To Life."*

We said goodbye. But to anybody who ever knew him, he is still
alive. I do not mean merely that he lives in both of us or in the
trees at Deerfield or in anything he touched truly, but that the
influence, the impact, of a heroic personality continues to exert
itself long after mortal bonds are snapped. Johnny transmits permanently something of what he was, since the fabric of the universe
is continuous and eternal. . . .

The whys of this story, why Johnny should have been struck just
in that part of him that would have been most fruitful . . . the why
above all whys which is why any child should die, the whys and
wherefores of the celestial bookkeeping involved, if any, I will not
go into here. There are other criteria for measuring a life as well as
its duration—quality, intensity. But for us there is no compensation,
except that we can go to him though he cannot come to us. For
others, I would say that it was his spirit, and only his spirit, that
kept him invincibly alive against such dreadful obstacles for so
long—this is the central pith and substance of what I am trying to
write, as a mournful tribute not only to Johnny but to the power,
the wealth, the unconquerable beauty of the human spirit, will and
soul.

## LOVING LIFE MORE, BEING MORE AWARE

*Frances Gunther*

*Johnny's mother wrote the last chapter in* Death Be Not Proud. *The passages which follow are taken from that chapter entitled "A Word From Frances."*

Death always brings one suddenly face to face with life. Nothing, not even the birth of one's child, brings one so close to life as his death.

Johnny lay dying of a brain tumor for fifteen months. He was in his seventeenth year. I never kissed him good night without wondering whether I should see him alive in the morning. I greeted him each morning as though he were newly born to me, a re-gift of God. Each day he lived was a blessed day of grace. . . .

He wasn't just dying, of course. He was living and dying and being reborn all at the same time each day. How we loved each day. "It's been another wonderful day, Mother!" he'd say, as I knelt to kiss him good night. . . .

Since Johnny's death, we have received many letters from many kind friends from all parts of the world, each expressing his condolence in his own way. But through most of them has run a single theme: sympathy with us in facing a mysterious stroke of God's will that seemed inexplicable, unjustifiable, and yet, being God's will, must also be part of some great plan beyond our mortal ken, perhaps sparing him or us greater pain or loss.

Actually, in the experience of losing one's child in death, I have found that other factors were involved.

I did not for one thing feel that God personally had singled out either him or us for any special act, either of animosity or generosity. In a way I did not feel that God was personally involved at all. . . .

During Johnny's illness, I prayed continually to God, naturally. God was always there. He sat beside us during the doctors' consultation, as we waited the long vigils outside the operating room, as we rejoiced in the miracle of a brief recovery, as we agonized when hope ebbed away and the doctors confessed there was no longer anything they could do. They were helpless, and we were helpless, and in His way, God, standing by us in our hour of need, God in

His infinite wisdom and mercy and loving kindness, God in all His omnipotence, was helpless, too. . . .

I wish we had loved Johnny more when he was alive. Of course we loved Johnny very much. Johnny knew that. Everybody knew it. Loving Johnny more. What does it mean? What can it mean now?

Parents all over the earth who lost sons in the war have felt this kind of question, and sought an answer.

To me, it means loving life more, being more aware of life, of one's fellow human beings, of the earth.

It means obliterating, in a curious but real way, the ideas of evil and hate and the enemy, and transmuting them, with the alchemy of suffering, into ideas of clarity and charity.

It means caring more and more about other people, at home and abroad, all over the earth. It means caring more about God.

I hope we can love Johnny more and more till we, too, die, and leave behind us, as he did the love of love, the love of life.

*Flora Elizabeth Hastings*

Grieve not that I die young. Is it not well to pass away ere life hath lost its brightness?

## GOD CALLED HIM

*James J. Metcalfe*

Your little boy was only five
When he was called away;
And in your dear parental hearts
It was a tragic day.

You heard him laugh and speak to you,
You saw him climb the stair,
And in your fondest memories
You find him everywhere.

You called to him, he called to you,
And you were not alone
Until that sudden moment when
God called him to His own.

But it was God, and only He
Who gave your baby life,
And who withdrew him gently from
The struggle and the strife.

He must have loved your boy so much
He did not want to wait
Until he grew to be a man,
However good and great.


*John Milton*

Think what a present thou to God has sent,
And render him with patience what he lent.


## THE JEWELS
### *Midrash*

While Rabbi Meir was holding his weekly discourse in the House of Study one Sabbath afternoon, his two beloved sons died suddenly at home. The grief-stricken mother carried them to her room and covered them with a sheet. When Rabbi Meir returned after the evening services, he asked his wife, Beruriah, about the boys whom he had missed in the Synagogue. Instead of replying, she asked him to recite the Havdalah service marking the departure of the Sabbath, and gave him his evening meal. When it was over, Beruriah turned to Rabbi Meir and said: "I have a question to ask you. Not long ago, some precious jewels were entrusted to my care. Now the Owner has come to reclaim them. Shall I return them?"

"But of course," said Rabbi Meir. "You know the Law. Naturally they must be returned." Beruriah then took him by the hand, led him to the bed and drew back the sheet. Rabbi Meir burst into bitter weeping. "My sons! My sons!" he lamented. Then Beruriah reminded him tearfully: "Did you not say that we must restore to the Owner what He entrusted to our care? Our sons were the jewels which God left with us and now their Master has taken back His very own."

## WEEP NOT FOR THOSE
### Thomas Moore

Weep not for those whom the veil of the tomb
In life's happy morning, hath hid from our eyes,
Ere sin threw a blight o'er the spirit's young bloom,
Or earth had profan'd what was born for the skies.

### Elbert Hubbard

Whom the gods love die young, no matter how long they live.

## WHEN THE FIG IS RIPE
### Midrash

In hot weather, a rabbi delivered his discourse to his disciples under the shade of a fig tree. They noticed that each morning the owner would pick his ripened figs. "Perhaps he fears that we will pick his fruit," they thought, and they moved to another place. The owner begged them to return. Believing that they had moved because his presence annoyed them, he resolved not to pick the fruit. In the evening, they beheld the figs dropping from the trees, spoiled by the heat of the sun. The disciples then appreciated why it was necessary for the owner to pick them in the morning.

The rabbi said: "The owner of the figs knows when his fruit should be picked, lest it be spoiled. Thus does God know when to summon His righteous children before they are spoiled. This is the reason why many good and gracious persons are sometimes called by God in their early manhood."

## NOTHING IS WASTED
### Zelda Popkin

He returned home drained and spent, his sunken eyes dazed and unbelieving. He had just watched a small white coffin being lowered into the earth. No parent in all his days performs a harder task than final farewell to a child.

"Why did it happen?" he cried. "If this is all there is to life, what's the use of going on?"

His father was there. His father had met bereavement before. He said, "Nothing is wasted, son. This is the experience through which you will grow." Then they sat down and quietly talked of the meaning of death.

## LOST LOVE

### Andrew Lang

In dreams she grows not older,
The lands of dream among,
Though all the world wax colder,
Though all the songs be sung,
In dreams doth he behold her
Still fair and kind and young.

## FROM "GONE"

### John Greenleaf Whittier

There seems a shadow on the day,
Her smile no longer cheers;
A dimness on the stars at night,
Like eyes that look through tears.

Alone unto our Father's will
One thought hath reconciled;
That He whose love exceedeth ours
Hath taken home His child.

Fold her, O Father! in Thine arms,
And let her henceforth be
A messenger of love between
Our human hearts and Thee.

## LINCOLN'S LETTER TO MRS. BIXBY

Dear Madam:

I have been shown in the files of the War Department a statement of the Adjutant General of Massachusetts that you are the mother of five sons who have died gloriously on the field of battle. I feel how weak and fruitless must be any words of mine which should attempt to beguile you from the grief of a loss so overwhelming, but I cannot refrain from tendering to you the consolation that may be found in the thanks of the Republic that they died to save. I pray that the Heavenly Father may assuage the anguish of your bereavement, and leave you only the cherished memory of the loved and lost, and the solemn pride that must be yours to have laid so costly a sacrifice upon the altar of freedom.

Yours very sincerely and respectfully,

Abraham Lincoln

## A CHILD'S EPITAPH

*Arthur Guiterman*

Above a low mound at the cedar tree's root
Is carved on a stone that is moldering dark
"The Dove found no rest for the sole of her foot,
And returned unto Him in the Ark."

## DO NOT FEAR FOR THE LITTLE LOVELY VOYAGER

*Leigh Hunt*

The little innocent face looks so sublimely simple and confiding among the terrors of death. Crimeless and fearless, that little mortal passed under the shadow and explored the mystery of dissolution. There is death in its sublimest and purest image; no hatred, no hypocrisy, no suspicion, no care for the morrow ever darkened that little one's face; death has come lovingly upon it; there yearnings of love, indeed, cannot be stifled; for the prattle and smiles, and all the little world of thoughts that were so delightful, are gone forever. Awe, too, will overcast us in its presence; for we are looking on death. But we do not fear for the little lovely voyager; for the child has gone, simple and trusting, into the presence of its all-wise Father. . . .

## AT A CHILD'S GRAVE

*Robert Ingersoll*

My friends: I know how vain it is to gild a grief with words, and yet I wish to take from every grave its fear.

Here in this world, where life and death are equal kings, all should be brave enough to meet what all the dead have met. The future has been filled with fear, stained and polluted by the heartless past. From the wondrous tree of life the buds and blossoms fall with ripened fruit, and in the common bed of earth, patriarchs and babes sleep side by side.

Why should we fear that which will come to all that is? We cannot tell, we do not know, which is the greater blessing—life or death. We cannot say that death is not a good. We do not know whether the grave is the end of this life, or the door of another, or whether the night here is not somewhere else a dawn.

Neither can we tell which is the more fortunate, the child dying in its mother's arms, before its lips have learned to form a word— or he who journeys all the length of life's uneven road, painfully taking the last slow steps with staff and crutch.

Every cradle asks us "whence?" and every coffin "whither?" The poor barbarian, weeping above his dead, can answer these questions just as well as the robed priest of the most authentic creed. The tearful ignorance of the one is as consoling as the learned and unmeaning word of the other. No man, standing where the horizon of a life has touched a grave, has any right to prophesy a future filled with pain and tears.

May be that death gives all there is of worth to life. If those we press and strain within our arms could never die, perhaps that love would wither from the earth. May be this common fate treads from out the paths between our hearts the weeds of selfishness and hate. And I had rather live and love where death is king than have eternal life where love is not. Another life is nought, unless we know and love again the ones who love us here.

They who stand with breaking hearts around this little grave need have no fear. The larger and the nobler faith in all that is, and is to be, tells us that death, even at its worst, is only perfect rest. We know that through the common wants of life—the needs and duties of each hour—their grief will lessen day by day, until at last this grave will be to them a place of rest and peace—almost of joy. There is for them this consolation: the dead do not suffer. If they live again, their lives will surely be as good as ours. We have no fear; we are all children of the same mother, and the same fate awaits us all. We, too, have our religion, and it is this: Help for the living—hope for the dead.

*Julianus*

Life's pleasure hath he lost—escaped life's pain,
Nor wedded joys nor wedded sorrows knew.

## THE SLEEP OF THE DILIGENT

*Midrash*

When Rabbi Bun died, Rabbi Zeira eulogized as follows: "To what is the case of Rabbi Bun like? To a king who has hired workmen for his garden, and he observes that one of them works expertly and efficiently. He calls him over and walks with him about the garden. In the evening, when the king pays his workmen, he gives to the capable man the same pay as to the others. The latter protest to the king: 'But he has worked only two hours, and we have worked for eight.' 'True,' answers the king, 'but he has accomplished more in two hours than you in eight.' Likewise, 'My beloved is gone down to His garden.' (Song of Songs 6:2) Rabbi Bun has labored in the Torah during his twenty-eight years more than another fine student in a hundred years. Therefore God summoned him to walk with Him. May 'the sleep of the diligent worker be sweet.'" (Eccl. 5:11)

*Robert Burns*

Here lies a rose, a budding rose,
    Blasted before its bloom;
Whose innocence did sweets disclose
    Beyond that flower's perfume.
To those who for her loss are griev'd
    This consolation's given,—
She's from a world of woe receiv'd
    And blooms a rose in Heaven.

### Leigh Hunt

Those who have lost an infant are never, as it were, without an infant child. They are the only persons who, in one sense, retain it always. . . . The other children grow up to manhood and womanhood, and suffer all the changes of mortality. This one alone is rendered an immortal child. Death has arrested it with his kindly harshness, and blessed it into an eternal image of youth and innocence.

## THE FLOWER PLUCKED BY THE MASTER

### Author unknown

A gentleman's gardener had a darling girl whom he loved dearly. At a tender age she was fatally stricken. The father was terribly distressed and murmured at the dealings of Providence.

The gardener had in one of his flower-beds a favorite rose. It was the fairest flower he had ever seen on the tree, and he daily marked its growing beauty, intending, when it was full blown, to send it to his master's mansion. One morning it was gone: someone had plucked it. Mortified at what he thought was the improper conduct of one of the servants, he tried to find out the culprit. He was, however, much surprised to find that it was his master who, on walking through the garden, had been attracted by the beauty of the rose, and, plucking it, had carried it to one of the beautiful rooms in the hall. The gardener's anger was changed into pleasure. He felt reconciled when he heard that his master had thought the flower worthy of such special notice.

"Ah, Richard," said the gentleman, "you can gladly give up the rose, because I thought it worthy of a place in my house. And will you repine because your heavenly Father has thought wise to remove your child from a world of trial and hardship to be with Himself in Heaven?"

## EPITAPH ON AN INFANT

### Samuel T. Coleridge

Ere sin could blight or sorrow fade,
Death came with friendly care;

The opening bud to Heaven conveyed,
And bade it blossom there.

## HE IS MORE ALIVE THAN WE ARE

*Canon W. H. Elliott*

We do not think of our Robin as dead—he who was always so much alive. He is not dead. He is much more alive than we are, his eyes on far horizons that we cannot see, his warm young heart aglow with love and hope, his whole eager nature intent already on the thrilling work that God is giving him to do.

He is not asleep, as some may think. What we have laid reverently away was his overcoat, as we describe it to his little brother Michael. He himself in his shining uniform—too full of light for eyes like ours to see it—has gone on.

Yet he has not gone from us. How we miss him in his coming and going, no words can tell. But we know that he does come and go—more than ever; that he is with us round the fire in a home circle still unbroken. But for his great shining we should see him. Nevertheless in his own way, he will make himself known and speak to us of his life and our life—more deeply shared than ever before—and of what the Wise Ones say.

We do not believe that God called him—even for some higher service. What we do believe is that, when a thing like this happens, God can take it and weave it so gloriously into the pattern of our lives that one day we shall shout when we behold it—for wonder and for joy. It is for us to see to it, that, in quiet faith and humility of heart and surrender of our wills to the Great Loving Will, we help and never hinder the hand of God which is at work upon us.

Being then so very confident of all this—that there is no death here, nor separation, nor loss—we do not feel that Robin's young life has been cut off in the fresh spring blossom of its promise. There is no "might have been" for him. If he might have been a great artist, as we think—for he drew and painted wonderfully—he will still be that. He will roam across wide landscapes, unknown as yet to any of us, where colors change and blend as no mortal eye can see them and sing themselves into music as they shine. There shall he "draw the thing as he sees it for the God of things as they are."

If, as both his schools had hoped, he might have been a leader of men, he still shall lead, and find the way for us and them the more easily from the high plane of his life. And in all that he was and is—his deep love for us, his strong sense of justice and fair play, his great compassion for suffering folk (including the animals), his will at every turn to be unselfish and to do his duty—he goes from strength to strength. For his young untiring energies and for his eager burning spirit he shall find wondrous scope both here on earth and in those wider ranges of the soul that we call heaven.

So we think of our very dear Robin. Help us to think that always. Our only picture of him is of a happy-hearted, laughing boy. That is what he was and still is. We shall never say, "How Robin would have laughed!" but, as we have said already, "How Robin must be laughing!" For he is not a proud and happy memory. He is a radiant, living, loving person, round about us. We know it.

That is our faith. So help us, God.

## THREE DUTIES

*Grace Perkins Oursler and April Armstrong*

Those who have lost a child have three great duties to the living: to husband or wife, to the rest of the family, and to children everywhere. These three duties are like sides of a great triangle, each one supporting the other.

No other can take your lost child's place, but by loving and caring for some needy little one, you can raise a lasting tribute to the spirit that did not need to live out the full years.

There are so many ways to do this! Think of the love-starved children in this lonely world who have lost their parents, or whose parents are too poor to care for them. Pour your love out on these friendless ones, in your own home, in their orphanages, by your financial, moral, or actual physical help! Even occasional visits and contacts are mutual blessings.

A parent's love does not die with the child. A mother's love is unquenchable: it is born of God, and in its eternal strength it demands an outlet. What, then, when the child is gone, when no longer there is a little one to tend, to wash and cook and mend for, to comfort? You cannot expect simply to take up life casually once he is gone. That love was given you for a purpose; use it wisely even when at first it seems that you are deprived of its main object.

If circumstances prevent actual adoption of a child, you might board one, work in a day nursery, support one. Even with other remaining children, people have found it wise to fill the place of the lost one. There was enough money, enough time, enough love before—there still is now.

In Miami there is an elderly couple who run a roadstand. They are a bit proud to be able to say: "We have sent five little Ellens through college," since they could never send their own Ellen. They had started her college fund the day she was born, but she was taken from them in a schoolyard accident in the eighth grade. Not all their five Ellens are actively grateful, but that doesn't seem to spoil their quiet pride and achievement. They are doing what they did—for Ellen.

## BE CAREFUL LEST YOU LOSE THOSE LEFT TO YOU

### Grace Perkins Oursler and April Armstrong

*Rebecca N. Porter, in an article in* Today's Woman, January, *1949, speaking from the schoolteacher's view, painted a vivid picture of the effect on one child of the loss of another. Ralph's parents had made a common mistake: to their dead son Earl they had attributed every virtue a boy could have. Earl had been talented, friendly, popular, good at baseball and studies. And Ralph?*

As Mrs. Porter says: "By spoken word, by implication, Ralph was made to feel that he fell short of what his parents would have had in their elder son. So he had come secretly to hate this dead brother. He fiercely resolved, perhaps unconsciously, to be unlike him in every way. Earl had been popular—Ralph would show people he could get along without them. He wouldn't even get as good grades as he knew he could. Struggling with his own sense of inadequacy, he may cry in his secret soul: 'I don't believe Earl was as perfect as that!' But he is forever helpless to disprove it.

"You parents who have lost a child, be doubly careful lest in other ways you lose those left to you. Let the brother or sister who is gone be, not an impossible paragon, an absentee tyrant, but a cherished memory of an imperfect but loved real child."

### William Wordsworth

Three years she grew in sun and shower,
Then Nature said: "A lovelier flower

On earth was never sown;
This child I to myself will make
A lady of my own."

## IN MY DARKEST HOUR—HOPE

### *Helen Hayes*

On each New Year's Eve the mail brings me a gift that is done up in ordinary brown paper, yet is precious beyond price. It is from Mr. and Mrs. Isaac Frantz, Brooklyn. To understand the value of this gift you must know something about the Frantzes.

They came into my life in 1949, just after my daughter, Mary, had died of polio and I was being tortured by the unanswerable question—Why? Mary had been so lovely and talented, so young and free from sin. Why had this happened to her? I could only feel that her death had been a cruel, senseless thing.

This was a self-destroying mood, for an artist needs the belief that life holds some beauty and meaning. I could not create beauty or meaning on the stage if there was none within me. So to save myself I began to search for God. I read St. Thomas Aquinas, explored the life and works of Gandhi, read the Bible. But the search failed. My daughter was dead! That brutal fact overwhelmed me, blinded my heart.

All during this time I accepted no professional or social engagements and saw only my family and most intimate friends. But, in this self-imposed isolation, I became aware that a Mr. Isaac Frantz was telephoning almost every day, trying to get through to me. My husband finally talked to him and reported: "He has just lost a little boy with polio and he seems to think it would help his wife if she could see you."

"Oh, Charles—no! I have no strength to give her. I have barely enough for myself. I simply can't do it."

"Of course, darling. That's what I told him."

But Isaac Frantz kept telephoning and we finally agreed to let him bring his wife to our home.

I steeled myself for the ordeal.

When they arrived in their Sunday best, they were ill at ease, but they had a quiet dignity that surmounted their painful self-consciousness. Coming face to face with us was obviously something that demanded all their courage. Charles and I tried to put them at ease.

Now I discovered the truth about their visit. It had been the husband's idea entirely and he had arranged it without his wife's knowledge. But he was so sure that a meeting would bring some comfort to his wife that he forced himself to ask it. As for his wife, she was appalled when she heard of the completed arrangements, but knowing how difficult it had been for her husband, and how important to him, she consented to come. Each was doing this for the other—in the moment of great need.

The Frantzes owned a tiny stationery store and obviously had to struggle for the necessities of life. Charles and I had never known anything but success, fame, luxury. And yet the four of us suddenly had one thing to share, the tragic loss of our children.

Mrs. Frantz soon began talking about her son in a most natural manner, and, before I quite knew what was happening, I had plunged into a series of stories about Mary. Then a glance at Charles's surprised face made me realize that I was actually mentioning her name for the first time since her death. I had taken her memory out of hiding, and I felt better for it.

Then Mrs. Frantz told us of her plans to adopt an orphan from Israel, and for a moment I was shocked.

"You are thinking I am letting him take my little boy's place?" she asked gently, guessing my thoughts. "No one could ever do that. But in my heart there is still love and maybe wisdom, too. Should I let these dry up and go to waste?"

"I—I don't know, Mrs. Frantz," I said.

"No, my dear, we cannot die because our children die. I should not love less because the one I loved is gone—but more should I love because my heart knows the suffering of others."

While she talked I thought about my child. Mary had been a big and wonderful part of my life. Even though that part had ended, I was a better human being for having had Mary, for having hoped and dreamed and worked for her. Tragic that it should have ended, but how much better than if it had never existed.

These were the things that Mrs. Frantz was saying, in her own way. These were the things that I now understood. Then I thought how ironic it was that I hadn't wanted Mrs. Frantz to come because I feared she would draw upon my feeble strength. It was I who drew upon hers!

When they finally rose to leave, I realized why my search for God had been fruitless—I had looked in the wrong places. He was not to be found between the covers of a book, but in the human heart.

We never met after that. Charles and I invited them back a couple of times, but they were always busy with their store and their new son. I think they understood that our worlds were meant to touch but briefly.

Every New Year's Eve since then I have received from them a box of candy wrapped in plain brown paper. Perhaps you can understand why it is so precious to me. For it was through these simple people that I learned humility, and God's pattern finally came clear. Now I know that when He afflicts the celebrated of the world, it is His way of saying, "None is privileged. In My eyes, all are equal."

## CAN I BRING HIM BACK?

### II Samuel

When King David's child became very ill, David prayed to God for the child. He also fasted and lay all night upon the earth. And the elders of his house arose and stood beside him to raise him up from the earth; but he would not, neither did he eat bread with them.

On the seventh day, the child died. And the servants of David were afraid to tell him that the child was dead; for they said: "Behold, while the child was yet alive, we spoke unto him, and he did not listen to us; how then shall we tell him that the child is dead? He may do himself some harm."

When David saw that his servants whispered together, David understood that the child was dead; and David said to his servants: "Is the child dead?" And they said: "He is dead." Then David arose from the earth and washed and anointed himself, and changed his apparel; and he came into the house of the Lord, and worshipped. Then he came to his own house; and when he requested it, they set bread before him, and he ate. Then his servants said to him: "What is this that you have done? You fasted and wept for the child while he was alive; but when the child died, you rose up and ate bread."

And David said; "While the child was yet alive, I fasted and wept; for I said: 'Who knows whether the Lord will not be gracious to me, that the child may live?' But now he is dead, why should I fast? Can I bring him back again? I shall go to him, but he will not return to me."

## BEREAVED

*James Whitcomb Riley*

Let me come in where you sit weeping—aye,
Let me, who have not any child to die,
Weep with you for the little one whose love
I have known nothing of.
The little arms that slowly, slowly loosed
Their pressure round your neck; the hands you used
To kiss. —Such arms—such hands I never knew.
May I not weep with you?
Fain would I be of service—say some thing,
Between the tears, that would be comforting,—
But ah! So sadder than yourselves am I,
Who have no child to die.

## ON A DEAD CHILD

*Richard Middleton*

Man proposes, God in His time disposes,
And so I wander'd up to where you lay,
A little rose among the little roses,
And no more dead than they.

It seem'd your childish feet were tired of straying,
You did not greet me from your flower-strewn bed,
Yet still I knew that you were only playing—
Playing at being dead.

I might have thought that you were really sleeping,
So quiet lay your eyelids to the sky,
So still your hair, but surely you were peeping,
And so I did not cry.

God knows, and in His proper time disposes,
And so I smiled and gently called your name,
Added my rose to your sweet heap of roses,
And left you to your game.

## LOVE AND SYMPATHY COUNT FOR SOMETHING
### Thomas H. Huxley

It is very sad to lose your child just when he was beginning to bind himself to you, and I don't know that it is much consolation to reflect that the longer he had wound himself up in your heart-strings, the worse the tear would have been, which seems to have been inevitable sooner or later. One does not weigh and measure these things while grief is fresh, and in my experience a deep plunge into the waters of sorrow is the hopefulest way of getting through them in one's daily road of life again. No one can help another very much in these crises of life; but love and sympathy count for something.

## ACCEPT THE VERDICT WITH HUMILITY
### Jerusalem Talmud

When Rabbi Abbahu's child died, he said: "We are taught that after the execution of a person condemned by an earthly court, where lies, deception, favoritism and bribery may have existed, whose judges are but mortal beings, the kinsfolk come and pleasantly greet the judges and witnesses to demonstrate that they have no grievance in their heart against them, because they have judged truthfully. How much the more then, after a person has surrendered his life according to the decree of the Heavenly Tribunal, where no human defects and shortcomings exist, should we not receive with humility and submission the verdict of Heaven."

### Wisdom of Solomon

Being found well pleasing unto God he was beloved of Him,
He was carried away lest wickedness should change his understanding,
Or guile deceive his soul.
Being perfect in a little while, he fulfilled long years;
For his soul was pleasing unto the Lord. . . .

It is better to go to the house of mourning, than to go to the house of feasting; for that is the end of all men, and the living will lay it to his heart.

—Ecclesiastes

# DEATH TEACHES LIFE

*The existence of death has ever served as a lesson to life. Man cannot for long evade the consciousness of his mortality nor fail to draw therefrom some fundamental attitudes on how his life shall be conducted.*

*Death, however, has not taught the same lesson to all people. To some, the presence of death has been a spur to unbridled self-indulgence and the uninhibited pursuit of pleasure. Thus among the Romans, a human skeleton was frequently exhibited among the celebrants at festive parties with the exhortation: "Let us enjoy life while we may." Herodotus tells us that a similar custom prevailed among the Egyptians. At joyous occasions, the image of a dead man carved in wood, or a coffin containing the embalmed remains of some ancestor, would be presented to each guest by a person whose function it was to pronounce distinctly as he did so: "Look upon this and be merry; for such as this, when dead, shalt thou be." The prophet Isaiah sums up the slogan of those to whom life's brevity is a stimulant to unrestrained hedonism in the words: "Let us eat and drink, for tomorrow we die."*

*This approach to life testifies to a failure of nerve and leads to moral bankruptcy. It is a philosophy of despair which not only fails to bring satisfaction but overlooks the many sources of real joy that life generously affords. Where the sole objective of living is reduced to an endless round of pleasure-seeking, the ultimate verdict must be a cynical refrain of disillusionment: "Futility of futilities, all is futility."*

*There are others whom death has instructed more wisely. To*

168

*them life's brevity has been an incentive to live more nobly, more generously, more creatively. They have recognized that while a limit has been set to the length of our days, we alone determine their breadth and their depth. Thus Joshua Loth Liebman counsels: "We must make up for the . . . brevity of life by heightening the intensity of life." Frances Gunther urges us to embrace life and those we love "with a little added rapture and a keener awareness of joy." Bertrand Russell, in a somewhat bleaker mood, realizes that we and our comrades alike are subject to "the silent orders of omnipotent Death." He would therefore have us "shed sunshine on their path . . . lighten their sorrows by the balm of sympathy . . . strengthen failing courage . . . instill faith in hours of despair." The Psalmist of an earlier age contemplated life's transiency and prayed: "So teach us to number our days that we obtain a heart of wisdom."*

*In the hour of bereavement the death of a loved one can teach us to pitch our lives at the highest level. Yes, life is brief, but we determine its quality. Indeed, precisely because of its brevity, we must be very discriminating as to what we put into it. We are like a man leaving on a journey with a small leather pouch. Shall he fill it with mud when he can take along diamonds? Shall we fill our days with selfishness and pettiness when close at hand is generosity and kindness? George Bernard Shaw's declaration might well serve as our watchword: "Life is no brief candle for me. It is a sort of splendid torch which I have got hold of for a moment and I want to make it burn as brightly as possible before handing it on to future generations."*

## DO NOT SQUANDER TIME

### *Benjamin Franklin*

Dost thou love life? Then do not squander time; for that's the stuff life is made of.

If time be of all things the most precious, wasting time must be the greatest prodigality; since lost time is never found again and what we call time enough always proves little enough. Let us then be up and doing, and doing to the purpose; so by diligence shall we do more with less perplexity. Sloth makes all things difficult, but industry all easy.

Employ thy time well, if thou meanest to gain leisure. Since thou are not sure of a minute, throw not away an hour.

# THE GOAL OF LIFE
*Joshua Loth Liebman*

The religion of Judaism can teach us . . . how to understand the goal of life in the presence of mortality. That goal is that we should create a pattern that will be a blessing and inspiration to those who come after us. When we die, those who have been touched and illumined by the flame of our being should rejoice to think of us with joyous reminiscence.

We can face death nobly when we resolve so to live and to work in the years allotted to us that no one shall cry in frustration or anger when we have gone, that no one shall silently curse the day of our birth but rather that they shall recall our day upon earth in the concert hall of memory and shall laugh, with the overbrimming joy that a dear one walked the earth bravely and lovingly once upon a time.

The thought of death need not fill us with dark and despairing anxiety but rather with a creative determination to be for the little world of which we are a part the center of the target toward which all the archers shall send the arrows of their aspiration, to be the oak tree, tall and stately, in the shelter of whose branches the young can sit and play and the old can find shade from the heat of the day. Let us live in such a way that our spirit shall be the rain causing the soil of other souls to grow moist and verdant, to be the sunlight making chlorophyll in the filigree leaves of other hearts and other minds, to be the star, the guiding North Star, by which the mariners and the navigators in our family and in our circle of friends can set their compass across the unchartered sea of being. This is the goal of life, so to live that men shall rehearse the story of our being with inspiration and with deep gratitude that we have walked the earth rejoicing to tell of our strong youth, the manliness of our maturity, the wisdom of our old age. Then indeed our memory shall be a blessing.

# LIFE IS WORTH LITTLE UNLESS . . .
*Eldad Pan (Translated from the Hebrew by the editor)*

*Eldad Pan was killed in Israel's War of Independence at the age of twenty, a veteran of many battles.*

Lately I have been thinking about what the goal of life should be. At best, man's life is short. His life may be kind or harsh, easy or difficult, but the time passes before he realizes it. An old person wants to live no less than a young person. The years of life do not satisfy the hunger for life. What then shall we do during this time?

We can reach either of two conclusions. The first is that since life is so short we should enjoy it as much as possible. The second is that precisely because life is short and no one can completely enjoy it (for we die with half our desires unsatisfied), therefore we should dedicate life to a sacred and worthy goal, to sacrifice it for something which will be valued above life. At times the first feeling is stronger and at others the second one. Of late, however, I think that the second feeling is dominant. It seems that I am slowly coming to the conclusion that life by itself is worth little unless it serves something greater than itself.

## LIFE IS TOO BRIEF

### W. M. Vories

Life is too brief
Between the budding and the falling leaf.
Between the seed time and the golden sheaf,
   For hate and spite.
We have no time for malice and for greed;
Therefore, with love make beautiful the deed;
   Fast speeds the night.

Life is too swift
Between the blossom and the white snow's drift,
Between the silence and the lark's uplift,
   For bitter words.
In kindness and in gentleness our speech
Must carry messages of hope, and reach
   The sweetest chords.

Life is too great
Between the infant's and the man's estate,
Between the clashing of earth's strife and fate,
   For petty things.
Lo! we shall yet who creep with cumbered feet
Walk glorious over heaven's golden street,
   Or soar on wings!

## TODAY IS THE DAY
### Grenville Kleiser

There are many fine things which you mean to do some day, under what you think will be more favorable circumstances. But the only time that is surely yours is the present, hence this is the time to speak the word of appreciation and sympathy, to do the generous deed, to forgive the fault of a thoughtless friend, to sacrifice self a little more for others. Today is the day in which to express your noblest qualities of mind and heart, to do at least one worthy thing which you have long postponed, and to use your God-given abilities for the enrichment of some less fortunate fellow traveler. Today you can make your life . . . significant and worth while. The present is yours to do with it as you will.

## THE TIME IS SHORT
### Phillips Brooks

You who are letting miserable misunderstandings run on from year to year, meaning to clear them up some day;

You who are keeping wretched quarrels alive because you cannot quite make up your mind that now is the day to sacrifice your pride and kill them;

You who are passing men sullenly upon the street, not speaking to them out of some silly spite, and yet knowing that it would fill you with shame and remorse if you heard that one of those men were dead tomorrow morning;

You who are letting your neighbor starve, till you hear that he is dying of starvation; or letting your friend's heart ache for a word of appreciation or sympathy, which you mean to give him some day;

If you only could know and see and feel, all of a sudden, that "the time is short," how it would break the spell! How you would go instantly and do the things which you might never have another chance to do.

### Louis D. Brandeis

I have only one life and it's short enough; why waste it on things I don't want most.

## HOW SWIFTLY ALL THINGS PASS AWAY
*Marcus Aurelius*

Think often of how swiftly all things pass away and are no more
—the works of man. The substance of the Universe, matter, is like
unto a river that flows on forever. All things are not only in a
constant state of change, but they are the cause of constant and
infinite change in other things. Upon a narrow ledge thou standest!
Behind thee, the bottomless abyss of the Past! In front of thee, the
Future that will swallow up all things that are now. Over what
things, then, in this present life wilt thou, O foolish man, be
disquieted or exalted—making thyself wretched; seeing that they
can vex thee only for a time—a brief, brief time!

*Wisdom of Ben Sira*

Remember that death will not tarry;
Do well unto thy friend before thou die;
And according to thy ability stretch out thy hand and give to him.

*Horace Mann*

Be ashamed to die until you have won some victory for humanity.

## WHAT WOULDST THOU BE FOUND DOING. . . ?
*Epictetus*

What wouldst thou be found doing when overtaken by Death?
If I might choose, I would be found doing some deed of true
humanity, of wide import, beneficent and noble. But if I may not
be found engaged in aught so lofty, let me hope at least for this—
what none may hinder, what is surely in my power—that I may be
found raising up in myself that which had fallen; learning to deal
more wisely with the things of sense; working out my own tranquillity, and thus rendering that which is its due to every relation
of life. . . .

If death surprise me thus employed, it is enough if I can stretch forth my hands to God and say, "The faculties which I received at Thy hands for apprehending this thine Administration, I have not neglected. As far as in me lay, I have done Thee no dishonour. Behold how I have used the senses, the primary conceptions which Thou gavest me. Have I ever laid anything to Thy charge? Have I ever murmured at aught that came to pass, or wished it otherwise? Have I in anything transgressed the relations of life? For that Thou didst beget me, I thank Thee for that Thou hast given; for the time during which I have used the things that were Thine, it suffices me. Take them back and place them wherever Thou wilt! They were all Thine, and Thou gavest them me." If a man depart thus minded, is it not enough? What life is fairer or more noble, what end happier than his?

*William James*

The great use of life is to spend it for something that will outlast it.

## INVOCATION OF THE DAWN
*Anonymous*
*From "Kalidasa"*

Look to this day!
For it is life, the very life of life.
In its brief course lie all the verities,
All the realities of existence:
The bliss of growth,
The glory of action,
The splendor of beauty;

For yesterday is already a dream,
And tomorrow is only a vision;
But today, well lived,
Makes every yesterday a dream of happiness,
And every tomorrow a vision of hope.
Look well, therefore, to this day!

## DEATH IS ALL WE HAVE MISSED
### *Israel Zangwill*

Whoever dies in the full tilt of his ambitions is buried alive, and whoever survives his hopes and fears is dead, unburied. Death for us is all we have missed, all the periods and planets we have not lived in, all the countries we have not visited, all the books we have not read, all the emotions and experiences we have not had, all the prayers we have not prayed, all the battles we have not fought. Every restriction, negation is a piece of death.

### *Wisdom of Ben Sira*

In all thy matters remember thy last end,
And thou shalt never do amiss.

### *James Russell Lowell*

Emerge thou mayst from the last whelming sea,
And prove that death but routs life into victory.

## FROM "IF WE KNEW"
### *May Riley Smith*

Strange we never prize the music
  Till the sweet-voiced bird has blown;
Strange that we should slight the violets
  Till the lovely flowers are gone;
Strange that summer skies and sunshine
  Never seem one half so fair
As when winter's snowy pinions
  Shake their white down in the air!

Let us gather up the sunbeams
  Lying all around our path;
Let us keep the wheat and roses,
  Casting out the thorns and chaff;

Let us find our sweetest comfort
In the blessings of today,
With a patient hand removing
All the briars from the way.


*Ralph Waldo Emerson*

Life wastes itself whilst we are preparing to live.


## TO CONTRIBUTE TO THE INHERITANCE
## OF MANKIND
*John Erskine*

Though I have little fear of death, yet I cannot contemplate with equanimity the fact that on this earth I shall some day be altogether forgotten, and my place shall know me no more. This sentiment is not peculiar with me. Every man and woman who thinks at all recoils from the prospect of mortal oblivion, even though confident of continued existence elsewhere.

The wish to live on men's tongues or on perpetual tombstones is ignoble and futile. But to contribute to the inheritance of mankind, and in our works to continue even after our names are lost, this is a kind of survival neither futile nor unworthy. The hope to gain it spurs us on. Let me correct myself—not the hope to gain but to deserve it.


*Henri F. Amiel*

Life is short and we have not too much time for gladdening the hearts of those who are traveling the dark way with us. Oh, be swift to love! Make haste to be kind!


## FROM "A FREE MAN'S WORSHIP"
*Bertrand Russell*

United with his fellow-men by the strongest ties of all ties, the tie of a common doom, the free man finds that a new vision is with him always, shedding over every daily task the light of love. The life of Man is a long march through the night, surrounded by invisible foes, tortured by weariness and pain, towards a goal that few can hope to reach, and where none may tarry long. One by one, as they march, our comrades vanish from our sight, seized by the silent orders of omnipotent Death. Very brief is the time in which we can help them, in which their happiness or misery is decided. Be it ours to shed sunshine on their path, to lighten their sorrows by the balm of sympathy, to give them the pure joy of a never-tiring affection, to strengthen failing courage, to instill faith in hours of despair. Let us not weigh in grudging scales their merits and demerits, but let us think only of their need—of the sorrows, the difficulties, perhaps the blindnesses, that make the misery of their lives; let us remember that they are fellow-sufferers in the same darkness, actors in the same tragedy with ourselves. And so, when their day is over, when their good and their evil have become eternal by the immortality of the past, be it ours to feel that, where they suffered, where they failed, no deed of ours was the cause; but wherever a spark of the divine fire kindled in their hearts, we were ready with encouragement, with sympathy, with brave words in which high courage glowed.

### Ethics of The Fathers

This world is like a vestibule before the World to Come; prepare thyself in the vestibule that thou mayest enter the Hall.

## A NEW AWARENESS OF THE VALUE OF LIFE
### Zelda Popkin

The understanding which grows out of personal loss is not merely in the ability to share the world's sorrows but in a new awareness of the value of life. "When my mother died," a man said to me, "my own children were at once closer and dearer to me."

"Losing my father," a young man said, "made us all realize how much we had wasted. We'd never gotten to know each other. There never seemed to be time. I hope to live differently with my own family. I've gotten a new sense of values from this."

*Ethics of the Fathers*

The day is short, the work is immense, the laborers are sluggish, the reward is great and the Master of the house is insistent.

## JOURNEY'S END

*Evelyn H. Healey*

We go from God to God—then, though
    The day be long,
We shall return to Heaven our home
    At evensong.

We go from God to God—so let
    The space between
Be filled with beauty, conquering
    Things base and mean.

We go from God to God—lo! what
    Transcendent bliss,
To know the journey's end will hold
    Such joy as this!

## NOW

*George H. Candler*

The clock of life is wound but once,
And no man has the power
To tell just when the hands will stop—
At late or early hour.
Now is the only time you own:
Live, love, work with a will.
Place no faith in tomorrow, for—
The clock may then be still.

*Marcus Aurelius*

Short is the little that remains to thee of life. Live as on a mountain!

## LIFE IS TOO SHORT TO BE LITTLE
### *Author unknown*

My favorite quotation is the sentence above, written by Disraeli. It has helped through many a painful experience. Often we allow ourselves to be upset by small things we should despise and forget. Perhaps some man we helped has proved ungrateful . . . some woman we believed to be a friend has spoken ill of us . . . some reward we thought we deserved has been denied us. We feel such disappointments so strongly that we can no longer work or sleep. But isn't that absurd? Here we are on this earth, with only a few more decades to live, and we lose many irreplaceable hours brooding over grievances that, in a year's time, will be forgotten by us and by everybody. No, let us devote our life to worthwhile actions and feelings, to great thoughts, real affections and enduring undertakings. For life is too short to be little.

## AS A TALE THAT IS TOLD
### *Psalms*

We bring our years to an end as a tale that is told.
The days of our years are three-score years and ten,
Or even by reason of strength four-score years;
Yet is their pride but travail and vanity;
For it is speedily gone, and we fly away.
So teach us to number our days
That we may obtain a heart of wisdom.

### *Goethe*

A useless life is only an early death.

## IN DYING . . . ONE GIVES SIGNIFICANCE
### *John Gardner*

If a soldier dies merely through the hazards of war, that is one thing. But if he dies for a cause to which his country has linked its destiny, such as human freedom or the maintenance of justice, he has linked himself to a cause which is great and glorious. If that cause is eternal, an eternal significance is given to his dying. But if not, his attachment to it gives him the distinction of a patriot and a hero, but not necessarily that of a saint. To die for justice or for freedom, links a man to something different from mere devotion to a flag. Justice is not temporal, it is eternal. In dying for it, one gives significance to his final act. If a man will link himself to the will of God and the reign of God over all human affairs; if he lives for it, dies for it, his life and death are merged in the life and purpose of God and therefore he is indestructible.

## Epictetus

Remind thyself that he whom thou lovest is mortal—that what thou lovest is not thine own; it is given thee for the present, not irrevocably nor forever, but even as a fig or a bunch of grapes at the appointed season of the year. . . .

## Deuteronomy

If they were wise, they would consider their latter end.

## THE SCHOOL OF ADVERSITY
### Joseph Krauskopf

Affliction is a stern teacher, but the best. From it alone we know how to value justly things below. He who wrestles with us strengthens our nerves and increases our skill. Our antagonist is our helper. He that has never known adversity is but half-acquainted with others or with himself. . . .

Much depends upon how we acquit ourselves under our crushing trials. . . . The sharpest sting of adversity is borrowed from our own impatience. . . . There are chemical solutions that deposit their precipitates in the shade and stillness of night; so in the dark hours of trouble the latent virtues of noble character are developed. . . .

## DEATH BRINGS AWARENESS
### Frances Gunther

All the wonderful things in life are so simple that one is not aware of their wonder until they are beyond touch. Never have I felt the wonder and beauty and joy of life so keenly as now in my grief that Johnny is not here to enjoy them. Today, when I see parents impatient or tired or bored with their children, I wish I could say to them, But they are alive, think of the wonder of that! They may be a care and a burden, but think, they are alive! You can touch them—what a miracle! All parents who have lost a child will feel what I mean. Others, luckily, cannot. But I hope they will embrace them with a little added rapture and a keener awareness of joy.

## BE PREPARED AT ALL TIMES
### Earl of Warwick

There is nothing more certain than death, nothing more uncertain than the time of dying. I will, therefore, be prepared for that at all times, which may come at any time, must come at one time or another. I shall not hasten my death by being still ready, but sweeten it. It makes me not die the sooner, but the better.

### Midrash

A man cannot say to the Angel of Death: "I wish to arrange my affairs before I die."

## PORTRAIT PAINTERS OF THE SOUL
### Joshua Loth Liebman

Judaism is the religion of life which makes no cult out of death, which seeks no private salvation from the grave, which accepts with confidence and trust both the miracle of birth and the mystery of death. Our faith does not close its eyes to tragedy and does not deny that we human beings shall never possess the everlastingness of stone, the silent perduring quality of the mountain peak, but we have other gifts, conscious minds, aspiring hearts, far-visioned souls. Our faith tells us that God has given to each human being the ability to paint a portrait large or small, beautiful or ugly, radiant or blooming, and our faith summons us to become a portrait painter of a soul-landscape that shall be worthy to be hung in any art gallery of the spirit. Judaism proclaims that God has arranged our journey so that in years brief or many we can find love, joy and the fruits of fulfilment, partial and relative though they be, and that when our day is finished, we should accept its final note with the same calm trust that we greet the skylark's song at sunrise. True, "each one of us has his toad to swallow every morning." Yet we can become what Goethe once said is the true task of man— "Life-worthy."

*Ecclesiasticus*

Remember thy last end, and cease from enmity.

## 'TIS A LITTLE JOURNEY

*Anonymous*

'Tis a little journey
This we walk;
Hardly time for murmurs—
Time for talk.

Yet we learn to quarrel
And to hate;
Afterwards regret it
When too late.

Now and then 'tis sunshine—
Sometimes dark;
Sometimes care and sorrow
Leave their mark.

Yet we walk the pathway
Side by side;
Where so many others
Lived and died.

We can see the moral,
Understand;
Yet we walk not always
Hand in hand.

Why must there be hatred?
Greed and strife?
Do we need such shadows
Here in life?

'Tis a little journey
Soon gone by;
Let's be friends together
Ere we die

## OPPORTUNITY

### Anonymous

I shall pass through this world but once.
Any good therefore that I can do or any kindness that I can show
to any human being let me do it now.
Let me not defer or neglect it, for I shall not pass this way again.

## ROB DEATH OF ULTIMATE VICTORY

### Jacob P. Rudin

Death will come. Its hand will not be stayed even an instant; nor
can we enter into judgment with it. Our question "Why?" will go
unanswered. But this does not mean that we are helpless in the
face of death. We can and we do rob death of ultimate victory,
by living life as long as it is ours to live. To ask of death that it
never come is futile, but it is not futility to pray that when death
does come for us, it may take us from a world one corner of which
is a little better because we were there.

When we are dead, and people weep for us and grieve, let it be
because we touched their lives with beauty and simplicity. Let it
not be said that life was good to us, but, rather, that we were good
to life.

## OF EVERY TEAR SOME GOOD IS BORN
### *Charles Dickens*

When Death strikes down the innocent and young, for every fragile form from which he lets the panting spirit free a hundred virtues rise, in shapes of mercy, charity, and love, to walk the world and bless it. Of every tear that sorrowing mortals shed on such green graves some good is born, some gentler nature comes. In the Destroyer's steps there spring up bright creations that defy his power, and his dark path becomes a way of light to heaven.

## A GOOD NAME IS BETTER THAN GOOD OIL
### *Talmud*

When Rabbi Johanan concluded the Book of Job, he said thus: The end of man is death, and the end of cattle is slaughter, and everything is designated for death. Blessed is he that has been reared in the Law, and whose toil is in the Law, and acts so as to please his Creator, and has grown up with a good name, and departed life with a good name, Concerning him, Solomon said (Ecclesiastes: VII, 1): "A good name is better than precious oil; and the day of death than the day of one's birth."

## TO LIVE FULLY, RICHLY, NOBLY
### *Joshua Loth Liebman*

And while we live, we should try to make each day a year as far as beauty, nobility, and a warm sense of brotherhood are concerned. In a time when there is so much cruelty abroad, we must generate the oxygen of love to keep the soul of the world still breathing. Religion should summon all of us to deepen the quality of life as a compensation for the diminution of its quantity, to treasure each other in the recognition that we do not know how long we shall have each other, to make life strong and brave and beautiful as our answer to the forces of death abroad in the world. We must make up for the threatened brevity of life by heightening the intensity of life. The crimes and sin for which there should be little forgiveness during this epoch are hardheartedness, selfishness, mutual cruelty, lovelessness—all of the little weapons which we use to shorten the lives of others. Our very understanding of each other can serve to deepen life even when we cannot lengthen it.

All men today need the healthy-mindedness of Judaism, the natural piety with which the Jew declares, "One world at a time is enough." For just as we can rely without fear upon the Power greater than ourselves during this earthly journey; just as we can rest and do rest securely upon the bosom of mystery every time we fall asleep at night—so we can trust the universe beyond time also, recognizing that it is the part of wisdom not to seek to remove the veil from before birth or after death, but to live fully, richly, nobly, here and now, and make possible a society where other men can so live.

*John Henry Newman*

Fear not that thy life shall come to an end, but rather fear that it shall never have a beginning.


# A RIGHTEOUS JUDGE

## *Ben Zion Bokser*

Simon mourned excessively for his departed friend. He was inconsolable in his grief. One night in a vision he heard a voice say to him reprovingly: "Why do you grieve so much? Is not death an inevitable incident in the cycle of life? Would you change the plan of the universe and make man immortal?"

Simon gathered courage and he talked back: "Why not, O Lord? Thou canst do all things. My friend—and others like him—why should there be an end to lives as wonderful as theirs?"

And the voice replied: "So you deny the service of death to the economy of life! Very well, then. We shall set you into a world where immortality prevails, and see how you like it."

Simon looked at the countryside and understood the meaning of his dream. All this magnificence will endure forever. Nothing of it will perish. And so it indeed turned out to be.

Not a flower died on its stalk. Not a blossom fell from the lilac bushes. Summer gave way and autumn came, but not a leaf withered, not a tree lost its foliage. The world in all its beauty had been given a kind of fixed permanence, and it shone in the self-same lustre. At last life seemed to be freed from the ravages of time and circumstance.

But gradually Simon felt palled. Nothing died in his world, but nothing was born in it either. He was spared the ravages of age, but he missed seeing the wondrous dance of youth. His eyes tired at the beauty of flowers forever the same in hue. He longed to witness the glory of a new flower's unfolding. He was ready to renounce the gift of immortality when he suddenly awoke from his dream.

He brooded for a while over his strange experience and then he said: "O Lord, I thank Thee that Thou hast made a mortal of flesh and blood. Someone died that I might be born and I am willing to die that there may be growth and the emergence of new life in Thy world. Thou art a righteous Judge."

### Madam Guyon

Our days are numbered: let us spare
Our anxious hearts a needless care:
'Tis Thine to number out our days;
'Tis ours to give them thy Praise.

## NOAM GROSSMAN

### (Translated from the Hebrew by Eliezer Whartman)

*Noam Grossman was born in Brooklyn. At an early age he was brought to Palestine, and later entered the Hebrew University, where he excelled in historical criticism. His career never came to full flower, for he was cut down at the age of twenty while on a mission in the Judean hills. . . .*

*One of the most heart-rending documents to come out of the war is Noam's will, the last message which his parents received. It was found among his things after his death. Upon the envelope was written: "To be opened only after my death."*

#### LAST WILL AND TESTAMENT

This will is written in haste without time to say goodbye.
1. Bury me in the Nahlat Yitzhak cemetery in Tel Aviv.
2. Do not print any tributes to me in the newspapers.

3. My salary and my money due me is to be turned over to my family to establish a fund with which to buy rifles for the Haganah.
4. My personal effects are to be forwarded to my family.
5. Do not mourn for me; I did only that which I was called upon to do.

### Ethics of the Fathers

It is not thy duty to complete the work but neither art thou free to desist from it.

## THE WATER MILL

### Sarah Doudney

Listen to the water mill, through the livelong day,
How the clanking of its wheels wears the hours away.
Languidly the autumn winds stir the greenwood leaves;
From the field the reapers sing, binding up the sheaves;
And a proverb haunts my mind, a spell is cast;
"The mill will never grind with the water that has passed."

Take a lesson to thyself, loving heart and true;
Golden years are fleeting by, youth is passing, too;
Learn to make the most of life, lose no happy day;
Time will never bring thee back chances swept away.
Leave no tender word unsaid, love while life shall last;
"The mill will never grind with water that has passed."

Work while the daylight shines, man of strength and will
Never does the streamlet glide useless by the mill.
Wait not till tomorrow's sun beams up the way;
All thou canst call thy own lies in thy today.
Power, intellect and health may not, cannot last;
"The mill will never grind with water that has passed."

Oh, the wasted hours of life that have drifted by,
Oh, the good we might have done, lost without a sigh;
Love that we might once have saved by a single word,
Thoughts conceived but never penned, perishing unheard,
Take a proverb to thine heart, take it, oh, hold it fast;
"The mill will never grind with water that has passed."

## Talmud

Blessed shalt thou be when thou comest in, and bless shalt thou be when thou goest out (Deuteronomy: XXXVII, 6). May thy departure from this world be like thy coming into this world. As thou didst enter into this world without sin, so mayest thou depart from this world without sin.

## Carroll Binder

I love life but I am not worried about death. I do not feel that I have lost my son and a host of others dear to me by death. . . . Death, I believe, teaches us the things of deathlessness.

## THE PURPOSE OF LIFE
### Albert Einstein

How extraordinary is the situation of us mortals Each of us is here for a brief sojourn; for what purpose he knows not though he sometimes thinks he senses it. But without going deeper than our daily life, it is plain that we exist for our fellow-men—in the first place for those upon whose smiles and welfare our happiness depends, and next for all those unknown to us personally but to whose destinies we are bound by the tie of sympathy. A hundred times every day I remind myself that my inner and outer life depend on the labors of other men, living and dead, and that I must exert myself in order to give in the measure as I have received and am still receiving.

## A THOUSAND YEARS IN THY SIGHT
### Psalms

Lord, Thou hast been our dwelling place in all generations.
Before the mountains were brought forth,
Or ever Thou hadst formed the earth and the world,
Even from everlasting to everlasting, Thou art God.
Thou turnest man to contrition;
And sayest: "Return, ye children of men."

For a thousand years in Thy sight
Are but as yesterday when it is past,
And as a watch in the night.


### Helen Keller

Each day comes to me with both hands full of possibilities, and in its brief course I discern all the verities and realities of my existence, the bliss of growth, the glory of action, the spirit of beauty.

## A ROSE TO THE LIVING

### Nixon Waterman

A rose to the living is more than
Sumptuous wreaths to the dead;
In filling love's infinite store,
A rose to the living is more—
If graciously given before the
Hungering spirit is fled,
A rose to the living is more than
Sumptuous wreaths to the dead


### Francis Quartes

If thou expect death as a friend, prepare to entertain it; if thou expect death as an enemy, prepare to overcome it; death has no advantage, but when it comes a stranger.

## I SHALL NOT PASS THIS WAY AGAIN

### Eva Rose York

I shall not pass this way again—
    Although it bordered be with flowers,
    Although I rest in fragrant bowers,
        And hear the singing
        Of song-birds winging
To highest heaven their gladsome flight;
Though moons are full and stars are bright,

And winds and waves are softly sighing,
While leafy trees make low replying;
Though voices clear in joyous strain
Repeat a jubilant refrain;
Though rising suns their radiance throw
On summer's green and winter's snow,
In such rare splendor that my heart
Would ache from scenes like these to part;
    Though beauties heighten,
    And life-lights brighten,
And joys proceed from every pain—
I shall not pass this way again.

Then let me pluck the flowers that blow,
And let me listen as I go
    To music rare
    That fills the air;
    And let hereafter
    Songs and laughter
Fill every pause along the way;
And to my spirit let me say:
"O soul, be happy; soon 'tis trod,
The path made thus for thee by God.
Be happy, thou, and bless His name
By whom such marvellous beauty came."
And let no chance by me be lost
To kindness show at any cost.
I shall not pass this way again;
Then let me now relieve some pain,
Remove some barrier from the road,
Or brighten someone's heavy load;
A helping hand to this one lend,
Then turn some other to befriend.

    O God, forgive
    That now I live
As if I might, sometime, return
To bless the weary ones that yearn
For help and comfort every day—
For there be such along the way.
O God, forgive that I have seen
The beauty only, have not been

Awake to sorrow such as this;
That I have drunk the cup of bliss
Remembering not that those there be
Who drink the dregs of misery.

I love the beauty of the scene,
Would roam again o'er fields so green;
But since I may not, let me spend
My strength for others to the end—
For those who tread on rock and stone,
And bear their burdens all alone,
Who loiter not in leafy bowers,
Nor hear the birds nor pluck the flowers.
A larger kindness give to me,
A deeper love and sympathy;
          Then, O one day
          May someone say—
Remembering a lessened pain—
"Would she could pass this way again."

## Talmud

Rabbi Eliezer declared: "Repent one day before your death." Whereupon his disciples asked: "How does one know which day that is?" "Exactly," answered the Sage, "for that reason we ought to live every day as though it were our last."

## Edward Capel Cure

What a man has is too often the standard of worth while a man is living; what he has done is the ultimate standard of the world; what he has been is God's standard.

## DEATH SERVES LIFE

In the University of Oxford, above the entrance to the Department of Anatomy, there is the following inscription: "This is the place where death serves life."

## FROM "THE CHOIR INVISIBLE"
### George Eliot

Oh, may I join the choir invisible
Of those immortal dead who live again
In minds made better by their presence; live
In pulses stirred to generosity,
In deeds of daring rectitude, in scorn
For miserable aims that end with self,
In thoughts sublime that pierce the night like stars,
And with their mild persistence urge man's search
To vaster issues!
                              This is life to come,
Which martyred men have made more glorious
For us to strive to follow. May I reach
That purest heaven, be to other souls
The cup of strength in some great agony,
Enkindle generous ardor, feed pure love,
Beget the smiles that have no cruelty,
Be the sweet presence of a good diffused,
And in diffusion ever more intense.
So shall I join the choir invisible
Whose music is the gladness of the world.


### George Eliot

If endless morrows had stretched before man's vision
He would never have accomplished anything today.


## FORGIVENESS
### John Greenleaf Whittier

My heart was heavy, for its trust had been
  Abused, its kindness answered with foul wrong;
So, turning gloomily from my fellowmen,
  One summer Sabbath day I strolled among
The green mounds of the village burial-place;
  Where pondering how all human love and hate

Find one sad level; and how, soon or late,
Wronged and wrongdoer, each with meekened face,
And cold hands folded over a still heart,
Pass the green threshold of our common grave,
Whither all footsteps tend, whence none depart,
Awed for myself, and pitying my race,
Our common sorrow, like a mighty wave
Swept all my pride away, and trembling I forgave!

## THE MEASURE OF MAN

*Anonymous*

Not—"How did he die?" But—"How did he live?"
Not—"What did he gain?" But—"What did he give?"
These are the units to measure the worth
Of a man as a man, regardless of birth.

Not—"What was his station?" But—"Had he a heart?"
And—"How did he play his God-given part?
Was he ever ready with a word of good cheer,
To bring back a smile, to banish a tear?

Not—"What was his shrine?" Nor—"What was his creed?"
But—"Had he befriended those really in need?"
Not—"What did the sketch in the newspaper say?"
But—"How many were sorry when he passed away?"

## MAN CARRIES NOTHING AWAY EXCEPT . . .

*Talmud*

A hungry fox was eyeing some luscious fruit in a garden, but to his dismay, he could find no way to enter. At last he discovered an opening through which, he thought, he might possibly get in, but he soon found that the hole was too small to admit his body. "Well," he thought, "if I fast three days I will be able to squeeze through." He did so; and he now feasted to his heart's delight on the grapes and all the other good things in the orchard. But lo! when he wanted to escape before the owner of the garden would find him, he discovered to his great distress, that the opening had again become too small for him. Poor animal! Again he had to fast three days, and as he escaped, he cast a farewell glance upon the scene of his late revels saying: "O garden, charming art thou, delicious are thy fruits! But what have I now for all my labor and cunning?"

So it is with man. Naked he comes into the world, naked must he leave it. After all his toil therein he carries nothing away with him except the good deeds he leaves behind.

*Benjamin Franklin*

A long life may not be good enough but a good life is long enough.

*Stephen Vincent Benét*

Life is not lost by dying!
Life is lost minute by minute, day by dragging day
In all the thousand, small, uncaring ways.

## BEHOLD, O EARTH

*Saul Tchernichovsky (Translated from the Hebrew
by Sholom J. Kahn)*

Behold, O Earth, what spendthrifts we are
indeed!
Where blessing dwells, in your hidden lap, we
have buried seed . . .
Not grains of heavy wheat, pearls of spelt with
glossy coats,
No gold-sheathed barley seed, nor timid ears
of oats.

Behold, O Earth, what spendthrifts we are
indeed!
In you we have hid our choicest flowers, most
splendid of the breed,
Kissed by the sun's first kiss, concealing still

Their grace on lovely stalks, cups of incense
ready to fill.
Before they could know their noon, at innocent
sorrow's core,
Or drain the dew for dreams of light that their
sprouting bore.

Take you the best of our sons, youth's visions
of purest worth,
Pure of heart, clean of hands, not soiled with
filth of earth,
The fabric of their lives still weaving, with hopes
of a day more fair.
We have none that are better than these. Have
you? Then where?

And you shall cover all these. May the plant
arise at length!
To its homeland's people sacred, in hundred-
fold splendor and strength!
Blest be their offering of death, by whose glory
our lives are freed . . .
Behold, O Earth, what spendthrifts we are
indeed!

*Virgil*

Death plucks my ear and says, Live— I am coming.


## FROM "THANATOPSIS"
### *William Cullen Bryant*

So live, that when thy summons comes to join
The innumerable caravan, which moves
To that mysterious realm, where each shall take
His chamber in the silent halls of death,
Thou go not, like the quarry-slave at night,
Scourged to his dungeon, but, sustained and soothed
By an unfaltering trust, approach thy grave
Like one who wraps the drapery of his couch
About him, and lies down to pleasant dreams.

I walked a mile with Sorrow
And ne'er a word said she
But oh the things I learned from her
When Sorrow walked with me.

—Robert Browning Hamilton

# THE THINGS WE LEARN
# FROM SORROW

*The moment of bereavement is the most dreaded of all moments. So deeply do we fear separation from those we love that we try desperately to prevent the very thought of it from stealing into our consciousness. When in unguarded moments it succeeds in breaking through, we hasten to expel the unwelcome intruder. It is therefore not altogether strange that sorrow finds us emotionally unprepared and perhaps even rebellious and resentful.*

*If we are wise, however, we will accept sorrow courageously now that it has forced its way into our lives. Despite its forbidding countenance, sorrow possesses great potential power to expand our lives, to enlarge our vision and to deepen our understanding. It has played a beautiful and transforming role in the lives of countless bereaved who could say in a mood of melancholy gratefulness with Wordsworth: "A deep distress hath humanized my soul."*

*Through the portals of sorrow we can enter into the suffering of others. Our human compassion is kindled. Our sympathies are awakened. Grief can also help purge us of pettiness and selfishness. It can elicit from us powers of fortitude and patience which, but for it, might have never been quickened into life. Sorrow can thus bring us closer to our fellow man and help introduce us to ourselves. The recorded experience and testimony of poet, psalmist and philosopher all tend to confirm overwhelmingly the observation of Jean Paul: "There is a purity which only suffering can impart; the stream of life becomes snow-white when it dashes against the rocks."*

196

*The abundance of elegaic poetry and music in world culture points up another benevolent service which sorrow frequently renders. Where we do not permit it to embitter us or crush us, it often arouses deep latent powers of creativity by which the human spirit transmutes suffering into song, adversity into artistry, and pain into poetry.*

*Thus it is quite possible to emulate those of whom the Psalmist wrote: "They pass through a valley of tears and convert it into a life-giving fountain." Our sorrows can serve as "needles with which God sews our souls to eternal truths." If we face sorrow affirmatively and creatively we can use it to enhance life's meaning and beauty for others no less than for ourselves.*

*This truth seems to be symbolized by a strange tree which grows near Bombay. It is called "The Sorrowful Tree" because it has the remarkable characteristic of blooming only in the night. Just as soon as the sun sets, the flowers come bursting out. May not this also reflect our uniquely human endowment? Like that tree we can also bring forth flowers of surpassing beauty in the dark night of sorrow.*

---

## VICTORY IN DEFEAT

### Edwin Markham

Defeat may serve as well as victory
To shake the soul and let the glory out.
When the great oak is straining in the wind,
The boughs drink in new beauty and the trunk
Sends down a deeper root on the windward side.
Only the soul that knows the mighty grief
Can know the mighty rapture. Sorrows come
To stretch out spaces in the heart for joy.

## LOST AND FOUND

### George MacDonald

I missed him when the sun began to bend;
I found him not when I had lost his rim;

With many tears I went in search of him,
Climbing high mountains which did still ascend,
And gave me echoes when I called my friend;
Through cities vast and charnel-houses grim,
And high cathedrals where the light was dim,
Through books and arts and works without an end,
But found him not—the friend whom I had lost.
And yet I found him—as I found the lark,
A sound in fields I heard, but could not mark;
I found him nearest when I missed him most;
I found him in my heart, a life in frost,
A light I knew not till my soul was dark.


## I THANK THEE, GOD! FOR WEAL AND WOE

*Eliza Cook*

I thank Thee, God! for all I've known
Of kindly fortune, health, and joy;
And quite as gratefully I own
The bitter drops of life's alloy.

Oh! there was wisdom in the blow
That wrung the sad and scalding tear;
That laid my dearest idol low,
And left my bosom lone and drear.

I thank Thee, God! for all of smart
That thou hast sent; for not in vain
Has been the heavy, aching heart,
The sigh of grief, the throb of pain.

What if my cheek had ever kept
Its healthful color, glad and bright?
What if my eyes had never wept
Throughout a long and sleepless night?

Then, then, perchance, my soul had not
Remembered there were paths less fair;
And, selfish in my own blest lot,
Ne'er strove to soothe another's care.

But when the weight of sorrow found
My spirit prostrate and resign'd,
The anguish of the bleeding wound
Taught me to feel for all mankind.

Even as from the wounded tree
The goodly precious balm will pour;
So in the riven heart there'll be
Mercy that never flow'd before.

'Tis well to learn that sunny hours
May quickly change to mournful shade;
'Tis well to prize life's scatter'd flowers,
Yet be prepared to see them fade.

I thank Thee, God! for weal and woe;
And, whatsoe'er the trial be;
'Twill serve to wean me from below,
And bring my spirit nigher Thee.

## SHAPING THE RAW MATERIAL
## OF SORROW
### Charles Lewis Slattery

We may turn this gift of sorrow as men turn a diamond in the sun and see new shafts of light from it. We may think of sorrow as harsh raw material which God gives to us, asking us to cooperate with Him in His creative power and, by using our ingenuity and our faith, to make this raw material into something glorious, and so give it back to Him as our own gift for His happiness.

We may think of an earthly father who presents to his son a tree, and then, giving him certain tools, such as an axe and saw and chisel, bids him turn that tree into something beautiful. Through the years, with increasing strength and increasing skill and imagination, the youth fells the tree and makes its wood at last into a great chest, which he carves with the images of animals and plants. When the carving is all that he can make it, when he has filled every angle and curve with the love which he bears his father, he brings his finished gift home. The happiness on the father's face is beyond all description; this chest, he commands, shall be bequeathed from generation to generation as a precious heirloom as long as his family shall endure. So God's human children may take the raw material of sorrow and fashion it, by years of faithfulness and labor and love, into a glorious thing, a fitting gift for the loving Father on High.

## SORROW—THE SOLEMN INITIATION
### George Eliot

For the first sharp pangs there is no comfort. Whatever goodness may surround us, darkness and silence still hang about our pain. But, slowly, the clinging companionship with the dead is linked with our living affections and duties, and we begin to feel our sorrow as a solemn initiation, preparing us for that sense of loving, pitying fellowship with the fullest human lot, which, I must think, no one who has tasted it will deny to be the chief blessedness of our life.

### Leigh Hunt

We may conceive it possible for beings to be made entirely happy; but in our composition something of pain seems to be a necessary ingredient, in order that the materials may turn to as fine account as possible, though our clay, in the course of ages and experience, may be refined more and more.

## FRIEND SORROW
### Adelaide Ann Procter

Do not cheat thy heart and tell her
    "Grief will pass away.
Hope for fairer times in future,
    And forget to-day."
Tell her, if you will, that sorrow
    Need not come in vain;
Tell her that the lesson taught her
    Far outweighs the pain.

*Thomas Fuller*

That which is bitter to endure may be sweet to remember.


## A MESSAGE FOR BETSY ANN

*Fulton Oursler*

No other letter I have ever received was as hard to answer as the one from Betsy Ann. Here is what Betsy Ann wrote:

"My dog is named Jigger. I love him like a little brother. He got sick and the vet said he could never get well. So I prayed to God, but Jigger died early this morning, before I went to school. Please print the answer to that: Why on earth didn't God answer my prayer?"

Why on earth? Grownups know that we cannot understand the mind of God. But how do you comfort a grieving child?

For one thing, I hope Betsy Ann gives a home to some poor homeless dog. Of course, I know she feels there can never be another Jigger; she's right about that. But she has so much love to give, and there are little dogs that the kind people at the S.P.C.A. would hate to see wind up in the pound. And if Jigger had a soul, he could never be happy in a dog heaven while his little mistress was so lonely. He would bark his joy across the sky, if she would try to help some friendless little dog.

When sorrows come, we are all tempted to feel bitter and cry out: "Why should this happen to me? What did I do to deserve it?"

But there is an answer. Often, I am sure, Betsy asks a favor of her earthly father. She climbs up on his knee and pleads with him, perhaps to stay home tonight and play games. And sometimes Daddy has to refuse. His reasons for saying no may be too hard for a little girl to understand, but just the same she is perfectly sure that Daddy loves her. We must be sure of God's love, too.

And now that Betsy Ann has learned so young what heartache is like—knowing how it feels to lose something dear and precious—she will always feel sympathy for others in a world that has a lot of trouble in it. She can even try to make them happy again. For there are others who have suffered even more terribly—and Betsy Ann can feel with them, which is the meaning of the word "compassion. . . ."

The greatest miracle in the world is compassion for others, rather than grieving for ourselves. In human sympathy, there is healing for ourselves and power to change the world. People who learn that mystery help to make this a better life. If Betsy Ann can know that miracle, little Jigger will not have died in vain.

*Anonymous*

And yet these days of dreariness are sent us from above;
They do not come in anger, but in faithfulness and love;
They come to teach us lessons which bright ones could not yield,
And to leave us blest and thankful when their purpose is fulfilled.

*Author unknown*

Sorrow is the blackboard upon which God writes His promises.

## SORROW CAN ENLARGE THE DOMAIN OF OUR LIFE
*Morris Adler*

Our sorrow can bring understanding as well as pain, breadth as well as the contraction that comes with pain. Out of love and sorrow can come a compassion that endures. The needs of others hitherto unnoticed, the anxieties of neighbors never before realized, now come into the ken of our experience, for our sorrow has opened our life to the needs of others. A bereavement that brings us into the lives of our fellow-men writes a fitting epilogue to a love that had taught us kindliness, and forbearance and had given us so much joy.

Sorrow can enlarge the domain of our life, so that we may now understand the triviality of the things many pursue. We have in our hands a noble and refined measure for judging the events and objects we daily see. What is important is not luxury but love; not wealth but wisdom; not gold but goodness.

And our sorrow may so clear our vision that we may, more brightly, see the God, of Whom it was said, "The Lord is nigh unto them, that are of a broken heart." Beyond the hurry and turmoil of life rises the Eternal. There is God in a world in which love like ours could bloom. There is God in a world in which human beings could experience tenderness. There is God in a world in which two lives can be bound together by a tie stronger than death.

Out of that vision will come a sense of obligation. A duty, solemn, sacred and significant, rests upon us. To spread the love we have known to others. To share the joy which has been ours. To ease the pains which man's thoughtlessness or malice inflicts. We have a task to perform. There is work to be done and in work there is consolation.

Out of love may come sorrow. But out of sorrow can come light for others who dwell in darkness. And out of the light we bring to others will come light for ourselves—the light of solace, of strength, of transfiguring and consecrating purpose.

## SUFFERING IS A HOLY THING

### Richard C. Trench

O Life! O Death! O World! O Time!
O Grave, where all things flow!
'Tis yours to make our lot sublime,
With your great weight of woe.

Though sharpest anguish hearts may wring,
Though bosoms torn may be,
Yet suffering is a holy thing:
Without it, what were we?

## STARS MAY BE SEEN FROM THE BOTTOM OF A DEEP WELL

### Joseph Krauskopf

The precious diamond must be cut in order to show its lustre. The sweet incense must be burned in order to exhale its fragrance. Adversity is like the periods of the former and the later rain—cold, comfortless, unfriendly, yet from such seasons the flower and the fruit have their birth. Stars may be seen from the bottom of a deep well when they cannot be discerned from the top of a mountain. So in adversity are learned many things which the prosperous man dreams of. We ought as fervently to pray for a blessing upon our daily rod as upon our daily bread. Adversity has the effect of eliciting talents which prosperity would permit to lie dormant. Prosperity is a great teacher; adversity is a greater. Possession pampers the mind; privation trains and strengthens it.

### E. B. Pusey

God does not take away trials or carry us over them, but strengthens us through them.

## TEMPESTS AND TRIALS MAKE THE MAN
### Joseph Krauskopf

A smooth sea never made a skilful mariner; neither do uninterrupted prosperity and success qualify us for usefulness and happiness. Shallow and loose-rooted is the tree that has known only sunshine, that has never felt the wrench and shock of the gale. The storms of adversity, like those of the ocean, rouse the faculties—excite the invention, prudence, skill, and fortitude of the voyager. The martyrs of all times, in bracing their minds to outward calamities, acquired a loftiness of purpose and a moral heroism worth a lifetime of ease and security.

It is not the so-called blessings of life—its sunshine and calm, its comfort and ease—that make man, but its rugged experiences, its storms and tempest and trials. Early adversity is often a blessing in disguise. Wherever souls are being tried, there God is hewing out the pillars for His temple.

### Alphonse Lamartine

Grief knits two hearts in closer bonds than happiness ever can; and common sufferings are far stronger links than common joys.

## PASSING THROUGH THE VALLEY
### Rufus Jones

Nobody enjoys by preference going through tunnels, or what the beloved Psalmist called "valleys of shadow." And yet all the greatest guides of the soul have known that there are no detours which go around these "valleys of weeping." They must be travelled through. The great achievement is to so pass through them that one makes them "places of springs of water" for others who come there afterwards.

## THERE IS COMPENSATION FOR SUFFERING

### *Charles Louis Slattery*

I have . . . known intimately those who have passed through the various experiences of life, from serene safety in the quiet harbours out into the raging storms of suffering and sorrow and death. It has been my duty to observe the changes and the growth of the human soul through these vicissitudes. Again and again I have seen, in the hour of woe, the souls of men and women arise from a life of selfishness and complacency and worldliness into a life of self-sacrifice, the giving of the whole self for others. A beauty and a radiance have come into faces which had not been there before. Below the kindness and the unselfishness there was always the lingering, unforgetting sorrow, but it was sorrow transcended, transmuted into something "rich and strange."

People in trouble, and particularly youth in trouble, turned to these deep natures made kind and beautiful, and invariably found the help they longed for and feared they could not find. And so there was compensation for the suffering, a new sort of joy which was foreign to anything known in the gay past, a joy which was bought at the heavy price of sorrow.

Perhaps the power to help in the hard places was worth the suffering which they had gone through; for nothing lighter or easier would have fitted them for this final and greatest ministry to the human heart and the human soul. When love reaches its goal, it counts everything that contributes to that achievement an asset in life, and the man who loves to the end is ready to thank God for the power, however that power is given. The man who knows that he has the power looks down with a fierce contempt upon the easy years when his barns were bursting with plenty, when he had every luxury at his door, when all he loved were seated around his heavily laden table.

The ease, the freedom from worry, the exemption from human sorrow, now seem cheap. He was then in the lower grades of the school of life. He really did not know life at all. Now he has been burned as by fire; his soul is branded with hot irons; he has lived through sorrow, and he knows. Henceforth he is as the shadow of the great rock in a weary land. Men shall flee to him for peace. And in his understanding and his love they shall find it. . . .


## THE LESSON OF THE ROSE
### *Harriet Beecher Stowe*

It is said that gardeners sometimes, when they would bring a rose to richer flowering, deprive it for a season of light and moisture. Silent and dark it stands, dropping one faded leaf after another, and seeming to go down patiently to death. But when every leaf is dropped, and the plant stands stripped to the uttermost, a new life is even then working in the buds, from which shall spring a tender foliage and a brighter wealth of flowers. So, often, in celestial gardening every leaf of earthly joy must drop before a new and divine bloom visits the soul.


### *Fulton Oursler*

True and strange it is, that often, if we do not run away from our trials but face them and conquer them, the prize is ours.


## SORROW—A STIMULANT, NOT A NARCOTIC
### *H. Adye Prichard*

Our tears are often strengthening; they often fit us for higher aims and nobler aspirations; they often send us out more intent upon the work in hand; and the dead, it may be, know that, in the tears that are shed for them, there is something of that same great refining power which will make the mourner stronger, in the future, for his mourning. Perhaps they do not grieve as much as we are warned they do for the sorrow they leave behind them, provided they see that sorrow is being used as a stimulant and not a narcotic.

## WHAT HAVE I TO LIVE FOR?

### *Grace Perkins Oursler and April Armstrong*

The Rev. Margaret Blair Johnstone, Congregational minister of Groton, Connecticut, tells of a young widow who determined upon self-destruction because, she said, "I cannot go on without him. What have I to live for? This is the greatest blow in the world."

"Then," said Mrs. Johnstone, "why do you want to inflict it on your mother and your children?"

"But what have I to live for?" the woman moaned.

"You might turn to God and ask. He has a purpose. He is not aimless, I assure you. If you seek Him, he'll show you why He wants you to live."

Fourteen years later that same widow hurried to her nineteen-year-old daughter's bedside.

"I don't want to live," the girl moaned in her first shock of knowledge that her husband had been killed in a highway accident which terminated their honeymoon. "I can't take it," she repeated. "What have I to live for without him, tell me, Mother?"

It was then, and only then, that the older widow knew she had found her own answer.

## PSALMS

It is good for me that I have been afflicted, in order that I might learn Thy laws.

## I WEPT AND THEN BELIEVED

### *B. A. Levinson*

When the mind is clear of trouble and the body free of pain, most of us feel no call for superhuman comfort and support. The daily round, the common tasks and customary distractions appear to suffice. It is when pain and anguish wring the brow that the yearning comes for help beyond human providence. That yearning becomes with suffering so urgent that its answer follows. . . . As it is said in the Psalms, "They cry out unto the Lord in their trouble and He bringeth them out of their distresses."

So we often read in biographies of a newborn faith coming as a solace to a sufferer. Browning's succinct words are apt: "Knowledge by suffering entereth." One example, quoted because it is as simple as it is poignant, is that of Chateaubriand.—Till then an avowed unbeliever, yet when intense sorrow fell to him upon the death of a beloved sister, he wrote in deep sincerity, "I wept and then believed."

Belief that comes thus to a sufferer, whether it be a wounded heart or a tormented body, is as an "awakening from the dream of life." Is it not truly a revelation?

*Henry Ward Beecher*

Sorrows are often like clouds, which though black when they are passing over us, when they are past become as if they were the garments of God, thrown off in purple and gold along the sky.

## USING TROUBLE CREATIVELY

*Harry Emerson Fosdick*

Here . . . is the real tragedy with us, not that we suffer but that in a world where suffering is the common human lot, sure to come in one form or another to every son and daughter of man, we take toward it merely a negative and defensive attitude, get out of it such habits as resentfulness and self-pity, do not hear it calling with creative voice for those faculties and attributes which ease never asks for and no comfortable happiness ever can produce. If our vocabulary did not have in it words like "trouble," "adversity," "calamity," "grief," our vocabulary by no possibility could have in it words like "bravery," "fortitude," "patience," "self-sacrifice." He who knows no hardship will know no hardihood. He who faces no calamity will need no courage. Mysterious though it is, the characteristics in human nature which we love best grow in a soil with a strong admixture of trouble.

Do not misunderstand me in this. I am not saying that trouble alone brings out our best. . . . Trouble by itself is neutral. It can do almost anything to a man. It can make him bitter and resentful. It can make him hard and cruel. It can plunge his life into despair and wreck his faith on futility. But trouble does that only to people who take a negative attitude toward it and let it do that to them.

There are others . . . upon whom trouble fell as cruelly as on other men, yet who had in them something so creative that their calamity became their opportunity. Those who knew them best looked on them in amazement, saying, "We never guessed they had *that* in them until trouble called for it."

## THE CHASTISEMENTS OF LOVE
### Claude G. Montefiore

. . . If the good suffer, we may say that this suffering tends to make goodness more independent. It helps us to care for goodness for its own sake, to love it, and to love its Source, for themselves and only for themselves. But there is something more. Suffering brings out and develops character. It supplies a field for all sorts of virtues, for resignation, faith, courage, resource, endurance. It stimulates; it purifies. This is an old and familiar and never-to-be-forgotten truth. "The chastisements of love," of which the old rabbis spoke, are very real. The discipline of sorrow, the purification of adversity; preachers often preach about these, and they are right.

### Ian Maclaren

What Absalom, in his impulsive way, did with Joab is like what God sometimes does with His sons. Joab would not come to Absalom's palace; so Absalom set his corn on fire and then Joab came. So God sometimes burns our harvests that we may go to Him.

### Sir Philip Sidney

A noble heart, like the sun, showeth its greatest countenance in its lowest estate.

## A MEDITATION ON AFFLICTION
### From "Blessings and Praise"

The Psalmist recalls the somber days of his affliction, the sudden disaster, the dazed heart heavy with grief, then the gradual healing of the wounded spirit, the chastened soul, the deepened understanding, and the blessed sense of God's comfort and mercy. All this he recalls and praises the Lord: "It is good that Thou hast afflicted me, for thus have I learned Thy statutes."

When we live at ease we sail carelessly over the surface of life unaware of its deeper undercurrents. Then calamity overtakes us, and, in the struggle with the waves, we learn how precious is life, how deep is pain, how boundless our gratitude to our Deliverer and Preserver. God brings us to the very gates of death, in order that we may learn, manfully, how to choose life.

It is not only our own affliction which brings us blessing. Our fellowmen suffer for our benefit. From their tragedies we learn how to avoid misfortune. Even the material comforts of our life are largely due to the suffering of those who lived before us. The houses in which we live, the fuel we burn, the streets we traverse, all have a history of toil, suffering, danger, and even death. The musician who delights us with his art, the teacher who brings light to our minds, the physician who rescues us from pain, all have endured years of self-denial, toil and trouble. We live by the sufferings of the mother who bore us and the parents who reared us. The beautiful lives which inspire us have been wrought in the furnace of affliction. The call comes to all of us to bless as we have been blessed; to accept our share of this interblend of pain and benefit. We who profit by the vast linkage of human woe and weal cannot refuse the burden of pain. We must patiently accept the daily restraints of conscience, and walk the arduous way of virtue. Perhaps others may profit by our strivings and find in our humble lives a blessing.

### Ian Maclaren

The crushing sorrow is often the key that opens the door of God's treasure-house.

## SORROWS RIGHTLY USED
### Charles Lewis Slattery

. . We may accept it (sorrow) as gold accepts the fire which refines it . . . if rightly used, it will mean much to us. We observe what it may mean when we examine certain of our friends. Here is a man who was harsh in his judgments, cynical concerning the virtue of humanity, often cutting and unkind in his wit. One day news was brought that the son he loved best had been killed in a drunken brawl. The old man almost died of the grief. But gradually he came back to life; and when he had made a full return to normal living he was altogether a changed man. None was so generous as he before human failure; none so ready to believe in the ultimate good of questionable character; and henceforth his humour only healed wounds, it never again made them. I knew that man.

Here, again, is a woman who was clever, with charm, limiting her friendship to a few, self-indulgent, just missing being selfish. One day her baby died—a child full of promise. It seemed as if she would never smile again; but for her, too, life came back in its normal phases, and when it came she was a changed character. Her old friends had difficulty in finding her, for she was busied over lonely and desolate people, particularly mothers of little children. Her old self-sufficiency had gone, and in its place appeared a beauty of unselfishness, which shone through her face, especially when she was moved to sympathy. The old charm was still one of her characteristics, but it was lifted into a rare graciousness which made people forget to admire her, because instinctively they gave her their love. That person, too, I knew.

Not all sorrow, you will object, has such effects. You will say that you know how it has turned a blithe man into a crabbed misanthropist; how it has turned a pleasant woman into a moping, dismal hag whom no one willingly sees. No doubt you have seen sorrow which thus disfigured its victims. No doubt, too, the story could be repeated through many examples. But the difficulty is that sorrow with this diabolic power to maim the human soul has been received not as a gift of God, but as a curse from the devil. It has been resented, and fought against, and hated as the final ill in life. It is bathed in darkness, and it remains dark; no light can shine through it. When, on the other hand, sorrow is accepted as an inevitable part of God's order . . . I am confident that it can have only one effect, transforming the spirit which dutifully receives it into a new life, and that life beautiful, radiating the deeper joys.

## TALMUD

As the drug gives out its perfume when it is crushed,
So the soul yields its fragrance when it is chastened.

## LIFE WOULD BE WORTH LITTLE WITHOUT SUFFERING

### *Maltie Babcock*

Present suffering is not enjoyable, but life would be worth little without it. The difference between iron and steel is fire, but steel is worth all it costs. Iron ore may think itself senselessly tortured in the furnace, but when the watch-spring looks back, it knows better. David enjoyed pain and trouble no more than we do, but the time came when he admitted that they had been good for him. Though the aspect of suffering is hard, the prospect is hopeful, and the retrospect will start a song. . . .

### *James Somerville*

Adversity, sage useful guest,
Severe instructor, but the best,
It is from thee alone we know
Justly to value things below.

### *Washington Irving*

Great minds have purposes, others have wishes. Little minds are tamed and subdued by misfortune; but great minds rise above it.

## SORROW

### *Lawrence Binyon*

Woe to him that has not known the woe of man
Who has not felt within him burning all the want
Of desolated bosoms, since the world began;
Felt, as his own, the burden of the fears that daunt;
Who has not eaten failure's bitter bread, and been
Among those ghosts of hope that haunt the day, unseen.

Only when we are hurt with all the hurt untold
In us the thirst, the hunger, and ours the helpless hands,

The palsied effort vain, the darkness and the cold—
Then, only then, the Spirit knows and understands,
And finds in every sigh breathed out beneath the sun
The human heart that makes us infinitely one.


### Honoré de Balzac

The winter's frost must rend the burr of the nut before the fruit is seen. So adversity tempers the human heart, to discover its real worth.


## SUFFERING IS THE CORNERSTONE OF LIFE
### Anatole France

It is on the parched granite of pain that man has firmly established love and courage, heroism and pity. Suffering is the cornerstone of life. On it humanity is founded as on a firm rock. If it should disappear, it would take with it all that makes the worth of life, it would despoil the earth of its splendor and of its glory. It would tear from it the tremulous love of mothers and the piety of sons, it would banish knowledge along with study and would extinguish the lights of the mind.


### Deuteronomy

That He might afflict thee, and that He might prove thee, to do thee good at thy latter end. . . .


## HOW WE LEARN
### Horatius Bonar

Great truths are greatly won. Not found by chance,
Nor wafted on the breath of summer dream,
But grasped in the great struggle of the soul,
Hard buffeting with adverse wind and stream,

Not in the general mart, 'mid corn and wine,
Not in the merchandise of gold and gems,

Not in the world's gay halls of midnight mirth,
  Not 'mid the blaze of regal diadems,

But in the day of conflict, fear, and grief,
  When the strong hand of God, put forth in might,
Plows up the subsoil of the stagnant heart,
  And brings the imprisoned truth-seed to the light.

Wrung from the troubled spirit in hard hours
  Of weakness, solitude, perchance of pain,
Truth springs, like harvest, from the well-plowed field,
  And the soul feels it has not wept in vain.


*Epictetus*

Difficulties are the things that show what men are.


*Leo Tolstoy*

It is by those who have suffered that the world has been advanced.


## RISING ON THE STAIRS OF PAIN
### S. Alfred Adler

Heaven is not to be won by rest and ease and quiet. Only those who have suffered and endured greatly have achieved greatly. The world's greatest workers, thinkers, and teachers have only reached the pinnacle of fame by surmounting obstacles which to ordinary men, content with the lower slopes, would have seemed insuperable. Man has ever risen nearer to God by the altar stairs of pain and sorrow—those altar-stairs which lead through darkness, forever upwards, towards the very Throne of God.


### A. Gordon

Sorrow is only one of the bass notes in the oratorio of our blessedness.

## HOW SUFFERING SHOULD BE MET
### *Harry Emerson Fosdick*

However much in doubt a man may be about the theory of suffering, he knows infallibly how suffering practically should be met. To be rebellious, cursing fate and hating life; to pity oneself, nursing one's hurts in morbid self-commiseration—the ignobility of such dealing with calamity we indubitably know. Even where we fall feebly short of the ideal, we have no question what the ideal is. When in biography or among our friends we see folk face crushing trouble, not embittered by it, made cynical, or thrust into despair, but hallowed, sweetened, illumined, and empowered, we are aware that noble characters do not alone bear trouble; they use it. As men at first faced electricity in dread, conceiving toward it no attitude beyond building lightning-rods to ward away its stroke, but now with greater understanding harness it to do their will, so men, as they grow wise and strong, deal with their suffering. They make it the minister of character; they set it to build in them what nothing save adversity can ever build—patience, courage, sympathy, and power. They even choose it in vicarious sacrifice for the good of others, and by it save the world from evils that nothing save someone's suffering could cure.

### *Aughey*
God's corrections are our instructions; His lashes our lessons, and His scourges our schoolmasters.

### *Midrash*

One thing acquired through pain is better for man than one hundred things easily achieved.

### *Confucius*

The gem cannot be polished without friction, nor man perfected without trials.

## EVIL CAN BE CONVERTED INTO GOOD
### *Louis Binstock*

Sorrow is as much a part of life as is joy. To live is to suffer as well as to rejoice. Sorrow cannot be avoided; it can only be conquered.

. . . One of the great teachers of Israel, recognizing the inevitability of sorrow and reconciling himself to it, adopted as the maxim of his life the famous phrase, "This also for good." His maxim has become a vital, necessary part of the religious philosophy and program of Israel throughout the ages—yea, of every Jew; sometimes it is his only source of salvation. It teaches that every experience of man may be of value, that even as the darkness eventually changes into light, so evil may be converted ultimately into good.

## STARS IN DARKNESS
### *Peter A. Lea*

Darkness makes us aware of the stars,
And so when dark hours arise,
They may hold a bright and lovely thing,
We might never have known otherwise.

### *Horace*

Adversity has the effect of eliciting talents which, in prosperous circumstances, would have lain dormant.

### *Midrash*

God's word recorded in Scripture, "Behold it is very good," refers to the suffering which occurs in the world. But how can the words "behold it is very good" be applied to suffering? Because through it men attain immortality. For go forth in life and see which path leads man to eternity. Surely it is the path of sorrow.

*Talmud*

As salt sweetened the sacrifices of old, so tribulation purifies the devout soul.

## SORROW CREATES SYMPATHY

### *James M. Barrie*

*James M. Barrie, the author, tells how his mother returned home after the death of her eldest son. He describes her reaction to the sorrow:*

"She came back to her desolate home and bowed herself before God. But she never recovered from the blow. From that time she sat in the chair by the window, tended by her noble daughter Jess. That is how my mother got her soft face," says Barrie, "and her pathetic ways, and her large charities; and how other mothers ran to her when they had lost a child."

## HIGH SORROWING

### *Richard Monckton Milnes*

A grace within his soul hath reigned
Which nothing else can bring;
Thank God for all that I have gained
By that high sorrowing.

### *David Mallet*

Affliction is the wholesome soil of virtue, where patience, honor, sweet humanity and calm fortitude take root and strongly flourish.

### *Goethe*

Who ne'er his bread in sorrow ate,
Who ne'er the mournful midnight hours
Weeping upon his bed has sate,
He knows you not, ye Heavenly Powers.

### Henri Frédéric Amiel

Those who have not suffered are still wanting in depth.

### Alphonse de Lamartine

Thou makest the man, O Sorrow!—yes, the whole man—as the crucible gold.

## A PRAYER

### Morris Joseph

O God, who healest the broken-hearted and bindest up their wounds, to Thee I turn in trust and submission in this dark hour....
O teach me so that I may get insight, and knowledge, and healing from Thy correction. . . . Send forth Thy light so that amid this shadow of death . . . I may see the path to Thee, to a better use of my powers, to a better understanding of life. I do not ask Thee to take this sorrow from me altogether, but to aid me in purging it from all taint of selfishness. . . . May my own pain make me more heedful of human woe, more responsive to it, more resolute in my endeavour to assuage it!

Fix my thoughts not only on this lower life, but on life with Thee; not only on the things of Time, but on the joyous promise of Eternity. . . . Strengthen my faith in my higher self . . . in my soul which . . . will unite me to Thee hereafter in blissful and endless communion. Then will all things be made plain. Then will the veil that hides Thee from me be torn away, and I shall see Thee clearly. . . . Then shall love come by its own—my dear one's which has been my joy in the bygone years, Thine which has blessed me all my life long. *Amen.*

### Arabian Proverb

All sunshine makes the desert.

### Author unknown

God sometimes puts us on our back so that we may look upward.

*Robert Browning Hamilton*

I walked a mile with Pleasure
She chattered all the way
But left me none the wiser
For all she had to say.

I walked a mile with Sorrow
And ne'er a word said she
But oh the things I learned from her
When Sorrow walked with me.


*Romain Rolland*

You don't know what things are real in art until you come to them in pain. Sorrow is the touchstone.


*John Ruskin*

When God shuts a door, He opens a window.


A  PRAYER

*Marion Franklin Ham*

I pray not for the joy that knows
No saving benison of tears;
The placid life of ease that flows
Untroubled through the changing years.

Grant me, O God, the mind to see
The blessings which my sorrows bring;
And give me, in adversity,
The heart that still can trust and sing.

It is for us, the living, rather, to be dedicated here to the unfinished work they have thus far so nobly advanced . . . that we here highly resolve that the dead shall not have died in vain.

—Abraham Lincoln

# IT IS FOR US THE LIVING . . .

*In describing the death of David, the Bible says: "And David slept with his fathers." This expression induced a Talmudic sage to ask why the Bible employed the word "slept" rather than "died," which the Bible used elsewhere. The answer he gave to his own question was that since David was survived by a son who cherished the same high ideals and values which were dear to him, David did not really die. He lived on in his progeny. Therefore David "slept."*

*Rabbi Phineas bar Hama, the Sage in question, was not alone in calling attention to the power of the survivors to confer a measure of immortality upon the departed. Men have always felt that they perpetuate the pulsating influence of their beloved dead when they identify themselves with their pursuits and reach out for their goals. By extending the impact of the remembered personalities beyond the span of their days, the survivors attest to the deathlessness of their loved ones. In a very real sense, it is the living who determine whether or not the departed live on.*

*In our own war-filled years, this interdependence of the generations has become more pronounced. Our liberty, our security, our very right to exist have been dearly purchased. On far-flung battlefields young men have died in unprecedented numbers in the cause of Freedom and Democracy. To them we feel an obligation too sacred to be discharged by mere rituals of remembrance. To them we owe the fulfilment of the vision which lured them on to their premature deaths. To them we owe a world united in peace and brotherhood, a society in which diverse political systems, religious orientations and racial groups live and work together for the common good. To the extent that we strive to achieve these difficult yet attainable goals, do we redeem their deaths from futility and we invest our lives with high purpose.*

*Whether we mourn the honored dead who fell in the cause of peace or grieve over the loss of someone who stood near to us, we would do well to hear and heed the wise words the poet spoke on behalf of the dead to the living:*

*"Complete these dear unfinished tasks of mine
And I, perchance, may therein comfort you."*

---

## ADDRESS AT GETTYSBURG

### Abraham Lincoln

Four score and seven years ago our fathers brought forth upon this continent a new nation, conceived in liberty, and dedicated to the proposition that all men are created equal.

Now we are engaged in a great civil war testing whether that nation, or any nation so conceived and so dedicated, can long endure. We are met on a great battlefield of that war. We have come to dedicate a portion of that field as a final resting place of those who here gave their lives that that nation might live.

It is altogether fitting and proper that we should do this. But in a larger sense we cannot dedicate, we cannot consecrate, we cannot hallow this ground. The brave men, living and dead, who struggled here, have consecrated it far above our power to add or detract.

The world will little note, nor long remember what we say here, but it can never forget what they did here. It is for us, the living, rather, to be dedicated here to the unfinished work they have thus far so nobly advanced. It is rather for us to be here dedicated to the great task remaining before us, that from these honored dead we take increased devotion to that cause for which they here gave the last full measure of devotion; that we here highly resolve that the dead shall not have died in vain, that this nation, under God, shall have a new birth of freedom; and that government of the people, by the people and for the people shall not perish from the earth.

# WEEP NOT FOR THEM

*Daniel A. Poling, father of one of the chaplains*

In the Chapel of the Four Chaplains which stands in the city of Philadelphia, there is a Book of Remembrance. Its first page tells us that the chapel "is a memorial to John P. Washington, George L. Fox, Alexander D. Goode and Clark V. Poling, the four young clergymen of three faiths—Catholic, Jewish and Protestant—who gave their life-belts and their lives that others might live when the *S. S. Dorchester* was sunk by enemy action in the North Atlantic just after midnight on February 3, 1943. . . ." After these words of dedication, there are the last two stanzas of the following poem:

On coral isles, on desert sands,
Beneath the swelling tides,
They sleep their long, untroubled sleep—
Their hard won rest abides.

They do not rise to meet the dawn,
Nor heed the battle call;
For they have finished with the fight,
These who have given all.

They lived and loved, their time was youth,
And youth they gave to time—
Now they have won eternity,
These warriors, yours and mine.

Weep not for them, nor for their cause,
Our sons who faltered not;
Weep only for ourselves who failed,
Who vowed the vow—forgot.

Weep for ourselves, but vow again,
Pledge in our children's blood,
To keep the faith, to win the peace
To make the world a Brotherhood.

## PLANTING TREES
### *Talmud*

A rabbi was once passing through a field where he saw a very old man planting an oak-tree. "Why are you planting that tree?" he asked. "Surely you do not expect to live long enough to see the acorn grow into an oak-tree?"

"Ah!" replied the old man. "My ancestors planted trees not for themselves, but for us, in order that we might enjoy their shade or their fruit. I am doing likewise for those who will come after me."

## MIND THE LIGHT
### *Author unknown*

In New York Harbor, between Manhattan Island and Staten Island, is a sunken shoal called Robbins Reef. A small lighthouse stands there, and for many years the keeper was an elderly widow, Mrs. Jacob Walker. One day she told her story to a reporter, who gave it to the world.

"I was a young girl living at Sandy Hook, New Jersey," she said, "when I first met my husband. He was keeper of the Sandy Hook Light, and took me there as his bride. I was happy there, for the lighthouse was on land and I could have a garden and raise flowers. Then one day we were transferred here—to Robbins Reef. As soon as we arrived I said to my husband, 'I can't stay here! The sight of water wherever I look makes me too lonesome. I won't unpack. . . .' But somehow all the trunks and boxes got unpacked.

"Four years later my husband caught cold while tending the light. The cold turned to pneumonia, and they took him to the infirmary on Staten Island.

"I stayed behind to tend the light. A few nights later I saw a rowboat coming through the darkness. Something told me the message it was bringing. The man in the boat said, 'We're sorry, Mrs. Walker, but your husband's worse.' 'You mean he's dead,' I answered; and there was no reply.

"We buried my husband on a hillside on Staten Island. Every morning when the sun comes up I stand at a porthole and look across the water toward his grave. Sometimes the hill is green, sometimes it is brown, sometimes it is white with snow. But it always brings a message from him—something I heard him say more often than anything else. Just three words—'Mind the light!' "

## LET US NOW PRAISE FAMOUS MEN

*Ecclesiasticus*

Let us now praise famous men,
And our fathers that begot us.
The Lord hath wrought great glory by them
Through his great power from the beginning . . .
But these were merciful men,
Whose righteousness hath not been forgotten.
With their seed shall continually remain a good
    inheritance,
And their children are within the covenant.
Their seed standeth fast,
And their children for their sakes.
Their seed shall remain for ever,
And their glory shall not be blotted out.
Their bodies are buried in peace;
But their name liveth forevermore.
The people will tell of their wisdom,
And the congregation will show forth their praise.

## TURN AGAIN TO LIFE

*Mary Lee Hall*

If I should die and leave you here awhile,
Be not like others, sore undone, who keep
Long vigil by the silent dust and weep.
For my sake turn again to life and smile,
Nerving thy heart and trembling hand to do
That which will comfort other souls than thine;
Complete these dear unfinished tasks of mine,
And I, perchance, may therein comfort you.

## WE CAN GRANT RENEWED LIFE
*Jacob J. Weinstein*

Whatever science or reason may ever say about the nature and persistence of matter, the profounder wisdom of the heart will guarantee the immortal life of our dear ones. But how they live—the quality of the influence they radiate—depends not alone on the kind of life they lived. It depends as much on us. We, the living, can determine the kind of immortality our beloved shall have. We can be more selective than they were when they lived among us. They had to compromise with the needs of the flesh and of the hour. Their good was mingled with the bad; the fine with the gross. We can sift the dross. We can recreate them as the fury and heat of their earthly life would not permit. We can grant renewed life to their nobler insights and their finest visions. We can act as their personal representatives to the living. Where they lifted the burden of worry from a fellow man, we can give encouragement and help; where they brought cheer and care and loyalty, we can be instead. That is how we can bind them into the bundle of eternal life, and build for them a memorial more enduring than stone, sweeter than the rose.

## VALLEY OF THE SHADOW
*John Galsworthy*

God, I am travelling out to death's sea,
    I, who exulted in sunshine and laughter,
Dreamed not of dying—death is such waste of me!
    Grant me one prayer: Doom not the hereafter
Of mankind to war, as though I had died not—
    I, who in battle, my comrade's arm linking,
Shouted and sang, life in my pulses hot,
    Throbbing and dancing! Let not my sinking
In dark be for naught, my death a vain thing!
    God, let me know it the end of man's fever!
Make my last breath a bugle call, carrying
    Peace o'er the valleys and cold hills forever!

## THE LEGACY OF INFLUENCE
*Joseph I. Weiss*

There is no death when one is held fast in the imagery of the mind. The sharp, stunning blow of sudden loss is relieved through time, as soft and fond memories begin to take their shape out of the bewildered haze of bereavement. Let our memories be full. They will make us strong if from them we can gain the inspiration to ennoble our own lives. What greater tribute can we pay to the dead, and what greater good can come to us than to activate their memories into living deeds of worth? Let our legacy of influence, through our own conduct in life, become increasingly great, that they may walk the earth again through us, and we and all of them through the years that are yet to be.

## A PLEDGE FROM THE LIVING
*Leo Jung*

The father's heart beat no more. The kindly eye was closed forever. . . . The son had stepped into the parent's shoes. He had undertaken the responsibilities for the honor of his house. And there at the open grave . . . he stood in the presence of the whole congregation of friends and strangers, before those of the age passing and those who were to lead in the age after him, and there at the saddest moment of his life he recalled neither sorrow nor his loss, but his duty. As a real Jew he knew the holiness of the moment, and he framed his resolution in the words holiest to Jewish hearts; there he opened his lips and made a pledge, a holy promise: "Yissgadal Veyisskadash Sh'meh Rabbah, Lord God, I do not murmur against Thy decree, I am a child of Jewry. Lord God, hear my voice at this moment. As my father lived for Thee, as his life was dedicated to Thy glory and Thy name, so do I declare Yissgadal Veyisskadash, 'that Thy great Name may be magnified and sanctified' as the promise for my future. So do I undertake to remember his fidelity, and never to forget my own duty."

That was the meaning of Kaddish in the times when Jews were Jewish. That is the meaning of the words today when said for mother and father. Not a prayer for the dead, but a pledge from the living; not a superstitious phrase, but a man's motto of life.

## IN FLANDERS FIELDS
*John McCrae*

In Flanders fields the poppies blow
Between the crosses, row on row,
That mark our place; and in the sky
The larks still bravely singing fly
Scarce heard amid the guns below.

We are the Dead. Short days ago
We lived, felt dawn, saw sunset glow
Loved and were loved; and now we lie
In Flanders fields.

Take up our quarrel with the foe:
To you from failing hands we throw
The torch; be yours to hold it high.
If ye break faith with us who die
We shall not sleep, though poppies grow
In Flanders fields.


## DEEDS OF LOVE TO THE DEAD
*Talmud*

The rabbis taught: In three things are deeds of love greater than charity. Charity is done at the mere sacrifice of money, deeds of love are performed with one's money and with one's person. Charity is only for the poor, deeds of love are for the poor and the rich, Charity is only for the living, deeds of love are for the living and the dead.


## WATER SPILT ON THE GROUND
*Beryl D. Cohon*

"For we must needs die, and our lives are as water spilt on the ground, which cannot be gathered up again; neither doth God respect any person" (II Samuel 14:14).

It is an ancient truth ever new. It has been voiced by saint and cynic alike, by the wisest of men and by the simple-minded. Life is like water spilt upon the thirsty ground. It sinks into the sands and is no more. Never may it be recalled; never may it be enjoyed again. . . .

Granted that this is true. Are our lives futile therefore? Is water spilt upon the ground lost? Is it not true that it is precisely this submerged water that makes life possible? It is the rain and the dew that fall on the ground and cease to be that make for life. Without it we perish.

Even so, is it with the life of the spirit. Our fathers and the many generations that went before them have poured out the red, sweet wine of their dreams and ideals and high hopes, and have been absorbed by the hungry earth of life; you and I are the harvest. They have given us not only our bodies; they have given us our minds, our appreciation of the good and the true, our will to live and achieve. We have absorbed into our personalities the spilt waters of their lives, just as we in turn, will be absorbed in the lives of our children and children's children. Teachers will be absorbed in the lives of their students and disciples; poets will be absorbed in the lives of the sensitive who appreciate their writings; the heroes and the martyrs of our social life will be absorbed in the lives of those who fight for the right. Thus the cycle runs its course.

Withhold this water from being spilt on the ground—if we can—and the world perishes; withhold the influences of parents, teachers, preachers, artists, and the life of the spirit is parched. A menacing dust bowl will develop in one generation. It is precisely in this absorption that we realize ourselves and achieve immortality. Alas for those who are not absorbed in someone's else life!

Is there nobility in our lives? Do we cherish high hopes? Is there strength, dignity, loyalty, capacity for whatever the cup of life may hold for us? That, largely, is the harvest with which our fathers have endowed us; it is the submerged water of their lives transformed within our souls.

Are we continuing the cycle? Are we bringing nobility, high hope, courage, loyalty into the lives of those dear to us? Are we pouring out fresh, sweet water that yields a harvest of goodness?

*Wisdom of Ben Sira*

A man shall be known through his children.

## THE CHALLENGE TO FULFILL
## THE PLEDGES
*Joshua Loth Leibman*

All over the world today there are fathers, mothers, and young wives who remember the songs of youths whose lives were brief in duration—songs of freedom defended and of humanity guarded. While we can never minimize the sadness of young melodies cut off in the first stanza, we are also quite certain that the singers of those songs, young aviators and sailors and brave young soldiers at their posts of freedom, would wish the living not to weep too long, but would remind us that there was a kind of fulfillment in their fleeting days of courageous and sacrificial living better than the futility of cowardly decades, and at the same time would challenge us to fulfill the pledges for which they have been called upon to die.

## MONUMENTS MORE BEAUTIFUL
## THAN THE TAJ MAHAL
*Louis I. Newman*

Let me tell you of one family, which, in the wilderness of its grief, was helped to discover a secret spring of healing and consolation. When her father died in the very prime of his years, a young girl received a letter from her high-school companions which I am privileged to impart to you in all its eloquent simplicity and beauty:

"Once there was an Indian Maharajah who had a beautiful and loving wife, Mehal. All his dreams and ambitions were wrapped up in her. When she died, he was bewildered and lost. He felt that his soul had died, too. One day an aged wise man came to him, saying: 'Oh, great Rajah, if you would keep the memory of your wife alive, build to her a monument of jewels, marble and ivory; a monument that would make all men remember Mehal, the beautiful.'

"The Maharajah took the wise man's advice and built a monument lovelier than any other. Mehal's memory was preserved forever in the exquisite beauty of the Taj Mahal.

"You, our friend, can make your life an everlasting monument to those who gave it to you. The monument can be made of materials more beautiful and precious than those of the Taj Mahal. Materials such as courage, faith, honor and work are infinitely more beautiful than any precious jewel. As you build this monument slowly and tediously, remember that we are always at your side, in your struggle against sorrow."

## AT YOUR GRAVE, MY BROTHER EPHRAIM

*Tsvi Guber (Translated from the Hebrew by the editor)*

*Ephraim died on the battlefield in Israel's War for Independence. He had not quite reached his twenty-first birthday.*

Good brother, I still cannot believe that you whom I followed constantly are gone. You were better and stronger than I, so why didn't I fall instead? . . . I stifle the cry of my pain with gritted teeth and restrain my tears with clenched fists. . . .

Mother, do not weep! Our dear one is still alive! He lives in the youthful joy of his friends and comrades in our homeland; he lives in the clear eyes of children, in the buds of this land which was soaked with his blood; he lives in the merry blossoms of spring and in the green growth of our fields; he lives and breathes in everything that throbs and grows under these skies! . . .

Can a leaden bullet destroy courage and purity of soul, an impish smile overflowing with jokes, longings, hopes and the love of a twenty-year-old heart? No! The soul does not die! Who knows—perhaps it flies like a summer butterfly or like a bee thirsty for the honeycomb? Or perhaps, Mother, the earth which swallows the soul returns to its bosom, sends it forth again in the blades of grass and in the roots of trees. And the soul which once sprouted forth from the depths of sparkling eyes now laughs from the cups of flowers.' . . .

Mother, do not cry! If he has fallen, I have remained to carry his burdens on my shoulders as much as is humanly possible. And if I, too, shall fall on the battlefield—you still have many sons left. Know this, Mother: Every lad who goes out at night to stand guard in the darkness where terror lurks; every youth who seals with his body the breach in the wall which the enemy made; every boy who rides among the horrors of the road of death; and everyone who fights on the battlefield against the jaws of danger and death with a youthful song which is gay and filled with faith—he is your son, Mother! . . .

My brother, I vow to you: My heart will be the candle of your soul and I shall cherish your memory within me like a priceless treasure! In the very path where you met your death I shall go, even though it be filled with pain and anguish, even if I knew for certain that it is my last road! . . .

By the holiness of the pain and by the holiness of my love for you I swear to you; by the sacredness of everything worth living for and the sanctity of everything worth dying for! . . .

*He fulfilled this promise which he made to his brother at the age of sixteen-and-a-half. He enlisted immediately in the Palmach and was killed a little while later after some heroic exploits. A year went by before his remains were discovered and brought to the military cemetery in the village of Warburg where he was born. He was buried in the same grave with his brother Ephraim, according to his own request in one of his letters. In honor of the two brothers the village was named "The Village of The Brothers."*

## Zohar

"A son honoreth his father." This is true during his lifetime. Is he exempted from honoring him after his death? No! Although he is dead, the son is duty-bound to honor him still more. If the son walks in the proper path, and improves his deeds. this certainly gives the father honor in the other world before the Holy One, praised be He.

## A PRAYER

### *From "Rabbinical Assembly Manual"*

Almighty God, whose mercies are from everlasting to everlasting, to Thee alone do Thy children turn for refuge in their affliction, for comfort from the grief that burdens the spirit, for peace from the sense of solitude and loss, and for strength of the soul in trouble.

O Thou, divine Comforter, Who lovest us with an everlasting love and Who turnest the shadows of night into the cloudless day that dawns, help these mourners wait upon Thee with reverent and submissive hearts. As we read the words of promise of eternal life, let them be filled with hope that love dies not, that righteousness is mightier than the grave and that the legacy of a good name is the most enduring memorial we can leave behind.

Let them return to their tasks with new cheerfulness and hope, gladly to accept whatever Thou dost give us to do or to endure, that neither sorrow nor death shall have dominion over us. Let this hour be for them a time of consecration, to resolve so to act that through their conduct and behavior, they may reflect honor upon him who was so dear to them in life. *Amen.*

## MY KID BROTHER LOSES A HEROIC FIGHT

### *Bob Considine*

Just before midnight Saturday, My Kid Brother, name of George, got a better offer. He took it, leaving this world for what surely can't be a worse one.

I have not seen many people die, and none as close to me as was this quiet, abundantly witty fellow I had known for so much of my life—and had presumed would outlive me by many years.

George didn't have much hair left when he finally tired of battling his cancer. The long hard pull had taken so terribly much out of him in other ways, too. But I kept thinking of him as I remembered him on his second birthday—a July 2, by the way—when we lived in the swamp-poodle section of Washington and he had long yellow curls. On that birthday, I remembered, he was happy with an apple pie with two little American flags stuck in it. George never asked for much.

My brother lay there at the Washington Sanitarium, a place as gentle as he himself was, and fought for his life with majestic determination. At times his pulse became imperceptible and he barely breathed. And holding his hand, when his wonderful girl wasn't, I thought of the hilarious and semi-violent tournament tennis we once had played in the stifling Washington heat. And I marveled at the hidden springs of strength in so shattered a vessel. And, by turn, I was proud—and wishful that his ordeal would end. . . .

My brother lived as cleanly as anybody I ever met. His appetite for the fleshpots was all but nil. But one morning he woke up with a pain in the stomach. No warning. No alarm. No reason. Just a pain in the stomach. And in a few swift and awful months it was to kill him as only cancer can kill. Almost everything else takes you. Cancer is just plain killer, unless met militantly.

I write about my brother not only because my mind is filled with the memory of his inherent goodness but because I watched him play a fearsome role in the great tragedy of our time, the appalling incidence of cancer. I write, too, because of the mountains that were moved by the staff of Memorial Hospital in New York. In vain, as it turned out. Yet what prodigious efforts and ever-inching progress!

Some day a man in a white coat will speed down the hall from Sloan-Kettering Institute or some such place in the world, and he will bear triumphantly in his hand that for which the world has searched since man became a thinking animal—a cure for this horrid thing that now attacks one in five. My brother and many others could not wait for him. But he will come, this man, if we give him the tools with which to fashion this cure. There is always a heart-lifting, searching, praying chance that he has already taken his first step down the hall, and if the stricken can hang on a bit longer, well, maybe. . . .

## THE PUREST DEMOCRACY

### Roland B. Gittelsohn

*Sermon on the Dedication of 5th Marine Division Cemetery on Iwo Jima.*

This is perhaps the grimmest and surely the holiest task we have faced since D-Day. Here before us lie the bodies of comrades and friends. Men who until yesterday or last week laughed with us, joked with us, trained with us. Men who were on the same ships with us, and went over the sides with us as we prepared to hit the beaches of this island. Men who fought with us and feared with us. Somewhere in this plot of ground there may lie the man who could have discovered the cure for cancer. Under one of these Christian crosses, or beneath a Jewish Star of David, there may rest now a man who was destined to be a great prophet . . . to find the way, perhaps, for all to live in plenty, with poverty and hardship for none. Now they lie here silently in this sacred soil, and we gather to consecrate this earth in their memory.

It is not easy to do so. Some of us have buried our closest friends here. We saw these men killed before our very eyes. Any one of us might have died in their places. Indeed, some of us are alive and breathing at this very moment only because men who lie here beneath us had the courage and strength to give their lives for ours. To speak in memory of such men as these is not easy. Of them, too, can it be said with utter truth: "The world will little note nor remember what we say here. It can never forget what they did here."

No, our poor power of speech can add nothing to what these men and the other dead of our division who are not here have already done. All that we even hope to do is follow their example. To show the same selfless courage in peace that they did in war. To swear that, by the grace of God and the stubborn strength and power of human will, their sons and ours shall never suffer these pains again. These men have done their job well. They have paid the ghastly price of freedom. If that freedom be once again lost, as it was after the last war, the unforgivable blame will be ours, not theirs. So it is we "the living" who are here to be dedicated and consecrated.

We dedicate ourselves, first, to live together in peace the way they fought and are buried in this war. Here lie men who loved America because their ancestors generations ago helped in her founding, and other men who loved her with equal passion because they themselves or their own fathers escaped from oppression to her blessed shores. Here lie officers and men, Negroes and whites, rich men and poor . . . together. Here are Protestants, Catholics, and Jews . . . together. Here no man prefers another because of his faith or despises him because of his color. Here there are no quotas of how many from each group are admitted or allowed. Among these men there is no discrimination. No prejudices. No hatred. Theirs is the highest and purest democracy.

Any man among us "the living" who fails to understand that will thereby betray those who lie here dead. Whoever of us lifts his hand in hate against a brother, or thinks himself superior to those who happen to be in the minority, makes of this ceremony and of the bloody sacrifices it commemorates, an empty, hollow mockery. To this, then, as our solemn, sacred duty, do we the living now dedicate ourselves: to the right of Protestants, Catholics, and Jews, of white men and Negroes alike, to enjoy the democracy for which all of them have here paid the price.

To one thing more do we consecrate ourselves in memory of those who sleep beneath these crosses and stars. We shall not foolishly suppose, as did the last generation of America's fighting men, that victory on the battlefield will automatically guarantee the triumph of democracy at home. This war, with all its frightful heartache and suffering, is but the beginning of our generation's struggle for democracy. When the last battle has been won, there will be those at home, as there were last time, who will want us to turn our backs in selfish isolation on the rest of organized humanity, and thus to sabotage the very peace for which we fight. We promise you who lie here: we will not do that! We will join hands with Britain,

China, Russia—in peace, even as we have in war, to build the kind of world for which you died.

When the last shot has been fired, there will still be those whose eyes are turned backward, not forward, who will be satisfied with those wide extremes of poverty and wealth in which the seeds of another war can breed. We promise you, our departed comrades: this, too, we will not permit. This war has been fought by the common man; its fruits of peace must be enjoyed by the common man! We promise, by all that is sacred and holy, that your sons—the sons of miners and millers, the sons of farmers and workers, will inherit from your death the right to a living that is decent and secure.

When the final cross has been placed in the last cemetery, once again there will be those to whom profit is more important than peace, who will insist with the voice of sweet reasonableness and appeasement that it is better to trade with the enemies of mankind than, by crushing them, to lose their profit. To you who sleep here silently, we give our promise: we will not listen! We will not forget that some of you were burnt with oil that came from American wells, that many of you were killed by shells fashioned from American steel. We promise that when once again men seek profit at your expense, we shall remember how you looked when we placed you reverently, lovingly, in the ground.

Thus do we memorialize those who, having ceased living with us, now live within us. Thus do we consecrate ourselves, the living, to carry on the struggle they began. Too much blood has gone into this soil for us to let it lie barren. Too much pain and heartache have fertilized the earth on which we stand. We here solemnly swear: this shall not be in vain! Out of this, and from the suffering and sorrow of those who mourn, this will come—we promise—the birth of a new freedom for the sons of men everywhere. *Amen.*

The tomb is not a blind alley. It
is an open thoroughfare. It closes
in the twilight to open with the
dawn.

—Victor Hugo

# DEATH IS NOT THE END

*O*urs *is an age in which theological matters do not occupy too
prominent a role in our thinking. We are nonchalant about beliefs
and doctrines over which former generations speculated abundantly
and in which they believed passionately. The belief in immortality
is one such doctrine towards which we display conspicuous indifference. Our emphasis has been largely humanistic, underscoring the
importance of leading worthy lives here and now and letting the
hereafter take care of itself. We normally presume that it makes
little difference one way or another whether the soul survives death
or not.*

*In the time of bereavement, however, it matters profoundly
whether we believe that death is "a period which brings the sentence of life to a full stop" or whether we believe that "it is only a
comma which punctuates it to loftier significance." It makes an
enormous difference whether we believe that the essence of our
loved ones has been totally erased from the slate of life or whether it
survives with the Author of Life, Himself. Our personal indifference
departs when sorrow enters. Thus even so confirmed an agnostic as
Robert G. Ingersoll, speaking at the funeral services for his brother,
felt constrained to add this comforting assurance: "But in the night
of death Hope sees a star, and listening Love can hear the rustle of
a wing."*

*It is not without significance that this section is among the largest
in the book. It contains but a fraction of the abundant literary harvest which is available on this theme in mankind's library. From
ancient man with his naïve beliefs down through the long corridors*

236

of time reaching into the present most sophisticated faiths, men have persistently and in decisive numbers held the human soul indestructible. Nor has this belief been limited to religious thinkers alone. Philosophers, poets, scientists, physicians are all included in the throng who answer "present" when the roll is called among the believers that death is not the end. The more we have learned about the universe in which we live, the more persuasive have grown the intimations of our immortality. Robert Millikan spoke for a host of his scientific colleagues when he declared: "The Divine Architect of the Universe has not built a stairway that leads to nowhere."

When death separates us from a loved one, the pain of parting can be assuaged in no small measure through our faith that the essence of our beloved lives on not only in our hearts and in our memories but more especially with the inexhaustible source of all life. We can be sustained by what the philosopher Santayana called "the Soul's invincible surmise." It is this faith which burst forth out of Emerson after the passing of his little son. "What is excellent," he wrote, "as God lives is permanent."

This was the conviction that welled up in the heart of Charlotte Brontë as she lay dying. "God will not separate us now; we have been so happy." Our craving for eternity in a world which responds to our every other fundamental yearning and need points to a God who, in the words of the Hebrew prayer-book, "implanted within us everlasting life."

Simple parables illustrate great truths. Little David found a bird nest near his home which contained some speckled eggs. He visited it for a few days and then had to leave on a trip to the city. Upon his return he rushed to the nest to look at the eggs. To his deep dismay he found that the beautiful eggs were no longer there. Indeed, there were only broken, empty shells. With tears in his eyes he ran to his father and cried: "Father, they were such beautiful eggs. Now they are all spoiled and broken." "No, son," his father reassured him, "they are not spoiled. The best part of them has taken wings and flown away."

## THERE IS NO DEATH—THERE'S IMMORTALITY

*Anonymous*

There is a plan far greater than the plan you know;
There is a landscape broader than the one you see.
There is a haven where storm-tossed souls may go—
You call it death—we, immortality.

You call it death—the seeming endless sleep;
We call it birth—the soul at last set free.
'Tis hampered not by time or space—you weep.
Why weep at death? 'Tis immortality.

Farewell, dear voyageur—'twill not be long.
Your work is done—now may peace rest with thee.
Your kindly thoughts and deeds—they will live on.
This is not death—'tis immortality.

Farewell, dear voyageur—the river winds and turns;
The cadence of your song wafts near to me,
And now you know the thing that all men learn:
There is no death—there's immortality.


*Henry Wadsworth Longfellow*

The grave itself is but a covered bridge leading from light to light, through a brief darkness.


## OUR HOPES ARE NOT DELUSIONS

*From "Blessings and Praise"*

The hope of immortality is the strength of our life on earth. Whenever we yield to the fear that our earthly labor will some day cease forever, we lose the courage to overcome circumstance, and lack the will to resist failure. If our toil is but for a day, we cannot build. But if, as our sages assure us, we may labor on beyond the accident of death into eternity, then no failure is irreparable, no task is too great. When we may include infinity in our plans then no aim is unattainable, no vision is too exalted.

We tend to doubt our immortality whenever life defeats us. When our plans go awry and our efforts fail, when friends disappoint and solitude grows bitter, then our strength seems to vanish, a sense of our frailty overpowers us and there comes the dread that all our hopes will soon be quenched in an eternal darkness. Our disappointments and our discouragements engender the fear that our life will end in a final defeat and the grave will win its ultimate victory. The terror of death grows from our failures in life.

Yet when each morning dawns and our strength is renewed, when our efforts succeed and the spirit of God, calling to our souls, reveals our innate divinity, then our life again seems triumphant and indestructible. Hope revives and we see our spirit entering, beyond the grave, into the gateway of greater life. Death loses its sting and the grave its victory. When life is strong we foresee our immortality.

We are poised between despair and hope. Each day our failures bring the terror of the grave and our victories bring intimations of immortality. We have ever before us both life and death. It is for us to choose the hope of life eternal; to depart from fear and to be strong in faith; to assert to our failing hearts that we shall not die, but live, and declare forever the wonders of God.

Our hopes are not delusions, for God is just and merciful. He would not bid us toil in His name, and then deny us the joy of completing our work. He would not bid us prepare in this antechamber of eternity, and then close against us the doors of His eternals halls. Since His mercies endure forever, He would not bid us sow in tears, without permitting us to reap in joy. We may trust in His love. We have known bereavement and the pain of death. He will comfort us. He will destroy death forever and wipe the tears from every face. Though the cords of death encompass us, we will yet walk before Him in "the land of the living."

*Sir Walter Scott*

Is death the last sleep? No, it is the last and final awakening.

## BOOK OF LIFE
### *John Donne*

All mankind is of one Author, and is one volume; when one Man dies, one chapter is not torn of the book, but translated into a better language; and every chapter must be so translated; God employs several translators; some pieces are translated by age, some by sickness, some by war, some by justice; but God's hand is in every translation; and His hand shall bind up all our scattered leaves again, for that Library where every book shall lie open to one another.

### *Psalms*

Into Thy hand I commit my spirit;
Thou hast redeemed me, O Lord, Thou God of Truth.

## DEATH MAY GIVE US MORE
### *Sir Edwin Arnold*

Birth gave to each of us much; death may give very much more, in the way of subtler senses to behold colors we cannot here see, to catch sounds we do not now hear, and to be aware of bodies and objects impalpable at present to us, but perfectly real, intelligibly constructed, and constituting an organized society and a governed, multiform State.

## A COMRADE RIDES AHEAD
### *Douglas Malloch*

Time brings not death, it brings but changes.
I know he rides, but rides afar,
To-day some other planet ranges
And camps to-night upon a star
Where all his other comrades are.

## IMMORTALITY
### Solomon Solis-Cohen

I dreamed my spirit broke the bars of sense
That hold the gates of consciousness shut fast,
Threw off the prison-garb of Self, and passed
Into the wonder of Omniscience.

I saw mists rise from ocean and condense
In clouds; in million raindrops melt, and at last,
Through brooks and rivers join again the vast
Primeval sea. And thus I read the Whence
And Whither of the soul.
When stream meets sea,

Is the swift river wave forever gone?
When souls rejoin All-soul, cease they to be?
Nay, there where All is Thought and Thought is One,
Within the Infinite All, eternally,
The thought once bound in me, lives boundless on.

## FROM "CONTEMPLATIONS"
### Anne Bradstreet

When I behold the heavens as in their prime,
    And then the earth, though old, still clad in green,
The stones and trees insensible of time,
    Nor age nor wrinkly on their front are seen;
If winter come, and greenness then do fade,
A spring returns, and they more youthful made;
But man grows old, lies down, remains where once
        he's laid.

By birth more noble than those creatures all,
    Yet seems by nature and by custom cursed—
No sooner born but grief and care makes fall
    That state obliterate he had at first;
Nor youth, nor strength, nor wisdom spring again
Nor habitations long their names retain,
But in oblivion to the final day remain.

Shall I then praise the heavens, the trees, the earth,
  Because their beauty and their strength last longer?
Shall I wish therefore never to had birth,
  Because they're bigger and their bodies stronger,
Nay, they shall darken, perish, fade, and die,
And when unmade so ever shall they lie;
**But man was made for endless immortality.**


*I Samuel*

The Lord killeth, and maketh alive;
He bringeth down to the grave, and bringeth up.


## A UNIVERSAL AND PERSISTENT LONGING

### *Ralph W. Sockman*

Just as science postulates a gas to explain the phenomena of the laboratory, or a new planet to explain the movement of the stars, or a body of water to explain the existence of fish, why is it not the part of wisdom to believe that there must be a land which "eye hath not seen and ear hath not heard" in order to explain the presence in man of the persistent and universal inclination towards it? For "this longing after immortality" is a normal appetite of the human soul, felt by the best minds in their healthiest moments. It is universal, being found among all races. It is persistent, haunting the twentieth-century sage as well as the primitive savage. Can it be that the universe which keeps faith with the instincts of the bird by providing air in which to fly, and with the instincts of the fish by furnishing water in which to swim, has played most cruelly false to man by endowing him with this craving for eternity only to deny its gratification? A heavenless universe would seem to be as deceptive and dishonest as a foodless one. And if this is a nonmoral world order, how can we explain the rise of moral aspiration in man? It needs a moral universe and immortal life to explain man.

## FROM "SNOW-BOUND"

### James Greenleaf Whittier

Henceforward, listen as we will,
The voices of that hearth are still;
Look where we may, the wide earth o'er
Those lighted faces smile no more. . . .
Yet Love will dream, and Faith will trust
(Since He who knows our need is just)
That somehow, somewhere, meet we must.

## WHENCE THIS LONGING AFTER IMMORTALITY?

### Joseph Addison

It must be so. . . .
Else—whence this pleasing hope, that fond desire,
This longing after immortality?
Or whence this secret dread and inward horror
Of falling into naught? Why shrinks the soul
Back on itself, and startles at destruction?
'Tis the Divinity that stirs within us:
'Tis Heaven itself that points out an hereafter
And intimates Eternity to Man.

## FROM "ODE TO THE SETTING SUN"

### Francis Thompson

For birth hath in itself the germ of death,
But death hath in itself the germ of birth.
It is the falling acorn buds the tree,
The falling rain that bears the greenery,
The fern-plants moulder when the ferns arise.
For there is nothing lives but something dies,
And there is nothing dies but something lives.
Till skies be fugitives,
And Time, the hidden root of change, updries,
Are Birth and Death inseparable on earth;
For they are twain yet one, and Death is Birth.

*Benjamin Franklin's Own Epitaph*

The body of
B. Franklin Printer,
(Like the cover of an old Book
Its Contents torn out
And stript of its Lettering and Gilding)
Lics heie, Food for Worms,
But the Work shall not be lost;
For it will (as he believ'd) appear once more
In a new and more elegant Edition
Revised and corrected,
By the Author.


## EPITAPH

*Composed by Dorothy Kahan Bar-Adon (1907–1950) and engraved on her tombstone in Merhavia, Israel.*

I, Dorothy Ruth, am in this ground,
Roots and rich soil close around,
Growth, creation, taking and giving
So life was death and death is living.


## DEATH IS NOT SEVERANCE

*Sir Oliver Lodge*

I tell you, it pains them to be thought dead. They have passed through the physiological process we call death; they have shuffled off the mortal body; but they themselves have more life than ever. If the bereaved and sorrowful could only realize that, the pain of parting would be greatly alleviated. I believe one of the outcomes of the war will be to make people realize the fact, much more vividly than before, that death is not severance, it is a change of condition but not of personality. Bullets and shells injure the body, but they are not amongst those things which assault and hurt the soul. The soul continues after death, and, by our love and affection, we can give some joy to those on the other side who have their lives before them, a different life from ours, but as helpful and as useful and more happy.

*Cicero*

I consider this world as a place which Nature never designed for my permanent abode; and I look upon my departure out of it, not as being driven from my habitation, but as leaving my inn.

## MY SUN SETS TO RISE AGAIN
### *Robert Browning*

*From "At the Mermaid"*

Have you found your life distasteful?
My life did, and does, smack sweet.
Was your youth of pleasure wasteful?
Mine I save and hold complete.
Do your joys with age diminish?
When mine fail me, I'll complain.
Must in Death your daylight finish?
My sun sets to rise again.

## THE SEA HAS ANOTHER SHORE
### *Harry Emerson Fosdick*

Death is a great adventure, but none need go unconvinced that there is an issue to it. The man of faith may face it as Columbus faced his first voyage from the shores of Spain. What lies across the sea, he cannot tell; his special expectations all may be mistaken; but his insight into the clear meanings of present facts may persuade him beyond doubt that the sea has another shore. Such confident faith, so founded upon reasonable grounds, shall be turned to sight, when for all the dismay of the unbelieving, the hope of the seers is rewarded by the vision of a new continent.

## IMMORTALITY
### *Cicero*

There is, I know not how, in the minds of men, a certain presage, as it were, of a future existence; and this takes the deepest root, and is most discoverable, in the greatest geniuses and most exalted souls.

*James D. Burns*

I have been dying for years: now I shall begin to live.

## IT CANNOT BE

*David Banks Sickels*

It cannot be that He who made
This wondrous world for our delight,
Designed that all its charms should fade
And pass forever from our sight;
That all shall wither and decay,
And know on earth no life but this,
With only one finite survey
Of all its beauty and its bliss.

It cannot be that all the years
Of toil and care and grief we live
Shall find no recompense but tears,
No sweet return that earth can give;
That all that leads us to aspire,
And struggle onward to achieve,
And every unattained desire
Were given only to deceive.

It cannot be that, after all
The mighty conquests of the mind,
Our thoughts shall pass beyond recall
And leave no record here behind;
That all our dreams of love and fame,
And hopes that time has swept away,
All that enthralled this mortal frame,
Shall not return some other day.

It cannot be that all the ties
Of kindred souls and loving hearts
Are broken when this body dies,
And the immortal mind departs;
That no serener light shall break
At last upon our mortal eyes,
To guide us as our footsteps make
The pilgrimage to Paradise.

## FROM "THRENODY"

### *Ralph Waldo Emerson*

*When Emerson lost his young son, he wrote to Carlyle: "My son, a perfect little boy of five years and three months, has ended his earthly life. You can never sympathize with me; you can never know how much of me such a young child can take away."*

*His grief found creative expression in that poetic masterpiece, "Threnody," from which the following lines are taken.*

> Wilt thou not ope thy heart to know
> What rainbows teach, and sunsets show?
> Verdict which accumulates
> From lengthening scroll of human fates,
> Voice of earth to earth returned,
> Prayers of saints that only burned,
> Saying, What is excellent,
> As God lives, is permanent;
> Hearts are dust; hearts' loves remain;
> Hearts' love will meet thee again.

## AWAY

### *James Whitcomb Riley*

> I cannot say, and I will not say
> That he is dead! He is just away!
> With a cheery smile, and a wave of the hand,
> He has wandered into an unknown land.
> And left us dreaming how very fair
> It must be, since he lingers there.
> And you—O you, who the wildest yearn
> For the old-time step and the glad return.
> Think of him faring on, as dear
> In the love of There as the love of Here.
> Think of him still as the same, I say;
> He is not dead—he is just away!

### *Sir Rabindranath Tagore*

Death is not extinguishing the light; it is putting out the lamp because the dawn has come.

## COMFORT
### William Morris

From out the throng and stress of lies,
From out the painful noise of sighs,
One voice of comfort seems to rise:
"It is the meaner part that dies."

## THE SPIRITUAL SELF CANNOT PERISH
### Felix Adler

Vast possibilities suggest themselves to us of an order of existence wholly different from all that we have ever known; what may be the nature of that other life it is impossible to know and it is useless to speculate. . . . Only this I feel warranted in holding fast to—that the root of my selfhood, the best that is in me, my true and only being, cannot perish. In regard to that the notion of death seems to me to be irrelevant. . . . I let go my hold on the empirical, transient self. I see it perish with the same indifference which the materialist asserts, for whom man is but a compound of physical matter and physical force. It is the real self, the eternal self, upon which I tighten my hold. I affirm the real, the irreducible existence of the essential self, though I know not the how or where of its survival. I affirm that there verily is an eternal divine life, a best beyond the best I can think or imagine. What I retain is the conviction that the spiritual self is an eternal self, and cannot perish.

## TIS LIFE BEYOND
### Anonymous

I watched a sail until it dropped from sight
Over the rounding sea. A gleam of white,
A last far-flashed farewell, and, like a thought
Slipt out of mind, it vanished and was not.
Yet to the helmsman standing at the wheel
Broad seas still stretched beneath the gliding keel.
Disaster? Change? He felt no slightest sign,

Nor dreamed he of that far horizon line.
So may it be, perchance, when down the tide
Our dear ones vanish. Peacefully they glide
On level seas, nor mark the unknown bound.
We call it death—to them 'tis life beyond.


*Robert Browning*

And I shall thereupon
Take rest, ere I be gone
Once more on my adventure brave and new.


## ON THE DEATH OF AN AGED FRIEND
*Roselle Mercier Montgomery*

You are not dead—Life has but set you free!
    Your years of life were like a lovely song,
    The last sweet poignant notes of which, held long,
Passed into silence while we listened, we, who loved
        you listened still expectantly!
And we about you whom you moved among would
        feel that grief for you were surely wrong—
You have but passed beyond where we can see.

For us who knew you, dread of age is past!
You took life, tiptoe: to the very last:
It never lost for you its lovely look;
You kept your interest in its thrilling book;
To you Death came no conqueror; in the end
You merely smiled to greet another friend!


*Joseph Addison*

How can it enter into the thoughts of man, that the soul, which is capable of such immense perfections and of receiving new improvements to all eternity, shall fall away into nothing almost as soon as it is created?

*Robert Louis Stevenson*

He is not dead, this friend; not dead,
But, in the path we mortals tread,
Got some few, trifling steps ahead,
    And nearer to the end;
So that you, too, once past the bend
Shall meet again, as face to face this friend
You fancy dead.

## DEATH CANNOT BE THE END OF LIFE

*Milton Steinberg*

Death cannot be and is not the end of life. Man transcends death in many altogether naturalistic fashions. He may be immortal biologically, through his children, in thought through the survival of his memory; in influence, by virtue of the continuance of his personality as a force among those who come after him, and, ideally, through his identification with the timeless things of the spirit.

When Judaism speaks of immortality it has in mind all these. But its primary meaning is that man contains something independent of the flesh and surviving it; his consciousness and moral capacity; his essential personality; a soul.

## HE IS A PORTION OF THE LOVELINESS

*Percy Bysshe Shelley*
*From "Adonais"*

He is made one with nature; there is heard
His voice in all music, from the moan
Of thunder, to the song of night's sweet bird,
He is a presence to be felt and known
In darkness and in light, from herb and stone
Spreading itself where'er that Power may move
Which has withdrawn His being to its own;
Which wields the world with never wearied love
Sustains it from beneath, and kindles it above.
He is a portion of the loveliness
Which once he made more lovely.

*Charles Darwin*

Believing as I do that man in the distant future will be a far more perfect creature than he now is, it is an intolerable thought that he and all other sentient beings are doomed to complete annihilation after such long-continued slow progress.

## EVOLUTION
*John Banister Tabb*

Out of the dusk a shadow,
    Then a spark;
Out of the cloud a silence,
    Then a lark;

Out of the heart a rapture,
    Then a pain;
Out of the dead, cold ashes,
    Life again.

## DEATH, BE NOT PROUD
*John Donne*

Death, be not proud, though some have called thee
Mighty and dreadful, for thou art not so;
For those whom thou think'st thou dost overthrow
Die not, poor Death; nor yet canst thou kill me. . . .

One short sleep past, we wake eternally,
And Death shall be no more: Death, thou shalt die!

## TRIUMPH OF THE DEFEATED
*Lord Byron*

They never fail who die
In a great cause. The block may soak their gore;
Their heads may sodden in the sun; their limbs
Be strung to city gates and castle walls;

But still their spirit walks abroad.
Though years
Elapse and others share as dark a doom,
They but augment the deep and sweeping thoughts
Which overpower all others and conduct
The world, at last, to freedom.

## THE OVERWHELMING MAJORITY SAYS "AYE"

*Sir James Frazer*

The question whether our conscious personality survives after death has been answered by almost all races of men in the affirmative. On this point sceptical or agnostic peoples are nearly, if not wholly, unknown. Accordingly, if abstract truth could be determined, like the gravest issues of national policy, by a show of hands or a counting of heads, the doctrine of human immortality, or at least of a life after death, would deserve to rank among the most firmly established of truths; for were the question put to the vote of the whole mankind there can be no doubt that the "ayes" would have it by an overwhelming majority. The few dissenters would be overborne; their voices would be drowned in the general roar.

## A REASONABLE FAITH

*Julian Huxley*

We do not know all. For instance, I have studiously avoided ever mentioning the word *immortality*, since I believe that Science cannot yet profitably discuss that question. But the discovery of unity in all that has so far been studied gives me reasonable faith that its wings will reach out to cover all that we shall still be enabled to learn, while the unbroken continuity of evolutionary direction gives us the same sort of right to believe that it will continue tomorrow and on into time as we have to believe that apples will continue to fall to the earth.

## GOD GRATIFIES OUR CRAVINGS
### F. W. Robertson

We wish for immortality. The thought of annihilation is horrible; even to conceive it is almost impossible. The wish is a kind of argument: it is not likely that God would have given all men such a feeling, if he had not meant to gratify it. Every natural longing has its natural satisfaction. If we thirst, God has created liquids to gratify thirst. If we are susceptible of attachment, there are beings to gratify that love. If we thirst for life and love eternal, it is likely that there are an eternal life and an eternal love to satisfy that craving.

### Edward Young

Still seems it strange, that thou shouldst live forever?
Is it less strange, that thou shouldst live at all?
This is a miracle; and that no more.

## SOLO
### Corporal Harold Applebaum

You cannot hear me now, my voice is lost
In thunder. The song of me is drowned
In the earth's grim symphony like the sound
Of violins all beaten flat and tossed
Against a cliff of brass. You cannot hear me,
But I am singing still beneath the clash,
Below the metal chorus and the lash
Of trumpets at the sky. I will be
But a tiny voice, saying there is yet a dawn,
Stars to dream at and the world beyond.
I will hold my keening note until the wand
Waves back the brasses and the drums are gone,
And brave against the stillness sing my part—
The deathlessness of beauty in the heart.

*Leigh Hunt*

Doth this soul within me, this spirit of thought, and love, and infinite desire, dissolve as well as the body? Has nature, who quenches our bodily thirst, who rests our weariness, and perpetually encourages us to endeavor onwards, prepared no food for this appetite of immortality?

## THE REASONABLENESS OF GOD'S WORK
*John Fiske*

I believe in the immortality of the soul, not in the sense in which I accept the demonstrable truths of science, but as a supreme act of faith in the reasonableness of God's work.

## THE BUTTERFLY
*Alice Freeman Palmer*

I hold you at last in my hand,
Exquisite child of the air.
Can I ever understand
How you grew to be so fair?
You came to my linden tree
To taste its delicious sweet,
I sitting here in the shadow and shine
Playing around its feet.
Now I hold you fast in my hand,
You marvelous butterfly,
Till you help me to understand
The eternal mystery.
From that creeping thing in the dust
To this shining bliss in the blue!
God give me courage to trust
I can break my chrysalis, too!

*Henry van Dyke*

The cry of the human for a life beyond the grave comes from that which is noblest in the soul of man.

## THE GIFT OF NEW LIFE

### *Grace Perkins Oursler and April Armstrong*

. . . We know the horrors of birth in similar manner. The pain, responsibility, possible loss of health, of looks, and of a measure of youth, even the risk of death. We know the forfeit of time, comfort, money, calling for selfless sacrifice. There are some who avoid parenthood and all it entails, many who cannot rise to it, even more who cannot live up to the full contract. But those who do know the beauty and the rewards, the joy and the glory, are in the millions, and the rewards far overshadow the losses. Everyone recognizes that the agony of labor is discounted in the gift of new life. The pain and goriness are soon gone, and what remains is joy in the product of union. That we experience and understand and welcome.

How do we dare to guess the same is not with death?

## THOU WILT RESTORE IT TO ME

### *Hebrew Prayer Book*

O my God, the soul with which Thou didst endow me is pure. Thou didst create it and fashion it; Thou didst breathe it into me and Thou preservest it within me. Thou wilt reclaim it from me but Thou wilt restore it to me in the life to come. So long as the breath of life is within me, I will give thanks unto Thee, O Lord my God and God of my fathers, Master of all works, Lord of all souls. Blessed art Thou, O Lord, who restorest life to mortal creatures.

## FOREVER

### *John Boyle O'Reilly*

Those we love truly never die,
Though year by year the sad memorial wreath,
A ring and flowers, types of life and death,
Are laid upon their graves.

For death the pure life saves,
And life all pure is love; and *love can reach*
*From heaven to earth,* and nobler lessons teach
Than those by mortals read.

Well blest is he who has a dear one dead;
A friend he has whose face will never change—
A dear communion that will not grow strange;
*The anchor of a love is death.*

## THERE IS SOMETHING . . . THAT CANNOT WHOLLY PERISH

### *George D. Prentice*

. . . In the beautiful drama of Ion, the hope of immortality . . . finds deep response in every thoughtful soul. When about to yield his young existence as a sacrifice to fate, his Clemantha asks if they should meet again, to which he replies: "I have asked that dreadful question of the hills that look eternal—of the clear streams that flow forever—of the stars among whose fields of azure my raised spirit has walked in glory. All were dumb: but as I gaze upon thy living face I feel that there is something in the love that mantles through its beauty that cannot wholly perish. We shall meet again Clemantha."

## A FORCE THAT CANNOT DIE

### *Louis Pasteur*

There are two men in each one of us: the scientist, he who starts with a clear field and desires to rise to the knowledge of Nature through observation, experimentation and reasoning; and the man of sentiment, the man of faith, the man who mourns his dead children and who cannot, alas, prove at all that he will see them again, but who believes that he will, and lives in that hope, . . . the man who feels that force that is within him cannot die.

### *Robert Browning*

Fool! All that is, at all,
Lasts ever, past recall;

Earth changes, but thy soul and God stand sure:
What entered into thee,
That was, is, and shall be:
Time's wheel runs back or stops; Potter and clay endure.

## CAN HE HAVE BECOME NOTHING?

### Charles Lewis Slattery

Our first intimation of the necessary idea of a future life comes in the presence of the death of a truly great man at the height of his power and influence. Again and again, through the centuries, a man to whom thousands look for inspiration falls by the wayside. An hour ago his eye flashed hope, his smile cheered, his word gave knowledge, his love gave confidence. He was like a dynamo, giving force to his whole wide environment as it lay about him. Then, a moment ago, without warning, he died.

What has become of him? Can he have become nothing? If we talk calmly of the conservation of energy in the physical world, can we fail to go one step farther and say a word of belief in the conservation of energy in the spiritual world? Is not such abounding life living somewhere, though its manifestation in this world has ceased? The wide-eyed disciples of Socrates, who knew the wisdom and love and strength of their master in that room in Athens where he drank the hemlock, and then saw him die, could not possibly believe that such wisdom and love and strength as his had stopped. A nation exulting in the great heart of Abraham Lincoln, which had by sheer strength and love and pity brought a warring people together and had won peace, received the sudden news that Abraham Lincoln had been fatally shot. Could anyone who had entered fully into the emotions of that hour believe for one instant that so mighty a personality could thus suddenly stop living? Somewhere, all thinking men said to themselves, that heart of love and pity and infinite patience must be living still.

## A PARABLE OF SOME GRUBS

### Walter Dudley Cavert

In the bottom of an old pond lived some grubs who could not understand why none of their groups ever came back after crawling up the lily stems to the top of the water. They promised each other

that the next one who was called to make the upward climb would
return and tell what had happened to him. Soon one of them felt
an urgent impulse to seek the surface; he rested himself on the top
of a lily pad and went through a glorious transformation which
made him a dragon fly with beautiful wings. In vain he tried to
keep his promise. Flying back and forth over the pond, he peered
down at his friends below. Then he realized that even if they could
see him they would not recognize such a radiant creature as one
of their number.

The fact that we cannot see our friends or communicate with
them after the transformation which we call death is no proof that
they cease to exist.

### Edwin Markham

The few little years we spend on earth are only the first scene in
a Divine Drama that extends on into Eternity.

### William Wordsworth

Our birth is but a sleep, and a forgetting;
The Soul that rises with us, our life's Star,
Hath had elsewhere its setting,
And cometh from afar;
Not in entire forgetfulness,
And not in utter nakedness,
But trailing clouds of glory do we come
From God, who is our home.

## TIME AND ETERNITY
### Yedaya Penini

God, the source of life, has placed in our nature the blessed hope
of immortality, by which we may console ourselves for the vanity
of life, and overcome the dread of death. Use thy time as thou
wouldst a doubtful companion: extract the good and avoid the
evil. Avail thyself of the few opportunities of improvement in his
company, and use thy discretion so that thou mayest suffer no
injury from thy association with him. And remember that the

companionship of time is but of short duration. It flies more quickly than the shades of evening. We are like a child that grasps in his hand a sunbeam. He opens his hand soon again, but, to his amazement, finds it empty and the brightness gone.

## HE IS NOT DEAD
### *Percy Bysshe Shelley*
### *From "Adonais"*

Peace, peace! he is not dead, he doth not sleep—
He hath awakened from the dream of life—
'Tis we who, lost in stormy visions, keep
With phantoms an unprofitable strife. . . .
He has outsoared the shadow of our night;
Envy and calumny, and hate and pain,
And that unrest which men miscall delight
Can touch him not, and torture not again. . . .
The One remains, the many change and pass;
Heaven's light forever shines, Earth's shadows fly;
Life, like a dome of many-colored glass,
Stains the white radiance of Eternity.

## HEAR THE IMMORTAL SYMPHONIES
### *Victor Hugo*

You say the soul is nothing but the resultant of bodily powers. Why, then, is my soul more luminous when my bodily powers begin to fail? . . . The nearer I approach the end, the plainer I hear around me the immortal symphonies of the worlds which invite me. It is marvelous yet simple. It is a fairy tale and it is a fact.

### *Charles Mackay*

There is no such thing as death.
In nature nothing dies.
From each sad remnant of decay
Some forms of life arise.

## THIS EARTH IS BUT THE PROLOGUE
*Joshua Loth Liebman*

. . . The very reasonableness of the world demands immortality. . . . Nature could not have placed mind in man like a candle to be gutted in a passing wind. The human soul is not a bit player, condemned to say one brief line upon the stage of time and then make a final exit. The Divine Playwright surely could not have written His drama so poorly—prepared all the resplendent scenery of the earth as a prelude to the appearance of the hero, Man, only to permit him the stammering sentence of a brief moment of time— this life—and then make both him and the drama of existence ludicrous by eternal silence. . . .

. . . This earth is but the prologue and many a rich act has been prepared for Man in other worlds. Reason demands it, and morality cries out that our human strivings, for justice, for love, for peace, require some eternal denouement, some immortal stage upon which all the perplexities and inequities of the prologue shall be solved and human destiny find both reconciliation and fulfillment. . . .

*George MacDonald*

I came from God and I'm going back to God, and I won't have any gaps of death in the middle of my life.

## PRAYER IN APRIL
*Sarah Henderson Hay*

God grant that I may never be
A scoffer at Eternity—
As long as every April brings
The sweet rebirth of growing things;
As long as grass is green anew,
I shall believe that God looks down
Upon his wide earth, cold and brown,
To bless its unborn mystery
Of leaf, and bud, and flower to be;
To smile on it from tender skies—

How could I think it otherwise?
Had I been dust for many a year,
I still would know when Spring was near,
For the good earth that pillowed me
Would whisper immortality,
And I, in part, would rise and sing
Amid the grasses murmuring.
When looking on the mother sod,
Can I doubt that this be God?
Or when a primrose smiles at me,
Can I distrust Eternity?

## HIS PROVIDENCE WILL FOLLOW ME
### *Moses Mendelssohn*
### *From "Phaedon"*

As for myself, I am content with the conviction that God's eyes
are ever upon me, that His providence and justice will follow me
into the future life as it has protected me in this, and that my true
happiness consists in the development of the powers of my soul. It
is such felicity that awaits me in the life to come. More I do not
desire to know.

### *Cawdray*

As he that is to pass over some broad and deep river must not
look downward to the current of the stream, but must set his foot
sure, and keep his eye on the bank, on the farther shore; so he
that draws near death must look over the waves of death, and fix
his eye of faith on eternal life.

### *Max Muller*

Without a belief in personal immortality, religion surely is like
an arch resting on one pillar, like a bridge ending in an abyss.

## TO POETS ALL
### *Thomas Curtis Clark*

We shall not wholly die.
Perhaps some truth

That we have sung
Shall linger on,
And from some tongue
More eloquent
Shall hail the dawn
That we have glimpsed.
Though we be spent,
We shall be well content.

*Helen Hunt Jackson*

Oh, write of me not "Died in bitter pains"
But "Emigrated to another star!"

## LIFE IS EVER LORD OF DEATH

*James Greenleaf Whittier*
*From "Snow-Bound"*

Alas for him who never sees
The stars shine through his cypress trees!
Who, hopeless, lays his dead away,
Nor looks to see the breaking day
Across the mournful marbles play!
Who hath not learned, in hours of faith,
The truth to flesh and sense unknown,
That Life is ever lord of Death,
    And Love can never lose its own!

*Abba Hillel Silver*

Death is the peak of a life-wave, and so is birth. Death and birth are one.

## MIND CANNOT BE MORTAL

*Cicero*

When I consider the wonderful activity of the mind, so great a memory of what is past, and such a capacity of penetrating into the future; when I behold such a number of arts and sciences and such a multitude of discoveries thence arising; I believe and am firmly persuaded that a nature which contains so many things within itself cannot be mortal. . . . But if I err in believing that the souls of men are immortal, I willingly err; nor while I live would I wish to have this delightful error extorted from me; and if after death I shall feel nothing, as some minute philosophers think, I am not afraid lest dead philosophers should laugh at me for the error.

*Sir Thomas Browne*

There is surely a piece of divinity in us, something that was before the elements, and that owes no homage to the sun.

## DEATH, OR LIFE ETERNAL?
### Arthur H. Compton

. . . Though it is true that science presents no weighty evidence for life eternal, it is only fair to point out also that science has found no cogent reason for supposing that what is of importance in a man can be buried in a grave. The truth is that science cannot supply a definite answer to this question. Immortality relates to an aspect of life which is not physical, that is, which cannot be detected and measured by any instrument, and to which the application of the laws of science can at best be only a well-considered guess.

If one is to have either a positive faith in a future life or a conviction that death is the end, such beliefs must, it seems to me, be based upon religious, moral, or philosophical grounds rather than upon scientific reasoning. It is primarily to clear the way for such metaphysical thinking that it seems desirable to consider certain scientific aspects of death. Few of us living in the present age would accept a doctrine which is demonstrably contrary to scientific fact or to the spirit of scientific thought. On the other hand, our lives would be exceedingly narrow if we based our thoughts and actions solely on facts that can be subjected to scientific test. Science, that is, erects a foundation on which our emotional and religious life, if it is to be stable, must be built. The strength and form of the foundation, however, by no means determines the architectural merit of the structure that is to be erected. If a belief in immortality is found to be of value to man, it will not be because of any scientific basis on which the belief rests, but because certain important ideals toward which men are striving can be attained only by a more complete life than is possible in the flesh.

### Howard Lee McBain

There is no more mystery or miracle or supernaturalness . . . in the wholly unproved fact of immortality than there is in the wholly unexplainable fact of life or in the unimaginable fact of the universe.

## 'TIS LIFE BEYOND

### John Bowring

If in the material world
No atom ever perished—though
In multitudinous changes hurl'd
Upwards and downwards, to and fro;
And all that in the present orb'd,
From silent growth and sudden storms,
Is but a former past absorb'd
In ever-shifting frames and forms—
If He who made the worlds that were,
And makes the worlds that are to be,
Has with all-wise, all-potent care
Preserved the smallest entity
Imperishable—though it pass
From shape to shape, by heat or cold
Dispersed, attracted, monad, mass—
A wind-blown sand, a solid mass—
Shall He not save those nobler things,
Those elements of mind and thought,
Whose marvellous imaginings
Have the great deeds of progress wrought?
Those instincts, be they what they may,
Of which the soul of man is made,
By which he works his wondrous way
Up to the light's very fountain head? . . .
If in the cycle of the earth
No atom of that earth can die—
The soul, which is of nobler birth,
Must live—and live eternally.

## LIFE HAS AN OUTLET

*Charles Lewis Slattery*

The vigor of life on earth is such that we must find ourselves convinced that it has an outlet. If it had no outlet, life here would become choked and heavy. It is no forced analogy to compare such a possible picture of life with the Dead Sea. The Dead Sea receives the waters of the Jordan, but it keeps those waters in its dreary basin, and only the sun takes them away by evaporation. And so that body is sterile, lifeless.

I think, by way of contrast, of the five inland seas of North America. From the enormous Superior, the living water is poured and the falls of Niagara, down through the rapids of the St. Lawrence, through a broadening stream till it reaches the wide Atlantic.

You know the destiny of the waters of Superior and Huron and Michigan and Erie and Ontario because their waters are alive. You know the hopelessness and limitation of the waters of that sea in Palestine because it is dead. When I see the sparkle and the endless hope, in spite of all adversity and calamity, in the countless generation of earth, I know that the waters of our life are not hemmed in by the earthly banks of time, but flow out through that narrow stream, between the rocks on either side, called death, through whatever course I know not, at last into the wide, sunlit sea, called eternal life.

*Wisdom of Ben Sira*

Have regard to thy name;
For it continueth with thee longer than a thousand great treasures
   of gold.
A good life hath its number of days;
But a good name continueth forever.

## THE UNBELIEVABLE

*Edwin Markham*

Impossible, you say, that man survives
The grave—that there are other lives?
More strange, O friend, that we should ever rise

Out of the dark to walk below these skies.
Once having risen into life and light,
We need not wonder at our deathless flight.
Life is the unbelievable; but now
That this Incredible has taught us how,
We can believe the all-imagining Power
That breathed the Cosmos forth as a golden flower,
Had potence in his breath
To plan us new surprises beyond death—
New spaces and new goals
For the adventure of ascending souls.
Be brave, O heart, be brave:
It is not strange that man survives the grave:
'Twould be a stranger thing were he destroyed
Than that he ever vaulted from the void.


*Proverbs*

In the way of righteousness is life, and in the pathway thereof
there is no death.


## DIVINE RHYTHM

*Henry Meade Bland*

Clouds, then the glory of sunset;
Darkness, then burst of the morn;
Dearth, then the gentle shower;
Sacrifice—Truth is born!
The earth-throe, then comes the harvest;
Silence, and then the word;
Mist, before the full starlight;
Discord, ere music is heard!
Erring, and then the forgiveness;
Heart's-ease after the strife;
Passion, and then the refining—
Death, then the wonder of life!

## I WILL BE AS MUCH ALIVE
### *Israel Davidson*

To those who will study my books a hundred years hence, I will be as much alive then as I was to those who studied them yesterday. So please do not mourn. . . . Glorified be the spirit—the pure spirit.

## KINGSLEY'S EPITAPH

The epitaph over Charles Kingsley's grave consists of three Latin words which he chose: "Amavimus. Amamus. Amabimus." (We have loved. We love. We shall love.)

## THERE IS NO REAL DEATH
### *Wilfred Thomason Grenfell*

It has been my lot in life to have to stand by many deathbeds, and to be called in to dying men and women almost as a routine in my profession. Yet I am increasingly convinced their spirits never die at all. I am sure that there is no real death. Death is no argument against, but rather for, life. Eternal life is the complement of all my unsatisfied ideals; and experience teaches me that the belief in it is a greater incentive to be useful and good than any other I know. . . .

Immortality may be the complement of mortality as water becomes steam and steam becomes power, and power becomes heat and heat becomes light. The conclusion that life beyond is the conservation of energy of life here may be as scientific as the great natural laws for material things. I see Knowledge become Service, Service become Joy. . . . (I have seen) hope bring back color to the face and tone to the blood. . . . I have seen love do physical things which mere intellectual convictions cannot. . . . I prefer to stand with Moses in his belief in the Promised Land and that we can reach it. . . .

### *Herman Melville*
Life is a voyage that's homeward bound.

# I CANNOT SUSPECT THE ANNIHILATION OF SOULS

## Benjamin Franklin

. . . When I see nothing annihilated and not even a drop of water wasted, I cannot suspect the annihilation of souls, or believe that He will suffer the daily waste of millions of minds ready made that now exist and put Himself to the continual trouble of making new ones. Thus finding myself to exist in the world, I believe I shall, in some shape or other, always exist; and, with all the inconveniences human life is liable to, I shall not object to a new edition of mine; hoping, however, that the errata of the last may be corrected.

## Ralph Waldo Emerson

The blazing evidence of immortality is our dissatisfaction with any other conclusion.

# DEATH IS ONLY A NEW BEGINNING

## J. H. Jowett

Death is not the end; it is only a new beginning. Death is not the master of the house; he is only the porter at the King's lodge, appointed to open the gate and let the King's guests into the realm of eternal day. And so shall we ever be with the Lord. The range of our threescore years and ten is not the limit of our life. Our life is not a land-locked lake enclosed within the shore lines of seventy years. It is an arm of the sea. And so we must build for those larger waters. We are immortal!

## Ecclesiastes

Before the silver cord is snapped asunder,
And the golden bowl is shattered,
And the pitcher is broken at the fountain,
And the wheel falleth shattered into the pit;
And the dust returneth to the earth as it was,
And the spirit returneth unto God who gave it.

## FROM "THERE IS NO DEATH"

### *John Luckey McCreery*

There is no death! The stars go down
To rise upon some fairer shore;
And bright, in heaven's jeweled crown,
They shine for evermore.

There is no death! The dust we tread
Shall change beneath the summer showers
To golden grain or mellow fruit,
Of rainbow-tinted flowers.

There is no death! The leaves may fall,
And flowers may fade and pass away;
They only wait through wintry hours
The coming of May-day.

There is no death! An angel-form
Walks o'er the earth with silent tread;
And bears our best-beloved things away,
And then we call them "dead."

He leaves our hearts all desolate,
He plucks our fairest, sweetest flowers;
Transplanted into bliss, they now
Adorn immortal bowers.

And ever near us, though unseen,
The dear immortal spirits tread;
For all the boundless universe
Is life—there are no dead!

## THE ROSE STILL GROWS BEYOND THE WALL

### *A. L. Frank*

Near a shady wall a rose once grew,
  Budded and blossomed in God's free light,

Watered and fed by morning dew,
  Shedding its sweetness day and night.

As it grew and blossomed fair and tall,
  Slowly rising to loftier height,
It came to a crevice in the wall,
  Through which there shone a beam of light.

Onward it crept with added strength,
  With never a thought of fear or pride.
It followed the light through the crevice's length
  And unfolded itself on the other side.

The light, the dew, the broadening view
  Were found the same as they were before;
And it lost itself in beauties new,
  Breathing its fragrance more and more.

Shall claims of death cause us to grieve,
  And make our courage faint or fail?
Nay! Let us faith and hope receive:
  The rose still grows beyond the wall.

Scattering fragrance far and wide,
  Just as it did in days of yore,
Just as it did on the other side,
  Just as it will forevermore.

### The Kotzker Zaddik

Death is merely moving from one home to another. If we are wise, we seek to regard the latter as the abode of beauty.

## CONCERNING IMMORTALITY
### Adelaide Love

Freely He lets us look upon some pages,
Bidding us read as best we can the preface.
Over and over we ponder words and phrases,
Slow to interpret.

Just as the meanings grow a little clearer
And the eager mind would turn to the coming chapters,

Would any God exclaim: "Here endeth the lesson!"
Closing the volume?

## BACK HOME

*May Williams Ward*

To live is to go on a journey,
To die is to come back home.
My shoe-soles are thin with wandering,
Sticky with clay and loam;
There are marks of stones and of brambles,
The leather is scuffed and torn,
And I must not have walked quite straight, I think,
For the heels are unevenly worn.
I shall take off my shoes, and sleep, and rest . . .
If I dream, shall I dream that I roam?
To live is to go on a journey.
To die is to come back home.

## TURNING THE CORNER

*Arthur B. Rhinow*

I often saw you
When I turned the corner
Into your street.

A while ago I followed you
As you bent to meet the storm
Along the one-way street.
And then you turned the corner
Where the shadows lie,
And I lost sight of you.

And I must still go on,
But when I turn the corner
I hope to see you again.

### *Proverbs*

A good man leaveth an inheritance to his children's children

'Tis well to learn that sunny hours
May quickly change to mournful shade;
'Tis well to prize life's scattered flowers
Yet be prepared to see them fade.

—Eliza Cook

# TO HOLD WITH OPEN ARMS

*This chapter does not contain brief excerpts from a variety of sources on a central theme. Instead it presents a slightly condensed version of a single, sustained development of a basic thought by one author—Milton Steinberg. This is not a chance occurrence.*

*In the opinion of the editor, Steinberg's inexhaustible human compassion has combined with his penetrating brilliance to frame a message of abiding worth. As a prescription for a mature appreciation of life and a courageous acceptance of death it is unexcelled. Here out of the stubborn substance of his own tribulation he has chiseled a work of uncommon spiritual art and literary beauty. Like Job, he saw God out of his own flesh.*

*The message was first spoken as a sermon to his congregation at the Park Avenue Synagogue in New York City. Too soon thereafter it was to become a source of solace and comfort to a bereaved family and an impoverished Jewish community when Milton Steinberg's noble heart stopped beating at the untimely age of forty-six.*

---

## TO HOLD WITH OPEN ARMS

*Milton Steinberg*

There are texts in us, in our commonplace experiences, if only we are wise enough to discern them.

One such experience fell to my lot not so long ago. There was nothing dramatic about its setting nor unusual in its circumstances. And yet to me it was moment of discovery, almost of revelation.

Let me recount it very briefly, as befits a text. After a long illness, I was permitted for the first time to step out of doors. And, as I crossed the threshold, sunlight greeted me. This is my experience—all there is to it. And yet, so long as I live, I shall never forget that moment. It was mid-January—a time of cold and storm up north, but in Texas, where I happened to be, a season much like our spring. The sky overhead was very blue, very clear, and very, very high. A faint wind blew from off the western plains, cool and yet somehow tinged with warmth—like a dry, chilled wine. And everywhere in the firmament above me, in the great vault between earth and sky, on the pavements, the buildings—the golden glow of the sunlight. It touched me, too, with friendship, with warmth, with blessing. And as I basked in its glory, there ran through my mind those wonder words of the prophet about the sun which some day shall rise with healing on its wings.

In that instant I looked about me to see whether anyone else showed on his face the joy, almost the beatitude, I felt. But no, there they walked—men and women and children, in the glory of a golden flood, and so far as I could detect, there was none to give it heed. And then I remembered how often I, too, had been indifferent to sunlight, how often, preoccupied with petty and sometimes mean concerns, I had disregarded it. And I said to myself—how precious is the sunlight but, alas, how careless of it are men. How precious—how careless. This has been a refrain sounding in me ever since.

It rang in my spirit when I entered my own home again after months of absence, when I heard from a nearby room the excited voices of my children at play; when I looked once more on the dear faces of some of my friends; when I was able for the first time to speak again from my pulpit in the name of our faith and tradition, to join in worship of the God who gives us so much of which we are so careless.

And a resolution crystallized within me. I said to myself that at the very first opportunity I would speak of this. I knew full well that it is a commonplace truth, that there is nothing clever about my private rediscovery of it, nothing ingenious about my way of putting it. But I was not interested in being original or clever or ingenious. I wanted only to remind my listeners, as I was reminded, to spend life wisely, not to squander it.

I wanted to say to the husbands and wives who love one another: "How precious is your lot in that it is one of love. Do not be, even for a moment, casual with your good fortune. Love one another while yet you may."

And to parents: "How precious is the gift of your children. Never, never be too busy for the wonder and miracle of them. They will be grown up soon enough and grown away, too."

We human beings, we frail reeds who are yet, as Pascal said, thinking reeds, feeling reeds, how precious are our endowments—minds to know, eyes to see, ears to listen, hearts to stir with pity, and to dream of justice and of a perfected world. How often are we indifferent to all these!

And we who are Jews and Americans, heirs of two great traditions, how fortunate our lot in both, and how blind we are to our double good fortune.

This is what struggled in me for utterance—as it struggled in Edna St. Vincent Millay when she cried out:

"O world I cannot hold thee close enough."

I want to urge myself and all others to hold the world tight— to embrace life with all our hearts and all our souls and all our might. For it is precious, ineffably precious, and we are careless, wantonly careless of it.

And yet, when I first resolved to express all this, I knew that it was only a half-truth.

Could I have retained the sunlight no matter how hard I tried? Could I have prevented the sun from setting? Could I have kept even my own eyes from becoming satiated and bored with the glory of the day? That moment had to slip away. And had I tried to hold on to it, what would I have achieved? It would have gone from me in any case. And I would have been left disconsolate, embittered, convinced that I had been cheated.

But it is not only the sunlight that must slip away—our youth goes also, our years, our children, our senses, our lives. This is the nature of things, an inevitability. And the sooner we make our peace with it the better. Did I urge myself a moment ago to hold on? I would have done better, it now begins to appear, to have preached the opposite doctrine of letting go—the doctrine of Socrates who called life a "peisithanatos"—a persuader of death, a teacher of the art of relinquishing. It was the doctrine of Goethe who said: *"Entsagen sollst, du sollst entsagen"*—"Thou shalt renounce." And it was the doctrine of the ancient rabbis who despite their love of life said: He who would die let him hold on to life.

It is a sound doctrine.

First, because, as we have just seen, it makes peace with inevitability. And the inevitable is something with which everyone should be at peace. Second, because nothing can be more grotesque and more undignified than a futile attempt to hold on.

Let us think of the men and women who cannot grow old gracefully because they cling too hard to a youth that is escaping them; of the parents who cannot let their children go free to live their own lives; of the people who in times of general calamity have only themselves in mind.

What is it that drives people to such unseemly conduct, to such flagrant selfishness except the attitude which I have just commended—a vigorous holding on to life? Besides, are there not times when one ought to hold life cheap, as something to be lightly surrendered? In defense of one's country, for example, in the service of truth, justice, and mercy, in the advancement of mankind?

This, then, is the great truth of human existence. One must not hold life too precious. One must always be prepared to let it go.

And now we are indeed confused. First we learn that life is a privilege—cling to it! Then we are instructed: Thou shalt renounce!

A paradox, and self-contradiction! But neither the paradox nor the contradiction are of my making. They are a law written into the scheme of things—that a man must hold his existence dear and cheap at the same time.

Is it not, then, an impossible assignment to which destiny has set us? It does not ask of us that we hold life dear at one moment, and cheap at the next, but that we do both simultaneously. Now I can grasp something in my fist or let my hand lie open. I can clasp it to my breast or hold it at arm's length. I can embrace it, enfolding it in my arms, or let my arms hang loose. But how can I be expected to do both at once?

To which the answer is: With your body, of course not. But with your spirit, why not?

Is one not forever doing paradoxical and mutually contradictory things in his soul?

One wears his mind out in study, and yet has more mind with which to study. One gives away his heart in love and yet has more heart to give away. One perishes out of pity for a suffering world, and is the stronger therefor.

So, too, it is possible at one and the same time to hold on to life and let it go, provided—well, let me put it this way:

We are involved in a tug of war: Here, on the left, is the necessity to renounce life and all it contains. Here, on the right, the yearning to affirm it and its experiences. And between these two is a terrible tension, for they pull in opposite directions.

But suppose that here in the center I introduce a third force, one that lifts upward. My two irreconcilables now swing together, both pulling down against the new element. And the harder they pull, the closer together they come.

God is the third element, that new force that resolves the terrible contradiction, the intolerable tension of life.

And for this purpose it does not especially matter how we conceive God. I have been a great zealot for a mature idea of God. I have urged again and again that we think through our theology, not limping along on a child's notion of God as an old man in the sky. But for my immediate purpose, all of this is irrelevant. What is relevant is this: that so soon as a man believes in God, so soon indeed as he wills to believe in Him, the terrible strain is eased; nay, it disappears, and that for two reasons.

In the first place, because a new and higher purpose is introduced into life, the purpose of doing the will of God, to put it in Jewish terms, of performing the "Mitzvoth." This now becomes the reason for our existence. We are soldiers whose commander has stationed them at a post. How we like our assignment, whether we feel inclined to cling to it, or to let it go, is an irrelevant issue. Our hands are too busy with our duties to be either embracing the world or pushing it away.

That is why it is written: "Make thy will conform to His, then His will be thine, and all things will be as thou desirest."

But that, it might be urged, only evades the problem. By concentrating on duty we forget the conflicting drives within ourselves. The truth is, however, that, given God, the problem is solved not only by evasion but directly; that it is solved, curiously enough, by being made more intense. For, given God, everything becomes more precious, more to be loved and clung to, more embraceable; and yet at the same time easier to give up.

Given God, everything becomes more precious.

That sunshine in Dallas was not a chance effect, a lucky accident. It was an effect created by a great Artist, the Master Painter of Eternity. And because it came from God's brush it is more valuable even than I had at first conceived.

And the laughter of children, precious in itself, becomes infinitely more precious because the joy of the cosmos is in it.

And the sweetness of our friends' faces is dearer because these are fragments of an infinite sweetness.

All of life is the more treasurable because a great and Holy Spirit is in it.

And yet, it is easier for me to let go.

For these things are not and never have been mine. They belong to the Universe and the God who stands behind it. True, I have been privileged to enjoy them for an hour but they were always a loan due to be recalled.

And I let go of them the more easily because I know that as parts of the divine economy they will not be lost. The sunset, the bird's song, the baby's smile, the thunder of music, the surge of great poetry, the dreams of the heart, and my own being, dear to me as every man's is to him, all these I can well trust to Him who made them. There is poignancy and regret about giving them up, but no anxiety. When they slip from my hands they will pass to hands better, stronger, and wiser than mine.

This then is the insight which came to me as I stood some months ago in a blaze of sunlight: Life is dear, let us then hold it tight while we yet may; but we must hold it loosely also!

And only with God can we ease the intolerable tension of our existence. For only when He is given, can we hold life at once infinitely precious and yet as a thing lightly to be surrendered. Only because of Him is it made possible for us to clasp the world, but with relaxed hands; to embrace it, but with open arms.

There are three ways in which a man expresses his deep sorrow; the man on the lowest level cries; the man on the second level is silent; the man on the highest level knows how to turn his sorrow into song.

—Abraham Joshua Heschel

# TURNING SORROW INTO SONG

*The closing chapter of this volume is one of the major additions introduced into the expanded edition of this book. It borrows its title from the quotation cited at the top of this page, and it contains passages which remind us that sorrow cannot only be confronted and endured; it can be used constructively and creatively. In the words of Abraham Joshua Heschel, we can indeed turn sorrow into song. Another author cited in this chapter affirms this truth in his own words: "A rich harvest can ripen from the dark seeds of pain."*

*But there will be other themes as well. This chapter differs from all the preceding ones in one vital respect—it is not confined to a single theme. In fact, it may be considered a kind of summary of all that has preceded it. It contains new statements fortifying ideas with which we have already become familiar, recapitulating the lessons our assembled authors sought to impart in the earlier chapters.*

*Grace Noll Crowell will give us strength in our darkest moments by the firm assurance that the gentle fingers of time will indeed sew together the ragged edges of our wound, that this grief too,*

> *"will pass as surely as passed before*
> *The old forgotten pain, and the other sorrows*
> *That once you bore."*

*George Santayana, in his poignant poem addressed to a departed friend, will remind us how memory enables us to retain forever a*

*vital part of those whose lives have touched our own. In Diogenes'
sharp reply to Alexander the Great we will be reminded of the
democracy of death; our common vulnerability to suffering and
sorrow will underscore the basic oneness that unites us with our
fellow man.*

*We shall hear once more the strengthening counsel urging us not
to be afraid of death but to face it "with valiant head uplifted to
the sky." In the midst of grief we will hear the voice of gratitude
as we are reminded not only of what we have lost but also of what
we have had and retain.*

*We shall be reminded too of the goodness of God in the time of
bereavement, His nearness to "the broken vessel," the lacerated
heart. Scarred veterans of the struggle with grief will impart to us
their hard-earned counsel on how to face sorrow, the strategy to be
employed to avoid being overcome by despair. We will be given
added consolation in the bitterest of hours, when we mourn the
death of the young, and it will come to us among others, from Helen
Keller—no stranger to life's severest handicaps. Once again, we will
try to absorb the wisdom which our mortality imparts in our endeavor to add meaning to the days and years at our disposal. We
will hear repeated some of the painful but priceless lessons which
are learned in the school of adversity.*

*New and persuasive voices will share with us their faith that
death is not the end, that precisely at the moment when we face the
dark gloom of the unknown, a voice is heard crying with ringing
certainty: "The dawn! The beautiful dawn!"*

*And then, lastly, we shall revert to the theme which gives this
chapter its name as Dean Stanley comforts us in our sorrow with the
challenging reminder that "The sweetest songs on earth have been
sung in sorrow. The richest things in character have been reached
in pain."*

*If there is one special thought with which the editor would con-
clude the volume, a thought which best captures the essence of his
message, it is to be found in the wise counsel of Henry Van Dyke:
"There is only one way to get ready for immortality, and that is
to love this life and live it as bravely and faithfully and cheerfully
as we can."*

## THIS TOO WILL PASS
### Grace Noll Crowell

This, too, will pass. O heart, say it over and over,
Out of your deepest sorrow, out of your deepest grief,
No hurt can last forever—perhaps tomorrow
Will bring relief.

This, too, will pass. It will spend itself—its fury
Will die as the wind dies down with the setting sun;
Assuaged and calm, you will rest again, forgetting
A thing that is done.

Repeat it again and again, O heart, for your comfort;
This, too, "will pass as surely as passed before
The old forgotten pain, and the other sorrows
That once you bore."

As certain as stars at night, or dawn after darkness,
Inherent as the lift of the blowing grass,
Whatever your despair or your frustration—
This, too, will pass.


### Robert Burton

Hope and patience are two sovereign remedies for all, the surest reposals, the softest cushions to lean on in adversity.


## THE PAIN PASSES—THE BEAUTY REMAINS
### Adrian Anderson

For two decades the life of the great French artist Renoir was one of pain and misery. Rheumatism racked his body and distorted his fingers. Often when he held his brush between thumb and forefinger, and slowly and painfully applied his paints to the canvas, great beads of perspiration broke out upon his brow, because of his suffering.

Renoir could not stand at his work, but had to be placed in a chair, which was moved up and down to give him access to the various parts of his canvas. At intervals a physician administered sedatives, but the suffering was seldom allayed.

Yet the artist nobly persisted, painting in pain his masterpieces of beauty and enchantment.

"Master," his disciple Matisse pleaded one day, "why do you do more? Why torture yourself?"

Gazing at one of his favorite canvases, Renoir replied, "The pain passes, but the beauty remains."

### C. S. Robinson

There are times when God asks nothing of His children except silence, patience, and tears.

## WHAT MADE THE DIFFERENCE?

Someone once asked James J. Corbett what was the most important thing a man must do to become a champion. He replied, "Fight one more round."

The Duke of Wellington said that the British soldiers at the Battle of Waterloo were not braver than Napoleon's soldiers, but they were braver five minutes longer. That made the difference between victory and defeat.

## TWO TYPES OF STRENGTH
### Harold Phillips

Sometimes nothing is harder in life than just to endure. There are two types of strength. There is the strength of the wind that sways the mighty oak, and there is the strength of the oak that withstands the power of the wind. There is the strength of the locomotive that pulls the heavy train across the bridge, and there is the strength of the bridge that holds up the weight of the train. One is active strength, the other is passive strength. One is the power to keep going, the other is the power to keep still. One is the strength by which we overcome, the other is the strength by which we endure.

*William Cowper*

Beware of desperate steps; the darkest day,
Lived till tomorrow, will have passed away.

*Kahlil Gibran*

Remembrance is a form of meeting.

## THE DOMAIN OF MEMORY
### *Alexander A. Steinbach*

Memory is a master painter, lining indelible pictures upon the mind's canvas. Time pilfers our years, our hopes, even our griefs. But it cannot cross the threshold that leads to the domain of Memory. Here we resuscitate the past. Here we gather once more water lilies that died, but came to life again in the pool of remembrance.

## TO A FRIEND
### *George Santayana*

With you a part of me hath passed away
For in the peopled forest of my mind
A tree made leafless by this wintry wind
Shall never don again its green array.
Chapel and fireside, country road and bay
Have something of their friendliness resigned
Another, if I would, I could not find,
And I am grown much older in a day.
But yet I treasure in my memory
Your gift of charity and young heart's ease,
And the dear honor of your amity;
For these once mine, my life is rich with these
And I scarce know which part may greater be,—
What I keep of you, or you rob of me.

# THE WOMAN WHO WOULD NOT FORGET

## Ralph W. Sockman

According to an ancient Greek legend, a woman came down to the River Styx to be ferried across to the region of departed spirits. Charon, the kindly ferryman, reminded her that it was her privilege to drink of the waters of Lethe, and thus forget the life she was leaving. Eagerly she said, "I will forget how I have suffered." "And," added Charon, "remember too that you will forget how you have rejoiced." The woman said, "I will forget my failures." The old ferryman added, "And also your victories." She continued, "I will forget how I have been hated." "And also how you have been loved," added Charon. Then she paused to consider the whole matter, and the end of the story is that she left the draught of Lethe untasted, preferring to retain the memory even of sorrow and failure rather than to give up the memory of life's loves and joys.

## Henry Ward Beecher

What the heart has once owned and had, it shall never lose.

## Seneca

The comfort of having a friend may be taken away, but not that of having had one.

# RETURN

## Mildred Bowers Armstrong

When other hearts are tuned
To a glad singing
In the spring, ever new,
Ever song-bringing;
When other hearts are feeling
The joy I knew,
Let me come back again,
Singing, too.

I shall know
When the pale petals blow
And spring comes flashing back
Another year.
You must not search and call.
When the first petals fall
I shall be here.

If you cannot see
The hands and eyes of me
When petals fill the air
You will hear a song
The wind blows along—
I shall be here.

## SORROW PLAYS NO FAVORITES
### *Louis Binstock*

We must see that sorrow is a universal, not merely an individual experience. It comes to the young as well as to the old, to the learned as well as to the illiterate, to the strong as well as to the weak, to the rich as well as to the poor. It is to be found in every country, in every climate, among every people and within every nation. Sorrow is the most impartial and impersonal of forces. She plays no favorites. She is everywhere. She can climb the highest mountain and descend into the deepest valley. She can break into the mightiest fortress and silently slip into the open tent. She is a guest at the banquet table in the castle as well as a frequent visitor in the poor man's hut.

## ALL LIE EQUALLY LEVEL
### *Austin O'Malley*

Our lives are waves that come up out of the ocean of eternity, break upon the beach of earth, and lapse back to the ocean of eternity. Some are sunlit, some run in storm and rain; one is a quiet ripple, another is a thunderous breaker; and once in many centuries comes a great tidal wave that sweeps over a continent; but all go back to the sea and lie equally level there.

# MAN CANNOT BE EXEMPT FROM PAIN

*Voltaire*

Man, born to die, can no more be exempt from pain than from death. To prevent an organized substance endowed with feeling from ever experiencing pain, it would be necessary that all the laws of nature should be changed; that matter should no longer be divisible; that it should neither have weight, action, nor force; that a rock might fall on an animal without crushing it; and that water should have no power to suffocate, or fire to burn it.

# BEYOND

*Ella Wheeler Wilcox*

It seemeth such a little way to me
    Across to that strange country—the Beyond;
And yet not strange, for it has grown to be
    The home of those of whom I am most fond;
They make it seem familiar and most dear,
    As journeying friends bring distant
       regions near . . .

And so for me there is no sting to death,
    And so the grave has lost its victory,
It is but crossing, with abated breath,
    And white, set face, a little strip of sea,
To find the loved ones waiting on the shore,
    More beautiful, more precious than before.

# EPITAPH

*Carved on the tombstone of President James Garfield,
twentieth President of the United States.*

Life's race well run
Life's work well done
Life's crown well worn
Now comes rest.

## TERMINATION OF ACTIVITY IS NO EVIL

*Marcus Aurelius*

Termination of activity, cessation from movement and opinion, and in a sense their death, is no evil. Turn thy thoughts now to the consideration of thy life, thy life as a child, as a youth, thy manhood, thy old age, for in these also every change was a death. Is this anything to fear? Turn thy thoughts now to thy life under thy grandfather, then to thy life under thy mother, then to thy life under thy father; and as thou findest many other differences and changes and terminations, ask thyself, Is this anything to fear? In like manner, then, neither are the termination and cessation and change of thy whole life a thing to be afraid of.

*Charles Caleb Colton*

Death is the liberator of him whom freedom cannot release; the physician of him whom medicine cannot cure; the comforter of him whom time cannot console.

## AS TREES

*Gail Brook Burket*

Let me grow old as trees grow old, dear Lord,
With pliant boughs, made resolute and strong
By wrestling storms, extended to afford
The welcome shade which shelters woodland song.
As trees are harps for every breeze, keep me
Attuned to life. As trees are havens, give
My days the joy of constant ministry
To human need so long as I shall live.
As trees put forth green leaves for every spring,
Let me renew my hope throughout the years.
As trees become more stalwart, let age bring
Adversity unmarred by sapling fears.
Let me greet death, when it is time to die,
With valiant head uplifted to the sky.

## PAIN IS NOT PUNISHMENT
### Kenneth Hildebrand

On occasion I hear someone cry in anguish of soul, "What terrible thing have I done that God should punish me so?" The answer is: nothing! Suffering, except through the universal law of cause and effect, does not come as punishment. Once and for all, we should rid ourselves of the thought that the Creator of Life sends pain as punishment. This is the basic point in the Bible's Book of Job. He wanted to demonstrate that the idea is unsound theologically and philosophically. Yet a rich harvest can ripen from the dark seeds of pain. Not as punishment, but in order that we may grow in faith and in character. God has placed us in a world where there is the presence of suffering.

## THE HERITAGE OF A DIVINER LIFE
### Plutarch

Alexander the Great, seeing Diogenes looking attentively at a parcel of human bones, asked the philosopher what he was looking for. "That which I cannot find," was the reply; "the difference between your father's bones and those of his slaves."

A good man being asked during his last illness, whether he thought himself dying, "Really, friend, I care not whether I am or not; for if I die I shall be with God; if I live, He will be with me."

Not by lamentations and mournful chants ought we to celebrate the funeral of a good man, but by hymns, for in ceasing to be numbered with mortals he enters upon the heritage of a diviner life.

## HOW DO YOU KNOW?
### Randolph S. Foster

When you take the wires of the cage apart, you do not hurt the bird, but you help it. You let it out of its prison. How do you know that death does not help me when it takes the wires of my cage down?—that it does not release me, and put me into some better place and better condition of life?

## SONG

*Christina Georgina Rossetti*

When I am dead, my dearest,
    Sing no sad songs for me;
Plant thou no roses at my head,
    Nor shady cypress-tree:
Be the green grass above me
    With showers and dew drops wet;
And if thou wilt, remember,
    And if thou wilt, forget.

I shall not see the shadows,
    I shall not feel the rain;
I shall not hear the nightingale
    Sing on, as if in pain:
And dreaming through the twilight
    That doth not rise nor set,
Haply I may remember
    And haply may forget.


*Tryon Edwards*

This world is the land of the dying; the next is the land of the
living.


## DEATH IS A DOOR

*Nancy Byrd Turner*

Death is only an old door
Set in a garden wall.
On quiet hinges it gives at dusk,
When the thrushes call.

Along the lintel are green leaves,
Beyond, the light lies still;
Very weary and willing feet
Go over that sill.

There is nothing to trouble any heart,
Nothing to hurt at all.
Death is only an old door
In a garden wall.


## ADVERSITY AND RAIN

### Walter Scott

Adversity is like the period of the former and of the latter rain,—cold, comfortless, unfriendly to man and to animal; yet from that season have their birth the flower and the fruit, the date, the rose, and the pomegranate.


## I SHALL NOT GO ALONE

### Author unknown

I know not when I go or where
From this familiar scene;
But He is here and He is there,
And all the way between;

And when I leave this life, I know,
For that dim vast unknown,
Though late I stay, or soon I go,
I shall not go alone.


## FATHER, GENTLY LEAD ALL HEARTS

### Leslie Savage Clark

How hard for unaccustomed feet
Which only knew the meadow
Is this bleak road they now must tread
Through valleys dark with shadow.
Until they learn how sure Thy love
That girds each day, each morrow,
O Father, gently lead all hearts
That newly come to sorrow!

## THE BROKEN VESSEL
*Midrash*

A man of flesh and blood, if he has a vessel,
so long as the vessel is whole, he is happy with it;
broken, he does not wish it.
But not so the Holy One, blessed be He.
So long as the vessel is whole, He does not wish to see it;
broken, He wishes it.
And what is the favorite vessel of the Holy One,
   blessed be He?
The heart of man.
If the Holy One, blessed be He, sees a proud heart,
He does not wish it;
as it is said: "Every one that is proud in heart is an abomination to
   the Lord" (Prov. 16:5).
Broken, He says: This is mine;
as it is said: "The Lord is nigh unto them that are of a broken heart"
   (Ps. 34:19).

## WHEN THEIR HANDS TOUCHED
*Gene E. Bartlett*

Two children were overheard talking about the death of their
grandmother. The five-year-old girl was asking her seven-year-old
brother how "grandmother went to God." "Well," said the boy, "it
happened this way. First Grandmother reached up and up and up
as far as she could. Then God reached down and down and down.
When their hands touched, He took her."

## FOR ALL OF TROUBLED HEART
*A. Warren*

The snow is falling softly on the earth,
Grown hushed beneath its covering of white;
O Father, let another peace descend
On all of troubled heart this winter night.

Look down upon them in their anxious dark,
On those who sleep not for their fear and care,
On those with tremulous prayers on their lips,
The prayers that stand between them and despair.

Let fall Thy comfort as this soundless snow;
Make troubled hearts aware in Thine own way
Of Love beside them in this quiet hour,
Of Strength with which to meet the coming day.

*A. Powell Davies*

To see death gently pronounce its benediction upon a fullness of years, to see its merciful hand remove the infirmities of one who has traveled long and become weary of the journey, is a hallowed experience.

## EVER THE STERN RENEWAL

*Elias Lieberman*

Ever the stern renewal
   Beckons us when we tire;
Ever the gift of fuel
   Answers the faltering fire.

Call of an old obligation
   Signals from barracks of time;
Trumpets of new elation
   Sound a mandate to climb.

Now we shall start ascending
   High over yesterday's sorrow,
Urged by a never ending
   Faith in a better tomorrow.

*Edmund Burke*

Never despair; but if you do, work on in despair.

*Laura Lee Randall*

Out of the earth, the rose,
  Out of the night, the dawn:
Out of my heart, with all its woes,
  High courage to press on.

## TEST YOUR SELF-RESPECT

*Oscar Edward Maurer*

Waste not your strength trying to push shut doors which God is opening. Neither wear yourself out in keeping open doors which ought to be forever sealed. Some episode in your life, over which you are anxious, is closed. It is in the past. Whatever its memory, you cannot change it. But you can shut the door. Go into some silent place of thought. Test your self-respect. Ask your soul, "Have I emerged from this experience with honor, or if not, can honor be retrieved?" And if your soul answers, "Yes," close then the door to that Past; hang a garland over the portal if you will, but come away without tarrying. The east is aflame with the radiance of the morning, and before you stands many another door, held open by the hand of God.

## UNFAILING

*Frances Shaw*

When, like a flower, your loved one lies
  Beneath the grasses
  Sleeping the great sleep,
Go out unlonely to the folding hills—
  They will not let you weep.

When one by one your dreams have stolen by,
  And blackness fills the night,
  And pain and care
Reach up for comfort to the leaning sky—
  The coming of the dawn is still a prayer.

## FROM "THE WHITE CLIFFS"
### *Alice Duer Miller*

O, sad people, buy not your past too dearly,
   Live not in dreams of the past, for understand,
If you remember too much, too long, too clearly,
   If you grasp memory with too heavy a hand,
You will destroy memory in all its glory
   For the sake of the dreams of your head upon your bed.
You will be left with only the worn dead story
   You told yourself of the dead.


## THOSE WHO DIE IN THE SPLENDOR OF THEIR PRIME
### *Helen Keller*

Often when the heart is torn with sorrow, spiritually we wander like a traveler lost in a deep wood. We grow frightened, lose all sense of direction, batter ourselves against trees and rocks in our attempt to find a path. All the while there is a path—a path of Faith—that leads straight out of the dense tangle of our difficulties into the open road we are seeking. Let us not weep for those who have gone away when their lives were at full bloom and beauty. Who are we that we should mourn them and wish them back? Life at its every stage is good, but who shall say whether those who die in the splendor of their prime are not fortunate to have known no abatement, no dulling of the flame by ash, no slow fading of life's perfect flower.


## THE SOURCE OF ALL OUR TROUBLES
### *Plutarch*

When Anaxagoras was told of the death of his son, he only said, "I knew he was mortal." So we in all casualties of life should say, I knew my riches were uncertain; that my friend was but a man. Such considerations would soon pacify us, because all our troubles proceed from their being unexpected.

*Harriet Beecher Stowe*

When you get into a tight place and everything goes against you, till it seems as though you could not hold on a minute longer, never give up then, for that is just the place and time that the tide will turn.

## A PSALM OF LIFE
*Henry Wadsworth Longfellow*

Tell me not, in mournful numbers,
    Life is but an empty dream!
For the soul is dead that slumbers
    And things are not what they seem.

Life is real! Life is earnest!
    And the grave is not its goal;
Dust thou art, to dust returnest,
    Was not spoken of the soul.

Not enjoyment, and not sorrow,
    Is our destined end or way;
But to act, that each tomorrow
    Find us farther than today.

Art is long, and Time is fleeting,
    And our hearts, though stout and brave,
Still, like muffled drums, are beating
    Funeral marches to the grave.

In the world's broad field of battle,
    In the bivouac of life,
Be not like dumb, driven cattle!
    Be a hero in the strife!

Trust no Future, howe'er pleasant!
    Let the dead Past bury its dead!
Act,—act in the living Present!
    Heart within, and God o'erhead!

Lives of great men all remind us
  We can make our lives sublime,
And, departing, leave behind us
  Footprints on the sands of time.

Footprints, that perhaps another,
  Sailing o'er life's solemn main,
A forlorn and shipwrecked brother,
  Seeing, shall take heart again.

Let us then be up and doing,
  With a heart for any fate;
Still achieving, still pursuing,
  Learn to labor and to wait.

## HOW TO MEET AFFLICTION
### *Dinah Maria Mulock*

The only way to meet affliction is to pass through it solemnly, slowly, with humility and faith, as the Israelites passed through the sea. Then its very waves of misery will divide, and become to us a wall, on the right side and on the left, until the gulf narrows before our eyes, and we land safe on the opposite shore.

### *William Lyon Phelps*

For my own part, I live every day as if this were the first day I had ever seen and the last I were going to see.

## DIGNITY TO LIFE
### *Samuel M. Lindsay*

Belief in immortality gives dignity to life and enables us to endure cheerfully those trials which come to us all. As the thought of immortality occupies our minds, we gain a clearer conception of duty and are inspired to cultivate character. Living for the future is no coward's philosophy, but an inspiration to noble and unselfish activity.

*Joseph Conrad*

Facing it—always facing it—that's the way to get through. Face it! That's enough for any man!

## ABOVE THE THUNDERING SHELLS
### *Anderson M. Scruggs*

Grieve not that life was closed for him before
His ears could hear the ultimate applause
The future held in store. Grieve not because
In eager youth time closed an ebon door
Between him and his dream. There is no act
So great as his. No lines he might have conned
From Shakespeare's noblest dreams could reach beyond
This one achievement in the world of fact.

In that last scene with Death no swift acclaim
Surged toward him from the dark. No mortal stirred
To stay the curtain or to shout his name,
But deep within his heart, I know he heard
Above the thundering shells, the heaving sod,
The silent plaudits from the lips of God.

## THE GREAT MYSTERY OF HUMAN LIFE
### *Fyodor Dostoevski*

It is the great mystery of human life that old grief passes gradually into quiet, tender joy. The mild serenity of age takes the place of the riotous blood of youth. I bless the rising sun each day, and, as before, my heart sings to meet it, but now I love even more its setting, its long slanting rays and the soft, tender, gentle memories that come with them, the dear images from the whole of my long, happy life—and over all the Divine Truth, softening, reconciling, forgiving!

My life is ending, I know that well, but every day that is left me I feel how my earthly life is in touch with a new infinite, unknown, but approaching life, the nearness of which sets my soul quivering with rapture, my mind glowing and my heart weeping with joy.

*Jonathan Edwards*

Resolved never to do anything which I should be afraid to do if it were the last hour of my life.

*Peter A. Lea*

Darkness makes us aware of the stars,
And so when dark hours arise,
They may hold a bright and lovely thing,
We might never have known otherwise.

*Frances M. Lipp*

So brief the hour
For work or play,
Why grieve the night
Or waste the day?

# DON'T WAIT

*Author unknown*

Friends, in this world of hurry
And work and sudden end
If a thought comes quick of doing
A kindness to a friend
Do it this very instant!
Don't put it off—don't wait;
What's the use of doing a kindness
If you do it a day too late?

*Henry Van Dyke*

Some people are so afraid to die that they never begin to live.

## DO IT NOW
*Author unknown*

If you have hard work to do,
   Do it now.
Today the skies are clear and blue,
Tomorrow clouds may come in view,
Yesterday is not for you;
   Do it now.

If you have a song to sing,
   Sing it now.
Let the notes of gladness ring
Clear as song of bird in Spring,
Let every day some music bring;
   Sing it now.

If you have kind words to say,
   Say them now.
Tomorrow may not come your way.
Do a kindness while you may,
Loved ones will not always stay;
   Say them now.

If you have a smile to show,
   Show it now.
Make hearts happy, roses grow,
Let the friends around you know
The love you have before they go;
   Show it now.


## THE DAWN! THE BEAUTIFUL DAWN!
*Archibald Rutledge*

As a personal experience, none of my own ever surpassed in moving power that beautiful and dramatic scene which, though it lies years back in the moonlit land of the past and of memory, is vividly alive to me now. It happened at sunrise, and it was of a sunrise.

One dearer to me than all else in life had, for days, lain helpless, speechless. Consciousness was gone. We knew that the mortal mists were fast gathering; that the irremediable river must soon be crossed. The last morning of our watching was misty; the day emerged so wanly that we hardly knew that it had come. Suddenly the one we loved so dearly sat up in bed, a strange light on her face of a happiness past all our mortal joy. She stretched abroad her arms, crying in the radiant abandon of spiritual certainty, "The Dawn! The beautiful Dawn!"

Those were her dying words—glad, triumphant. And for me they hold the eternal promise of the sunrise. They glow with immortality. In every sense, our mortal dawn that day was anything but beautiful; but she saw the beginning of an immortal day. Believing in a God of infinite love and of infinite power, I find it natural to believe that death is not a disastrous sundown but rather a spiritual sunrise, ushering in the unconjectured splendors of immortality.

### Johann Wolfgang Von Goethe

Life is the childhood of our immortality.

### Henry Van Dyke

There is only one way to get ready for immortality, and that is to love this life and live it as bravely and faithfully and cheerfully as we can.

## PREPARING FOR DEATH
### Bonaro W. Overstreet

When Socrates was told that the time had come for him to prepare for his death, he asked reasonably, "Know ye not that I have been preparing for it all my life?"

### Kahlil Gibran

Your pain is the breaking of the shell that encloses your understanding.

## THINGS THAT NEVER DIE
*Charles Dickens*

The pure, the bright, the beautiful
    That stirred our hearts in youth
The impulses to wordless prayer,
    The streams of love and truth,
The longing after something lost,
    The spirit's yearning cry,
The striving after better hopes—
    These things can never die.

The timid hand stretched forth to aid
    A brother in his need;
A kindly word in grief's dark hour,
    That proves a friend indeed;
The plea for mercy softly breathed,
    When justice threatens high,
The sorrow of a contrite heart—
    These things shall never die.

Let nothing pass, for every hand
    Must find some work to do,
Lose not a chance to waken love—
    Be firm and just and true.
So shall a light that cannot fade
    Beam on thee from on high,
And angel voices say to thee—
    "These things shall never die."


## THE ARROW OF SORROW
*T. DeWitt Talmage*

When Prometheus was assaulted by an enemy, an arrow struck a swelling which had threatened his life. The swelling was opened, and so the life of Prometheus was saved. So I think it is the mission of the arrow of sorrow to open great swellings of pride and to cure the diseases of the soul. You never feel your dependence on God, and you never feel your own weakness until you have trouble.

## TO DIFFUSE ITS LIGHT
*Johann Wolfgang von Goethe*

I am fully convinced that the soul is indestructible, and that its activities will continue through eternity. It is like the sun, which, to our eyes, seems to set in night; but it has really gone to diffuse its light elsewhere.

### *Josh Billings*

As the flint contains the spark, unknown to itself, which the steel alone can awaken to life, so adversity often reveals to us hidden gems, which prosperity or negligence would forever have hidden.

### *Swami Sivananda*

Life is a school in which every sorrow, every pain, every heartbreak brings a precious lesson.

### *Yiddish Proverb*

Not to have had pain is not to have been human.

## THE GREATEST TRUTHS ARE SEEN THROUGH TEARS
*John C. Van Dyke*

Rembrandt's domestic troubles served only to heighten and deepen his art, and perhaps his best canvases were painted under stress of circumstances and in sadness of heart. His life is another proof, if needed, that the greatest truths and beauties are to be seen only through tears. Too bad for the man! But the world—the same ungrateful, selfish world that has always lighted its torch at the funeral pyres of genius—is the gainer.

*Ralph G. Ingersoll*

Our hope of immortality does not come from any religions, but nearly all religions come from that hope.

*John Milton*

Death is the golden key that opens the palace of eternity.

## LIFE JOINED ETERNITY
*Samuel T. Coleridge*

How well he fell asleep!
Like some proud river, widening toward the sea;
Calmly and grandly, silently and deep,
Life joined eternity.

## THEY ARE NOT LOST
*Hugh Robert Orr*

They are not gone who pass beyond the clasp of hand, out from the strong embrace. They are but come so close we need not grope with hands nor look to see, nor try to catch the sound of feet. They have put off their shoes softly to walk by day within our thoughts, to tread at night our dream-led paths of sleep.

They are not lost who find the sunset gate, the goal of all their faithful years. Not lost are they who reach the summit of their climb, the peak above the clouds and storms. They are not lost who find the light of sun and stars and God.

*Mark Twain*

I have never seen what to me seemed an atom of proof that there is a future life. And yet—I am strongly inclined to expect one.

## NOTHING DISAPPEARS WITHOUT A TRACE
### *Wernher von Braun*

Many people seem to feel that science has somehow made "religious ideas" untimely or old-fashioned. But I think science has a real surprise for the skeptics. Science, for instance, tells us that nothing in nature, not even the tiniest particle, can disappear without a trace. Nature does not know extinction. All it knows is transformation.

Now, if God applies this fundamental principle to the most minute and insignificant parts of His universe, doesn't it make sense to assume that He applies it also to the human soul? I think it does. And everything science has taught me—and continues to teach me—strengthens my belief in the continuity of our spiritual existence after death. Nothing disappears without a trace.

### *Jean Richter*

Each departed friend is a magnet that attracts us to the next world.

## I ERR GLADLY
### *Cicero*

If I err in my belief that the souls of men are immortal, I err gladly, and I do not wish to lose so delightful an error.

## WILL HE NEGLECT THE SOUL?
### *William Jennings Bryan*

If the Father deigns to touch with divine power the cold and pulseless heart of the buried acorn and make it burst forth from its prison walls, will He leave neglected in the earth the soul of man made in the image of his Creator?

304 • TREASURY OF COMFORT

## THERE SHE COMES!

### Anonymous

I am standing upon the seashore; a ship at my side spreads her white sails to the morning breeze and starts for the blue ocean. She is an object of beauty and strength, and I stand and watch her until—at length—she hangs like a speck of white cloud just where the sea and sky come down to mingle with each other. Then some-one at my side says, "There! She's gone."

Gone where? Gone from my sight—that is all. She is just as large in mast and hull and spar as she was when she left my side and just as able to bear her load of living freight to the place of destination. Her diminished size is in me, not in her; and just at the moment when someone at my side says, "There! She's gone," there are other eyes watching her coming and other voices ready to take up the glad shout, "There she comes!" And that is dying.


### Robespierre

Death is not an eternal sleep! Citizens, erase from the tomb this inscription put there by sacrilegious hands, which casts a pall over the face of nature. Engrave rather this upon it: Death is the be-ginning of immortality.


## HE HAS FOR ME A GLAD SURPRISE

### Lyman Abbot

I think of death as a glad awakening from this troubled sleep which we call life; as an emancipation from the world which, beau-tiful though it be, is still a land of captivity; as a graduation from this primary department into some higher rank in the hierarchy of learning . . .

I neither know nor wish to know what the future life has for me. I would not, if I could, stand at the open window and peer into the unknown beyond. I am sure that He whose mercies are new every morning and fresh every evening, who brings into every epoch of my life a new surprise, and makes in every experience a new disclosure of His love, who sweetens gladness with gratitude, and sorrow with comfort, who gives the lark for the morning and the nightingale for the twilight, who makes every year better than the year preceding, and every new experience an experience of His marvelous skill in gift-giving, has for me some future of glad surprise which I would not forecast if I could.

### Thomas Binney

Nature is the most thrifty thing in the world; she never wastes anything; she undergoes change, but there's no annihilation—the essence remains.

### Nathaniel Hawthorne

Our Creator would never have made such lovely days, and have given us the deep hearts to enjoy them, above and beyond all thought, unless we were meant to be immortal.

### Oliver Wendell Holmes, Jr.

Life seems to me like a Japanese picture which our imagination does not allow to end with the margin. We aim at the infinite and when the arrow falls to earth it is in flames.

## IMMORTALITY
### Harry K. Zeller, Jr.

The stars look down on the earth,
The stars look down on the sea.
The stars look up to the infinite God,
The stars look down on me.
The stars will live for a million years,
For a million years and a day,
But God and I will live and love
When the stars have passed away.

## MAN WILL PREVAIL
### William Faulkner

I decline to accept the end of man. It is easy enough to say that man is immortal simply because he will endure; that when the last ding-dong of doom has clanged and faded from the last worthless rock hanging tideless in the last red and dying evening, that even then there will still be one more sound: that of his puny inexhaustible voice, still talking. I refuse to accept this. I believe that man will not merely endure: he will prevail. He is immortal, not because he alone among creatures has an inexhaustible voice, but because he has a soul, a spirit capable of compassion and sacrifice and endurance.

### Joseph R. Sizoo

The history of the world is in reality the story of tears transformed into triumphs.

### Bernard Baruch

The art of living lies not in eliminating but in growing with troubles.

## ALCHEMY
### Sara Teasdale

I lift my heart as spring lifts up
A yellow daisy to the rain;
My heart will be a lovely cup
Altho' it holds but pain.

For I shall learn from flower and leaf
That color every drop they hold,
To change the lifeless wine of grief
To living gold.

*Thomas Bailey Aldrich*

What is lovely never dies, but passes into other loveliness.

## WE ARE BORN FOR A HIGHER DESTINY

*Edward Bulwer-Lytton*

We are born for a higher destiny than that of earth; there is a realm where the rainbow never fades, where the stars will be spread before us like islands that slumber on the ocean, and where the beings that pass before us like shadows will stay in our presence forever.

## FROM "CATO"

*Joseph Addison*

It must be so . . .
Else—whence this pleasing hope, that fond desire,
This longing after immortality?
Or whence this secret dread and inward horror
Of falling into naught? Why shrinks the soul
Back on itself, and startles at destruction?
'Tis the Divinity that stirs within us;
'Tis Heaven itself that points out an hereafter
And intimates Eternity to Man.

## THE MAN WHO LIVES IN THAT HOPE

*Louis Pasteur*

There are two men in each one of us: the scientist, he who starts with clear field and desires to rise to the knowledge of Nature through observation, experimentation and reasoning; and the man of sentiment, the man of faith, the man who mourns his dead children and who cannot, alas, prove at all that he will see them again, but who believes that he will, and lives in that hope. . . . The man who feels that force that is within him cannot die.

## FROM "VERSES WRITTEN IN 1872"
*Robert Louis Stevenson*

He is not dead, this friend; not dead,
But, in the path we mortals tread,
Got some few, trifling steps ahead,
    And nearer to the end;
So that you, too, once past the bend
Shall meet again, as face to face this friend
You fancy dead.


## IMMORTALITY
*Francesca Falk Miller*

And there shall come a day . . . in Spring
When death and winter
Loose their chill white hold
Quite suddenly. A day of sunlit air
When winging birds return,
And earth her gentle bosoms bare
So that new, thirsty life
May nurture there.
That breathless hour . . .
So filled with warm, soft miracles
That faith is born anew.
On such a day . . .
I shall return to you!

You may not touch me . . . no,
For you have thought of me as dead.
But in the silence lift believing eyes
Toward the dear infinity
Of skies. And listen . . .
With your very soul held still . . .
For you will hear me on some little hill,
Advancing with the coming of the year.
Not far away . . . Not dead . . .
Not even gone.

The day will suddenly be filled
With immortality and song,
And without stirring from your quiet place,
Your love will welcome mine . . .
Across the little space,
And we will talk of every lovely thing . . .
When I return . . . in Spring!

## THE DIVINITY THAT STIRS WITHIN US
### *Joseph Addison*

Whence this pleasing hope, this fond desire,
  This longing for immortality?
'Tis the divinity that stirs within us;
'Tis heaven itself that points out a hereafter,
  And intimates eternity to man.

## THE SWEETEST SONGS HAVE BEEN SUNG IN SORROW
### *Dean Stanley*

There is a story of a German baron who made a great Aeolian harp by stretching the wires from tower to tower of his castle. When the harp was ready he listened for the music. But it was in the still air; the wires hung silent. Autumn came with its gentle breezes and there were faint whispers of song. At length the winter winds swept over the castle, and now the harp answered in majestic music.

Such a harp is the human heart. It does not yield its noblest music in the summer days of joy, but in the winter of trial. The sweetest songs on earth have been sung in sorrow. The richest things in character have been reached in pain.

### *Henry Ward Beecher*

Sorrows are often like clouds, which, though black when they are passing over us, when they are past, become as if they were the garments of God, thrown off in purple and gold along the sky.

## A GROWING PAIN TOWARD JUNE
### *Robert Hillyer*

I believe in my survival after death. Like many others before me, I have experienced "intimations of immortality." I can no more explain these than the brown seed can explain the flowering tree. Deep in the soil in time's midwinter, my very stirring and unease seem a kind of growing pain toward June.

## CLOSING THE DOORS
### *Irene J. McKeehan*

I have closed the door on Doubt,
I will go by what light I can find,
And hold up my hands and reach them out
To the glimmer of God in the dark, and call—
I am Thine, though I grope and stumble and fall,
I serve, and Thy service is kind.

I have closed the door on Fear.
He has lived with me far too long.
If he were to break forth and reappear,
I should lift up my eyes and look at the sky,
And sing aloud, and run lightly by;
He will never follow a song.

I have closed the door on Gloom.
His house has too narrow a view;
I must seek for my soul a wider room
With windows to open and let in the sun,
And radiant lamps when the day is done,
And the breeze of the world blowing through.

For centuries political theorists, philosophers, and historians have asked why war occurs. Innumerable books have been published on the question, yet none has proved authoritative. In this book, Kalevi Holsti approaches the issue from a new perspective. He asks three interrelated questions that have not previously received systematic analysis. What issues generate conflict? How have attitudes toward war changed? And what attempts have been made historically to create international orders and institutions that can manage, control, or prevent international conflicts and crises?

Professor Holsti begins by assessing the achievements and shortfalls of the voluminous literature of war, and outlines the model of international politics that informs his study. Then, starting with the Treaties of Münster and Osnabrück of 1648, he examines 177 international wars from the European and global states systems. Through these cases, he identifies a range of conflict-producing issues and how these, as well as the attitudes of policy-makers to the use of force, have changed over the last 350 years. He demonstrates how the great peacemaking efforts of 1648, 1713, 1815, 1919, and 1945 involved implicit and explicit theories of international relations. The new orders established in those watershed peace conferences attempted to solve the issues of the past, yet few successfully anticipated those of the future. Indeed, some created the basis of new conflicts.

*Peace and war: armed conflicts and international order 1648–1989* is a major study of the origins of war and the foundations of peace in the last 350 years. It will be an important text for students of and specialists in diplomatic history, war and peace studies, international relations, international conflict, and political studies.

# PEACE AND WAR: ARMED CONFLICTS AND INTERNATIONAL ORDER 1648–1989

*Cambridge Studies in International Relations* is a joint initiative of Cambridge University Press and the British International Studies Association (BISA). The series will include a wide range of material, from undergraduate textbooks and surveys to research-based monographs and collaborative volumes. The aim of the series is to publish the best new scholarship in International Studies from Europe, North America and the rest of the world.

## CAMBRIDGE STUDIES IN INTERNATIONAL RELATIONS

# PEACE AND WAR: ARMED CONFLICTS AND INTERNATIONAL ORDER 1648–1989

KALEVI J. HOLSTI

*Professor, Department of Political Science, University of British Columbia*

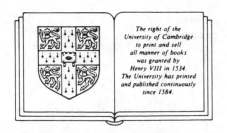

The right of the
University of Cambridge
to print and sell
all manner of books
was granted by
Henry VIII in 1534.
The University has printed
and published continuously
since 1584.

CAMBRIDGE UNIVERSITY PRESS

Cambridge

New York   Port Chester

Melbourne   Sydney

Published by the Press Syndicate of the University of Cambridge
The Pitt Building, Trumpington Street, Cambridge CB2 1RP
40 West 20th Street, New York, NY 10011, USA
10 Stamford Road, Oakleigh, Melbourne 3166, Australia

First published 1991

Printed in Great Britain by Redwood Press Limited, Melksham,
Wiltshire

*British Library cataloguing in publication data*

Holsti, K. J. (Kalevi Jacque), *1935–*
Peace and war: armed conflicts and international
order 1648–1989.
1. Foreign relations. Conflict, history
I. Title   II. Series
327.1609

*Library of Congress cataloguing in publication data*

Holsti, K. J. (Kalevi Jacque), 1935–
Peace and war: armed conflicts and international order
1648–1989/Kalevi J. Holsti.
    p.      cm. – (Cambridge studies in international relations: 14)
Includes bibliographical references and index.
ISBN 0 521 39048 6. – ISBN 0 521 39929 7 (pbk.)
1. War   2. World politics.   3. Military history, Modern.
4.   International relations.   I. Title.   II. Series.
U21.2.H627   1990
355.02 – dc20   90–2110   CIP

ISBN 0 521 39048 6 hardback
ISBN 0 521 39929 7 paperback

RP

For Marilyn

# CONTENTS

# FIGURES

# TABLES

# PREFACE

Why war? The question is asked in literature, poetry, and drama, and in innumerable studies by philosophers, historians, and political and strategic analysts. The answers have ranged from the nature of international systems to the genetic make-up of man. None is authoritative and so the question continues to be raised.

This study offers no answers, but provides some clues to understanding, clues which have not been investigated in the significantly large literature on war that has emerged in the last several decades. Instead of asking "why war?" it poses three interrelated questions: what do men fight about? how have their attitudes toward war changed? and to what extent have they succeeded in creating international orders and institutions that manage, control, or prevent international conflicts and crises from breaking out into war? We are concerned with issues, attitudes, and orders, how they are related, and how they affect the propensity of states to employ armed force in international relationships.

At least two assumptions inform the investigation. Sharing the Enlightenment's perspective on politics, I am reasonably convinced that man can build diplomatic institutions, norms, and procedures that will at least reduce the incidence of war. I do not share those pessimistic views that see war as a necessary concomitant of man's genetic make-up, a perpetual "struggle for power" among nations, or an inevitable consequence of international anarchy. Throughout the history of the nation-state system, a major opportunity for undertaking the task of doing something about war came after the conclusion of world war or major regional wars. Wars are learning experiences, and most efforts to create postwar orders are designed to prevent the recurrence of the previous war and possibly other types of wars as well. But sometimes efforts to resolve problems can also make them worse. In international relations, the way a peace is ordered may in fact sow the seeds of new conflicts. Nevertheless, I do not share Rousseau's pessimistic generalization that "all the horrors of war stem from men's efforts to prevent it" (Vaughan, 1915: I, 365). Some attempts to build international orders have been more successful than others. While it is impossible to identify how things might have turned out if *other* arrangements had been made, we can evaluate the great peacemaking efforts in terms of their intellectual and political foundations, and how they affected the subsequent profiles of war activity.

The peacemakers have undertaken the task of creating postwar institutions and norms on the basis of explicit and implicit theories of international relations and war. Whether Mazarin, Castlereagh, Wilson, Roosevelt, or Stalin, they all approached the task with some notions of the general causes of war and the conditions of peace. This book concentrates on theories of peace – not those of academics and philosophers, but of the peacemakers themselves.

The second assumption is that warmaking is essentially a rational activity, a means designed to protect or achieve certain known ends. Men do not go to war for the sake of battle, but to resolve issues that cannot be reconciled by other means. War may be rational in the sense that it is goal-oriented and is based on rough or carefully crafted calculations of costs, risks, and advantages. How these calculations are made also depends in part on policy-makers' general attitudes toward armed conflict. Chapter 1 justifies this perspective and contrasts it with competing conceptions of war.

This study was made possible by a Canada Council National Killam Fellowship which provided a year's leave of absence and funded part of a sabbatical leave from the University of British Columbia. I wish to thank Michael Brecher, J. David Singer, and Janice Stein for their early support for the project. Grants from the Military and Strategic Studies Programme of the Canadian Department of National Defense and from the Canada Donner Foundation helped defray many of the research and manuscript preparation costs. I am particularly grateful to Mark Zacher, Director of the Institute of International Relations at the University of British Columbia, who administered the DND and Donner grants and provided many other forms of support. Grants from the Humanities and Social Sciences Research Fund at the University of British Columbia aided in bibliographical research and covered some of the manuscript preparation costs.

My sincere thanks to Adam Abaghoushe, Mary Goldie, Karen Guttieri, Birte Hunter, Deepa Khosla, and Marilyn Wan, who assisted with various research chores and helped provide the data for many of the wars discussed in the study. I also acknowledge the punctual and cheerful word processing performed by Carol Zacher, and the excellent copy-editing of Pauline Marsh.

Professor Chihiro Hosoya of the International University of Japan kindly invited me to spend a semester at the lovely campus in Yamato-machi, Niigata Prefecture. This offered a perfect opportunity for meeting students from around the world, presenting some of my ideas in classes and seminars, and writing in an ideal environment. I am also grateful to Professors Raimo Väyrynen and Osmo Apunen of the Universities of Helsinki and Tampere, respectively, who arranged through the Academy of Finland a lecture and seminar tour in the autumn of 1988. Most of the presentations there focused on this book.

Professor A. P. Rana and his colleagues, aided by a Ford Foundation grant, invited me to present a series of lectures that were derivative of parts of this study, at the University of Baroda, India, during December 1989. I am grateful for their generous hospitality and for the opportunity to explore some ideas with the Baroda faculty and students.

Marilyn Wan and Professor Peter Nailor generously read the manuscript, much to my advantage. Both made numerous helpful suggestions that have improved the quality of the study, but they deferred to my judgments on the main themes. I remain responsible for them and for the peculiarities of historical interpretation. I am grateful to them for their efforts on behalf of this work.

# 1  ON THE STUDY OF WAR

The analysis of war is too important to be left to the intuitionists.
Quincy Wright

[We] turn to history and only to history if what we are seeking are the actual causes, sources, and conditions of overt changes in patterns and structures of society. Conventional wisdom to the contrary, we shall not find the explanations of change in those studies which are abstracted from history.                    Robert Nisbet

Analytical studies of war can be traced back at least to the great work of the historian Thucydides, but systematic exploration of war as a unique but generic form of behavior between political communities was undertaken initially by political philosophers. Machiavelli, Rousseau, Kant, Hobbes, Hegel, and others had significant things to say about the etiology and consequences of war, but their insights were suggestive and prescriptive rather than empirical. They could enumerate the reasons wars are likely, but their causal statements were mostly hypothetical. Few had systematic evidence to support them.

The search for patterns and generalizations based on accumulated evidence is of more recent vintage. Today there is a large literature that has a common focus on the "causes of war." It is not my purpose to examine in detail this important corpus of work, but it may be appropriate to reflect on some of its achievements and shortfalls because yet another book on war must be justified either as filling a gap or extending in significant ways existing bodies of knowledge.

Descriptive studies of the incidence, location, and costs of war have advanced significantly over the past few decades. Today, comprehensive lists of wars, rebellions, civil wars, and other categories of violence are available (Wright, 1942; Perré, 1962; Bouthoul and Carrère, 1976; Small and Singer, 1982; Levy, 1983; Luard, 1986). Although there are methodological debates about contenders for inclusion and exclusion (Duvall, 1976; Luard, 1986), researchers can take satisfaction in the knowledge that only minor tinkering or marginal additions would be

1

necessary to satisfy the requirements of comprehensiveness in time and location. While most data admittedly come from Western sources, dealing with armed contests between the nation states of the modern era, there are no compelling reasons to postpone research until, let us say, we have a full catalogue of data on inter-tribal wars in Africa during the thirteenth century. Today we know what we are talking about – the phenomenon to be explained – which was not the case until fairly recently.

In the realm of explanation, however, the record is more sketchy. The causes of war, which are *the* subject of speculation in international relations over the last four centuries, remain obscure, but less obscure than previously. Modern research has still left a trail of uncertainty, partial clues, contradiction, and continued mystery. This is not unexpected, since the scientific enterprise never moves along a straight path. All avenues and possibilities have to be explored, and we would expect many of them to lead to intellectual dead ends or to findings of only weak significance. That there is no answer to the ancient question "why war?" is not the fault of the scientific method per se. But how questions are posed, which questions are raised, which are neglected, what assumptions are made about causation, and how we select levels of analysis and individual explanatory variables vitally affect the quality of results. Inconsistent results are another problem. For example, studies assert that arms races lead to war or that they do not lead to war. Some argue that balances of power are critical foundations for peace. Others argue, marshaling equally impressive evidence, that preponderances are a necessary condition for peace. Alliances have been linked both to war and to peace. This state of affairs prompted J. David Singer (1979:14) to write that the systematic study of war has failed to "achieve any significant theoretical breakthrough." There is, he suggested, no "compelling explanation" for war. His solution to the problem was to shift from the concept of causality to that of explanation: the latter implies a plurality of possible explanations rather than the identification of a single cause. This, of course, is an important insight. Yet, Singer did not raise other fundamental concerns about the nature of causality or explanation in contemporary war and peace research. He did not, for example, examine the dominant sociological mode of analysis that emphasizes the explanatory potential of broad systemic factors and national attributes, what I will call ecological variables. The assumption is that somehow these background conditions are translated into disputes and wars through actions and interactions. If there is causality, then it lies through a complex chain of conditions and events, but the ecological variables, which are often

2

operationalized in dichotomous terms, stand out as the sources of explanation in most studies.

## EXPLANATORY CONFIGURATIONS

Investigators of conflict, crises, and war reached a consensus years ago that monocausal explanations are theoretically and empirically deficient. Kenneth Waltz' (1957) classic typology of war explanations convincingly demonstrated various problems arising from diagnoses that locate war causation exclusively at the individual, state attribute, or systemic levels. He also illustrated how prescriptions based on faulty diagnoses offer no solution to the problem. Even Rousseau's powerful exploration of the consequences of anarchy, updated by Waltz (1979), remains full of insights, but it only specifies why wars recur (there is nothing to prevent them) and offers few clues that help to predict when, where, and over what issues. Blainey (1973), in another telling attack on monocausal theories, continues where Waltz left off. He offers, on the basis of rich historical illustrations, both logical and anecdotal rebuttals of facile explanations of war that dot academic and philosophical thought on the subject. But rebuttals of the obvious are not sufficient. We presently have myriads of theories of war, emphasizing all sorts of factors that can help explain its etiology. As Carroll and Fink (1975) note, there are if anything too many theories, and even too many typologies of theories. Quoting Timasheff approvingly, they point out that anything *might* lead to war, but nothing will *certainly* lead to war.

Table 1.1 sets out the location of explanatory variables in some of the theoretical and empirical literature. More elaborate classification schemes are available (e.g., Deutsch and Senghaas, 1971; Carroll and Fink, 1975), but our purpose is not to add yet another typology or to produce so many cells that virtually every study has a niche of its own. The studies are categorized according to the well-known "levels of analysis" scheme, but include only those that emphasize ecological/attribute variables; according to a static–dynamic dichotomy (or more properly, a dimension); and according to an attribute or relational configuration of the independent variables.

Several conclusions emerge from this illustrative rendering of the field. First, a significant proportion of the studies continue to employ single independent variables. While most reason in terms of associations and correlations, they are intended to be causal: variations in $a$ cause changes in $b$, usually defined as variations in the incidence of war. Second, the location of possible sources of war is infinitely expan-

3

Table 1.1 *Ecological, attribute, and relational correlates of war: selected studies*

| | Attributes | | Relations | |
|---|---|---|---|---|
| | Static | Dynamic | Static | Dynamic |
| SYSTEM-LEVEL | *Power concentration and war*<br>+ Singer et al. (1972)<br>− Levy and Morgan (1986)<br><br>*Alliances and war*<br>+ Ostrom & Hoole (1978)<br>− Levy (1981) | | *Status inconsistency and war*<br>+ Wallace (1973)<br>− Gochman (1980)<br><br>*Arms races and war*<br>+ Wallace (1979)<br>− Wilkinson (1980) | *Power transition and war*<br>+ Organski (1968)<br>− Bueno de Mesquita (1981a) |
| NATIONAL-LEVEL | *Democracies and conflict*<br>+ Rummel (1983)<br>− Weede (1984)<br><br>*Capitalism and war*<br>+ Lenin (1939)<br>− Wright (1942) | *War contagion*<br>+ Davis, Duncan & Siverson (1978)<br>− Levy and Morgan (1986)<br><br>*Domestic conflict and war*<br>+ Tanter (1966)<br>− Wilkenfeld (1969) | *Power parity and war*<br>+ Naroll et al. (1974)<br>− Bueno de Mesquita (1981b)<br><br>*Attribute distance and war*<br>+ Wright (1955)<br>− Rummel (1972) | |

+ = positive association.
− = no association.

dable (we would have to add an extraterrestial analytical level to include one study – whose author I prefer not to reveal – that correlated sunspot activity with the incidence of war). The range of explanatory variables runs from the genetic (not considered here) to the cosmic. Some ordering of the comparative significance of these types of variables is long overdue. Third, most studies employ variables from only one level of analysis. This leads to a number of problems, among which is the perennial issue of determinism and free will. Explanatory systems that emphasize structural and ecological variables such as the degree of power concentration in the international system are largely deterministic, as are genetic explanations of war. Studies that emphasize decision-making, values, and perceptions of policy-makers come closer to the free will end of the spectrum. How can the two be reconciled?

The prevalence of contradictory findings is the final problem. There are some important areas of consensus – what Singer has termed "reliable knowledge" – that have emerged from replication and modification of research designs and data. Great powers are more war-prone than other kinds of states. Studies have confirmed Woodrow Wilson's hypothesis (Shaw, 1924:I, 379) that democracies do not go to war against each other. The hypothesis of systemic war contagion processes has been disconfirmed in numerous studies (Geller, 1988:366). At least two studies have demonstrated persuasively (though not without challenge, based on other data and methodologies) that, not surprisingly, borders play a role in conflict. Both alliance membership and contiguity increase the probabilities that any given state will become involved in a war should its neighbour and/or alliance partner be at war (Siverson and Starr, 1990). Some theories of relative power cycles among the great powers show rather impressively how, at certain "inflection points" in the relative rise and decline of great powers, serious wars are more likely to occur than at other times. The problems of adjusting foreign policies to new roles consistent with new power positions in some ways lead to a higher probability of war participation (Doran, 1983). Beyond these and a few other areas of general agreement, explanations of variation in war remain contested either because there have been no findings meeting various tests of significance or because findings have been contradictory. In a significant proportion of the systemic studies of war, there is no verdict.

Is there the prospect that if we heed the perennial cry for more research we will uncover exciting new possibilities? Will the addition of new independent variables increase the storehouse of reliable knowledge? How should researchers deal with the problems of

5

chronic incompatibility of findings? Are the solutions to these difficult-ies to be found primarily within the context of quantitative analysis? There is a common assumption that with adjustments here, a little methodological tinkering there, and the compilation of ever more studies, researchers will eventually uncover the numerous mysteries that remain. But perhaps more fundamental questions need to be raised. Two in particular come to mind. First, is the emphasis on single ecological variables appropriate to the problem to be investigated? Second, what areas of investigation have been overlooked in the re-search agenda? This study examines three areas of pronounced ne-glect: (1) what are the issues that initially generate international conflict? what do men fight about? (2) what is the "meaning" of war to those who resort to it? and (3) in what ways do the arrangements of peace serve as a source of future international conflict? We will exam-ine each of these questions and the relationships between them below, but first we should explore in more detail the issue of ecological variables as explanations of war.

## THE PROMISES AND PITFALLS OF ECOLOGICAL VARIABLES

Sociological analyses of war generally link broad background variables of the international system or of its member states to the incidence of international violence. Typical variables include the degree of power concentration in an international system, numbers and types of alliances, balances and imbalances of power, relative rates of power change among key states, the presence or absence of arms races, degrees of status inconsistency, and the like. Other studies have concentrated on the link between national attributes (size, location, type of political system, and the like) and conflict/war. A derivative avenue of inquiry has examined the nature of relationships between attributes of nations. Most continue to employ single independent variables, even though at the theoretical level, monocausal theories of war have been proven inadequate for a long time. The usual answer to this problem is that correlational findings are not causal. They only indicate that the probabilities of war involvement or war initiation increase or decrease under certain specified systemic conditions or attribute profiles. Such results are not only interesting but potentially of theoretical significance. The combination of certain specified systemic and attribute conditions could certainly indicate which sorts of configurations increase or decrease international stability and the overall incidence of war in a particular era. But it does not tell us much

6

about the sources of individual wars. Not many wars begin because there is a parity or preponderance of power, or because two parties share a frontier, or because they have differential growth rates (consider the unlimited and unknown numbers of wars that did *not* begin under such conditions). Knowledge of change in probabilities is important, but is it sufficient? Let us use a domestic analogy to make the point that statistical associations between relatively static variables such as system structure or national attributes, and war incidence, while they may reveal certain patterns, do not in most cases offer a satisfactory form of explanation.

I do not have a quarrel with my neighbor because he or she is older, is more wealthy, or has a larger house. All of these attributes are in most cases irrelevant to the neighborly relationship, whereas behavior is critical. If my neighbor throws his garbage on my porch, a quarrel is likely to ensue. We have an *issue* that generates conflict. The fact of contiguity and our attribute differences offer less satisfactory possibilities. The probabilities of a quarrel with a neighbor are no doubt greater than they would be with an unknown person living on the other side of town. But a probability difference is not a very satisfactory explanation, much less a cause. Some of the studies that link attributes to war incidence face this same problem. It is interesting to know, for example, that great powers are more war-prone than other kinds of states, but this fact can be explained also on a simple probability basis: great powers have more relationships and more interests to advance and protect, and hence we should expect them to resort to armed force more frequently than smaller states. An individual with a broad network of relationships is more likely to be involved in conflicts than is a hermit.

But these are relatively technical problems. More significant is the determinism implied in many of the studies, the presumed relevance and priority of ecological variables. Researchers assume that somehow, through decision-making and other processes, these systemic and other-nation conditions are translated into foreign policy outputs and decisions to employ force. But how? And how are we to estimate their significance compared to more immediate stimuli (behaviors)? Of what relevance was the degree of systemic power polarization to the Argentine generals who decided to invade the Falkland Islands; or to President Nasser, who decided to have another go at Israel? or to the Iraqi president who launched a war against Iran in 1979? There is an element of the ecological fallacy in these questions (explaining an individual event in terms of general system properties), and yet they should be asked.

7

Many of the studies cited here assume a high degree of constraint imposed by system characteristics, national attributes, and relational variables. They are reminiscent of the early voting behavior studies that linked socio-economic variables such as class, education, religion, and income to voting choices. But those early studies failed to ask voters *why* they voted in a particular way. The view of man in these studies is that of an automaton forced to behave in certain ways because of environmental characteristics or individual attributes. There is no acknowledgment that people have purposes, ideas, preferences, and dislikes; that they have concerns for personal welfare and sometimes even a calculated concern with the welfare of the broader society and its political system. What are the limits of choice? Peter the Great, Louis XIV, Charles XII, Bismarck, Wilson, and Hitler, just to mention a few, did as much to create system characteristics as they were constrained by them.

Why is it that some countries that share numerous attributes nevertheless have substantially different foreign policies? And why do some countries that share few attributes nevertheless have many foreign policy features in common? Libya and Tunisia share many characteristics and inhabit a common global system and regional subsystem. But for years their foreign policies have been fundamentally different except that they both sympathize with the plight of the Palestinians. Burma and Albania have virtually nothing in common, but in the 1960s and 1970s their foreign policy orientation of extreme isolation was almost identical. The list of examples could be elaborated at length, certainly enough to raise questions about the presumed critical importance of ecological variables (or as is often the case, dichotomies) in explaining variations in the incidence of war.

Of the many people who have authored studies of the genre, J. David Singer is among the few who have directly addressed some of the questions raised above. He has argued that the contexts in which nations behave must be examined initially and their explanatory power discovered, because it will not be possible to gauge otherwise how much freedom of choice decision-makers enjoy. Singer's strategy of choosing to focus on ecological and structural background variables appears initially to be a matter of preference rather than one of the probable weight of explanation. Yet, Singer also argues that ecological variables are fundamental and institutional, while decision-making and other approaches concentrate on more immediate concerns. His distinction follows Thucydides' separation of the underlying and proximate causes of war. The underlying causes in Singer's view are clearly more important.

8

So that there may be no misunderstanding of Singer's position on the critical importance of ecological variables, it is best to let him speak for himself. In 1970 he wrote (Singer, 1970:536; cf. Singer, 1981:4–5):

> While fully concurring that an "ecological" theory of war would be incomplete at best, I would urge that serious attention to these attributes and relational variables is absolutely essential. To look at behavioral events alone, or as parts of interaction sequences, is to court disaster unless they are examined along with – and in the context of – the physical, structural, and cultural setting within which they occur ... Government decisions and behavior represent the intervening variables between a set of ecological incentives and constraints (domestic and global) on the one hand, and war or no war as the outcome of conflict, on the other; they can only be understood in that sort of context ... Until we can get at the discrepancies (if any) between the objective incentives and constraints and the way in which they are perceived, we will be far from understanding the behavior which leads toward or away from war ... Until certain of the key ecological variables are identified and their own explanatory power ascertained, we will never know exactly how much control remained in the hands of the decision-makers and how much of the variance is accounted for by their behavior.

Singer's general strategy is laudable, and there are numerous grounds for exploring the explanatory power of ecological variables. But until recently, few have followed all of Singer's admonitions. Only within the last several years have researchers begun to assess the *comparative* explanatory power of ecological and decision-making variables. This concern has already produced findings in explaining probabilistically the process of war diffusion (Siverson and Starr, 1990), with alliance membership (representing choice) having a greater impact on war participation than contiguity (representing an ecological variable). The results of another recent study suggest that ecological variables as explanations of war incidence fare rather poorly compared to approaches that employ Thucydides' notion of "proximate" causes (Bueno de Mesquita and Lalman, 1988). Students of war are finally beginning to abandon single-variable and single-level types of analyses – twenty years after Singer pinpointed the problem. The pioneering work is as yet a mere trickle, but it is moving in an appropriate direction. However, the cultural context of war, noted by Singer as a critical research area, remains largely ignored (Singer, 1981).

### THE MEANINGS OF WAR

One of the problems of quantitative studies of war is that in

9

order to obtain statistically sufficient universes of the dependent variable, they must remain fairly insensitive to different kinds of war. This is not the problem of legal definitions, or cut-off points in the number of casualties required to be included in the data set, or duration of hostilities. These are relatively technical issues, and since there have been so many wars since 1492, 1648, 1740, or 1816 (the usual starting dates for various data sets), the addition of several wars that had, let us say, 750 casualties instead of the usual 1,000 would probably not alter most findings.

The real difficulty is that through history the use of force in statecraft has had different meanings, and if this is so, the sources, causes, or correlates of war in one period cannot be easily transferred to another. Russia was at war against Turkey in 1713. Pakistan was at war against India in 1971. Both wars satisfy the usual criteria for inclusion in a data set. Similarly, two patients are "ill" when they both have fevers significantly above normal body temperatures. But one has a severe rash and acute lung congestion while the other has severe stomach pains. Both share one symptom – fever – which places them both in the "ill" category. But the other symptoms suggest entirely different causes. The "meaning" of the first illness is likely death; for the second, it is several more hours of discomfort until a medicine produces a cure. In 1713, the war arose because Russia was not fulfilling the terms of peace to which it had committed itself in a war the previous year. Turkey began the war in order to compel Russia to meet those terms. The stakes in the war were not very significant, however, and neither side believed that it was risking much in undertaking a contest of arms. In 1971, Pakistan fought for its survival (defined as East and West Pakistan). The meaning of the war for it was fundamentally different than it had been for either the Ottoman Empire or for Russia in 1713.

Statistical studies have generally avoided classifications of types of war in terms of their cultural and historical meaning. They have distinguished wars by the nature of participants, the track record of war participation by individual states, by geographical location, and the like. These have produced interesting and significant descriptive findings. But does it not seem possible that war is significantly rooted in its social and cultural context? Would it not make a difference in terms of war incidence whether decision-making elites view it as a duel, an avenue for fame, glory, and honor, an act of self-defense, the execution of a judgment, a crime, a technique of persuasion, or as an act of mutual suicide (Wright, 1942:II, 877)? Should it not make a difference in terms of war causes and frequency that Louis XIV in his youth regarded war as an alternative to the joys of the hunting season and

10

that Frederick the Great saw it as an instrument for gaining personal reputation and glory, while Neville Chamberlain regarded it as a diplomatic and moral catastrophe? The commitment to search for regularities through statistical techniques over long periods of time, and the constraints imposed by the necessity of formal quantification render these and other significant differences of little scientific interest. Discriminating between wars on the basis of their "meaning" would no doubt require all sorts of arbitrary and "soft" judgments, but this is not a sufficient ground for excluding the exercise.

Richard Mansbach and John Vasquez (Mansbach and Vasquez, 1981; Vasquez, 1987) have suggested a rather different form of explanation. They point out that there are identifiable *processes* that lead to war. They present an explanation for the rise of contentious issues, identify variables that can explain under what circumstances they get placed on the global agenda, and how they are eventually resolved authoritatively including through the use of force. The "paths of war" include many of the symptoms located in the traditional and quantitative literatures, including arms races, misperception, the "Peloponnesian syndrome" of preventive war, and negative affect of the parties toward each other. These combine in various ways to produce an increased likelihood of war. As such, the processes are not "causes" in the ordinary $a \rightarrow b$ model. Rather, the variables may link in complex ways. No single factor, whether structural, attribute, or relationship, can be isolated and identified as *the* cause. Any model of explanation that emphasizes dynamics and the interplay of variables across levels of analysis and over time is a distinct step forward.

Yet, one is still troubled by the lack of contextual factors and the assumptions that all wars are equal. There may be many paths to war, diverse patterns of behavior that eventuate in contests of arms. And contexts do matter. Consider the Franco-Dutch War of 1672–79. The war certainly became a process, but its origins do not fit well with the "paths to war" model. Louis XIV had been planning the war for almost four years prior to his aggression against the United Provinces. The war was not preceded by an arms race; there was no bargaining in a crisis situation; there were rough calculations of military capabilities, but no evidence of misperceptions. Although Louis and Colbert had their reasons for disliking the Dutch, none of them was sufficient to explain the outbreak of a major war. The "roi soleil" disliked many regimes with which he did not go to war. The "paths to war" in 1672 – and in many cases subsequent to then – were fundamentally different than those of 1914 or of the American intervention in Vietnam. These examples suggest the need for careful historical research, for studies

11

employing the "focussed comparison" method (George and Smoke, 1974), and for the development of more discriminating independent *and* dependent variables.

## WHAT MEN FIGHT ABOUT: ISSUES AND INTERNATIONAL CONFLICT

Notice that in most of the studies of the genre reviewed here there is a gap – namely human behavior – between the independent and dependent variables. Preponderances favor peace; arms races lead to war, as do resource shortages, the uneven development of capabilities among the great powers, status inconsistency, and many other things. Nowhere do we find the issues that excite men's passions and fears, those stakes that predispose them to take up arms to pursue or defend their causes and purposes. True, older studies of war classified the sources of war as political, religious, economic, and the like, but with the significant exception of Luard's study (1986) and the recent work of Mansbach and Vasquez, no one has taken up the challenge of exploring this difficult terrain. Why? Perhaps it is because issues are difficult to define and even more difficult to measure. However, to leave out issues is to leave out the stuff of politics. Adding issues to the research agenda may not tell us why some conflicts end in wars, while others do not – an important area of contemporary research – but it tells us what men are likely to fight about and how issues change over time. It is hard to see how this critical question, even if posed only in descriptive terms, can be ignored any longer.

One of the reasons that it has been ignored, in my opinion, is the general social perspective toward war during much of the twentieth century, certainly since 1918. Academic researchers, peace movements, and many politicians for quite understandable reasons have depicted war variously as a disease, as a catastrophe, as a crime, in brief, as a form of *deviant* behavior. This perspective on war has arisen from the horrible experiences of twentieth-century war, the anticipated consequences of nuclear war, and the liberal nineteenth- and twentieth-century belief in human and humane progress. To many, war is an irrational activity, representing a rejection of politics for an entirely different domain of behavior. It must be, therefore, structures and processes that lead to war, and not the deliberate calculations of policy-makers who might be bent on conquest. Our generally liberal views toward the purposes of states and regimes underestimates the extent to which there may be, as Leon Bourgeois argued during the debates on the League of Nations Covenant during the Paris peace

12

conference in 1919, *états de mauvaise foi*, states committed to the use of force to achieve various purposes that are inconsistent with the safety and vital interests of other states.

A Clausewitzian approach does not regard war as a form of deviant behavior. War, rather, is characterized in instrumental terms as a rational, if not desirable, means of achieving or defending known purposes. It is "an act of violence intended to compel our opponent to fulfill our will . . . War is not merely an act of policy but a true political instrument, a continuation of political intercourse, carried on with other means" (Clausewitz, 1984:75, 87). Issues become immediately relevant in this view of war.[1] "The political object – the original motive/issue for the war – will thus determine both the military objective to be reached and the amount of effort it requires" (ibid., 81). This perspective on war approaches the free will end of an ecological/determinist – free will continuum. Politics and war are in the realm of constrained volition rather than in the realm of ecological determination. Policy-makers, whether princes, kings, Politbureaus, cabinets, or presidents, generally seek to defend, extend, or achieve certain objectives. When these purposes and the means to implement them are incompatible with the values and interests of other actors, the probability of the use of force increases. Governments must then consider whether or not the stakes are worth all the risks entailed in war.

Stakes are not exactly the same as issues (cf. Rummel, 1976:275). The United States intervened in Vietnam in order to achieve a stated set of purposes. The issue was defined in Washington as the continued independence of a political entity called the Republic of Vietnam. The issue for North Vietnam was the unification of a historic state and the construction of socialism in it. At stake for the United States, however, was its credibility, its prestige, and its sense of commitment to its allies. The issues generated the conflict, but the probability of the use of force by the United States increased dramatically only after North Vietnam and the Viet Cong had decided to achieve the unification of the country through military means. A number of choices were made along the way; there was nothing inevitable about American intervention. However, it is difficult to see exactly how ecological or attribute variables were compelling. The issues were necessary conditions for the intervention, and the issues combined with the stakes and the behav-

---

[1] Clausewitz also discussed the development of war into an "absolute war," in which "there is not a trace of an overlap with the process of bargaining, or persuasion, or of non-military pressure of any kind" (Gallie, 1978:52).

iors of North Vietnam and the Viet Cong were, taken together, sufficient conditions.

If we grant the validity of this perspective, then we may reverse the usual structure of explanation. Rather than looking at antecedent conditions, whether ecological, structural or attributional, we search for purposes and objectives. The explanation then becomes teleological: wars occur not "because of" but "in order to." Others have mentioned this form of analysis but have seldom explored its implications in the study of war (Howard, 1983:12–16; Wright, 1942:II, 1236, 1291; Eagleton, 1972:16–17; Rummel, 1976:245). While we recognize that we may be speaking of two sides of the same coin, the emphasis on purpose steers us at least part of the way around the hurdle of the assumed explanatory power of ecological, genetic, and relational variables or dichotomies. Purposive behavior between two or more parties may lead to contention over certain values, or as most people use the term, over issues. The underlying problem for investigation is not "why do nations fight?", which is the usual way the question is put, but "what are they fighting about or over?". To borrow from Mansbach and Vasquez (1981), we are less concerned with the issue of power than with the power of issues.

Such a formulation entails some difficulties. Here, let us raise the question posed by authors such as Geoffrey Blainey and Michael Howard, who argue that all issues can be boiled down to one mega-issue: whatever the window dressing, propaganda lines, and self-serving justifications for the use of force, the basic issue is always a power contest between two or more protagonists in which, according to Raymond Aron, the stakes are the "existence, the creation, or the elimination of states" (quoted in Howard, 1983:16). While the historical record shows numerous examples of the "Peloponnesian syndrome," where states go to war preventively because they face an impending hegemony or preponderance of power by their main rival, there are many more instances when no such stakes were involved. Governments choose to employ force because they value interests and make claims against others that cannot be adjusted or compromised through diplomacy or other non-violent means. Preventive war does occur (Levy, 1987), but in many instances state survival is not at stake. Other sorts of issues, implying considerably more limited values, are the source of most wars.

It is difficult to see, as just two illustrations of this conclusion, how the Somalia–Ethiopia War of 1978 or the Falklands War of 1982 can be explained satisfactorily as power contests. They were contests of power in the trivial sense that any trial of arms includes the application

14

of military power. But state survival was neither the issue nor the stake that generated the war. If we "explain" war by reducing the phenomenon's origins to contests of power, then we simply avoid the critical questions, since clearly not all power contests end in war. Howard and Blainey, like so many others, have identified a necessary condition for war, but not a sufficient one.

I have left out of the analysis consideration of the many studies that focus on psychological, perceptual, and organizational variables. The vast literature has significantly increased our knowledge of the problems of decision-making processes in crisis situations, and the ways that information, organizational mores, misperceptions, and a variety of personality characteristics can increase the probability of making suboptimal decisions. But even this literature contains some difficulties. There are at least three issues of note. First, most of the literature defines or assumes that decisions to employ force or to go to war are suboptimal. There is more than a hint of the Western twentieth-century view of war as deviant, irrational behavior. At a minimum, this literature depicts the use of force as an exceptional form of statecraft. Second, like the ecological and attribute studies, the policy-making studies of war focus on processes and ignore issues. They concentrate on information flows, the role of stereotypes and other psychological phenomena, bureaucratic in-fighting, and the like, but do not discuss the stakes involved in the contentious issues. And third, the literature has been strongly influenced by two notable crises, the events of August 1914 and Cuba in October 1962. A more recent source of data has been the numerous decisions that led ultimately to the American armed intervention in Vietnam. These cases have often been portrayed as paradigmatic examples of decisions to use force (or in Cuba, to avoid it). Yet, these examples are taken from an immense domain of possibilities. There is no evidence that they are typical or representative of the universe of cases. Most notable by their absence are decisions to employ force by national liberation movements and other groups that seek to establish states. Comparative studies across historical eras and geographical locations are needed.

There has been some significant work to correct the distorting effects of an extremely narrow sample of cases. Jervis (1976) has used an extensive catalogue of historical evidence to examine the problems of crisis decision-making, while Lebow (1981) has been one of the few to compare explicitly across a number of cases taken from the nineteenth and twentieth centuries. The state-centric bias remains, however.

15

## A MAP OF A MAP

I have raised questions, not provided answers. The purpose of this book is to complement previous work by demonstrating the importance of three problems that have been largely neglected in the study of war:

1. The role and types of issues that generate international conflict.
2. The change in socio-historical-intellectual milieux in which war is undertaken and which can sometimes help explain probabilistically why decisions to go to war are made. This is the "meaning" of war, identified through attitudes toward the use of force among those who guide state policy.
3. The link between peace settlements and war. Peace settlements deal primarily with issues; how they deal with them may have a profound impact on the character and incidence of war in the postwar period. We are concerned here with the problem of building international orders – who defines them, how they were designed, on what sorts of diagnoses of the etiology of international conflict they were based, and how they operated.

The model of international politics that underlies the study of these neglected areas of war is as follows. All governments face certain sets of problems that they must solve, learn to live with, or adapt to. These include state-formation and nation-building; provision for the general welfare, broadly conceived; defense of the realm; maintenance of independence and autonomy; and perpetuation of the regime (K. J. Holsti, 1990). Some governments have other purposes, which may include regional or global imperialism, ideological proselytization and conversion, search for prestige and status, and many others. In most cases purposes can be identified.

Decisions and actions are taken within certain socio-economic and diplomatic contexts. These offer both constraints and opportunities, but they are seldom determinative of individual decisions. Attributes offer fewer fruitful avenues of investigation. If they were significantly determining or highly constraining, we would expect states sharing them to behave in roughly similar fashion. Yet, as we look around the world, we can see many instances where states sharing both contexts (e.g., system polarity) and attributes (e.g., size, culture, economy, regime, and the like) have different foreign policies and profiles of war activity.

A model which assumes a fairly rational ordering of means to ends, which places purpose at the centre of analysis, does not preclude folly (Tuchman, 1984), misjudgment, wishful thinking, poor prediction, unanticipated consequences, and other foibles and shortcomings of governments and their caretakers. Apart from the problem that one's short-run folly can always be a blessing in the long run, and vice versa, these shortcomings do not vitiate the view that politics is an essentially purposeful activity.

The reader will see the ghost of Clausewitz in these comments. If foreign policy is a purposeful activity, then, in most cases so is war (I will reserve the problem of nuclear war for the concluding chapters). It is one of many ways of wielding influence, of compressing change into a relatively short period of time, of resolving issues that were not amenable to other techniques of settlement. Purposive behavior between two or more parties usually leads to contention over certain values, or as most people use the term, over issues.

Issues are not sufficient conditions for war. There are contentious issues facing governments daily, yet only a small proportion are contested or resolved through armed force. The critical problem of why some conflicts eventuate in war while others do not is a recent and critical avenue of inquiry, but is beyond the scope of this study. Each case rests on a complex calculus of costs, advantages, degrees of threat, risk, and the like. However, policy-makers' attitudes toward the use of force and how they "define" war will critically affect those calculations.

## DEFINING ISSUES

The investigation proceeds inductively. The typology of issues developed as the result of studying 177 wars and major armed interventions. This seemed a preferable strategy over deductively defining abstract categories of issues, such as those of Rosenau (1966) and Mansbach and Vasquez (1981). There are two reasons for this choice. First, the purpose of this part of the study is descriptive rather than explanatory. The categories of issues are those used by historians who report the activities of policy-makers. Abstract categories remove the researcher even one step further from the perspectives of those who make decisions to go to war. Second, some of the typologies of issues really define procedures such as log-rolling, or outcome properties such as distributional results, rather than the values or stakes in contention. There is not always a very good fit between the typologies of academics and the issues as they were defined by the actors involved in conflict.

Working inductively does not necessarily simplify the matter, however. Many conflicts involve multiple issues; issues change over time, particularly as a war progresses; disputants do not place the same value, or even identify the same values, as being in contention or

17

jeopardy; some issues are so intermixed that attempts to separate them become arbitrary if not impossible; and weighing the relative importance of different issues injects the investigator's judgment as a substitute for the operating frames of reference of the decision-makers. Evidence can often lead to several interpretations.

I am aware of these problems and some others of less import as well. Were our concern chiefly to offer a precise issues synopsis of every single war in the European and global states system since 1648, more modesty would be displayed. Since the purpose is to draw a rough map of issue change over time, however, some differences of interpretation, some omissions, and some arbitrary judgments may be less lethal. A portrait or characterization is more important than detail.

Mansbach and Vasquez (1981) distinguish between *objectives* under contention, *values* to be satisfied by their allocation, *proposals* (statements of, or claims for, potential outcomes), and *stakes* and *positions*. Issues include all of these. They may involve several stakes and values, including status, prestige, security, honor, and the like. For our purposes, an issue can be defined as the stakes over which two or more parties contend. It includes values, but it is often difficult to identify or measure those. Mansbach and Vasquez also identify stakes as the core of the concept. Issues are the "contention among actors over proposals for the disposition of stakes among them." They include "the characteristics of the stakes involved" (1981:59).

Stakes are usually fairly concrete – a piece of territory, the protection of an ethnic minority, the creation of a new state, the end of apartheid, and so forth. Values are more difficult to pinpoint, and their analysis always includes the formidable problem of ends and means. They are, moreover, usually a by-product of conflict rather than the stake that gives rise to the conflict in the first place. The stakes in Louis XIV's attack on the United Provinces in 1672 involved territorial gains. At issue were specific pieces of territory Louis wanted to add to his domains. An important value at play in this conflict was the king's *gloire*. It was an important consideration in the court at Versailles and among all of Europe's ruling monarchs and princes. *La gloire* increased or diminished with the fortunes of war, but it was not the stake involved in the planning for the war. Similarly, Lyndon Johnson defined the American stakes in Vietnam as the freedom of South Vietnam and the security of the United States via the maintenance of a non-communist southeast Asia. American prestige, status, and reputation for meeting commitments to allies were no doubt important considerations or values, but they were perceived more as the *consequences* of particular policies than as the issues which led to American

18

intervention and the bombing of North Vietnam. We can assume that all conflicts involve calculations of status, prestige, and reputation, but they might be more relevant in helping to explain why wars continue rather than why they start. I will include such values only where they are designated as a bone of contention between the parties.

In the chapters that follow, statements by the parties involved, as reported in standard historical accounts, identify the issues. If they are unavailable, historians' judgments will serve as the basis for the data. In every case, at least two historical accounts have been used. In some instances the position of a government or other policy-making body is not possible to identify given the usual research constraints. Why, exactly, the Tatars joined Turkey in its war against Poland from 1671 to 1676 is not listed in standard English- and French-language diplomatic histories. Many cases of small partners joining a warring state, when no alliance commitment is involved, suggest simple opportunism. They go to war, or join an ongoing contest of arms, in order to get in on the spoils. Some of the histories are deficient in specifying all war participants' stakes. The operating rule guiding research is therefore to identify only the issues that generated the conflict between the *original* combatants. States that entered wars later are omitted from the analysis.

The distinctions between issues are usually clear, but in some instances rough judgments are required. There is also the problem of instrumentality and the lack of concordance between parties' perceptions of stakes. How, for example, would we classify the following situation as described by Boccalini in discussing the foreign policy of Venice in the fifteenth century?

> The Venetians have as the ultimate purpose of their existence peace .... For the Venetians it is enough to have territorial possessions large enough to assure Venice its freedom. They want to have power not out of ambition, to command others, but out of their striving not to become the subject of others (quoted in Ranum, 1975:28).

A Veronese claim to Venetian lands would raise a territorial issue for Verona. Yet the ultimate stake for Venice, as the quotation implies, would be to prevent itself from becoming the subject of others. Territory is instrumental; the Venetian stake is *autonomy*, not just a piece of land. In this case, we would classify the issue as one of autonomy for Venice and territory for both Venice and Verona.

If we enter the labyrinth of instrumental stakes, attempting to classify some as means, and others as ends, we might never emerge to make any conclusions. Others have mentioned the difficulties in-

19

volved (Wright, 1942:II, 722–23, 857, 1290; Blainey, 1973:146–51, 248–49), and seem to have been scared off by the task. Bouthoul and Carrère (1976) use a simple classification scheme, but its categories are too coarse. In my view, the best way to proceed is to define the issues as the policy-makers defined them, allowing for the limits of historical evidence.

### DATA SOURCES: GEOGRAPHICAL AND TEMPORAL DOMAINS

The cases used as the basis for this study come from the European and global states systems from 1648 through 1989. There is a consensus among scholars of international relations that a single states system, or society of states, has existed since the treaties of Westphalia. It is defined by the security interdependence of its members, meaning generally that the foreign policy activities of one actor had some impact on others in the system. What the United Provinces' agents said and did in 1655 was noted and responded to by Venice, Brandenburg, Sweden, and many others in continental Europe and Britain. The Burmese–Thai Wars of the 1760s, on the other hand, had no impact in the European states system. The states system became global only in 1945 in the sense that conflicts on any continent were noted by and responded to by international institutions and by many individual states throughout the world.

In all, there are 177 cases, which form a reasonable sample compared to the 118 interstate and extra-systemic wars chronicled by Small and Singer (1982) for the shorter period 1816–1980, and the 154 interstate wars, 1740–1975, listed by Bouthoul and Carrère. It is also a reasonable proportion of Luard's comprehensive list of violence that includes a massive total of 470 cases from 1648. These include numerous rebellions, civil wars, and wars where little or no documentation in a major European language is available in the standard histories. Until the post-1918 period, all wars involved 1,000 or more casualties; some major interventions were less costly in lives, but involved the physical occupation by one country's armed forces in a foreign jurisdiction for a minimum of two weeks. Further discussion of the choices for the post-1918 period is contained in chapters 11 and 12.

The selection of 1648 as the starting point is less contentious than the selection of cases. That date is commonly recognized as the official birthday of the modern states system. The principles of sovereignty and legal equality were enunciated in the Treaties of Osnabrück and Münster. The principles became major legal and philosophical pillars in the struggles to create modern states, and provided the basic norms for the conduct of their mutual relations.

## ATTITUDES TOWARD WAR

The "meaning" of war refers to the policy-makers' conceptualizations of war – what type of activity and ethical connotations it involves, for example – and their attitudes toward the use of force. Most of the literature on this subject examines popular, philosophical, or academic opinions about war (e.g., Gooch, n.d). Public moods may indeed act as a constraint on or support of policy-makers: witness the strong sentiments of pacifism in Great Britain during the 1930s. But since public participation in matters of war and peace is a phenomenon of only the last two centuries, and only in a few states, it is not a sufficient guide to officials' attitudes. Nor is it safe to assume that public and governmental attitudes always coincide.

Attitudes do not always lead directly to actions. However, they offer rationales and justifications for the use of force. They also influence the calculus of costs, risks, and benefits when it comes time to decide whether or not to unsheath the sword. The attitudes toward the use of force by Japanese leaders in the 1930s offer a stark contrast, for example, to those of their British colleagues in the same era. I will not try to explain the origins of those attitudes. Description at this stage will have to suffice.

## ISSUES, WAR, AND PEACE: CREATING INTERNATIONAL ORDERS

Most wars end with formal negotiations leading to peace treaties. These treaties perform several functions. They establish, in most cases definitively, the losses and gains suffered or achieved in the contest of arms. They specify the outcome of war, or as Mansbach and Vasquez (1981, ch. 8) put it, they represent "decisions" that authoritatively allocate values. Many of the issues that generated the preceding war are resolved. The agreements also legitimize war outcomes in the sense that the parties are expected to meet the commitments undertaken in the negotiated or imposed documents. Subsequent efforts to evade commitments then justify reprisals, sanctions, and possibly further war. Finally, peace treaties often reaffirm international norms and conventions, including prior peace treaties (cf. Randle, 1973).

But some peace treaties represent more than the settlement of the issues that generated a previous war. They are expressions of the fact

21

that, despite the rather dismal record of war occurrence, wars are great learning experiences. The costs, strains, and often the negative outcomes for all parties encourage governments to think about methods of preventing resort to arms in the postwar world. Peace treaties may thus include new sets of principles, procedures, or territorial distributions upon which to organize the postwar relations between states. These efforts reflect both the nature of the issues that gave rise to previous wars, and significant changes in the attitudes of diplomatic elites toward the use of force in subsequent international relationships. Expressions such as "permanent amity," "the permanent repose of Europe," and "a just and lasting peace" are sprinkled throughout major peace treaties. They are not only ritual statements, but acknowledgments that there should be better ways than through armed combat to resolve international conflicts. They are also statements of hopes and expectations that the character of international relations will change fundamentally as a result of the lessons learned through costly wars. The great multilateral peace conferences were, in brief, attempts to build new international orders. The main elements of these orders include the definition of norms regarding the use of force; systems of governance for the society of states; conflict-resolving mechanisms and procedures; the resolution of war-producing issues; specific terms of settlement that will preclude wars of revenge by the losers (assimilation); and some consideration of the types of issues that may generate conflict in the future. I will evaluate each peace in terms of these criteria, leaving a more developed discussion for the last chapter.

Chapters on the great attempts to erect more pacific international relationships are interspersed with the chapters on conflict-generating issues. My purpose is not to present yet another historical account of peace conferences, but to assess the designs, plans, and assumptions about war and international order that were in play at them. Theories of peace at the conferences and the resulting treaties were usually based on policy-makers' explicit or implicit theories of war, or at least on their evaluation of the causes of the most recent war. These conferences represented the learned diplomatic wisdom of the day about war and peace. It was not the writings of academics and philosophers, which were notoriously ignored in most peacemaking efforts, but the ideas of the policy-makers themselves that mattered. They were the ones who not only settled the terms of the preceding war, but who also tried to hammer out – never ignoring their own state's vital interests – some sort of system or set of procedures that would either prevent future armed conflict or that could help manage or limit it. In brief, we will explore the theories of international relations of the peacemakers.

22

Exercises in international order building have seldom been typical of bilateral peace conferences, or even in diplomatic gatherings following multilateral wars that were limited in time, location, and/or costs. Moreover, those peace treaties that were basically armistices seldom contained provisions for ameliorating or accommodating the issues that generated a war. Some peace treaties, after all, were designed not to allocate values authoritatively, but to provide a pause until the next round of war could be undertaken to try to finish the job. They were stratagems and phases in continuing conflicts over unresolvable issues. Many of the peace treaties between Russia and the Ottoman Empire in the eighteenth and nineteenth centuries, for example, were of this kind, as were the treaties that slowly brought to an end the Swedish Empire of the seventeenth century.

The great peace conferences that attempted to come to grips with the fundamentals of war and peace include Osnabrück and Münster, 1644–48, the more limited conferences that resulted in the treaties collectively known as the Peace of Utrecht (1713–15), the two Treaties of Paris and the Congress of Vienna that succeeded the Napoleonic Wars, the conference of Paris in 1919, and the 1945 San Francisco conference, including its antecedents, during the Second World War. These constitute the focus of the inquiry.

The analytical framework for the study can be characterized as a

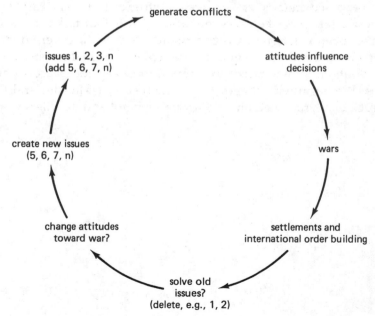

Figure 1.1   The peace and war cycle

23

peace–war loop. Issues generate conflict, when two or more governments seek to achieve incompatible objectives (e.g., a piece of territory) or stake out mutually exclusive positions on a particular problem (e.g., rights of neutral shipping and trade in wartime). In any era, some types of issues will predominate as conflict-producers.

Whether or not the contests over the issues eventuate in war is in part a function of policy-makers' attitudes and conceptualizations of war. The hypothesis is that the more favorable the attitudes toward war, the greater its incidence. But the kinds of issues also affect incidence. Contests over strategic territory, for example, are more likely than disagreements over trade policy to generate contests of arms. Security is a more important value in most eras than is welfare. The succeeding chapters identify the issues in each era that were most prominent as sources of war.

Wars end in peace. Peace treaties and agreements usually resolve the issues that gave rise to the previous war. Some also try to create new international orders, and they develop new norms, reflecting changes in attitudes, regarding the future use of force. An even smaller number try to anticipate issues of the future and develop means for dealing with them. How these conferences deal with past issues and with the defeated combatants may also be critical in influencing the nature of postwar international relationships. In some instances the great peace settlements set the stage for future eras of conflict and war. In these cases, peace becomes the father of war. Our task is to assess each conference in terms of its contribution both to the order-building enterprise and to the subsequent pattern of warfare in the system. The periodization is thus based on intervals between the peace conferences. We begin with the lengthy conferences at Münster and Osnabrück that terminated one of Europe's longest and deadliest wars.

# 2 MÜNSTER AND OSNABRÜCK, 1648: PEACE BY PIECES

> [The Peace of Westphalia] is null, void, invalid, unjust, damnable, reprobate, inane, empty of meaning and effect for all time.
>
> Pope Innocent X

The Pope's reaction to the Treaties of Münster and Osnabrück is understandable. The Thirty Years War had raged across Bohemia, Germany, Italy, France, and the United Provinces, pitting nascent states against empires, rebellious princes against the Holy Roman Emperor, free cities against imperial cities, and Catholics against Protestants. The Pope condemned the outcome of four years of negotiations that led to the Peace of Westphalia because it confirmed the religious schism begun by Luther and significantly reduced the political authority of the Holy Roman Emperor and the other great symbol of Christian unity, the papacy. The Peace of Westphalia organized Europe on the principle of particularism. It represented a new diplomatic arrangement – an order created by states, for states – and replaced most of the legal vestiges of hierarchy, at the pinnacle of which were the Pope and the Holy Roman Emperor.[1]

The Congresses of Münster and Osnabrück, which produced the Treaties of Westphalia, were the first of their kind. Europe had not previously witnessed a multilateral diplomatic gathering that was designed both to terminate a pan-European war and to build some sort of order out of the chaos into which Europe had increasingly fallen since the late fifteenth century. The congresses brought together the main heterogeneous political units of Europe at that time. There were 145 delegates representing 55 jurisdictions, including the Holy Roman Empire and all the major kingdoms except Great Britain, as well as significant duchies, margraves, landgraves, bishoprics, free cities, and imperial cities (Combes, 1854:235). Here was an opportunity to do more than barter over territory or extract spoils. This was a veritable

---

[1] The Treaties of Münster and Osnabrück contained clauses renouncing curial protest; these clauses "finally and officially did away with Rome's possibility to decisively alter the course of secular politics in Europe" (Rietbergen, 1980:37).

25

Estates-General of Europe, something akin to the vision of Henry IV, an opportunity to establish a new order for the continent. Hopes and expectations ran high; intentions were great. They included the creation of a pan-European diplomatic system based on the new principles of sovereignty and legal equality (Combes, 1854:269), and a balance of power that would prevent drives for hegemony.

Much indeed was accomplished. Without a pan-European settlement that provided the established and nascent dynastic states with a period of peace in which they could further consolidate authority over challenges from sub-national units such as duchies and free cities, it is easy to speculate that major conflicts involving the incompatible principles of fragmentation and hierarchy would have continued to break out, perhaps with the result that the Ottoman Empire, taking advantage of an exhausted Europe, would have successfully expanded into the continental heartland. Westphalia paved the way for a system of states to replace a hierarchical system under the leadership of the Pope and the Hapsburg family complex that linked the Holy Roman and Spanish Empires. But it did not provide a set of authoritative principles, effective system of governance, or conflict-resolving institutions upon and through which the aspiring dynasts of the postwar period could conduct their mutual relations on a pacific basis. Westphalia set free the dynasts to pursue whatever interests motivated them, with few guidelines as to how these interests might be moderated. It helped create a society of states, if by that term we mean a sense of propinquity and interdependence. But such a society can resemble more a Hobbesian state of nature than a gentlemen's club with strictly defined entrance requirements and well-articulated "rules of the game" that effectively regulate mutual relations. Without Westphalia, matters might have been much worse; but the delegates and their governments were able to build only a piece of a peaceful order.

## THE THIRTY YEARS WAR

Starting initially in Bohemia as an uprising of the Protestant aristocracy against Spanish authority, the war escalated rapidly, eventually incorporating all sorts of issues (Parker, 1984:ch. 1). Questions of religious toleration were at the root of the conflict, but other important stakes soon became involved. These included the relationship between the Holy Roman Emperor and the Electors, princes, free cities, and other political units of the Empire; the struggle for independence by the United Provinces against Spanish rule; the extent and shape of Sweden's Baltic Empire; and the search for hegemony throughout Europe by the Hapsburg family complex.

All the major political actors in continental Europe felt threatened by the hegemonic aspirations of Ferdinand II, the Holy Roman Emperor, and his fellow Hapsburg, Philip IV of Spain. Imperial and Spanish armies in the Rhineland, the Valtellina, and in the Spanish Netherlands threatened France. The Hapsburgs had already conquered Savoy and held most of Italy as well. Gustav Adolph, taking up the causes of the Protestant faith and its supporters among the German Electors and principalities, issued a manifesto in 1630, signaling Sweden's formal entry into the war. He did not mention Hapsburg aspirations to expand imperial influence to the Baltic coast, thereby threatening Sweden's supremacy in the area, but he was well aware of the threat. He justified the Swedish intervention in more global terms:

> It will be sufficient to say that the Spaniards and the House of Austria [Holy Roman Empire] have been always intent upon a Universal Monarchy, or at least designed the conquest of the Christian states and provinces in the West . . . That House has made such a progress, that if this brave and generous northern prince [Gustav Adolph] had not bestirred himself, and opposed that torrent, she had pushed her ambition and arms to the most distant kingdoms and provinces, which have hitherto preserved and maintained their liberty . . . This is what has given occasion to His Majesty of Sweden to put fleets to sea and bring armies into the field, in order to preserve his friends; being thereto invited by several princes and states of the Empire, before they were entirely reduced to servitude and misery, wherein they now find themselves shackled (text in Symcox, 1974:103–105).

Gustav Adolph did not mention the religious issue in his manifesto, despite his personal Protestant piety. He could not launch propaganda attacks directly against the forces of Catholicism, since he anticipated and eventually received funds and support from Catholic France. The perceived threat of Hapsburg "universal monarchy" was reason enough to justify the Swedish intervention.

The religious cleavage was expressed in its clearest diplomatic form in the warring between the Protestant Union, made up mostly of the principalities of northern Germany and Bohemia, and the Catholic League, which carried on the cause in the name of the Empire and the faith. But by the 1630s, the war involved a jumble of conflicting stakes, with all sorts of cross-cutting dynastic, religious, and state interests involved. Protestant entities were frequent allies of Catholic counterparts; Catholic Spain provided aid for French Huguenots; France supported the Protestant United Provinces against Catholic Spain.

27

Richelieu, on behalf of the "Most Catholic" King of France, Louis XIII, leagued with Protestant Sweden, and in 1635 declared war on co-religionist Spain.[2] The Peace of Prague (1635) resolved some of the local religious issues, but unabashed pursuit of state interests extended the war throughout Europe. As Gustav Adolph put it, "All the wars of Europe are now blended into one" (Roberts, 1967:202). Europe was fighting its first continental war.

The fighting had followed a path of increasing destructiveness and callous disregard for restraints. Religious conflicts, which had taken increasingly violent forms since the middle of the sixteenth century (Nef, 1952:114–16), were typically prosecuted by torture, witch-burning, massacres, and wholesale destruction of civilian populations and their properties. In the sack of Magdeburg in 1631, for example, Catholic forces slaughtered most of the population of thirty thousand and razed the buildings. Protestants committed similar atrocities. Michael Howard (1986:37) describes the character of the war:

> A soldier . . . was well described as a man who had to die so as to have something to live on. His condition was no better than that of the peasants he tormented. Armies were in a continual state of deliquescence, melting away from death, wounds, sickness, straggling, and desertion, their movements governed not by strategic calculation but by the search for unplundered territory. It was a period in which warfare seemed to escape from rational control; to cease indeed to be "war" in the sense of politically-motivated use of force by generally recognized authorities, and to degenerate instead into universal, anarchic, and self-perpetuating violence.

Wallenstein's "living off the land" and Gustav Adolph's "swath of destruction" were tactics that had never been equaled in destructiveness in one thousand years of previous European history (Rabb, 1975:76).

Historians disagree on the costs of the war. Some suggest that the destruction of lives amounted to about one-third of Germany's population. Perré (1948:409) argues that Germany's population in fact declined from 13 million to 4 million, or by 69 percent. Some 12,000 towns and villages were destroyed. Ward (1906:417) provides even more grim

---

[2] Vigorous debates on the question of alliances and religion took place in France during the war. Richelieu argued that state interests are not to be confused with questions of individual religious choice. The state has special responsibilities for preserving peace and general welfare, and its authority is divinely appointed. To the extent that relations with Protestant entities serve the interests of a Catholic state, they are both necessary and desirable. Richelieu's critics replied that his policies aided and abetted heretics. A prominent Jansenist asked: would Louis XIII 'dare to say to God: Let your power and your glory and the religion which teaches me to adore You be lost and destroyed, provided my state is protected and free from risks?' (Church, 1972:388)

figures: of some 35,000 villages in Bohemia, "it is stated that hardly more than 6000 were left standing." About 400,000 troops died in battle. The rest of the depopulation of central Europe resulted from starvation, disease attributed to malnutrition, the deliberate slaughter of civilians, and emigration. Whatever the exact costs, by the 1630s Europe's populations had borne an unprecedented burden of excessive taxes, decline in food production, and the more direct costs of injury and death.[3]

The war came to an end not because of any great commitment to peace in the abstract or because of decisive military victories and defeats. Rather, the parties exhausted themselves. Their treasuries were depleted, the mercenaries who constituted the bulk of the military forces refused to fight without pay, and since the huge armies and their hordes of campfollowers had to live off the land, inflicting great cruelties among the peasantry, they began to run out of the means of survival. During the course of the war, then, some of the political leaders had to begin giving thought to the postwar order. These were elaborated in general memorandums, as well as in the specific instructions relayed to ambassadors abroad. Gustav Adolph, Richelieu, and Mazarin provided the major ideas about the conditions they thought would be necessary for creating a lasting peace.

### PLANNING FOR PEACE

Gustav Adolph's ideas on peace evolved from his wartime experience as leader of the Protestant forces. Two components of his thinking stand out in particular: the hatred and distrust of the Catholics, and the need to enforce a peace. The former derived from his pious commitment to the Protestant cause; the latter from his strenuous and not always successful efforts to maintain a league of Protestant princes in war. In fact, Gustav Adolph's peace plan was little more than the extension into peacetime of the wartime coalition he led. He believed that any peace-enforcing coalition required dynamic and strong leadership. There was more than just a hint that he would provide it himself. That leadership was necessary in order to contain and over-

[3] Mazarin, by 1644, was unable to increase taxes to pay off previous loans to finance the war. He had to resort to selling offices and creating new government positions. Asked to approve his measures to continue the war, the *Parlement* in Paris rebelled, forcing Mazarin to extricate France from the German theater and to agree to peace negotiations. Mazarin, however, was able to continue the war against Spain for another fifteen years. Throughout the 1630s and 1640s, there were peasant uprisings in France to prevent imposition of onerous taxes. Most of France's peasantry in the North was reduced to extreme poverty through taxation to pay for the war effort (Pages, 1949:239–40; Burkhardt, 1971:ch. 11).

ride the petty jealousies of the German princes (Gustav Adolph had not been impressed by the backsliding and lack of commitment of several of his erstwhile German allies). It was necessary, moreover, to command a standing peacetime army whose task it would be to police the terms of settlement. The imperialists were to be disarmed; hence, the peace project looked like little more than a plan for the permanent subordination of the Catholic portions of the Empire to the Protestants. As with many victorious military leaders, Gustav Adolph's chronic suspicion of the enemy "was betraying him into the grievous error of thinking that the only permanent solution was total victory" (Roberts, 1958:II, 664).

Under the pressures of war and keeping together a ragged coalition, Gustav Adolph did not have much time to speculate on the abstract requirements of a general peace and of a postwar diplomatic order. He concentrated on a particular type of peace, verging on a *diktat* policed by his victorious armies. In his view, the cause of the war had been imperial aspirations to European hegemony and subversion of the rights of Germany's Protestant princes. The solution he proposed followed logically from the diagnosis: the purpose of the peace must be to prevent a recurrence of the Hapsburg hegemonic drive. Hence, his proposed strategy for peace looked suspiciously like a mode of domination; it was to be a particular peace to solve the problems of the past, a peace of the victors' preponderance and deterrence.

The peace plan, whose institutional form was to be a coalition *corpus bellicum* (army) and a collective *corpus politicum*, or assembly of Protestant princes, possibly modeled on the governmental structure of the United Provinces, died with Gustav Adolph on the battlefield of Lützen (1632). But other components of the programme were incorporated in the Swedish diplomats' negotiating positions at the congress of Osnabrück. These included significant territorial claims, all designed to protect Swedish imperial interests, to establish a permanent Swedish voice in imperial affairs, and to obtain Swedish guarantees for the peace (Roberts, 1958:II, 657–69).

Cardinal Richelieu, Louis XIII's prime minister, foreign minister, political tutor, and major adviser, was not burdened by the tasks of battlefield leadership against the Empire and Spain. He had more time to speculate about the requirements for a successful general peace. As early as 1637, in his instructions to the French ambassadors attending an abortive peace conference in Cologne, Richelieu outlined his plans for the construction of a peaceful order in Europe.

Richelieu's diagnosis of the European problem was roughly similar to that of Gustav Adolph. France declared war on Spain in 1635, justifying its decision in part on the grounds that Spain sought "universal empire." There was sufficient evidence to support such a view, although that evidence would seem to provide a case of potential rather than actual hegemony. Philip III of Spain had treated his fellow dynasts as inferiors. He had sought election as Holy Roman Emperor in 1600, 1609, and 1613, all with a view to continuing the imperialist policies of Charles V. His successor, Philip IV, along with Ferdinand II (the Holy Roman Emperor) had already conquered Savoy. Imperial and Spanish forces threatened the United Provinces and controlled the Rhine River and most of Italy. By 1635 France was surrounded and Spain was heavily subsidizing the Huguenot dissidents in France (Bourgeois, 1901: 44–45). A defeat of the Protestant forces throughout Germany would have left France and Holland at the mercy of the Hapsburg family complex.

Richelieu's strategic purpose was to protect the small states of Italy and Germany against this threatened hegemony. His tactics were to annex territories that could be used by his enemies against France or that would enable France to intervene militarily into Italy and Germany to enforce the peace. To fulfill the role of the protector of the "security and liberties" (Dickmann et al.,1962:53) of the Holy Roman Empire's constituent units and to create a balance between them and the Hapsburgs, France had to gain control over Pinerolo and Lorraine. In his 1637 instructions, Richelieu insisted that the former was "necessaire au Roy comme une porte pour le secours de l'Italie." Annexed territory was not considered French aggrandizement but as necessary to create a general European security system. French arms, of course, had made other conquests as well. Richelieu had his advisers dredge up old legal claims to them. On hindsight, this might appear as little more than self-serving justification for territorial expansion. But again, a larger purpose was in Richelieu's mind. In order to create a stable European order, France would have to operate from a position of strength. Its leading position in Europe would have to be based more on trust and reputation than on arms; and an integral part of that reputation was to lay claims that derived from dynastic rights of inheritance. Richelieu was not even willing to compromise historical French claims against Spain in order to secure a peace. He might easily have agreed to the "natural" frontier in the Pyrenees, but to do so he would have abrogated outstanding French claims to territory under Spanish control (Dickmann, 1963:66–67). The rest of the peace plan would not work, in his opinion, were France to compromise for political expediency all the rights it claimed in law.

In addition to the territorial features of the general settlement, Richelieu also spelled out (Dickmann et al., 1962:47–50) his plan for a collective security system. The idea was to create two leagues of states, one for Germany, the other for Italy, providing mutual guarantees for the peace treaty, and mutual obligations to "use arms against a party that seeks to disturb the peace." Richelieu saw the leagues as deterrents, primarily against Spain. But perhaps more important, he saw them as substitutes for an alternative peace strategy, which was to break up the Hapsburg domains, that is, to eliminate two essential actors, Spain and Austria, from the emerging states system. Instead, the ostensible or anticipated losers of the war were to be assimilated into the postwar system, thereby precluding wars of revenge. Revisions of the general peace were to be made only with the consent of the collectivity. Underlying the edifice of assimilation, collective responsibility, and French capacity to enforce the peace through military intervention would be a general commitment to respect ancient and negotiated legal rights.

Some of Richelieu's thoughts survived his death in 1642. His successor, Mazarin, virtually copied Richelieu's words in his own 1643 instructions to the French delegation for the Münster conference (Mazarin's instructions are reproduced in Dickmann et al., 1962:58–123). Mazarin, however, went into more detail on the territorial and other claims to be made, and discussed more extensively the concept of "natural frontier" that would incorporate the Spanish Netherlands into France to serve as an "impregnable boulevard around Paris" (Bourgeois, 1901:44). He also elaborated France's claims to great portions of Alsace, Luxemburg, and Franche-Comté. Mazarin was more interested in French aggrandizement and less concerned with constructing a general peace system for Europe.

Gustav Adolph, Richelieu, and Mazarin were not to see all of their plans come to fruition. The war continued through the four years of the peace negotiations, and some of the bolder conceptions of collective security and general commitments to respect historic and negotiated rights were to be left out. On the other hand, some of the divisive issues that had given rise to the Thirty Years War, but which Richelieu did not contemplate in his peace plan, were successfully resolved.

## NEGOTIATIONS AT MÜNSTER AND OSNABRÜCK

The major war participants had been professing a desire for peace for several years, always to find pretexts for delay in the expectation that a little more warfare would strengthen their bargaining positions. Plans for a congress had evolved as early as 1636, but

Richelieu hesitated, and Sweden refused to attend any conference mediated, as was the plan at that time, by a representative of the Pope. Subsequent mediation attempts by Denmark, Brandenburg, and Luxemburg failed, as did the proposals of the new Holy Roman Emperor, Ferdinand III, to settle issues within the Empire. However, Sweden, the Empire, and France negotiated a preliminary treaty in Hamburg, signed on Christmas Day 1641, with the expectation that negotiations for a final treaty would start in the spring of 1642 (Ward, 1906:396–98). But the major parties procrastinated. Richelieu died in December 1642, and his successor, Mazarin, did not yet hold effective authority in France. Possibilities on the battlefields offered further reasons for delay.

A glittering procession through the town of Münster on December 4, 1644 heralded the opening of the conference between the Catholic parties. The conference in Osnabrück, which included the delegates of Sweden and other Protestant negotiators, did not get under way until 1645. The two-conference format was the initiative of Richelieu, a device to circumvent Sweden's refusal to participate in meetings that included papal representation.

The complex format of the congress matched its extensive agenda. The two towns were located fifty kilometers apart, which necessitated the use of couriers to send proposals back and forth between the Catholic and Protestant delegates. Issues of status and precedence took up a large amount of time. These matters were not mere trifles. They reflected the competing principles of order in Europe: hierarchy versus dynastic state equality. The Empire's representative sought to enforce the ancient principles of vertical authority, declaring publicly that the King of France, like other princes, "was of right, and must forever remain subject to the Roman Emperor" (Gross, 1948:31). The French ambassador, rejecting any hint of subordination in his dealings with the imperial or papal delegates, insisted on all the trappings of equality. A personal meeting between the French and imperial ambassadors at a neutral site at the beginning of the conference already represented a defeat for the Empire.

Ceremonial meetings were carefully staged. This required considerable time in planning logistics, costumes, numbers of servants, questions of precedence of coaches maneuvering through the narrow streets, and even obtaining safe conduct passes for some of the delegates into the temporarily neutralized towns of Münster and Osnabrück. The French and Swedish ambassadors waited each other out to see who would first pay a courtesy call upon the other. Jean Oxenstierna, son of the Swedish Chancellor, finally went to visit his

French counterpart, accompanied by twelve hallbardeurs and numerous pages and servants in livery (Pages, 1949:229). Ever conscious of his importance, he announced to the townspeople and fellow delegates his awakening, meals, and retiring by means of a chorus of trumpets and cymbals. Given the continuation of the war, the lack of enthusiasm of several key players, the gargantuan agenda, and the prickly questions of diplomatic etiquette and precedence, one can wonder that anything at all was resolved.

Yet, thanks to increasing financial exhaustion, to the effective mediation efforts of Contarini (Venice) and Chigi (representing the Pope), and to the declining passions aroused by the religious issue, three years and ten months later the Treaties of Münster and Osnabrück were signed, signaling the first successful attempt in European history to establish a continental diplomatic order that was to be based on the sovereign state.

### OUTCOMES

The two critical issues of the war had been religious toleration – freedom of conscience, the education of children, and civil status – and the hegemonic ambitions of the Hapsburg family complex. The negotiations at Osnabrück dealt extensively with the first issue. As the leader of the Protestant coalition, Sweden insisted upon a settlement that would leave these matters to the jurisdiction of the individual princes and to other members of the Empire. The formula for settlement was borrowed from the Peace of Augsburg of 1555: *cuius regio, eius religio*. This was not an entirely satisfactory basis for universal religious tolerance, as it left the matter of regulating religious practice to the state and excluded tolerance in the Hapsburg family territories. However, the relevant articles did confirm the right of private worship, and any subsequent change of religion by a ruler was not to affect that right. Finally, subjects could educate their children in conformity with their faith, and they were not to suffer any civil discrimination or be denied religious burial because of their private beliefs. With these latter provisions, the settlement went beyond the principles of 1555. Indeed the congress also recognized Calvinism as a legitimate branch of the Christian faith, and established a Lutheran Church with bishops, titles, and honors modeled on the Churches of Sweden and England, though its head was not to be a crown.

On the question of hegemony, the outcome generally reflected the main objectives of Sweden and France: to split the Hapsburg family complex that united Spain, the Empire, and various territories

34

throughout Italy and central Europe. Under the terms of the Münster Treaty, the Emperor renounced his right to provide assistance to Spain, with whom France was still at war. Both treaties included formal disavowals of imperial ambitions by Ferdinand III and his successors, and granted both Sweden and France the right to intervene in imperial affairs to enforce this undertaking (Droz, 1959:10).

The main technique for putting an end to imperial hegemonic possibilities was to establish the rights of the individual units of the Empire and to provide for their control over imperial foreign policy. The Treaty of Osnabrück in effect rewrote the constitution of the Empire, bringing the Emperor's prerogatives over foreign policy under the scrutiny and effective control of the Imperial Diet. Article 64 reads:

> To prevent for the future any differences arising in the politic state, all and every one of the Electors, princes, and states of the Roman Empire, are so established and confirmed in their ancient rights, prerogatives, liberties, privileges, [and] free exercise of territorial right ... that they never can or ought to be molested herein by any whomsoever upon any manner or pretense. (Symcox, 1974:46–47)

Article 65, in addition to defining a concept that implied sovereignty, established the controls:

> [The members of the Diet] shall enjoy without contradiction, the right of suffrage in all deliberations touching the affairs of the Empire; but above all, when the business at hand shall be the making or interpreting of laws, the declaring of wars, levying or quartering of soldiers, erecting new fortifications in the territories of the states, or reinforcing the old garrisons; as also when a peace or alliance is to be concluded, and treated about, or the like, none of these, or the like things shall be acted for the future, without the suffrage and consent of the free assembly of all the states of the Empire; above all, it shall be free perpetually to each state of the Empire to make alliances with strangers for their preservation and safety; provided, nevertheless, such alliances be not against the Emperor, and the Empire.(Symcox, 1974:48–49)

Through this single article, the pattern of international relations in Europe was drastically changed: over three hundred political entities were now entitled to conduct foreign relations (make alliances), and the Holy Roman Emperor could not employ force in the conduct of foreign policy, or even make alliances, without the consent of the individual members of the Empire. In other articles, France and Sweden were granted the right to intervene in imperial affairs to enforce the principles of these two articles, among others.

While these provisions took care of the question of hegemony, the

35

delegates also outlined procedures for managing conflicts in the future (Turretini, 1949:63–65). The Treaty of Münster (Articles 113 and 124) obliged the signatories to submit conflicts to "friendly" mediation or to legal means. There was a further obligation to act jointly after a three-year delay, to assist the party which had received injury, "being advised by the injured that gentle Means and Justice prevailed nothing." In this case, armed force could be used against the party that had caused "injury." The critical shortcoming of the obligations was that it failed to designate a body that could determine if and when an "injury" had been committed. The delegates put no teeth into Richelieu's idea of a collective responsibility to protect the general peace against future usurpations.

A number of other general matters were resolved as well. These included freedom of navigation on the Rhine and the formal recognition of the sovereignty of the Swiss Confederation and the United Provinces. This recognition was an important indicator of the existence, by 1648, of at least a nascent society of states. States were not just created by their own efforts, but were to gain international recognition by the acts of the collectivity: the society ratifies (or withholds) the independence of individual states. There were, finally, the dozens of territorial settlements that recorded the outcomes of hundreds of battles and numerous campaigns. The major issues here concerned the immediate and critical security requirements of France and Sweden.

Under the conventions of the day, states had the right to demand *satisfactio* and *assecuratio*. Victors could require the enemy to pay for the costs of war. For Gustav Adolph, Sweden's *satisfactio* was to be cash, Pomerania, Silesia, Mecklenburg, Wismar, the bishoprics of Verden and Bremen, and several German ports on the Baltic. The purpose of these demands, ostensibly as payments for the considerable financial and human effort the Swedes had made on behalf of the Protestant cause, was really to secure Sweden's commercial and naval supremacy in the Baltic and to create the legal basis, as a holder of German properties, for Sweden's admission into the Imperial Diet. As an Elector of the Empire, Sweden would have a permanent *droit de regard* into imperial affairs. In order to gain this *satisfactio*, Sweden, as *assecuratio*, held on to the numerous territories it had under its control toward the end of the war. These maximum demands were substantially reduced through the course of negotiations, but the critical concerns of Sweden were met. Through the Treaty of Osnabrück, it received approximately one-half of Pomerania – the remainder going to Brandenburg – the two bishoprics, and several ports on the Baltic. It became a member of the Empire and a guarantor of the treaty.

As the fortunes of France's armies grew after 1638, so did French demands for *satisfactio*. It initially claimed international recognition of its century-long occupation of Metz, Verdun, and Toul, and at Münster, France successfully negotiated their transfer to French sovereignty. It also received Breisach, a strategically important post commanding a bridge on the Rhine. French claims included Alsace, an area technically belonging to the Empire, but governed under a complicated set of medieval arrangements. In general, France came close to realizing Mazarin's ideas of "natural frontiers," suggesting a predominantly defensive orientation for the future. But French territorial gains could also become the cause of the German states' insecurity. The territorial arrangements of the Treaty of Münster opened virtually the whole Rhineland to potential French invasion. From the French point of view, as outlined in Richelieu's peace programme, this was a necessary condition for guaranteeing the peace. But for an expansionist France, it was an opportunity that could be exploited at the expense of both the German states and the 1648 settlement.

France had intervened in the war as the champion of the German states' "liberties." Along with Sweden, it had borne the great costs of fighting both imperial and Spanish forces. The delegates could therefore well afford to concede France's claims to *satisfactio*. Given certain assumptions about France's future behavior, they were not unreasonable concessions. After all, France was exhausted and on the eve of civil war. Moreover, after almost four years of negotiations, the delegates no doubt wanted to put an end to the affair. Some territorial issues were left unresolved; others were to create new problems in later years. The Treaty of Münster did not provide a comprehensive, authoritative territorial settlement, but in 1648, it did not seem to matter. The Hapsburg hegemony and religious questions had been resolved, and they were the critical issues. No one could anticipate Louis XIV, to whom the details of France's eastern frontiers were more than just a question of *satisfactio*.[4]

## A NEW ORDER FOR EUROPE?

The outcomes negotiated at Osnabrück and Münster achieved much of what Richelieu, Gustav Adolph, and Mazarin had sought. They successfully ended the Hapsburg family complex's designs for "universal monarchy" and at the same time preserved and strength-

---

[4] Doran (1971:ch. 8) provides a thorough examination of the outcomes and diplomatic implications of the Peace of Westphalia. He discusses a number of details that are not, however, of immediate concern to this analysis.

ened the "liberties" of the German states. They built a constitution for central Europe that was to last until 1806.

The religious issue, the overriding source of increasing chaos, brutality, and intolerance throughout Europe for the preceding century, was resolved according to principles with which the rulers and dynasts of the day, if not the Popes, could live. No war occurring after 1648 – wars against the Ottomans excepted – derived primarily from religious issues. The Westphalia religious formula, moreover, was so successful that it served as a model for numerous other treaties, such as the Peace of Oliva (1660) ending a Swedish–Polish war (Ruyssen, 1958:8–9). Westphalia, in brief, resolved an issue that had generated numerous wars in the past. Domestic intolerance continued in many countries and caused frequent diplomatic frictions, but the dynasts never again went to war against each other carrying the banners of the Protestant or Catholic faiths. The delegates of Münster and Osnabrück achieved in this realm a historic turning point.

The formula for resolving the hegemony issue was no less successful. The Hapsburg family complex was broken up. The treaties contained guarantees and the right of intervention to enforce their terms. Through its annexation of the larger part of Pomerania, Sweden became an Elector of the Empire; it secured a *droit de regard* and a means of monitoring imperial affairs. Swedish influence over Protestant princes in the Imperial Diet also assured that the Emperor could not use his arms to threaten any of the guarantor's interests in Germany. The delegates constructed mechanisms to ensure that the terms of the treaties would be faithfully carried out in the future. And France emerged with both the right and the capacity to act, unilaterally or collectively, as the policeman of the peace.

The peacemakers at Münster and Osnabrück also drafted an instrument that largely precluded revenge as a possible motive for future war (Doran, 1971:chs. 8–9). In their propaganda, France and Sweden constantly referred to their efforts to *restore* the rights and "liberties" of the Protestant princes. Their purpose was to reconstitute the Empire in a less threatening mold, not to destroy it. Thus, no party at the congresses was at the mercy of another, and no party enjoyed a position from which it could impose its own form of hegemony (Dupuis, 1909:20). Though Sweden and France obtained the greatest territorial gains from the war, their purposes were essentially defensive and order-constructing: to provide themselves either with defensible frontiers (France) or with hinterland that would protect an existing empire (Sweden). The French territorial gains were also designed to provide avenues for military intervention to uphold the peace should its provisions be threatened by the Emperor or any other party.

The peace legitimized the ideas of sovereignty and dynastic autonomy from hierarchical control. It created a framework that would sustain the political fragmentation of Europe. The reverse of the coin was that it delegitimized all forms of hegemony and the vestiges of hierarchical controls. During the next three hundred years, European states repeatedly invoked the principles of Westphalia to safeguard themselves against those who had different visions of European order. By sanctifying Europe's centrifugal forces, by providing a legal basis for the developing territorial particularisms of Europe, and by terminating the vestiges of relations between superiors and inferiors, with authority emanating downward from the Emperor and the Pope, the documents licensed an anarchical dynastic states system and the internal consolidation of its members. But in their desire to subvert the principles and trappings of hierarchy, they did not understand all the consequences of its alternative, anarchy and fragmentation. The peace had constructed some of the requisites for a reasonably stable international order, particularly in fashioning a system of governance through the right of Swedish and French intervention to uphold the terms of the treaties, and by assimilating the Hapsburgs into the order, thus pre-empting potential wars of revenge. But an effective mechanism of order requires more than governance and assimilation of the defeated.

While historians generally agree on the processes that led to the weakening of imperial and papal authority – the impact of the Renaissance and Reformation, and the rise of individualism, for example – there is no consensus on what, exactly, took its place. According to Turretini (1949), the Peace of Westphalia was notable for inculcating the idea of solidarity, for underlining the interdependence of Europe. This is the idea of a society of states, a type of body politic with communitarian characteristics, including reciprocal obligations based on equality, that falls about midway between a strucure of hierarchical authority and a system of pure anarchy. The idea of community solidarity was indeed expressed in the preambles of the treaties, by the guarantees, and by the collective grant of recognition to the Swiss Confederation and the United Provinces. The obligations of pacific settlement and collective action against usurpers also constituted significant components of an international order. Finally, all states were theoretically given legal protection, regardless of size, lineage, or religion. For some analysts, then, Westphalia represented "the starting point for the development of modern international law," "the first

39

faint beginnings of an international constitutional law;" and the first instance of "deliberate enactment of common regulation by concerted action" (Gross, 1948:26, citing Paul Fauchille, F. S. Dunn, and P. H. Winfield).

A different interpretation seems better supported by subsequent events. Westphalia did not really erect an order characterized by communitarian norms and effective conflict-resolving or managing mechanisms. It successfully destroyed or at least recorded the decay of norms associated with hierarchy. But it did not replace them with any similarly authoritative system involving lasting reciprocal obligations and a distribution of power that could effectively check the new dynastic states against their expansionist proclivities. Westphalia produced a peace and a type of order designed to guarantee *that* particular peace, but not peace in general. The peace was effective in terms of the Hapsburg hegemony problem, but it was based on the assumption of relatively benign French and Swedish behavior in the postwar period. It was not designed to cope with a different set of assumptions. Should the purposes of either of those powers, or indeed of any great power, change over time, the new order, whose "repose" was based on a particular distribution of power, would no longer be effective or stable.

Furthermore, the delegates at Münster and Osnabrück, in their zeal to destroy the structure (or pretensions) of hierarchy and to legitimize the centrifugal forces of Europe, did not take the opportunity to build a general legal regime whose authority lay in intergovernmental or supranational institutions. The *liberty of states*, championed by Gustav Adolph, Richelieu, Mazarin, and a host of German principalities, was the fundamental objective of the negotiations. Professions of solidarity, mutual guarantees, and a semblance of a balance of power were not sufficient foundations for regulating effectively the consequences of that liberty. The Peace of Westphalia did not build a *general* system of reciprocal obligations, including limitations on the use of force. War was proscribed only as a means of altering the 1648 settlement. The delegates did not grasp Grotius' idea that true peace requires *organized* cooperation (Clark, 1958:13) to cope with generic, and not just specific, issues.

The architects of Westphalia thought in terms of statics. The solutions to the religious and hegemony problems were to be permanent. The balance of power was based on the assumption of permanent Swedish and French predominance. The settlement was to be frozen forever. The idea of dynamic changes in the relative power of the dynasts was not yet entertained seriously. Thus, when power changed and postwar solidarity evaporated in the face of a host of new contentious issues, the foundations of the new order weakened. The men of Westphalia had not anticipated the rise of a Louis XIV, the incorporation of colonial conflicts into the European states system, the precipitous decline of Sweden, and the rise of Prussia and Russia. With the possible exception of Richelieu, the negotiators of the peace were more backward than forward looking. The problem for them was to solve the problems of the past and not to anticipate the changes of the future.

At a less theoretical level, the Peace of Westphalia carried with it the seeds of new conflicts. Spain withdrew from the congress in 1646, having negotiated the independence of the United Provinces, but it could not tolerate the Swedish and French outlines of a comprehensive peace. It remained committed to its goal of crushing France. The treaties did nothing to control this axis of conflict, leaving Louis XIV to fashion other means of resolving the ancient enmity, ones that would give rise to the next great European war. The division of Pomerania between Brandenburg and Sweden created a new enmity. Some of the territorial issues were left unresolved or were resolved in such an ambiguous fashion that disputes over their interpretation were to mar the tranquillity of Europe for the next five decades. It may be an exaggeration to claim, as has Victor Tapie (in Hatton, 1976:30), that the ambiguities, claims, and counter-claims resulting from the treaties were critical sources of the Great Northern and Spanish Succession Wars of the eighteenth century, but it is certainly correct that the Peace of Westphalia was neither definitive nor universally authoritative.

The peace was thus incomplete on both particular and general levels. It failed to resolve some issues or left them in an indeterminate state, inviting revisionist aspirations among some key actors. It failed to construct a legal-institutional system for regulating the relations among the increasingly powerful and centralized sovereignties of the continent, that is, to articulate a set of rules that were to extend beyond the particularities of the 1648 settlement. Dynastic claims, the source of so much international conflict and war throughout the sixteenth and seventeenth centuries, were not addressed as a generic problem of the system. Colonial and maritime issues, both of which were emerging as critical items on the international agenda, remained without guidelines for resolution. Westphalia produced no consultative mechanisms, no system of regular conferences, none of the features normally associated with an authoritative system of legal obligations, and no firm basis for international collaboration. The resolution of the religious and hegemony problems was a signal achievement, as was the system built to guarantee against their recurrence as major sources of international conflict. But this was only a piece of a general peace. An effective international order requires, at a minimum, a system of governance, general limitations on the use of force, sets of conflict-resolving procedures and institutions, and other components. Westphalia provided some of them, but not enough to reduce the incidence of war effectively in the postwar period. Perhaps the tasks of the peacemakers were too broad, maybe even incompatible. Can one simultaneously lay the foundations for an anarchical system *and* build in the restraints that are necessary for international moderation and order? Perhaps not, but Westphalia did leave some important legacies that helped to form the foundations of order, if not lengthy periods of peace. They will be evaluated in the next chapter.

# 3 WAR AND PEACE IN THE ERA OF THE HEROIC WARRIORS, 1648–1713

> We know only too well from sad and frequent experience that predominant States rarely fail to trouble their neighbours, to oppress them, and even to subjugate them completely, when they have an opportunity of doing so with impunity. Emmerich de Vattel

> I have loved war too much. Louis XIV

The Peace of Westphalia failed to establish a comprehensive order, but it did include some elements of a hypothetical international order. There was a primitive system of governance (Swedish and French guarantees), the assimilation of the Holy Roman Empire, and in particular, some important territorial allocations that were to provide benchmarks of legitimacy.

Did Westphalia provide important sources of stability for international politics in succeeding decades? The reality probably lies somewhere between Giraud's claim that post-Westphalia Europe constituted "a community of destinies and of interests," a "system, born of facts but consecrated by law," (1847:12–13), and Zeller's comment (1955:III, 16) that Westphalia did not reveal "the shadow of a constructive idea," and that the statesmen and diplomats of the later seventeenth century had no conception of a common good, or of a concern for the future of Europe. Westphalia sanctified anarchy, to be sure, but it also drew a map of Europe that defined the bounds of legitimacy, one that was commonly regarded as drawn for eternity (Rabb 1975:78). The peace served as a point of reference, a measure to evaluate states' actions to see whether or not they were consistent with the undertakings of the Treaties of Münster and Osnabrück. Even if the balance of power created in the settlement came apart, no state could seek to alter the terms of the treaties without incurring strong opposition from the rest of Europe.

There was, then, a part of an order, in particular the various territorial settlements that were assumed to be legitimate and long-lasting. The ambiguous parts of the settlement provided loopholes for consequent annexations and aggressions, but most dynasts of the period kept their claims within those areas of ambiguity.

The influence of the territorial elements of the order can be seen in the constant attempts to fashion peace settlements for bilateral and multilateral wars in Western Europe on the basis of the Westphalia peace. At the peace negotiations of Nijmegen (1676–79), Sweden, and even France as the aggressor, insisted that the final treaty be based on the 1648 settlements (Pillorget, 1980:231; Pages, 1948:216). Article 2 of the Treaty of Nijmegen refers to the Münster and Osnabrück conventions as the basis for the peace which terminated Louis XIV's attempt to crush Holland. Similarly, the French delegates to the negotiations at Ryswick, yet another conference to settle one of Louis XIV's aggressive wars, were instructed to base their demands on the Westphalia settlement (Commission des Archives Diplomatiques, 1922:XX, 515). The "grand alliance" of 1689, which united Holland, the Empire, and Great Britain against France, specified that the purpose of the coalition was to restore the terms of the Westphalia settlement against Louis's attempts to overturn their provisions regarding the left bank of the Rhine and other areas. In brief, the settlement of 1648 served as a critical benchmark for defining the limits of the powers' foreign policies and for providing the framework and contours of peace settlements in the 1648–1713 period.

Without such a standard, dynastic claims could have been limitless, leading to an epidemic of war-causing conflicts. In the 1630s, Richelieu had instructed his officials to research all possible French claims, going back to the time of Charlemagne. Had Louis XIV chosen to pursue these, French annexations would have extended to a large part of Germany, Italy, and Spain. By accepting most of the Westphalia outcomes as a legitimate settlement, he implicitly limited the scope of his claims. Where his claims constituted significant revisions to the settlement, he still employed, albeit in a rather tortured way, the Peace of Westphalia as a legitimating source for them. The wars of Western Europe during the latter half of the seventeenth century were thus basically adjustments to Westphalia, notwithstanding the fact that Louis XIV had aspirations for a French-centred European order that would have been largely inconsistent with the 1648 settlement. When he went beyond its terms, he was kept in check by a coalition of states that *was* committed to maintaining the basic contours of the 1648 settlements.

In the rest of Europe, the influence of Westphalia was less pervasive. The Peace of Oliva, as suggested, applied Westphalian principles to Swedish–Danish–Polish relations, but the states of the Baltic littoral, including Russia, were determined to dismember the Swedish Empire. Hence, this area was to constitute a major zone of war until 1721. Russia became a major actor in the northern system by the end of the century, and its ambitions, personified by the modernizing zealot, Tsar Peter, were inconsistent with the integrity of the Swedish Empire, a guarantor of the Westphalia settlement. Finally, Ottoman Turkey was a critical player in the European games of power politics but was not yet accepted as a member of the club. The expansion of Muslim power into the central European heartland constituted a severe crisis for "Christendom," and particularly for the Pope and the Austrian Hapsburgs. While Turkey was expanding into Hungary and all the way to the gates of Vienna, it was on the defensive in the East, trying to fend off Peter's drive to gain access to the Black Sea. None of these zones of conflict was affected by the Westphalia settlement. Whatever the rules of the game in Western Europe, they did not apply in the North and the East. These areas contained virtually autonomous international systems, where anarchy was not moderated by elements of society.

A system of anarchy is moderated when its members have some conception of a *community interest*, some notion of a common destiny and need for self-restraint for the sake of a more inclusive community goal. While allowing for propaganda, there is some evidence that the dynasts of the Westphalian core were aware of this larger community and were willing to limit their claims and the use of force for its sake. The diplomatic documents of the era are sprinkled with references to the compromises or policy changes taken for "the tranquillity of Europe," the "repose of Europe," or the "peace of Christendom." Louis XIV, according to diplomatic instructions his officials sent to the French delegates at Ryswick, was willing to make important concessions to his adversaries "pour le repos général de la Chrétienté" (Commission des Archives Diplomatiques, 1922:XX, 510). In his own testament and memoirs, Louis acknowledged that he had on several occasions "sacrificed advantages that I gained in the war . . . to [the needs] of public tranquillity" (Wolf, 1968:487). Giraud points out (1847:46) that the Holy Roman Emperor, Leopold, was willing to abandon his claim to the Spanish throne in favor of his son, thereby averting possible war. According to the decree announcing the decision, Leopold chose in consideration of "the welfare of our peoples and the health of the European community."

The Westphalian settlements thus provided some moderating elements for postwar international relations. These were largely implicit and informal, rather than the more institutional components of order identified in the previous chapter. On the other hand, the balance of power and the guarantees, both significant elements of a system of governance in an anarchy, languished or were destroyed through Louis XIV's wars and the decline of the Swedish Empire. The post-Westphalia order was punctuated by frequent war; our conclusion must be that the order included some elements of stability, but it did little to reduce the incidence of war.

### ISSUES THAT GENERATED WARS

Several methodological problems confront the researcher when reviewing the information on wars and issues. Some of these were introduced in chapter 1. Here we can elaborate in the context of the particular diplomatic histories of one era. First, there is the problem of different stakes involved for different parties. If two opponents have significantly different views on those stakes, they are noted separately. For example, France's attack on Holland in 1672 revolved around French designs on significant Dutch territories. For France, strategic and commercial stakes were involved (Colbert in particular saw great opportunities for French trade were Antwerp to become part of the kingdom). On the other hand, the territories coveted by France were critical to the survival of Holland as an independent state. The stake for Holland, then, was national survival – a stake which proved very accurate when Louis XIV's armies tried to capture Amsterdam. In the Russo-Turkish War of 1694–1700, in contrast, the stake is the same for both parties (territory), so the issue is recorded only once. However, Peter was also interested in obtaining access to the Black Sea for commercial purposes. For Russia, then, a commerce/navigation issue is added.

A second difficulty arises over coalition wars, where there are different arenas of conflict. The rule guiding research is that wars are counted separately if they are fought for essentially different purposes, involving different stakes for each of the participants. The Great Northern War, 1700–21, is usually treated by historians as a single conflict. During drinking bouts and target-shooting sessions, Peter of Russia and August of Saxony planned their alliance to dismember Sweden. They were joined by Denmark. Yet, each of the aggressors had different purposes in mind, and each fought and made peace separately. The theatres of warfare were broadly separated; the alliance was merely a convenient maneuver to provide the three parties with seemingly greater strength. Otherwise there were no bonds between them (Wolf, 1951:55). In the research, each is counted as a separate war. Indeed, Denmark and Sweden fought two entirely different wars within the twenty-one-year period.

In contrast, the War of the Spanish Succession, even though not all the participants joined the fighting simultaneously, was fought as a genuine coalition. Purposes and stakes were broadly similar, and the parties remained united until the British defected to negotiate a preliminary peace with France. In those negotiations, however, Great Britain pushed hard to advance the interests of its allies.

Finally, there is the problem of defining limits to issues. This is where individual judgments have to be made and where there is substantial room for disagreement and perhaps error. How does one, for example, distinguish between territorial and dynastic issues, when in the diplomacy of the day almost all territorial claims were based on some version or other of dynastic rights? As we will see in the discussion of the individual issues of the era, in some cases it is impossible to separate them. In these circumstances, both are listed as issues generating war. For example, in the "War of Devolution" between France and Spain, 1667–68, Louis XIV made claims to territories in the Spanish Netherlands, Luxemburg, and the Franche-Comté. He found ancient laws pertaining to inheritance in the Spanish Netherlands and used them to justify his claims, which were actually based on the rights of his wife. Though he was committed to fulfilling the obligations of his patrimony, he was also interested in obtaining territories of critical strategic importance. When he unleashed the French army, it was not portrayed as an army of conquest, but as the army of Maria Theresa occupying territory that was rightfully hers (Wolf, 1968:200–10). Thus, both strategic territories and dynastic claims are listed among the issues that generated the war.

For the period 1648–1713, there were twenty-two wars.[1] A total of 51 issues are identified as sources of those conflicts.

Contests over territory constitute the most significant source of war, accounting for 24 percent of all the issues. They are followed by commercial/navigation issues (16 percent), dynastic/succession claims (14 percent), contests over territories having particular strategic significance, including British claims to sovereignty over the oceans (10 percent), and stakes involving dynastic/state survival. Wars involving religious stakes, treaty enforcement, colonial competition, national liberation, balance of power/hegemony, commerce/resources, and

---

[1] Luard counts twenty-seven wars. Some of his wars were really campaigns fought in the context of a larger war (e.g., France–Genoa, 1684–85) or interventions to quell rebellions. Some of the wars in my list are not included in his (e.g., the War of Devolution). See Luard (1986:431–33).

47

Table 3.1 *Wars and issues, 1648–1713*

| Wars/interventions[a] | Issues for original combatants |
|---|---|
| 1. Great Britain–Holland 1652–1654 | 1. commerce/navigation<br>2. strategic territory<br>3. commerce/resources |
| 2. Russia–Poland 1654–1657 | 1. territory |
| 3. Sweden–Poland 1655–1660 | 1. dynastic/succession claims (P.)<br>2. strategic territory (S.)<br>3. commerce/navigation (S.) |
| 4. Great Britain–Spain 1655–1659 | 1. colonial competition<br>2. other |
| 5. Turkey–Holy Roman Empire 1663–1664 | 1. state/regime survival (H.R.E.) |
| 6. Great Britain–Holland 1665–1667 | 1. dynastic/succession claims (H.)<br>2. commerce/navigation<br>3. colonial competition |
| 7. France–Spain 1667–1678 | 1. dynastic/succession claims (F.)<br>2. commerce/navigation (F.)<br>3. strategic territory |
| 8. France–Holland 1672–1679 | 1. strategic territory<br>2. commerce/navigation (F.)<br>3. protect religious confrères (F.)<br>4. state/regime survival (H.) |
| 9. Turkey–Poland 1672–1676 | 1. territory<br>2. protect religious confrères (P.) |
| 10. Denmark–Sweden[b] 1675–1679 | 1. territory |
| 11. Turkey–Holy Roman Empire 1682–1697 | 1. territory (T.)<br>2. protect religious confrères (H.R.E.)<br>3. state/regime survival (H.R.E.) |
| 12. France–Spain 1683–1684[b] | 1. strategic territory<br>2. enforce treaty terms (F.) |
| 13. France–Holy Roman Empire, Great Britain, Holland, Spain 1689–1697 | 1. territory (F.)<br>2. balance of power (allies)<br>3. dynastic/succession claims (F.) |
| 14. Russia–Turkey 1694–1700 | 1. territory<br>2. commerce/navigation (R.) |
| 15. France–Spain, Great Britain, Holland, Denmark, 1702–1713 | 1. dynastic/succession (F., S., H.R.E.)<br>2. balance of power/hegemony (allies)<br>3. territory (F., S., H.)<br>4. commerce/navigation (G.B., H.)<br>5. state/regime survival (H.) |
| 16. Denmark–Holstein-Gottorp (Sweden) 1699–1700 | 1. dynastic/succession claims (D.)<br>2. territory (D., H.-G.)<br>3. state/regime survival (H.-G.)<br>4. protect/defend ally (S.) |

Table 3.1 *continued*

| Wars/interventions[a] | Issues for original combatants |
|---|---|
| 17. Saxony (Poland)–Sweden 1700–1706 | 1. territory<br>2. dynastic/succession claims<br>3. national liberation/state creation (P.) |
| 18. Russia–Sweden 1700–1721 | 1. territory<br>2. commerce/navigation |
| 19. Denmark–Sweden[b] 1709–1720 | 1. territory |
| 20. Turkey–Russia 1710–1711 | 1. territory |
| 21. Turkey–Russia 1711–1712 | 1. enforce treaty terms (T.) |
| 22. Turkey–Russia 1712–1713 | 1. enforce treaty terms (T.) |

[a] State starting and/or declaring war first is listed first.
[b] Indicates wars of revenge, attempts to reverse outcome of previous war.

protecting a dynastic ally appear in descending order. The "other" category covers the Ottoman intervention in a 1663 Hungarian uprising.

The relative importance of the different issues is apparent when we count the number of times an issue was involved in generating war. The figures are listed in table 3.3. Again, territorial issues stand out. More than one-half of the twenty-two wars for the period had a general territorial issue as a major stake for at least one of the original combatants. Questions of commerce and navigation are also prominent, figuring in more than one-third of the wars. Dynastic claims are only

Table 3.2 *Distribution of issues that generated wars, 1648–1713*

| Issues | Frequency | % of all issues |
|---|---|---|
| Territory | 12 | 24 |
| Commerce/navigation | 8 | 16 |
| Dynastic/succession claims | 7 | 14 |
| Strategic territory | 5 | 10 |
| State/regime survival | 5 | 10 |
| Protect religious confrères | 3 | 6 |
| Enforce treaty terms | 3 | 6 |
| Colonial competition | 2 | 4 |
| Balance of power/hegemony | 2 | 4 |
| National liberation/state creation | 1 | 2 |
| Defend/support ally | 1 | 2 |
| Commerce/resources | 1 | 2 |
| Other | 1 | 2 |
| Total | 51 | 102 |

slightly less conspicuous. Although our period saw the development of limited forms of warfare (see below), five of the participants were literally fighting for their lives. National or dynastic survival was the stake for one of the parties in 23 percent of the wars. Religious issues, usually the attempted protection of religious confrères under alien (often Muslim) rule, figured in 14 percent of the wars, as did efforts to enforce previous treaty terms. Colonial competition was only beginning to generate inter-state wars, and two grand coalition wars against Louis XIV involved conscious attempts to maintain a balance of power.

These figures do not contain any great surprises. They confirm the conventional historical wisdom about the decline of religion as a factor in international politics after the Westphalia settlement, and they underline the importance of dynastic claims, a distinct continuity with the pre-Thirty Years War international system. Perhaps it is startling to see how quickly territorial possession not deriving from distinct legal/historical claims became a major goal of the dynastic state after the Westphalia settlement. This reflects the growing solidity of the dynastic state, and its expanding needs for developing sources of taxation revenue, largely for the purpose of creating large standing armies (Finer, 1975:86–141; Braun, 1975:311). Territory was the critical foundation for these new revenues. The rise of commercial issues was also notably rapid. Economic considerations were relatively unimportant in previous periods of warfare; of all the issues settled in Münster and Osnabrück, only a small proportion dealt with questions of trade and navigation. But in the succeeding period, there were three wars

Table 3.3 *Issues that generated wars, 1648–1713*

| Issues | As sources of war | % of wars |
|---|---|---|
| Territory | 12 | 55 |
| Commerce/navigation | 8 | 36 |
| Dynastic/succession claims | 7 | 31 |
| Strategic territory | 5 | 23 |
| State/regime survival | 5 | 23 |
| Protect religious confrères | 3 | 14 |
| Enforce treaty terms | 3 | 14 |
| Colonial competition | 2 | 9 |
| Balance of power/hegemony | 2 | 9 |
| National liberation/state creation | 1 | 4 |
| Defend/support ally | 1 | 4 |
| Commerce/resources | 1 | 4 |
| Other | 1 | 4 |
| Total | 51 | |

between England and Holland (only two listed in table 3.1 because the third was subsumed in a larger war) where commercial and navigation competition and rivalry not only constituted factors in war decisions but were sufficient conditions explaining the outbreak of violence. Finally, although many historians have underlined the importance of balance of power considerations in the warfare of this period, the actual percentage is relatively low. The explanation is that balance of power considerations did not figure in the wars of north, east, and southeast Europe. All the states there, except Sweden, sought expansion simultaneously, and there is no evidence that the key policy-makers of the areas thought in terms of balances. In western Europe, by contrast, two wars were fought by coalitions against France; in each case, the coalitions were formed to check the presumed "universal monarchy" ambitions of Louis XIV. The diplomats of the period functioned exactly as the theory postulated.

It is now appropriate to examine each of the issues in turn, to note their significance in the general practice of diplomacy, and also to identify any changes that occurred in them during the period. The analysis will also help the reader understand the research decisions that formed the bases of the tables. Finally, I am interested in exploring why dynasts and their advisers placed such great value on the different stakes that they were willing to go to war to resolve contests over them.

### General territory

At the beginning of the post-Westphalia period, dynasts and their counselors did not generally think of frontiers in lineal terms. The typical kingdom was made up of complicated hierarchies of subunits. Territorial expansion thus initially took the form of claims for specific political jurisdictions such as provinces, duchies, free cities, and smaller fiefs. Contiguity was unimportant. The values of duchies, cities, and provinces had a great deal to do with the king's *gloire*, his patrimony, and the link of personal loyalty between a king and his subjects. A noble or peasant of Burgundy, for example, owed fealty to Louis XIV not as King of France but as Duke of Burgundy. The pursuit of dynastic claims thus had state-building, centralization, and loyalty values that were more important than land or government revenues. Hence, conflicts over them are classified as dynastic/succession claims rather than territory.

As demands for revenues increased, however, largely as a result of the costs of building and maintaining permanent military establishments, dynasts began seeking new sources of funds. Colonial terri-

51

tories offered one major source – Spain's heyday as an imperial power in Europe was funded almost entirely by gold and silver from the New World – but neighboring space offered similar opportunities for those states that were not engaged in overseas expansion. Peasants, commercial establishments, and trade offered lucrative sources for the kings' tax collectors. The Danish–Swedish Wars and the repeated wars between Russia and the Ottoman Empire were almost pure territorial wars; that is, the contests over territorial jurisdiction were sufficient causes of war. Dynastic claims and other legalities were absent, or at most were used as post hoc justifications for territorial aggrandizement. Thus, by the end of the period, boundaries had become increasingly important and concepts of territory had changed. The lineal frontier surrounding a contiguous national domain began to replace the concept of a realm made up of diverse historic jurisdictions, many of them located hundreds of kilometers from the national core area. There was a new assumption that conquests of territory were final, that the dynastic state had a defined territorial base, not just a foundation of historical rights and prerogatives, or a congeries of feudal elements, all sheltered under the royal patrimony. This generalization applies unequally throughout Europe – it was not generally understood in Russia, for example – but there is a noticeable trend toward its recognition.

### Issues of commerce and navigation

Montesquieu claimed that "the natural result of commerce is to promote peace" (Earle, 1986:240). This idea, which remains fashionable today, was certainly not appropriate for the late seventeenth century. Under the influence of mercantilist thought and developing rivalries in the colonies, commercial competition became a major source of antagonism between states and in at least three instances was sufficient to cause war between Great Britain and Holland, despite strong religious and dynastic ties between the two countries. Those wars were among the first in which the representatives of fishermen, traders, and manufacturers demanded that the state employ military force to resolve outstanding commercial/navigational disputes. The genesis of the Anglo-Dutch War of 1652–54 offers insight into the role that economic issues played in international relations during the post-Westphalian period.

Though aggressive in its pursuit of colonial wealth through the very successful Dutch East India Company, Holland generally followed a peaceful foreign policy orientation, based on the recognition that war would disrupt trade. In part, it could afford such a policy because it held a predominant position in the Baltic trade and elsewhere. Its predominance was a major source of grievance to the British, however. Fisheries added another issue. About 20 percent of the Dutch population were involved in the herring fisheries industry, and a significant portion of the fish came from Dutch vessels operating off the coast of England. Not unexpectedly, British interests demanded a diminution of Dutch fishing activities; this was done, in part, by making extensive claims to territorial sovereignty over the seas. Thus a fisheries issue was transformed into an issue of territory, one which had not only repercussions for the extent of territorial jurisdiction, but also great strategic and commercial implications.

Rights of neutrals during war – another commercial problem – added to the Anglo-Dutch difficulties. France and Great Britain in the immediate post-Westphalia period were engaged in informal maritime warfare (including the predatory practices of privateers). Great Britain insisted on the right of search and contraband, intercepting Dutch vessels sailing to and from France, and impounding their cargoes. The Dutch championed the rights of neutrals to trade freely with all states. A variety of British restrictions on trade and fishing, including the famous Navigation Act of 1651, led to extreme tensions between the two countries. London's prohibition against all imports from France (Clark, 1934:87) indicated to the Dutch that Great Britain's policies posed a general threat to international trade and commerce. The Act stipulated that all merchandise imported into England must be brought directly from the country of origin (thus bypassing Dutch entrepôts), and in British ships (thus breaking up the Dutch hegemony over Baltic trade). No goods from Asia, Africa, or the Americas could come to Great Britain in foreign vessels. Finally, the Act prohibited the import of salted fish and reserved for British fishermen vast tracts of ocean used predominantly by Dutch fishermen. The Dutch sought the repeal of most of the provisions, but without success. They then took measures to protect Dutch commercial and fishing vessels operating in their traditional modes and locations. The almost inevitable naval incident followed, and the war was on (Wilson, 1957).

Commercial considerations were also significant in decisions to go to war by France, Russia, Spain, and Sweden. Tsar Peter expanded to the south and northwest primarily to open up channels of trade and communications with Europe. In so doing, he ran up against the Ottoman and Swedish Empires, which at that time dominated the Black and Baltic Seas and monopolized trade in their littorals. Given the zero-sum assumptions about trade and the predominant objective of creating monopolies over both shipping and trade, it was almost inevitable that commercial and navigation issues would become important sources of international conflicts. This was generally a new area of diplomacy, and the belligerents had not yet begun to learn of the advantages of maximizing mutual trade opportunities. Moreover, governments were learning that trade could be used as an adjunct to, or as a substitute for, war. As the commercial stakes in the Americas and the East Indies grew in importance, the strategy of attacking the overseas trade of rivals became increasingly attractive (Nef, 1952:164).

Despite the increasing importance of trade issues in the genesis of war, at no time did commercial matters assume the importance of "high policy" for most of the actors. Holland and Great Britain were exceptions, but for the other countries, the dynasts were not very interested in these matters. Mazarin had taught Louis XIV that the tasks of a king centred upon great political goals; these did not include matters of commerce. Louis did not need to be encouraged in this regard. He had no education in commercial matters, nor was he particularly interested in them. He was vitally interested in, and informed about, all the political problems of Europe, and this meant court gossip throughout the realms, the administration of the army, diplomatic strategies, and all the myriads of dynastic issues that required daily attention (Wolf, 1968:183). Louis listened much more carefully to Louvois, who was preaching a policy of dynastic annexations, than he did to Colbert, whose main task was not so much to advise the king on what he should do, as to contrive ways of finding the means to pay for them once the king had decided on his projects (Zeller, 1955:56). Thus, an economic interpretation of the diplomacy of the era would diverge seriously from the realities. Commercial issues assumed a new importance in the latter half of the seventeenth century, but they commanded far less attention, and hence were less important in generating international conflicts, than were other sorts of issues. They played a role in more than one-third of the wars, but only in three could it be claimed that they constituted sufficient conditions for those wars. Territorial contests loomed more important.

### Dynastic and succession issues

I have frequently used the term "state" to describe the essential actors of international politics during and after the Congresses of Westphalia. To understand the nature of dynastic claims, which formed such an important part of late seventeenth-century diplomacy, it is necessary first to describe what we mean by state. It was not a territorially based unit, much less one encompassing a distinct ethnic group, language, or religion. Though there are important exceptions to the generalization – Sweden and Holland are particularly important in this regard – states were primarily family patrimonies. Sovereignty was the possession of a person, the king, queen, or prince, and territory was just part of the realm, almost a personal estate. "Those who held it," wrote George Clark (1958:93), "were subject to all the influences which make the owner of any kind of property, or the holder of an office, apt to magnify it and desirous at least of handing it on undiminished to his successor." Mazarin taught Louis XIV the critical importance of passing on to his successors the complex of rights, prerogatives, and powers that inhered in the throne.

According to the theories of the day, the basis of sovereignty was an act of God. The king represented a hereditary order that God had intended for the world. Thus, to forego making claims for titles to which there was some legal basis was to deviate from God's plan. Claims to provinces, duchies, crowns, cities, and other political units were not therefore primarily territorial in nature. Contiguity or non-contiguity were irrelevant. Claims were part of an obligation to fulfill a divinely inspired order.

One consequence was that people commonly regarded any act of a monarch as just, no matter how capricious and arbitrary it may seem to contemporary observers. The king can do no wrong – including launching aggressive wars – if his authority derives from God's will (Church, 1972:39). Thus, while on hindsight many of Louis's claims may seem to have been motivated purely by strategic considerations or territorial greed, in fact Louis believed he was acting in his capacity as trustee of the patrimony. In delivering instructions to Louis's diplomats at Ryswick, his secretary underlined the divine sanction for the Most Christian King's claims: "Dieu protège la justice de la cause de Sa Majesté." Diplomacy was not just a matter of bargaining over real estate; claims were of the greatest significance. They were an obligation to do God's work (Commission des Archives, 1922:XX, 510).

This proprietary view of the state vitally affected perceptions of interest, and hence of the kinds of issues that generated international conflict. The interests were as much those of a family as those of a state. The Peace of the Pyrenees, 1659, which terminated twenty-four years of Spanish–French hostilities, was as much a compact between the Hapsburg and Bourbon families as a treaty between two states. It included the betrothal of the infanta, Maria Therese, to Louis, thus sealing a bond between the two great families of Europe (Pages,

1948:216). Inter*national* politics is thus somewhat of a misnomer, or at least it is incomplete. Interconnections between state and dynastic interests were strong, but often separable. In the late 1600s, for example, the usual way to describe or understand international affairs was to enumerate the rights and pretensions of dynasts (Clark, 1958:92) rather than to analyze the clash of strategic or commercial interests. The category of dynastic claims as a source of international conflict can thus stand separately from others, particularly from the category of territory.

Yet subtle changes occurred during the period. The rigid adherence to family inheritances and rights deriving from ancient conquests and marriages began to give way to, or be complemented by, concerns of a more pragmatic nature. In the various peace negotiations of the era, one begins to see an increased willingness to conclude bargains where territories and political jurisdictions could be exchanged if roughly equivalent strategic and commercial values were involved. Both peace conferences at Nijmegen and Ryswick incorporated "exchanges and equivalents." Their justification was based on "reason and common sense" rather than on inheritances or dynastic principles (Hatton, 1980:8–9). This change was to continue into the eighteenth century, when partition and exchange became normal formulas for resolving international conflicts. The point is that territory increasingly became an exchangeable commodity. It did not remain throughout the period a sacred patrimony that rested upon uncompromisable legal and historical claims.

Despite the importance of conflicting dynastic claims as issues generating conflicts and wars, there are no examples where dynastic claims were a sufficient condition for war. In the twenty-two wars of the period, combinations of stakes were involved, even where dynastic concerns were significant. The greatest war of the period, the War of the Spanish Succession (1702–13), centred around the issue of joining the Spanish and French thrones through Philip V, Louis's grandson. A purely family affair might have been tolerable to the rest of Europe. But the joining of the Spanish Empire, with its vast holdings in Italy and the Western hemisphere, to the Bourbon state was also a critical threat to the European balance of power. None of the dynasts could have felt secure on a continent where France's power would have been greater than that of all the other states combined. Significant commercial issues were also involved. The British, in particular, could not tolerate the prospects of losing their markets in Spain, to say nothing of their lucrative trade opportunities in Spain's colonial holdings in the New World. There were multiple issues that caused the formation of the

56

anti-French coalition; the succession issue was paramount, but it was not exclusive.

### Strategic territory

Strategic territory is placed in a separate category. It could be subsumed under the broader category of territory, but the stakes are rather different. Attempts to gain territory were connected with state building and expanding tax revenues and, in a few cases, providing space for particular types of economic activities (the Cossack and Tatar requirements for grazing land, for example). Territory also offered prestige, and population resources were a factor to consider in an era when armies were becoming significantly larger.

Strategic territory, on the other hand, involved specific points that were considered important in helping to solve the dynastic states' security problems. Over the period, notions of linear defense were beginning to develop. It was a standard part of French military thought in the late seventeenth century to control the "gateways" to France, territories through which France had been invaded in the past. Many of Louis XIV's claims to territories in the Spanish Netherlands and along the Rhine, though ostensibly justified by inherited titles or ancient conquests subsequently surrendered, were really an attempt to build a series of fortified points, constituting a perimeter that could make France impregnable. Likewise, a cardinal objective of Dutch foreign policy was to garrison key fortresses in the Spanish Netherlands (the so-called barrier fortresses) as a means of providing a forward defense against French aggression. Swedish or Danish control over the Baltic sounds was critical not only for regulation of navigation and obtaining tolls for the state treasury, but also to control the passage of naval vessels. He who controlled the sounds basically controlled the whole of the Baltic area. In the Russian–Turkish zone of conflict, control over the Sea of Azov in effect controlled access to the Black Sea. Finally, British claims to territorial jurisdiction on the oceans, but particularly in the Channel, were incompatible with the commercial and naval needs of Holland, whose economy depended very heavily upon foreign trade, shipping, and fisheries. For the Dutch, access to ocean territory was not just a question of providing more advantageous conditions for solving its security problem; it was a "core interest," vital for national survival.

### Dynastic/state survival

Some of the wars of the post-Westphalian period were fought

57

over issues that were directly linked to national survival. Russia, Sweden, Turkey, or France could lose a province, a city, or a duchy without incurring significant costs to the rest of the realm. The consequences were relatively insignificant, and in any case there was always the expectation that a future war might recoup those losses. But had the Ottoman Turks succeeded in their sieges of Vienna in 1663–64 and twenty years later, the consequences would have been disastrous for the Holy Roman Empire and perhaps for all of "Christendom." We have already noted the French and British wars against Holland; a series of decisive naval and/or land victories by either power would have rendered Holland little more than a weak dependency of the victors (Mowat, 1928:157; Bourgeois, 1901:231). And Danish king Frederick IV's claims against the Duchy of Holstein-Gottorp in 1700, had they not been checked by the timely intervention of Sweden, would have eliminated one of the smaller actors of the European states system. The duke (who was Charles XII of Sweden's brother-in-law) faced the elimination of his patrimony. But to the Danes, of course, no such stake was involved; Frederick simply wanted to expand his domains, as any good king of the period might seek to do.

### Protecting religious confrères

Westphalia put an end to wars of religion. The settlement drew up not only a territorial and dynastic map of Europe, but a religious map as well. There were specific areas of religious uniformity and areas of toleration. Matters of residence, worship, church property, and civil rights were more or less well defined and no longer burdened diplomacy to the extent that they had in the previous era. Religion as a political issue did not disappear with the signing of treaties, however. Matters of succession remained contentious for many more decades, particularly in the case of England, where the struggle between the Catholic James II and the Protestant Stuarts were to invite French intervention, Dutch concern, and general animosity between regimes. In addition to Louis's strategic and commercial concerns vis-à-vis Holland, he felt considerable personal animosity toward the Dutch Republic, led by revolutionaries who had founded their order by a revolt against a hereditary ruler, Louis's great-great-grandfather. As the "Most Christian King," he had no love for the Protestant Dutch, who were practicing their own brand of intolerance against the Catholic minority. Louis would probably not have gone to war against Holland merely to protect his religious confrères, but the religious issue was at least one that, when combined with the other stakes, made war much more likely.[2] The wars between Turkey and Poland, and Turkey and the Holy Roman Empire, originated in part over religious issues. In the former, Poland resorted to arms to intervene on behalf of Catholics under Muslim rule, and in the latter religious incompatibilities were instrumental in launching the war. Indeed, Pope Urban VII made a vast effort to mobilize all of Europe to protect itself against the expanding Ottoman armies; both sides became engaged in a holy war.

But throughout the rest of Europe, religious considerations were generally put aside. One sees no evidence of their importance in the construction of coalitions, in the various peace negotiations, or in most of the dynastic claims that were pressed. At the Congress of Nijmegen, Catholics and Protestants sat together in conference, whereas just thirty years earlier they had to inhabit entirely different venues. Alliances were based solely on strategic considerations, and shared non-religious interests and the desire to get in on the spoils. A coalition of Lutheran Denmark, Catholic Poland, Calvinist Brandenburg, and Orthodox Russia sought to dismember Lutheran Sweden. During the early days of Louis XIV's reign, his chief adviser, Mazarin, the "foreign minister" of Catholic, monarchical France, made an alliance with Oliver Cromwell, the Protestant regicide responsible for the death of Louis XIV's uncle. Religion may have played a modest role in exacerbating or alleviating conflicts; but it was not, with the several exceptions noted, determinative of war and peace in the post-Westphalian era.

### Colonial competition

Wars between colonial powers were not yet an important feature of the international relations of the dynasts. For most of the seventeenth century, colonial issues were largely separate from the diplomatic problems of the continent. The colonies formed a separate military and political sphere (Symcox, 1974:14), largely because (with the significant exception of Spain) the spearhead of colonial activity resided in the great private trading companies, modeled upon the highly successful Dutch East India Company founded in 1602. These non-state actors, although chartered by royal decree, really conducted their own foreign policies. They had their own armaments, built their own fortresses, and engaged in various predatory practices against each other and against many of the indigenous peoples upon whose

[2] In fact, Louis offered Spain's Charles II substantial sums to join him in a war against Holland, ostensibly for the purpose of converting that country to Catholicism.

territories they operated and expanded. They were virtually independent powers whose conflicts did not significantly disturb the "high politics" of the royal courts. As late as 1686, notes Symcox (1974:14), Louis XIV and James II reached an agreement isolating their respective North American colonies from conflict that might break out between them in Europe.

But as the commercial stakes expanded, and as manufacturers and traders began to wield political influence, particularly in London and Amsterdam, the two spheres became increasingly coupled. The development of large-scale plantation agriculture, particularly in the West Indies, added greatly to the value of colonies, making them increasingly a focus for rivalry and for various forms of economic and semi-official naval warfare. Colonial competition was a significant factor only in the second Anglo-Dutch War, but it continued to exacerbate interdynastic relations until it was more than just a peripheral consideration in the War of the Spanish Succession. By that time, in Great Britain, Spain, and Holland, the state had transformed the interests of the charter companies into national interests, to be defended and expanded by the use of official military force. For our period, however, colonial competition as an issue area could be counted only twice as significant sources of warfare. Colonies had not yet emerged as components of "high policy."

## Balance of power/hegemony

The Nine Years War (1688–97) originated with further territorial claims and annexations by Louis XIV. Whatever Louis's purposes, he was widely regarded as having ambitions for creating a French-centred "universal monarchy," the same spectre that had hung over Europe in the sixteenth and early seventeenth centuries. Historians disagree on Louis's aspirations. Some deny his hegemonic ambitions and emphasize instead his concerns with particular territorial and dynastic "adjustments" to the Westphalia settlement (Legrelle, 1900:VI, 356). Others, citing some of Louis's own comments, argue that he sought, if not a universal monarchy, at least a hegemonic position in which he could become the arbiter of Europe. Whatever the case, the important point is not what may or may not have been his consistent concerns, but rather the perceptions of them that predominated in the courts of Europe. And there, Louis's ambitions were generally interpreted as extending beyond minor territorial rectifications and the pursuit of historical claims (Giraud, 1847:27–28; Mowat, 1928:157).

France, after all, was the epitome of the great power. Its population of sixteen million was almost four times that of England. Louis's royal pretensions were grandiose in almost every respect. Moreover, he seriously entertained ambitions to become the Holy Roman Emperor. Following the Peace of Nijmegen, when the Empire, England, Holland, Spain, Cologne, Prussia, and Savoy (originally an ally of France) coalesced against seemingly inexhaustible French military victories, Louis concluded treaties with the Electors of Bavaria, Brandenburg, Saxony, and Cologne, each containing clauses requiring the Electors to vote him, or his candidate, to the imperial throne in the next election (Wolf, 1968:414). This was not a modest proposal, and certainly not one that was met with sympathy in Vienna and the other capitals of Europe.

The event did not take place, but upon the death of the Spanish king, Charles II, a severe crisis with fundamental consequences for the distribution of power in Europe developed. Charles II's testament of October 2, 1700 read: "for the well-being of my subjects and for the peace of Christendom and all of Europe, this [Spanish] monarchy must always remain separate from the Crown of France" (Giraud, 1847:33). Charles, only too aware what would happen to the "peace of Christendom" were the Spanish crown to be joined either with the Austrian Hapsburgs or the Bourbons, did accept a Bourbon as King of Spain. But he and his fellow monarchs could not accept that the Duke of Anjou, Louis's grandson, who was to become Philip V of Spain, would also succeed Louis on the *French* throne.

Louis, having sounded Spain for cession of the Spanish Netherlands to France, and failed, attacked the Dutch barrier forts in the territory. This may not have been a sufficient *casus belli* for a European war. But by letters patent, Louis next announced that Philip V would also become the next King of France. France and Spain would thus be united, and the entire Spanish Empire would become available to the court at Versailles. Here was a clear case of impending French hegemony, a gross violation of the assumptions and intentions underlying the Westphalia settlements. Not only would the balance of power be destroyed, but significant British and Dutch commercial interests would be threatened (Vast, 1899:4–9). The combined French and Spanish navies could close the Mediterranean to British shipping, and French sovereignty over the Spanish Netherlands would reduce or block British access to central Europe. French domination of the Spanish Netherlands would constitute a mortal danger to the Dutch, who were also concerned about safeguarding their navigation rights against a French threat.

61

The declarations of war of 1702 and the terms of the "Grand Alliance" uniting the British, Dutch, and the imperials starkly outlined the stakes involved. There were, in the first place, Louis's pretensions to "universal monarchy." Also at stake were the territorial security of both the Empire (the areas along the Rhine contested by France) and Holland, freedom of commerce and navigation, the joining of the two crowns, and finally, the clear statement "que les Français ne prendront jamais possession des Indes espagnoles, qu'ils n'auront pas le commerce exclusif de ces colonies' (Giraud, 1847:43). In 1702, Louis presented the most comprehensive challenge to the Westphalian order of the entire postwar period. While he may have thought that the union of the two crowns was a family affair, he must have known that he could not act without consulting the rest of Europe. In fact, Louis deliberately provoked the war, and the balance of power issue would have been sufficient to start hostilities. The territorial and commercial issues were perhaps more the anticipated consequences of allied inaction than the issues that caused the conflict.

### Other issues

The remaining issues were of significantly less import, at least in their frequency and consequences. Wars of national liberation were not yet on the international agenda, but in 1700 Augustus of Saxony was inveigled by a Lithuanian noble to launch a war of liberation against the Swedish imperial possessions on the Baltic coast. The local nobility were mobilized and, joined by Poland, this first modern war of liberation began. It ended ignominiously with Charles XII's crushing campaign against Augustus, and with the instigator's capture, torture, and execution.

The final issue involved Sweden's military support for the beleaguered Duke of Holstein-Gottorp. In Copenhagen, this was considered a *casus belli*, and Sweden launched a successful war against Frederick IV, ending the threat to the duchy for the time being.

We end with the observation that the quest for territory was the issue that was most often involved in the outbreak of war. But it was seldom a sufficient condition. Most of the wars of the period had multiple sources; territory stands out only because it was so frequently involved. Dynastic claims were also significant, and commercial competition emerged as a major source of conflict in western Europe.

Balance of power wars were few, but they involved many more participants and lasted longer than wars whose origins lay in incompatible positions over territory, strategic points, and dynastic claims. At stake was the system of political fragmentation and the continued independence of some states, particularly of Holland. Louis XIV presented a formidable threat to the rest of Europe despite his great concerns for legalities and his care to act according to the royal conventions of the day. Europe was not to see another attempt to gain hegemony over the continent until Napoleon.

With France's defeat in the War of the Spanish Succession, the value of state autonomy had shown its resiliency. The balance of power became a means of maintaining state independence and preventing hegemony. All the other kinds of issues, however, were to continue to cause friction and war throughout Europe. We may ask, nevertheless, were there not other reasons for the recurrence of war in the states system between 1648 and Louis's defeat by 1713? We have already noted the weaknesses of the Treaties of Münster and Osnabrück. These were certainly important sources of continuing conflict. There were wars because Westphalia designed only a few artifacts to prevent or control them. But attitudes were also important.

### ATTITUDES TO WAR

Attitudes do not determine whether or not force will be used; but they can influence the calculation of risks, costs, and advantages, and they may also be reflected in the manner in which wars are fought. In the late seventeenth century, public attitudes on war had little influence on most dynasts' policies, although in the Dutch Republic, Sweden, and Great Britain, various social groups, particularly commercial classes, had significant inputs into policy-making. They were not necessarily more pacific than the nobility and court officials, although in the case of Holland, the burghers generally saw peace as a necessary condition for commercial prosperity. Public attitudes became more significant *after* wars had been launched; taxpayers carried the burden, and at times they refused to carry it any further. The lack of financial capabilities was a significant constraint on the prosecution of war, but it was less significant in decisions to go to war.

To the extent that broad publics thought about problems of war and peace, they were generally resigned to war as a fixed characteristic of human life, or as a divine punishment for the sins of people (Clark, 1958:7). War was taken for granted; causes and consequences were not the object of study or speculation. Writers were more interested in the details of diplomatic maneuvers and military campaigns (Symcox, 1974:2). The few schemes for peace that existed (Sully, Crucé, and the like) may have been known in certain circles, but they had no influence in high places. They all prescribed "action by states which those states, by their very nature, were incapable of taking" (Clark, 1958:13).

War was an institution, not just a series of disconnected events. It was a regular and accepted means of achieving and defending objectives, almost a regularized means of property acquisition (Hale, 1985:22–23). Dynastic claims had to appear just because dynasts often had to mobilize their populations, through means of propaganda, to pay for the campaigns. Popular loyalties were directed not to the nation, or even to the state, but as had been the case for almost a millennium throughout Europe, toward the royal figure.

The period under review was not especially violent. Twenty-two wars over a sixty-five-year period, in an international system of about two dozen major players, represented a decline of the incidence of armed combat compared to previous eras (Perré, 1962:II, 379–87).[3] The elements of order in the Westphalian settlements, as well as European war weariness, may have contributed to the trend. Moreover, the character of war changed in some significant ways.

Most important was that the state increasingly gained control over the instruments of violence. In the 1630s, war often created policy; by the end of the seventeenth century, war had become an instrument of policy. Standing armies commonly replaced mercenary forces. Increasingly, professional officers raised through merit systems replaced the nobility, whose military concerns were predominantly part-time. Actual campaigns became models of discipline and limited action compared to their predecessors in the Thirty Years War. There was general repugnance toward uncontrolled violence and cruelty. Etiquette and strict rules of warfare, including care for the wounded, replaced the butcheries of the first half of the seventeenth century. In 1705, Louis XIV issued orders on the holding and surrender of forts. He authorized their governors to surrender, with honor, after a small breach had been made in the walls, and a single assault had been beaten back. These instructions replaced those issued three generations before by his father, Louis XIII, forbidding a commander to surrender until a wide breach had been made in the main wall, and until several assaults had been repulsed. A century later, Carnot, a famous general of the French Revolution, worried that "what was taught in the military schools was no longer the art of defending strong places, but that of surrendering them honourably, after certain conventional formalities" (Nef, 1952:156–57). Louis's famous expert on

---

[3] Perré presents interesting figures on annual "actions de guerre" in Europe going back to A.D. 1250. The annual average for the period 1620–59 was 16. Between 1660 and 1715, the figure declined to 10.6.

siege warfare, Vauban, designed rules for warfare that were specifically designed to minimize civilian casualties. Despite some flagrant breaches of the conventions of the day by Louis's forces in the Palatine and against Genoa – through literal scorched earth policies – the sack of cities and towns became relatively rare occurrences (Symcox, 1974:3; Rabb, 1975:122).

War was an exclusive undertaking of armies and navies. Trade between nations at war was the rule rather than the exception. There was no concept of civilian responsibility for dynastic wars. Travel remained unimpeded, and passports were regularly issued for voyages to countries that were legally in a state of war. War was limited not only in terms of casualties and destructiveness, but also in social "depth." There were enemy crowns, but not enemy nations (Treasure, 1985:206).

The declining destructiveness of war is reflected in casualty figures. In the battle of Nordlingen in 1634, 58,000 troops joined the combat; about one-third died. At Oudenarde more than seventy years later (1708), 160,000 troops fought a major engagement. Fewer than 5 percent (8,000) were killed. In many instances, after sieges, the defenders were allowed to leave peacefully, taking their possessions, wives, and families, often accompanied by formal farewell ceremonies. They only left their arms behind. Given the relatively low incidence of war and the declining scale of violence, it is not surprising that general attitudes were either supportive of war or fatalistic. Certainly major military victories were highly popular. They were times of celebrations, Te Deums, and fireworks. It was only after wars had dragged on and begun to impose severe hardships on the taxpayers that opposition to particular wars developed. No general current of pacifist thought flourished in the Europe of the late seventeenth century. In general, then, public attitudes toward war did not enter the policy-makers' decision calculus.

In contrast, there is a direct connection between attitudes and war when we examine those who ultimately decided whether or not to unsheathe the sword. We look briefly at two of the heroic warriors of the day, Louis XIV of France and Charles XII of Sweden. Much of the war of the period was initiated and/or carried on by these figures. While they were perhaps not typical princes of the day, some of their colleagues – Peter of Russia in particular – modeled their own practices on the French and Swedish leaders. They also articulated and expressed the general ethos of governing circles regarding the use of force in diplomacy.

For Louis, military leadership was the quintessential role of the

65

dynast. It was the prime *métier* of the prince, the avenue through which he gained *la gloire*. A painting on the ceiling of the Hall of Mirrors at Versailles shows him flying over the waters of the Rhine in an airborne chariot wafted by angels and cherubs. This depiction of France's attack in the Palatine symbolized the heroic nature of the military undertaking. War was more than just a matter of organizing campaigns and sieges. It was a reflection of the prince's mystique, of his reputation. The prince who did not fulfill the role of the warrior was not a complete ruler. Louis's aptitude for martial undertakings was well developed. For him, war was a hobby, a sport, a Christian and patrimonial duty, and always a source of considerable pleasure (Zeller, 1955:9).

From his early youth, he was trained in military matters, above all, in the need to instill discipline, organization, and morale among the officers and troops. He took great delight in attending to the details of marches and maneuvers, and easily adapted to the rigors of long marches, hours on horseback, and deporting himself among his soldiers. His mother wrote: "[Louis] shows the greatest passion for war, and is in despair when he is prevented from going [to the front] . . . He has as much courage as anyone can have" (Wolf, 1968:182). Among his troops, Louis learned that his presence generated courage and enthusiasm; his soldiers idolized him. Even during times of peace, he would take his entourage, mistresses and all, for regular reviews of military units, much as wealthy ranchers today like to take visitors for guided tours of the "spread."

In 1661 France was at peace. The war with Spain had ended two years earlier, borders were secure, the threat of internal rebellion had receded, and the arts and commerce were flourishing. But Louis noted that it was "undoubtedly a little unfortunate to enjoy such tranquillity . . . at a time when my age and the pleasure of being at the head of my armies made me wish for a little more activity abroad" (Wolf, 1968:182). Those around him were no less hospitable to the idea of war. Among the nobility, war brought adventure and reputation. Fame, wealth, and women were the prizes to be won in battle. Those concerned with less heroic activities, including commerce, were not prominent in the royal entourage, and those who were wedded to the idea of peace as a condition to be sought were nowhere to be seen or heard. The prince who came to the throne at a time when there were no wars to be fought, no battles to be won, and no reputation to be earned was not considered fortunate for his time.

For the typical prince, then, war was instrumental, a means to many ends, and particularly to the ends of reputation and *gloire*. For Louis, these were important, but he genuinely enjoyed most aspects of war

on their own terms. News of military victories spread quickly throughout Europe, and the prestige and status of the king was intimately
connected to his fortunes on the battlefield.

In at least a few cases, concerns of *gloire* and reputation were as
important in decisions to threaten or use force as were the issues that
provided reasons for launching his armies. In his *Mémoires* (p. 123)
written for his son, Louis confessed that some of his wars had constituted a "vast field for me to distinguish myself and to fulfill the
great expectation that I had for some time inspired in the public."
On numerous occasions he let it be known that war was the most
brilliant way to win glory. Though Louis may have been puffed up
with self-importance, he was expressing ideas that were fairly
common among the dynasts and aristocrats of the late seventeenth
century.

But even on these occasions, Louis could link his personal reputation with reasons of state: reputation was an essential ingredient of
diplomatic influence. It could achieve as much or more than large
armies. He wrote: "A king never need be ashamed of seeking fame, for
it is a good that must be ceaselessly and avidly desired, and which
alone is better able to secure success of our [state and dynastic] aims
than any other thing" (Wolf, 1968:185).

Given Louis's pronounced interest in and knowledge of military
matters, as well as his commitment to the search for greater reputation
for himself and his state, it is not surprising to see that he launched
most of his wars with considerable enthusiasm. He of course made
careful calculations of costs and benefits – he was seldom reckless – but
he did not regard war as an abnormal state, something to be avoided if
at all possible. On the contrary, he had a "quick trigger," and was
persuaded on several occasions to threaten or use military force where
princes with different attitudes might well have chosen otherwise.
Tempestuous and forever concerned about his *gloire*, Louis broke off
relations with his father-in-law (Charles II of Spain), canceled all Spanish passports (a breach of the conventions of the times), and prepared
for war, all because the Spanish ambassador in procession to the Court
of St. James had hired hundreds of soldiers as personal retainers, and
sought to precede the French ambassador, who had far fewer flunkies
in attendance. An ensuing melée resulted in several deaths; Louis was
horrified. His reputation, he thought, was seriously compromised and
could be resuscitated only through war or a formal apology from
Spain. Mobilization of the French military machine was sufficient to
obtain the latter, and war was avoided. On several other occasions,
Louis was prepared to use force to vindicate his honor. The victims of

his wrath included the Pope, who, like Charles II, had to make a formal apology to the Sun King as the price for peace (Wolf, 1968:186–87).

This is not to say that Louis was a warmonger, that he had a lust for bloodshed, much less that he displayed particular pathological traits reflecting unresolved emotional conflicts. While Louis was quick to employ force, he was no nihilist. He usually thought that his wars were just. He had dynastic claims that were rooted in history and treaties. He acted according to the postulates of the political morality of the times, though perhaps with greater zeal than was typical of his peers. According to Corvisier (1979:299), Louis was profoundly religious and was imbued with the notion of just war. On hindsight (and also among many of his contemporary opponents), he may appear to have been an aggressive imperialist. His aims were by no means modest, and on his deathbed he conceded that he "had loved war too much." But he believed that he fought for the right causes, and when his wars went badly, he was often willing to make notable compromises in order to achieve peace for the "tranquility of Europe."

Louis's personality, his martial enthusiasm, and the ethos of the warrior prince constitute sufficient conditions to explain his *tendency* to threaten or use force in diplomacy. Combined with the relevant issues, they can largely explain his recourse to war in particular situations. Broad systemic conditions and the attributes of states in the system offer few compelling explanations for the wars of the late seventeenth and early eighteenth centuries. France was directly involved in 7 of the 22 wars of the period and was the instigator or aggressor in 5. Under another king, a different personality, all five of those wars might never have taken place. Louis was attempting to achieve specific objectives, and his attitudes and political style made it *likely* that he would use force to achieve them. A teleological, Clausewitzian analysis, combined with a certain pattern of attitudes congenial to the use of force to achieve or defend foreign policy and dynastic purposes, will provide us with a better understanding of the etiology of war in the period than will other models of explanation.

Charles XII of Sweden, Louis's much younger contemporary, offers a stark contrast. He had been taught by his father to avoid war "until you are dragged in by your hair" (Hatton, 1968:127). This was appropriate advice, since Sweden had reached the limits of empire and could have few further designs for expansion. The advice was essentially to keep hold of what you have. Charles himself expressed horror at the idea of aggressive war. Yet, he identified closely with his predecessors Gustav Adolph and Charles XI, both renowned warriors. Charles XII had fixed ideas about royal obligation. He was often impetuous and daring in his youth and trained himself to "be tough in mind and body and disciplined to face fatigue and danger with stoical calm" (Wolf, 1951:56). He was prepared to be a warrior, but unlike Louis, he did not go looking for action. Charles was also imbued with a high sense of morality and self-righteousness – or at least with a sense of righteousness for Sweden. He may have not sought war, but if it was inflicted on Sweden, he was merciless in his quest to avenge "unjust and treacherous invasions." These started in 1700 with the Danish–Russian–Saxon attacks on the Swedish Empire and on Sweden's ally, the Duke of Holstein-Gottorp.

Charles was to devote the rest of his life to undoing the injustice of 1700. At the age of eighteen, he led his troops in an invasion of Zeeland and canceled a siege of Copenhagen only because the Danes agreed to terms. He crushed the Russians and Saxons in their own backyards but he rejected peace offers of both Tsar Peter and Augustus and continued the war into the heart of Russia, where he suffered the disastrous defeat at Poltava. He always led his troops, but not just in administrative and logistics matters, organizing marches and supervising sieges. He actually led the charges and personally maintained the discipline and morale of his troops in battle. He was not a bureaucratic/strategic warrior like Louis. By any standards, he was extraordinarily brave.

His inflexibility was his downfall. He could not compromise. He could not accept terms unless they were of his own devising. He ruled Sweden mounted on horseback, in the Russian steppes, in barracks, tents, or fortresses, or while staying several years in semi-captivity as a guest of the Sultan after his ignominious defeat at Poltava. Charles was killed (1719) by a bullet while inspecting fortifications in Norway during his second war with Denmark. He had had numerous opportunities to terminate his wars on conditions that would have saved the Empire. He rejected all of them, despite suffering an increasing number of military defeats. Viscount Bolingbroke, the British Secretary of State, wrote to his ambassador in Utrecht, summarizing well the connection between Sweden's disasters and Charles' attitudes:

> The Heroism of the King of Sweden and the absolute Resignation of his subjects to his will, are the original causes of this disastrous [decline of Sweden]. The inflexible obstinacy which this Prince has shewn, and the high terms he has insisted upon, even at the lowest ebb of his fortunes, have made it impossible for his true friends to speak and act on his behalf. (Legge, 1925:68)

Here was a prince, then, whose personal inclination was to *avoid* war, who made no particular hobby of the martial enterprise, and who

69

sought no expansion. There is no link between his upbringing, his early attitudes toward war, and his subsequent behavior. In responding to the appeal of an ally and in fighting initially a defensive war to protect the Empire against the Russian–Danish–Saxon alliance, he acted as any prince might. But once at war, he made it his premier occupation, and nothing could turn him away from his "grand design" of severely chastising those who had unjustly aggressed against him. The "in order to" logic explains adequately the origins of his wars (use force to defend the imperial realms), but personality becomes a critical variable in explaining the duration and outcomes of those wars. The "meaning" of war for Charles was something more than a Clausewitzian concern for using arms to accomplish what other means could not. War became not just a means to protect the Empire, but a full-time profession, almost an obsession. Louis went to war easily and in his youth enjoyed the military life; but he could terminate a war as easily as he started it. Charles was initially a very reluctant warrior, but once engaged in a contest of arms, he could not end it.

# 4 ACT TWO OF THE HEGEMONY DRAMA: THE UTRECHT SETTLEMENTS

The French–English preliminaries of peace are addressed to the view of satisfying, according to the rule of reason, the security requirements and frontiers, as well as the freedom of commerce, of all parties to the conflict, and to regulate the same so that these two issues will not again trouble the European peace. It is on this basis that the treaty of peace must be founded.

Instructions for the plenipotentiaries of France at Utrecht, 1713

Three major multilateral peace conferences took place in the aftermath of Westphalia: Nijmegen, Ryswick, and Nystadt. The first two terminated Louis's wars against Holland; the latter brought to an end the Great Northern War(s). There were also bilateral settlements between France and Spain, Great Britain and Holland, Denmark and Sweden, Russia and Turkey, and several others. Nijmegen and Ryswick stand out because they introduced some diplomatic conventions and best exemplified practices such as compensation, exchange, and the role of mediation in conflict resolution. They also reconfirmed the importance of the Westphalia settlements as an outline of order for western Europe.

But they were not significant learning experiences; they dealt with particulars rather than with the generic sources of war. Following each conference, Louis XIV continued his annexations and provocations against neighbors. Individual issues were resolved, compromised, or left unsettled. It is hard to see any "authoritative allocation of values" in those conferences. None of the participants regarded the treaties as lasting solutions to the problems that had generated war in the first place (Rystad, 1980:142). The diplomats terminated wars, but they did nothing to resolve the types of issues that were leading to war. They provided no mechanisms for adjustment or peaceful change. They did not produce outcomes that carried with them a sense of legitimacy, justice, or community. They laid no foundations for cooperation. Most of the major actors remained dissatisfied. The Empire was unrecon-

71

ciled to the Westphalian solutions to territorial problems along the Rhine. France had not achieved control over all of the "gateways" to the kingdom. And the innovation of drawing lineal frontiers showed that France's defense perimeter in the north was constituted of little more than some distant strong points. This was an invitation to straighten out the lines – at the expense of the Spanish Netherlands and Holland, of course. Holland thus remained threatened by any French attempt to establish for itself a lineal defensive perimeter. Great Britain was in constant conflict with France over Louis's meddling in its domestic affairs.

The outcomes of other major settlements were hardly more constructive. Swedish–Danish hostilities continued, and Turkey and Russia regarded their peace negotiations as little more than armistices that would allow them to regroup for the next round. In the period there were three wars of revenge, where parties resorted to armed force to undo previous peace settlements. In brief, the practice of making peace in the second half of the seventeenth century offered no improvements, no concern with war as an endemic characteristic of the international system, and no formulas for bringing more "tranquillity" and "repose" to Europe. Several of the peace settlements, indeed, were the direct causes of new wars.

The Utrecht settlements provided some new insights into the problems of international relations in an environment of anarchy. Unlike the other multilateral conferences that preceded, the diplomats who organized peace following the long, exhausting War of the Spanish Succession were concerned with order and stability. There had been, in other words, something of a learning experience. There was a conscious desire to negotiate a peace that would prevent a recurrence of a certain kind of war.

But none of the governments of the day came to believe that they had to do something about the more general problem of war. No statesman or dynast presented a comprehensive diagnosis of war causation, and therefore none developed a theory of peace. The most general theoretical insight developed through the war was that the essential purpose of a peace is to protect the independence of the dynastic sovereigns by limiting hegemonic designs and policies. The purpose of the Utrecht settlements was not so much to avoid future wars as to resolve the issue of hegemony – a replay of the Westphalian drama.

There was no formal coalition planning for the peace settlement. Each state, with two significant exceptions, had its own narrow concerns and claims (Doran, 1971:119–22). For the Dutch it was a question of constructing some sort of defensive system against French aggrandizement. For the Austrian Hapsburgs, there were territorial issues in the Rhineland, namely recovery of territories lost to the French during the war, and claims in Italy. The smaller allies had the usual spoils of war in mind.

Only the French and British had broader perspectives. The former wanted to minimize their territorial losses and were generally successful in this endeavor. But more important, since they did not consider themselves aggressors and did not expect a harsh peace, they thought in terms of postwar arrangements in which they would play a central role. The keys to the French plans were to design territorial settlements that would provide each state with security, and to fortify the principle of freedom of navigation. The instructions of the French plenipotentiaries at the Utrecht negotiations insisted that the final settlement must "meet the legitimate security requirements and frontiers, as well as the freedom of commerce, of all the parties to the conflict, and to regulate the same so that these two issues will not again trouble European peace" (Legrelle, 1900:391). The instructions further noted the critical importance of the Spanish succession problem. The French also planned a postwar alliance with Great Britain, thus implying that the centrepiece of any general settlement in the western European arc of conflict must be British–French reconciliation. Although subsequent observers have noted the importance of the concept of balance of power in the settlement (e.g., Giraud, 1847:60), the French design for peace really amounted to a British–French condominium.

The British, largely through the leadership of Huxley and the Earl of Stanhope, had somewhat more elaborate plans, also dependent upon a reconciliation with France. Indeed, they defected from the wartime coalition, and contrary to the terms of the grand alliance of 1701–1702, began secret negotiations with the French in 1709. They did not have by that time a definitive scheme for peace; it developed more fully through the course of negotiations in Utrecht, but already by the time of the discussions leading to the preliminary peace, the outlines of the settlement were in place. They were contained in the 1709 instructions to Marlborough and Townshend, Great Britain's interlocutors with the French on the shape of a preliminary peace.

## THE BRITISH "PLAN"

The British plan for the pacification of Europe offered formulas for resolving four critical problems: (1) the Spanish succession; (2) security for France's neighbors; (3) the construction of a British–French

73

alliance involving mutual guarantees; and (4) the neutralization of Italy.

The diplomatic correspondence of the period makes it clear that Stanhope saw the Spanish succession question as the heart of the peace problematic. It had been the main source of the recent war, and the British considered that "the fate of Europe in general turns upon this hinge" (Legge, 1925:71). Article 27 of the preliminary peace provided the formula. Britain would recognize Philip V as the legitimate heir of Charles II of Spain on condition that Philip renounce his claims to the French inheritance. This was somewhat of a concession by the British. During the war, the allies had offered Louis XIV peace terms including the demand that he order French troops to march into allied Spain to unseat the Bourbon king – his own grandson. They also insisted that France accept a permanent prohibition against *any* connection between the French and Spanish thrones. Louis was shocked by this assault on the traditional rules of dynastic succession, and continued the war. He reluctantly accepted the more modest formula for Philip's renunciation put forth by the British in the secret negotiations (Giraud, 1847:57–58), although he was very unhappy that one of his opponents could dictate Spain's laws of succession.

Philip's attitude was predictable. Initially he refused to renounce his claim to the French inheritance. The issue was decided on the battlefield. In 1712, he signed an Act of Renunciation. The Treaty of Utrecht includes reference to it, in exchange for British recognition of Philip V as the rightful heir to the Spanish throne.

The British "Plan" (the term is used throughout the diplomatic correspondence) also included the French idea of territorial arrangements that would provide security for the states of Europe. However, the core of the arrangement was not one to the liking of the French. The centrepiece was to hem in France in the north (facing Holland), in the east (on the Rhine), and in the south. Through technical arrangements negotiated in Utrecht and Baden and through an Austro-Dutch Barrier treaty, Holland was given the right to garrison eight strong points in the Austrian Netherlands (Spain having ceded the Netherlands to Austria), and thus provided with forward defense against French expansion. In the Baden treaty, France returned its military conquests on the right bank of the Rhine to the Empire. And in the south, the frontier between France and Savoy was adjusted among Alpine peaks and plateaus in such a manner that Savoy became a significant barrier against French military movement into Italy (Ward, 1908:437–59; Legge, 1925:360–67). By this means, Austria and France became effectively separated, and Richelieu's project of the 1630s to provide France with an avenue for intervention into Italy was formally terminated. Utrecht thus implicitly revoked France's status as the primary guarantor of the Westphalia settlements.

The third component of the British scheme of pacification was a set of mutual guarantees of the territorial and succession settlements, combined with an alliance of the Big Four: Great Britain, France, Holland, and the Empire. Through a series of secret negotiations, France and Great Britain created the core of the alliance (1716). The essential terms of the reconciliation was French recognition of the British succession to the House of Hanover and official abandonment of support for the Catholic James II. This aspect of the general European pacification thus depended upon the prior settlement of British–French dynastic conflicts.[1]

As early as 1712, British diplomats had realized that the "Plan" would be incomplete without Austrian participation. Through diplomacy and a series of promises for support of Austrian claims in Italy, the Empire was brought into the alliance (Quadruple Alliance, 1718), and thus made to appear as an organization of the powers devoted to upholding the Utrecht settlements against the revisionist policies of Spain (Chance, 1909:29).

The final component of the pacification scheme was the neutralization of Italy. In the Utrecht settlements, Austria received Naples, Milan, and Sardinia, and Savoy received Sicily, Nice, and a slice of Milanese territory. The rest of Italy was placed under the guarantee of the signatories (Bourgeois, 1901:241). For the British, the idea was ostensibly to "preserve the liberties of the [Italian] princes and states for which the Queen [Anne] has expressed a very tender concern" (diplomatic instructions to Bishop of Bristol and Earl of Stafford, November 11, 1712, in Legge, 1925:45). Sentimentality aside, the idea of neutralization was a device to prevent future French–Austrian conflict over Italy, and thereby to help obtain Austrian adherence to the Utrecht settlements and to the Triple Alliance.

In the British "Plan" and throughout the peace discussions there was only minor concern with commercial questions. Britain made significant territorial demands and ultimately received Minorca and Gibraltar from Spain, and Newfoundland and Nova Scotia from France. However, these were not critical components of the "Plan." Although they were later to provide important bases for British naval

[1] A more cynical interpretation (Bourgeois, 1909:I) is that rather than attempting to create a pan-European security system, George I and his first minister, Stanhope, were really attempting to enlist French support for George's Hanoverian claims against Sweden; the French Regent, the Duc d'Orleans, was only seeking to obtain British support for his own succession to the French crown should the sickly Louis XV die.

power in the Mediterranean, they also produced rivalry and conflict with France in the New World. Overall, however, the commercial dimension of the War of the Spanish Succession was not at the forefront of the designs for pacification. One gains the impression that most of the governments were seized by territorial and dynastic issues, not with trade (Legrelle, 1900:408–409). There were, finally, some other territorial adjustments reflecting the fortunes of the battlefield. These were not directly connected to the British plan for pacification, whose territorial contours were designed primarily to impose restraints on France and to provide borders of the major powers with maximum defense value.

The final negotiations were held in Utrecht during 1712 and 1713. They resulted in six bilateral treaties (Great Britain–France, Great Britain–Spain, France–Holland, France–Prussia, France–Savoy, and Savoy–Spain). It took a further year to arrange peace between France and the Empire (the Treaties of Rastadt and Baden), and even more time to arrange the settlement between Spain and Holland, and Spain and Portugal (1715).

### OUTCOMES

The succession issue was not entirely resolved through the Utrecht settlements. Charles VI, the Holy Roman Emperor, also had a claim to the Spanish throne and refused to consider Philip V as the rightful heir to Charles II. This issue was not resolved for several years, but the spirit of the Utrecht Treaties made it clear that neither the French nor the British would countenance the reunification of the Spanish and Austrian branches of the Hapsburg family. The Treaty of Baden (1714), though not definitive on this point, in effect reconfirmed the Westphalia settlements.

To the extent that dynastic politics remained an important ingredient of international conflict, the Utrecht settlements were simply a replaying of the Thirty Years War drama. No family was going to dominate European politics, and no settlement would be fashioned that provided any possible opportunity for a dynast again to seek "universal monarchy." The resolution of the family question thus ensured that some sort of balance of power rather than a form of hierarchy would provide the context of international politics in the future. The settlement excluded both the Austrian Hapsburgs and French Bourbons from Spain; regardless of who would succeed Philip V, it could not lead to a union of French and Spanish crowns.

One sees in the method of settlement an important erosion of the dynastic principle and a precedent for the formal intervention of the great powers into national laws of succession. In addition to the dynasts determining international political relationships, the Powers would jointly determine the dynastic issues of each state (Bourgeois, 1901:239). This was a practice that was to extend into the nineteenth century. It became both a source of international conflicts and a means of reconciling them. But in this settlement, it was the critical formula for peace.[2]

Compared to Westphalia, the Utrecht settlements generated only partial compliance and legitimacy. While the British were generally lenient toward the French – in part to stop French meddling in British succession questions, and also to enlist French adherence to an alliance–Austria and Spain, in differing degrees, did not accept the outcome of the war and postwar negotiations. Charles VI, the Holy Roman Emperor, maintained his claim to the Spanish crown and initially refused to accept the division of Spain's Italian holdings, of which he was a major beneficiary (McKay, 1977:158). He still had unrequited claims for the expiring Medici dynasty in Tuscany, and he would not accept Savoy's spoils in Milan, where he had his own ambitions. Indeed, Britain and France ultimately had to support some of Austria's claims in Italy as the price of getting it to adhere to the Triple Alliance (Bourgeois, 1909:I, 464–68). This policy was incompatible with the notion of Italian neutralization and was to become a source of conflict, not a means of preventing it. By 1718, Austria had become reconciled to most of the principles and provisions of the Utrecht settlements, but it was a reluctant partner at best.

Spain was the big loser of the war and the settlements. Although it signed a series of treaties with its military opponents, it never accepted their terms until forced to do so in 1719–20. As soon as the Succession War was over and the Utrecht Treaties signed, Spain set out to undo the entire settlement. It had been stripped of the Netherlands, all of its Italian holdings, and Gibraltar and Minorca. It was compelled to grant British participation in the Asiento trade, shipping African slaves to Latin America and to the Spanish West Indies. Philip V had been forced to renounce his claim to the French throne. The settlements were thus a major national and dynastic humiliation. Whereas the French, the initiators of the war, had survived with relatively mild

[2] In another innovation, the Utrecht settlements recognized Frederick William, Elector of Brandenburg, as King of Prussia. Again, the powers determined the status of one of Europe's rulers. Though Louis abhorred the Utrecht succession formula as a gross intervention in French and Spanish Salic Law, he was congenial to the plan to raise the status of Prussia's ruler.

77

territorial concessions, and had emerged with a British alliance, Spain was stripped of all of its non-contiguous European territories, its succession was determined by outside powers, and it remained diplomatically isolated. The assault on the settlement came quickly.

Shortly after signing the Act of Renunciation, Philip V resurrected his claim to the French throne, causing the British government to instruct its ambassador in Paris to "show how scandalous, how infamous a violation of the publick Faith, and of all which we ought to hold sacred either as Christians or as men, such an attempt [to reclaim the French throne] would be ... nor what fatal consequences must necessarily and immediately follow" (Legge, 1925:74). In 1717 Spain attacked to recover Sardinia. The following year it invaded Sicily, again to recover territory lost under the Utrecht settlements.

The Quadruple Alliance, a semblance of a system of governance for the system, had failed to deter Spain. Now it was used for coercion, to enforce the Utrecht settlements. Again, it was Stanhope who was the main architect of this peace-keeping coalition (Chance, 1909:31). After obtaining Austria's adherence to the Triple Alliance through the promise of support for its further Italian claims, Great Britain went to war against Spain (1719) on behalf of the alliance. A British fleet destroyed the Spanish naval opponent, convoyed Austrian troops to Sicily, and generally oversaw the defeat of Spain's attempt at retribution and revenge. In 1719, French armies invaded Spain proper. The whole issue was ultimately resolved through the Hague Treaty of 1720, in which Spain renounced most of its Italian claims. Philip V's ambitious wife, Elizabeth Farnese, however, was to seek royal seats in Italy for her sons for several more years.

The Triple and Quadruple Alliances were thus both a primitive system of governance and an enforcement organization. But their domains were limited to the terms of the Utrecht settlements. There is the germ of an idea here: with the congresses of the powers at Cambrai and Soissons in the 1720s, we may see a forebear of the nineteenth-century Concert system (those congresses accomplished little; they were mostly devices for consultation and stalling for time). At a minimum, there is a recognition that any conflict issue on the continent is now a legitimate matter for great power consultation. There is a component of a society of states or international order in the sense that anybody's business had become everybody's business. But that is about as far as it went.

Westphalia had set up the outlines of a European order. It failed to provide any mechanism for ensuring it, aside from the rights of the main guarantors, France and Sweden, to intervene in the Empire to enforce the terms of settlement. But as we have seen, it was France that became the main postwar revisionist power; there was no provision in the settlement to take care of this eventuality. Hence, ad hoc coalitions had to be formed to defend the settlement and the principle of particularism against Louis's challenges. The idea of coalition politics to maintain a particular distribution of power thus became strongly ingrained in European thinking about peace. The British idea for enforcement of the Utrecht settlements was to incorporate mutual guarantees, and ultimately to provide 6,000 troops as a contribution to the defense of Holland. Guarantees were included in the major treaties and alliances, but they were insufficient mechanisms for ensuring the continuity of the peace, just as they had been insufficient after 1648. It took a military coalition to compel the Spaniards to accept the war settlements.

## ANALYSIS

Penfield Roberts (1947:240) has noted that the men who fashioned the Utrecht settlements were not thinking like their successors of 1814, 1919, or 1945. They were not self-consciously aiming at some sort of permanent international organization, much less at a federal solution to the problem of particularism. Yet, the British "Plan" for pacification had some order-building elements to it. The recipe combined ingredients that would resolve the outstanding succession issues, provide for the legitimate security interests of the western European states, buttress those with mutual guarantees and alliances, and remove a major arena of confrontation by the device of Italian neutralization. This was a rather sophisticated plan, in some ways more advanced than the ideas incorporated in the Treaties of Osnabrück and Münster. In particular, it envisaged the use of *community* power to enforce the settlement, rather than sanctioning unilateral intervention, as had been provided for in Westphalia. There is thus the idea that the entire community of states has a stake in preserving the peace settlement.

The diplomatic correspondence of the time also reflects the negotiators' sensitivity for, and understanding of, the security concerns of the major actors. The statesmen of the postwar period were not concerned solely with maximizing national or dynastic spoils. To be sure, the Empire and Holland did not see much beyond their narrow concerns, and they certainly did not display any enthusiasm for a diplomatic restructuring of the continent. It was British leadership, supported more or less enthusiastically by the French, that served as the "educator" of the Utrecht settlements. Like Richelieu, Stanhope and George I could rise above the clamor of immediate "satisfactions" (though these were never lost sight of; George was as interested in aggrandizing his Hanoverian domains as he was in constructing a peace system) to try to fashion something more than just another armistice, a waiting period in which the powers would regroup for the next fray.

Despite these positive points, the potential for constructing an enduring peace system was not fulfilled. There was no general condemnation of the use of force. The treaties established no consultative mechanisms or institutions for managing or resolving international conflicts in general. The Quadruple Alliance was designed to enforce only the particulars of the Utrecht settlements. Although the practices of the early 1700s with regard to dynastic succession issues had been internationalized, there was no attempt to come to grips with the phenomenon of persistent and conflicting dynastic claims. The War of the Spanish Succession had taught no lessons in this regard. No sooner had the treaties been signed than the dynasts were back to pleading their causes, intriguing among each other, signing aggressive and defensive alliances, and making plans to rewrite the map of Europe. In this domain Great Britain was as predatory as the rest. George's beloved Hanover had designs on Sweden's Bremen and Verden. Prussia was on the move to relieve Sweden of its Pomeranian possessions. Elizabeth Farnese pushed her claims to Italian thrones for her sons, to the point of war. Austria was not content with its sizable territorial and dynastic spoils from the war against France; it had to have even more. Of the European powers, only Holland and France seemed to be satisfied.

Nothing in the Utrecht negotiations or settlements addressed the continuing problem of dynastic and national aggrandizement. The settlements sought, through mutual guarantees and alliances, to provide means of security for most of the system's members. But they did little to diagnose or prescribe remedies for the *sources* of insecurity. There could obviously not be any permanent peace because the settlements had done nothing to locate the permanent sources of war. Like Westphalia, Utrecht looked to the past. It solved a particular problem posed by France and Spain, but it failed to address the more generic problems associated with a system of independent sovereignties driven by dynastic ambitions.

The terms of settlement imposed on Spain prevented rather than encouraged assimilation of the defeated power. The settlements thus lacked legitimacy and immediately gave rise to plans for a war of revenge. Another building-block of an international order was thus left out.

The preliminary negotiations of 1709 and the treaties signed at Utrecht were the first to mention explicitly the importance of the balance of power (Donnadieu, 1900:75). The territorial adjustments and the Quadruple Alliance were designed to prevent the recurrence of hegemonic drives by any of the powers. This aspect of the settlements worked throughout the remainder of the century. It was an order-building device of sorts because it sustained the independence and autonomy of the individual powers; it was an essential component for perpetuating international anarchy. The statesmen of the day, however, did not see it as a solution to the problem of war. Thus, we cannot link it to any variations in war incidence in subsequent years.

The settlements were static rather than dynamic. There were no provisions for peaceful change. Like Westphalia, they sought to freeze a moment in history: the results of the war against France and Spain. They also assumed the extension of wartime collaboration into the postwar period. The plan for pacification anticipated that the main foreign policy goals of the victors, and of the assimilated French dynasty, would be to preserve the settlement. The assumptions proved incorrect. Once the settlements had been fashioned and Austria and Spain had been inveigled or coerced to accept them, the sense of common purpose dissipated. Once again, each dynast went on a rampage of particularistic claims, each designed to increase dynastic and state power, none consistent with the assumptions and spirit of the Utrecht settlements. It is for this reason that Bourgeois (1909:I, 239) argued that the Triple and Quadruple Alliances were less peace-keeping or peace-enforcing instruments (institutions of order) than systems for mutual support of territorial and dynastic claims; they were alliances that bred rather than managed conflict.

Finally, the architects of the settlements were mainly backward-looking. They concentrated on preventing a recurrence of French expansionism rather than examining the kinds of issues that were likely to spawn international conflicts in the future. Theirs was more an act of restoration than of creation.

The reasons for the incapacity of the peace settlements of 1713–15 to bring about a declining incidence of war and to build the bases of collaboration also include those attitudes toward war outlined in the previous chapter. The peacemakers at Utrecht did not yet consider that war was an endemic problem of the system of states. War, despite the exhaustion of state treasuries it caused, was not yet regarded as an evil, much less a threat to other dynastic or national values. Indeed, the limited nature of war in the late 1600s and early 1700s may well have made it a very practical and attractive instrument of policy, one not to be avoided, but to be used. It is for this reason that the purpose of peacemaking was not to devise means to modify, control, or eliminate the use of force, but rather to resolve the immediate problems that had brought on the previous war.

Almost seventy years later, Rousseau explained why princes could never use the community interest as a guide to policy. In a system of anarchy they are compelled to pursue immediate and particularistic concerns, even when they know that in the long run this will not only damage the common interest, but their own security as well. The Utrecht settlements and their aftermath confirmed Rousseau's insight. Even those, like the British, who were firmly committed to the settlements and who created the alliances that would enforce their terms soon began to conduct their foreign policies in violation of their spirit and principles. After 1717, they were once again making dynastic and territorial claims, engaging in colonial competition, and plundering the smaller territories of Europe or the declining empire of Sweden. Utrecht had taken care of Louis and his grandson. It did little to reform the system in which Louis was only playing a typical, if exaggerated, role. The issue of hegemony was resolved for almost another century. However, resolving the problem of endemic war and establishing the basis of international cooperation were not among the achievements of the Utrecht settlements. Like Westphalia, these settlements were a victory for the principle of anarchy against hegemonical designs; they were not a victory for peace.

# 5 THE LETHAL MINUET: WAR AND PEACE AMONG THE PRINCES OF CHRISTENDOM, 1715–1814

It is certainly a remarkable occurrence, that in the course of three most eventful centuries, amid so many bloody wars, so various and decisive negotiations, so frequent changes of power . . . , amid a general anarchy of all social, civil, religious, and political relations, not one independent state was annihilated by violent means.

Emmerich de Vattel

Powerful sovereigns succeed only too often in winning for themselves partisans and allies who are blindly devoted to their designs. Dazzled by the glitter of a present advantage, seduced by their greed, deceived by unfaithful ministers, how many princes become the instruments of a power which will one day swallow up either themselves or their successors.

Friedrich von Gentz

The War of the Spanish Succession did not suggest that something may have been wrong with the structure, actors, or processes of the new system. Quite the contrary: it demonstrated that it was working very well. The international problem of the late seventeenth and early eighteenth century was not war. It was hegemony, Louis's version of the old drive for domination that had animated Charles V and the Spanish imperialists. It was the success of the system in solving that problem, via the operation of the balance of power, that helps account for the absence of concern about the problem of war. No one in authority, as a result of the recurring wars of the post-Westphalia system, believed yet that a new kind of thinking about war and peace was required. No one appealed for new attitudes or new institutions. The system of states was still in its infancy. Any peace had to confirm sovereignty, not limit it. The system's main actors were not yet ready for reform. It was enough to reconfirm the Westphalian formulas, albeit with a few new twists.

The peacemakers at Utrecht, despite their limited achievements, failed to recognize that Louis, for all his idiosyncrasies, represented a type of behavior that was likely to recur in a system of anarchy. They managed to resolve the succession problem and they built a set of territorial fetters around France, but they did not even consider that the typical modes of princely behavior, the ambitions for expansion and state centralization, would guarantee the recurrence of war. Utrecht thus represented more continuity than change in the habits and patterns of diplomacy and war. No new international system came into being, either in structure or process. The consequences of anarchy and the attitudes toward the use of force underwent no transformation.

Nevertheless, there were some interesting changes that occurred slowly in the issues that generated international conflict in the post-Utrecht international system. Table 5.1 lists the wars for the period 1715–1814.[1]

There were thirty-six conflicts, or one every 2.85 years. This represents no significant change from the one war each three years, on average, for the immediate post-Westphalia period. There are, however, some differences that are not immediately apparent from the list of wars.

The number of militarily active powers in the European system declined significantly in the eighteenth century. Prior to the War of the Spanish Succession, small sovereignties, such as Cologne, Württemburg, Hesse, Holstein, Münster, Bremen, and Genoa, were active participants in the wars of the latter half of the seventeenth century. These actors – as allies, objects of territorial plunder, or suppliers of armed forces – virtually disappeared from the scene of international war after the Utrecht settlements. For the entire century, only Sardinia, Saxony, Bavaria, Venice, Naples, and Savoy, as minor powers, became involved in the wars of the period, and only infrequently.

War became, then, primarily a great power activity, and a very frequent one at that. Russia was an original combatant (or military intervenor) 14 times during the century, followed closely by Austria and France (12 each), Great Britain (11), Prussia (8), and Turkey (7). Holland was at war only twice (once the victim of Prussian intervention), as was Naples. Sardinia and Venice were original combatants only once in the one hundred-year period. One sees, then, a pattern to military activity in the sense that it is essentially the same cast of

---

[1] The number of wars in table 5.1 differs from those offered by Luard and others, although not in significant proportions. The differences are accounted for by the way general wars have been handled, and by other rules of inclusion and exclusion. Luard, for example, counts the wars of the French Revolution and the Seven Years War as single conflicts. I list each original war, even though the wars eventually became blended into a single conflict. I have included wars of national liberation only if they became internationalized through external intervention. Thus, the list includes the Polish uprising against Russia and Prussia in 1794 and the American colonies' war against Great Britain which eventually involved French intervention. The Irish uprising against England in 1798 is not included, because it remained an intra-empire problem.

Table 5.1 *Wars and issues, 1715–1814*

| Wars/armed interventions | Issues for original combatants |
|---|---|
| 1. Turkey–Venice, 1715–1718[a] | 1. territory |
| 2. Austria–Turkey, 1716–1718 | 1. territory |
| 3. Austria, France, Great Britain, Holland–Spain, 1718–1719[a] | 1. dynastic claims (S.)<br>2. strategic territory (S.)<br>3. enforce treaty obligations (allies)<br>4. honour of crown (G.B.) |
| 4. Spain–Great Britain, 1727–1729[a] | 1. dynastic claims (S.)<br>2. strategic territory (S.)<br>3. commerce/navigation |
| 5. Russia–Poland; France, Spain, Sardinia–Austria, 1733–1735 | 1. dynastic/succession (R., P., F.)<br>2. territory (F., Sar., S.)<br>3. strategic territory (S., Sar.) |
| 6. Russia–Turkey, 1736–1739 | 1. territory<br>2. commerce/navigation (R.) |
| 7. Great Britain–Spain, 1739–1740 | 1. commerce/navigation |
| 8. Prussia–Austria, 1740–1742 | 1. territory<br>2. national unification/consolidation (Pr.) |
| 9. Russia–Sweden, 1741–1743[a] | 1. territory<br>2. dynastic/succession |
| 10. Prussia–Austria, 1744–1745[a] | 1. territory<br>2. defend/protect ally (Pr.)<br>3. dynastic claims |
| 11. Austria–France, 1744–1748 | 1. territory<br>2. dynastic claims |
| 12. France–Great Britain, 1744–1748 | 1. commerce/navigation<br>2. colonial competition |
| 13. France–Great Britain, 1754–1763 | 1. commerce/navigation<br>2. colonial competition |
| 14. Prussia–Austria, Russia, 1756–1763 | 1. territory<br>2. state/regime survival (Pr.) |
| 15. Sweden–Prussia, 1757–1762 | 1. territory |
| 16. Russia–Poland, 1764 | 1. dynastic/succession<br>2. protect religious confrères (R.) |
| 17. Turkey, Poland–Russia, 1768–1774 | 1. territory<br>2. commerce/navigation (R.)<br>3. protect religious confrères (R.) |
| 18. Spain–Portugal, 1776–1777 | 1. territory (boundary dispute)<br>2. colonial competition |
| 19. American colonies–Great Britain, 1776–1783 | 1. national liberation/state creation (col.)<br>2. maintain integrity of empire (G.B.)<br>3. commerce/navigation |

Table 5.1 *continued*

| Wars/armed interventions | Issues for original combatants |
|---|---|
| 20. France–Great Britain, 1778–1783 | 1. colonial competition<br>2. territory<br>3. commerce/navigation |
| 21. Austria–Prussia, Bavaria, 1778–1779 | 1. dynastic/succession<br>2. territory<br>3. defend/support ally (Pr.) |
| 22. Great Britain–Holland, 1780–1783 | 1. enforce treaty terms<br>2. commerce/navigation |
| 23. Prussia–Holland, 1787 | 1. government composition |
| 24. Russia, Austria–Turkey, 1787–1792 | 1. territory<br>2. state/regime survival (T.)<br>3. protect religious confrères (R.)<br>4. empire/state creation (R.) |
| 25. Sweden–Russia, 1788–1792[a] | 1. territory<br>2. government composition<br>3. state/regime survival (Sw.) |
| 26. Russia–Poland, 1792–1793 | 1. government composition<br>2. maintain regional dominance (R.) |
| 27. France–Austria, Prussia, 1792–1797 | 1. government composition (A., Pr.)<br>2. state/regime survival (F.)<br>3. protect/defend ally (A., Pr.) |
| 28. Russia, Prussia–Poland, 1794–1795 | 1. national liberation/state creation (P.)<br>2. territory (Pr.)<br>3. government composition |
| 29. France–Great Britain, Austria, Prussia, Portugal, Turkey, 1798–1802 | 1. territory<br>2. ideological liberation (F.)<br>3. strategic territory<br>4. empire/state creation (F.) |
| 30. Great Britain–France, 1803–1807 | 1. enforce treaty terms (G.B.)<br>2. territory<br>3. commerce/navigation |
| 31. Turkey–Russia, 1806–1812[a] | 1. territory<br>2. state/regime survival (T.)<br>3. strategic territory (T.)<br>4. commerce/navigation<br>5. protect religious confrères (R) |
| 32. Russia–Sweden, 1808 | 1. territory<br>2. commerce/navigation<br>3. strategic territory |
| 33. Great Britain, Spain–France, 1808–1814 | 1. national liberation/state creation (S.)<br>2. defend/support ally (G.B.)<br>3. balance of power/hegemony (G.B.)<br>4. maintain integrity of empire/state (F.) |

Table 5.1 *continued*

| Wars/armed interventions | Issues for original combatants |
|---|---|
| 34. Austria–France, 1809[a] | 1. territory<br>2. maintain integrity of empire/state (F.) |
| 35. France–Russia, 1812–1814 | 1. commerce/navigation (R.)<br>2. territory<br>3. empire/state creation (F.)<br>4. state/regime survival (R.) |
| 36. United States–Great Britain, 1812–1814 | 1. commerce/navigation<br>2. territory |

[a] Wars of revenge (8 = 23%).

characters that reappears in the diplomatic contests that led to wars.

Finally, the wars of the continent became intermingled. Whereas in the latter half of the seventeenth century there were two or three distinct theatres of military conflict, the events in one not significantly affecting the others, by the mid eighteenth century isolated wars often became joined. The War of the Polish Succession (1733–35) involved, among others, Russia in the East and France in the West. Most of the major powers were at war with each other in the latter 1740s, and the Seven Years War (1756–63) was pan-European, although it began as a set of distinct conflicts, with France versus Great Britain and Prussia versus Austria as the main pivots. From St. Petersburg to Paris, Stockholm to Sicily, and the Crimea to Lisbon, all of Europe constituted a single zone of conflict, a distinct international system which even included, albeit as a distinct anomaly that had not really joined the club, the Ottoman Empire (Naff, 1984).

### ISSUES THAT GENERATED WARS

Table 5.2 lists the distribution of issues for the thirty-six wars of the period. They represent the stakes for which the original combatants were willing to go to war. The percentages do not reveal any significant discontinuities, nor do the rankings. Territory and commerce/navigation continue as the issues that most often generated conflicts. The percentage of dynastic claims and succession issues declines from 14 to 9 percent, certainly not a trend, but as we will see, of some significance nevertheless.

There is an increase in the number of different issues that appear, even though four of them are sources of war in only one instance. The total for the eighteenth century is seventeen different issues, com-

Table 5.2 *Distribution of issues that generated wars, 1715–1814*

| Issues | Frequency | % of all issues | Previous period % |
|---|---|---|---|
| Territory | 24 | 26 | 24 |
| Commerce/navigation | 13 | 14 | 16 |
| Dynastic/succession | 8 | 9 | 14 |
| State/regime survival | 6 | 7 | 10 |
| Strategic territory | 6 | 7 | 10 |
| Government composition | 5 | 5 | — |
| Colonial competition | 4 | 4 | 4 |
| Protect religious confrères | 4 | 4 | 6 |
| Empire/state creation | 4 | 4 | — |
| Defend/support ally | 4 | 4 | 2 |
| National liberation/state creation | 3 | 3 | 2 |
| Enforce treaty terms | 3 | 3 | 6 |
| Maintain integrity of state/empire | 3 | 3 | — |
| Other | 4 | 4 | 2 |
| Total | 91 | 97[a] | |

[a] Rounding error.

pared to twelve for the post-Westphalia period. One of them is particular to the wars of the French Revolution (ideological liberation), but the other new entries came from wars in the pre-1792 period. This may mean that international relations are becoming more complex, as new values and stakes become the object of competition and quarrel, adding to those that were already present in the age of Louis XIV. Several new issues are significant and will become even more important as sources of international conflict in the nineteenth and twentieth centuries: government composition, state creation, ideological liberation, and the indicator of the "hardening" of sovereignties, quarrels over the exact location of national boundaries.

Table 5.3, which counts the number of times that a particular issue served as a source of war, gives a somewhat different impression, where we begin to detect the outlines of possibly significant changes. The attempt to gain or hold territory, *qua* territory, was a significant source of conflict in two-thirds of the wars, an increase of twelve percentage points over the post-Westphalia period. Commerce and navigation issues maintain their second place ranking, with no change between the two eras. Confirming the impression gained from the percentage distribution of issues in table 5.2, dynastic and succession claims show a decline of nine percentage points. We see here the beginning of an important shift in international politics. An essential purpose of state diplomatic and military activity was to expand territory. This was for both state-building and military security purposes. In contrast, the pursuit of titles, once the hallmark of all sovereigns' patrimonial concerns, began to abate. Interstate or international relations are taking the place of interdynastic relations. There is no sudden transformation, to be sure, but the pattern which was to become distinct in the nineteenth and twentieth centuries already appeared years before the French Revolution.

None of the other figures provides reason for extensive comment. Wars in which state or regime survival were at stake decreased in percentage, but as I will suggest below, the behavior of the main states in the eighteenth century was often predatory. Strategic territory as a bone of contention declined a little, probably because of Sweden's secure control over the Baltic straits after the end of the Great Northern War. Although this problem was resolved more or less permanently, new strategic issues that bedevilled international relations emerged from the Utrecht settlements, in particular British control of Minorca and Gibraltar. We now turn to an examination of those sources of war that changed in some important ways during the eighteenth century.

### Territory

Territory in the eighteenth century provided the essential ingredients for national power – population from which to conscript, shanghai, or purchase soldiers; a base of productivity that could gener-

Table 5.3 *Issues that generated wars, 1715–1814*

| | As source of war | % of wars | Previous period % |
|---|---|---|---|
| Territory (including boundaries) | 24 | 67 | 55 |
| Commerce/navigation | 13 | 36 | 36 |
| Dynastic/succession | 8 | 22 | 31 |
| State/regime survival | 6 | 17 | 23 |
| Strategic territory | 6 | 17 | 23 |
| Government composition | 5 | 14 | — |
| Colonial competition | 4 | 11 | 9 |
| Protect religious confrères | 4 | 11 | 14 |
| Empire/state creation | 4 | 11 | — |
| Defend/support ally | 4 | 11 | 4 |
| National liberation/state creation | 3 | 8 | 4 |
| Enforce treaty terms | 3 | 8 | 14 |
| Maintain integrity of state/empire | 3 | 8 | — |
| Other | 4 | 8 | 4 |

ate taxes and raw materials; and control over trade routes. Whether for domestic or external reasons, the policy-makers of the day commonly saw territory as the essential component for meeting general welfare and security objectives and for creating modern centralized states. Many of the dynasts ceased to think of territory in terms of family patrimony, regarding it instead as a commodity that could be employed for a variety of domestic and foreign policy purposes, particularly for cementing alliances and for providing "compensations" in peace settlements.[2] These practices provided a certain amount of flexibility in the international system – territories could be traded to avoid, prosecute, and terminate wars – but they represented a departure from previous eras, when territorial ownership was deeply rooted in legal rights, family compacts, ancient marriages, and feudal titles.

For some, territory became an essential basis for state consolidation and state-building. Non-contiguous family holdings became highly vulnerable to predation in a system where compact state territories increasingly became the rule. Prussia, for example, was throughout most of the eighteenth century a congeries of territories, separated by Polish provinces, bisected by minor principalities, and basically devoid of resources aside from sand and forests. Silesia, the object of Frederick II's aggression in 1740, resolved a number of pressing problems for a dynast whose ambitions were to model Prussia on the centralized states of France, Great Britain, and Spain. It provided Frederick with a number of valuable benefits: consolidating state boundaries, a greater population from which to fashion a disciplined professional army, a tax base to pay for that army, and domains extensive enough to match Frederick's notions of what constituted great powerhood (Gooch, 1947:12; Cowie, 1963:191).

Russia was the second great expansionist power of the era. It waged a series of wars against Turkey to gain access to the Black Sea and to bring the Tatars and Cossacks under effective control from Moscow. The extent of Russian territorial expansion was so great that by the end of the century Catherine the Great could dream of creating a Russian Empire that stretched from the Pacific to the Greek Islands. The foundation for this vast empire lay in the territories that Peter the Great, his successors, and Catherine annexed through their many wars against

[2] In 1742, for example, Cardinal Fleury offered Charles Emmanuel of Sardinia the Duchy of Milan as a bribe to join France in an alliance. France, of course, did not own Milan at this time. Following the War of the Polish Succession, Tuscany was given to the Duke of Lorraine as a form of compensation for having been unsuccessful in obtaining the Polish throne. In 1812, Metternich offered Prussia most of Saxony as a reward for joining the anti-Napoleon coalition. The King of Saxony, of course, was not consulted on the matter. There are many other examples of territorial arrangements made without regard to laws of succession, much less to the wishes of the local population.

the Ottoman Turks and Sweden. In the Russian case, territorial expansion seemed to feed upon itself. As the victories grew, so did the appetite for even greater annexations. This was in marked contrast to Frederick who, having snatched Silesia from Austria and carved slices off Poland, was content to devote the rest of his days to protecting those valuable gains.

Throughout the period contests over territory generated more wars than any other issue.

### Commerce and navigation

The issues of commerce and navigation underwent some significant changes during the eighteenth century. In the previous period, governments could disassociate themselves from some of the questions typically seen as matters of "low policy." In the eighteenth century the linkages between trade, navigation, and state interests became firmly established. Problems of trade monopoly, privateering, the rights of neutrals during war, and smuggling all combined to produce the War of Jenkins's Ear in 1739. The war was sought by a faction in the Parliament which, despite earlier agreements between Spain and Great Britain, wanted to acquire Spanish possessions in the West Indies, longed to break the Spanish monopoly of trade in the area, and claimed that despite the huge British naval supremacy in the Caribbean, the Spanish version of a coast guard was harassing British shipping (a typically silly incident which cost a Captain Jenkins his ear in a scuffle with Spanish officials provided the excuse to declare war on Spain). The critical issue related to navigation: the right to search versus the right of free navigation.

The Anglo-Dutch War of 1780–83 was fought around similar problems – this time it was the Dutch who championed the rights of neutrals to trade with belligerents (the American colonists). In the eastern part of the system, Russia's attempts to control the Crimea were rooted in the stake of commerce and navigation on the Black Sea. The Turks were simply not willing to allow Russia a foothold in an area they considered their backyard. It was only through a series of wars that, by the end of the century, Russia was sailing fleets not only on the Black Sea, but into the Aegean and Mediterranean as well. It would only be a matter of time until the Bosporus and Dardanelles would become another source of friction between the two empires.

If problems of navigation contributed frequently to crises and wars, views on trade were beginning to change. By the middle of the century, even the major rulers and their advisers were beginning to abandon mercantilist doctrines which taught that the best way of enriching the society and the state treasury was to impoverish neighbors. Under the influence of the Physiocrats and others, the new wisdom of the late eighteenth century was that economic welfare is better served by promoting agriculture, industry, and commerce within the state's borders than by attacking the trade of foreign countries. The commercial issue that was a contributing factor to wars was not so much trade in general, as the attempts of the colonial powers to maintain monopolies of trade with their overseas territories (Nef, 1952:265). Until Napoleon instituted his continental system, trade declined in importance as an issue generating war.

### Dynastic claims and succession

This issue underwent profound changes in the 1715–1814 period. Rights of succession had been at the core of international conflict for several centuries. Ancient titles, marriages, cessions, and annexations not only provided a dynast with a patrimony, but also established the *right* to rule. They were the bases of regal political legitimacy. The territories that reverted to a prince, king, or queen were less significant than the rights that inhered in them.

In the eighteenth century, as territory took on increasing importance for state-building, defense, and general foreign policy purposes, concerns for succession began to relate less to the right to rule (who has the better claim to succeed in a particular jurisdiction; who is the true king, queen, or prince?) than to other values derived from territorial possession. As Luard puts it (1986:101, 156), territory no longer resulted from a claim; the claim resulted from the demand for territory. Dynastic rights were systematically violated in the numerous territorial exchanges of the period. Even the selection of monarchs became a matter of strategic and diplomatic calculation, for the convenience and interests of the powers, and not a matter of discovering the correctness or priority of competing legal claims. Matters of succession, in other words, had become fully internationalized, and the means for selection were either negotiated agreements among all parties concerned or the verdicts of the battlefield.

Legal claims were often trotted out, but not in the same way that they had been in the latter half of the seventeenth century. Louis XIV may have cooked up far-fetched claims in the War of Devolution, but they were believable claims, and he was a prince who believed strongly in inherited rights. To leave them in abeyance was to neglect patrimonial duties. In contrast, Frederick the Great never hid the fact that his legal claims to Silesia were pure fiction. After deciding to launch his war against Austria, he directed one of his subordinates to work up a case that Silesia really belonged to Prussia. The official contrived a case, much to the surprise and amusement of Frederick, who lauded him for being an excellent charlatan (Luard, 1986:101). The ambitious Elizabeth Farnese, wife of Philip V of Spain, sought for almost twenty years to obtain thrones for her sons. Failing to do so through war (1718), she kept pressing her claims until in 1727 and 1735, she succeeded in getting the powers to provide them with duchies in Italy. She had a family claim to Parma and Piacenza, but her sons received their titles in other jurisdictions. Napoleon completed the perversion of the dynastic principle by appointing his commoner relatives to Italian, Belgian, and Spanish thrones. There was no question of legal inheritance or of rightful succession. In brief, the dynastic principle, if not dynasticism, underwent a process of dilution or corrosion in the eighteenth century to the point that it seldom contributed to wars. Hereditary rights were now fig leaves for other kinds of claims, usually territorial.

But in another sense succession problems were critical in contributing to the wars of the period. They offered unique opportunities for predation. As Blainey points out (1973:68–69) in his analysis of "death watch wars," eight wars in the eighteenth century were "heralded or influenced by the death of a monarch." The explanation is that the impending or actual death of a prince created a period of uncertain succession, or succession by a weak and inexperienced leader. Opportunities for aggression increased in these circumstances. Aggressors may have stated that they were fighting on behalf of the "right" successors, but in fact they were usually fighting for other spoils.

### State/regime survival

It is part of the conventional wisdom about the character of eighteenth-century diplomacy that dynasts and governments pursued limited aims with limited means (Cowie, 1963:126). Vattel, as the quotation at the beginning of this chapter suggests, was among the first to propose this view. This was supposedly an era of balance, of proportion, of a pan-European culture, of a society of states, the prime rule of which was to respect the privileges and obligations of sovereignty. In many ways this characterization is correct, and certainly so in relation to the conduct of warfare. But how limited were state objectives?

93

In the course of most wars, states sought marginal gains, a little territory here, a title there, the reconquest of territory lost in a previous war, control over key areas of strategic or commercial importance, the breakdown of monopolies over colonial trade and the like. But with a frequency that belies the popular image of restraint and constraint, the dynasts and princes also sought to destroy each other. With some frequency, they developed plans and projects literally to dismember each other. This was the practice of "partition," a euphemism for predation. During the period under review, there were at least eight planned and three executed "partitions."

1. In 1742, France, Prussia, and Bavaria, all ready with trumped up legal claims (Bavaria claimed *all* of the Hapsburg holdings except Hungary) planned to partition Austria.
2. Under the Treaty of Warsaw (1745), Saxony and Austria, with the complicity of Russia, planned to downsize Frederick's Prussia to the original pre-1713 borders of Brandenburg, with the king reduced to his former status as an Elector within the Empire.
3. At the beginning of the Seven Years War, Austria, Saxony, and Russia almost succeeded in partitioning Prussia.
4. Russia, Austria, and Prussia partitioned Poland in 1772.
5. Russia, Denmark, and Prussia planned a partition of the remnants of the Swedish Empire in 1773–74.
6. In 1787, as part of Catherine's "Greek Project," Austria and Russia planned to partition all of Turkey's European territories.
7. Poland was further partitioned in 1792.
8. Poland was eliminated as a sovereign state in 1795.

If we add to these cases the attempts by Napoleon to redraw the map of Europe, the incorporation of Belgium into France, and particularly his rearrangement of Italy into a set of "Republics," thereby eliminating actors rooted in ancient titles and laws of succession, the idea that state aims were strictly limited has to be amended substantially. Many of the monarchs did seek to destroy each other, and had not fortune (e.g., the death of Tsarina Elizabeth and her replacement by the Frederickophile Peter III when Frederick was at the point of military defeat) and the alliance system worked fairly well to preserve many states' independence, some of the major actors would have been eliminated from the states system.

If all the plans for partition had succeeded, not only would European history have been quite different, but the notion of moderation would never have developed. Von Gentz' emphasis on predation, quoted at the beginning of this chapter, would seem to be a more accurate depiction of eighteenth-century international relations than the conventional view. Napoleon may have had unusually great aspirations, and he was blatant in his disregard for questions of succession and other traditions, but what he sought was not entirely unique. In many ways his ideas represented a continuity with the aspirations of Philip V, Joseph II, and Catherine the Great. The stakes in 17 percent of the wars of the period involved state/regime survival.

### Colonial competition

Colonial competition continued unabated during the eighteenth century. The difference from preceding eras was that the tangle of actors and interests – privateers, smugglers, colonists, overseas troops, and commercial spokesmen in courts and legislative assemblies – all became embroiled in the development of state policy. Colonial politics frequently became "high politics" even if they never commanded as much attention as did continental affairs (Cowie, 1963:211). It was no longer a question of conflicts between private trading companies and a few settlers. Colonial governors, national navies, forts, and garrisons representing the monarchies were all involved. As the economic stakes in the colonies increased, so did the commitments of the sovereigns to promote and protect those interests. Colonial policy now became national policy, and the linkage between colonial wars and continental wars became firmly established. The War of Jenkins's Ear melded into the War of the Austrian Succession. The operations of French and British armies and navies during the Seven Years War extended from remote regions of Canada to the battlegrounds of central Europe. Incidents in the nether reaches of colonial and settler areas, once of little note or significance in the royal courts, now became *causes célèbres* among parliamentarians, lobbyists, and royal advisers. It was the parliamentary spokesmen of commercial interests who goaded Walpole into recommending war against Spain in 1739. And various commercial interests in Great Britain strongly supported George III's policy of coercing the American colonists to behave like good British subjects, that is, to maintain the monopolistic and mercantilist trade structure between colonies and the mother country.

In comparison to other issues, however, colonial competition did not constitute an important source of war. It was an issue in 11 percent of the wars (9 percent in the previous period), and embroiled primarily Spain, France, and Great Britain. The other powers were not involved. They were busy seeking to expand their territorial holdings closer to home and remained largely indifferent to the colonial activities of the "Western" great powers.

95

## Government composition

Another common view of the characteristics of eighteenth-century international relations was that, like religious differences, government composition did not seriously affect diplomatic alignments and wars. Monarchies and republics not only coexisted, but regularly made alliances (Austria–Venice, 1718, France–United Provinces throughout the post-Utrecht period, French support for the American colonists, and the like).

Yet the composition of governments had a major impact on strategic interests, and the dynasts frequently intervened militarily to impose certain constitutional arrangements that would benefit parties that were more or less sympathetic to their own interests. Russia's constant intervention in Polish affairs throughout the century may have been unusual in its frequency, but it was by no means unusual as a type of coercive activity. In 1733, for example, the Polish Diet had elected Stanislas Leszczynski, father-in-law of Louis XV, to the throne. His competitor, August III of Saxony, called in Russian troops to install him instead. Later, among her first official acts, Catherine installed her former lover, Stanislaus Poniatowsky, on the Polish throne, contrary to the wishes of the Poles and to the constitutional arrangements of the country. In 1772–73, Sweden and Russia came to the brink of war following a royal *coup d'état* by Gustavus III in Stockholm. In the Peace of Nystadt (1721) Russia had guaranteed the integrity of the Constitution of Sweden. This offered a pretext for Catherine to pose as the protector of Swedish constitutional arrangements against royal usurpation. Catherine was not, of course, interested in the domestic affairs of Sweden as such, but saw in Gustavus III a threat to Russian interests in the Baltic (Bain, 1984:I, 145).

The Declaration of Pillnitz (August 1, 1792) is often considered the first ideological diplomatic manifesto of the eighteenth century. The Duke of Brunswick, acting on behalf of the Austro-Prussian alliance, issued this famous statement threatening intervention against France if the revolutionary regime caused harm to Louis XVI – the king who had already sought to escape from the odious tasks he was facing in confronting the revolutionary leadership by his flight to Varennes. This statement was the immediate cause of the first of the French Revolutionary Wars, but it was not the first time that a power intervened on behalf of a particular constitutional order abroad.

Six years earlier, a Dutch popular party had deposed the Stadtholder, William V, Prince of Orange, for alleged maladministration. This action started a civil war, into which Prussia intervened. Frederick

96

William II espoused the cause of the deposed Stadtholder and demanded instant satisfaction from the rebels, who rejected it. In 1787 a Prussian army overran Holland and reinstated William at The Hague. This was all done in the name of maintaining a "legitimate" ruler against the demands of a popular assembly.

The French revolutionaries thus did not inaugurate the practice of breaching the rights of sovereign nations to order their domestic affairs. Again, the notion of an international politics of moderation is not entirely warranted by the practices of the post-Utrecht era. Whereas it had been customary for centuries to contest royal successions, a practice that continued throughout the eighteenth century, the installation or maintenance of regimes by foreign bayonets was a relatively new feature of eighteenth-century international politics, although it had been practiced occasionally by the Holy Roman Emperor and by the British and French in India. The "age of sovereignty" did not preclude violations of its principles. Domestic politics was already becoming internationalized. Fourteen percent of the wars in the century following the Utrecht settlements had government composition as one of the main contributing sources. This is an issue that gained increasing prominence as a source of international conflict in the nineteenth and twentieth centuries.

### National liberation

In the previous period, only one war of national liberation took place: this was the uprising of the Livonian nobility against Swedish rule. By the late eighteenth century, two more international wars occurred as the result of national uprisings. In both cases, the rebellions were genuinely popular and not just the cause of the landed gentry. The American colonial rebellion was broadly based (though there were significant numbers of British loyalists as well). The Polish uprising against the partition of the country by Austria, Prussia, and Russia was just the first of a series of futile and tragic attempts at the assertion of autonomy and independence by the Poles.

The third war of national liberation took place in Spain (the Peninsular War), in which Great Britain, for its rather more extensive purposes against the Napoleonic system, intervened on behalf of the Spanish guerrillas who sought to expel the French and their imposed Bonaparte king. A particularly vicious war, it demonstrated that not all European populations would remain passive in the exchange, purchase, and conquest of territories that were arranged to suit state and dynastic purposes. Henceforth, the views of the population, which

97

were seldom of concern to the diplomats of the eighteenth century or during most of the wars of the French Revolution, were going to make an impact on the formulation of foreign policy and major peace settlements. Only 8 percent of the wars of the post-Utrecht period were conflicts of national liberation, but the issues that underlay them soon join territory as one of the most important sources of international conflict in subsequent eras.

### State/empire creation

Territorial expansion was an integral part of the state or empire-building enterprise in Europe (I keep it distinct from territorial expansion-by-discovery elsewhere; most colonial annexations were unrelated to the state-building enterprise except that they often provided revenues for the royal treasury). Prussia and Russia in particular linked their territorial claims to their need to build centralized states on the French model.

As the successor to Brandenburg, Prussia was initially a hopeless state. Its territories were spread throughout northern Germany, many of them non-contiguous. For the most part, these were non-defensible and offered numerous opportunities for opponents to press claims of sovereignty and inheritance over them. The Silesian aggression and Frederick's championing of the partition of Poland were really attempts to create a state in the image of Great Britain or France: an organization that was geographically, economically, commercially, administratively, and militarily viable.

One can have perhaps somewhat more sympathy for Catherine the Great's grandiose ambitions when we understand that throughout the eighteenth century, as in preceding eras, Russia remained not much more than a vast marshland subject to constant invasion from Sweden, from Poland, by the Ottomans, the Tatars, Cossacks, and others. Peter I had made great strides in creating a modern state fashioned upon European lines, but it remained extremely vulnerable to foreign incursions. There was, then, as after 1939, a certain defensive motivation in Russian territorial expansion, as well as an effort to create a political organization that could compete on equal terms with the Europeans. If Russia was going to have contacts with the West, as Peter insisted, it had to be able to operate on the basis of national strength. This would require, above all, a modern military establishment and access to European markets and sources of supply. To be constantly interdicted by the Swedes, Poles, and Ottomans was inconsistent with the state- and military-building enterprises.

Yet, to impute such far-seeing objectives is to indulge in post hoc explanation. Certainly Peter understood the long-range requirements for modernizing Russia, but even he became concerned primarily with securing bits and pieces of territory for the immediate advantages they offered. Most of the wars against the Turks also had these narrow purposes, and hence are listed in table 5.1 as wars in which specific territories are at issue. But when we come to Catherine, in addition to these narrower concerns, she did develop a great project for creating (or recreating) a Byzantine Empire, nominally independent, but really under control of the Russian throne. There were religious questions involved – Russia throughout the eighteenth century posed as the champion of Orthodox rights in the Muslim Ottoman Empire – but Catherine was more concerned with a vast military-commerical-ethnic enterprise. The war of 1787–92 was initially undertaken to bring this vast plan into effect. As in the case of so many wars of the eighteenth century, however, long-range plans were scuppered by short-term tactical necessities, by the vagaries of usually unreliable allies (Austria), and by the opportunities available to other states. While Russian forces were tied down in the south, Sweden took retribution against earlier losses. Sweden's attack on Russia in 1788 put an end to Catherine's empire-building project. If Sweden had not gone to war, others might well have stepped in to prevent Catherine's planned partition of the Ottoman Empire. As in so many cases, the system of many great powers worked in various combinations to prevent those with seemingly excessive ambitions from achieving their objectives.

We need not dwell on the importance of empire creation during the Napoleonic period. Where Catherine failed, Napoleon succeeded – almost. For the first time since Louis XIV's plan to unify the Spanish and French crowns, the major power of the system was committed to a fundamental transformation of international politics. Napoleon assaulted virtually every value and stake for which nations had been fighting over the last several centuries: rights of dynastic succession (which Napoleon violated repeatedly); national survival (the virtual dismemberment of Prussia in 1806, and Napoleon's invasion of Russia in 1812); commerce and navigation (the continental system); territory (France's extensive annexations at the expense of Belgium, the Rhineland, Switzerland, and Italy); colonial competition (battles fought throughout the West Indies, in North America, Mauritius, the Mediterranean, and elsewhere) and the numerous means Napoleon employed in his conquests to sustain his continental hegemony and his system of plunder that could pay for the costs of sustaining France's imperial armies abroad.

The ultimate stake of the early French Revolutionary and Napoleonic Wars was the survival of the states system. Thus, while state and empire creation accounted for or contributed to only 11 percent of the wars of the period, they were in fact major sources of international conflict. They were wars to create new imperial orders, pitting the principles of hierarchy against political pluralism. In the Revolutionary and Napoleonic Wars, some of the pre-Westphalia issues were resurrected; and as in 1648 and 1713, the forces of pluralism, via the operation of the balance of power, were to prevail. Napoleon's defeat laid the issue to rest for another century.

### Ideological liberation

This was a new issue in international politics. It arose initially from the French revolutionaries' response to the threat of externally sponsored counter-revolution. By 1792, Austria and Prussia had become moderately concerned about the fate of the French monarchy. But acting as traditional great powers of the era, they were not overly concerned about the domestic political arrangements of France. This was the case even after French émigrés had urged Leopold of Austria to intervene on behalf of Louis XVI, who was in virtual captivity in Paris. A series of incidents and mutual exchanges of insults between Vienna and Paris ultimately led to the Pillnitz declaration, designed to protect the French king, but in fact viewed in Paris as the harbinger of Prussian and Austrian intervention against the revolution. Several months after the declaration was received in Paris, the revolutionary regime declared war on Austria and Prussia. France's stated purpose was to protect the revolutionary regime against impending outside intervention. The facts were somewhat otherwise.

> Inflaming the revolutionary imagination with a threat of a collective counterrevolutionary crusade, the members of the Coalition were primarily concerned with anything but the destruction of the French Republic. The most significant event in their eyes was the partition of Poland, the ramifications of which seemed to be infinitely more crucial for the general balance of power in Europe than the rise of a democratic regime in France. Here was a classic case of mismatched stakes and misperceptions. (Kim, 1970:74)

In the revolutionary atmosphere of Paris in 1792, what was to start essentially as a defensive war to save the revolution soon became transformed into a war of ideological liberation. This was not to be expected, since those who made the revolution neither desired nor expected to use war as an instrument of national policy. Quite the contrary. The publicists of the day had been raging against the "bad" wars of the king, the greedy annexations, the balance of power, and all that smacked of hypocrisy and futility in dynastic diplomacy. It was commonly thought that the foreign policy of a free people would be pacific, and as democracy spread, a major result would be international peace (Best, 1982:72). In 1790, the Constituent Assembly had even renounced all wars of conquest. But after some initial and unexpected victories (Valmy, Jemappes), French revolutionary foreign policy sought to spread the blessings of liberty, equality, and fraternity to the oppressed peoples of Europe. In November 1792, the Convention offered "fraternity and assistance to all peoples who seek to recover their liberty." With a nation now in arms, France had the military means to liberate others – not, however, without insisting that those who were to be liberated had to help pay for the costs. And those who did not welcome French liberation were forced to be free (only the Savoyards really embraced the French Revolution as their own cause and requested French annexation). In one speech enthusiastically received in the Convention, a speaker noted that the Belgians (Austrian Netherlands) were too slow and stupid to know what was good for them; they should be compelled to be free. Ideological liberation was supported by ideas of "natural borders" for France, so annexations were not always undertaken solely for humanitarian or ideological reasons. Concerns of state security operated no less during the expansionist phase of the revolution than they had during the times of the Bourbons.

The zeal for ideological liberation did not last very long. For both domestic and international reasons, Robespierre and the revolutionary regime by late 1793, abandoned messianic revolutionary expansionism. There were no more conquests in the name of spreading the revolutionary articles of faith, and the government declared that it was ready to coexist with monarchical regimes so long as they did not threaten France or its revolutionary regime (Kim, 1970:88–89). But slowly the French armies of liberation or occupation were turned into instruments of imperial expansion. The Thermidorians annexed the Austrian Netherlands in 1795, and two years later Napoleon, ostensibly in the name of the revolution, but more in order to plunder and pay for the maintenance of French armies and navies abroad, undertook his Italian campaign, creating "states" in Italy as he went along.[3] Ideological liberation continued to play a role in Napoleonic conflicts, but the ideas of the revolution were more fig leaves to cover up less

[3] These included the Cisalpine Republic, the Ligurian Republic, the Roman Republic, and, except for Geneva, which was annexed to France, the Helvetic Republic.

commendable foreign policy purposes. I therefore list ideological liberation as a source of only one war, the War of the Second Coalition, and even here it is only a marginal issue (it is not listed in the War of the First Coalition because liberation did not become an objective until *after* the war was underway).

### WAR IN THE POST-UTRECHT INTERNATIONAL SYSTEM

Though the objectives of states in the eighteenth century were not always limited, the conduct and consequences of war were substantially muted. There were high casualties in many wars – often due to disease – but by historical standards they were in no way exceptional. One of the reasons war was not considered a serious problem requiring systematic diagnosis and prescription was that it was not highly destructive.

Wars were limited in the style of operations and the focus of planning. The Thirty Years War had featured marauding armies living off the land, looting, pillaging, and in general lacking any discipline. In contrast, the armies of the eighteenth century (including the early French revolutionary wars), in keeping with the philosophies of elegance, poise, and balance of the age, fought according to strategies of incremental gains and maneuvers. They did not seek to annihilate the opponent, and in any case they had not developed techniques of destructive pursuit. Prudence was not solely a result of the temper of the times, however.

Professional armies cost money. Even if they were constituted from the "scum" of society (as was commonly acknowledged),[4] they still had to be paid for. They were an asset that could not be risked in great pitched battles. Even a victory in a great decisive battle could prove to be a loss if the casualties were too high. Campaigns were thus organized to secure maximum advantages compatible with the security of one's forces. In military planning the arts of siege warfare, fortification, marches, maneuvers, and logistics took precedence over preparations for mass battles and annihilations. Naval warfare, given the conditions of the eighteenth century, also proved to be indecisive and often not particularly destructive (Palmer, 1986:94–95; Nef, 1952:165; Howard, 1986:72).

[4] According to the strategist Guibert, the profession of the soldier was abandoned to "the most vile and miserable class of citizens – a soft and timid multitude." Frederick II remarked that if his soldiers began to think, "no one would remain in the ranks" (Nef, 1952:306–07).

Restraint was not only a characteristic of eighteenth-century battles and strategy. Attitudes toward civilians also changed significantly in the years after the slaughters of the Thirty Years War. Military planners and commanders made serious attempts to preserve society from the ravages of war. Certainly there was no attempt to involve civilians in the conduct of warfare, and in most spheres of life commercial and other contacts between societies continued much as in peacetime. It was Frederick the Great's ideal that, when engaged in war, the civilian population should not even be aware that a state of war existed (Treasure, 1985:207). Until the French Revolutionary and Napoleonic Wars, looting was an exceptional feature of the military–civilian relationship. Cities were not sacked if they capitulated before a final assault, and even where they held out to the last, soldiers were given strict time limits on the rampaging they could carry out after victory.

The level of military technology and costs of forces explain in part the character of war in the post-Utrecht period; but they provide only a portion of the explanation. A more important part of the explanation lies in the role of manners in eighteenth-century society. Attitudes toward war reflected the ideas of the age, particularly those in France, which were usually imitated by almost all other Europeans. Manners and *politesse* inclined rulers, ministers, ambassadors, and military leaders to exercise great decorum and restraint. Most military officers came from the aristocracy, where manners were a *sine qua non* for developing any sort of reputation. Through the officers, as exemplars, the rules of etiquette extended to the battlefield. Above all, this meant dignified and humane treatment of the defeated and wounded (Nef, 1952:393). Illustrations are readily available from the military history of the period.

Nef (1952:393) describes the battle of Fontenoy, just east of the river Scheldt, during the War of the Austrian Succession:

> There . . . a French army . . . defeated an Anglo–Austrian–Dutch army commanded by the Duke of Cumberland, in one of those battles of slow movement characteristic of the age of limited warfare . . . Before the fighting started, Captain Lord Charles Hay, of the Grenadier Guards, ran in front of the allied line, doffed his hat to the French enemy, drank to them out of a pocket flask, shouted a taunt, and called for three cheers from his men. The salute and the cheers were returned by the French, who waited for the English to fire the first shots after Hay had rejoined his company. Thus, as a prelude to battle, officers went through respectful formalities, understood and accepted by both sides, after the fashion of two gentlemen approaching a doorway.

The termination of battles was no less ritualized, as provision was

103

made for the exchange of prisoners, care of the wounded, and drafting terms of surrender. Formal parades and other ceremonies often marked the end of a battle or siege.

Although matters changed significantly during the French Revolutionary and Napoleonic Wars, the officers' code of conduct did not. Officers commonly regarded military leadership as an honorable profession, and reputation in the guild was based as much on observance of gentlemanly manners as on heroic leadership in battle. During the Peninsular War, where the Spanish guerrillas fought a particularly brutal war against the French army of occupation (and thereby invited reprisals), French and British officers – opponents in the field – regularly consorted with each other after battle. They enjoyed the fellow-feeling of officers and had much more in common with each other than with Britain's erstwhile ally, the Spaniards, whose brand of guerrilla warfare they both loathed (Best, 1982:179).

The transformations in the art of warfare wrought by the French Revolution and Napoleon are well known and need no elaboration here. It is sufficient to point out that the changing nature of warfare in the last years of the eighteenth century had little to do with technological innovation, and much to do with the formation of a citizens' army and the development of ideological foreign policy goals. The *levée en masse* of 1793 was prompted by a series of French military defeats at the hands of the Prussians and English. Although the French revolutionary leaders had already created a volunteer civilian army, it was not up to the task of parleying early victories in 1792 into a general peace favorable to French national and revolutionary interests. Robespierre's government thus took the radical action of mobilizing the entire country on a war footing. This was not just a question of instituting conscription – that was already an unprecedented novelty – but also of instilling the idea that all citizens were obliged to assist in the prosecution of the national war effort. Other measures included economic mobilization, government control of prices and wages, and a system for requisitioning matériel. Nothing of this kind had been seen previously in Europe. Here was the citizen soldier replacing the "scum" that had populated the ranks of dynastic armies. He was fighting not to survive, to overcome the effects of unemployment, or for adventure, but for his country. His emotional and material stakes in the army would be crowned by his personal share in its politics (Best, 1982:56). There was to be tremendous military potential not so much in the size of the army, but in its enthusiasm. Already the ideas of Jacques de Guibert, who had written several years earlier about the great potential for national wars and who criticized ideas of limited war, were coming into effect.

The creation of the citizen army (or more accurately, the blending of the volunteer, conscription, and regular armies) made possible a number of military innovations. Brigades and divisions numbering thousands of troops could be arrayed in long lines. Movement could replace maneuver; and perhaps most important, the availability of reserve troops reduced significantly the risks involved in massive battles. Casualties could easily be replaced. The citizen army was thus to be *used* in controlled violence, and not to be spared for fear of having no reserves. Plentiful human resources, motivated by patriotic and ideological fervor, provided a margin of safety that the mercenary armies lacked. Desertions declined, indeed became rare, and while casualties rose significantly, conscription and the policy of making the victims of French "liberation" pay for the costs of war provided an almost limitless capacity to conduct campaigns. The creation of a national army "could not but add to the increasing dynamism of violent contacts between nation-states" (Kim, 1970:91).

There was now an inseparable connection between the purposes of diplomacy and the means available. During the French Revolutionary and Napoleonic Wars, the French state acted not only in terms of defined interests (liberation, territorial annexation, and empire-building) deriving from ideology and national needs, but increasingly in terms of what was possible. The means began to dictate ends (Kim, 1970:94–95).

The French armies lived off their conquests, and the prospect of loot helped to supplement ideological fervor. The armies could not subsist on French territory, so they were kept abroad, their costs covered by taxes and special levies on those whom they occupied. The careful tailoring of means to ends, characteristic of international politics in the post-Utrecht system, gave way to ceaseless war, at times without any seeming objective beyond loot and plunder; enrichment of *la grande nation* was sufficient reason to undertake military activity (Howard, 1986:82; Best, 1982:92–93).

### THE MEANING OF WAR

Many of the political writers of the century between the Utrecht settlements and the Congress of Vienna abandoned the fatalism and apathy that characterized perspectives on war in the post-Westphalia period. Consistently with many of the assumptions of the Enlightenment, they argued that permanent peace was possible. They had confidence in the power of the mind to alter, build, or control political conditions so as to achieve desired ends. The works of the

Abbé de Saint-Pierre, Vattel, and Kant are known for their analyses of war causation and their proposals for reordering the international system. In the case of Kant, it was a less mechanistic approach, the argument being that man, through the sufferings of history, could learn his way out of the predicament of perpetual warfare. There were at least two reasons for the writers' optimism.

There was, above all, the growth of the common European culture, a common universe of customs, beliefs, and concepts that transcended the multiplicity of languages and sovereignties. The multiple ties that bound the Europeans underlined their affinities rather than differences. Listening to Burke, one would have thought that the inheritors of the traditions of Christendom had more or less resolved the problem of war: "Nothing is so strong a tie of amity between nation and nation as correspondence in laws, customs, manners, and habits of life . . . They approximate men to one another without their knowledge and sometimes against their intentions" (quoted in Nef, 1952:268). In a multinational society of common manners, political institutions, intellectual tastes, and artistic fashions one could indeed assume that these constituted sufficient conditions for creating leagues of princes and other types of international organizations to deal with the problem of war.

The second source of optimism was commercial. The old mercantilist ideas were rapidly disappearing under the assault of new economic theories that celebrated the rewards of international trade. Rousseau was the significant exception; he thought that increased trade would lead to increased international conflict. His ideal society of states was one of isolation and autarky among its members. But among the others, including Montesquieu and Kant, trade was an important pacifying factor.

The sense of a European society and optimistic views of the century's great thinkers may have helped to limit the nature of war, and perhaps even the purposes of foreign policy (Nef, 1952:268–69). But in general, the progress of civilian thought on war and peace was not matched in diplomatic practice, either before, during, or after the French Revolution. We have already seen how, prior to 1792, wars recurred; how rulers plotted to destroy each other; how smaller actors were bartered like so much real estate, and in the case of Poland, eliminated; how dynasts interfered in the constitutional arrangements of their neighbors; and how many monarchs (Catherine in particular) and their advisers pursued goals that were hardly limited.

The limited nature of warfare may have been the problem. The costs of war were so negligible compared to previous eras that the dynasts were not prepared to regard the military enterprise as any sort of aberration or exception to the norms of the day, much less an evil that required reforms of international practices and customs. The policy-makers may have been aware of the writings of philosophers and publicists, but they were not prepared to accept the messages in them. Despite recurrent wars, the leading figures of Europe appeared to be satisfied with the state system created in 1648 and reconfirmed in the Utrecht settlements, even if they were not always content with their own position in that system.

Among the groups that ultimately decided on questions of war and peace, there was no hint of pacifism, much less the idea that war was some sort of social ill or a social institution that could be eliminated through reason and international institutional devices. Quite the contrary. The reigning monarchs of Europe were in the service of the nobility, and the political values and interests of the nobility heavily influenced the outlook of the key decision-makers.

Since the Middle Ages, the principal occupation of the nobility throughout Europe had been warfare. This did not change in the eighteenth century. War to the French or Swedish nobleman of 1740 meant opportunity, financial gain, reputation, and many other things. As Dorn (1940:5) explains:

> [The nobility's] psychological orientation, their traditions, their ambitions, their sense of honor, their very language were military. Everywhere they constituted a more or less highly integrated military caste, everywhere a considerable number of them found in military activity their only outlet and their natural source of political influence. It was a rooted tradition that the proper occupation of a nobleman was to serve as officer in the army ... and all of them accepted war as a necessary part of the system. In this sense warfare became a function, if not an actual necessity, of the structure of European society. For the aristocracy an extension of frontiers signified a multiplication of offices and an improvement of their chances of advancement. Nobles were in need of occasional wars to distinguish themselves; their class interests coincided with the tradition of the crown, which had made warfare a legitimate and necessary occupation of kings ... The specific causes for which the monarchy went to war were often indifferent enough, for the nobility and ruling classes were satisfied with any war.

The recurrence of war must be set against the intellectual background of the aristocrats and dynasts who, although they took for granted that peace was preferable to war, usually chose war to the non-achievement of valued objectives. War avoidance was not a maxim of good government. Certainly the general attitudes prevailing among the

107

intelligentsia of Europe placed some constraints on types of warfare, and perhaps even on its incidence, but no dynast was ready to concede yet that in the hierarchy of political values peace was at the top. The commitment to peace, if there was one at all, was supremely conditional. In the matrix of policy calculation, distaste for war ranked far below expectations of gains and fear of defeat. General commitment to Europe's "repose" did not mean that war should be avoided except in highly exceptional circumstances. Wars had to appear just, but it was not difficult to find reasons for engaging in it. Frederick the Great revealed frankly the numerous circumstances in which the use of violence was justified:

> All wars whose sole design is to guarantee against usurpation, to maintain unquestionable rights, to guarantee the public liberty and to ward off the oppression and violence of the ambitious, are agreeable to justice. When sovereign states engage in wars of this kind, they have no reason to reproach themselves with bloodshed; they are forced to it by necessity and in such circumstances war is a lesser evil than peace.

(quoted in Luard, 1986:346–47)

To Frederick, preventive and pre-emptive wars were also acceptable, a view he put into practice in 1756. Before he became king, he wrote:

> A prince ought rather to engage in offensive war than wait till desperate times come on . . . It is a certain maxim that a prince should rather prevent than be prevented; great men have always been successful when they make use of their forces before their enemies take such measures as tie their hands and suppress their power.

(Luard, 1986:349)

The presumption in favor of peace was thus precarious; it was seriously tested by Frederick's attack on Silesia in 1740. Although his behavior was roundly condemned by his peers, they could not fail to see that he had won an important prize by organizing a deceitful military blitzkrieg (he planned the attack while professing his pacific intentions toward, and admiration of, the new young Empress, Maria Theresa). Rather than drawing the conclusion that steps ought to be taken to curb this kind of activity, they began to emulate it. Frederick's early penchant for the sword was soon enough copied by Maria Theresa, sworn to revenge her loss, by Joseph II of Austria, and by Catherine the Great.

Decisions to declare war were seldom the result of some unforeseen crisis, the end product of misperceptions, faulty decision-making processes, or lack of mutual understanding (though there were examples of all of these). Most wars were carefully planned, sometimes years before the event. Austria organized for almost two years before attacking Turkey in 1715. Elizabeth Farnese and her main adviser, Alberoni, plotted for many months before undertaking to reverse the results of the Utrecht settlements. Maria Theresa spent more than ten years preparing to reverse the loss of Silesia. Russia devoted the better part of the century organizing to fight a series of wars against the Ottomans for control of the Crimea and the Black Sea. Decisions to go to war were made in light of the armies' stage of readiness, the lineup of diplomatic support and opposition, and the opponent's strengths and weaknesses. Not infrequently, royal advisers engaged in complicated scheming to get their royal masters to agree to war (e.g., Marshal Bellisle's maneuvers to get in on the planned partition of the Austrian Empire in 1741).

Of all the wars of the post-Utrecht period, perhaps the only ones that resulted from an unanticipated crisis were the War of Jenkins's Ear (1739) and the French revolutionary government's declaration of war against Austria and Prussia in 1792. Most of the remainder were carefully prepared, designed to protect or further dynastic and state interests. They fit in well, of course, with the expectations of the nobility, and there were few powerful voices to oppose them.

There was one factor in royal decision-making on questions of war and peace that did change significantly in the century of international relations following the Utrecht settlements. With the significant exception of Frederick the Great and the less significant command of Hanoverian troops at the battle of Dettigen by George II of Britain, monarchs ceased to pose as heroic warriors. After Louis XIV, no French king was to take to the battlefield; nor did his Austrian, Russian, or Swedish counterparts. Their international prestige rested on other foundations (victories by armies did count, of course), not the least of which was patronage of the arts and literature. The monarchs of the eighteenth century no longer had a personal and individual stake in war; they were not required or expected to go to war to be considered "good" princes. Reasons of state rather than personal pride or ambition provided the only justification for deciding in favour of war.

Frederick was the significant exception. His purposes in invading Silesia, as we have seen, had a great deal to do with state-building and consolidation. But in the tradition of Louis XIV, he also found military leadership an important avenue to fame, glory, and building the status of Prussia into that of a great power. In a letter of March 1741, some months after his aggression against Maria Theresa, he wrote: "My youth, the fire of passion, the desire for glory, yes, to be frank, even curiosity, finally a secret instinct, has torn me away from the delights of

109

tranquillity. The satisfaction of seeing my name in the papers and later in history has seduced me" (Gooch, 1947:12). It is confessions such as these that render generalizations about the causes of war so problematic. But whatever the role of glory, reputation, and curiosity, they were not sufficient conditions for the war of 1740. Given the importance of the stakes involved, it is doubtful that vanity "caused" the war. In any event, Frederick was to learn quickly that his reputation as a military leader could be compromised by his reputation as an aggressor; and in later years he learned that reputation could be gained by many means other than those of war.

The French Revolution fundamentally changed attitudes toward war, not only in their content, but also in their social depth. Even though some of the eighteenth-century wars were genuinely popular – royal propagandists invariably presented military activity as an attractive and admirable undertaking – the ideas of the masses counted for little either as inputs into policy-making or as constraints on the latitude of choice (Holland was an exception: the burghers remained strongly pacifist throughout the eighteenth century, and their attitudes counted). The perspectives of the nobility were by far the most significant: war was not only right as a means of vindicating royal claims, but also a right of the class.

The French revolutionaries came to power bathed in optimism, and enthusiastically embraced the view of man's inherent goodwill and the idea of social and philosophical progress. As far as war was concerned, the key idea was that it was just if enough people supported it. Justice in international relations was to be determined by numbers, not by state power or the quality of legal claims. So the common man was given the opportunity to take to the battlefield on behalf of justice, as interpreted by popular assemblies initially, and later by a single man, Napoleon.

The rights of princes, which were often matters of popular indifference, were now replaced by the rights of peoples. The heroic view of war was now buttressed by the notion of moral right, of political certitude, a kind of mystical faith in the judgment of the many (Perré, 1962:19). The revolutionary regime exalted the "peoples'" martial spirits, copying in form if not exactly in content the nobility's view of the military profession. Indeed, the whole French attitude toward international relations changed fundamentally as a result of the revolution. In the revolutionary credo, there were universal principles of right and wrong. These cannot be compromised, so even if Robespierre could enunciate a doctrine of peaceful coexistence, to remain a revolutionary and to play the game of international politics according to the classical rules was logically impossible. International relations, in the French view, was no longer a question of the vindication of legal and hereditary claims, based on the assumption that there may be different interpretations to these claims, and thus room for compromise. It was simply a question of right and wrong, where compromises were at best tactical necessities that could later be ignored. Broad public faith in the righteousness of a national cause was a fundamental discontinuity with the style of post-Utrecht international politics.

## THE PROBLEM OF PEACE

The peace treaties of the era reflect the paradox of the stability of the *system* (until 1792), and the profound insecurity of its *members*. They were commonly regarded as little more than war-terminating instruments, mere cease-fires, this despite their flowering terminology of "perpetual amity" and concern for the "tranquillity of Europe." They were seldom genuine settlements or "authoritative allocation of values." Louis XV had imagined that the peace of Aix-la-Chapelle (1748) would indeed be a perpetual peace, but he was naive in thinking that the termination of the wars of the Austrian Succession had really resolved the underlying issues of Prussian–Austrian, Russo-Turkish, Russo-Swedish, and French–British competition and conflict. Choiseul, the principal French negotiator at the Treaty of Paris, 1763, considered that peace only a respite, an armistice in the continuing conflict over empire. Shortly after signing it, he began to rebuild the French armed forces for yet another round of war with Great Britain (Gershoy, 1944:2, 166–67).

The developing practice of mediation might suggest at least some concern with the problem of war. Mediation became a normal and admired diplomatic practice, not only because it helped terminate conflicts, but also because it brought prestige to those dynasts or agents who acted as the intermediaries. George I was the official mediator of the Peace of Nystadt (1721), gaining through it prestige and reputation, just as he had in helping arrange the peace of Passarowitz (1718) between Austria and Turkey. The maritime powers mediated the war between Spain and Austria in 1735, Cardinal Fleury helped to bring an end to the Russo–Austrian war against Turkey in 1739, Great Britain mediated the end of the first Austro-Prussian War in 1742, and Russia successfully mediated the War of the Bavarian Succession in 1779. These were some of the more notable accomplishments, but there were many others.

While not denying the importance of this practice, we have to acknowledge that mediation was a device – often a face-saving device at that – to terminate wars, not to prevent them. The issues had already been resolved on the battlefield, and the combatants, usually mutually exhausted and with no further prospects of stunning strategic victories, began looking for ways out of their impasses. Accepting mediation offers provided the perfect means. There are no cases on record where formal mediation actually prevented a war. The provision of mediating services to terminate wars is no mean achievement. The practice almost became an institution, but no one thought that it might be extended systematically into the realm of conflict prevention. While most sovereigns might have conceded that peace was preferable to war, none would have acknowledged the right of others to intercede in their disputes to try to prevent the use of armed force. This idea had to wait many more years before it was recognized as a possible practice in international relations. We have to notice as well that all the mediations were individual initiatives. They were not undertaken on behalf of a community. They did not reflect the consciousness of a common interest, the idea that the combatants had to terminate their quarrels in order to maintain the "tranquillity and repose" of Europe. The powers between 1713 and 1814 developed little capacity to act in concert, unless one wants to claim that the partitions of Poland represented a plan to save the peace of Europe (this claim has been made by many, including the main author of the scheme, Frederick II; see Mowat, 1928:273). Even the coalition wars against Napoleon offer slight evidence of a sense of community. The coalitions were forged during war, out of vital necessity. They were not a planned means of preventing war, a system of collective security and deterrence. They fell apart as quickly as they were formed. Even the final drive against Napoleon in 1813–14 almost collapsed because of rifts between the main collaborators.

Thought on the questions of war and peace, of paths to peace, were thus confined to a small group of philosophers. They had profound insights into the causes of war (Rousseau in particular), but there is no evidence in diplomatic practice that the rulers and their advisers devoted similar attention to the problem. Their insights were strategic and immediate rather than systemic and long-range. They were guided by the requirements of the moment. With at least nine powers, none stably in the camp of the other, with the rise and death of sovereigns, their incessant claims, and the shuffling back and forth of territories for the resolution of pressing diplomatic quandaries, there was little time for theoretical speculation about the state of the world and what could be done to make it better. The memoirs of the dynasts and their counselors are largely devoid of thought about the fundamentals of a system of anarchy and of proposals about things that might be done to create a peaceful world. War was regarded as a fact of life and as a useful instrument of diplomacy, not as a problem. Peace, considered as an essential condition of international relations, was no preoccupation of the princes of Christendom.

# 6  PEACE THROUGH EQUILIBRIUM: THE SETTLEMENTS OF 1814–1815

> We flattered ourselves . . . that the congress [of Vienna] would crown its labours, by substituting for these fleeting alliances (the result of necessities and momentary calculations) a permanent system of universal guarantees and general equilibrium . . . the order established in Europe would be placed under the perpetual protection of all the parties interested, who by wisely concerted plans, or by sincerely united efforts, would crush at the outset, any attempt to compromise it.
> Talleyrand

The peacemakers at Utrecht confronted the problem of hegemony. In addition to the usual spoils of war, some of them had sought to create a system that would prevent the recurrence of French designs to "lay down the law" to the rest of Europe. In this objective, they succeeded, but they failed to create an order that would effectively reduce the incidence of war. One hundred years later, as the allied forces of Russia, Prussia, Austria, and Great Britain bore down upon Napoleon – yet another figure who pursued the vision of "universal monarchy" in Europe – the leaders of the great powers once again had to consider how they could prevent a recurrence of this type of threat to the states system. There was a major difference this time, however. In 1713 the delegates at Utrecht and in subsequent peace negotiations did not consider war a significant international problem. By 1813, twenty-one years of incessant warfare and revolutionary turmoil, conquered territories under direct French rule, assaults on the principles of legitimacy, the strained economic capacity of states to carry on war on a large scale, and mounting casualties and destruction encouraged the statesmen of the day to consider that war as an institution was a problem requiring attention. The peacemakers of 1814–15, reflecting the optimism of the Enlightenment that man could create and mold political institutions, thought that rather than negotiate just another territorial settlement apportioning the spoils of war among the victors, they could construct a *system* or order for security that would embrace the entire European "family." It included several but not all of the elements necessary for

114

an international order that could significantly control or reduce the future resort to arms.

The designs for bringing "repose" to Europe were the work of three leaders: Tsar Alexander, Prince Von Metternich, and Viscount Castlereagh. Prince Talleyrand became an important participant in the postwar settlements, but his role was primarily to negotiate the restoration of France to the status of an equal in the arrangements that were to govern postwar Europe. These men were not burdened by bureaucratic advisers, interest groups, or opinion polls. In the last months of the war against Napoleon and during the negotiations for peace and the subsequent congress at Vienna, they almost single-handedly created a new security system and fashioned, after intense haggling and bargaining, a territorial settlement that provided the equilibrium necessary to make the system work. It was a relatively mechanical task, unencumbered by economic considerations or the special claims of peoples and communities whose territories were to be distributed to create the equilibrium. This was still an age when diplomats could draw lines on maps, carve up territories and barter them off against each other without worrying unduly about the opinions of the populations concerned, or even about the rights and titles of dynasts. The goal was to create an equilibrium of power; the means was the redistribution of continental and overseas territories and populations.

A standard interpretation of the outcome is that it was disastrously old-fashioned, that it addressed the wrong problems, and that it sought to restore an eighteenth-century world that no longer existed. A typical criticism holds that the negotiators' fatal mistake "was the willful disregard of the principle of nationality." The architects "calmly set aside all national considerations and, true to the international usages of the seventeenth and eighteenth centuries, ... proceeded once more to treat European peoples as so many pawns in the game of dynastic aggrandizement" (Hayes, 1924:9).

That the peace was not perfect, or that it failed to incorporate important new political ideas, is clear. For example, they concentrated on producing a power equilibrium, suggesting a rather static, mechanical approach to the task of creating a security system, and generally ignored major social and intellectual changes that the French Revolution had inaugurated. It is less clear, however, that the architects had nothing more in mind than turning back the clock. In fact, some of the plans for peace contained ideas that were significant departures from the diplomatic practices of the eighteenth century. As one example, the architects of peace shared the idea that any international order had to be *managed* by a consultative process, and that the treaty-making procedures of the eighteenth century had been deficient.

The security system fashioned by the allied victors encompassed the Treaty of Chaumont (March 9, 1814,) the first Treaty of Paris (May 30, 1814), the second Treaty of Paris following Napoleon's defeat at Waterloo, the Holy Alliance (September 15, 1815), and the Quadruple Alliance (November 20, 1815). The conferences at Aix-la-Chapelle (1818), Troppau (1820), Laibach (1820), and Verona (1822) constituted the major efforts to interpret the previous agreements. In assessing the contribution of these diplomatic arrangements and meetings, we must understand how the players of the game approached the task: what assumptions they made about the causes of war, and what sorts of explicit or implicit theories about the requisites of a peace system they entertained.

### DIAGNOSES

Castlereagh, Metternich, and Alexander understood that the international politics of the eighteenth century provided little in the way of "repose."[1] They talked or wrote critically about the unstable and unsatisfactory "fleeting alliances" of the eighteenth century, and of the endless wars of "princely caprice" (Chevallaz, 1964:120–21). And because Castlereagh and Metternich were devotees of the principle of balance and equilibrium, they critically assessed the eighteenth-century balancing mechanisms of aggandizement with compensation, and judged them to be ineffective ways of producing stable results (Craig and George, 1983:30).

The real problem in 1814–15 was not the inadequacies of the eighteenth century, however. Facing the task of reconstructing Europe, the peacemakers were concerned primarily with the sources of the most recent wars, and these were clearly identified as revolution. As practical men rather than theorists, they came together in Paris and Vienna primarily to prevent the recurrence of the French revolutionary and Napoleonic experiences. Any international order they could construct would have that as its main task. Managing international conflict in general was only a secondary purpose.

To Castlereagh, the root of the problem was republicanism and military Jacobinism. A pronounced critic of the French Revolution, he was above all concerned with its external manifestations. It was the

[1] Some leaders did pine for the good old days. Lord Liverpool, Castlereagh's prime minister, hoped at the close of 1814 that after two or three years of peace, popular feelings would calm down and diplomats could then contrive, without peril to the established order of society, a "war not different in its characteristics and its effects from any of the wars which occurred in the seventeenth and eighteenth centuries" (Halévy, 1924:93).

coupling of nationalism with Jacobinism that produced the problem. Any solution to it must therefore concentrate on setting up a system that muted both impulses. That could be achieved by restoring the Bourbon dynasty within France and designing a territorial arrangement in Europe that would constitute an effective "arc of constraint" against any future French expansionism. To cap the system, the allies would have to agree to act cooperatively to police the peace, and to be prepared to take military action should revolution anywhere in Europe threaten to upset the settlements. Writing in December 1815, he noted that the immediate objective of the various treaties had been

> to inspire the States of Europe . . . with a sense of the dangers they have surmounted by their union, . . . to make them feel that the existing Concert is their only perfect security against the revolutionary embers more or less existing in every state of Europe; and that their true wisdom is to keep down the petty contentions of ordinary times, and to stand together in support of the established principles of social order. (Schenk, 1947:120)

While he saw France as the source of the problem, he was convinced that revolutions were not national events. They had become transnational phenomena that respected no frontiers: "one revolution was made the means of giving birth to another" (Nicolson, 1946:155).

Castlereagh and his Tory colleagues did not see revolution as a product of deep social forces, institutionalized injustices, the rise of the bourgeoisie, or of any other social phenomenon. It arose, rather, from a set of false ideas and principles that had led to regicide, terror, and aggressive war. The British foreign secretary did not make a distinction between French nationalism and republicanism. Thus, his proposed solutions, as we shall see, did not incorporate a realistic response to either. Instead, any disturbance that threatened the peace regardless of its forms or sources had to be suppressed by a concert of the great powers who alone had a proper understanding of the principles of equilibrium internationally and correct government domestically (cf. Lockhart, 1932:264-65; Webster, 1922:519).

These views coincided closely with those of Metternich, who, however, did not make any distinction between domestic revolution and its external manifestations. To Metternich, the French Revolution had brought Austria to the brink of dissolution. The wars against Napoleon had been wars of state survival – which was not the case for Great Britain – and thus any stable peace had to contend primarily with *preventing* revolution, and should that prove impossible, snuffing it out wherever it occurred whether or not it took an externally expansive form. Metternich viewed Europe as a single cultural and religious unit, and the course of domestic politics in any of its parts would be of concern to all, particularly to a realm that was physically impossible to isolate. Liberal and nationalist ideas, he predicted accurately enough, were fundamentally incompatible with the ancient and decrepit political institutions of an autocratic, multinational Austria. Whatever the faults of eighteenth-century diplomacy, the immediate problem of 1814–15 was to prevent a recurrence of the French revolutionary experience. There could be no European repose, and a society could not function internally, "if it is constantly on the defensive against forces attacking its myths" (Kissinger, 1957b:31). For Metternich, the nightmare was permanent revolution.

Alone among the peacemakers, Tsar Alexander pitched his diagnosis at the systemic level. Already by 1804 he was convinced that the diplomatic practices of the eighteenth century led to recurrent wars. These practices, he suggested, had ignored such basic guiding principles as the "rights of humanity," and had been utterly arbitrary. Kings and princes, he believed, had acted both domestically and externally without principle. In particular, they were indifferent to the nationality principle. Impressed by the works of Montesquieu, Rousseau, the Abbé de Saint-Pierre, and other eighteenth-century rationalist thinkers, he believed that the victors over Napoleon would have to construct a new international system in which the old practices were replaced by principles derived from liberalism and Christianity. Napoleon was just one manifestation of an international order that had gone awry. In Alexander's early diagnosis, the fault lay in the system, or more properly, in the processes that permeated the system, and not in a single man or even in the revolution. Revolution was abhorrent, but it was the rational response of people acting against the arbitrariness of despots. The Tsar's views on these matters were to change frequently; he made several intellectual voyages of discovery between Tilsit and Verona. But it is significant that he diagnosed the sources of war as both within and between states, rather than attributing the evil solely to the false ideas of French revolutionaries.

On hindsight, it is perhaps surprising that none of the diagnoses attributed the chaos of the previous two decades to Napoleon himself. Had not the fortunes of war favored the allies in 1813–14, they would have made peace with him on the basis of dismantling his European empire and forcing him to disgorge most of France's territorial conquests since 1792. The Emperor would have remained on the French throne. Napoleon's vanity prevailed, however. He rejected these terms, and so allied war aims expanded to include restoration of the Bourbons to the French throne. But in none of the diagnoses of the problem do we see analyses that focus on this unique personality. For the Tsar, the problem was the international system and its traditional practices; for Metternich and Castlereagh, the problem was revolution. In these differing diagnoses we can see the roots of the fundamental disagreements over the paths and plans designed to bring Europe to an era of repose. Ultimately, by 1822, Alexander came to share the revolution-as-cause-of-war thesis, driving it to its furthest point, the necessity of military intervention anywhere in Europe where the principle of legitimacy was under assault. But until his late conversion to the reactionary cause, he worked hard but ineffectively to convince his colleagues that his prescriptions for a reconstituted international order based on liberal principles would bring an era of peace to Europe. The others were content to rely upon the older conception of equilibrium, bolstered by an allied monitoring and decision-making system that could deter or suppress any disturbances that threatened the revived monarchical order of Europe.

### SOLUTIONS

What did the young Alexander have in mind as an alternative to the practices of the eighteenth-century princes? The Tsar spelled out his thoughts in a set of instructions he sent to the Russian ambassador in London in 1804. They were based on a memorandum written the previous year by the Italian, Scipione Piatloli, for the Russian Foreign Ministry. The three essential ideas were: domestic constitutionalism; the independence of Europe's nations, based on the principle of nationality; and a federation of Europe.

If despotic arbitrariness had been the main cause of revolution, according to Alexander, then the solution was to fashion legal procedures that would replace the individual whims and caprices of dynasts and princes. Constitutions are the necessary means. The purpose of the war was not just to defeat Napoleon or to liberate France, but to promote the universal triumph of the "rights of humanity." These he interpreted to mean self-determination. The constituent units of the European states system would have to be reorganized on the basis of the nationality principle. At the international level, there would have to be a European confederation or league, including a prohibition against the use of force by its members until diplomatic procedures and remedies, including international arbitration, had been exhausted. A new code of international law was also required to establish a set of restraints on arbitrary behavior. Perhaps the most radical idea was that the institutions of a European confederation could

119

interfere in the constitutional issues of its members; the line between domestic and international questions, clearly demarcated in Castlereagh's mind, was virtually eliminated in the Tsar's analysis. This might not be surprising, since the Tsar looked upon Europe as 'one big family.' Pending the reconstruction of Europe on these principles, the immediate task was to make certain that the wartime coalition against Napoleon would continue into the postwar period, and that the great powers would mutually guarantee any settlement (Phillips, 1907:3; Renouvin, 1930:6–7; Schenk, 1947:28–30; Kuehl, 1969:34).

These ideas, some of which reappeared in 1919, contained a greater appreciation of the new intellectual currents sweeping Europe in the early 1800s than did the analyses of Castlereagh and Metternich. The Tsar understood – at least until he faced some domestic difficulties of his own – that severe injustices underlay the revolutions of the era, and that the way to deal with them was through constitutionalism rather than through a return to royal absolutism. His instructions to the ambassador in London also argued the case for the nationality principle: "il serait nécessaire ... de composer chaque état de peuples homogènes qui puissent se convenir entre eux, et s'harmoniser avec le gouvernement qui les régit" (Schenk, 1947:28). In brief, the Tsar anticipated two main sources of domestic and international conflict during the nineteenth century, and his early peace program was explicitly designed to solve those problems – through constitutionalism and self-determination – before they became new sources of war. His peace plan contained both preventive and curative dimensions: undermine the causes of war, and should that fail, construct a policing system.

Alexander's ideas made litle impact on Prime Minister Pitt in 1804, to whom they were first presented, nor did he promote them consistently a decade later in Paris and Vienna. There he was just as interested in promoting purely Russian interests as in establishing an international order. His handling of the Polish issue suggested a significant discrepancy between his professed liberal ideas and his diplomatic actions. The Tsar was committed in principle to the rebirth of a Polish state, but his policy was to create a Polish satellite under Russian suzerainty.[2]

---

[2] The following discussion between Talleyrand and the Tsar in November 1814 illustrates the latter's "schizophrenia." The Tsar: "How are affairs now, and what is your position in them?" Talleyrand: "Always the same, sire. If your Majesty is willing to put Poland in a state of complete independence, we are ready to second you." Alexander: "I desired at Paris [1814] the restoration of Poland, and you approved of it. I desire it still, as a man, and as always being faithful to liberal ideas, which I will never abandon. But in my position, the desires I have as a man cannot guide me as a sovereign. Perhaps the day will come when Poland will be once again on a footing of complete independence. At present it cannot be thought of" (de Broglie, 1891:II, 321).

On other issues, he could maintain his liberal demeanor. The Anglo-Russian Treaty of April 11, 1805 included a statement that in setting up new governments in countries that were to be liberated from Napoleon, "the will of the people is to be decisive" (Schenk, 1947:31). In facing the greatest dilemma during the Congress of Vienna, the problem of Saxony, the Tsar strongly opposed carving up this pro-Napoleon kingdom among several powers, arguing that its population preferred it to become part of Prussia. Not coincidentally, however, this application of the principle of self-determination met the Tsar's wartime commitment to Prussia. The other allies were prepared to settle the issue by recourse to arms, and Alexander eventually relented. In an interview with Francis II, the Austrian Emperor, the Tsar continued to hold out for his principles, rather disingenuously reconciling his wartime commitment to Prussia with the principle of self-determination. Alexander stated, as reported by Talleyrand: "At the present time, we sovereigns are obliged to conform to and obey the wishes of the people. The wish of the Saxon people is not to be divided. They prefer to belong to Prussia, rather than be divided or parceled out." To this, Francis replied: "I do not understand that doctrine at all. This is mine: a Prince can, if he wishes, surrender a portion of his dominions . . ." The Tsar retorted that Francis' view was not consistent with modern ideas. "It is my opinion," replied Francis, "that it ought to be that of all sovereigns, and consequently yours. As for me, I will never depart from it" (de Broglie, 1891:II, 355).

The Tsar's liberal ideas met stiff resistance from Metternich, Talleyrand, and Castlereagh. The plan for creating a territorial equilibrium was inconsistent with application of the principle of self-determination. On this issue Alexander remained a minority of one.

Constitutionalism and a confederation of Europe was never placed on the agenda either in Paris or in Vienna. They did not appeal to the Tsar so much in 1815 as they had in 1805. The only ideas of Alexander that survived the bargaining were the continuation of the alliance into peacetime and periodic meetings of the leaders of the great powers. As for reconstituting the principles guiding inter-state relations, the negotiations led only to the Holy Alliance, an innocuous sop to the Tsar's wounded feelings.

That document has been condemned by generations of historians as a charter for great power intervention against national-liberal revolutions that were beginning to appear on the European landscape. At the time, however, all the signatories, as well as the British, who did not sign it, dismissed the document as so much nonsense, of no practical importance (Metternich referred to it as a "high-sounding

121

nothing"; Talleyrand termed it a "ludicrous contract," and Castlereagh thought it no more than a "piece of sublime mysticism and nonsense"). In fact, the Holy Alliance derived from the Tsar's desire to reform the international system, not from his later concern with revolutions. The original draft of the treaty reflected his idealism and liberalism, but by the time it was made acceptable to Metternich and the others it had been reduced to little but platitudes. All references to liberal ideas had been effectively deleted, leaving little but vague commitments of the powers to conduct their mutual relations according to Christian principles. For the Tsar, the project must have been a resounding failure.

But he did not cave in entirely to his colleagues' indifference. Shortly after introducing the project for the Holy Alliance, he approached Castlereagh and the others for a project on disarmament. Again the colleagues politely dismissed the idea, Metternich relying on a justification that has a distinctly twentieth-century flavor: the powers would have difficulty obtaining reliable evidence on force levels in Russia (Schenk, 1947:215). At the conference at Aix-la-Chapelle in 1818, his disarmament scheme having failed, the Tsar proposed creating a European army, directed by a permanent Allied General Staff, primarily to protect small states and to deter aggression. By 1818, however, the Tsar had converted to reaction, and so he came to see this project as a means for a coordinated crusade against liberal-national revolutions.

Overall, the Tsar's solutions to the problem of war were of a decidedly modern character. They went beyond an attempt to create a particular peace, to create a more peaceful international order. He acknowledged the social and institutional roots of revolution, the inadequacies of eighteenth-century diplomatic practices, and the intellectual currents of his age. He saw that the best formula for creating an international order was to combine domestic harmony *within* the members of the European family by the devices of constitutionalism and self-determination, with guarantees, consultations, and international principles to regulate relations *between* states. He was concerned with a generic problem of the international system and not just with the particulars of the French revolutionary and Napoleonic eras. His colleagues were less interested in that question and sought to deal primarily with the source of the latest war, namely the French Revolution. The Tsar sought to create a general system of peace; his colleagues focused on the principle of equilibrium, with little else. The Tsar anticipated the ideas and problems of the nineteenth century; his colleagues wanted to avoid them or, should they manifest themselves through revolution, to crush them.

To Metternich, a balance of power was the beginning and end for protecting against both revolutionary upheavals and French imperialism. Repeatedly, both in his public pronouncements and in the agreements he negotiated (e.g., the draft of preliminary peace terms he offered Napoleon in February 1814), Metternich employed the terms "balance of power," "durable equilibrium," and "reestablishment of the political equilibrium." The formula for establishing this state of affairs included territorial rearrangements, notably stripping territories France had conquered or "liberated" since 1792, building up Prussia as a counterweight to Russia, and extending Austrian dominions in Italy. Like his colleagues, Metternich thought of power primarily in terms of population. In his detailed and laborious negotiations on territorial redistribution at Vienna, he mastered all the information about the populations of territories that were available for barter. As for mechanisms for maintaining the postwar territorial settlement, he was an enthusiastic supporter of periodic meetings among the Big Five, seeing them as the guarantors of future stability and repose.

What is significant about Metternich's solution to his diagnosis of the problem is that the former did not derive logically from the latter. If domestic revolutions and nationalism were the sources of the international problem, then an international balance of power seems hardly an adequate response. Instead of ignoring the sources of revolution, he should have thought seriously about them. His mind seems to have focused on the purpose of achieving international "repose," for which a balance of power would have been appropriate if the problem were defined as defense against hegemonic drives. But it is not clear how a territorial balance of power could deal with the problem of domestic revolution.

Perhaps Metternich inverted the causal direction. Certainly he feared the "epidemic" of revolution, seeing that there were no natural barriers to contagion. And it is understandable that the main policymaker of a realm made up of Germans, Magyars, Czechs, Poles, Ruthenians, Slavs, Romanians, and Italians, should wish to avoid discussion of the nationality principle (Jane, 1910:14–15). If he granted any legitimacy to it, he would be promoting the destruction of the Austrian Empire. In these circumstances, he may have surmised that a period of international peace and stability would undercut domestic revolutions. Perhaps, in his view, it was international conditions that determined or influenced domestic trends rather than the reverse. If that was the logic of his analysis, it proved to be incorrect. Within five years of the Congress of Vienna, during a period of exceptional international repose, three major nationalist/liberal revolutions took place in Europe.

Like Metternich, Talleyrand was a tinkerer rather than one committed to a transformation of the international system. He, too, was committed to the reestablishment of a balance of power in Europe, as long as France, having suffered military defeat and occupation, was quickly restored to the ranks of the "governors" of Europe. Although in Napoleon's service, he was convinced that "rank, primacy, and preponderance [hegemony] were but the reefs upon which the Empire must ultimately suffer shipwreck" (Lockhart, 1932:61). To Talleyrand, war was a confession of diplomatic failure. Sharing the optimism of eighteenth-century thought, he believed that human efforts could overcome the less savory consequences of structural anarchy and dynasticism. A far-seeing and careful plan for creating equilibrium could significantly reduce the incidence of war. The edifice of equilibrium had to be built on a foundation more secure than the "fleeting alliances" based on necessities and momentary calculations that were typical of the eighteenth century. Though not a main architect of the proceedings at Vienna (technically he was the plenipotentiary of a defeated power, but he successfully inveigled himself to be dealt with as an equal), he was sympathetic to the main outlines of Castlereagh's schemes for peace, notably a territorial distribution approximating a balance of power, mutual guarantees, and a monitoring and managing system. He shared the belief that the settlements of 1814–15 were fundamentally non-negotiable in the future and were to set the legitimate framework for conducting international relations in the postwar era. In his words, the "order established in Europe [will] be placed under the perpetual protection of all the interested parties, who by concerted plans, or by sincerely united efforts, [will] crush at the outset, any attempt to compromise it" (de Broglie, 1891: II, 141).

Like Metternich, Talleyrand assumed that an internationally tranquil Europe would reduce the probabilities of domestic rebellion. International peace would create domestic tranquillity: "Governments would be able to devote their time to home administration and real reforms, in conformity with the needs and wishes of the people, and in the execution of numerous salutary schemes, which, owing to the dangers and convulsions of past times, had unfortunately been in abeyance" (de Broglie, 1891: II, 141).

Talleyrand's forte was in delineating the requirements for an effective balance of power – ignoring, of course, the language, ethnic, or religious characteristics of those whose territories would be shifted around to create the balance. His thinking was based on the assump-

124

tion that imbalances create wars, yet his solution looks more like a preponderance than a balance. He did not believe that absolute equality of power between states was either necessary or desirable. He classified states as either satisfied or expansionist. In order to maintain peace, the minimum resisting power of the smallest status quo coalition has to be greater than the maximum power of an aggressive state. But any territorial equilibrium would be artificial and precarious. The main ingredient in success must be a relative equilibrium that is *maintained* by states that are "motivated by a spirit of moderation and justice" (de Broglie, 1891: II, 173). The balance is thus not an automatic mechanism that results from policy. It is to be a diplomatic creation that requires constant monitoring and managing.

This meant a coalition of France, Great Britain, and Austria. Unlike Metternich, Talleyrand foresaw accurately that one great problem of the future would be the growing military strength of Prussia. Prussia was indeed an important counterweight to Russia (in 1814–15, almost everyone was concerned with Russia's "pretensions"), but an overly powerful Prussia would be even a greater threat to all.

On hindsight, his recipe for peace was prophetic. But for the system to work, all three conservative states had to act together. By the 1820s, however, Great Britain had become uninterested in continental affairs, and following Castlereagh's death in 1822, it was unwilling to make any lasting commitments of the kind envisaged in the Quadruple Alliance. Castlereagh's policy did not outlive him, but until his death it provided at least some support for the kind of equilibrium Talleyrand had in mind.

Castlereagh's thought on peace and war paralleled that of his colleagues as far as the question of an equilibrium was concerned. But in a more modern vein, and echoing some of the Tsar's thoughts, he wanted to set up a security system based on enduring commitments. He, too, thought in terms of a created and managed international order, and not just a division of spoils following a war, or a contrived balance of power.

Castlereagh's recipe for a postwar system included four main ingredients: (1) a territorial balance of power, basically directed against any future French attempt at hegemony; (2) the reincorporation of France into the European system, via a lenient peace (Hafner, 1980:73); (3) mutual guarantees among the peacemakers, that is, commitments to support the settlements against those who might assault it; and (4) a decision-making or governance system that could monitor threats to the established order and, if necessary, act collectively to enforce the peace.

125

The territorial equilibrium represented not so much a balance as a distribution of lands and domains to hem in France, somewhat along the lines of the Utrecht settlements. Castlereagh planned on using some of Britain's colonial conquests of the Napoleonic Wars, plus his personal persuasiveness, to purchase the consent of his colleagues. He had in mind a series of "barriers" that would place impediments against any future French plans for expansion and hegemony. These included the creation of a greater Holland, incorporating into it the former Austrian Netherlands that had been annexed to France in 1795. On the Rhine, Castlereagh argued for an extension of Prussian realms to the left bank, thus replacing some of the weak mini-states of the region. Baden and Bavaria were to be strengthened. In the south, Genoa was to be incorporated into Sardinia, thus creating an impediment against French incursions into Italy. Castlereagh also advocated reestablishing an independent Poland, not for reasons of nationality, self-determination, or liberalism, but as a barrier against Russian expansion into the heart of Europe. The final product of this territorial arrangement was a rough equilibrium, to be sure, but one which would prevent either French or Russian revisionism or expansion. He looked upon Prussia, Austria, and Great Britain as the "conservative" states of the balance. Like Talleyrand, his scheme amounted to a preponderance of power, and not a true balance if by that term we assume an equal distribution of power. Castlereagh did not share Talleyrand's concern about the future of Prussia.

The British foreign minister was adamant in his argument that, even after Napoleon's one hundred days, France must be dealt with leniently. The reason did not arise out of sentimentality. Castlereagh above all feared revolution, and he wanted to provide no grounds for future French discontent. If the restored Bourbons were to be at all secure, France would have to be both a pacified and a pacific power. Were the French to regard the peace as punitive and unjust, Bonapartism (indistinguishable in his mind from revolution and Jacobinism) would have an important rallying cry. "The great object," Castlereagh wrote his prime minister, "is to keep the King [Louis XVIII] on the throne. A moderate [peace], I believe, is the best chance for doing so." (Schenk, 1947:47). Throughout the negotiations of the first and second Treaties of Paris, Castlereagh repeated that the purpose of the peace was future security, not revenge. He was essentially successful in this regard, deflecting the covetous claims of the victors, particularly those of Prussia. The whole idea, deriving from his diagnosis of Europe's problems, was to destroy the aggressive revolutionary spirit of France and to prevent any possibility for a return of Napoleon or any of his relatives. A strong, stable French monarchy, territorially satisfied, but also hemmed in, would prove to be a beneficial factor for Europe's repose. As a relatively satisfied state, France could also act effectively as a counterweight to Russia (Webster, 1934:139; Marriott, 1936:246–47; 270–71; 300–301).

Castlereagh further insisted that any peace settlement must incorporate a set of mutual guarantees and the continuation of the wartime coalition into the postwar era. The Treaty of Chaumont, March 9, 1814, stipulated that the alliance was to continue for twenty years after the end of the war, and provided for mutual guarantees against a French attempt to undo the forthcoming peace settlement. His idea, at this stage, was not so much a multilateral European concert to police the peace, but a league against a revolutionary France. Somewhat later he became a proponent of a general set of guarantees to enforce the entire peace settlement against any disruptions, but on this question he failed to bring along his colleagues. The final settlements reflected three of Castlereagh's formulas for a lasting peace. The missing element proved to be its undoing.

### FORGING THE SETTLEMENT

France was given a generous peace and, thanks to Talleyrand's diplomatic skills, was in effect reassimilated into the big power club by the early stages of the proceedings at Vienna. Napoleon's escape from Elba and subsequent defeat at Waterloo resulted in a somewhat harsher peace, including military occupation and an indemnity, but that one-hundred-day interlude did not disrupt the process of incorporating France into the condominium. Castlereagh's reasoning about the necessity of French assimilation under a Bourbon restoration proved congenial to Metternich in particular, and obviously to Talleyrand. On this, the position of the three prevailed against Prussia and Russia, which thought more in terms of revenge and spoils.

Fashioning a territorial redistribution that could at once hedge in France and yet build counterweights against Russia proved to be a more difficult task than assimilating France and, indeed, nearly led to war in the early winter of 1815. The most intractable issues surrounded Poland and Saxony. We need not recount the tortured history of the negotiations that led to a final settlement, or to the drafting of a secret treaty between Austria, France, and Great Britain (January 1815) that successfully coerced Russia and Prussia into agreement upon the Saxony issue. The results from the point of view of creating an equilibrium were generally satisfactory, except that Russia succeeded in creating a new Poland under its suzerainty, thus extending its power deep into the heart of continental Europe. Prussia received most of Saxony as well as territories on the Rhine. Baden, Bavaria, and Westphalia were strengthened, and upon Great Britain's insistence and at the cost of some of its naval conquests from the recent war – as exchanges – the former Austrian Netherlands were attached to Holland, making it an effective barrier against France. Genoa was given to Sardinia. Thus, Castlereagh's "arc of containment" was created around France, Austria received extensive spoils in Italy, and Prussia constituted some sort of counterweight to Russia. In effect, the negotiators sought to satisfy rather than stifle the desire for expansion on the assumption that if one could create a group of "satisfied" powers, future wars could be avoided and jealousies removed (Jane, 1910:12).[3]

The question of allied collaboration in the postwar period proved more difficult to resolve than the territorial issues. The Treaty of Chaumont (March 9, 1814), negotiated while Europe was still at war with Napoleon, set forth the principles of unity: the purpose was to enforce the upcoming peace treaty with France and to safeguard the general territorial redistribution that would be fashioned in Vienna. It was commonly understood, moreover, that the postwar governance of the system was to reside exclusively among the great powers. Already at the conference of Chatillon (February 1814), Metternich and his colleagues had publicly declared that "they did not come to the conference as mere envoys of the four courts, . . . but as men entitled to treat for Peace with France in the name of Europe, which is but a single entity" (quoted in Chevallaz, 1964:123). Their role as the future policemen of Europe was further established in a secret article of the first Peace of Paris (June 1814): the Vienna Congress would establish "the relations from whence a system of real and permanent balance of

---

[3] Castlereagh and the Liverpool cabinet in London never thought in terms of creating a British hegemony. The whole purpose of the allied war against Napoleon was to destroy French hegemony on the continent. The victors were not disposed to replace France with England. The British, it is true, were unwilling to discuss questions of maritime law at the Congress of Vienna. They successfully insisted on maintaining freedom of navigation, and thus their leading role as a commercial power. But the continentals were never much concerned with the issue, and concentrated on the problem of land-based hegemony. The territorial settlement legitimized British overseas conquests during the Napoleonic Wars, but at this time British politicians did not see these as having any particular commercial value. Their importance was strategic.

The idea of Great Britain's hegemony is mostly a fiction of recent international relations scholars who seem to argue that economic factors determine the nature of politics. In 1815 and during the next half-century, European statesmen were magisterially indifferent to economic questions. Throughout the conversations held in Paris and Vienna in 1814–15, one searches in vain for any reference to economic issues or to the notion of British hegemony. The territorial settlements and the concert system were based on security considerations.

power in Europe is to be derived, [and] shall be regulated at the Congress upon the principles determined . . . by the Allied Powers amongst themselves" (Webster, 1934:45).

On the question of guarantees, the diplomats failed, and thus the peace settlement was incomplete. The Tsar had proposed a general statement of principles to regulate the mutual relations of the great powers in the postwar world. The document included references to the "wishes of the people" and to the principle of nationality. Partly as a means of avoiding the Tsar's proposals, but also to set up a system against Russian ambitions in the Balkans, Castlereagh came up with another project: a set of mutual guarantees, a general commitment by all the powers to respect the rights of their neighbors, and an undertaking to oppose by joint means any threat to the peace, no matter from what quarter it materialized. This of course implied possible joint action against one of the peacemakers. The Tsar was initially enthusiastic about the project, until Castlereagh let it be known that among the territories which, if disturbed, would constitute a threat to the general peace, were those of the Ottoman Empire. At this suggestion, the Tsar lost interest in the project, and the delegates at Vienna went home without so much as a public declaration of joint action to secure and protect the outcomes of the congress negotiations (Renouvin, 1930:8).

Castlereagh later settled for the Quadruple Alliance (November 20, 1815), which renewed the Treaties of Chaumont and Vienna and excluded Napoleon or any member of his family from the throne of France. Should revolution again convulse France and thereby endanger the repose of other states, the signatories agreed to consult and to take those measures "they may judge necessary . . . for the safety of their several states, and for the general tranquillity of Europe." This treaty stipulated consultations and joint measures only in the event of *French* revolutionary disturbance. There was no specific mention of the territorial arrangements fashioned in Vienna, or of threats to peace emanating from other European quarters. The Quadruple Alliance thus constituted a league to enforce the peace against France, and not a system for the governance of Europe or for general conflict resolution. On the other hand, it did incorporate Castlereagh's idea, like the Tsar's, for a permanent mechanism for monitoring compliance with the peace settlement. The signatories agreed to hold meetings "for the consideration of the measures which shall be considered the most salutary for the repose and prosperity of nations and for the maintenance of peace in Europe." Through this article, the mandate of the great powers was expanded beyond that of simply policing France.

129

And thus the Concert of Europe was built, but with serious cracks in the edifice.

In all their deliberations and despite numerous relevant articles in the many treaties that constituted the settlements of 1814–15, the statesmen never formed a consensus on the following critical issues: (1) against whom they would act in case of a disturbance to the peace; (2) what, exactly, constituted a threat to the peace; and (3) what they would do about it should it occur. In other words, these exemplary and, in some cases, far-seeing leaders failed to define the very essence of all security agreements, the *casus foederis* and the nature of obligations of the signatories toward each other in the event of a breach of the peace. That the leaders believed strongly in unity is beyond dispute. To the Tsar, this unity was just one aspect of the new principles to guide postwar diplomacy, and in practice he frequently passed up opportunities for meddling against the Ottoman Empire in order to placate the allies: "tout avec mes Alliés, et rien sans eux" was his password (Schenk, 1947:211). Castlereagh was of a similar opinion, even if his cabinet colleagues and many fellow Tory parliamentarians were not. Both Metternich and Talleyrand were firm believers in the territorial redistribution, and they both understood that henceforth their governments could not act on critical international issues, even those involving their core interests, without the explicit or tacit consent of the other great powers. The bargaining during and after the war proceeded on the assumption of postwar collaboration. But these statesmen who had carefully counted every head in Saxony, Poland, and indeed in any territory that was up for barter (through the Statistical Commission of the Congress of Vienna), forgot to enumerate the issues over which they would collaborate in the future.

## ALLIED UNITY UNRAVELED: DEFINING THREATS TO PEACE

Wartime allies frequently assume that the heavy burdens they share in a common struggle are sufficient to cement unity into the postwar period. The diplomats of 1814–15 were no less under the spell of this assumption than were those of 1919 and 1945. As we have seen, most of the peace planners in Paris and Vienna diagnosed the problem of international relations of the two previous decades as the military and aggressive manifestations of revolution. The allies disposed of Napoleon, but it was obvious that their military victory did not solve the problem of revolution. And as I have argued, a territorial balance of power is not a solution to the problem of revolution unless we assume, as Talleyrand and Metternich did, that international instability causes or abets revolutions. Castlereagh's conception of a *casus foederis* was fundamentally different from that of his continental allies. Throughout the postwar period, at the Congresses of Aix-la-Chapelle, Troppau, Laibach, and Verona, he or his representatives argued that allied armed action could take place only in the event of an overriding external danger, that is, of an expansive Bonapartism. In one of the most famous state papers in British history (Temperley and Penson, 1938:47), Castlereagh carefully spelled out, mostly in negative terms, his conception of the situation that could trigger joint action. He argued (May 1820) that the Quadruple Alliance was never intended "as a Union for the Government of the World, or for the Superintendance of the Internal affairs of other States." The Alliance was designed to respond to revolutionary power in its *military* character, "against which it is intended to take precautions, rather than against Democratic Principles . . . spread throughout Europe." Castlereagh, in other words, would countenance joint action only in the clear-cut case of external aggression by a revolutionary power. To him, the consequences of acting "to embrace subordinate, remote, and speculative cases of danger" would prove the undoing of allied unity. (cf. Hafner, 1980:78–80).

In a fundamental disagreement with his colleagues, made clear at the Troppau Congress, he took the position that no state could interfere in the internal affairs of another, even against national-liberal revolutions, unless that revolution took on a clearly aggressive character. "The principle of a state interfering by force in the internal affairs of another . . . is always a question of the greatest possible moral as well as political delicacy . . . [To] generalize such a principle and to think of reducing it to a System, or to impose it as an obligation, is a Scheme utterly impractical and objectionable" (Temperley and Penson, 1938:61). No doubt Castlereagh strongly believed these words, but he was also responding to strong political currents in England which were not sympathetic with any scheme to maintain a high level of diplomatic involvement in continental affairs.

The attitudes of the continental leaders were unabashedly anti-revolutionary and cautious. To them, the *casus foederis* was any revolution, anywhere. It would be necessary to act jointly before any disturbance had an opportunity to take an externally aggressive form. In Kissinger's words (1957b:228), their "crucial battle was the first, not the last; their effort was to prevent an overriding danger from materializing."

Thus, we see essentially contending versions of the postwar order.

Castlereagh wanted a Concert to respond only to those revolutions that threatened to upset the general peace of Europe as embodied in the 1814–15 settlements. The others wanted an allied response, armed if necessary, to *any* domestic turmoil in Europe, whether or not it threatened any particular peace, or the general peace. In the end, their position prevailed, but at the cost of British participation in the Concert. At Laibach, Metternich orchestrated Austria's intervention against the liberal uprising in Naples. At Verona, France obtained Russian support for its forthcoming intervention against a liberally inspired but totally unthreatening uprising in Spain. These actions, along with an Austrian intervention against a revolt in Piedmont in 1821, were ostensibly legitimized by the Troppau Protocol (November 19, 1820, vigorously opposed by Great Britain), which declared that any revolution that threatened the tranquillity of Europe would justify individual or collective action. None of the three revolutions in question threatened either the peace of Europe in general or any of the provisions of the Vienna Treaty, but by 1820 it was clear that what was left of allied unity was directed against revolution and liberalism, and not against threats to the international peace.[4] Those who had made peace had forgotten their main purpose in coming together in Vienna: to create a pan-European security system.

### ASSESSMENT

Among historians there is no consensus concerning the contribution of the 1814–15 settlements to international peace and security. For some, the Congress of Vienna and the peace treaties with France launched a century of relative peace. Despite the deep fissures among the allies, the Concert system survived, and the great powers effectively managed the great historical changes that took place in the nineteenth century. To others, the peacemakers willfully sought to suppress all the ideas, good or bad, that emanated from the French Revolution, and thus avoided most of the issues that were to succeed them.

Implicit in these judgments are numerous "measures" of success and failure, rarely spelled out, and even more rarely supported with systematic evidence. Both views – and there are others as well – are of course correct. It all depends upon our conceptions of international peace and security, whether peace is defined as the absence of a major

[4] In fairness to the Tsar, he was not against liberal constitutions, but against revolution. He supported Austria's restoration of the King of Naples, but insisted that the latter institute reforms and promulgate a liberal constitution. Metternich sought no such promises from the king.

pan-European war, or the absence of all warlike activity. If the former, the architects of 1814–15 were eminently successful; if the latter, they failed. But let us assess the accomplishments of the peacemakers according to some of the criteria employed in evaluating Westphalia and Utrecht.

According to classical international theory, peace is not the normal condition resulting from the interaction of many sovereign units. In anarchies, wars recur. To reduce their incidence, therefore, some party or parties in the system have to take it upon themselves, preferably with the consent of others, to define the limits of tolerable international behavior. Aside from certain territorial settlements, neither Westphalia nor Utrecht did this. In contrast, the great powers at Paris and Vienna clearly arrogated for themselves the responsibility for managing the international system, at least as far as questions of war and peace on the continent were concerned. They had in mind a system of governance. They established a system of monitoring and decision-making with regard to developments on the continent, and initially they were prepared to take joint action against any threat to the peace. Neither the wishes of Europe's small states nor the principle of non-interference in domestic jurisdictions were to stand in the way. But there was not consensus on what, exactly, would constitute a challenge to the system of governance and to the general peace that emerged in 1815. And governance would amount to little if the governors failed to agree on the nature of their tasks, and if they failed to prepare for the eventuality that one of the governors might itself become a major threat to international peace and security. Moreover, by 1822 it was clear that four of the five original governors shifted their definition of the task. It was no longer to monitor and police the peace settlement, but to root out revolution wherever it might occur regardless of its potential to disturb international tranquillity. They thus put themselves in a legally and morally untenable position: their ostensible purpose was to provide international security, meaning the security of individual states. But to do this, they proposed to violate one of the fundamental legal guarantees of security, namely sovereignty. They would destroy regimes in order to save a narrow, class-defined system of order rather than international peace in general.

The system of governance established in 1815 was really a great power condominium, more or less accepted by all of Europe,[5] but only the Big Five defined its tasks. By 1822, many in Europe no longer supported those tasks, and so the system of governance lost much of

[5] Even as late as 1820, the Tsar argued that the Concert must include all the states of Europe. He alone supported an egalitarian conception of a security organization.

its legitimacy. The governors operated solely by virtue of their superior military power, and one of them, Great Britain, had more or less defected from the condominium.

A second requirement of an effective peace system is a territorial distribution of power that enjoys substantial acceptance among the key actors in the system. This was accomplished at Paris and in Vienna. France lost only its recent conquests. The restored Bourbons had no difficulty defining the limits of France as those that had prevailed prior to 1792 (in fact, France did keep some territory acquired after 1792, particularly in Savoy). Austria received generous compensation in Italy; Prussia expanded and effectively replaced Austria as the leader of the new German Confederation; and Russia hung on to its Polish acquisition. The map of Europe was substantially redrawn. The losers were the small states of Germany which had no hopes, anyway, of surviving in an age of large territorial states. But the Vienna Congress failed to incorporate the volatile Balkan and Aegean territories as part of the European balance, and this area was to prove a major source of war in succeeding years.

The territorial rearrangement did significantly increase the costs of hegemony-seeking and/or reduced the costs of defense. France was effectively hemmed in. Great Britain sought no hegemony on the continent. Its problem was relative indifference to the governance system that it had been instrumental in constructing in 1814 and 1815. Prussia now constituted at least a minimal counterweight to Russia, and Austria through its Italian compensations resided among the "satisfied" states of Europe. None of the smaller countries, including even the relatively powerful Spain, could conceivably upset the postwar equilibrium. The great problem lay in Russia. It alone had the resources and will to undo the peace edifice. But Alexander, as one of the architects of the peace, took its obligations seriously and seemed content with his acquisition of Finland (1809) and the Duchy of Poland. In any event, the Russians had the whole Balkan area to exploit for further expansion. The problem of hegemony, in short, was resolved as it had been in 1648 and 1713. Those who would stoutly defend the territorial settlement of 1814–15 far outnumbered and outweighed those who might seek to rearrange it.

A third element for an international order is a set of rules to guide future change. Here, the architects of the post-Napoleonic settlement essentially failed. They concocted a static formula to enforce the peace in a dynamic world. Their conception of an equilibrium was mechanical; the motivation was safety through permanence (Kissinger, 1957b:143) rather than through adjustment to inevitable change. The repose which all sought with such fervor was defined essentially in fixed terms: mildly autocratic governments, simple, natural, and fixed frontiers, and a monitoring system made up of royalty and foreign ministers who could decide the fate of Europe far from the crowds and parliamentary nit-picking (cf. Lockhart, 1932:264–5). In their many deliberations, Alexander, Metternich, Talleyrand, and Castlereagh failed to contemplate or discuss the problem of change. They assumed that the only significant problem was revolution, and if they could successfully deal with it, the repose of Europe would continue indefinitely. The territorial distribution was designed to last forever; any significant change would obviously constitute a deviation from the equilibrium that had been fashioned. And as for change that led to different ratios of power among the great powers, this was not considered either. Power was still measured by the number of troops a regime could field, by state (and generally static) population, and by the extent of territorial holdings. That power could be altered through industrialization was not yet contemplated. The statesmen of the period therefore saw power ratios as relatively fixed, provided the territorial distribution created in 1815 remained unaltered.

In another sense, however, the peacemakers established at least implicit procedures for change. They had arrogated for themselves the governance of Europe. They were convinced that in all their plans and actions, they had in mind the interests of the entire continent and not just those of the state they happened to represent.[6] If there was to be change, emanating from whatever quarter, it was to be accomplished with the consent of the five great powers. The idea of periodic meetings for consultation implied the institutionalization of multiple factors in decision-making. All powers, but particularly the great powers, now had to face the opinions of their peers before they could undertake any major foreign policy initiative, including of course, war. In the postwar world, foreign policy was to be formulated within a system of consent and consensus. This is what the Tsar had sought, but the practical application of the idea did not come to fruition until long after his

---

[6] All the diplomats in Paris and Vienna spoke of a European interest and of a European "public law." While they were charged with the task of advancing their own state's interests, they were also conscious of operating within a European order, a larger interest to which they were occasionally willing to subordinate purely national concerns. Metternich wrote: "Politics is the science of the vital interests of States, in its widest meaning. Since, however, an isolated State no longer exists . . . we must always view the Society of States as the essential condition of the modern world. The great axioms of political science proceed from the knowledge of the true political interests of all states; it is upon these general interests that rests the guarantee of their existence. The establishing of international relations on the basis of reciprocity under the guarantee of respect for acquired rights . . . constitutes in our time the essence of politics" (quoted in Nicolson, 1946:39).

death. By the middle of the nineteenth century, the Concert was working more or less as originally envisaged, no longer as an instrument of reaction, but as an international institution to manage the important affairs of the European system.

The assimilation of the defeated power – unsuccessfully sought at Utrecht – is an important ingredient in establishing a postwar international order. Upon Castlereagh's insistence and Talleyrand's diplomacy, this purpose was achieved quickly and helped to make France a satisfied power well into the next generation.

The various treaties constituting the settlement of 1814–15 included a mechanism for monitoring and controlling (potentially) international conflicts. This distinguished it from its predecessors of 1648 and 1713. The periodic meetings of the representatives of the Big Five were designed particularly for the monitoring function, but also provided opportunities to decide on those steps that the powers would take individually or collectively to handle threats to the peace. This was not yet an institutionalized mechanism for peaceful conflict resolution.

The language of the relevant treaties, particularly the Quadruple Alliance, suggested the use of coercion as the primary means of enforcing peace. There was no mention of mediation or of any other relatively disinterested process which the great powers would simply manage. Thus, the conflict-resolving mechanism was both primitive, confined to deterrence or coercion, and limited in scope to those problems that constituted a threat to the previous peace settlement. There was no indication that the mechanism was to be employed to resolve relatively minor problems or to manage issues other than those arising from liberalism, nationalism, and revolution. For example, all the disturbing difficulties in the Balkans were outside the purview of great power monitoring and conflict management.

A further requirement of an effective peace system is the anticipation and consideration of issues that are likely to generate international conflict in the future. Here the architects of 1814–15 failed. With the possible exception of the Tsar, they were all obsessed by the long years of war against French imperialism, the source of which, they assumed, was domestic revolution. Their purpose was to solve this problem of the past rather than to anticipate sources of future disturbance. Even though they acknowledged that revolution was an international problem, they did not seek to understand its sources. Nor did they contemplate the problem of nationalism. In general, the peace settlement was backward-looking. The problem of the future was assumed to be the problem of the past: French revolutionary expansionism. It is little wonder that the wartime alliance broke up by 1822 when the main reason for its being no longer existed. The drafters created a successful system to cope with the problem of hegemony-seeking. That is not an insignificant accomplishment, but the threat of hegemony was not to arise for many more decades. In the mean time, the problems of national liberation, national unification, and liberal constitutionalism were already on the horizon. They would become the most important sources of war throughout the nineteenth century, but the 1814–15 settlements ignored them. The statesmen of the great powers created a static system for a world of change, an equilibrium of power that did not derive logically from their own diagnoses of the sources of international conflict (revolution), and a peace system that anticipated for the future little more than a recurrence of a problem that they had already resolved.

# 7 CONFLICT AND CONSENT, 1815–1914

> [The] external relations of the states are ordered and settled for a long time to come; the political peace in Europe is secured better than it has been for centuries.
>
> Friedrich von Gentz

The international order created in 1814–15 was from the beginning controversial. The main participants did not agree on all of its fundamental contours and on the tasks they were to fulfill to maintain it. Detractors had many targets for criticism. They challenged the elitist structure of the system, the presumption of the policeman roles by the great powers. The statements of dynastic solidarity appeared to liberals as little more than commitments to reaction. Whatever the line of criticism, there was an underlying consensus that the peace had firmly joined domestic and international issues. The two were inextricably combined: royal legitimacy and international peace (cf. Holbraad, 1970:15).

Whether the condominium of the great powers was essentially an instrument to crush challenges to the principle of legitimacy (as Prussia and Austria were to interpret it), or an organization to guarantee the territorial settlements, that is, the balance of power (as the British generally interpreted it), the diplomats of the period commonly regarded the outcomes of the Paris and Vienna negotiations as watershed events. Like the Treaties of Westphalia, they were the yardsticks against which all change in individual countries' domestic and foreign policies were to be measured. The authors of the 1814 and 1815 agreements had in fact created a new order for Europe, and the policy-makers of succeeding governments assumed that any deviation from that order would be a cause for common concern. As late as 1863, Napoleon III could write approvingly that the order that emerged from Paris and Vienna constituted "the foundations upon which the political edifice of Europe now rests" (Oakes and Mowat, 1918:255).

This order contained a particular set of territorial and domestic political arrangements, a set of "governors" to monitor, regulate, sanction, or prevent change, and certain procedures, rules, norms, or conventions to regulate their individual and mutual behavior. It did not, however, include formal conflict-resolving institutions. The purpose of the order was more to maintain a particular territorial balance of power than to prevent wars. Wars, in fact, would be just one of several means to maintain the balance.

Castlereagh, Talleyrand, Alexander, Metternich, and the Prussian representatives (mostly Stein) had in effect created a system to check or regulate their own ambitions. But in imposing a system from the top, they had little impact on those who sought national liberation or on those who worked for the democratization of their societies. The nineteenth century featured the rise of nationalities and the decline of empires, leading to a fundamental reconstitution of the principles upon which the political units of the European society of states would be based. The balance of power order created in 1815 was based on a system of *historic* states and empires. But what emerged through the remainder of the century was a collection of *popular* states. An order appropriate for the first kind of system was not necessarily appropriate for the other. The Concert was relatively effective in maintaining the order through the first fifty or sixty postwar years. But by the 1880s, or even earlier it was fast unraveling.

## WAR AND INTERVENTION IN CONCERT EUROPE

The list of wars and significant interventions in table 7.1 includes only those armed contests that had an impact on the interdependent European security system. I exclude wars in the peripheries and wars that were essentially self-contained and isolated. The Mexican–American War, the numerous wars of nineteenth-century Latin America, and the Sino-Japanese War of 1894–95, for example, are excluded. Wars fought by European states in areas not properly part of the system of mutual relations are also excluded. This category contains a significant population of armed violence, mostly connected with European imperialism in the Middle East, Africa, and Asia. Some of the wars were historically notable (the Anglo-Burmese Wars, Opium Wars, Sepoy Mutiny, and the like), but their effects were confined to the new peripheries.

The list does include, however, several marginal cases: the Egypt–Ottoman Wars, the Boxer Rebellion, the Boer War, and the Russo-Japanese War. They are noted because they had immediate repercussions throughout Europe and/or because they brought the Concert into operation. By the late nineteenth century, the dividing line between intra- and extra-European wars became increasingly blurred,

Table 7.1 *Wars and issues, 1815–1914*

| Wars/major armed interventions | Issues for original combatants |
|---|---|
| 1. Austria–Naples, 1820–1821 | 1. Government composition |
| 2. Austria–Piedmont, 1821 | 1. Government composition |
| 3. France–Spain, 1822–1823 | 1. Government composition |
| 4. Russia (Greece, Great Britain, France) – Turkey, 1828–1829 | 1. National liberation/state creation (R., Gr., G.B., F.)<br>2. Protect religious confrères (R.)<br>3. Commerce/navigation (R., T.)<br>4. Protect ethnic confrères (R.)<br>5. Maintain integrity of empire (T.) |
| 5. Belgium (France)–Holland, 1830–1833 | 1. National liberation/state creation (B., F.)<br>2. Maintain integrity of state (H.) |
| 6. Turkey–Egypt, 1832–1833 | 1. Territory<br>2. Empire creation (E.)<br>3. Maintain integrity of empire (T.) |
| 7. Turkey–Egypt, 1839–1847 | 1. Dynastic claims<br>2. Territory<br>3. Empire creation (E.)<br>4. Maintain integrity of empire (T.) |
| 8. Prussia–Denmark, 1848 | 1. Dynastic/succession claims (D.)<br>2. Territory<br>3. National unification/consolidation |
| 9. Sardinia–Austria, 1848–1849 | 1. Territory<br>2. National unification/consolidation (S.)<br>3. Ideological liberation (S.)<br>4. Maintain integrity of empire (A.) |
| 10. France–Roman Republic, 1849 | 1. Government composition<br>2. Maintain regional dominance (F.) |
| 11. Russia (Austria)–Hungary, 1849 | 1. National liberation/state creation (H.)<br>2. Maintain integrity of empire (A., R.) |
| 12. Turkey (Great Britain, France, Austria)–Russia, 1853–1856 | 1. Protect religious confrères (R.)<br>2. National liberation/state creation (Wallachia, Moldavia) (R.)<br>3. Balance of power (G.B., F., A.)<br>4. Maintain integrity of empire (T., G.B., F., A.)<br>5. Strategic territory (R.) |
| 13. Sardinia (France)–Austria, 1859 | 1. Territory (F., S.)<br>2. National liberation/state creation (S.)<br>3. Ideological liberation (S.)<br>4. Maintain integrity of empire (A.) |

140

Table 7.1 *continued*

| Wars/major armed interventions | Issues for original combatants |
|---|---|
| 14. German Confederation (Prussia)–Denmark, 1863–1864 | 1. Dynastic/succession claims<br>2. Protect ethnic confrères (P.)<br>3. Strategic territory (D.)<br>4. Enforce treaty terms (P.)<br>5. National unification/consolidation<br>6. Territory<br>7. Ethnic unification/irredenta |
| 15. Russia–Poland, 1863 | 1. National liberation/state creation (P.)<br>2. Maintain integrity of empire (R.) |
| 16. Austria–Prussia (Italy), 1866 | 1. Territory<br>2. National unification/consolidation (P., I.)<br>3. Maintain regional dominance (A.) |
| 17. Italy–Roman Republic, 1870 | 1. National unification/consolidation (I.)<br>2. Regime/state survival (R.R.) |
| 18. France–Prussia, 1870 | 1. National honor (F.)<br>2. Test of strength<br>3. National unification/consolidation (P.) |
| 19. Serbia, Montenegro–Turkey, 1876–1878 | 1. Territory<br>2. National unification/consolidation (S., M.)<br>3. Maintain integrity of empire (T.) |
| 20. Russia–Turkey, 1877–1878 | 1. Protect religious confrères (R.)<br>2. Territory<br>3. National liberation/state creation (Wallachia, Moldavia) (R.)<br>4. Protect ethnic confrères (R.)<br>5. Commerce/navigation (R.)<br>6. Maintain integrity of empire (T.) |
| 21. Bulgaria–Turkey, 1885 | 1. Ethnic unification/irredenta (B.)<br>2. National unification/consolidation (B.)<br>3. Maintain integrity of empire (T.) |
| 22. Serbia–Bulgaria, 1885 | 1. Territory |
| 23. Turkey–Greece, 1897 | 1. Protect ethnic confrères (G.)<br>2. National liberation/state creation (Crete)<br>3. Maintain integrity of empire (T.) |
| 24. Spain–United States, 1898 | 1. Ideological liberation (U.S.)<br>2. Commerce/navigation (U.S.)<br>3. Maintain integrity of empire (S.)<br>4. National liberation/state creation (Cuba, U.S.) |

Table 7.1 *continued*

| Wars/major armed interventions | Issues for original combatants |
|---|---|
| 25. Russia, Great Britain, Germany–Chinese rebels, 1898–1900 | 1. Maintain regional dominance<br>2. Commerce/navigation<br>3. Autonomy (C.) |
| 26. Boer Republics–Great Britain 1899–1902 | 1. Strategic territory (G.B.)<br>2. Autonomy (B.)<br>3. Protect nationals/commercial interests abroad (G.B.) |
| 27. Japan–Russia, 1904–1905 | 1. Empire creation (R.)<br>2. Colonial competition<br>3. Strategic territory (J.) |
| 28. Italy–Turkey, 1911–1912 | 1. Territory<br>2. Maintain integrity of empire (T.) |
| 29. Montenegro, Bulgaria, Greece, Serbia–Turkey, 1912–1913 | 1. Territory<br>2. Maintain integrity of empire (T.) |
| 30. Bulgaria–Serbia, Greece, 1913 | 1. Territory |
| 31. Austria–Hungary–Serbia, 1914 | 1. National honor (A.)<br>2. Maintain integrity of empire (A.)<br>3. Protect ethnic confrères (S.)<br>4. Regime/state survival (A.) |

but it is reasonable to claim that until the First World War, most armed conflicts in non-European areas had only limited effects on the mutual relations of the European-centered system.

Often described as a century of peace, the ninety-nine years after the Congress of Vienna had a 13 percent lower occurrence rate of war and armed interventions than the previous period (one war every 3.3 years compared to one every 2.8 years for the 1715–1814 period). Early in the period there were armed interventions to quell or support constitutionalist/liberal/nationalist revolutions in Italy, Spain, Belgium, and the Ottoman Empire. Toward the late nineteenth century, new, small states became significant war participants, often launching fairly blatant aggressions. But except for the three brief wars of German nation-building and Russia's armed interventions into Hungary and Poland at mid-century, the center of Europe running from London, through Paris, Berlin, and Vienna constituted a significant zone of peace. The populations of this area were to know only a few months of war during the entire century. The order constructed in 1814–15 was in part the source of the notably low incidence of intra-great power wars in the nineteenth century. The architects of the order, and their successors who corrected some of its deficiencies, succeeded where their predecessors of 1648 and 1713 had largely failed. The figures are something of a testimonial to the system of great power collaboration that was launched in the great war against Napoleon and formalized in the Quadruple Alliance: in the subsequent century, there were only four wars among the peacemakers of Paris and Vienna. Of these, three were brief and resulted in no fundamental restructuring of great power relationships. Only the Franco–Prussian War was to leave a residue of hostility and help polarize the continent. But if the measure of success is a significant diminution of *all* war, then the order did not dramatically improve the tenor of international politics.

The Balkans, and to a lesser extent Italy, were almost chronic arenas of crisis and war. These were the areas where the forces of nationalism favoring the creation of ethnically based nation states ran head on into the imperial structures of Austria-Hungary and Turkey. Russia was the main champion of "national liberation" against the Ottomans, while Napoleon III posed as the patron of Italian liberation and unification. The forces of change, in the form of national liberation and/or unification, could not be contained successfully within the old imperial structures, and war was the result.

The distribution of issues throughout the post-Vienna period reflects the great socio-political cleavages of the century. National liberation and unification/consolidation issues constituted 19 percent of all the issues that generated wars and armed interventions. The other side of the coin is the 18 percent where, for defenders, maintenance of imperial integrity and unity were the issues. Together, these accounted for 37 percent of all issues for the period, a significant increase from the 7 percent in the previous century. In contrast, issues of previous eras began significant declines: struggles over territory declined from one-quarter of all issues to 14 percent in the nineteenth century. Commerce and navigation issues diminished from 14 to 4 percent, and dynastic/succession issues declined by a more modest six points. Wars involving stakes of state/regime survival and colonial competition also have figures significantly lower than in the preceding century.

Table 7.3, which divides the number of wars and armed interventions (31) by the number of times a particular issue appeared as a source of war, confirms the impressions gained from table 7.2. More than one-half of all the wars (55 percent) involved problems of state creation. In these cases, the integrity of existing empires was at stake. The percentage increases from the previous period are dramatic, rising from 8 to 55. The nineteenth century was, par excellence, the era of nation-state creation and, as a concomitant, of the destruction of empires.[1]

[1] It may be one of the paradoxes of the era that while the peoples of Italy and the Balkans were attempting to liberate themselves and to create political structures based on ethnic/language/ and religious bases, France, Great Britain, Russia, Germany, and the United States set about to create or expand overseas empires. The two processes were almost simultaneous: empire disintegration and empire creation.

Table 7.2 *Distribution of issues that generated wars, 1815–1914*

| Issues | Frequency | % of all issues | Previous period % |
|---|---|---|---|
| Maintain integrity of state/empire | 17 | 18 | 3 |
| Territory | 13 | 14 | 26 |
| National liberation/state creation | 9 | 10 | 3 |
| National unification/consolidation | 8 | 9 | 1 |
| Protect ethnic confrères | 5 | 5 | — |
| Government composition | 4 | 4 | 5 |
| Strategic territory | 4 | 4 | 7 |
| Commerce/navigation | 4 | 4 | 14 |
| Dynastic/succession claims | 3 | 3 | 9 |
| Ideological liberation | 3 | 3 | 1 |
| Protect religious confrères | 3 | 3 | 4 |
| Maintain regional dominance | 3 | 3 | — |
| Empire creation | 3 | 3 | 4 |
| Regime/state survival | 2 | 2 | 7 |
| Ethnic unification/irredenta | 2 | 2 | — |
| National/crown honor | 2 | 2 | 1 |
| Autonomy | 2 | 2 | 1 |
| Balance of power | 1 | 1 | 1 |
| Enforce treaty terms | 1 | 1 | 3 |
| Test of strength | 1 | 1 | — |
| Colonial competition | 1 | 1 | 4 |
| Protect nationals/commercial interests abroad | 1 | 1 | — |
| Total | 92 | 96[a] | 94[a] |

[a] Rounding error.

The rise of national liberation/state creation and national unification issues that generated wars in the nineteenth century was accompanied by the significant decline of many of the issues that were the sources of war prior to the French Revolution. Contests over territory continued to be a major conflict issue, but declined from 67 to 42 percent for the previous period. Commerce/navigation, dynastic/succession, and regime/state survival issues also diminished by significant proportions. Colonial competition gave rise to a number of international crises at the end of the period (Fashoda, Algeciras), but only one war resulted from the clash of imperial ambitions (the Russo-Japanese War, 1904–1905). Let us now examine in more detail some of the characteristics of war-generating issues. We begin with comments on new and rising issues.

Table 7.3 *Issues that generated wars, 1815–1914*

| Issues | Frequency | % of wars | Previous period % |
|---|---|---|---|
| Maintain integrity of state/empire | 17 | 55 | 8 |
| Territory | 13 | 42 | 67 |
| National liberation/state creation | 9 | 29 | 8 |
| National unification/consolidation | 8 | 26 | — |
| Protect ethnic confrères | 5 | 16 | — |
| Government composition | 4 | 13 | 14 |
| Strategic territory | 4 | 13 | 17 |
| Commerce/navigation | 4 | 13 | 36 |
| Dynastic/succession claims | 3 | 10 | 22 |
| Ideological liberation | 3 | 10 | 1 |
| Protect religious confrères | 3 | 10 | 11 |
| Maintain regional dominance | 3 | 10 | |
| Empire creation | 3 | 10 | 11 |
| Regime/state survival | 2 | 6 | 17 |
| Ethnic unification/irredenta | 2 | 6 | — |
| National/crown honor | 2 | 6 | 3 |
| Autonomy | 2 | 6 | — |
| Balance of power | 1 | 3 | 3 |
| Enforce treaty terms | 1 | 3 | 8 |
| Test of strength | 1 | 3 | — |
| Colonial competition | 1 | 3 | 11 |
| Protect nationals/commercial interests abroad | 1 | 3 | — |
| Total | 92 | | |

NEW WAR-GENERATING ISSUES

## National liberation/state creation

Blainey (1973:70) suggests that "increasingly in Europe [during the nineteenth century] the royal funeral was replaced by civil strife as a dangerous disturber of peace." This was the case. The nightmares of the Paris and Vienna architects – the principles of liberalism and nationality – were the major sources of both civil and international wars between 1815 and 1914. In fact, the two issues often became joined. The bonds between rebel groups and outside patrons, usually one or more of the great powers, proliferated. Starting with the armed contest over Greek independence, the great powers often found themselves caught between conflicting principles: support for liberalism and "national" rights versus non-intervention. And these principles soon became entangled with more traditional problems of great power rivalry. While British public opinion, for example, may have

145

sympathized with the national aspirations of the Balkan peoples, the collapse of the Ottoman Empire could result in Russian hegemony in the region, a position that would pose a direct strategic threat to Great Britain's growing commercial interests in the Middle East and to its lifeline to India. The dilemmas of conflicting principles were daunting even by contemporary standards. Despite the fears of Castlereagh, Talleyrand, and Metternich, by the 1830s the great powers became increasingly sympathetic to the nationality principle, even if they could not usually tolerate tendencies toward liberalism and democracy on the home front. In fact, they often became midwives to the birth of new states. They collaborated to coerce the Ottomans to grant independence to Greece. France intervened on behalf of Belgian rebels and the Concert powers jointly created and legitimized the birth of that nation, separating it in 1831 from the Dutch kingdom. Napoleon III conspired with Sardinia's Cavour in 1859 to launch a war of liberation and Italian unification against Austria-Hungary. Russia constantly championed the cause of Slavic nation-building and acted as the protector of the often-persecuted Christians of the Ottoman Empire. Greek, Romanian, Bulgarian, and Serbian statehood was as much the result of Russian diplomacy and military activity as it was of indigenous movements for national liberation.

The nineteenth century, then, represented the "nationalization" of international issues. The international politics of the seventeenth and eighteenth centuries revolved largely around princely claims, based on law, ancient titles, and more pragmatic concerns of power politics. By the nineteenth century, the rights of princes were increasingly replaced by the "rights of peoples." As much as the policy-makers may have remained faithful to notions of power balancing and to the requirements of a stable international order, they could not ignore this great process of national consciousness and state-formation that was taking place throughout the continent (Perré, 1962:19). Yet, to the extent that, like Russia and France, they actively promoted the process, they were unwittingly undermining the bases of the order that had been created after the Napoleonic Wars.

### Maintain integrity of the state/empire

More than one-half of the wars of the period revolved wholly or in part around efforts to create nation states. With the exception of German unification and Belgium's birth, these efforts were at the expense of imperial integrity. The process had begun with the revolt of the American Colonies, but accelerated rapidly after the Napoleonic

Wars. The Greek cause aroused considerable sympathy throughout Europe, and with the success of that effort, the message of imperial vulnerability had been sent. The Egyptian Pasha, Mehmet Ali, attempted to create his own empire from Ottoman lands; the cause of Italian liberation and unification soon followed, then came Prussia's turn to create a German state, and finally the peoples of the Balkans tore themselves out of the Ottoman Empire.

The issue of imperial integrity is not classified as state or regime survival because few of the beleaguered imperial crowns or courts saw the loss of a province as a mortal threat. The Ottomans attempted to forestall the process of Balkan state formation by alternating between violent repression and mild reforms – the latter usually imposed on them by the Concert – and the Austrians sought compensation for imperial losses in Italy by extending their influence into the Balkans. Typical Ottoman and Austrian leaders did not regard imperial collapse as imminent until the eve of the First World War. They had managed to maintain the façade of imperial integrity through annexations (Bosnia in 1908), periodic military victories (the Turkish repression of a Cretan rebellion, supported by Greece, in 1897), and external support (Great Britain in the case of Turkey and Germany in the case of Austria–Hungary). By 1914, however, the situation was no longer tenable, particularly in Austria-Hungary. The strong will of Chief of Staff Conrad and Foreign Minister Berchtold to crush Serbia was born out of a sense of desperation. The Empire could no longer survive with a continuation of nationalist agitation and subversion emanating from the Balkans. Metternich's nightmare had come to pass.

### National unification/consolidation

The process of national liberation did not always result in the fulfillment of the nationality principle. Often a discontinuity between the new state (e.g., Sardinia, Prussia) and the larger language community remained. Portions of those communities persisted as a congeries of small independent states or as political jurisdictions under foreign imperial control. In addition to national liberation movements, therefore, there were also movements for national unification and consolidation of territories inhabited by ethnic kin. The 1850s and 1860s constituted the great era of national unification wars in Germany and Italy. In both cases, they were primarily at the expense of Austria–Hungary and thus further undermined the order established in 1814–15.

147

### Ethnic unification/irredenta

This category derives as well from the nationality principle. It is a new phenomenon of international relations and played a role in 6 percent of the wars of the period. The new states responded to pleas from their ethnic kin residing in neighboring jurisdictions to incorporate them. The struggle between Denmark and Prussia over Schleswig-Holstein, which generated two wars, represented from the Prussian point of view generous (if cynical) assistance to help a people join their ethnic kin. Within the German-speaking areas of the Danish provinces, there was vigorous agitation for unification with the German Confederation, on whose behalf Prussia was formally acting. Similarly, in 1885, the eastern Rumelians rose up against Turkish rule and requested Bulgarian intervention and eventual annexation. This issue is distinguished from national unification/consolidation by the fact that agitation for unification comes initially and primarily from the irredentist groups abroad.

### Protect ethnic confrères

Throughout the post-Vienna period, Russia acted as the protector of Slav (and also Romanian) ethnic groups throughout the Balkans. The Ottomans typically confronted nationalist agitation and rebellion by massacres and systematic persecution, and only less frequently by reforms and the granting of greater autonomy. Though the Russians could be equally harsh in dealing with Polish nationalism, they went to war with Turkey twice in part to protect and support Slav populations against Ottoman oppression.

### Government composition

Thirteen percent of the wars and armed interventions of the 1815–1914 period concerned in whole or in part attempts of external actors to suppress civil disturbances arising over republicanism. The post-Napoleonic War coalition was severely strained by the problems posed by liberal constitutional revolutions in Naples, Piedmont, and Spain. In each of the instances a great power intervened to sustain the forces of royal legitimacy. We must recall the tremendous impression the French Revolution had made on most European governments. Their first priority after 1814 was to restore domestic and international order. Any alternative to discipline and "repose" was a threat – and the forces of constitutionalism, liberalism, and nationalism often believed that armed violence was a legitimate means of achieving their

148

purposes. In this situation, royal regimes regarded armies as necessary to undertake domestic and international police duties, of preventing unrest and insurgency (Best, 1982:205).

There were minor interventions by Spain and Great Britain in Portugal's domestic disturbances in the 1830s and 1840s (not included in the list of cases), but for the latter half of the nineteenth century and until the First World War armed interventions to effect the outcomes of domestic political contests no longer took place. The doctrines of constitutionalism and republicanism had become sufficiently widespread, and since they were no longer coupled with revolutionary imperialism of the Napoleonic kind, most courts no longer saw them as threats to the peace in general or to the balance of power in particular.

### Protect religious confrères

Statistically there is no significant change in the frequency of this issue compared to the previous period. Until 1856, Russia remained the official protector of the Christian populations and holy places in the Ottoman Empire. The Ottomans had granted this status and implied right of intervention to the Russians in the Treaty of Kutchuk-Kainardji (1774). Religious persecution by the Turks attracted the attention of Russia's policy-makers throughout the nineteenth century and was one of several problems that kept Ottoman–Russian relations at a high level of hostility. Religion was seldom an issue sufficient in itself to lead to war, although on one occasion Alexander II was so enraged at Turkish actions against Orthodox Christians in 1877 (as reprisals against Greek-sponsored rebellion in Crete and elsewhere) that he might have acted militarily even in the absence of other issues, had not his advisers' views prevailed. Elsewhere in Europe, religious differences failed to create major international tensions. The secularization of international politics, begun in 1648 and virtually completed by the conclusion of the War of the Spanish Succession, continued without change.

### National/crown honor

This issue refers to statements by policy-makers that they must go to war to preserve or vindicate the honor of the state/regime. In modern parlance we would probably refer to the value at stake as reputation or status, as in the case where America's reputation for meeting its "commitments" was a value underlying the decisions to escalate involvement in Vietnam. No doubt all wars involve these

149

values at least implicitly; this would be particularly the case of an actor defending the status quo. It must respond by the use of force lest the initiator see a weak reaction as an opportunity for escalating demands and/or actions. In two cases, concerns of honor or status were important considerations in the policy-making process. The challenges were in themselves not critical. The first case was the French response to the Prussian project of placing a Hohenzollern on the throne of Spain in 1870. The second was Austria-Hungary's response to the assassination of the Archduke Ferdinand in Sarajevo in 1914. In both instances the challenge and provocation were interpreted as direct assaults on the honor of the state.

Nineteenth-century concepts of honor were rather broader than the contemporary notions of reputation and prestige. They contained not only a strategic calculation (the costs of retreating or ignoring a challenge or provocation), but also a moral value. Honor had been and remained throughout the nineteenth century the moral basis for leadership. It was grounded in tradition, caste, and conscience, and it formed the ultimate basis for the military profession: honor among officers within an armed force, and honor among combatants in time of war (Pearton, 1982:29). The diplomats had their own counterpart: certain kinds of diplomatic actions went beyond any of the explicit or implicit "rules of the game" among the powers. Such actions did not have to constitute threats to national security (the Hohenzollern withdrew his candidacy upon French objections). It was enough that Bismarck had treated France in such a deliberately provocative manner as to constitute a fundamental deviation from the diplomatic norms of the time. As in a duel, France declared war in 1870 as much to vindicate honor as to achieve any specific political or security objective. Similarly, the Austrian policy-makers judged that the assassination of 1914 was sufficiently outrageous to justify a humiliating ultimatum against Serbia. It was just one of several issues that precipitated the war, but from the perspective of the times, it was an important one.

Now let us examine issues that showed significant declines in incidence during the 1815-1914 period.

## OLD AND DECLINING ISSUES

### Territory

The quest for territory declined as a source of international conflict. Contests over territory appeared in thirteen of the thirty-one wars (42 percent), but that is a significant change from the 67 percent figure for the 1715-1814 period. The value of territory as a basis for national power, status, and prestige did not diminish notably; it is only that the issues generated by constitutional, liberal, and national causes underlay more of the conflicts of the era.

In the nineteenth century, territory continued to be the main indicator of a nation's power, as it had been since the days of Louis XIV. The architects of Paris and Vienna constructed a *territorial* (including population) balance of power, and not a balance defined in terms of the size of armies, the number of garrisons and forts, or the number of vessels in navies. For most of the policy-makers throughout the century, economic assets and industrial capacity counted for little. For example, the military advisers of the Austrian Emperor, Francis Joseph, were oblivious to and uninterested in the opportunities offered by German and Austrian financiers to build railways through the Balkans. The military were only interested in territorial gains in the Balkans as a means of compensating for earlier losses of Italian territory (Taylor, 1954:231). They also considered partitioning the whole area with Russia as a means of maintaining the balance of power.

Throughout Europe, conservatives, many of whom held high positions in the governments of Germany, France, Great Britain, Italy, and Russia, regarded the state and its territories as critical elements of an organism, a social whole that had to expand or otherwise succumb to others. These officials, under the influence of social Darwinism and the ideas of German philosophers, regarded national power as a tangible substance, the primary component of which was territory. While losses of other tangible assets such as population could be tolerated if necessary, a cession of territory was comparable to an operation on the body of the state. Conversely, territorial acquisition was a physical manifestation of the organic need of the state to enlarge itself (Petersson, 1964:36). In the nineteenth century, then, territory assumed several critical functions in strategic and diplomatic thought: as a measure of the balance of power, as the primary index of national power, as the critical component of the organic body politic and thus for many, as the primary prize in war. Its significance went far beyond the resources and population that it contained. These were only of secondary importance and seldom in themselves an asset worth a war.

The successors to the peacemakers of 1814–15 generally maintained the view that the balance of power was defined in terms of a particular territorial distribution, and most agreed in principle that territorial balancing was necessary to maintain peace in Europe. The post-Napoleonic territorial settlements constituted the mental frame of reference for them. Any significant deviations from it would be a cause for concern and perhaps a *casus belli*. Deviation invariably was defined as

151

any attempt by a nation to appropriate to itself territory which belonged to another. Lord John Russell typified attitudes of nineteenth-century policy-makers: "We are connected . . . with the general system of Europe, and any territorial increase of one power . . . which disturbs the general balance of power in Europe could not be a matter of indifference to this country" (quoted in Hinsley, 1966:224). Thus, a political economy interpretation of nineteenth-century international politics does not reflect the realities. The world of diplomacy and the world of finance and production remained largely separate at least until the end of the century.

### Dynastic/succession issues

Dynastic and succession issues declined notably as sources of international conflict and war. Royal legitimacy was constantly challenged by constitutional, liberal, and national principles, but these involved questions not so much of *who* would rule as *how* peoples would be ruled. No longer was the death of a monarch a cause of international instability, nor could royal marriages by themselves cement military alliances. Only three wars of the period (Egypt–Turkey and the two wars over Schleswig–Holstein) involved important dynastic/succession issues. The Hohenzollern candidacy for the Spanish crown in 1870 instigated a serious Franco-Prussian crisis, but the candidacy was withdrawn and, as suggested, other issues of honor and national unification served as the purposes over which the two parties reverted to war. Selecting monarchs for some of the new states of Europe such as Greece, Belgium, and Bulgaria caused some diplomatic frictions, but after the 1820s no government actively went in search of crowns, and "death watch" wars, so prominent in the previous 150 years, became a thing of the past.

### Colonial competition

Colonial competition, the struggle to create exclusive zones of economic activity and settlement, ceased to generate armed conflicts for more than sixty years after the Congress of Vienna. That settlement had distributed colonies between Great Britain and France, primarily in North America and the Caribbean, and for a variety of reasons the French accepted the settlement as final. France was not a colonial-revisionist power after the Bourbon restoration in 1814, although there were serious quarrels with the British over the Levant and Egypt in the late 1830s. Napoleon III's adventure into Mexico was a cause of alarm in the United States, but mostly a cause of incredulity in Europe. Russian expansion and influence-seeking in Persia caused conflict with Great Britain during the latter part of the nineteenth century, and British occupation of Egypt in 1882 was a source of some concern on the continent. But the nineteenth century did not witness a continuation of the great Anglo–Spanish–French armed rivalries of the previous century. The post-Napoleon settlements were authoritative in this issue area for more than fifty years.

The new age of imperialism starting in the 1870s remained for the most part peacefully competitive for the next decades, but once the territory of Africa, the Middle East, and the South Pacific became appropriated, competition turned into conflict, as the gains of one party were commonly regarded as losses for others. Crises over the Sudan and Morocco almost caused great power wars, while Russia's expansion into Japan's sphere of influence in Korea ended in war.

Among others, Lenin was impressed by the new imperialism and came to attribute its causes to the increased concentration of capital and to the production of surplus. He uses a standard $a$ causes $b$ type of analysis: governments were "pushed" abroad by internal economic processes. As a monocausal theory, it failed to assess all the other types of explanations, including the international competitiveness of the times (keeping up with the Joneses syndrome), humanitarian sentiments to bring Christianity and civilization to the "backward" peoples of the world and to terminate the Arab slave trade, strategic necessities and opportunities and, as in the case of Russia's highly belligerent behavior in the Far East, getting involved in a "nice little war" to stifle revolutionary activity at home. Whatever the explanations, the diplomatic and military behaviors associated with imperialism added a new dimension of conflict to international politics, both between the major competitors and between the imperial nations and the subject peoples. The Cuban uprising against Spain and the Boxer Rebellion in China were early indications that Westernization and economic exploitation of the "backward" peoples would not go unchallenged. The great outward thrust of European civilization at the end of the nineteenth century sowed the seeds of the greatest single issue that would lead to war and violence in the post-1945 period.

### Commerce/navigation

One of the most dramatic declines among the issues that generated wars in the European states system involved commerce and navigation. Matters of trade monopolies, privateering, fishing rights,

rights of neutrals in wartime, and territorial jurisdiction over the seas had been significant sources of conflict and war during the seventeenth and eighteenth centuries. By the nineteenth century, many of these issues had been resolved through the development of customary law, international treaties, or obsolescence. The Peace of Paris in 1856 was a particularly notable landmark in developing law governing river navigation, establishing an international regime for the Turkish straits, and defining the rights of neutral shipping during war. America's naval action against the Barbary pirates in the early 1800s also helped in making the Mediterranean Sea a relatively safe avenue for commerce and transportation.

Liberal opinion in the 1820s and 1830s commonly regarded international commerce as an "ally of peace" (Nef, 1963:336) and as a factor that generally promoted progress and tied nations together. But perhaps more important, for most of our period commercial activity was not directly tied to the power of the state. With the exception of Great Britain and less so of France, commercial figures did not have significant influence among the key policy-making groups. This was to change somewhat in St. Petersburg, Vienna, and Berlin around the turn of the century, but for the most part commercial activity remained "low politics" throughout the continent. The international politics of nineteenth-century Europe revolved around questions of territory, state creation, balance of power, alliances, and colonial rivalry. Commercial and navigational problems excited little attention at the highest levels of government.

The 13 percent of the wars in which they figured significantly all involved the problem of the Turkish straits. The positions of Russia and Turkey were straightforward and fundamentally incompatible: Russia wanted free access through the straits for both commercial and naval vessels during peace and war; Turkey maintained and fought to maintain full control over all vessels transiting the Dardanelles and Bosporus waterways. The Turkish position prevailed in the Treaty of Paris (1856), but the issue continued to cause frictions and was not authoritatively resolved until after the Second World War.

### Balance of power

Commitment to the maintenance of the balance of power on the continent remained significant for most of the policy-makers of the great powers at least until the turn of the century. In virtually all the crises of the period, policy-makers estimated their adversaries' behavior against the yardstick of the 1814–15 settlement. The balance, however, was seldom a critical issue that generated war. It could be maintained by means other than force. The British position on the "Eastern Question" that so frequently upset the repose of Europe was to restrain Russian pressure against the Ottomans. The Vienna Congress did not include discussion of the Ottoman problem, and although Alexander I strongly believed that Russia should not act in the region without the consent of his fellow monarchs, his successors did not feel so committed. By ignoring the problem, the peacemakers failed to provide ground-rules for the future. But this lacuna could be covered by the general principle of power balancing through alliances or by other means. It was generally understood throughout Europe that the destruction of the Ottoman Empire and a corresponding extension of Russian power into the region would be inconsistent with the general balance. Thus Great Britain, and to a lesser extent France and Austria, sought to support the Turks against Russian pressures. They did this by helping to train the Sultan's armies and navies; by advising him to introduce domestic reforms; and by cajoling or coercing him to provide greater religious freedom and political autonomy for the Orthodox Christians and Slavic populations. In 1853–56, they fought on the Sultan's side against Russia. British policy-makers in 1853 made explicit references to the maintenance of the balance of power as one of the main issues under contention.

By the late nineteenth century, the meaning of the term "balance of power" had changed significantly. During the 1880s and 1890s it began to refer primarily to the *military balance* of the two alliances, or of two individual states such as France and Germany. There were no longer frequent references to a particular distribution of territory throughout Europe or to a general principle that preserved the peace of Europe. Although Bismarck had been a champion of balance in this older sense, his successors were not. German industrial and military might were so highly developed by the end of the century as to encourage thinking in terms of predominance and world leadership rather than balance. Eyes were now cast almost exclusively on levels of armaments and manpower. Territory no longer served as the measure of balance or imbalance.

### Other issues

The remaining issues are for the most part self-explanatory, and their incidence is sufficiently low that no upward or downward trends are apparent. The category "test of strength," however, needs a comment. The Franco-Prussian War was in some ways unique, particularly because there were few concrete issues dividing the two nations. Bismarck believed that he would have to defeat France militarily in order to consolidate and conclude the great project of German unification. This was his purpose, and he had to concoct an issue (as Napoleon III and Cavour had done in 1859 before going to war against Austria) to justify the resort to arms. French honor was involved, but once the Hohenzollern candidacy had been abandoned no concrete issue remained between Berlin and Paris. Like two gunslingers, one of whom had been challenged by a relatively petty incident (the Hohenzollern candidacy and the infamous Ems telegram), the Germans and French seemed compelled to find out which was superior through a test of arms. This unfortunate and eminently avoidable war was essentially a test of strength and reputation. The analogy of the duel is particularly appropriate here.

## THE CHARACTER OF WAR PREPARATION

The French revolutionary and Napoleonic regimes introduced vast social, organizational, and ideological changes in the arts, organization, and strategies of warfare. Technological changes, in comparison, were relatively minor. After the Congress of Vienna, however, military dispositions tended to revert to pre-revolutionary patterns. Most governments did not introduce or maintain conscription, and most important, they did not deploy their troops in a threatening manner. Diplomacy was left to the diplomats and military advisers came into the decision-making process only after war had been declared. Military planning did not constrain diplomatic action. Options were left open, although some governments did anticipate the most likely avenues of attack. Russia had no concentration of troops in the south as a permanent threat to Turkey. Austrian and Russian garrisons were posed mostly against Poland, ready to intervene against any revolutionary activity there. The bulk of the Prussian army was on the Rhine, deployed there on the common assumption of the time that the main threat to Europe remained a French revolutionary onslaught of the 1792 and 1798 models (Taylor, 1954:3).

Military forces were not of such a size, in any event, as to constitute a significant threat to neighbors and adversaries. The great powers had only vague notions of each others' land and naval military resources (Bridge and Bullen, 1980:8). The task of the military was to win wars after they had been declared, and not to direct diplomatic events to accommodate military plans. Policy-making remained firmly in the hands of the civilians. Finally, both military and civilian leaders anticipated short wars.

The military experience of the first three quarters of the nineteenth century was characterized by unusually brief contests of arms, usually terminated after one or two decisive battles. Important battles such as Solferino, Sadowa, and Sedan settled the issue, sometimes only weeks after the war had been officially declared. The contrary experiences of the Crimean War and the American Civil War did not suggest other possibilities. Nor, once military planning became a major governmental enterprise, did the expectation of brief wars change. Schlieffen explicitly rejected a strategy of attrition on the grounds that protracted struggle would be "impossible at a time when the existence of the nation is based on an uninterrupted functioning of commerce and industry. . . A wearing-out strategy cannot be undertaken at a time when the maintenance of millions calls for billions" (quoted in Vagts, 1959:349). It was also on this assumption that civilian leaders and parliamentarians throughout Europe were willing to commit the necessary resources for largely expanded armies and their increasingly costly weapons system (Rosecrance, 1963:163; Bond, 1983:27).

In the 1870s and 1880s, the character of war preparation, military planning, and threat perception changed significantly. Military plans, of which Schlieffen's is only the most famous, became increasingly detailed and based on fixed views about the identity of the enemy. Options became increasingly narrower as railway timetables, mobilization plans, and logistics problems all had to be worked out in detail ahead of the first battle. Efficiency and speed were the values to be maximized, and the plans had to incorporate roles for all sorts of new weapons systems. Many of these weapons supported short war expectations by enhancing the capacity to achieve strategic surprise and quick concentration. By the turn of the century, conscription was the rule rather than the exception in Europe (Bridge and Bullen, 1980:9).

The emphasis on creating mighty and efficient military machines escaped close civilian scrutiny. Particularly in Wilhelm's Germany, civilian control over the military was eroded badly. Between the 1860s and the turn of the century, for example, the Reichstag lost the right even to debate or discuss the military budget except for special occasions usually spaced as far apart as every seven years. The civilian war minister became a figurehead, a man who had no authority or influence over the army or the navy. The Kaiser made the key decisions, and he looked for advice primarily to his own military cabinet and to the general staff (Bond, 1983:58). In France, Italy, Austria-Hungary, and Russia, civilian controls remained more effective, but at the ultimate moment in 1914, the Tsar had to accept Russian plans for full mobilization – meaning war – because there were no options for partial mobilization.

It was also after mid-century that the estimation of power became increasingly connected to military capabilities rather than to territory. With the application of modern technology to war-making capacities, and with advanced planning that maximized speed and efficiency in mobilization, deployment, and attack, the distinction between peace-time and wartime became less prominent. By the 1870s military estab-lishments were perpetually poised for combat, swaggering, and display. In the pre-industrial era, cabinets and courts could carefully attune military responses to the unique nature of threats and chal-lenges. By the end of the century, the options had been reduced primarily to doing nothing and mobilizing fully (Pearton, 1982:133). Bismarck likened the Europe of his time to a railway carriage, in which five strangers, all heavily armed, are placed in the same compartment. The slightest movement toward a firearm would be cause for a pre-emptive shot (Bond, 1983:27).

Under the balance of power system in the first half of the century, marginal territorial gains or losses were not generally evaluated as threatening to the whole system. Where calculations of power are based on rapidly changing military capabilities, however, the notion of balance tends to be more stringent and less flexible. The sensitivity of the British and Germans during the naval arms race prior to the First World War demonstrates how finely power calculations were made. Virtually every dreadnought launched provided evidence either of a mortal threat or of an increasing and significant margin of safety. In the 1820s and 1830s, the arming of a garrison was seldom newsworthy.

### THE MEANING OF WAR

After the Napoleonic Wars, political leaders and diplomats continued to see the military in instrumental terms. Armed forces had a distinct diplomatic purpose: to coerce, warn, or deter opponents for specific political ends. Clausewitz' view of the military operating in a defined political context was the conventional wisdom of the day. Force was an adjunct to, and not a replacement for, diplomacy. Although the nature of warfare had changed considerably during the Napoleonic period, its functions in international relations had not. The wars of the first half-century after the Congress of Vienna had very clearly understood purposes defined in terms of the issues discussed above. Once the purposes had been achieved, or if a stalemate and/or military exhaustion developed on the battlefield, the war terminated. Once the Russians had extracted by military means promises on the part of the Sultan to provide freedom of conscience and worship, and security of church property, for his Orthodox Christian subjects, and once they had helped the Greeks obtain their independence in the 1820s, the war ended. In 1859, the plot of Cavour and Napoleon III to seize Lombardy and Venice from Austria and to begin the process of Italian unification was carried out by the military. Once the clearly specified and limited objectives had been achieved through the defeat of the Austrians at Solferino, the war ended. Though Napoleon was shocked and sickened upon witnessing the carnage of the battlefield, he did not cease to make cost-benefit calculations. The sacrifice of French and Italian lives was, in his view, justified by clear political gains, namely the liberation and political unification of Italy (the nationality principle) and French territorial gains in Savoy and Nice.

For the first half-century after the Congress of Vienna, the distinction between war and peace and between civilians and the military remained clear-cut. War was partly the antithesis of peace, but it was also the continuation of peacetime processes albeit in different form. War was conducted in a framework of moral ideas, specific purposes, and assumed limits. International relationships did not stop with the onset of war; neither diplomats nor civilians across nations ceased speaking to each other. During the Crimean War, the British government permitted its military opponent, Russia, to raise a loan on the London money market, and the French invited the Russians to participate in an international exhibition of industry and the arts.

By the turn of the century, this rational and limited view of war changed. The Franco-Prussian "test of strength" seemed to many unnecessary and wasteful. The purposes of the military action were ephemeral: they involved humiliating rather than merely defeating an enemy army in battle. The publics of the nations concerned viewed the war as national undertakings to demonstrate superiority over the other. It was not only a contest between armies, but a struggle of societies. Even though the war was relatively short, it gave some important clues about what to expect as the means of destruction became increasingly effective.

Prophetic analysts, such as Ivan Bloch, began to write about the nature of war under industrial conditions. Unlike earlier wars, they argued that wars of the future would be great struggles between civilizations, wars of national survival and of supremacy. They would manifest the great spiritual and moral virtues of armed combat. The issues that separated nations were of secondary importance. National-

159

ism, jingoism, militarism, the mechanization of warfare, and the increasingly significant role of the professional military in diplomacy all combined to create a new phenomenon in international relations: the war between entire societies for unknown or obscure purposes.

As the nineteenth century progressed, popular attitudes toward the use of force in international relations became increasingly divided. For the majority among the educated classes and to a large extent among the new industrial working classes the ideas of liberalism and pacifism ran strong. War was now defined as a continuing problem of concern, requiring political action to restrict its use.

Liberals were optimists. They assumed that as civilization and commerce progressed, the problem of war would largely resolve itself. "If barbarism had cropped out in the community of European nations [as in 1870] it was not because of the ways in which Western peoples were becoming civilized. It was because they were not civilized enough" (Nef, 1963:336). The message of the liberal optimists was that wealth and progress would come through industry and trade, not through war. Indeed, much of Montesquieu's argument that war was incompatible with trade and wealth remained throughout the nineteenth century. According to Auguste Comte and many others, the pursuit of economic advantage was likely to improve human manners, customs, and laws, and as a consequence, to reduce the incidence of war.

Liberal and pacifist views flourished in Great Britain and on the continent and took institutional form in numerous peace societies and in some of the social democratic parties – notably in Germany, where by 1912 it had become the largest party in the Reichstag, supported by 4.5 million voters. By the end of the century transnational peace groups met frequently and urged governments to institute arbitration plans. Their sentiments were shared by such well-known personages as Alfred Nobel, Andrew Carnegie, Bertha von Suttner, Ivan Bloch, and Leon Bourgeois. Many leading professionals of the times also adhered to cosmopolitan and anti-war attitudes.

Another stream of thought developed simultaneously. Many influential individuals came to regard war as a desirable and constructive social activity. Their image of war was of short, decisive battles between armies. Few correctly predicted what war under industrial conditions would really be like. Nevertheless, these individuals became champions of the "struggle between nations" conception of war.

It is not possible to gauge to what extent such ideas formed the images of war of the men and women in the streets, but they no doubt helped to make credible the increased jingoism of the press in many countries of Europe during the late nineteenth and early twentieth centuries. And it is clear that the "meaning" of war for millions throughout Europe became fundamentally different from what it had been and what it has become during the late twentieth century. These people did not view war as a result of diplomatic breakdown; nor was it a social disease, a tragic mistake, a failure of conflict management, or an indicator of moral insensitivity. It was, rather, an inevitable and constructive consequence of the eternal struggle between nations and civilizations. Millions anticipated that its consequences would be beneficial, at least to the winners. All the traditional virtues that seemed to be assaulted by growing materialism, class warfare, secularism, and pragmatism would be strengthened and redeemed through war. These included social cohesion and group solidarity, commitment to a cause greater than the self or family, patriotism, and moral-cultural improvement. War was to be welcomed, not avoided. For its advocates, it was a philosophical and moral good, as much an agent of progress as commerce and scientific discovery were for the liberals and pacifists. Allegiance to the nation and the doctrine of the national state as the final end of existence and as the justification for war replaced earlier conceptions of philosophy in which man was the primary concern (Nef, 1952:405).

Numerous writers and politicians took up these themes throughout the latter half of the nineteenth century. These included Treitschke, Proudhon, von Bernhardi, and the many social Darwinists who argued that the survival of the fittest provides a justification for war and a means of social, cultural, and moral progress. To Steinmetz, for example, war "is an institution ordained by God, who weighs the nations in its balance . . . Its dread hammer is the welder of men into cohesive states and nowhere but in such states can human nature adequately develop its capacity. The only alternative is degeneration" (quoted by Dunn, 1974:228).

To Treitschke, among the most notable historians and social philosophers of the late nineteenth century, war not only gave birth to and preserved states, as Hegel had maintained, but was also a tonic for peoples, an agent of creation and a means of cultural progress. It also consolidates peoples, sweeps away factionalism and group selfishness, and intensifies patriotism (cf. Rosecrance, 1963:163). This was not only an empirical description of outbursts of enthusiasm that typically greeted the first days of war, but also a justification for the use of force without any particular political purpose. War would have beneficial social consequences. These would be more important than diplomatic goals.

161

Armed with these images and ideas, publics and many political and military leaders abandoned earlier conceptions of war in its instrumental sense. If war is good as well as inevitable, then the problem of the diplomat is not how to avoid it but how to choose the appropriate time. If international relations are no longer viewed as the adjustment of states within an overarching balance of power, but as a struggle for social, economic, and cultural supremacy and expansion, then compromise, conflict resolution, and moderation can only be seen as signs of weakness. The external purposes of society no longer concern particular issues, but nothing less than mastery over other peoples in an endless struggle for survival.

We have already argued that favorable elite attitudes toward war are neither necessary nor sufficient conditions that will lead policy-makers to choose armed force in any particular situation (see chapter 1; Lebow, 1981:248). Yet, when top policy-makers, supported by broad publics and a vigorous press, regard war as a philosophical good and as a necessary condition for national survival and moral and cultural progress, then fear of its consequences and the calculation of its costs are not so likely to act as constraints against choosing this course of action. In the Hegelian, Nietzschean, social Darwinist view, the overall calculation of costs and advantages, including favorable social by-products of war, tilted dangerously toward the "war pays" end of the spectrum.

Policy-makers in the generation after 1815 did not see war in apocalyptic terms, although they were conscious of the possible revolutionary consequences of lengthy wars. Their concern was, rather, that war had to be undertaken within the context of certain rules, assumptions, and standards that were articulated in the post-Napoleon settlements and through numerous subsequent meetings of the Concert powers. Wars should be consistent with the general principles of the balance of power or they should serve some reasonably noble or collective purpose such as protecting Christian minorities against repression by the Ottomans. As late as the 1860s, both the broad public and numerous policy-makers saw war as the last choice, to be used only when other means had failed.[1] Napoleon III (though he did not regularly follow his own advice) wrote that war could be used only for the defense of the weak and for the maintenance of law and justice against wrongdoing. In his view, national aggrandizement was not an adequate moral basis for bloodshed (Pearton, 1982:29). There was the final consideration of

[1] The Treaty of Paris (1856) made the first reference to the pacific settlement of disputes since the Treaty of Westphalia. Protocol 23 of the treaty included a general statement to the effect that governments should resort to mediation through a third power before they could legitimately use force. This implied a presumption against military solutions to diplomatic problems (Hinsley, 1967:233).

proportionality. Force had to be consistent with the advancement or defense of some reasonably concrete purpose. Policy-makers, like Napoleon III, explicitly condemned general wars of aggrandizement that would destroy the balance of power or that violated established rights and conventions. Through the mid-century, the moral, diplomatic, and customary constraints against the use of force were substantial and reasonably effective.

These attitudes changed dramatically in the last decades of the century. Advocates of war were to be found in high levels in most of the governments of Europe. Although European foreign offices had frequently issued threats as a means of signaling opponents their commitments to certain positions, this was commonly understood to be a normal practice of diplomacy, necessary for defining the limits of tolerance. In contrast, German officials after the demise of Bismarck and under the tutelage and exemplar of the Kaiser regularly issued threats of force, even when no important stakes were involved in a conflict. Many of the Kaiser's utterances were unnecessarily bellicose and echoed the German redemption-through-war school of thought. In 1912, for example, he referred to the "struggle for existence which the German people . . . will eventually have to fight against the Slavs, supported by the Latins" (Luard, 1986:357). His advisers were devotees of such views and did not hide their beliefs behind the façade of military professionalism. Colmar von der Goltz asserted that war had become the nation's way of doing business. Von Moltke virtually quoted Hegel and Treitschke in arguing that "without war, the world would stagnate and lose itself in materialism" (Bond, 1983:26–27).

In St. Petersburg, officials constantly cajoled the Tsar to act aggressively against the Chinese and Japanese in Manchuria and Korea. Advisers like von Plehve argued that a war would relieve some of the pressures of revolutionary agitators and unite the country against a foreign enemy. Tsar Alexander III publicly declared the necessity of "crushing" Germany at the first opportunity. Throughout the courts of the three monarchies, and even in Paris, military officials were constantly clamoring for war during the thirty years prior to the events of July–August 1914; in some cases they took unauthorized steps to make certain that an opportunity to go to war would present itself.

Nowhere were pro-war attitudes more clearly crystallized and articulated than in Vienna. Baron Franz Conrad von Hotzendorf, Chief of Staff of the Austrian army after 1906, passionately believed that the monarchy had to strike down Italy and Serbia. His ideas were both philosophical and strategic: war was a good in itself, and significant victories would rejuvenate the monarchy. On the other hand, displaying all the symptoms of the Peloponnesian syndrome, he argued that Italy's growing military power and Serbia's agitation among Austria's Slavic populations constituted mortal threats to imperial survival. Preemptive war was the solution to the problem. By 1912, he had convinced Count Berchtold, the foreign minister, of the necessity of such a war. It was only a question of finding the right opportunity, which came in July 1914. By this time, policy-makers had ceased advancing claims of rights or general rules of law to justify war. Under the philosophies of state supremacy and the moral, curative powers of war, no justification had to be made. The state had the absolute right to make war.

Austria planned the war but arguably would not have acted without German support. Germany did not plan for a war in the summer of 1914, but welcomed it when a *casus belli* was presented to the Austrians. In Bond's view (1983:95), "in most of the belligerent countries, excluding Britain, the service leaders . . . forced the issue, and everywhere politicians willingly surrendered a large amount of political responsibility to them." War had become sufficiently popular that most of the constraints against the use of force had effectively been eroded. The liberal and pacifist conscience remained, but its voice was nowhere heard among the top ranks of military officialdom in Europe's major capitals. To the professional military, pacifist sentiments were part of the problem. They were profound evidence of the growing cancer of national weakness, moral degeneracy, and lack of patriotism. These military leaders saw themselves as the vehicles of progress and regeneration. It was the liberals and particularly the socialists who were the real reactionaries, for their visions of a feeble cosmopolitanism undermined national will and strength. The militarist attitudes were not a direct source of war, but the behaviors of many leading figures and their civilian sympathizers vastly exacerbated the tensions that were arising from more fundamental historic and structural changes in the European-centered international system. By the 1860s the order created in 1814–15 was already beginning to crumble, and as it dissolved the regeneration-of-society-through-war school of thought replaced the Clausewitzian, instrumentalist view of war.

## THE PROBLEM OF PEACE

Clemenceau, a veteran of the breakdown of the European system in the early twentieth century, once quipped that war is easier to make than peace. While there were many wars in Europe after the Napoleonic period, none was general and a majority were of remarkably short duration. Many ascribed this state of affairs to the growth of civilization, to industry, commerce, and science. This was an age when, despite the gloomy pessimism of those who decried the growth of materialism and decline of moral fibre, most people assumed or took for granted social, political, and aesthetic progress, concomitants of the economic and scientific progress that was visible to all. Liberals, socialists, and pacifists offered varied diagnoses of the causes of war, but they were all general, such as human nature, the continued existence of despotisms, feudal holdovers, and colonialism. This was the pantheon of war-causing evils for thinkers such as Bentham, Mill, Cobden, Comte, and others. Few attributed the relative peace of the half-century after Vienna to the contrivances of 1814–15 and to the operations of the Concert. Peace for them was the result of some automatic historical process.

Chief among the contrivances was the territorial balance of power. We must recall that, as in 1713, the great fear of European statesmen was not war but hegemony. Added to this was the spectre of revolutionary imperialism. Napoleon's vision was a Paris-centered empire, a centralized order which maintained a semblance of international pluralism but which was in effect organized as a political and military hierarchy under a Napoleonic family complex. It was this vision of order rather than mere territorial aggrandizement that the allies sought to destroy. In the Declaration of Frankfort (1813), they stated clearly that their war was not against France, but against "pretensions to hegemony." France had to be reincorporated into the European balance of power because "French power is one of the fundamental bases of the [European] social order" (Donnadieu, 1900:256). It was largely because of the commitment to the balance, particularly by Great Britain, that the Ottoman Empire and a few other political entities survived through the nineteenth century.

Attempts to impose political uniformity by suppressing revolutions wherever they occurred had failed by the 1830s, but the balance of power implemented through the Concert system survived to constrain, to modify, and to provide the bases of collaboration to maintain general peace. In addition to the general distribution of territory contrived at Vienna, what were the operating assumptions underlying the foreign policies of the great powers in the post-1815 world?

In the first place, the idea of a general European interest, of an organic society of states, continued as a holdover from the eighteenth century. In the 1820s and 1830s it largely took the form of the brotherhood of monarchs, a "family of kings," as Alexander I had called it. But even with the slow erosion of the dynastic principle the idea of common responsibilities to a good greater than individual national interests remained firmly entrenched in the thought of most policy-makers. The concept was summarized in numerous policy pronouncements and was engraved, for example, in the nineteenth protocol of the conference dealing with the Belgian problem in 1831: "chaque nation a ses droits particuliers; mais l'Europe aussi a son droit" (Hinsley, 1966:55).

This vision of Europe as a unique and distinct international society diverged substantially from the anarchic world of states portrayed in the analyses of Hobbes and Rousseau. The vision had a critical impact on both the substance of policy and on the procedures of diplomacy. The policy-makers of the post-Vienna period were conscious of the benefits of stability within Europe as a whole, and often tailored their individual policies to make them consistent with the requirements of its order and stability. The powers acted with restraint at least until the Crimean War and again during the 1870s and 1880s. They rarely acted arbitrarily or capriciously, and major decisions usually followed only after mutual consultations. It was not until the 1850s that one of the allies provoked a major diplomatic crisis – Russia did it in its occupation of Moldavia and Wallachia – but had it not been for some failures of communication, that war might have been avoided.

Revolutionary and national liberation struggles provoked most of the diplomatic problems of the times, in addition to the perennial "Eastern Problem" that had not been handled at Vienna. The response of the powers to these disturbances was to try to contain them, allowing for change when necessary, but not pushing solutions contrary to the interests of any one of them. They helped to prop up the Ottomans in their wars against Egyptian secession and empire-building in the 1830s. The powers sanctioned change – or sometimes merely ratified it if they could do nothing to prevent it – but only change they saw as consistent with the balance and the "rights" of Europe. If we can put the ideas of Europe and the balance of power in the context of their concrete application to diplomatic scripts of the times, the question the crowns and foreign ministers explicitly or implicitly asked in many decision-making situations was this: is course of action $x$ or $y$ consistent with the Paris and Vienna settlements and with the balance of power? Is it in the interest of the European order as well as in our own interest? The ideas of balance and of European rights were guides to policy, not only to protect against hegemony, but also to help manage changes to the status quo.

The second set of ideas and practices critical to the balance of power derived from Article VI of the Quadruple Alliance, the provision for periodic summit meetings. What is significant here is not the frequency of meetings (twenty-five between 1830 and 1884), or the distinction between conferences (meetings of ambassadors) and congresses (meetings of heads of state and/or foreign ministers, of which, after Verona, there were only two: Paris in 1856 and Berlin in 1878), but the following unofficial rules or conventions that justified or served as bases of those meetings:

1. The Powers have a common responsibility for maintaining the Vienna settlement, and for monitoring, managing, and sanctioning any deviations from it.
2. No change should be made unilaterally.
3. No change should be to the significant disadvantage of any power in particular or to the balance of power in general.
4. Change can come only through consent; unilateral behavior without consultation and implied or explicit consent is evidence of aggressive intent.
5. Consent means consensus, but votes are not to be taken (cf. Hinsley, 1966:53).

Together, these practices and norms were termed the Concert of Europe. The informal association of the powers, to which Turkey was admitted only in 1856, survived the unraveling of the anti-Napoleon coalition at the meetings in Aix-la-Chapelle, Troppau, Laibach, and Verona. As an idea, set of assumptions, informal norms, and guides to policy, however, the Concert retained a high place in European international relations until the end of the nineteenth century (cf. Holbraad, 1970:3). It had its failures, and many proposed conferences never met — refusal to attend or various delaying tactics were one form of a veto — but on the whole the successors of the 1814–15 peacemakers built upon the foundations of Vienna and largely accepted the assumptions and commitments of the Quadruple Alliance. As one measure of relative success, none of the wars of the nineteenth century threatened to become general. Another measure of the Concert's effectiveness as a system governor is the number of authoritative decisions its members made collectively. Many of those decisions resolved conflicts or legitimized their outcomes. The Concert consecrated the independence of Belgium, Romania, Serbia, and Montenegro. It freed Bulgaria and Crete. It provided guarantees and protection for the Maronites in the Levant. In 1839, it prevented a war between Belgium and Luxemburg, and on several other occasions rescued Holland and Belgium from war. It gave the Ionian islands to Greece, but prevented Greece from going to war against Turkey in 1886. It sanctioned the incorporation of eastern Rumelia into Bulgaria. All of these actions, taken against or in support of the small states of Europe, were decided in the name of the general European interest. Many were also decisions which prevented war among the powers. The governors dictated to the weak in order to maintain the relative harmony of the strong (Dupuis, 1909:504).

The Concert did not function effectively solely because of the pan-European sentiments or diplomatic self-abnegation that submerged national or dynastic aspirations to the general welfare, defined as the balance of power. The constraints in the system arose also from the particular distribution of power and the impossibility of creating permanent coalitions. The balance of power worked because it was flexible. "[Each power] was too divided from the rest, by intent or ideology, or both, to permit alliance formation; yet each was deterred from taking too much risk alone by the lack of preponderant power. Also, because in the first half of the century, there was continuous upheaval. All faced a common peril at home [e.g, the 1830 revolutions] . . . Fear of disorder brought them together" (Hinsley, 1966:51–54). There was also the factor of an emerging British predominance if not hegemony. British policy-makers, particularly Palmerston and Russell, thought consistently in balance of power terms, and they usually interpreted this to mean keeping Europe divided.

The Vienna settlement gained substantial legitimacy throughout the century, although there were numerous initiatives to improve it. These never succeeded, largely because of British opposition, based on considerations such as those enumerated by Castlereagh. In 1836, Louis Philippe proposed a congress to draft a treaty according to which "no change, no alienation of territory, would take place without the concurrence of all the Powers to settle all questions with a general and European interest" (Hinsley, 1966:215). Thirteen years later, Louis Napoleon suggested a general congress for the revision of the 1815 treaties, a call he reissued, again unsuccessfully, in 1863. The French Emperor, who himself had championed Italian nationalism at the expense of Austria-Hungary, saw Prussia's drive for German unification as the most serious threat to the diplomatic order created in 1814–15. He was concerned not so much to improve the concert system but to save it. He wrote Queen Victoria in 1863: "the foundations upon which the political edifice of Europe now rests . . . are crumbling to pieces on all sides . . . It is impossible not to admit that on all points the treaties of Vienna are destroyed, modified, disregarded or menaced. Hence there are duties without rules, rights without title, pretensions without restraint" (Oakes and Mowat, 1918:225). It did not occur to him, apparently, that in these words he was describing some of his own policies.

Napoleon III was not the only one who, by the 1860s, was concerned about the state of the European order. In addition to lapses from the rules and norms of the Concert system, there were underlying sociological, ideological, and technological changes taking place that were not consistent with many of the visions and assumptions of 1815. At the diplomatic level, the habits and practices of occasional collaboration, consent, and limits were being eroded rapidly. The tenor of international relations changed from a reasonable moderation to increased national rivalry and competition.

## NATION-STATE CREATION AND SYSTEM BREAKDOWN

The architects of the Paris and Vienna settlements ignored the principle of nationality. States were abolished, created, partitioned, and "adjusted" in terms of an overall conception of rough parity and equilibrium, with appropriate territorial defenses against any future French ambitions. Strategic rather than ethnic considerations dominated the planning. Yet, support for the nationality principle among policy-makers in succeeding years became an increasingly important strategy for managing change and resolving conflicts. It was applied to Greece and to Belgium within several years of the last summit meeting in Verona, which had been dedicated to organizing plans for crushing liberal/nationalist outbursts. Palmerston stressed the importance of recognizing the importance of nationalism during the troubles of 1848, and Napoleon III subsequently became its most vigorous advocate in relation to the Italian question. The struggles of the Hungarians and Poles at mid-century were viewed with much sympathy throughout Europe, and what the Russians were unwilling to grant to the Poles, they promoted throughout the Balkans. Lord Russell rejected the application of the principle in the Schleswig-Holstein conflict during 1864, arguing that it was "too new" for Europe and that the "Great Powers had not the habit of consulting populations when questions affecting the Balance of Power had to be settled" (Taylor, 1954:151). Russell was speaking in the old tradition. What mattered was the balance of power and the general European order, not the aspirations of ethnic minorities. His comment suggests, in fact, that the balance of power and the nationality principle were incompatible, and in this view he was largely correct.

The Europe of 1815 comprised the five great powers, a potential power in the Ottoman Empire, and about seven other actors which counted for something. The process of state creation culminated in

169

1914 with fifteen European non-great power states. In the post-1815 diplomatic environment the powers managed or controlled the activities of the smaller units in the system. By 1914 they had great difficulty in so doing. Moreover, many of the new states in the Balkans became allies and accomplices of Russia or Austria-Hungary, pawns in the growing rivalry of the two great powers.

The growth in the number of lesser powers was not necessarily incompatible with a balance of power system, provided they did not essentially alter the balance between the great powers by coalescing with one of them, or that they were not used by the same powers as Trojan horses for their own aggrandizement. But here we come to the fundamental incompatibility between the European order as conceived and developed in the first half of the nineteenth century, and the principle of nationality. For applied to its fullest extent, that principle was incompatible with the continued existence of two essential actors, the Ottoman Empire and Austria-Hungary. The Ottoman Empire could check Russian expansion to the south into the Balkans. With the loss of virtually all of its European holdings by the turn of the century, and with the growing importance of pan-Slavism, Russian influence and predominance stretched far beyond anything envisaged in 1815 or even 1856. Russia's interests, moreover, were bound to clash with those of Austria-Hungary, which saw in the Balkans the only area in which it could seek compensation for the losses of its Italian territories.

Those who, like Bismarck, believed that the Hapsburg monarchy was essential to the European balance could not help but be concerned about the turn of events in the Balkans. Ottoman power was replaced by a collection of small states, all seeking added territory, several fundamentally antagonistic to Vienna. The state-creating exercise, successful in part through Russian support, in Romania, Serbia, Montenegro, Albania, Bulgaria, and Bosnia–Herzegovina was the exemplar for the Slovenes, Magyars, Poles, Czechs, and other remaining ethnic minorities in the Empire. Their agitation for autonomy or independence, combined with Vienna's sclerotic political system, rendered the continued survival of Austria–Hungary problematical.

Could there be an effective balance of power without the Ottoman and Austro-Hungarian Empires? The Austrians might have crushed their Serbian tormentors without precipitating a world war. It is less probable that the Hapsburg Empire could have survived under the weight of the nationality principle without causing severe diplomatic problems and perhaps general war. Regardless of changing ideologies, growing militarism, and the polarization of Europe into two hostile alliances, the structural changes in the balance of power that occurred between the late 1870s and 1914 as a result of the nation-state creation process would have been sufficient to create great uncertainty and danger. Those changes were incompatible with the outlines of the European order drafted in 1815 and more or less observed for the following six decades.

That order, in addition to the commanding principle of territorial balance, was also based on the principle of great power consensus. That consensus had pretty well collapsed by 1822, but it revived in less formal ways, as in the periodic meetings to manage conflicts. In fact, the lack of consensus may have created more flexibility in the system. Between 1815 and 1871, there were fourteen main great power alignments on issues that brought states into conflict and sometimes to war. After 1871, there were only two fulcrums of conflict: France and Germany and Russia and Austria-Hungary (Pearton, 1982:95).

The loss of Alsace-Lorraine, demanded by Prussia almost as an afterthought (and largely on the insistence of the Prussian military), struck a great blow to the flexibility of the system. It ruled out any prospect of future Franco-German collaboration, and provided the French with a sense of grievance and humiliation that cried out for revenge. The Peace of Frankfurt assured Franco-German antagonism and provided just one of several bases for the eventual Franco-Russian alliance, which in turn created the belief that Germany was like a man living among deadly enemies, only able to survive by being sufficiently armed to defeat and to anticipate all attacks (Mowat, 1930:332–33).

One final change helps account for the breakdown of the system created after the Napoleonic Wars. This was not a structural change, but alteration in the way that policy-makers calculated power. During the first half of the century, the balance of power was estimated in terms of a particular distribution of territory, command of strategic points, the defensibility of barriers, and the like. Military manpower differentials, to the extent that they were even known, were relatively less significant than command of territory. By the late nineteenth and early twentieth centuries, in contrast, policy-makers commonly calculated power in terms of some combination of manpower, railways, and naval vessels. Population growth rates were also a matter of great concern, but the critical question was how many men could be put under arms and transported to the battlefield in a minimum amount of time to initiate the decisive battles that everyone thought would determine the outcome of the war (Howard, 1983:16–17). Increments to these variables caused considerable insecurity among those whose growth rates and efficiency of mobilization and transportation were

171

not keeping up. The new speed of the crisis-mobilization-war sequence, and the number of soldiers that could be brought to the battlefield, made the man or woman in the street in Paris, Berlin, or Vienna probably more fearful of impending attack than has been the case for hostage populations during the era of the nuclear balance of terror.

The growth of the arms race also gave the appearance of rapid changes in relative power. There had been no similar phenomenon in the half-century following the Paris and Vienna settlements. Taylor (1954:56) has calculated that German arms expenditures quintupled between 1880 and 1914, while those of England and Russia trebled, and France's almost doubled. In 1815 all knew who the great powers were, and nothing in the succeeding fifty years significantly changed the rough distribution of territory and military capabilities between them. In contrast, during the fifty years prior to the First World War, the development of railways and the vastly increased national capacity to produce new quantities and qualities of arms created significant and rapid changes in relative power, *all without any significant territorial redistributions*. The Peloponnesian complex was the result: the urge to go to war preemptively to avoid being left behind. The policy-makers of the last forty years of peace may seem to have been preoccupied obsessively with matters of status, prestige, and national chauvinism. But all of these behaviors were indicators of insecurity born of rapid but non-parallel power shifts.

With the collapse of the flexible balance of power system based on the existence of at least five coherent and solid great powers who were mutually committed to a European order, with the polarization of the continent by the early 1900s, and with the increased sense of insecurity, the remaining elements of order disappeared or fell into disuse. In 1906, for example, France and Great Britain settled the destiny of Morocco without consulting Germany, a signal violation of the norms of the Concert system and also a violation of the Convention of Madrid (1880), which required any change of those terms to be arranged only with the assent of all treaty powers, of which Germany was one. A conference was ultimately held on the Moroccan issue, but the alliance structures were already determining national positions on the substantive issues, and Germany remained isolated. In 1908, Austria-Hungary announced the annexation of Bosnia, an action that was also taken unilaterally and contrary to the terms of the Treaty of Berlin (1878). The old norm of no change without Concert consent was being systematically abused or ignored. After the Algeciras and Bosnian crises, all governments began seriously to contemplate war, and war not so much in the instrumental sense of a continuation of policy, but war to reduce tensions, to stave off ultimate defeat, to test the mettle of nations, to break up isolation and encirclement. According to Howard (1983:16), the Germans and British – and he might have added the French and Russians – felt

> justified in going to war, not over any specific issue that could have been settled by negotiations, but to maintain their power; and to do so while it was still possible, before they found themselves so isolated, so impotent, that they had no power left to maintain and had to accept a subordinate position within an international system dominated by their adversaries.

The examination of issues offers only a few clues to the origins of the Great War. There were identifiable stakes that helped to generate contests of arms, but after examining the structural and attitudinal changes that occurred in the last forty or fifty years prior to 1914, one has the feeling of war inevitability.

The Treaty of Utrecht attempted to create a security system that would take care of the problem of hegemony. It did that, but it did not create a general security system. The behavior of the princes before and after 1713 did not change; only the cast of characters did. In the case of the Paris and Vienna settlements, they did change diplomatic behavior, and their impact was more lasting. They resulted in common assumptions about the requirements of order (if not peace), including self-restraint, mutual consultation, and respect for the territorial balance of power. The norms of the Concert system were innovations, and their frequent observance for more than a half-century stands in stark contrast to the atomistic, Hobbesian behavior of the eighteenth-century dynasts.

But the policy-makers of the late nineteenth century did not stop to ponder how they could redesign a balance of power based on legitimist and traditional territorial principles into one that could operate after the disappearance of two key actors and the appearance of eight new states, all flexing their nationalist muscles. Technological and demographic changes were taking place more rapidly than at any previous time, coincidentally with the great structural changes in the balance of power wrought by the wave of state creation and empire collapse.

The architects of the post-Napoleon order avoided the nationality question, in part because they feared it, but perhaps also because they did not take it seriously. It was a new and potentially revolutionary idea. Up to a point, their successors managed the problem successfully. Beyond that point, after approximately 1870, the state-creation enterprise became a zero-sum game: new states could only be born at the expense of two of the major pillars of the balance of power, the Ottoman and Austro-Hungarian Empires, and ultimately at the expense of general peace.

# 8  1919: PEACE THROUGH DEMOCRACY AND COVENANT

> I offer my apologies to the memory of Attila and his congeners, but the art of arranging how men are to live is even more complex than that of massacring them.
>
> Georges Clemenceau

When the guns on the western front fell silent on November 11, 1918, there had been fifty months of unprecedented slaughter and destruction. The Great War was the longest European armed struggle in more than a century, and it resulted in more than eight million fatalities (Bouthoul and Carrère, 1976:211), millions more maimed, and vast property and industrial destruction throughout Belgium and northeast France.

For most Europeans, the Great War had been a source of disillusionment. The nineteenth-century assumption of the moral and material progress of civilization was shattered. Those who had thought that, thanks to the invention of new weapons systems, future wars would be rapid and decisive learned that more probably they would develop into deathly stalemates. Those who had thought that international institutions, including the Hague Conventions, the Concert mechanisms, and the growing interdependence of societies through trade, investment, and communications, would guarantee peace learned that they were ineffective. And those, including Woodrow Wilson, who had admired Germany for its contributions to science, technology, art, literature, and music also learned that such a civilized society could arrogantly violate international norms and treaties, seek unprecedented imperial expansion in Europe (as revealed by the vast territorial gains made at the expense of Russia and Romania in the Treaties of Brest-Litovsk and Bucharest), and attempt to establish for itself a position of continental and possibly global hegemony. When it was all over, few remained to be convinced that such a war must never happen again. Among vast populations of Europe there was a strong conviction that this time the parties had to plan a peace that would not just terminate another war, but a peace that would change attitudes

175

and build a new type of international order. There were thus two problems, separate, yet connected: the terms of settlement between the belligerents of the Great War, and the creation of international institutions that would both guarantee the preservation of that settlement and prevent new wars.

The issues of war settlement and constructing a new international edifice were not confined to the musings of government leaders as they had been in 1814. Throughout the Great War, citizens' groups in France, Great Britain, the United States, and in the Central Powers debated the outlines of the postwar settlement and the shape of new international institutions. The French Society for an Association of Nations sponsored debates and publications on these themes. In Great Britain, the League of Nations Society, the Fabian Society, and the Bryce Group, among others, carried on the work of the pre-war peace movement (Egerton, 1978:ch. 1). Throughout Scandinavia and southern Europe, and even in Asia, other groups gathered to draft programs for a postwar international organization to maintain peace and security.[1]

None was instrumental as far as the future shape of the League of Nations was concerned, but these publics made the general point vigorously and effectively: after the slaughter and destruction of the previous four years, there could be no return to the old, pre-war style of diplomacy. New principles and institutions were needed. As the Allied and Central governments began to publish their war aims in 1917 and 1918, it was clear that political leaders shared these public sentiments at least in part. In a speech of January 5, 1918, Prime Minister Lloyd George argued that the "crushing weight of modern armaments and the evils of conscription remain as blots on western civilization." That nations are compelled to live under the threat of war because "men are dominated by ambition and passion" is sufficient reason to make a great attempt to establish some international organization as an alternative to war. In addition to such an organization, a lasting peace would have to meet two other essential conditions: some system for establishing the sanctity of treaties, and a postwar territorial settlement based on the right of self-determination. Acknowledging that this principle had been ignored in previous great postwar settlements, he suggested that "the days of the Treaty of Vienna are long past" (Egerton, 1978:61).

Four days later President Woodrow Wilson made his famous Four-

---

[1] An extensive collection of these plans and programs – remarkably similar whatever their continent of origin – is contained in Conférence des Préliminaires de Paix, Commission de la Société des Nations, 1919a.

teen Points speech to the American Congress. It was significantly more radical than Lloyd George's talk. It enunciated principles for a wholesale reconstruction of the international system and of the foreign policy practices of its members. Wilson shared the broad public's concern for institutional reform, but he went much further: the guarantee of peace does not lie in the modification of international institutions or in drawing up constitutions for a League of Nations. More important is a fundamental transformation of attitudes toward international relationships. Policies are to be based on right and justice, and the sanctions for correct behavior would derive from morality and world public opinion, not from a balance of power. Most publics, as well as leaders such as Lloyd George, were mere institutional tinkerers. They sought reform. Wilson sought a revolution, the replacement of one kind of international system with an entirely different one. The League of Nations was to be the expression of this revolution, and not a source of it.

Wilson gave substantially more, and more profound, thought to the postwar order than did his European colleagues. Already in 1916, before the United States had entered the war, Wilson announced that

> if this war has accomplished nothing else for the benefit of the world, it has at least disclosed a great moral necessity and set forward the thinking of statesmen of the world by a whole age . . . [T]he principle of public right must henceforth take precedence over the individual interests of particular nations, and . . . the nations of the world must in some way band themselves together to see that that right prevails as against any selfish sort of aggression; . . . henceforth alliance must not be set up against alliance, understanding against understanding, but . . . there must be a common agreement for a common object, and . . . at the heart of that common object must lie the inviolable rights of peoples and of mankind. (Shaw, 1924:I, 273)

By January 1917, Wilson had also announced the basis for a settlement of the war. It was to be "peace without victory," a peace that would win the approval of mankind and not one that "merely . . . will serve the several interests and immediate aims of the nations engaged" (Shaw, 1924:I, 350). If the peace is to endure, it must be a peace made secure by "the organized major force of mankind." That force would support a new doctrine underlying international relationships, the doctrine of President Monroe "that no nation should seek to extend its polity over any other nation or people, but that every people should be left free to determine its own polity, its own way of development, unhindered, unthreatened, unafraid, the little along with the great and powerful" (Shaw, 1924:I, 355).

Throughout 1918, after the United States joined the Entente as an

Associate power, Wilson continued to elaborate the principles upon which the peace should be made and upon which a new international order would be constructed. The peace must be an act of justice, and not just another bargain between sovereigns. In major speeches on July 4 and September 27, he spelled out in ever-greater detail his analyses of the causes of the war and the necessary conditions for peace, both theoretical and practical. As he did so, he came to command both the moral and political high ground and to establish for himself a position of leadership in developing the agenda and substance of the forthcoming peace conference.

Like the situation a century earlier, the basic outlines of the 1919 settlement were the work of just a few leaders: Wilson, Lloyd George, Georges Clemenceau, Robert Cecil, and Léon Bourgeois. But unlike their predecessors, these leaders worked in a fundamentally different environment. Metternich and his colleagues not only operated on their own, but with the exception of Castlereagh, they faced few if any domestic constraints. They were largely free agents. In 1919, by contrast, the leaders were sensitive to the state of public opinion, and each was constantly looking over his shoulder to see what the parliamentarians and interest groups at home were saying. Wilson's great project for peace was in important ways diluted to appease the isolationists in the American Senate. Despite large majorities in the House of Commons and the Chamber of Deputies, Lloyd George and Clemenceau could only agree to what they thought could be sold to their legislatures. All the peacemakers had their diagnoses and prescriptions, but none was entirely free to press his personal preferences.

The architects of the 1814–15 settlement agreed broadly on the sources of international instability and what to do about it. The military strategy of the anti-Napoleonic coalition had been developed since 1812 with a view to creating a postwar balance of power, and all agreed that France must be reincorporated into the postwar order. In 1919, in contrast, the peacemakers came to Paris with fundamentally different perspectives about the nature of international politics, significantly diverging diagnoses of the causes of the Great War, and largely incompatible recipes for constructing an enduring peace. Each had his own agenda, theories, priorities, visions, and prescriptions. The only thing that unified them was their understanding that they must not just terminate a war, but must construct a peace that had some chance of surviving. Beyond that, there had to be a great deal of hard bargaining and the peace necessarily had to be a compromise.

Through his articulation of the preconditions of peace and the outline of a suitable postwar international order, Wilson preempted the

178

Allies' agenda. While Clemenceau, as the chapter's opening quote indicates, understood that there was much more to building peace than merely settling accounts with Germany, and while Lloyd George and his cabinet colleagues enunciated some general principles underlying British war aims, neither claimed for himself a historic mission or argued that he had some sort of mandate that transcended his nation's interests.

From the beginning of the war, Wilson sought to pose as the champion of humanity and as the person chosen to help bring to fruition America's historic mission in reorganizing the world along the lines of justice and freedom. By the time he had delivered his famous "Peace without Victory" speech in January 1917, he had become the hero, the leader, and the spokesman of pacifist, liberal, and socialist groups throughout Europe (Link, 1971:106). Wilson believed that he had a special mandate for leadership because in the forthcoming peace settlement only the United States was relatively disinterested. It had no territorial or other spoils in mind, no secret treaties to implement, and no special understandings. It could dispassionately seek to found the peace on general principles of justice, freedom, and self-determination. Moreover, Wilson strongly believed that his mandate came from world public opinion. He would serve as the champion of the peoples' wishes. No continental leader who had to act on the basis of narrow national interests could make similar claims. In a speech in Manchester just prior to the opening of the peace conference in Paris, Wilson claimed that "there is a great voice of humanity . . . in the world . . . which he who cannot hear is deaf . . . We are not obeying the mandate of parties or of politics. We are obeying the mandate of humanity" (Temperley, 1920:III, 59). Wilson was using the plural pronoun to refer to himself.

In addition to a global mandate, Wilson saw his task in terms of a uniquely American historical mission in the world. For him, the Covenant (he invented the title) represented more than just another international treaty. It was the vehicle for fulfilling America's mission to lead the Old World away from its traditional war-producing diplomacy of secrecy and balance of power into a new international order, one based on American political thought and constitutional practices. He projected on to the world at large these values and principles. The bases of peace, he intoned in his January 1917 speech, "are American principles. And they are also the principles and policies of forward-looking men and women everywhere, of every modern nation, of every enlightened community. They are the principles of mankind and must prevail" (Shaw, 1924:I, 356).

179

Why should the United States have a special mandate to leadership? Why should it claim special authority? Wilson believed that the American people had a particular historic mission because they were in so many ways unique, and unique in a manner that was particularly relevant to the construction of a peaceful international order. Americans had created a democracy, but so had many other societies. What was unique to Americans was their radical affirmation of equality and their historic repudiation of all forms of social hierarchy that were typical of the caste- and class-ridden societies of Europe and Asia. Since Wilson believed that class-based political orders were inherently aggressive, Americans were better able to lead and to implement egalitarian ideas at both the domestic and international levels. Moreover, the United States had successfully created a federal system encompassing a vast continent, and Wilson saw this great experiment as the model for world organization. Finally, Americans represented a unique morality. The United States had been created with the express purpose of making mankind free. Americans, he suggested, were the "custodians of the spirit of righteousness, of the spirit of even-handed justice, of the spirit of hope which believes in the perfectibility of the law and the perfectibility of human life itself" (quoted in Link, 1971:78). America's mission in the world was not to gain wealth, privilege, and power, but to serve mankind.

Having arrogated for himself a universal mandate to pursue an historic mission, Wilson had to deal carefully with his allies. After all, they had borne the brunt of fighting, casualties, and destruction. The main problem, as he saw it, was to get them to agree in principle to his conceptions of peace and to avoid any premature commitments to theirs. Thanks in large part to Colonel House's diplomacy in London in 1918, the British largely went along with Wilson's general ideas. The French avoided comments on, or commitments to, Wilson's principles and programs. They adhered to a joint declaration of war aims that the Allies issued on January 10, 1917, and privately rejected the Fourteen Points as too vague to guide concrete negotiations (Walworth, 1977:95–97). When the French submitted a general agenda for the upcoming peace conference to Wilson in late November, 1918, he never acknowledged it (Bruun, 1968:184–85; Gonda, 1981:102). Wilson had his own agenda, the chief item of which was his Covenant for a League of Nations.

Wilson kept his ideas on the League mostly to himself. In part this was because he believed that any international organization would have to grow organically and that a set of firm commitments and mutual guarantees for political independence and territorial integrity was more important than elaborate constitutional structures: better to work out the Covenant in general form and trust to experience and individual cases to guide future action. This was a typical Anglo-Saxon approach to the development of law (Walworth, 1977:132). But there were political considerations as well. Wilson wanted the discussions in Paris to focus on his ideas and not on those of the British or French. To publicize the details of his ideas prior to the conference would invite criticisms and counter-proposals, not only from his allies but even more so from his opponents in the United States Senate. As for the Allies' general proposals, Wilson either politely dismissed them or remained silent. He acknowledged that his and the Allies' views on the peace differed, but as the spokesman of humanity he was convinced that he had a superior mandate and that his agenda should and would prevail. And just in case the Allies were not open to moral suasion, there was always American power: "When the war is over we can force them to our way of thinking, because by that time they will, among other things, be financially in our hands" (quoted in Wimer, 1982:162). Wilson never had to employ such crude pressures. His status as the incarnation of world public opinion was sufficient to ensure an outcome that was reasonably consistent with his expectations and plans. We turn now to an examination of the intellectual foundations of peacemaking in 1919. We remain concerned primarily with the statesmen's diagnoses of war causation and their prescriptions for peace, the conditions they thought were necessary to create both a specific settlement that could endure and an international arrangement that would prevent new wars.

## WOODROW WILSON: THE MORAL–POLITICAL UNIVERSE

Wilson had been a professor of government prior to entering politics, and he had taught and thought about the problems of democracy for decades prior to 1919. His vision of the postwar international order was based primarily upon his understanding of the origins and uniqueness of the American political experience, the moral roots of democracy, and the stages of political growth. His views on the causes of war and the conditions of peace thus derived more from his analysis of American domestic politics than from any deep familiarity with the practices or history of European international relations. What he did know of the latter, he rejected. The new order would have to be based on fundamentally different principles, and these would come from the American experience which he regarded as historically unique. There could be no mere modification of traditional and conventional diplomatic practices.

Wilson, a Presbyterian of pronounced religious faith, believed in a moral universe; its rules derive from God and govern nations as well as men. In this view of the universe, there is scant room for cultural or moral relativism. There are universal standards of right and wrong, good and bad. Democracy represents the most advanced, humane, and Christian form of government. It is the ultimate phase in four stages of political development, toward which all peoples are moving (Link, 1971:76–77). In the first stage, government is master, the people are subjects. Government rules by force, coercion, and religious-based authority. In the second, the relationship remains between master and subject, but authority is increasingly based on "insight and sagacity" and on leadership qualities. In the third stage, the masters begin to fail and are confronted with the leaders of the people, who are bent on controlling the levers of power. This is a period of deep agitation and revolutionary potential. In the final period, the leaders of the people themselves become the government and institute democracy. It will take either the English parliamentary or American presidential form.

But even in a mature democracy, there are special interests that are bent on capturing influence for selfish ends. The task of democratic government is to organize the common interest against the special interests (Johnston, 1982:196–97; 228).

The parallels between Wilson's understanding of politics in the United States and his vision of the postwar world are striking. Wilson believed that, as in the United States, there is a latent global common interest – the interest of humanity, as he termed it. It was his task to articulate that interest and to defend it against the special interests represented by the European nations that sought territorial and other spoils. Equally important, he assumed that as among individuals in a democratic polity, there is an underlying harmony of interest among the nations. This credo of early nineteenth-century liberalism was a fundamental link between Wilson's analyses of domestic and international politics. In the United States, the common interest finds expression because people are free and there are constitutional guarantees for that freedom. The global underlying harmony cannot find expression if the constituent units of the international system are represented by autocratic and militarist governments. The principle of self-determination is thus crucial for forging a peaceful world order. Just as in a democracy where people are free, the world must be made up of free nations, and as those free nations are organized around mutual recognition and mutual guarantees for their freedom, the underlying harmony of free people will prevail over all special interests. A blueprint for peaceful world order is, in a sense, a United States writ large.

Wilson's penchant for using concepts dichotomously was striking: masters and subjects, democracy and autocracy, special interests and the common interest, the old and the new, the retrograde and the progressive, the good and the bad. Wilson's world view was imbued with opposites and the clash between them. It is this characteristic of his political and moral thought that led him to adopt a strategy of replacement rather than of reform. To him, there could be no question of amelioration, of pragmatically adjusting the old diplomatic practices to the new times. His statements and speeches were crammed with dichotomous contrasts, with vigorous denunciations of everything that represented the old diplomacy. His diagnoses of the causes of the Great War were merely more precise statements of general causes, and these were located in every facet of non-democratic politics at the domestic level and the practices of the old diplomacy at the international level. Wilson did not always make an explicit link between them, but the connection is clear from many of his statements: bad domestic polities make bad international relationships. Any strategy of peace must first smash both types of old systems:

> Our object now . . . is to vindicate the principles of peace and justice in the life of the world as against selfish and autocratic power and set up amongst the really free and self-governed peoples of the world such a concert of purpose and of action as will henceforth ensure the observance of those principles . . . The menace to that peace and freedom lies in the existence of autocratic governments backed by organized force which is controlled wholly by their will, not by the will of their people . . . We have no quarrel with the German people. We have no feeling towards them but one of sympathy and friendship. It was not upon their impulse that their government acted in entering this war . . . It was a war determined upon as wars used to be determined upon in the old, unhappy days when peoples were nowhere consulted by their rulers and wars were provoked and waged in the interest of dynasties or of little groups of ambitious men who were accustomed to use their fellow men as pawns and tools . . . Only free peoples can hold their purpose and their honour steady to a common end and prefer the interests of mankind to any narrow interest of their own. (Shaw, 1924:I, 378–79)

Wilson repudiated all of the maxims, assumptions, and prescriptions of the traditional realist school of international relations: self-(national) interest, alliances, balances of power, secret diplomacy, and wars to maintain the balance. There was nothing at all to be learned from the European diplomatic experience except that it had resulted in one disaster after another and served only the interests of small groups of men. He insisted that there be "no odor of the Vienna settlement" at Paris (Walworth, 1977:95). He also insisted that the new attitudes that would have to serve as the basis of an enduring peace were totally inconsistent with the "turgid, selfish, greedy relationships of the old diplomacy." He was convinced that "no real peace, no real justice is ever again possible upon the old basis of interest" (Baker, 1923:I, 181–82). His diagnosis was simple and authoritatively stated: the old order, both autocratic states and systems of autocratic states, is the cause of war.

In his demonology, the professional military were the main culprits. In a statement of the Council of Four, he argued that "military men, with their strategic, military, and economic arguments, had been responsible for the Treaty of 1815. Similarly, military men had been responsible for Alsace-Lorraine. It was military men who had led Europe from one blunder to another" (Baker, 1923:I, 169). The American people would thus repudiate any peace settlement that smacked of the old order.

In presenting to the delegates of the peace conference the completed Treaty of Versailles that included the Covenant of the League of Nations, Wilson took the position that he and his colleagues had created something entirely new. Peace would be guaranteed because all of the old practices and principles of European diplomacy had been excised from the new international politics. How?

## REPLACING THE OLD WITH THE NEW: THE MORAL AND POLITICAL FOUNDATIONS OF ENDURING PEACE

Wilson approached the combined problems of fashioning a settlement to the war and constructing a new type of international system at three levels of descending specificity. The essential foundations of the peace and of peace are moral: they must be based on justice, defined as the equality of rights and the preservation or creation of individual and national liberties. At the next level, certain political principles derive from the moral maxims: a peace negotiated between equals (peace without victory), self-determination, non-acceptance of special interests, and the "consent of all nations to be governed in their conduct towards each other by the same principles of honor and of respect for the common law of civilized society that govern the individual citizens of all modern states in their relations with one another: to that end all promises and covenants may be sacredly observed" (Shaw 1924:I, 500). Finally, these political principles lead to specific policies, such as freedom of the seas, open diplomacy, basing territorial settlements or adjustments on the consent of those who are affected ("no right exists anywhere to hand peoples about from sovereignty to sovereignty as if they were property"), and, foremost, a "community of power" in the League of Nations. None of this program, in Wilson's view, was negotiable. There could be discussion of details, of course, but principles could not be diluted because they flowed from each other and all were requisites of a lasting peace. Compromise one, and the whole edifice would collapse.

The principle of justice is most fundamental because it is the essential basis of political stability and personal contentment. "This world can be at peace only if its life is stable, and there can be no stability where the will is in rebellion, where there is not tranquillity of spirit and a sense of justice, of freedom, and of right" (quoted in Johnston, 1982:204). Peace could not be achieved through just another bargain between governments. It could be achieved only through righteousness.

### THE POLITICAL FOUNDATIONS OF THE NEW INTERNATIONAL ORDER: DEMOCRACY, COVENANTS, AND ARMS CONTROL

Wilson did not seek to transcend the states system. In today's parlance, Wilson's international theory was state-centric. He was fully committed intellectually and emotionally to a world of states, but of particular kinds of states: democracies founded on the principle of nationality. He diagnosed as a major cause of war the lack of fit between nations and states. The peace would have to redraw the map of Europe so that nations and states coincided. That was to be the first step. Beyond this, the great transformation to a peaceful international order was to be achieved by (1) changing the bases of national behavior – from the pursuit of narrow state interests to devotion to the common interest and to the right – and by (2) changing national capabilities (Johnston, 1982:204). These are two distinct, but clearly related, avenues of change. How are they to be achieved?

Wilson's analysis of the first problem relied on classical democratic theory. States are in varying stages of development. But all aspire under the impulse of self-determination to a condition of nationhood and democracy. If the nation is freely determined under conditions of

185

classical democratic theory, it will become non-aggressive, law-abiding, and a responsible and moral member of the world community (Nicholas, 1982:182). If the world is composed of such self-determined democracies, there will be a natural harmony between them – a Lockian vision applied to the world at large. Why? Because in democracies, governments only aspire to meet their peoples' welfare needs, primarily through trade. A government committed to the national, general interest will threaten no one. In Wilson's view, it was the impulses to empire, to hegemony, and to territorial annexations that were the precursors of war. These were pursued only by small cliques of selfish rulers and by the atavistic urges of the military. Replace such regimes with democracies, and the interests of the peoples will emerge. They will pursue those interests internationally through commerce and other peaceful means. A community of democracies would thus replace the Hobbesian state of nature that was characteristic of pre-war international politics, where nations could find security only through armaments and the balance of power.

The League of Nations must therefore be composed of "all the great free peoples of the world." By this he meant (though he got into some difficulties of definition when he negotiated with his partners in Paris) all "self-governing nations."

> A steadfast concern of peace can never be maintained except by a partnership of democratic nations. No autocratic government could be trusted to keep faith within it or observe its covenants. It must be a league of honour, a partnership of opinion. Intrigue would eat its vitals away; the plottings of inner circles who could plant what they would and render account to no one would be a corruption seated at its very heart. Only free peoples can hold their purposes and their honour steady to a common end and prefer the interests of mankind to any narrow interest of their own. (Shaw, 1924: I, 379)

But Wilson was not convinced that the problem of war and international conflict could be resolved solely through domestic political transformations and the application of the self-determination principle in postwar territorial settlements. There would still be legal disputes, and even in democracies, as he himself had seen in the United States, private (narrow) interests could combine against the general interest. There must be as well an international organization that would guarantee the changes in behavior and changes in capabilities. Wilson did not seek a traditional alliance of victors. His preponderance of power was to be based on right and justice, not on armaments or other traditional indicators of power. The democracies would "all band together for the protection of the integrity of each" (Nicholas, 1982:180). What are the means for banding together?

The instrument for establishing the "community of power" is the Covenant, a social contract among democratic nations. The Covenant includes two essential features:

1. A mutual pledge of the members to guarantee each other's independence and territorial integrity. This was to become Article 10 of the League Covenant.
2. A mutual pledge to substitute public discussion and peaceful modes of conflict resolution for the use of force (Articles 12–16).

Changes in behavior would thus come through democratization at the national level and guarantees contained in an international covenant.

The second avenue of change was to reduce national military capabilities "to the lowest point consistent with domestic safety" (Article 8). This would include abolishing compulsory military service and the manufacture of munitions for private profit. Essentially, then, Wilson's formula for peace was simple: take away the things governments have traditionally fought about through democratization, and take away the means for fighting over them through disarmament. For the remaining cases of conflict, there would be procedures for peaceful settlement.

These foundations for a peaceful international order derived from Wilson's diagnosis of the "old diplomacy" and from his understanding of the American historical experience. The heart of the Covenant came from Lockian ideas of a social contract contained in the colonies' Articles of Confederation, from the Constitution of the United States, and from the Monroe Doctrine. Peaceful methods of resolving international conflicts represented the *modus operandi* of all constitutional democracies; right replaces might as the basis of political authority and change. And the disarmament and arms control provisions derived from the American tradition of state militias: no state needs to have more than a militia to preserve domestic order when the union of all guarantees the safety of each (Baker, 1923:I, 346).

In developing his ideas, Wilson faced but never resolved an important logical difficulty. If all the members of the League are "good," then a League of Nations may be superfluous. Wilson's answer was that the great Covenant was more a symbolic affirmation of the "rightness" of democracies in their mutual relations than an obligation that had to be secured by threats against deviant behavior. But what if democracies violated their covenants, an improbable but not impossible event? The bases of good international behavior must come from within states, through democracy. Wilson repeatedly emphasized that his edifice of peace was based on good faith and a sense of moral obligation, and not on coercion or military deterrence. Yet, he had to confront those who argued that in international politics, even in relations among democracies, good faith and conscience might not be sufficient to guarantee good behavior. In reply, Wilson fell back upon the effectiveness of world public opinion, the opinion which he believed always represented morality. If democratization, the obligations embodied in Article 10, and disarmament were not sufficient to guarantee peace, world public opinion would act as the great enforcer.

> Through this instrument we are depending primarily and chiefly upon one great force, and that is the moral force of public opinion of the world – the pleasing and clarifying and compelling influence of publicity . . . so that designs that are sinister can at any time be drawn into the open, so that those things . . . may be promptly destroyed by the overwhelming light of the universal expression of the condemnation of the world". (quoted in Temperley, 1920:III, 63)

In his explanations of the Covenant to the members of the Senate Foreign Relations Committee and to the American public, after his return from Paris in June 1919, Wilson conceded that some organized form of coercion might be necessary to supplement public opinion. He had been impressed by the effectiveness of Allied economic warfare against Germany, claiming that it, as much as the Allied armies, had brought about Germany's desire for an armistice. The economic boycott built into the Covenant (Article 16) was to go into effect when any member of the League resorted to war in disregard of the obligations of peaceful conflict resolution in Articles 12, 13, or 15. Wilson saw the boycott as sufficient to coerce even the most committed aggressor. "When you apply that boycott, you have got your hand upon the throat of the offending nation, and it is a proper punishment. It is an exclusion from civilized society. That is the remedy that thoughtful men have advocated for several generations . . . The boycott is an infinitely more terrible instrument of war . . . The boycott is what is substituted for war" (quoted in Foley, 1923:71–72). Many in Paris remained skeptical. What about the role of force, the ultimate sanction of a collective security system?

Wilson had a repugnance of physical force, and even after the United States entered the war against Germany he remained sensitive to the brutalizing and intoxicating effects of war fever and the desire for overwhelming victory (Nicholas, 1982:184). From the outset of the war, Wilson had sought to mediate between the belligerents and to protect American shipping rights through peaceful means. He had enunciated the doctrine of peace without victory, and in Paris he resisted his allies' pressures for military intervention in Russia (Johnston, 1982:193). Though he acknowledged that in some very unusual though unspecified circumstances the League might have to use force, he placed all his faith in the moral undertakings, in the procedures for peaceful conflict resolution, in world public opinion, and in economic sanctions. His constant theme was that the League of Nations was to be a league for peace, and not a league for war.

He was sufficiently confident in the pacifying effects of democratization and in the force of public opinion and non-military sanctions that he could proclaim to the plenary of the Paris Peace Conference, on presenting the final draft of the Covenant, that it "is a definite guarantee of peace. It is a definite guarantee against aggression" (Temperley, 1920:III, 63). In saying this, he of course knew that the United States Senate would never approve a document that would obligate the United States to use force upon the determination of an international body. But aside from such constitutional problems, Wilson did not believe that such a situation was likely to arise. In his world of democracies, with its underlying harmony of interest, with states reduced in armaments to levels which would preclude wars of conquest and imperialism, and with solemn oaths of guarantee buttressed by world opinion, the problem of war and aggression would be resolved. The changes of foreign policy behavior through democratization and the lowering of military capabilities would make the international use of force superfluous. In his view, the power of right was always much more effective than the power of guns.

## PEACE THROUGH A PREPONDERANCE OF POWER: CLEMENCEAU

The French shared neither Wilson's diagnoses nor his prescriptions. To them, the problem of international relations was not autocracy or democracy, the transformations of foreign policy brought about through self-determination or constitutionalism, or the efficacy of covenants. The problem was German power, under *any* regime, and France's security. A League of Nations constituted a new and possibly marginal way of dealing with the problem. But to Clemenceau, the French premier, and to Léon Bourgeois, who was charged with overseeing France's policy on the drafting of the Covenant, Wilson's ideas were hopelessly naive and contributed little or nothing to France's immediate problem. Wilson was clothing his ethnocentrism in a global vocabulary of liberal platitudes. France must remind him that the traditional elements of power in international relations had not become obsolete just because the American president wished them away.

Understandably, French public opinion was vigorously hostile to Germany. There was little question in France as to which party had started the war, which party had hegemonic ambitions in Europe – the French cited the treaty of Brest-Litovsk as compelling evidence – and what sorts of peace terms the Germans would have imposed on France had Ludendorff and his associates won the war. Unlike the Americans, who suffered only 65,000 casualties and no destruction of their homeland, the French counted 1.5 million killed, many more maimed and wounded, and the whole northeast of the country systematically razed and plundered by the Germans. While Wilson was toying with Lockian ideas of political philosophy, the French could focus on little else than constructing a peace that would never allow 1914 to happen again. Typical of all great peace settlements (but not typical of Wilson), the French sought to prevent a recurrence of the past rather than constructing a system for resolving the problems of the future.

Georges Clemenceau, "the Tiger," as he was affectionately and not so affectionately called by his admirers and many opponents, had been president of the Council of Ministers (premier) since February 1917, and had an immodest reputation for being the "destroyer of ministers," an often-lethal politician who determined the fate of numerous French governments prior to the war. He had been strongly influenced by the shame of the Treaty of Frankfurt ending the Franco-Prussian War, and like most Frenchmen, he was committed to rectifying its injustices. But in the long run, the problem was more than just settling scores. A peace would have to center upon the guarantee of French security. How long could such a peace last?

Clemenceau did not share Wilson's vision of a warless world, much less of an underlying harmony between democratic societies. His vision of political life was not one of transformation, but of continuity. All existence, in his view, is a struggle, and no peace will put an end to that perpetual condition. Any peace will leave many burdens, vexations, and even miseries (Ratinaud, 1958:217). "To live in society is always to be in a perpetual state of confrontation, with fleeting periods of mutual agreement" (Clemenceau, 1930:181). The duty of the statesman is to put his people in the most advantageous position in the always renewed struggle between nations. There was no question that Germany could be permanently pacified, regardless of type of regime. But Germany could be deterred: that was the task of the peace. Wilson's vision of a postwar world depended upon the restraint of

190

state ambitions through domestic transformation and mutual covenants. Clemenceau's vision was the realization of maximum French ambitions vis-à-vis Germany (Johnston, 1982:221) through a clear power preponderance. Wilson's was a global perspective; Clemenceau's was national and European. The American president thought in terms of abstract principles based on right and justice, from which all political programs flowed. The Tiger cared little for principles. He cared only for what would work, and that could be established only on empirical grounds.

The solution to the problem of war arises from its diagnosis, and Clemenceau's diagnosis of the causes of war was simple: "All wars . . . have been wars of conquest . . . The nations are forever in search of a satisfactory frontier, and perhaps the most remarkable thing is that they have never found it" (Clemenceau, 1930:357). The war of 1914 was just another of this same type. Germany sought territorial annexations, the extent of which would have resulted in the domination of Europe. (We see again the old problem of hegemony in Europe, the problem that the settlements of 1648, 1713, and 1814–15 sought to resolve.) Clemenceau could not accept Wilson's analytical distinction between Germany's military circles and its peoples. The struggle between nations went on regardless of type of regime:

> What after all is this war, prepared, undertaken, and waged by the German *people* [my italics], who flung aside every scruple of conscience to let it loose, hoping for a peace of enslavement under the yoke of militarism destructive of all human dignity? It is simply the continuation of the recrudescence of those never-ending acts of violence by which the first savage tribes carried out their depredation with all the resources of barbarism. The means improve with the ages. The ends remain the same . . . Germany was unfortunate enough to allow herself (in spite of her skill at dissimulation) to be betrayed into an excess of candor by her characteristic tendency to go to extremes. *Deutschland über Alles.* That, and nothing else, is what she asks . . . Not only does she make no secret of her aims, but the intolerable arrogance of the aristocracy, the servile good nature of the intellectual and the scholar, the gross vanity of the most competent leaders in industry, and the widespread influence of a violent popular poetry conspire to shatter . . . honored traditions of individual, as well as international, dignity".                    (Clemenceau, n.d.:100–101)

To Clemenceau, there was no Germany of "good" population and "evil" autocrats, of the innocence of the many and the guilt of the few, of the passivity and gullibility of the masses, and the plottings of the militarists. German war guilt was national, and the peace would have to be based on that conclusion.

In seeking a mandate from the French Chamber of Deputies, Clemenceau conceded that the pre-war system of alliances, arms racing, and balance of power had failed. But as mechanisms they had been used for centuries with some success, and certainly no alternative plan had worked better. Wilson's schemes were novel and interesting, but Clemenceau did not share the American president's faith that the League of Nations could preserve peace. He stated this in courteous tones to the Chamber, and his peace program for weakening Germany received a 398–93 majority vote. In private, he was much harsher with Wilson. The American president's ideas were dangerous illusions, and no responsible French government could base its future security on vague principles such as the Fourteen Points or on international organizations whose sole guarantee lay in good faith and public opinion. Wilson's peace program represented "a certain number of abstractions that might fall into the domain of Utopia" (Ratinaud, 1958:189; cf. Renouvin, 1969:52). The League of Nations, Clemenceau was to argue later, was a "simple organization for peace," with emphasis on the first word. "There are probably few examples of such a misreading and disregard of political experience in the maelstrom of abstract thought" (Clemenceau, 1930:162).

French planning for the peace was delegated to a Ministry of Foreign Affairs *Comité d'études* that circulated proposals several days after the armistice. The committee looked to previous European peace conferences for both procedural and substantive precedents, and concluded that this peace must rest on three principles: (1) self-determination and protection of minority rights; (2) the renunciation of all secret treaties; and (3) the inviolability of Allied territory. A significant point was that the upcoming conference was to be a *preliminary* peace negotiated between the Allies whose results would then be given to the Germans. A general congress of all belligerents, to construct the postwar order and to discuss a league of nations, would follow.

On the question of the league, Clemenceau had appointed a committee under the chairmanship of Leon Bourgeois. In June 1918 it issued its report for a *Société des nations*. This was largely the creation of Bourgeois, as he had committed most of his adult life's work to this project. A former French premier – in whom Clemenceau had little confidence[2] – Bourgeois had spent two decades searching for an alternative to the old European diplomatic system. He had led France's delegations to the two Hague conferences, and he stumped the coun-

---

[2] At the Paris peace conference, Clemenceau was asked how he, as France's president, had once selected Bourgeois to be premier. He replied that as he had sacked so many others there was no one left to fill the post (Bonsal, 1944:212–13).

try constantly exhorting his followers on behalf of the idea of a permanent international organization that would offer a variety of mechanisms for the peaceful settlement of international disputes. As president of France's League of Nations Society during the war, he had numerous opportunities to expand his ideas and to reflect on the experience of the Hague system. His ideas were in some ways similar to those of Wilson, but less rooted in political philosophy. He sought the transformation of international politics not through national democratization and international covenant, but through a powerful international organization, that is, through collective security and collective deterrence.

He saw such an organization as eminently realistic. There are, he suggested, only two roads to enduring peace: realism (organization) and balance of power. The Great War had shown the bankruptcy of the latter. It was perhaps not intrinsically flawed, but balances require alliances, and alliances escalate local conflicts. Arms racing is another result. But power has to remain a component of diplomatic life. The trick is to collect power into a global decision-making authority that could both deter aggression and impose sanctions should deterrence fail. Like Wilson, Bourgeois emphasized the issue of rights. The task of international organization is to protect rights, not just interests. Rights have both a legal and moral meaning. Ultimately the organization of peace depends upon justice. Bourgeois also posited an interest that was common to all states. That interest was defined in terms of justice, order, and legal rights. When this interest is internationalized, a system of collective security becomes possible. Without it, there can be only a Hobbesian world of selfish states, each pursuing its purposes at the expense of the others. "Pas d'harmonie sans l'ordre, pas d'ordre sans la paix, pas de paix sans la liberté, pas de liberté sans la justice" (Bourgeois, 1910:16).

In Bourgeois's scheme, international arbitration would be compulsory. The international executive authority would have the right to establish the maximum size for national armies, and would be provided with authority and capacity to monitor national implementation of disarmament levels. The organization, finally, would create an international army under an international general staff. Its tasks would include executing decisions of the international tribunal and defending member states against aggression (Bourgeois, 1919:113–19; text of the French draft for a league is in Baker, 1923:III, 152–67).

Since the great powers would dominate the organization, the scheme looked in some of its details like little more than a highly organized continuation of the wartime alliance. Germany would not belong to the organization, and Bolshevik Russia was beyond the pale of civilization. This left the United States, Great Britain, France, Italy and Japan: all the victors of the Great War.

Wilson indicated his attitudes toward the French proposals by refusing to answer French diplomatic communications that outlined them. In Great Britain, Lord Robert Cecil, who was preparing a British draft of a league, rejected Bourgeois's plan as a new Holy Alliance (Egerton, 1978:75). Clemenceau had little enthusiasm for his colleague's ideas, but he appointed him and Professor Larnaude, a legal scholar, to handle the issue at the peace conference. Their unenviable task was to fight for Bourgeois's version of an international organization against Wilson's ideas, those of the British, and Clemenceau's indifference and skepticism.

## PEACE THROUGH CONFLICT RESOLUTION MECHANISMS: THE BRITISH CONTRIBUTION

The roots of British thinking about the postwar order in general and about the League of Nations in particular were historical and pragmatic. While Wilson was speculating about the universalization of the American constitutional and historical experience, about the foundations of right and justice in international life, and about the nature of the global interest, British authorities were looking at the events of August 1914 and at the European congresses of the nineteenth century for their inspiration. Sir Edward Grey, the foreign secretary in 1914, was profoundly influenced by the failure of his efforts to preserve the peace after the assassination in Sarajevo. He was convinced that if the Concert of Europe had had some machinery for obligatory consultations, the Great War might have been avoided (Tillman, 1961:102). There was nothing fundamentally wrong with the Concert system; what was needed in a crisis situation was time, consultation, and delay. While Wilson wanted to jettison the whole edifice of nineteenth-century diplomacy, the British wanted only some institutionalized reforms of it.

The task of thinking systematically about the League of Nations was delegated to a committee chaired by Lord Phillimore. The results of its deliberations were sent to the Americans. Some of Colonel House's ideas on a league derived from the Phillimore report, but Wilson stuck to his own advice. Prime Minister Lloyd George left the task of further development and detailed analysis to General Smuts and to Lord Cecil, parliamentary secretary of state for foreign affairs and member of the cabinet in his capacity as blockade minister. Cecil, like Grey, located the sources of the Great War in the voluntaristic features of the Concert system. Chief among them was the lack of time and communication in an era where rapid mobilization of forces had outstripped the capacity of diplomats to consult each other. He reminisced about the "desperate attempts . . . by Sir Edward Grey to induce Austria to agree to refer her dispute with Serbia to an international conference" (Cecil, 1941:47). A theme of all subsequent British plans was that disputants should be forbidden to resort to war until all measures short of war had been exhausted. Any future League of Nations must include compulsory conflict-resolution procedures.

The British prime minister agreed that it would make a difference if the world's leaders could meet to discuss matters. Lloyd George was skeptical of Wilson's idea of mutual guarantees – no state could tie its hands through an abstract commitment – but he was attracted to the notion of lessening the burdens of armaments. As for an international executive authority with the power to impose sanctions, he thought it would take generations for an organization of this kind "to acquire the necessary authority to dictate the actions of independent nations charged with angry emotions and moved by interests as well as patriotism" (quoted in Egerton, 1978:159). Certainly he knew that despite some radical public opinion to the contrary, no British parliament would approve anything like the ideas contained in Bourgeois's draft of the League of Nations. Reflecting the tone of Castlereagh's famous memorandum of a century earlier, he argued that

> the probable effect of including in the constitution of the League of Nations obligations to go to war in certain stated conditions will be to make it impossible for any nation to join the League, for no nation will commit itself in such a vital manner except by the free decision of its own Government and of its own Parliament, and no Government and no Parliament can come to such a decision except after an examination of the facts at the time when the decision has to be made. The attempt to impose obligations of this kind . . . will either end in their being nugatory or in the destruction of the league itself. The thing that really matters is that the nations should remain in continuous consultation under a system which enables them to come to prompt decisions on world problems as they arise from day to day.
>
> (quoted in Egerton, 1978:122)

Lloyd George wanted little more than a Concert system of the old type with loose guarantees of consultations in crisis situations. There is no idea that the consultations should be among others than the great powers either. While the British government found ways to collaborate with the Americans, there was little in Lloyd George's thinking about the postwar order that matched in scope or depth either that of Wilson or of Bourgeois. Lloyd George's perspective on international relations was as steeped in traditional national interests as was that of Clemenceau. The major difference was that the prime minister wanted a relatively lenient peace with the Germans. Yet, in appointing Robert Cecil as the British representative to the League of Nations Commission at the Paris conference, he made it almost certain that Wilson's conception of the League would prevail. Cecil had his own ideas about how to translate the lessons of 1914 into more than a mere voluntaristic, casual set of consultations between leaders. Colonel House had warned Wilson that Cecil was the only man in the British government who really had the League at heart (Egerton, 1978:128). House might have mentioned General Smuts as well, but his observation was generally correct. Lloyd George's entourage and the Conservative leaders, including Churchill, were not bold thinkers. For them, the Great War had changed very little, and no international organization was likely to alter the eternal verities of international politics and the commanding strategic interests of the British Empire. None of Great Britain's official leaders saw the League as an *alternative* to traditional strategies for managing Great Britain's imperial security. The League, however, might mobilize the United States on behalf of a new European balance of power. A league of democracies could complement rather than supplant traditional British strategies (Egerton, 1978:109).

## PARIS 1919: THE IMPORTANCE OF PRELIMINARIES AND PROCEDURES

Following Wilson's first of fourteen points, the peace conference in Paris was to epitomize the processes of the new diplomacy: open covenants openly arrived at. All of the Allied and Associated powers were to negotiate a peace treaty with the Central Powers, or what was left of them. In addition, representatives of all the peoples seeking the right of self-determination were invited to send delegates or spokesmen, and they did so in profusion. Non-governmental organizations were active as well. They sought and for the most part received audiences with the premiers, presidents, and foreign ministers of the major actors, all pleading their special causes and importuning the policy-makers to include statements of principle in the Covenant of the League of Nations (Walworth, 1986:ch. 2). The leaders of the conference were also assisted by hundreds of experts mobilized in advance to advise on the details of the settlement. The agenda was huge, literally thousands of issues that needed decision. This was the first scientific peace conference, where decisions were to be made on the basis of the popular will and on relevant data, and not on the whims and calculations of a small group of men. The consent of the governed was the first principle to be applied; all other considerations would have to be subordinated to it. The scientists – historians, lawyers, geographers, and economists – had the unenviable task of reconciling this principle with political, economic, and strategic realities and necessities. In some cases, as in a zero-sum game, the gains secured for one polity via the principle of self-determination were at the expense of the same principle for another nation. For example, the Four could not resurrect Poland and provide it with an outlet to the Baltic Sea through Gdynia without incorporating into Poland some two million Germans who had no wish to become Poles. Prussia was cut off from the rest of Germany by the Polish corridor. Wilson, in particular, was to learn that the practical application of general principles necessitated some very unpalatable compromises.

The ultimate authority of the conference was the plenary. In reality, the leaders of the United States, France, and Great Britain, and to a much lesser extent, Italy, made the decisions. The meetings began under the auspices of the Council of Ten, the four leaders and their foreign ministers, plus Japan's delegates, but even this concentration of talent and authority was found to be too cumbersome. Clemenceau, as president of the conference, eagerly accepted Colonel House's suggestion of informal meetings of the Four, and it was in the dozens of informal gatherings of Clemenceau, Lloyd George, Wilson, and Orlando – the "steering committee" – that the real decisions were taken. The plenary met only to receive those decisions. It decided nothing itself, nor was it a forum for debates and discussion. The text of the Treaty of Versailles was submitted to the plenary only one day before it was presented to the Germans. Despite all the trappings of parliamentary diplomacy, the role of experts, and the glare of publicity, the Paris peace conference was not essentially different in decision-making procedures from its nineteenth-century predecessor. Wilson had wanted "no odor" of 1815 to permeate the Paris gathering, but it was there.

By late 1918 he had also abandoned one of his critical moral maxims: peace must be based on justice. In practice, this meant that the peace would have to be negotiated between all the belligerents; it must be a peace between equals. But Wilson insisted by the end of the war that the peace would be negotiated only between the victors. Its terms would then be offered to the defeated Central Powers on a take-it-or-resume-the-war basis. In deciding to move ahead in this manner, Wilson not only compromised his theoretical foundations for a new

197

international order, but circumvented nineteenth-century European practice. That practice had been to hold a preliminary peace conference *between the belligerents*. The preliminary peace device was meant to reestablish diplomatic relations between the war participants and to prepare a program for the final conference. Frequently, the general conference, because it took place in a somewhat changed diplomatic environment, altered the terms of the preliminary peace to make them more consistent with the security requirements of all of Europe. What was critically important was that in each stage all the belligerents negotiated with each other. This had been the case in Utrecht, at Paris in 1814, after the Crimean War (the Treaty of Vienna, the preliminary peace, was followed by the Congress of Paris in 1856), and in 1878, when the Congress of Berlin ratified, but also changed, the terms of the Treaty of San Stefano that had terminated the war between Russia and Turkey. In other words, a peace negotiated directly between the participants in a war ultimately had to obtain the approval of the European community of states. This procedure was commonly recognized as a fundamental requirement for establishing legitimacy to a peace settlement and for assimilating the defeated power(s) into the postwar order. European practice was consistent with some of the theoretical prerequisites for creating international order.

Initially, the Paris conference was to adhere to the traditional format. Its official title was the Conférence des Préliminaires de Paix. But in a speech of September 27, 1918, Wilson ruled out German participation in any peace conference:

> We are all agreed that there can be no peace obtained by any kind of bargain or compromise with the governments of the Central Empires ... They have convinced us that they are without honor and do not intend justice. They observe no covenants, accept no principle but force and their own interest. We cannot "come to terms" with them ... Germany will have to redeem her character, not by what happens at the peace table but by what follows. (Shaw, 1924:I, 522)

The installation of a parliamentary government in Germany in late 1918 was not sufficient to change Wilson's decision to negotiate a peace of victors.

The French also deviated from past practice. They proposed to Wilson in a note of November 29, 1918 (text in Baker, 1923:III, 55–66) that the Allied and Associated powers meet in Paris to develop the preliminaries for peace that would be "imposed severally on the enemy without any discussion with him." However, this preliminary peace would be followed by a general peace congress where all of the belligerents would be represented. The French position was, of course, contradictory: it proposed to *impose* a preliminary peace, and then to *negotiate* a final peace. But the contradiction hardly matters. Wilson never bothered to reply to the French note and, once in Paris, he managed the agenda in such a manner that the negotiations there became the final peace.

Wilson wanted a single text. He had to tie in the Covenant with the terms of the settlement with Germany in order to have any chance of saving his dream of a League of Nations from Senate cannibalism. He never took seriously the advice of House and Clemenceau that ultimately the peace terms would have to be negotiated with Germany (Gonda, 1981:13; Tardieu, 1921:116–17). The Paris peace conference became the first European multilateral war settlement that was not negotiated between all the belligerents. Whatever the pretensions of the peacemakers that their work represented leniency and justice and that it could serve as a basis for an enduring peace, it was a *diktat* – as most Germans were to claim from the day it was signed.

The Germans were invited to Paris to sign the treaty, but the conference provided them only fifteen days to review the text (meanwhile treating the members of the German delegation as virtual prisoners) and to submit written comments. The Allied leaders reviewed the numerous German protests and disagreements, which emphasized the incompatibility between Wilson's publicly stated peace principles and the actual terms of the treaty. They made a few modest changes, but altered neither the spirit nor the substance of the treaty significantly.

The punitive impulses of the peacemakers prevailed over the traditional understanding that an enduring peace must be based on legitimacy which, as Wilson often noted prior to 1919, can only be achieved through free negotiations between equals and through the assimilation of the defeated power(s) into the international society. There were further debates respecting Germany's membership of the League of Nations, the French adhering to a vigorous punitive line, with the Americans somewhat more lenient. The outcome was that Germany and the other defeated belligerents would have to serve a probationary period, earning their way to membership through their foreign policy behavior, even though they otherwise met the only specific membership requirement in the Covenant, that a state be "self-governing."

### THE DRAMA OF THE LEAGUE OF NATIONS COMMISSION

The League of Nations Commission was charged with the task

of drafting the Covenant of the new international organization. Woodrow Wilson served as chair; Colonel House served as the second American delegate. Robert Cecil and General Smuts represented the British Empire. Bourgeois and Larnaude worked for the French vision of a league. The Italian prime minister, Orlando, and Senator Scialoja represented Italy. Other original members of the Commission included Japan, Brazil, Serbia, Belgium, China, and Portugal. The Commission met for the first time on February 3, 1919, and immediately the Americans and British preempted the agenda. The Italians and French had prepared drafts of a League of Nations, but these were neither translated into English (the working language of the Commission) nor submitted to the members. The Anglo-American draft, a hybrid of various proposals developed in the preceding months by Wilson, Colonel House, Cecil, Smuts, and drafted into formal language by the American and British legal advisers, David Miller and Cecil Hurst, served as the basis of the discussion in the Commission. Wilson presented it to the members without first having circulated it. The French and Italians wanted twenty-four hours to review it before commencing discussions of principles and details (the draft had not even been translated into French or Italian), but Wilson and Cecil prevailed in their view that discussions of detail must begin immediately. They insisted that there be no prior discussion of principles.[3]

The contest between the visions of a postwar international organization was dramatic and heated, and there were few compromises on fundamentals. Wilson and Cecil prevailed, and the French were confirmed in their view that they could never rely upon the new League of Nations for their security. The four fundamental areas of disagreement were (1) the nature of international crises; (2) decision-making rules; (3) war avoidance through deterrence or persuasion; and (4) disarmament and how it was to be achieved.

The Hurst–Miller draft represented British and American responses to the processes that had led to the Great War. The conflict-resolving procedures outlined in the Hurst–Miller and final versions of the Covenant were lengthy and detailed. The underlying image of conflict was that it originates from lack of communication and misperceptions. It was an image of conflict through error, of parties that behaved aggressively because they were ill- or misinformed. There was no

---

[3] The discussion that follows is based on two sets of minutes taken during the Commission meetings: Conférence des Préliminaires de Paix, Commission de la Société des Nations, 1919b, and Miller, 1928:I, 130–472. Stephen Bonsal's *Unfinished Business* (1944) also summarizes some of the discussions. For details of the negotiations in Paris prior to the meetings of the League of Nations Commission, see Walworth (1986:ch. 6).

assumption of guilt or possible malevolence attached to the parties to conflict, except in rare cases where a state refused to follow League procedures or where, once having accepted them, it went to war in defiance of League Council recommendations. The articles in the Covenant were based on a view of government reason and restraint, and on the belief that a careful examination of the facts of any dispute would change the behavior of the conflict parties. Again, the theme of conflict through misunderstanding. Wilson's faith in public opinion was also evident; the light of publicity would alter diplomatic behavior. Economic, diplomatic, and military sanctions – the former obligatory, the latter voluntary – were built into the League, but could be used only where one of the parties to a dispute circumvented the conflict-resolving procedures through the use of force.

The French argued vehemently that this image of international conflict and of state behavior in crisis situations was, if not totally erroneous, at least incomplete. There are, Bourgeois maintained presciently, *états de mauvaise foi*, states that have aggression and conquest in mind. What could a League of Nations modeled upon the Anglo-American plan do in case of a surprise attack by such a state? An aggressor would present the League with a *fait accompli*. With slow conflict-resolution procedures and voluntary armed sanctions only, the League could not force the aggressor to withdraw from its territorial or other gains. What could the League do if sanctions not only required the unanimous approval of the Council, but also had to be debated in the legislatures of all member states? A determined aggressor could conquer half a continent before the League could come to any decision. And what if the legislatures of key states were in recess at the time of aggression? Further delays would result, leading to ever-increasing security of gains made by a country that resorted to the use of force.

The League's decision-making rules derived from the Anglo-American optimistic view of the character of international conflict, as well as from concern over the traditional rights of sovereignty. Wilson and Cecil, always alert to parliamentary sentiment at home, argued that substantive decisions of the League Council would have to be unanimous. The French, supported by the small powers on the Commission, argued for majority votes. The British reaction to this idea was one of horror: Great Britain could never base its foreign policy decisions on the vote of a group of small powers. The Anglo-American team saw the League in terms of exclusive great power leadership. It was only through the vigorous diplomacy of the Belgians, Greeks, and others, that they consented to include *any* small powers on the Council. The French, on the other hand, placed more trust in the small states as potential allies than they did in the United States and Great Britain. If Wilson and Cecil were willing to accept a watered-down international debating society as a basis for international peace and security, it would be better to rely on countries such as Belgium, countries that had suffered most under Germany after 1914.

Léon Bourgeois and his colleague saw the League of Nations as a collective deterrent system. The League had to be more than a ponderous set of conflict-resolving procedures designed to cope with well-meaning but misinformed parties who almost accidentally went to war. It had to include more than a vague set of mutual guarantees. Potential aggressors had to know in advance that the League, representing the community of nations, had at its disposal a permanent military force, organized and directed by a League of Nations general staff. This international army had to be superior to the armed might of all nations combined. The purpose of the League must be not only to resolve conflicts, but to prevent them. It would not be sufficient to recommend, after the fact, that member states combine voluntarily to impose military sanctions against a state that had violated the provisions and principles of the Covenant. The French argued persistently for amending the Hurst–Miller draft so as to provide the League with a deterrent capacity. To no avail, however. Lord Cecil simply could not envisage "putting a portion of the British army under the command of a general who was not a British subject" (Bonsal, 1944:187). Wilson, aside from any constitutional and political problems such a League would create at home, opposed on principle: he could not countenance "substituting international militarism for national militarism" (Conférence des Préliminaires de Paix, Commission de la Société des Nations, 1919b:70). After heated debates, the French amendments to the Hurst–Miller draft failed to receive unanimous support (they did receive a majority, however) and Wilson, as chair, ruled that unanimity was required to approve amendments of this import. Bourgeois lamented to Colonel House that his life's work had just been wiped out (Bonsal, 1944:152).

The disarmament issue left one remaining possibility. If the League's deterrent capacity was to be based on little more than good faith and world public opinion, security might be gained at least by reducing the armed forces of the member states. This possibility was consistent with Wilson's principle that the armed forces of members must be reduced to the lowest point consistent with domestic safety. The Hurst–Miller draft in fact (Article 6) stipulated that no state would be admitted to the League except on condition that its army and naval forces and armaments would conform to standards and levels pre-scribed by the League. The Council (Article 8) would determine the levels of armed forces for all members and applicants. But there was nothing to guarantee that any League plan (which would require unanimous approval by the Council) would in fact be implemented. In Wilson's view, good faith and the light of publicity could take care of that problem. Cecil rejected the ideas of the Hurst–Miller draft altogether. Great Britain would not accept limits on the size of its armed forces. The French proposed a Commission of Control and Verification. Its task was to make certain that armaments levels defined by the League would in fact be carried out, and also to report on the military deployments of member states – a power, in other words, to warn of impending attacks. The French again failed to carry the Com-mission against the opposition of Wilson and Cecil. Even the Hurst–Miller proposals were eliminated. Disarmament in the final draft of the Covenant was left as a statement of hope for the future rather than as an obligation of the present.

The Commission debated many other problems, but the outcome of these four critical issues determined the nature of the organization and, to a certain extent, the nature of international politics in the 1920s and 1930s. There was one final issue, important mostly for its symbolic meaning, but it added significantly to the French disillusionment with the entire peace settlement. The question was, should the Covenant include a provision for withdrawal from League membership? This issue was perhaps even more important than defining the qualifi-cations for membership. The United States Senate Foreign Relations Committee insisted that the Covenant include provision for with-drawal. Wilson proposed a period of two years' notice. But how could a member withdraw from a Covenant of almost sacramental status? Could Article 10, the mutual guarantee of a political independence and territorial integrity, mean anything if members could renege so easily on their solemn undertakings? With the right of withdrawal, the Cov-enant would become just another treaty, and the security provisions were further diluted. The French insisted on the principle of perma-nent membership, and thus of permanent obligations. Their position accorded with Wilson's own beliefs, but the president had to bend to Senate opinion. He sacrificed one of his most treasured principles, the perpetual mutual guarantee, and successfully resisted the French. Among the delegates, no position Wilson took throughout the debates so compromised his prestige and standing (Bonsal, 1944:165). Wilson readily bent to the realities of America's legislative politics, but he had demonstrated no similar sensitivity to the realities of France's security and French public opinion.

The Covenant that emerged from the Commission represented a victory for the Anglo-American vision of international organization. It was to be a league for peace, essentially a covenant of mutual guarantees of political independence and territorial integrity, combined with a set of conflict-resolving procedures to be applied to states that were assumed to be essentially benevolent. Sanctions remained in the background, possibilities that relied on the principle of voluntarism. Disarmament remained little but a vague pledge, and the ultimate escape from international responsibility, withdrawal of membership, was guaranteed.

The final text of the Covenant was introduced to the plenary of the peace conference on April 28, 1919. Clemenceau was in the chair and adroitly preempted some criticisms that were in the offing. The prime minister of Australia was ready with an anti-League and anti-Japan speech; the Portuguese delegate was primed with a speech complaining that his country had never since the days of Pedro the Cruel signed an international treaty that did not include a reference to the Holy Trinity. Wilson explained the main provisions of the text and how discussions had proceeded in the Commission. He then moved adoption of the Covenant, whereupon Bourgeois made one last effort to mobilize support for his concept of an effective League of Nations. By this time everyone in Paris was thoroughly familiar with Bourgeois's views on the matter. Stephen Bonsal recorded the proceedings:

> Colonel House's face was a study . . . it was a dark moment. The President [Wilson] slumped wearily in his chair, Mr. Balfour [the British Foreign Secretary] gazed intently at the ceiling. Clemenceau [the chairman of the conference] closed his eyes, and the delegates prepared to listen once again to the thoughts and the fears that the father of the French League of Nations Society expresses in such halting phrases . . . "I do not conceal from you the fact that if we are to have a League, and thereby security for all, sacrifices will have to be made. Some of our historic traditions and our long-accustomed rights will have to be abandoned, but how insignificant is this loss of independent action when you contrast it with the menace that will hang over us all – if the League is not established *with force behind it*" [Bonsal's italics]. M. Bourgeois had talked along this line for about ten minutes when, unwisely, he stopped for breath and dived into the pyramid of manuscript notes before him. Suddenly Clemenceau opened his eyes wide and rapping sharply with his gavel . . . in a loud, clear voice announced: "As I hear no objections, I declare that the

Conference has considered and adopted the revised Covenant as presented by the Commission of the League". (Bonsal, 1944:211–12)

Bourgeois's last effort to provide a league that could resolve France's security dilemma was undercut by the French chairman – much to the amusement and relief of the assembled delegates. The world was not ready for more than moral obligations and procedures for the peaceful settlement of international conflicts.

Wilson's evaluation of his great efforts in Paris was positive. He understood the weaknesses of the League Covenant, but he thought that as an institution it would grow, develop, and change to meet the circumstances of the times. The critical point was that the members of the conference had accepted the key mutual guarantees of Article 10, plus commitments to employ conflict-resolving mechanisms and to lower levels of armaments. Article 10 indicated that governments were willing to build their foreign policies on new foundations, on the bases of right and liberal principles of internationalism. The League, he suggested, would be the "eye of the Nations to keep watch upon the common interest, an eye that does not slumber, an eye that is everywhere watchful and attentive" (Levin, 1972:44).

## THE GERMAN SETTLEMENT

Clemenceau, reflecting French parliamentary and public opinion, consistently sought to guarantee against a new German attack by making Germany weak and France strong. This meant restoration of Alsace-Lorraine, stripping Germany of its colonies, and dismantling its navy – in brief, destroying Germany as a world power. France would also take over the Saar basin as compensation for the German army's systematic destruction of French coal mines in the northeast. Many others in France were clamoring for the dismemberment of Germany, reconstituting its old sovereignties such as Bavaria, Württemburg, Hesse, and the like. But for Clemenceau, the essential task was to prevent the Germans from ever again using the Rhineland as a staging area for an invasion of western Europe. There were numerous means to that end, of which French occupation in the name of the Allies was only one.

Lloyd George took exception to the French approach to Germany. He was concerned above all that a harsh peace would drive the Germans to Bolshevism and Europe would then be divided between the Bolshevik bloc of Russia, Germany, and several eastern European states, arrayed against France, England, and the Benelux countries. The peace with Germany must be one that a responsible German government could sign "in the belief that it can fulfill the obligations which it incurs." It must be a peace "which will contain in itself no provocations for future wars, and which will constitute an alternative to Bolshevism" (quoted in Baker, 1923:III, 454).

Clemenceau's response was devastating. He implied that by sequestering the German fleet, by taking Germany's merchant navy as part of the reparations, and by stripping Germany of its colonies – all parts of the Armistice provisions – Great Britain's security concerns had been resolved. If there was any element of injustice to Germany arising from French security requirements, even greater injustices had already been committed in order to satisfy British interests. Lloyd George, he implied, had expressed magnanimity toward the Germans only after Great Britain's main objectives had been achieved. France's territorial concerns were defensively motivated and also drawn up with a view to the application of self-determination in eastern Europe. One could not have a just peace as defined solely by the Germans. The justice of the victors and the new states of Europe had to be fulfilled as well. France would not be swayed by the bogey of German Bolshevism. The critical point remained the building of a secure Europe, and this could only be accomplished by measures that would effectively preclude any future German attack (Baker 1923, III, text of a letter to Wilson responding to a memorandum by Lloyd George, March 25, 1919, pp. 249–52).

Wilson's position lay somewhere in between. The president desired to make the German settlement an example of the "harsh wages of international sin' (Levin, 1968:107). He was concerned about justice, and in his conception of justice, punishment played a role. Despite his wartime distinction between the evil German autocrats and militarists and the good German people, he was not willing to absolve the latter for the sins of the former. Germany would have to be stripped of its great power status, it would have to admit its guilt in starting the war, it would have to pay reparations, and it would have to endure a probationary period before it could be considered for membership in the League of Nations. Wilson feared that the moderate German regime that succeeded the Kaiser had not really destroyed the reactionary roots of German militarism. Hence, he was willing to support most of the French positions on the settlement, as well as those of the Poles and Czechs: "Until we know what the German government was going to be, and how the German people were going to behave, the world has a moral right to disarm Germany, and to subject her to a generation of thoughtfulness" (quoted in Levin, 1968:123–25).

Wilson did not, however, share Clemenceau's position with regard to the occupation of the Rhineland, French discussion of restoring

France's eastern borders to those of 1814, and the virtual annexation of the Saar. An impasse developed on these and other issues, and Wilson threatened to leave for Washington. Lloyd George and Wilson saved the situation by proposing to resolve France's security problem through American and British guarantee treaties. They would come to the assistance of France should Germany make yet another military assault. Clemenceau also agreed to a fifteen-year occupation of the Rhineland by an Allied army, control over the Rhine bridgeheads, and, at his insistence, a stipulation that the period of occupation could be prolonged indefinitely if Germany failed to meet any of its responsibilities in the Treaty of Versailles. France was to run the coal mines of the Saar for a similar period of time, and the ultimate fate of the territory would be determined by plebiscite.

Under the final version of the Versailles Treaty, France would have three lines of defense: (1) Allied occupation of the strategically critical Rhine area, an occupation that would be reduced by stages to coincide with German fulfillment of all the terms of the settlement; (2) the long-term American and British guarantees against a renewed German attack; and (3) the League of Nations, whose membership Germany would eventually seek, and which meant that it would commit itself to honor France's political independence and territorial integrity. For Wilson and Lloyd George, this constituted a foolproof security system. It would ensure both the endurance of the peace treaty with Germany and French security.

For Clemenceau, the peace was a necessary compromise, an essential ingredient for postwar Allied harmony. He had no faith in the future of the League of Nations, but he did view optimistically the possibility of extending long into the postwar period the wartime alliance of the democracies. The key lay in firmly holding the Germans to their commitments under the Treaty of Versailles while giving life to the Anglo-American guarantee treaties.

As for the settlement with Germany and the rest of Europe, Wilson was less pleased. He had had to compromise some of his principles, he was uncertain about the future of German democracy, and there was turmoil and warfare in eastern Europe and the Soviet Union. But he believed that if there were any injustices in the settlement, they could be taken to the League for correction. The Paris conference had built the foundations for peace. It would take years to fill in the details, for the League to grow in authority, and for all the forces of democracy to rid the world of the old diplomacy.

Wilson returned to the United States to find a substantially hostile Senate Foreign Relations Committee. He stumped the country attempting to build up public enthusiasm for the Versailles Treaty. In his speeches, however, he was forced to emphasize the voluntary character of League obligations: the Council could only advise member states to take action against an aggressor. He acknowledged that the necessity of unanimous voting in the Council weakened the organization, but there remained the essential covenant and the power of public opinion:

> Unless you get the united concerted purpose and power of the great Governments of the world behind this settlement, it will fall down like a house of cards. There is only one power to put behind the liberation of mankind, and that is the power of mankind. It is the power of the united moral forces of the world, and in the Covenant of the League of Nations the moral forces of the world are mobilized . . . And what do they unite for? They enter into a solemn promise to one another that they will never use their power against one another for aggression; that they will never impair the territorial integrity of a neighbor; that they never will interfere with the political independence of a neighbor . . . They consent . . . to submit every matter of difference between them to the judgement of mankind, and just so certainly as they do that . . . war will be in the far background, war will be pushed out of that foreground of terror in which it has kept the world for generation after generation, and men will know that there will be a calm time of deliberate counsel . . . We have accepted the truth and we are going to be led by it, and it is going to lead us, and through us the world, out into pastures of quietness and peace such as the world never dreamed of before. (Cronon, 1965:517–19; 531)

After this peroration in Pueblo, Colorado, Wilson suffered a collapse that was to incapacitate him for most of the remainder of his presidential term. As best he could, he fought the Senators who demanded reservations to the treaty. Ultimately, the treaty failed to gain approval in the Senate by six votes. Not only would the United States remain outside the League of Nations, but the project for a guarantee treaty with France lapsed. The British also reneged on their commitment, arguing that a British guarantee was contingent upon an American guarantee. Two of France's three lines of defense never materialized; it is easy to understand why Clemenceau felt betrayed.

### EVALUATION

For the first time in history, broad publics and the peacemakers shared a conviction that war was a central problem in international relations. Previously, hegemony, the aggressive activities of a particular state, or revolution had been the problem. In 1648, 1713, and 1815, the peacemakers had tried to resolve issues of the past and to construct orders that would preclude their reappearance. But in 1919 expectations ran higher. The sources of the war were less important than the war itself. There was a necessity to look more to the future than to the past. The problem was not just to build a peace, but to construct a peaceful international order that would successfully manage all international conflicts of the future.

Wilson thought he had the blueprint for such an order: the transformation of societies via the principle of self-determination, coupled with a universalization of the ideas of the American political tradition and the Monroe Doctrine. The British thought they could take care of the problem by establishing conflict-resolving mechanisms and consultative international machinery. And the French thought they could achieve it through a combination of German weakness and Allied strength, through a preponderance of power built upon the foundations of the wartime coalition. Despite the diverging conceptions of postwar order, all peacemakers were essentially optimistic about the future, although given the turmoil and violence taking place in Russia and eastern Europe at the time, the actual outlook was hardly salutary.[4]

We need not enumerate the many reasons for the failure of the peace. This is common historical knowledge, although still a matter of debate. Looking at it more abstractly, however, we can see that some of the theoretical requisites for an enduring peace and a pacific international order were missing already in 1919.

In previous peace congresses, all the major powers were included, even those that had suffered defeat on the battlefield. In 1919, by contrast, Russia remained on the sidelines. Though the peace conference nullified the *diktat* of Brest-Litovsk to the great advantage of the new Soviet Republic, the Allied military intervention and assistance to the anti-Bolshevik forces in the Russian Civil War made a greater impression in Leningrad and Moscow. The Russians were no friends of the Versailles Treaty, nor were their ideological goals of world revolution consistent with the philosophies inherent in the Covenant.

Germans of many political persuasions found the treaty humiliating, onerous, offensive, and a betrayal of Wilson's peace principles (Schwabe, 1985). From 1919 on, they were committed to changing its terms, either through diplomacy or through more aggressive means. Hitler did not create the issue; he simply exploited feelings that ran deep and broadly throughout German society. Allied efforts at ap-

---

[4] During the conduct of the negotiations in Paris, some fourteen civil and international armed conflicts were taking place.

peasement and change of the treaty terms throughout the 1920s and 1930s were only partially successful in changing German attitudes.

The United States retreated to isolationism and lost its stomach for any but the most modest involvements in European affairs. The British were diverted by imperial and economic reconstruction issues and found French security concerns unfounded and tiresome. The Italians remained unsatisfied with their territorial gains in the war. This left only France to uphold the settlement. The peace never enjoyed or earned legitimacy in many capitals.

Nevertheless, the League of Nations achieved some notable successes in disputes between small states. During its brief history, its organs considered 66 cases ranging from technical legal disputes to major cases of armed conflict. Twenty were referred to other agencies. Eleven cases resulted in military conquest contrary to League obligations. But it was successful in the remaining 35 cases (76 percent), making it significantly more effective as a conflict manager than its successor, the United Nations (data in Wright, 1942:II, appendix 34, 1429–31). This was a significant achievement, and it is possible to speculate that had those cases not been resolved, more general wars could have occurred. The diagnoses and expectations of Sir Edward Grey and Robert Cecil were at least partly correct.

But for dealing with major threats to peace, the theories underlying the Covenant were tragically flawed. The drafters of the Covenant insisted that the burden of enforcing the mutual guarantees would fall upon the great powers. Yet, the only really serious threats to peace could come from a great power, and the League could not act in these circumstances because the drafters also insisted on the principle of unanimity in decision-making. The League thus became not an organization to enforce the terms of Article 10, but a set of procedures for resolving conflicts between parties *that agreed or wished to resolve those conflicts short of conquest, that is, through compromise*. The Germans, Japanese, and Italians in the 1930s did not want to resolve conflicts, as Wilson and Cecil thought any power would, but were resolved on military victory. Bourgeois's predictions were all too correct: the League was irrelevant against *états de mauvaise foi*.

The theory of conflict resolution enunciated by Grey, Cecil, and Wilson assumed that national interests are malleable (Holsti, 1988:110–13). They estimated that through consultations and publicity, leaders can be persuaded to change their interests and goals. They erred fundamentally in assessing that in cost-benefit calculations, aggressive leaders would always place greater emphasis on the costs of bad world publicity than on the gains of achieving their goals. The quotation of

Wilson's speech in Pueblo, Colorado, clearly establishes this view of crisis behavior. In a world of perfect or even relatively malleable states, alterations of cost-benefit calculations may well take place. But in such a world there would be little need for international organizations.

Another fundamental problem with the theory of the Covenant was its unstated assumption of the durability of Allied unity. Wilson believed that alliances were incompatible with the principles of the League. They represented the "old diplomacy," special interests combined against the general interest. Yet, at times he spoke of the combined power of the democracies, and occasionally he made references to the League as an organization virtually run by France, Great Britain, and the United States (apparently he never speculated on how the League might function were it dominated by Germany, Russia, and Japan). He and his colleagues in Paris made the common error of all peacemakers: that the winning wartime coalition will continue into the new era of peace. Gustav Adolph, Mazarin, Stanhope, Metternich, and Castlereagh operated under the same assumption or illusion. Those who win the war will police the peace. But what if one or more of the winners becomes the great revisionist power? A coalition of great powers cannot coerce one of its own members without threatening another world war. It has never yet dawned on the leaders of winning coalitions that among the group there may lurk a potential or actual plotter. In the 1930s the plots would come from all directions: war losers (Germany), winners (Japan), and those who benefited little (Russia and Italy). What was left of the winning coalition did not have the power, much less the authority, to coerce the plotters of the 1930s.

Finally, the scientific peace of 1919 created as many problems as it solved. The peacemakers of 1919 were resolved not to repeat the presumed errors of their 1815 predecessors. Nationalism and the search for statehood were fundamental sources of conflict throughout the nineteenth century. The peace of 1815 ignored this problem, or more accurately, devised means to suppress it. The settlement of 1919 took it as the highest priority. Its authors responded positively to the issues they knew had created so much war during the previous century. Wilson can be properly applauded for being among the first statesmen to seek a durable international order by strengthening the elements of justice in that order (Johnston, 1982:227). The difficulty was that he and his colleagues placed such high priority on fashioning the new states from the collapse of the Russian and Austrian Empires on the basis of popular will that serious anomalies between economic, strategic, historical, and public opinion values arose. The settlement created economic improbabilities, security problems, restive minorities, and irredentist movements throughout eastern Europe. Many of the armed conflicts of the 1920s and 1930s were to derive from the territorial settlements of 1919. Perhaps no one could have done better. The experts went to great lengths to devise ways of squaring circles. Every boundary drawn created grievances somewhere. There was simply no way to reconcile all the possible criteria that should guide the process of state creation.

The settlement of 1919 created effective mechanisms for conflict resolution for certain kinds of international quarrels, and in many ways it democratized the processes of international relations. Wilson's hope that a growing and developing League of Nations could rectify some of the difficulties created through the territorial settlements was not misplaced. However, the treatment of Germany and the non-participation of Russia created problems the magnitude of which no League of Nations could resolve. The German settlement greatly increased the probabilities that the peace of 1919 would be the father of later tragedy. We can only speculate whether or not a peace negotiated between the belligerents and a quick assimilation of Germany into the ranks of the great powers would have altered the course of history. Clemenceau's strategy of insisting on the priority of French security through German weakness and a vigorous policing of the resulting terms of settlement might have worked as well. It is likely that neither of those paths would have had results worse than those that ensued from the Treaty of Versailles. The international order created in 1919 might also have operated according to expectations had one of Wilson's key ingredients to peace come into being: a world made up of democratic states. By the 1930s, only a minority of the great powers belonged to that category. The remainder were committed to destroying the order.

# 9  WAR AS THE AFTERMATH OF PEACE: INTERNATIONAL CONFLICT, 1918–1941

Mankind has grown great in eternal struggle and only in eternal peace
does it perish.                                                    Adolf Hitler

The task of creating a durable peace in the aftermath of the First World
War would have been beyond the intellectual and diplomatic capacities of most mortals. The process of imperial disintegration in
central Europe, Bolshevik revolution and civil war in Russia, and the
stirrings of nationalism in Africa, Asia, and the Middle East would lead
to armed conflict regardless of what the wise men of Paris did or did not
do. They might try to create nations on the basis of popular will, but
they could not do so without creating new minorities and in some cases
drawing frontiers that made little economic or historical sense. In the
period 1918–41, our list contains thirty interstate wars in the central
international system. Of these, at least eight (27 percent) had their
sources in the post-1918 settlements. The parties went to war or otherwise used force to alter the terms of the relevant peace treaties or to
enforce their provisions against challenges by military means.[1] From
the point of view of controlling or reducing the incidence of war, the
1814–15 settlements were far more successful. The thirtieth war or
armed intervention did not take place until 1913, ninety-nine years
after the first Peace of Paris, while after the Versailles settlements the
world was plunged into thirty wars in the twenty-two years after
Woodrow Wilson sailed home from Europe. Given the hopes and
expectations surrounding the negotiations at Paris, the subsequent
history of international relations represented not progress but
regression.

The thirty wars and armed interventions listed in table 9.1 need

[1] The cases are: Romania–Hungary (1919); Poland–Soviet Republic (1920); Greece–Turkey (1920–22); Poland–Lithuania (1920–27); Japan (Kwantung army)–China (1931–33);
the German remilitarization of the Rhineland (1936); Germany–Czechoslovakia (1938–
1939); and Germany–Poland (1939). In the latter two cases, revisions of the Versailles
Treaty to incorporate ethnic Germans into the Third Reich was more a pretext than a
source of military action.

Table 9.1 *Wars and issues, 1918–41*

| War/major armed intervention | Stakes for original combatants |
|---|---|
| 1. Soviet Republic–Finland (1918–1920) | 1. government composition (S.R.)<br>2. maintain integrity of state (S.R.)<br>3. national unification/irredenta (F.)<br>4. territory |
| 2. Estonia–Soviet Republic (1918–1920) | 1. national liberation/state creation (E.)<br>2. maintain integrity of state (S.R.) |
| 3. Latvia–Soviet Republic (1918–1920) | 1. national liberation/state creation (L.)<br>2. maintain integrity of state (S.R.) |
| 4. Lithuania–Soviet Republic (1918–1920) | 1. national liberation/state creation (L.)<br>2. maintain integrity of state (S.R.) |
| 5. Allied intervention–Soviet Republic (1918–1920) | 1. government composition (Allies)<br>2. protect nationals/commercial interests abroad (Allies)<br>3. regime survival (S.R.) |
| 6. Great Britain—Afghanistan (1919) | 1. autonomy (A.)<br>2. territory<br>3. strategic territory<br>4. maintain integrity of empire (G.B.)<br>5. maintain regional domination (G.B.) |
| 7. Romania (Czechoslovakia, Yugoslavia)–Hungary (1919) | 1. territory<br>2. enforce treaty terms (R., Cz., Y.)<br>3. state/regime survival (H.)<br>4. government composition |
| 8. Poland–Soviet Republic (1920–1921) | 1. territory |
| 9. Greece–Turkey (1920–1922) | 1. territory<br>2. protect ethnic confrères<br>3. revise treaty terms (T.) |
| 10. Poland–Lithuania (1920–1927) | 1. territory (boundary)<br>2. enforce treaty terms (L.)<br>3. protect ethnic confrères (P.) |
| 11. Moroccan tribes–Spain (France) (1921–1926) | 1. national liberation/state creation (M.)<br>2. maintain regional domination (S.) |
| 12. Italy–Greece (1923) | 1. compensation/reparation for incident (I.) |
| 13. Druse–France (1925–1927) | 1. enforce entry terms (D.)<br>2. maintain integrity of empire (F.) |
| 14. United States–Nicaragua rebels (1927–1933) | 1. government composition<br>2. protect nationals/commercial interests abroad (U.S.) |

Table 9.1 *continued*

| War/major armed intervention | Stakes for original combatants |
|---|---|
| 15. Paraguay–Bolivia (1928–1935) | 1. territory (boundary)<br>2. commerce/resources (B.) |
| 16. China–U.S.S.R. (1929) | 1. maintain national integrity (C.)<br>2. strategic territory<br>3. enforce treaty terms (C.)<br>4. compensation/reparation for incident (U.S.S.R) |
| 17. Japan (Kwantung army)–China (1931–1933) | 1. strategic territory<br>2. commerce/resources (J.)<br>3. protect nationals/commercial interests abroad (J.)<br>4. maintain national integrity (C.)<br>5. empire creation (J.) |
| 18. Peru–Colombia (1932–1934) | 1. territory<br>2. commerce/resources<br>3. enforce treaty terms (C.)<br>4. protect nationals/commercial interests abroad (P.) |
| 19. Saudi Arabia–Yemen (1934) | 1. territory<br>2. enforce treaty terms (S.A.) |
| 20. Italy–Abyssinia (1935–1936) | 1. commerce/resources (I.)<br>2. empire creation (I.)<br>3. strategic territory (I.)<br>4. state survival (A.) |
| 21. Spanish Civil War (Germany, Italy, U.S.S.R.) (1936–1939) | 1. regime survival (S.)<br>2. support ally (I., G., U.S.S.R.)<br>3. government composition |
| 22. Remilitarization of Rhineland[a] (1936) | 1. revise treaty terms (G.)<br>2. autonomy (G.) |
| 23. Japan–China (1937–1945) | 1. empire creation (J.)<br>2. state/regime survival (C.)<br>3. territory<br>4. protect nationals/commercial interests abroad (J.)<br>5. commerce/resources (J.) |
| 24. Germany–Austria[a] (1938) | 1. ethnic unification (G.)<br>2. ideological liberation (G.)<br>3. territory<br>4. strategic territory<br>5. empire creation (race) (G.)<br>6. state/regime survival (A.)<br>7. enforce treaty terms (A.) |
| 25. Germany–Czechoslovakia[a] (1938–1939) | 1. ethnic unification (G.)<br>2. strategic territory<br>3. ideological liberation (G.)<br>4. empire creation (race) (G.)<br>5. state/regime survival (C.) |

Table 9.1 *continued*

| War/major armed intervention | Stakes for original combatants |
|---|---|
| 26. Germany–Poland (1939) | 1. empire creation (race) (G.)<br>2. strategic territory<br>3. territory<br>4. revise treaty terms (G.)<br>5. state/regime survival (P.)<br>6. ethnic unification (G.) |
| 27. Great Britain–Germany (1939–1945) | 1. balance of power (G.B.)<br>2. support ally (G.B.)<br>3. enforce treaty terms (G.B.) |
| 28. U.S.S.R.–Poland (1939) | 1. territory<br>2. ethnic unification (U.S.S.R.)<br>3. state/regime survival (P.) |
| 29. U.S.S.R.–Finland (1939–1940) | 1. strategic territory<br>2. territory<br>3. ideological liberation (U.S.S.R.)<br>4. state/regime survival (F.) |
| 30. Japan–United States (1941–1945) | 1. maintain integrity of empire (J.)<br>2. state/regime survival (J.)<br>3. enforce treaty terms (Wilsonian principles) (U.S.)<br>4. support 'ally' (China) (U.S.)<br>5. strategic territory |

[a] Non-violent use of force.

some explanation. While the incidence of war increased dramatically in 1918–41 compared to other historical periods, the increase is explained in part by statistical probabilities. The number of states in the international system ballooned as a result of the break-up of the Austro-Hungarian, Ottoman, and Russian Empires. By 1921, the League of Nations had 41 members, whereas in 1914 the European central states system had only 22 members. For the first time in history, the states system, as symbolized in the League of Nations, had members from all continents in the world. We would expect, as in motor traffic, that as the number of actors increases, so will the number of accidents, conflicts, and wars. But even allowing for this increase in the number of actors in the new global system, the incidence of war expanded beyond mere probabilities. The 1919 settlements, the Russian imbroglio, and the rise of Fascism and Nazism combined to make the interwar years the most violent period in international relations since the Thirty Years War and the wars of the French Revolution and Napoleon.

The list includes all wars referred to the League of Nations, plus those armed contests that grew out of the Russian Civil War involving both Allied intervention and the birth of the Baltic states and Finland. I have included three spheres of influence wars (the Riff War, France's military suppression of the Druse, and the Anglo–Afghan War) because they involved sufficient battle casualties (minimum of 1,000) and were genuine wars between organized parties, not just the repression of unorganized rebellions in colonial territories. I have excluded two incidents that are usually contained in lists of wars in this period: the Changkufeng (1938) and Monohan (1939) incidents between Japanese troops and Soviet armed forces. Though the casualties were high, the evidence suggests that these were unauthorized incidents largely initiated by elements of the Japanese Kwantung army resistant to central control from Tokyo. These incidents represent examples of military insubordination and adventurism more than the deliberate use of force for foreign policy objectives. The Manchurian (Mukden) incident, on the other hand, while also instigated by the Kwantung army, ultimately came to be championed by the central decision-makers in Japan. The conspirators had their own initial purposes, but for the most part these coincided with official Japanese aspirations for the colonization of Manchuria (Peattie, 1975).

I have included three cases that are not found in most lists because, technically, they were not wars and did not meet the standard 1,000 casualty minimum. These were the German remilitarization of the Rhineland in 1936, Germany's *anschluss* with Austria in 1938, and the two-stage dismemberment of Czechoslovakia in 1938–39. These three incidents meet all criteria for war – except that no shots were fired. They were preceded by international crises, Hitler was committed to war to achieve his objectives had any resistance been offered, and Germany occupied the territories it had gained by coercion and extortion. These were all Clausewitzian uses of force for specified objectives; the victims were compelled to surrender by virtue of threats to employ violence on a mass scale.

## ISSUES THAT GENERATED WARS, 1918–1941

Table 9.2 lists the frequency and percentages of issues that surrounded the thirty uses of armed force listed in table 9.1. Several figures deserve comment.

Territory remained the single most important source of international conflict. The figures show no changes, in terms of percentages, between the two periods. The second conflict-producing issue was state/regime survival. Like the eighteenth century, the 1920s and 1930s were a period of pronounced international predation. State/regime

Table 9.2 *Distribution of issues that generated wars, 1918–41*

| Issues | Frequency | % of all issues | Previous period % |
|---|---|---|---|
| Territory | 14 | 14 | 14 |
| State/regime survival | 11 | 11 | 2 |
| Enforce treaty terms | 9 | 9 | 1 |
| Strategic territory | 9 | 9 | 4 |
| Maintain integrity of state/empire | 9 | 9 | 18 |
| Commerce/resources | 6 | 6 | — |
| Empire creation | 6 | 6 | 3 |
| Ethnic unification/irredenta | 5 | 5 | 2 |
| Government composition | 5 | 5 | 4 |
| Protect nationals/commercial interests abroad | 5 | 5 | 1 |
| National liberation/state creation | 4 | 4 | 10 |
| Ideological liberation | 3 | 3 | 3 |
| Revise treaty terms | 3 | 3 | — |
| Defend/support ally | 3 | 3 | — |
| Compensation/reparation for incident | 2 | 2 | — |
| Autonomy | 2 | 2 | 2 |
| Maintain regional dominance | 2 | 2 | 3 |
| Protect ethnic confrères | 2 | 2 | 5 |
| Balance of power | 1 | 1 | 1 |
| Total | 101 | 101[a] | |

[a] Rounding error.

survival was at stake in eleven of the conflicts, constituted 11 percent of all issues, and increased from only 2 percent in the nineteenth century. The third-ranking issue was treaty enforcement. This refers in most cases to attempts by one or more party to enforce through military means the various gains, losses, and distributions of the post-First World War settlements. This figure is stark evidence of the lack of widespread legitimacy of the Treaty of Versailles and its associated peace treaties. Armed challenges to the settlements were a major feature of the interwar period.

National liberation/state creation issues declined significantly from their high percentage in the nineteenth century. In Europe (Ireland excepted) the search for statehood based on ethnic/language divisions was played out with the creation of the central European succession states, the Baltic states, and Finland. Most of the armed and diplomatic conflicts of the 1920s in Europe were contests over precise definitions of boundaries and adjustments to the territorial boundaries drafted at the Paris conference.

The attempt to create empires constituted a significant new issue for the central system. Imperial expansion into areas considered "unciv-ilized" had been the case in the nineteenth century. Now imperial expansion was at the expense of sovereign states, all members of the League of Nations. The main protagonists were, of course, Germany, Italy, and Japan, in quest of the racially based Thousand-Year Reich, the modern Roman Empire, and the "Greater East Asia Co-prosperity Sphere."

Table 9.3, column 3, indicates the percentages of wars in which various issues played a role. These are compared with the percentages for the 1815–1914 period in column 4. Some interesting contrasts emerge from an examination of the two sets of figures. Struggles over territory increase slightly, but the most significant change is in the state/regime survival category. This statistic underlines, as suggested In table 9.2, the predatory nature of international politics in the inter-war period. In 37 percent of the wars, the survival of a state as a sovereign entity, or of a government, was at issue. These were not wars of territorial adjustment, campaigns to incorporate ethnic kin in an adjoining state, or defenses of particular territories against foreign intrusion (indicated in the "maintain integrity of state/empire" cat-

Table 9.3 *Issues that generated wars, 1918–41*

| Issues | Frequency | % of wars | Previous period % |
|---|---|---|---|
| Territory | 14 | 47 | 42 |
| State/regime survival | 11 | 37 | 6 |
| Enforce treaty terms | 9 | 30 | 3 |
| Strategic territory | 9 | 30 | 13 |
| Maintain integrity of state/empire | 9 | 30 | 55 |
| Commerce/resources | 6 | 20 | — |
| Empire creation | 6 | 20 | 10 |
| Ethnic unification/irredenta | 5 | 17 | 6 |
| Government composition | 5 | 17 | 13 |
| Protect nationals/commercial interests abroad | 5 | 17 | 3 |
| National liberation/state creation | 4 | 13 | 29 |
| Ideological liberation | 3 | 10 | 10 |
| Revise treaty terms | 3 | 10 | — |
| Defend/support ally | 3 | 10 | — |
| Compensation/reparation for incident | 2 | 7 | — |
| Autonomy | 2 | 7 | 6 |
| Maintain regional dominance | 2 | 7 | 10 |
| Protect ethnic confrères | 2 | 7 | 16 |
| Balance of power | 1 | 3 | 3 |
| Total | 101 | | |

egory), but struggles for survival. The Nazi, Fascist, and Japanese empire-builders may have allowed various fig leaves of sovereignty for those whom they conquered (e.g., Manchukuo, Slovakia), but the other states in the international community were for the most part unwilling to recognize satrapies and satellites as true sovereign states.

We have, then, the paradox that as the principle of self-determination became increasingly accepted as a major international norm, some governments were dedicated to the destruction of states and regimes. The list of potential or actual victims of predation is lengthy: the Bolshevik government in Russia, Bela Kun's socialist regime in Hungary, the republican government of Spain, and China. Abyssinia, Austria, Czechoslovakia, Poland, and Albania were eliminated as independent actors in the system, and Finland nearly suffered the same fate. In no other period since Napoleon's empire-building phase had members of the international community faced such serious and widespread threats to their existence.

Other significant changes in percentages include the increasing importance of conflicts over strategic territory, the relative decline of limited challenges over the integrity of a polity, the increasing importance of commercial issues, this time linked to access to raw materials and resource exploitation, the rise of conflicts over ethnic and irredenta problems, and the significant decline of armed movements for national liberation and state creation. The enforcement of treaty obligations, an issue of little importance in the nineteenth century, ranks third among the issues that underlay armed conflicts in the 1918–41 period. Some of the significant conflicts that arose over enforcement of the terms of the 1919 Paris settlement include the Vilna dispute between Poland and Lithuania and the United States' efforts to find an accommodation with Japan on the basis of Wilsonian principles of international relations. This was not, technically, the enforcement of a specific treaty. But Secretary of State Cordell Hull insisted that any overall settlement with Japan, which was a necessary condition for the avoidance of crippling American economic sanctions, would have to incorporate major Wilsonian principles such as the Open Door and the restoration of Chinese independence.

The protection of nationals and commercial interests abroad appears for the first time in any frequency in our list of issues. It was an issue in the origins of the Boer War and provided at least a pretext for American interventions in the Caribbean and Central America during the first two decades of the twentieth century. In the 1920s and 1930s, however, it appears with increasing frequency. It reflects the growth of international economic contacts during the late nineteenth century and the extension of imperialist practices into polities that were ostensibly sovereign. Providing protection to one's nationals abroad was a serious enough business, but it also served as one of several pretexts for more extensive forms of economic penetration. Chinese bureaucrats' attempts to maintain and establish legal and police jurisdiction of Japanese nationals residing in and around Mukden in Manchuria provided the Japanese Kwantung army leaders with an issue they could exploit to extend military control and economic penetration throughout northern China. The Mukden incident was actually staged by Japanese agents, but made to look like a provocation against Japanese civilians by the Chinese. Similarly, American intervention in Nicaragua in 1927 was ostensibly undertaken to protect American lives and property during another of the many violent changes of government in that Central American country. When the Sandino faction took up arms, the American Marines became fully involved on the side of the "constitutionalists" against the rebels. The United States was committed to a particular type of political order and set of personalities, but argued that its military action was necessary to safeguard American nationals and their economic activities in Nicaragua.

The range of issues that generated armed conflicts in the 1918–41 period did not increase over the previous century, but the distribution of types of issues symbolizes the breakdown of some of the norms and assumptions of the nineteenth-century states system. While territorial problems remained the largest single source of conflict, the prominence of state and regime survival, treaty enforcement, empire creation, and government composition indicates a great deal of systemic instability. The classical prescriptions against domestic interference, destruction of states, and forcible alteration of treaty obligations were frequently violated. Many of the restraints and assumptions of the Concert system – the practices of great power consultation, the principle of compensation, and the idea of limited wars for limited purposes – became quaint anachronisms. By the 1930s, there were three great powers that were fully committed to a reordering of the international system along hierarchical, hegemonic, and imperial lines. The implementation of those ideas constituted a fundamental challenge to the norms elaborated at Westphalia and confirmed and extended at Utrecht, Vienna, and Paris. We now examine in more detail some of the individual issues to illustrate how they were defined by the parties to conflict.

## Territory

Conflicts over territory have been an endemic characteristic of interstate relations since 1648. But as we have seen in previous chapters, the value and significance of territory has undergone substantial changes through the historical periods covered in this study. Territory initially offered the bases of dynastic legitimacy. Later it came to provide population and tax resources for state creation and the maintenance of professional armed forces. In the nineteenth century, territorial extent was the major indicator of the continental balance of power. Its economic potential was of significantly less importance. The commercial value of territory resided primarily in overseas colonies. By the twentieth century, the resources and economic opportunities attached to a specific piece of real estate began to grow in importance. Japanese expansion into Manchuria and China, the Chaco War, and the Leticia dispute were all fundamentally about territory, but the value of the territory was not intrinsic or symbolic: it resided in economic prospects and access to exploitable resources. In none of the thirty cases of armed conflict was territory sought for reasons of prestige, for increasing tax revenues, much less for regime legitimacy or population. It was either an asset of actual or potential commercial value, or an arena for racial expansion. Hitler's definition of territory was largely unique, but it was central to the ideology that justified and guided repeated German aggression. It is therefore worth further comment.

To Hitler, the fundamental unit of historical growth and decay was race. Hitler's image of historical processes centered around the struggle between races, not between nations. In *Mein Kampf* and in his conversations and speeches, Hitler emphasized that he was uninterested in the fate of nations, and certainly did not limit his aims to reestablishing the frontiers of pre-1914 Germany. In 1934, he told a colleague that the conception of the nation had become meaningless, that it was an expedient of liberalism, a creation of the French Revolution.

> The new order cannot be conceived in terms of the national boundaries of peoples with a historical past but in terms of race that transcends those boundaries ... I have to liberate the world from dependence on its historical past ... Just as the conception of the nation was a revolutionary change from the purely dynastic feudal states ... so our own revolution is a further step or rather, the final step, in the rejection of the historical order and the recognition of purely biological values ... The active section in the nations, the militant, Nordic section, will rise again and become the ruling el-

ement over these shopkeepers and pacifists, these puritans and
speculators and busybodies. (Rauschning, 1939:229–30)

But what were the limits of this racially based political order? The
most sacred of all human rights is the right to the soil. All races depend
upon territory. Trade, navies, colonies, and industrialization are no
substitute for soil (Maser, 1970:131). Germany did not have sufficient
soil so that every citizen of the state could be provided with a piece of
ground which he could call his or her own. The problem is that the
distribution of land for racial survival is not consistent with the distribution of land as defined by historical and political frontiers. Each race
can only obtain the soil necessary for its survival by conquering the soil
held by others. In *Mein Kampf*, Hitler made it clear that the historic
political frontiers of Europe would be changed radically in order to
accommodate Germany's land-for-survival:

> We National Socialists must hold unflinchingly to our aim in foreign
> policy, namely, to secure for the German people the land and soil to
> which they are entitled on this earth . . . Just as our ancestors did not
> receive the soil on which we live today as a gift from Heaven, but had
> to fight for it at the risk of their lives, in the future no folkish grace will
> win soil for us and hence life for our people, but only the might of a
> victorious sword . . . it certainly cannot be the intention of Heaven to
> give one people fifty times as much land and soil in this world as
> another. In this case we must not let political boundaries obscure for
> us the boundaries of eternal justice. If this earth really has room for all
> to live in, let us be given the soil we need for our livelihood. True, the
> [Slavs] will not willingly do this. But then the law of self-preservation
> goes into effect; and what is refused to amicable methods, it is up to
> the fist to take. (Hitler, 1943:138–39)

Hitler thus made no preset limits to his demands for territory.
Territory must expand to accommodate population growth. Germany,
racially defined, would continue growing. The people had to be able to
feed themselves from the products of their own soil. Germany could
not survive through trade or industrialization. Nations are defined
racially and territorially. The larger the race, the larger the territory it
needs to be self-sufficient. The right of territorial possession depends
solely upon the strength of the conqueror.

In practical terms, Hitler envisaged a Germany extending deep into
Russia and the Balkans. Poland was to be exterminated quickly and the
European parts of Russia colonized.

Hitler's conception of territory was fundamentally inconsistent with
notions of territoriality underlying the Westphalian order and the
principle of self-determination. The statesmen and diplomats of

223

Europe who analyzed Hitler's motives and purposes did so from the intellectual vantage of the traditional vocabulary and concepts of international relations, and from the notions of fixed territorial boundaries based on historical, ethnic, economic, and strategic validations. They failed to appreciate that Hitler was an intellectual revolutionary, that his view of the world, of its component units, of its space and historical actors, was fundamentally different. Hitler acted upon *his* philosophical, biological, and territorial theories, not on those of traditional Europe. The issue that generated more armed conflict than any other revolved around essentially incompatible conceptions of territory and territorial limits.

### Empire creation

The basis of Hitler's new Order was racial; state territory was to be the *consequence* of racial distribution, and not a constraint upon it. Politically, Hitler's purpose was to create a German continental empire. The Lebensraum for the German *Volk* would be provided in eastern Europe and Russia. "In the east, we must have mastery as far as the Caucasus and Iran. In the west, we need the French coast, we need Flanders and Holland. Above all, we need Sweden" (Rauschning, 1939:126; Hitler, 1962: 173). Germany, in Hitler's estimation, could not coexist with other great powers in Europe. It could not survive by a policy of alliances, or by seeking merely to throw off the shackles of the Versailles Treaty. The *Führer* estimated that Germany would have to rule all of Europe if it was to avoid degenerating into the historical particularisms of the Holy Roman Empire. "We cannot, like Bismarck, limit ourselves to national aims. We must rule Europe or fall apart as a nation, fall back into the chaos of small states. Now do you understand why I cannot be limited, either in the east or the west?" (Rauschning, 1939:126).

The broad vision of the Thousand-Year Reich was thus of a vastly expanded – and continually expanding – German core, extending deep into Russia, with a number of vassal states and regions, including France, the Low Countries, Scandinavia, central Europe and the Balkans, that would provide resources and labor for the core. There was to be no civilizing mission in German imperialism. On the contrary, the lesser peoples were to be taught only to do menial labor or, as Hitler once joked, educated sufficiently to read the road signs so they wouldn't get run over by German automobile traffic. The lowest of the low, the Poles and Jews, were to be exterminated. This was not an idle fantasy of a romantic revolutionary of the 1920s, who already at that

224

time claimed that if fifteen thousand German Jews had been gassed in 1914, Germany's losses in the Great War would not have been in vain (Hitler, 1943:117). It was a definite plan that only awaited the right opportunities to put into effect. His solution to the Jewish problem was already implicit in numerous speeches and actions in the 1930s. For the Poles, Hitler made his intentions unmistakably clear only several days before his attack. In the presence of the highest-ranking officers of the three military services, he announced (August 22, 1939) that "I have ordered to the east my 'Death Head' units with the order to kill without pity or mercy all men, women and children of Polish race or language." He added that the same fate awaited Russia (Wheeler-Bennett, 1964:448).

Where Louis XIV sought some sort of French hegemony in Europe, he saw it in terms of existing conventions and recognized the importance of maintaining the dynastic and sovereignty principles. He sought preponderance *within* a pluralistic system. Napoleon's French-centered empire was also a hegemonial system, but the Emperor did not fundamentally challenge the idea of political pluralism on the continent, and in some ways he was the champion of the nationality principle. The Germans in the early twentieth century sought something as vague as a "place in the sun" and arguably a predominant European and world position. These vague aims did not constitute a challenge to the fundamental principles of the states system. As with Louis XIV, the purpose of policy was to increase one's position *within* the system. To Hitler, in contrast, the purpose of policy was to destroy the system and to reconstitute it on racial lines, with a vastly expanded Germany running a distinctly hierarchical and exploitative order. Vestiges of sovereignty might remain, but they would be fig leaves covering a monolithic order. German occupation policies during the war, whereby conquered nations were reduced to satellites, satrapies, and reservoirs of slave labor, were the practical application of Hitler's conception of the new world order. They were not improvised or planned for reasons of military necessity. None of this was minimally consistent with the foundations and norms of a system of states.

The intellectual bases of Japanese empire creation were rather different. Japanese leaders in the 1920s had sought to incorporate the country into the liberal international order that developed in the nineteenth century and which was reformed by Wilsonian principles after 1919. Japanese welfare and security goals were to be achieved through the adoption of the gold standard and gaining tariff autonomy, and through arms limitation, export and emigration promotion, and, in general, international cooperation through multilateral institutions

(Bamba, 1972; Iriye, 1981:2). To this might be added Japan's unsuccessful efforts to establish racial non-discrimination as a major norm of international relations and domestic policy.

All of this changed under the impact of the world depression. Already in the late 1920s new types of leaders were emerging in Japan, people who rejected many aspects of the Westernization of Asia in general, and of Japan in particular. They were unhappy with the Paris settlements and with the severe constraints that the liberal international economic system imposed on Japan. The depression's impact was devastating to Japan's farmers and working class, and the politicians appeared unable to offer any solutions to the general suffering. The pat solutions to economic survival – trade, local industrialization, international collaboration, and emigration – were not working; and they were not working, according to these figures, because of the policies of the Western industrial states. Military and civilian traditionalist leaders such as Ishiwara Kanji and Prince Konoe argued that Japan could never survive under the rubric of Western internationalism and export-led growth.

They rejected everything connected with Western liberalism and the conventions of European and American diplomacy. They were convinced that the guiding principles of Japan's diplomacy should be the Imperial Way, the external expression of *kokutai*. In policy terms, this meant the creation of a new order in Asia, based on traditions such as absolute loyalty to the Emperor, paternalism, obedience, frugality, and other traditional values (Bamba, 1972:374). Japan was to become the lord of Asia, and autarky would replace international collaboration as the strategy for national survival. The colonization of Manchuria was the key to the strategy. It provided vast resources that were increasingly being denied from other sources, as well as land for Japan's rapidly growing population. For Ishiwara, who already in the 1920s anticipated a fateful protracted military conflict with the United States, control of Manchuria was essential for both the short-run task of making Japan self-sufficient and for the long-range necessity of building the military wherewithal to challenge the Americans. Only after a cataclysmic war with the United States could peace come to Asia (Peattie, 1975:96–97; Barnhart, 1987:270).

The imperial vision was thus born of disillusionment with Western international practices and norms, and the perceived threat to Japan's economic survival. Racial and biological factors were not significant components of imperial theory.

Prince Konoe, who was to head two cabinets in the late 1930s and early 1940s, was no militarist, but he saw no way out of Japan's dilemmas except through military means. In his view, the fundamental causes of war are the inequalities among nations. No international order can be based on a situation where some nations with growing populations have to remain closeted in narrow, resource-poor territories, while other sparsely populated nations enjoy vast territories and abundant resources. The precondition for peace in such circumstances is territorial redistribution. The peace of 1919 had been drafted to sustain the paramount economic positions of France, Great Britain and the United States, along with their empires. It was sanctimonious for these three great imperial powers to lecture the Japanese about the evils of territorial expansion and the exploitation of unused resources abroad when they themselves had pursued such policies throughout the nineteenth und early twentieth centuries. If the world order created in 1919 was to be permanent, then Japan and all other developing nations would be forever subordinated to the advanced nations (Oka, 1983:27, 37).

Other Japanese leaders, including the upper military echelons, shared these outlooks or variations of them, to the extent that options other than military conquest were seldom considered. The maldistribution of territory, resources, and population, along with the collapse of the liberal world trading order, created acute needs, and the needs provided both rights and justifications. Japan would create a new order in Asia. It would hold the leading position and would act as the agent for the regeneration of China. Western imperialism in Asia would be destroyed, and in its place a core of collaboration between Japan, Manchuria, and China would emerge. This would end the long tradition of dependency on and tutelage of the West.

The Greater East Asia Co-prosperity Sphere, announced as the great imperial plan in November 1938, was the design for Asian unity. On the ideological plane, this order was to replace Western ideas of nationalism, individualism, liberalism, materialism, selfishness, and imperialism with a system characterized by regional collaboration, harmony, selflessness, and subordination of the individual to the community (Iriye, 1981:4–5).

The intellectual roots of the imperial vision were numerous and varied (but mostly indigenous to Japan), but what is most important from the point of view of international relations theory is that the Japanese traditionalists viewed the world in terms fundamentally different from those of the West. To the Japanese leaders of the 1930s, Wilsonian principles were a rationalization for Western world domination. Whereas Wilson saw equality and reciprocity between peoples as the actual pattern of international relations – once the militarists and autocrats had been removed – the Japanese saw the practical application of those same principles in terms of tutelage, trade discrimination, protectionism, inequality of resources, racism, and Hobbesian anarchy. A proper basis for international relationships, in their view, was hierarchy, authority, and mutual respect. Japan would be at the top of the hierarchy, but in its liberation of Asia from Western domination it would perform a noble historical task. That the means would be primarily military was of no particular consequence. Japan had not really shared in the experiences of the Great War, and the strong strain of pacifism that was incorporated into the Covenant of the League of Nations had few strong adherents in the Japan of the 1930s. Quite the contrary: the significant victories of Japan in the wars with China (1894–95) and Russia (1904–1905) suggested that the military way was to be preferred over other means.

Other issues showed no significant changes from the previous period. We now turn to the question of changing and contrasting attitudes toward war. In the interwar period there was a particularly close connection between attitudes and the use of armed force.

## ATTITUDES TOWARD WAR

Many of the provisions of the League of Nations Covenant reflected attitudes commonly found among the populations of the liberal democracies. Force was to be used only in the service of the international community or under certain other carefully specified conditions. War as an instrument of policy in the Clausewitzian sense no longer enjoyed legitimacy, and the Kellogg–Briand Treaty of 1928 rendered it a criminal act. It was "outlawed." The norms of the international community had changed fundamentally in the aftermath of the war to end war. But the history of the interwar period shows that the flowers of anti-war sentiments had not taken root deeply or universally.

States of all kinds used force in the 1920s. But they were also restrained in some significant ways by the Wilsonian legacy and by League of Nations obligations. Conflicts between Finland and Sweden (the Aaland Islands), Greece and Bulgaria (border incidents), Italy and Greece (the Corfu incident), and Poland and Lithuania (Vilna) were more or less successfully managed or resolved through League of Nations action. The end of the Russian civil war presaged more conventional and less threatening forms of international relationships in eastern Europe, and the brief period of European harmony between 1925 and the full development of the depression suggested that once the dramas of the Great War, the break-up of the empires, and the Bolshevik Revolution had been played out, a new international era had begun, one that was based on the views of war and violence incorporated in the League Covenant and the Kellogg–Briand Pact. By 1929, few could anticipate a reversion to an unprecedented idolatry of violence and war as instruments of statecraft. We turn to a discussion of German and Japanese attitudes toward war during the 1930s, and conclude with some contrasts offered by the British.

### Hitler and armed violence

To understand Hitler's attitudes to the use of armed force, we have to outline his peculiar theory of the biological bases of historical development. His ideas came from a variety of nineteenth- and early twentieth-century scientists and writers, but the *Führer* was not one to acknowledge intellectual debts to others. Suffice it to remark that his biological and racial views drew extensively upon the theories of Gobineau, Houston Stewart Chamberlain, Thomas Malthus, Charles Darwin, Friedrich Nietzsche, Hegel, and many others.

Hitler's *Weltanschauung* (one of his favorite words) was based on the idea of struggle. All life is a struggle, whether at the fundamental biological level or at the levels of individuals and races. There is no underlying harmony between biological units. The struggle is not just an eternal competition with temporary winners and losers. In order to survive, all living units, from cells and bacteria to nations and empires, must destroy their enemies. Thus, there would be nothing new or unusual in creating the German Reich through the use of armed force and exterminating those who resisted. "We should remember," he told Walter Rauschning, "that we are merely doing unto others as they would have done to us" (Rauschning, 1939:141).

Conquest and annihilation are necessary for racial survival. The struggle never ceases because populations grow at different rates and peoples must expand territorially to survive. Moreover, biological and social virility depend upon ceaseless effort and action. "All passivity, all inertia, is senseless, is inimical to life. From this proceeds the divine right of destroying all who are inert" (quoted in Rauschning, 1939:222).

Racial survival depends upon genetic purity and adequate soil. Animals do not breed across species, and so it is with humans: they do not naturally breed between races (but if intra-species breeding is "natural" and breeding between species impossible, why worry about it among humans?). Not bothered by the illogic of his position, Hitler maintained that any mixing of blood of the Aryans with lower races would extinguish the culture-bearer (Jackel, 1972:89). He pointed to the decline of France as evidence of his racial theories. France was becoming "more and more negrified ... What France ... is doing in Europe today is a sin against the existence of white humanity and some day will incite against this people all the avenging spirits of a race which has recognized racial pollution as the original sin of humanity" (Hitler, 1943:624). The first requirement is therefore to maintain racial purity and to practice eugenics.

The question of soil, however, cannot be resolved by such benign means. Control of soil requires armed struggle because there is not a sufficient quantity available to provide the means of life for all races. There is a definite limit to the productivity of soil, and since population is increasing, nature has decreed the races to engage in a ruthless "free play of forces" in the battle for self-preservation. The productivity of soil can only be increased up to a certain point, whereas both population and the socially determined necessities of life are growing at a faster rate. Need outstrips capacity, and therefore territorial expansion offers the only solution (Maser, 1970:121).

Hitler did not seriously contemplate the variety of hypothetical solutions to the problem of racial survival. Whereas Malthus had considered sexual abstinence, late marriage, and intensive promotion of agriculture, Hitler's sole solution was ruthless wars of plunder and annihilation. In *Mein Kampf*, Hitler did acknowledge the alternatives of international trade and colonization on the British model, but he rejected these without examination. Already in 1923, then, Hitler was fully committed to a fundamental foreign policy line of expansion in the East after crushing France first.

Conquest of soil cannot be achieved by means other than violence, for violence in itself both assures the purity of the race and steels it for its perpetual struggle against other races. A peace policy through alliances, diplomacy, and multilateral institutions is passive and weak. It "leads to the destruction of a people, to the weakening of its flesh and blood," as he put it (Hitler, 1943:18). Armed force is not just an instrument of foreign policy in that Clausewitzian sense: it is an integral part of and requirement for racial survival.

Maser (1970:122) argues that Hitler did not glory in war. This is a doubtful proposition in so far as the *Führer's* entire political outlook was based on hatred and the need for destruction. His writings, speeches, and private diatribes are filled with references to annihilation, bodies swinging on gibbets, the gassing of undesirable and cancerous social elements, and the need to forego all pity and mercy in dealing with enemies. War is more than just a means to an end. It

230

is a joyful activity for its own sake, one that coincidentally develops characters and steels the racial pool. To get the flavor of Hitler's approach to the subject, it is best to let him speak for himself:

> war is the most natural, the most everyday matter. War is eternal, war is universal. War is life ... War is the origin of all things ... I shall shrink from nothing. No so-called international law, no agreements will prevent me from making use of any advantage that offers [sic]. The next war will be unbelievably bloody and grim. But the most inhuman war, one which makes no distinction between military and civilian combatants, will at the same time be the kindest, because it will be the shortest ... But I want war. To me all means will be right. My motto is not "Don't, whatever you do, annoy the enemy!" My motto is: "Destroy him by all and any means." I am the one who will wage the war.                    (quoted in Rauschning, 1939:16, 21)

The prosecution of war cannot be left to the professional military because, in Hitler's view, military leaders are cautious and prone to sentimentality. To be effective, violence requires a fanatical outlook and full appreciation that the "ultimate aim of politics is war" – an idea that few generals in the Third Reich could be trusted to support. Violence could not be just instrumental, it had to be philosophical: "Only in the steady and constant application of force lies [sic] the very prerequisites for success. This persistence, however, can always and only arise from a definite spiritual conviction. Any violence which does not spring from a firm spiritual base will be wavering and uncertain. It lacks the stability which can only rest in a fanatical outlook" (Hitler, 1943:171).

And so Hitler, after 1933, took many measures to assure that he, and not the generals of the Wehrmacht, would be the warlord. He required that they take a personal oath of allegiance: "I swear before God to give my unconditional obedience to Adolf Hitler, *Führer* of the Reich and of the German people, Supreme Commander of the Wehrmacht, and I pledge my word as a brave soldier to observe this oath always, even at peril of my life" (Wheeler-Bennett, 1964:339). By 1936, he was increasingly excluding the army from his plans and calculations. In November 1937, without prior consultation, he revealed to the military leaders his plans for the attacks on Austria and Czechoslovakia. The military chiefs did not object so much to the idea of aggression as to the low probability that it would succeed. But Hitler was determined to go to war. He recalled that the military had counseled against the invasion of the Rhineland in 1936. He accused the military leaders of lacking guts, of being willing to move only if the chances of success were better than 51 percent. The risk of defeat was no deterrent for him. If he could

231

win by coercion and extortion – as he did in 1938 and 1939 – so much the better, for then his forces would be primed for the campaigns against France and Russia. But any opportunity to use force also steeled the German people and soldiers and, if successful, would rally the recalcitrant generals behind him. Defeat was no overwhelming problem because the nature of modern war assured that all would suffer equally. Already in 1934, Hitler had told Rauschning that in general war, Germany could be defeated, "but if we are, we shall draw the world with us – a world in flames" (Rauschning, 1939:14; cf. Wheeler-Bennett, 1964:355).

In the case of Hitler's Germany, the links between attitudes and policies are direct and determining. Given the *Führer*'s historical and biological theories and his personal hatreds, there was no question whether or not he would use military force. This was made publicly clear already with the publication of *Mein Kampf* in 1924, reconfirmed in Hitler's "secret book" written in 1928, and underlined in hundreds of speeches, interviews, and diatribes delivered between his assumption of the German Chancellorship and the invasion of Poland in 1939. The only question was when he would attack.

Hitler abhorred everything that Wilsonianism and the 1919 settlement stood for. He had stated on numerous occasions that he would violate every current norm of international relationships and that he was fully committed to establishing the Thousand-Year Reich by means of total war. His philosophies, attitudes, and actions fit together perfectly. The structure of the international system, the attributes of states, the nature of Germany's relations with the other states, all of these things that have been sought as causes of war are irrelevant to an analysis of Hitler's policies. They could only help explain when he went to war, but they contribute little to an understanding of why he went to war.[2]

### War as an instrument of policy: Japan

In Japan, there was no single figure who spelled out a philosophy of history and of international relations that placed war and extermination at the center of action. Rather, it was a case where, despite serious rivalries between the military services, the middle

[2] An interesting if not entirely convincing psychological exploration of Hitler's hatreds, based on a content analysis of his speeches, is in Koenigsberg (1975). The author argues that the *Führer* made an unconscious connection between the cancer that killed his mother and the 'cancers' that he thought were destroying Germany – the Jews and Germany's foreign opponents. For Germany to survive, these cancers had to be destroyed. In this view, Hitler's policies were essentially defensive. Hitler's language is full of bacterial, biological, and medical metaphors.

echelons of the military bureaucracy came to make foreign policy for the country and had little understanding of, or sympathy with, traditional Western ideas of negotiations, compromise, and patience (Bamba, 1972:369). To make matters even more complex, the leadership of the armies in the field took military initiatives without the knowledge of the central authorities, or even against their advice. The military in the field organized and transformed the Mukden incident into an outright conquest of Manchuria, and resisted negotiation and conciliation with Chiang Kai-shek following the Marco Polo bridge incident in 1937. As a group, the military were men of action, not of negotiation, and they seldom contemplated policy options that did not include military coercion and warfare.

By the late 1930s, the civilian politicians had given way to the military on matters of foreign policy, and while some of the military leaders in Tokyo urged a conciliatory policy toward the Chinese (fearing that a war with China would invite Soviet military pressure against Manchukuo), by 1940 there was a consensus that Japanese objectives in southeast Asia would be pursued by military means only (Barnhart, 1987:269). The document "Main Principles Governing the Response to Changes in the World," drafted by the Imperial Headquarters in 1940, stated that Japan would seek to end the war with China but that issues relating to southeast Asia would be resolved by force. It anticipated and predicted war with both Great Britain and the United States (Oka, 1983:100). Civilian policy-makers had no input into these decisions and commitments.

Unlike Germany, where Hitler was in full control over the military, the picture in Tokyo was one of "complete paralysis, lack of [civilian] will, authority, and influence over military decision-making. The military made momentous decisions that involved diplomacy. All Army ministers . . . were little more than the mouthpieces of those under them . . . The cabinet had been continuously manipulated by the army" (Oka, 1983:7; cf. Peattie, 1975:372). No doubt the Japanese leaders of the depression era – some military fanatics aside – would have preferred constructing the new Asian order on the basis of peaceful collaboration with China, but the Japanese vision of the new order was incompatible with China's sovereignty, independence, and autonomy. Ultimately, the new order would have to be organized through the force of arms. By 1941, with Germany's stunning military victories in western Europe and in the Soviet Union as exemplars, the military solution appeared even more persuasive in Tokyo.

In contrast to Hitler, Japanese military leaders did not typically glorify war as an end in itself. Military victory was an important means of avoiding diplomatic humiliations – to which all Japanese were extraordinarily sensitive – but most leaders saw the use of force in instrumental terms: given Japan's economic vulnerability, the resulting foreign policy purposes, and Western opposition to them, there were not many remaining alternatives. There was much discussion in Tokyo of building a permanent peace once the new order had been created, whereas for Hitler, racial survival and population growth would require permanent warfare. Reflecting in part the samurai tradition, the military leaders "prepared themselves for death instead of what they perceived was a shameful escape from and surrender to the Western domination of the world" (Bamba, 1972:369).

The roots of Japanese militarism – if that is the right word – were thus located in the painful process of Japan's incorporation into the European states system. Wilsonianism had proved promising in the 1920s. By the time of the depression it was discredited among those who were to make Japanese foreign and military policy. Military solutions brought success in the early 1930s, and increasingly those policies commanded credibility. The civilians had no alternatives to offer, and thus were relegated to the sidelines. By the late 1930s, the policies of decision-making in Tokyo revolved around questions of preferred military strategies, inter-service rivalries, and whether to place priority on attacks to the south or against the Soviet Union in the north. It was not a question of war or peace, but what kind of war, where, when, and against whom. Attitudes are again fundamental in explaining behavior. Structural characteristics of the international system offered opportunities and constraints, but were not determining. Japan's attribute of economic vulnerability is, however, of considerable importance as an explanatory variable.

### Western liberal attitudes to war: Neville Chamberlain

There could be few greater contrasts in attitudes toward the use of force than between those of the Nazi leadership and the Japanese military on the one hand, and those among most members of the British government in the 1930s, on the other. To Hitler and his lieutenants, war was a biological necessity, an integral part of national morale, a means of liquidating inferior races, and an avenue for social revolution. To the Japanese military, war was an effective and rational instrument of policy, and should be used even in high-risk situations. But to large segments of the British population in the 1930s, war was a horror, a catastrophe, perhaps an instrument of policy, but one to be used only as the absolute last resort to defend carefully defined vital

234

interests, including national survival. The roots of those attitudes went back to the origins of the First World War.

Despite the flood of anti-German propaganda during the Great War, many in Britain regarded the origins of the war as evidence of the breakdown of diplomacy, of the runaway military mobilization systems, and of Balkan nationalism. Unlike the French, who tended to see German malevolence everywhere, many influential Britons attributed the sources of the war to arms manufacturers, secret treaties, faulty diplomatic communications, mobilization plans, and the like. A considerable number sympathized with the view that Germany had been surrounded by hostile states, and had struck out of desperation. By the 1920s, there was a growing belief that the war had been a mistake (Gilbert, 1966:29).

These diagnoses of the origins of the Great War motivated the British negotiators in Paris. As we have seen, Lloyd George fought a vigorous battle, via his Fontainebleau memorandum of March 1919, to secure a non-punitive peace, to impose limits on indemnities, and to prevent the incorporation of German minorities into the succession states. He believed a harsh peace, based on the assumption of German war guilt, would provide the sources for new troubles and probably a war of revenge and treaty revision. John Maynard Keynes, a member of the British delegation, resigned his post because he could not accept the generally punitive nature of the peace and, more specifically, the limitless reparation payments it incorporated. There were many, then, who from the day of the treaty's signature began to lobby for its revision in favor of defeated Germany.

The idea of a sympathetic reconsideration of the treaty came under the general rubric of appeasement, a diplomatic strategy that originally meant a voluntary elimination of injustices, from a position of strength. Given that many in Great Britain argued for the assimilation of Germany into a viable European order – made all the more necessary by the absence of Soviet Russia – the strategy of appeasement seemed both realistic and honorable.

The climate of opinion in Great Britain during the 1920s and until at least 1937 was strongly pacific, sympathetic to treaty revision and German assimilation, and in support of the League of Nations as an institution. There was little advocacy of the use of military force in the abstract, or for coercive enforcement of the Treaty of Versailles. Indeed, Anglo–French relations were often strained because of French insistence on holding Germany fully to its commitments.

Hitler's formal entrance into German government in January 1933 did not change these currents of British opinion. His declared aim of ignoring or overturning the restrictive terms of the treaty (reparations had been terminated in 1932) were met with indifference or sympathy among most political circles in London. Hitler's brutality against political opposition within Germany, as well as his anti-Semitism, raised doubts and hesitations, but these actions were usually dismissed as matters of German domestic jurisdiction and not sufficient reasons to prevent business-like diplomatic, commercial, and cultural relations between Berlin and London. There was a steady stream of skeptical British visitors to Berchtesgaden and the German capital, all provided with set interviews with the *Führer*. He put their hesitations at ease, emphasizing the justice of Germany's claims and his willingness and desire to act as a responsible statesman of the classical European mold. Good behavior could be guaranteed, he suggested, by universal recognition of the justice of Germany's demands. Most of the *Führer's* interlocutors were too timid to raise questions about the treatment of Jews, communists, and social democrats in Germany, about the restrictions placed on authors and artists, and about many other unsavory aspects of the new Reich. Hitler, in any case, while he could brook some argument, accepted no criticism – and few offered it (Gilbert, 1966:164). The popular impression in Great Britain was that Hitler wanted peace, but one based on the removal of the injustices of 1919. He also wanted the principle of self-determination applied to Germans throughout Europe.

Appeasement, then, was a diplomatic strategy born of the horrors of modern war, the unwillingness to accept the theory of German war guilt, and the proposition that an injustice to Germany had been committed in Paris. A fourth source was the fear of Bolshevism. A strong, rearmed Germany could offer a shield against the threat from the East. This was a theme that Hitler constantly emphasized, and it made strong impressions in many leading circles in Great Britain.

But Hitler's behavior at home and abroad continued to create suspicions, and Germany's rearmament required some adjustments to appeasement. By the mid 1930s that adjustment took the form of cautious rearmament. But the expectations that benefits conferred upon Hitler would change his behavior did not alter. In the British view, there were truly no *états de mauvaise foi*. If Hitler resorted to coercion with his own people and acted ungentlemanly in his dealings with many foreign governments, discussions and incentives could change all of that. Even the most irascible politician could be placated if treated with respect. Conciliation, negotiations, and understanding would suffice, because it did not occur to most of the British public that any sane politician would deliberately choose war over peace. And there was some evidence that Hitler's behavior could be changed. There was the Anglo-German naval agreement of 1935, and Hitler repeatedly expressed sincerity and goodwill in his personal interviews with British politicians, cultural figures, and journalists.

Prime Minister Chamberlain's strategy was to follow two tracks simultaneously: build up Great Britain's defenses – for which he was roundly condemned by the Opposition as a warmonger – and try to meet Germany's legitimate demands through negotiations. If there were international conflicts, they were based not on irreconcilable purposes, but on misunderstandings and suspicions. Diplomacy, and particularly personal meetings between government leaders, could allay those suspicions and clear away all misunderstandings. Domestically, Chamberlain's chief priority was to stem the growing fatalism in certain British circles, the idea that war with the dictators was inevitable. To Chamberlain, it was more likely that peace was inevitable.

Chamberlain was not a doctrinaire pacifist, but he personally abhorred war and he regarded the use of force as a confession of diplomatic failure, as an instrument of last resort. He dichotomized diplomacy and force: they were alternative means of pursuing objectives, not necessary companions. During the height of the Czech crisis, he could inform the members of the House of Commons that "we still intend to employ ourselves, and to urge others to employ, the methods of reason and diplomacy rather than those of menace and force" (Chamberlain, 1939:153–54). His faith in the power of reason and bargaining never wavered, and the Munich settlement proved to him and millions of his admirers that the way of negotiation could save the peace. Chamberlain epitomized the pragmatic, common-sense, shopkeeper British diplomatic style of the era, a style based on the assumption that all political leaders are reasonable men and that once suspicion and misunderstanding have been cleared away through personal discussions, bargains will be in the offing. In a 1937 speech to the Birmingham City Council, Chamberlain outlined his deep faith in the methods of diplomacy:

> When I served [on this Council] I learned one lesson which I have never forgotten, and that is that in this imperfect world a man cannot have everything his own way, and that those who get things done are those who are ready to work with and for others, and who are prepared to give up something themselves in order that they may receive something in return. There is always some common measure of agreement if only we look for it. (Chamberlain, 1939:22)

The problem was that Chamberlain never applied this principle of

237

reciprocity that resides at the core of the diplomatic method. Great Britain was acceding to Germany's demands, but asked only in return that Germany not use force. In November 1937, Chamberlain wrote his sister that he saw no reason why he couldn't simply tell Hitler that Great Britain would not use force to prevent him from accomplishing his goals in eastern Europe in return for a guarantee that Germany would not use force to achieve them (Fuchser, 1982:93). Moreover, had Chamberlain and his colleagues carefully analyzed Hitler's writings and some of his speeches, they might have surmised that this type of bargaining was exactly what the *Führer* loathed. It epitomized the democratic, liberal, and pacifist ethos, all chronic weaknesses of the post-Versailles German regime that Hitler despised. In none of the many parliamentary debates in England in the 1936–39 period did Chamberlain ever hint that Hitler might have views on diplomacy that differed from his own. Appeasement, by the 1930s, was a policy of hope, based on a trinity of beliefs: (1) the fundamental goodwill of political leaders; (2) misperceptions and suspicions as the sources of all international conflict; and (3) the efficacy of bargaining and discussion as means of changing behavior. Hitler held none of these.

Chamberlain understood that in a rearming world, Great Britain would have to prepare as well, and he believed that British defense measures would inject an element of stability and security in the international system, at least until mutual disarmament could be arranged. Rearmament was necessary, but Chamberlain lamented it because it represented the growing triumph of passion over reason: "I must confess that the spectacle of this vast expenditure upon means of destruction instead of construction has inspired me with a feeling of revolt against the folly of mankind" (Chamberlain, 1939:67). He found it difficult to understand how governments could deliberately resort to the use of force. Committed to his own government's priorities on the development of public welfare in Great Britain, he assumed that all governments had similar priorities. He could not fathom the reasoning behind Japan's war with China, or the brutalities of the Spanish Civil War. None of this slaughter made any sense to a man who personally abhorred war, and whose view of politics deeply reflected the Conservative Party's paternalistic concern for serving the people. "When I look round the world," he mused several weeks before the outbreak of the Czech crisis, "I must say I am appalled at the prospects. War, accompanied by horrible barbarities, is going on today . . . I wonder whether, since the world began, has it ever seen such a spectacle of human madness and folly" (Chamberlain, 1939:238).

Chamberlain's attitude toward war was based on two considerations: (1) the costs to the lives and property of ordinary citizens; and (2) its irrationality. The prime minister was familiar with the flourishing literature of the 1930s that depicted the disastrous nature of war in the industrial age. He argued that war was a social undertaking vastly different from what it had been in the days of Wellington. Industrialism had made war total. In the midst of the Munich crisis, Chamberlain described to his House of Commons colleagues why the use of force in international relations should be seen only as the last, desperate resort:

> people burrowed underground, trying to escape from poison gas, knowing at any hour . . . death or mutilation was ready to come down upon them. Remembering that the dread of what might happen to them or to those dear to them might remain with fathers and mothers for year after year – when you think of these things you cannot ask people to accept a prospect of that kind . . . unless you feel yourself, and can make them feel, that the cause for which they are going to fight is a vital cause – a cause that transcends all the human values, a cause to which you can point, if some day you win the victory, and say "That cause is safe." (Chamberlain, 1939:319)

To the prime minister, Czechoslovakia was not that cause. "However much we may sympathize with a small nation confronted by a big and powerful neighbour, we cannot in all circumstances undertake to involve the whole British Empire in war simply on her account. If we have to fight it must be on a larger issue than that" (radio broadcast, September 27, 1938, Chamberlain, 1939:276). Chamberlain added that he was a man of peace, "to the depths of my soul. Armed conflict is a nightmare to me . . . war is a fearful thing." Throughout the 1930s, the spectre of the First World War haunted Chamberlain and his colleagues. As Fuchser notes (1982:45), "from the early days of Britain's attempt to find an adequate policy toward Hitler, issues and policy options were raised, not with a view to what they might achieve against Hitler, but rather what they might have done to prevent the last war."

In addition to these humanitarian sentiments, Chamberlain regarded war as the last resort because it was ultimately irrational. In conditions of modern warfare, there were no winners, only losers.

Like most of his colleagues and the majority of the British public, the prime minister projected on to others – the Soviet Union excepted – British modes of diplomacy and British opinions and attitudes toward war. Hitler's betrayal, when he dismembered Czechoslovakia only months after making solemn obligations and assurances of no more territorial demands at Munich, was a bitter lesson for Chamberlain. He had publicly defended Hitler's reputation as a reasonable man of limited and justified demands; he had believed Hitler's promises; and he had assured his cabinet colleagues, in the wake of Anthony Eden's resignation as foreign secretary, that the *Führer* was a man who could both see reason and be trusted to keep his word. Only in 1939 did he realize that his conceptions of underlying harmony between nations, of the conflict-producing consequences of misperception and suspicion, and of the balming effects of personal diplomacy, were not shared universally.

Some have argued that because of its lagging armaments, there is little Great Britain could have done to save Czechoslovakia. To have declared war in 1938 would have led to military disaster. According to all terms of rational calculation, Chamberlain was wise to try to defer Hitler's plans through negotiations. He thereby allowed more time for Great Britain to rearm (cf. Kennedy, 1940; Hyde, 1976). This view from hindsight is not an accurate portrayal of Chamberlain's calculations, and it does not take into consideration the prime minister's attitude toward the use of force in international relations. In none of his speeches did he specify that Great Britain's rearmament was to be part of a deterrent strategy, that he would combine diplomacy with military threats as a means of altering Hitler's behavior. In none of his negotiations with Hitler did he threaten force; at most he expressed disappointment and concern. Chamberlain's unalterable priority was to avoid war, not to deter Hitler. Any policy that entailed the risk of war was rejected. During the Czechoslovakian crisis, there was discussion of going to the assistance of France, which had treaty obligations to the beleaguered Czechs. War could not be avoided, he suggested, if Germany marched into Czechoslovakia. But these statements were always made in the sense of a last resort, the ultimate option, the signal of diplomacy's failure; and subsequent statements were designed to nullify any threatening implication (Fuchser, 1982:128–29). Threats were not part of Chamberlain's diplomacy.

There was no attempt to deter Hitler through an explicit threat until March 1939, after the *Führer* had taken over the rump state of Slovakia. And that was only in the form of guarantee treaties with Romania and Poland. Hitler was not impressed with these. If there was an attempt to deter, it was implied rather than explicit.

The philosophy of appeasement prevailed more because of the strong attitudes against the use of force than because of any careful calculation of the relative military strength of Great Britain and Nazi Germany. Britain's policy was rooted more in choice than necessity, and the choices strongly reflected the prevailing attitudes of Chamberlain, of the party leaderships, and of the broad public. Chamberlain could have combined threats with conciliation, but he never attempted it; nor did he ever articulate a strategy of deterrence. It is unlikely that Chamberlain would have acted differently than he did even if Great Britain had possessed a substantial military lead over Germany (which it did have as far as naval strength was concerned). He was convinced until 1939 that his views of the world, of diplomacy, and of the sources of international conflict were correct. He thought he could change Hitler by reason, respect, and bargaining. It never occurred to him that he might reexamine his assumptions and theories of international relations in the face of an unchangeable dictator. A change of British policy, in other words, would have required much more than a preponderance of arms. It would have required a fundamental reconstruction of the theories, hopes, aspirations, and values of the prime minister, his colleagues, and most of the British public. And perhaps most important, it would have required a fundamental reevaluation of the causes and horrors of the Great War.

In the interwar period, there was a close correspondence between the attitudes toward war and the use of force in international relations. The roots of the favorable disposition toward the use of force were fundamentally different in Germany and Japan, but in both, military means were the first and preferred means of achieving objectives. For Hitler, violence had many redeeming qualities both for himself and, as he saw it, for the German *Volk*. For the Japanese, there was not so much high value in violence, except that it provided the most visible and therefore satisfying means of compensating for a history of humiliating subservience to the West. Some among the Japanese military counseled against going to war against China, and a few were willing to allow a chance for diplomacy to avert war with the United States. But for the majority, the military solution was a foregone conclusion by 1939.

Wilson's theories of international relations were both vindicated and demolished in the twenty-two years after the Paris peace conference. On the one hand, the history of the era supported the proposition that autocratic and/or military regimes are inherently warlike and thus not fit members of a liberal international community. International peace and domestic dictatorship are incompatible. On the other hand, Wilson's image of an underlying harmony between societies was shattered. The German people, as well as the Italians, were not for the most part coerced into supporting their dictators. The assumed benign and pacific aspirations of Wilson's world public opinion were shown to be incorrect. Under the influence of demagogic leaders and ideologies

241

based on hate, people could be aroused to an ardor for war that would have shocked Wilson. Yet, despite the overly optimistic assumptions in Wilson's (and Chamberlain's) theories of international relations, and despite serious flaws in the Paris settlement, the Wilsonian agenda for creating a more liberal, humane, and pacific world continued to dominate the thinking of Western statesmen. During and after the Second World War, they would try to reconstruct the world on many of the same principles enunciated in 1918 and 1919. To these would be added some of the great lessons learned from the democracies' experiences with the dictators.

# 10 PEACE BY POLICING

> I think the Crimea Conference was a successful effort by the three leading nations to find a common ground for peace . . . It spells – and ought to spell – the end of the system of unilateral action, exclusive alliances and spheres of influence, and balances of power and all other expedients which have been tried for centuries and have always failed.　　　　　　　　　　Franklin D. Roosevelt, March 1, 1945

> I confess to growing apprehension that Russia has vast aims and that these may include the domination of Eastern Europe and even the Mediterranean and the "communizing" of much that remains.
> 　　　　　　　　　　　　　　　Anthony Eden, March 1944

The memories of 1919 lay heavily upon the Allied leaders during the Second World War. A number of lessons had been learned, one of which was not to wait until the war was over before planning for the postwar world. While the Allies were hard pressed militarily through 1942 and 1943, the Soviet Union, the United States, and Great Britain had already put in place bureaucratic mechanisms to begin assessments, projections, and plans for the postwar order. The Atlantic Charter, negotiated by Roosevelt and Churchill on a naval vessel off the coast of Newfoundland four months before formal American involvement in the war, spelled out general political and economic principles that would constitute both war aims and guidelines for constructing the postwar order. It reiterated a number of Wilsonian principles: the right of self-determination, prohibition against any "aggrandizement, territorial or other" during the war, abandonment of the use of force in postwar international relations, a commitment to economic collaboration, and a reference to a postwar international security system. On September 24, 1942, the Soviet government notified London and Washington that "a consistent application of those principles will secure the most energetic support on the part of the Government and Peoples of the Soviet Union."

In the United States, Secretary of State Cordell Hull established a set of postwar planning committees shortly after America's entry into the war. British Foreign Office personnel were doing similar work. At the October 1943 Foreign Ministers Conference in Moscow, the Soviet Union, after considerable hectoring and pressure from Hull on the importance of postwar international cooperation and the necessity of not returning to a politics of spheres of influence, agreed to a set of principles (Four Power Declaration of October 30, 1943) regarding Allied unity and collaboration "into the period following the end of hostilities," as well as the establishment of a general international organization for the maintenance of international peace and security. One month later, at the Tehran Conference, Roosevelt and Stalin were able to discuss in more detail American thinking on the postwar international organization and several other issues of the post-hostilities international order. The foundations for the order would be strong Allied unity to police the world. The United States would provide naval and air contingents for policing in Europe, while Russia and Great Britain would provide land armies. Stalin concurred in these ideas (Russell, 1958:156).

The Big Four (including China) negotiated detailed outlines of the new international organization at Dumbarton Oaks, near Washington, D.C., in August–September 1944. The emerging draft served as the basis for the final negotiations among all the United Nations at San Francisco between April and June 1945. Before the Charter emerged, the Allies had forged a consensus on three critical issues: (1) keeping in mind the experience of 1919, they decided that the work of constructing the postwar international organization would be kept distinct from the task of forging settlements with the defeated Axis powers and their allies; (2) the postwar international order would be fashioned primarily by the Big Four, acting in concert but consulting when appropriate with smaller powers; and (3) Germany would be dismembered, de-Nazified, disarmed, and occupied.

Unlike 1919, when the victorious Allies converged on Paris, each with its own peace agenda, the leaders of the wartime anti-Axis alliance seemed to have established an intellectual and political basis for reconstructing the war-torn world on a foundation of great power collaboration, something akin to the consensus that animated the discussions in Paris and Vienna in 1814–15. But the consensus was made up of generalities, forged at a time when the outcome of the war was not yet certain, and when the necessities of military cooperation could help paper over wide and substantial political and ideological differences between the powers. In fact, the Allies were led by men who had fundamentally different approaches to the problem of peace and war in the international system.

## WILSON REVISITED AND REVISED: THE UNITED STATES

Most of the American officials who planned for the postwar order were staunch Wilsonians who rejected the "old" system of power politics, balances, and spheres of influence, and who believed that they could construct an alternative world order through international institutions and Allied unity. Cordell Hull was formally responsible for organizing the planning operations in the State Department. He was an admirer of Wilson, and his general pronouncements about war and peace generally coincided with the theoretical analysis put forward by the late American president. Hull's long-range vision was no less than the great tasks of "building human freedom and Christian morality on firmer and broader foundations than ever before" (United States, Department of State, 1950:94). The United States would lead the way in the great crusade to democratize the world. The purpose of fighting the war was enunciated in terms very similar to those expressed by Wilson between 1914 and the 1918 armistice. Hull was the intellectual driving force of postwar planning until his illness late in 1944. But he had numerous disciples in the State Department and his successor, Edward Stettinius, shared his general outlook and hopes for the postwar world. They parted company with Wilson in two important respects, however.

They insisted that the successor to the League of Nations must have enforcement powers. The organization must not only be able to help resolve international conflicts but also have a capacity for both deterrence and for military and economic coercion. Here, they were following the thought of Leon Bourgeois. Conceding to tenets of realism, the policy planners agreed that a covenant – a pledge of good behavior – was an insufficient foundation upon which to build an international security organization. The planners had surveyed and debated a full range of options for deterrence and enforcement, including the creation of a United Nations army, a UN air force (a Soviet proposal), or forces made up of national contingents (United States, Department of State, 1950:128; Russell, 1958:209). They assumed that the great powers at least would have to remain heavily armed after the war to fulfill their collective security obligations.

In the economic realm they also surpassed Wilson. They incorporated into various drafts of the document that was to emerge as the

Charter of the United Nations the idea that peace has economic as well as military foundations. Sumner Welles, the Undersecretary of State, had already announced in 1941 that "no peace ... would be valid or lasting unless it established fully and adequately the natural rights of all peoples to equal economic enjoyment" (Russell, 1958:33). President Roosevelt explicitly applied the philosophical underpinnings of the New Deal to the international sphere. In his annual message to Congress in January 1944 he suggested that the purpose of international organization was to provide not just military security for its members but also to secure

> economic security, social security, moral security, in a family of nations ... All our Allies have learned by bitter experience that real development will not be possible if they are to be diverted from their purpose by repeated wars – or even the threat of war ... An equally basic essential to peace is a decent standard of living for all ... Freedom from fear is eternally linked with freedom from want.
> (United States, Department of State, 1950:203)

The Secretary of State was the most articulate defender of this theory of war and peace. Like many others in Washington, he worked under the shadow of the experiences of the 1930s. The future was to be analyzed in terms of the events of the recent past, and of those events, none had made a greater impression on Hull than the depression. It had been a major cause of war and thus the essential condition for future peace would be international economic welfare:

> To me, unhampered trade dovetailed with peace; high tariffs, trade barriers, and unfair economic competition, with war. Though realizing that many other factors were involved, I reasoned that, if we could get a freer flow of trade ... so that one country would not be deadly jealous of another and the living standards of all countries might rise, thereby eliminating the economic dissatisfaction that breeds war, we might have a reasonable chance for lasting peace.
> (Hull, 1948:I,81)

General world prosperity came to be seen as an essential foundation of military security. It took vigorous American diplomacy during the war to convince the Russians and the British that this theory should find institutional expression in the postwar international organization.

This linkage of economic conditions and the sources of international conflict was a theoretical innovation of great subsequent significance. It was instrumental in forming the basis of the Economic and Social Council of the United Nations and in energetic American efforts during and after the war to create liberal international trade and finance regimes.

246

The American vision of the postwar world also included a strong anti-colonial dimension. Roosevelt in particular bridled at the thought of fighting the war in order to save the Europeans' colonies. Although he may have had some designs of replacing British and French tutelage with an American economic and moral presence among the colonial peoples (Campbell, 1973:5), his vision was somewhat more extended; it was part of the general American urge to replace the old system of international politics with a new one. Roosevelt's initial intention was to fight the war in part to liberate the colonies rather than "to help the [colonial powers] hang on to the archaic, medieval Empire ideas" (quoted in Fenno, 1955:74). The Atlantic Charter spelled out the principle of self-determination. Roosevelt intended to apply it globally and not only to territories liberated from the Axis. Among the State Department planners, anti-colonialism was linked to the broader problem of global welfare. The underlying assumption of the discussions surrounding the mandates system (renamed trusteeship) was that independence in itself would bring about an era of welfare and prosperity (Russell, 1958:211).

What is notable about this menu of theoretical propositions about the sources of international conflict is the linkage between all the issues: security, welfare, and national (colonial) self-determination. American leaders, unlike their allied counterparts, were presciently convinced that the demand for self-government and independence by colonial peoples was to be one of the great issues of the postwar order. Independence would lead to prosperity, and prosperity would lead to peace. The equation could run in the reverse direction as well, but the main point was that the causal variables were all inextricably linked. Thus, the postwar international organization would have tasks and roles far beyond those envisaged by Wilson.

While there was a general consensus about the sources of international conflict and the prerequisites of peace, there were significant differences on institutional details as these came to be developed by Roosevelt and by the various committees working in the State Department. Until the end of 1943 there was little coordination between the White House and the State Department. The main point of difference, although more one of degree than of kind, was over the extent of great power leadership. The president justified his enthusiasm for the Big Four police concept on his assessment of trends in the 1930s. Given the character of modern warfare, small powers, he believed, were no longer able to provide for their own security. The economic burdens of arming to deter or repel great power aggression would be ruinous. The small states, therefore, might just as well remain unarmed and delegate their security concerns to the care of the great powers. The Big Four would be the trustees of small power security. Prosperity would be more likely, moreover, to the extent that the majority of the world's states would not have to spend their productive resources on armaments. To take the edge off the anticipated outcry of great power domination, the United Nations (the wartime alliance as it was then called) would create a general international organization that could influence the policies of the policemen. The small states would use it as a watchdog to protect their concerns.

The four policemen, maintaining significant armed capabilities, would both deter and coerce. In the event of intractable conflicts between the minor powers, the policemen could dampen conflict through quarantine methods, that is, by starving the conflict parties of the means of conducting military operations. Beyond the quarantine, should that prove ineffective, the Big Four would bomb the aggressor until it capitulated. Since all but the great powers would be effectively disarmed at the end of the war, small aggressors would have no means of defending themselves against armed coercion by one or more of the Big Four. The disparity of armed capabilities would provide a significant deterrent effect as well (Russell, 1958:96–98; cf. Gaddis, 1972:24).

Roosevelt's image of the postwar security order resembled the Hobbesian domestic analogy: order through trusteeship and deterrence. The "people" of the world, the small states, delegate to the trustees – the four-power Leviathan – a monopoly of military capabilities and the right to use force and economic coercion in exchange for guarantees of security. Roosevelt did not speculate at length on the obvious lacuna: who polices the police? He had suggested an advisory role for the small powers in the universal international organization, but without any means of exercising any coercive capabilities they could control only by diplomatic persuasion. Moreover, the president did not resolve the most difficult dilemma: what if one of the Big Four were to be the aggressor? In Hobbes' Leviathan the authority is a single entity. The Big Four obviously constituted a plural authority. The whole edifice thus rested on a requirement of similar political perspective and an equal commitment to the maintenance of the postwar order among the policemen. Such a consensus had never existed in diplomatic history except perhaps during the brief interval between Waterloo and the Verona and Troppau congresses.

Roosevelt was aware of the dilemma and later acknowledged that great power unity had to be created rather than assumed. If Stalin did not choose to cooperate with the others, the world would be driven back to a balance of power system. It was Roosevelt's strong commitment to postwar unity that helps explain his great efforts to understand the Russians and his propensity to play down very troubling signals that were already appearing by late 1943. He felt compelled to disregard these in light of the great stakes that were involved in perpetuating the Allies' unity into the postwar period. The president was convinced that the Soviet Union had to be brought into the postwar period through patience and understanding. If Stalin could be persuaded to accept a constructive role in the world, Roosevelt's vision of the postwar order could come to fruition. Preemptory Anglo-American demands for impeccable wartime behavior, and particularly any policies that gave the impression of "ganging up" against the Soviet Union, might well jeopardize the whole enterprise. Roosevelt did not see the United Nations merely as the result of Allied unity. It was also to be a major instrumentality for resolving disputes and disagreements between the Big Four (Campbell, 1973:193), that is, for sustaining unity. Hence, Roosevelt and after his death, Stettinius, were committed to launching the organization before the termination of hostilities. They hoped that the international organization would not itself become a source of conflict between the victors.

Roosevelt's conception of a postwar security organization did not prevail, although important elements of it were to be embodied in the Charter. Rather, the careful preparation that had been going on in the State Department under the guidance of Hull and Welles eventually became official American policy. The Agenda Group of the State Department prepared a "Plan for the Establishment of an International Organization for the Maintenance of International Peace and Security" that was approved by Hull and sent to the White House on December 29, 1943. It came to be known as the Outline Plan, and with Roosevelt's approval on February 3, 1944 it became official policy. This was Hull's version of an international organization, with closer affinities to the League of Nations than to the president's more original concepts. It incorporated Roosevelt's thinking about the four policemen, but provided a significantly greater set of tasks and responsibilities for the small states. The General Assembly would have significant influence in the area of conflict resolution when and if the Security Council could not act. An important addition to the League model, the memorandum provided that the Security Council could formulate terms of settlement for any dispute where other procedures had failed. The United Nations, in this version, was to be judge as well as policeman (the text is in United States, Department of State, 1950: appendix 33). There was no mention of the position on disarmament enunciated in the Atlantic Charter, but the leading position of the policemen was clearly articulated. The Big Four "will maintain adequate forces and will be willing to use such force as circumstances require to prevent or suppress all cases of aggression." Pending the working out of specific arrangements for creating a United Nations military force, "the states parties to the Four Nation Declaration [Moscow, October 1943] and other states in a position to do so should provide . . . such forces and facilities as may be needed for establishing security and peace."

Hull's conservative approach to international organization can be explained in part by the careful examination conducted by the State Department committees of the League of Nations experience, but more important, by his concern with and awareness of public opinion in general and attitudes in the Senate in particular. Hull had made it a practice to consult broadly with key Senators of both parties throughout the preparatory stages, and it was clear in these discussions that the Senate would not sanction American involvement in any international organization that derogated from Congress's constitutional war powers. The idea of an international force that could be launched by the Security Council on its own initiative had no hope of being included. The Soviet proposal for a UN air force was rejected on similar grounds. If the postwar organization was going to be a policeman, the American Congress would determine when and if it could act.

As the American draft developed between 1942 and the Dumbarton Oaks Conference, the more radical ideas for empowering the organization were pruned down. All of the old dilemmas brought out in the American debates on the League of Nations, particularly the tension between the need for international authority and speedy collective decision-making and the demand for the exercise of sovereignty on all questions of war and peace, reemerged in the discussions of the new international organization. The document sent to the White House in December 1943 was therefore conservative in preserving the fundamental attribute of sovereignty, but it improved the decision-making procedures for the new organization. Decisions would be made by a qualified majority instead of unanimity (though with a necessary consensus among the permanent members of the Security Council), and the Council could develop terms of settlement. The draft also outlined the modalities of using coercive military power as a response to the determination of aggression. The elitist structure of the organization was clearly spelled out: the great powers were given primary responsibility for maintaining international peace and security. Wilson would have accepted this in fact, but as an idea he likely would have found it inconsistent with his more egalitarian sentiments.

## BALANCE OF POWER: GREAT BRITAIN AND THE POSTWAR ORDER

When he speculated about the nature of postwar organization, Churchill drew certain theoretical conclusions from the practice of the League of Nations. His main concern was that the theory of collective security did not translate into the foreign policy priorities of most states. States, he argued, were not equally concerned with international security. They tended to be preoccupied with their own problems or, at best, with problems of their particular regions. It would make more sense, therefore, to have several regional organizations – for the Americas, Europe, and Asia – and above these a supreme council made up of the Big Four exclusively. The regional councils would deal with local concerns ("to avoid having every nation poking its fingers into every other nation's business around the world"), and only in the event that the regional councils failed to resolve conflicts would those be taken to the supreme council for handling (Campbell, 1973:11). The supreme council would be an exclusive club of the military victors of the war, and its primary task would be to police the peace, defined as preventing a renewal of aggression by Germany and/or Japan. In this regard, Churchill looked backward and defined the future in terms of the past. Germany and Japan would be the likely trouble-makers in the postwar world – along with the Soviet Union – despite the Allies' commitment since 1943 to unconditional surrender and their clear purpose of purging the defeated nations of all traces of Nazism and militarism.

Churchill had promoted the idea of an international organization as early as 1941, but he did not conceive of it as a replacement for more traditional security devices. Great Britain's security ultimately would have to rely upon postwar cooperation between the victors and the resources of the British Empire, buttressed by an extension of the Anglo-Soviet alliance of 1942 and a possible alliance with the United States.

Most of Churchill's ideas on international organization were not translated into policy. Roosevelt was interested in them, but as in the United States the preferred vision of officialdom prevailed. British officials did not attribute to an international organization the system-transforming possibilities that the Americans saw in it. Those who were formally responsible for preparing outlines for a postwar international organization produced results that were rather similar to those emerging from the State Department in Washington. Eden supported them and added a few of his own ideas such as the military staff committee to be attached to the Security Council. Its task would be to coordinate and organize the military forces that member states would make available to the Security Council (Eden, 1965:514). At a meeting of the Commonwealth Prime Ministers in May 1944, Churchill's ideas of regional councils and a supreme council were subjected to critical review by the Australians, New Zealanders, and Canadians. They argued vigorously for a universal organization, and eventually officialdom's and Eden's ideas prevailed: the new United Nations would be a refurbished League of Nations, with greater powers and a clear division of responsibility for maintaining international peace and security between the great powers and others.

The relatively slight attention paid to problems of international organization in the memoirs of the British participants indicates the priority of the subject in wartime London. Even allowing for the pressing business of conducting the war and managing the increasingly difficult relationship with the Soviet Union, British officials did not seriously flirt with more imaginative ideas about postwar international organization. There was no formal coordination with the Americans (to say nothing of keeping in touch with the Russians) on these matters, only informal and sporadic conversations between Roosevelt and Churchill. Eden complained in his memoirs (1965:590–91) that when he met the Americans on the way to the Yalta conference "they seemed to give rather too much weight to the World Council and too little to Poland, in the sense that unless the Russians can be persuaded or compelled to treat the Poles with some decency there will not be a world council that is worth much." The British did not even have the postwar international organization as an item on their proposed agenda for the Yalta discussions!

The Americans wanted to use the international organization that had for all practical purposes been ironed out at the Dumbarton Oaks meetings to cement Allied unity. The British saw little need to hurry with the project solely on this account. The organization could not work unless unity was established and sustained prior to its launching. Churchill was likely rather bored with the whole issue. His mind focused on the immediate task of defeating Germany and on the implications of the rapid series of victories in the Balkans and central Europe by the Red Army. He was not about to wait to see if the proposed United Nations could somehow rescue the deteriorating wartime coalition (Campbell, 1973:192). The immediate priority was to make some deal with the Russians and perhaps an alliance with the United States. Russian activities in Poland were becoming increasingly alarming, and despite the Allies' "Declaration on Liberated Europe," in which they pledged to observe democratic procedures in establishing governments for the liberated European peoples and to cooperate with each other in this process, the Russians refused to cooperate, and their procedures for establishing governments in most of the areas liberated by the Red Army were hardly consistent with any Western understanding of the terms "democracy" or "self-determination."

Churchill's nightmare was coming to pass. Already in October 1942 he was talking about the "measureless disaster if Russian barbarism were to overlay the culture and independence of the ancient states of Europe" (quoted in Fenno, 1955:74). The Red Army's victories in 1944 convinced Churchill that the Russians were seeking a position of overwhelming power in Europe. It is on the basis of this assessment that he (1) sought to open a second front in the Balkans (always vetoed by the American military), (2) promoted a project for an East European federation, (3) took up the case for restoring France as a great power – the prospect of a power vacuum between the Soviet Union and Great Britain disturbed him – (4) began to think in terms of a permanent Anglo-American alliance, and (5) entered into the famous deal with Stalin (June and October 1944) whereby Britain and the Soviet Union agreed on dividing "spheres of responsibility" in the Balkans.

Churchill wanted to make certain that British and American troops would extend as far as possible into central Europe. By early 1945 it was clear to most in London that the Russians would not live up to the commitments of Yalta, as interpreted in London and Washington, unless they were pressured militarily to do so. Despite Eden's disclaimer (1965:517) that the idea of a postwar alliance of Western powers was solely for the purpose of preventing a renewal of German aggression, it is more likely that by 1944 Churchill was thinking in terms of east and west blocs after the war. Eden agreed to a hurried timetable to launch the United Nations discussions of the Dumbarton Oaks proposals not as a means of cementing unity with the Russians, as the Americans would have it, but in the expectation that "only by encouraging the formation of some World Organization are we likely to induce the Americans, and this means the American Senate, to agree to accept any European commitments designed to range America . . . against a hostile Germany *or against any European breaker of the peace* [my italics]" (Eden, 1965:517). Roosevelt had stated at Yalta that American troops would be brought home from Europe within two or three years of the defeat of Germany. The prospects of facing the Russians alone were no doubt daunting, but with a rejuvenated France and some American commitment to become a guarantor of European security there was a reasonable prospect for limiting Soviet ambitions. In other

253

words, the United Nations would become a means for playing the classical balance of power game. Great Britain could not stand alone; the long-range security of Europe could only be established on the basis of "special arrangements," meaning alliances. This is not to say that Churchill and his colleagues were indifferent to the German problem. The revival of German expansionism remained the most likely postwar threat. But in London in 1944 it was clear that an equally likely source of insecurity would be the Soviet Union. The United Nations, no matter what its constitutional outlines, would provide no adequate substitute for power balancing. While Roosevelt after Yalta could proclaim that the meeting of minds on the Crimea had made possible the transformation of international politics, Britain's leaders were becoming increasingly convinced that the more venerable practices of international politics were necessary.

## SECURITY THROUGH EXPANSION: STALIN AND THE POSTWAR ORDER

The mass of documentation available in the United States and Great Britain allows the analyst to trace the development of theoretical propositions about the causes of war and the conditions of peace among the key wartime policy-makers. This is not the case with Stalin and his colleagues. Interpretations of Soviet intentions abound. Most are based on selective evidence inferred from behavior rather than on documented statements and analyses. The interpretations range from the view that the Soviet Union sought to communize the whole European continent, to the idea that the Russians sought only a belt of "friendly" governments surrounding their nation.

It is reasonably clear that Soviet war aims and postwar plans remained fluid throughout most of the war. Reports of ambassadors in Moscow during the hostilities fail to reveal the existence of any Soviet master plan. On the contrary, the theme of uncertainty and choice pervades these reports. For example, the Canadian minister in Moscow wrote in 1942 that Stalin could choose either to veer toward cooperation with the Allies or he could turn the Soviet Union into a highly armed, isolated state. By February 1944, he suggested that Soviet priorities ran in terms of concluding the early military defeat of Germany, the dismemberment and de-Nazification of the country, the establishment of deferential governments through eastern Europe, and continued collaboration with Great Britain and the United States into the postwar period (Smith, 1988:48, 59). This assessment was reasonably typical of most Western evaluations of the time. By late

254

1944, however, many analysts were beginning to underline accumulating evidence of Soviet malevolence and violations of those norms of
consultation and policy coordination between the Allied leaders that
had slowly emerged during the war. Some read Stalin's treatment of
the Polish problem as a harbinger of what the rest of the areas liberated
by the Red Army could expect. Others, however, sympathized with or
at least understood the Russians' insistence on establishing "friendly"
governments in an area that had been used repeatedly as an invasion
route into Russia.

Stalin did not help clear up the uncertainties. He provided little
evidence of long-range thought or speculation on the nature of postwar international relations or on the types of issues that would or could
generate future international conflict – with one important exception
discussed below. He pressed his territorial claims, demanded a high
price for entering the war against Japan, and at the rhetorical level
generally subscribed to the norms of great power unity. He demonstrated an acute sensitivity to questions of status and the norm of
reciprocity, but little of this demonstrated theoretical wizardry. Foreign Minister Molotov, whom Stalin generally kept on a tight leash,
did not indulge in long-term speculation about theories of international relations or the causes of war and the conditions of peace in
the abstract. He shared Stalin's suspiciousness and was ready to identify Allied malevolence in both innocuous and not-so-innocent events.

If we can reconstruct Stalin's thoughts, the first conclusion would be
that the Soviet dictator was not generally concerned with problems of
international security in the abstract. He focused almost exclusively on
the immediate task of defeating Germany and establishing a postwar
order that would effectively prevent Germany or any other power from
invading the Soviet Union. His conceptions of postwar international
organization and general security were deeply colored by this problematic. He was convinced that Germany would attempt to restore its
might and launch new aggressions. Shortly before Yalta, he declared
that "History shows that a short period – some twenty or thirty years –
is enough for Germany to recover from defeat and restore her might"
(quoted in Deutscher, 1960:538). At Tehran, he predicted even a briefer
period for Germany's comeback. Stalin constantly repeated this theme
to his foreign interlocutors.

The essential task of the postwar international organization would
thus be to police whatever peace the victorious allies could impose on
Germany and Japan. Stalin looked at the future in terms of the past: the
perennial problem of international relations was Germany, although
by early 1945 he probably added Great Britain or the United States or a

255

combination of them to the agenda of potential threats. When Stalin embraced the necessity of wartime and postwar collaboration, he had in mind these problems – with emphasis on Germany – and not possible conflicts in Latin America, the desirability of constructing a liberal international economic order, or all those matters that were to come under the jurisdiction of UNESCO. Stalin shared nothing of traditional liberal theories of international relations, either of the Wilsonian or Hull varieties. To him, these excursions into the peripherals of international politics were more likely signs of growing American imperialism.

The bases of international relationships were power, not community. Power conferred status and international entitlements. Those who fought to crush Nazism were entitled to retribution and spoils. But most important, they were entitled to create, unilaterally if necessary, a set of conditions that would guarantee against reenactments of August 1914 or June 1941. In a speech of 6 November, 1944, Stalin argued that the task of any postwar international organization was to prevent "fresh aggression" by Germany (United States, Department of State, 1950:337). This organization must have the power to act with force. This must not be a refurbished League of Nations which had neither the right nor the means to avert aggression. Could we expect the actions of this world organization to be sufficiently effective? Yes, provided the great powers continued to act in a spirit of unanimity and accord. "They will not be effective if this essential condition is violated." Stalin was willing to face squarely the dilemma that many Americans avoided: the latter thought the UN could be used to create consensus. Stalin regarded the consensus as a necessary precondition of the organization. But the significant point is that in 1944 and 1945 Stalin defined the organization's tasks primarily in terms of the German problem. His postwar scripts and problematics were in the same mold as those of Gustav Adolph, Metternich, and Clemenceau: the problem of recurrence, seeing the future in terms of the past, and generally ignoring speculation about new kinds of issues that might arise on the international agenda and devising organizational and more informal diplomatic means of anticipating and dealing with them.

All Soviet wartime policy was animated by this concern for Germany. The evidence of terrible Nazi brutality and killing piled up as the Red Army advanced westward. Russian hatred for and fear of Germany was understandable. The solution to the German problem thus had to be extreme. In December 1941, Stalin had already revealed his intention of dismembering the country, and as the war continued he developed plans for extensive reparations, the virtual dismantling of German industry to pay for Nazi destruction in Russia, disarmament, and guarantees against any German resurgence. Those guarantees would have to be more than paper promises. They would include constructing Allied military bases within and along the borders of Germany and a string of strategic bases outside the area. Allied military installations on the Pacific islands would be used to contain Japan (Russell, 1958:156). The Soviet proposal for a United Nations air force was not just an abstract idea for general international security purposes. It was to be an instrument for keeping Germany and Japan in a state of docility. The policing of the peace was to be uniquely a great power activity. Indeed, the whole project of postwar reconstruction was defined in terms of the security interests and requirements of the Soviet Union. The demands of the small states – and they were beginning to be heard already in 1944 as they were liberated were to be subordinated to Soviet security concerns. As Stalin suggested at Yalta, he would "never allow any Allied action to be submitted to the judgement of the small powers." Roosevelt and Churchill agreed that those who had led the war must write the peace, and there was no question that the small states would dictate to the large. But Stalin reversed the proposition: the large must dictate to the small. Churchill came to the defense of the small: "The eagle should permit the small birds to sing and care not whereof they sang," to which Stalin retorted that small birds had better watch their step (Clemens, 1970:130). Stalin's attitude struck Eden (1965:563) as grim, "not to say sinister."

The practical application of Stalin's approach to the German problem had already begun to emerge in 1939. The Nazi–Soviet pact did not provide for a reconciliation of the two ideological enemies. It did provide the means whereby the Soviet Union might secure strategically important territories in anticipation of an ultimate war with Germany. By the end of 1940, the Soviet Union had annexed Bessarabia, northern Bukovina, the Baltic republics, a large slice of Poland, and most of Finnish Karelia. To most Western observers this expansion was a cynical carving up of spheres of influence. To Stalin it was a necessary prelude to an inevitable war with the Reich. Control over the eastern Baltic littoral provided defense for Leningrad while a portion of Poland would allow the Russians to position forces further to the west in anticipation of a German attack.

Throughout the war Stalin had unsuccessfully urged Great Britain and the United States to recognize these conquests. Since they were inconsistent with the Atlantic Charter, the western Allies were not willing to discuss territorial changes prior to the end of the war. They

257

regarded it as a matter of principle. Stalin thought it necessary to construct as many obstacles as possible between the Soviet Union and Germany – a Germany which by mid 1945 the Americans and British were increasingly defining in terms of reconstruction and reincorporation into the international community. The vision of postwar Germany that was developing in London and Washington was fundamentally inconsistent with Stalin's priorities, which were to dismember it, keep it permanently weakened, and plunder it for extensive reparations. The more these visions diverged the more emphasis Stalin seemed to place on constructing obstacles unilaterally – regardless of Allied objections. Whether or not Stalin had ever assumed that he could construct his security belt with British and American collaboration remains unknown, but it was perhaps prophetic that at the Moscow Conference in 1943, Molotov objected to the American draft declaration which included a statement that the Big Four act together in "any occupation of enemy territory and of territory of other states held by the enemy." Since Great Britain and the United States had not invited Soviet participation in the occupation of Italy in 1943, Stalin at least had a precedent for taking unilateral action in Poland.

The Big Three made a number of agreements at Yalta, but as the war reached its end in both Europe and the Pacific all the parties either tried to change those agreements or acted inconsistently with them. Great Britain and the United States pressed Stalin to treat Poland in a manner consistent with liberal standards of self-determination. Allied leaders and diplomats had repeatedly expressed understanding for Stalin's demand for a "friendly" government in Poland; but they also insisted on a democratic one. But the two criteria were politically inconsistent: any democratic regime in Poland would not have been friendly to Russia, a fact that Stalin acknowledged in 1945. The Soviet treatment of occupied Romania – where it installed a pro-communist regime under an ultimatum delivered by Deputy Foreign Minister Andrei Vishinsky – was equally inconsistent with Stalin's undertakings at Yalta, but he deflected American and British protests by suggesting that Great Britain's participation in the Greek Civil War was hardly consistent with the Yalta understandings. The Polish and Romanian cases, as well as the continued occupation of the Baltic republics and the harsh victor's armistice the Soviet Union imposed on Finland in 1944, indicated that Stalin was determined to create an extensive security belt between the Soviet Union and Germany whether or not Great Britain and the United States consented, and he would do it with little regard for general principles such as those enunciated in the Atlantic Charter or the Yalta Declaration.

Stalin's actions were fortified and justified by his views on the nature of war and victory. He was adamant that the peace should reflect the relative military efforts and suffering of the victors. At the height of the war effort after the Channel invasion, western Allied armies engaged only one-third of the total Nazi military forces (Clemens, 1970:75). The Red Army confronted most of the remainder. In the early years of the war Stalin had claimed that the Soviet Union was singlehandedly fighting Nazi Germany, and as the conflict continued he only grudgingly admitted a contribution by his allies. It was not, moreover, in the Russian military tradition to conquer territories and then to evacuate them. Victory created entitlements, both in the form of territory and reparations to pay for the aggressor's destruction. These gains should not be the subject of bargaining and haggling among the Allies.

Such views on war were fundamentally different from those that prevailed in Washington. To Americans, war was an immoral necessity. Its sole purpose was to defeat and punish the aggressor. It was not intended to establish entitlements beyond certain minimum sums in the form of limited reparations. There was a strong presumption that except for the defeated Axis, the world, territorially speaking, would return to its pre-1939 configuration.

If an essentially defensive and historical outlook animated Stalin's conception of a postwar European order, there is also evidence to suggest more ambitious designs. In 1940 Stalin had raised with the Germans the possibility of gaining control over the Kattegatt straits between Denmark and Sweden. In November of the same year, Molotov told Ribbentrop and Hitler that the Soviet Union intended to annex Finland in the same manner that it had dealt with the Baltic republics – ultimatums and the installation of a "friendly" government, followed by military occupation "requested" by that government (Metzger, 1984:216–17). Between 1939 and June 1941, Stalin went on a binge of territorial conquests and annexations that fed on each other and were not explained solely by defensive considerations.[1] At Yalta the General Secretary unveiled an extensive list of territorial claims in the Far East, arguing these were just demands for restoration of losses inflicted by Japan in 1905. In fact, the claims went considerably beyond the territorial adjustments of 1905 and constituted a serious compromise of Chinese sovereignty. Roosevelt's consent to these demands – the price of obtaining Russia's entry into the war against Japan – was funda-

---

[1] In 1988 a senior Soviet military historian acknowledged that Stalin's territorial acquisitions prior to June 1941 were not motivated solely by strategic/defensive considerations. The relative ease of some of the acquisitions whetted his appetite for even greater gains (Hyvärinen, 1989:42–44).

mentally inconsistent with his own principles and seriously undermined the credibility of his concerns about the right of
self-determination in Poland.

At Potsdam in July 1945, Stalin unveiled designs that extended far
beyond Russia's periphery. He proposed a Soviet trust territory in the
Mediterranean (with preference for Libya), his troops were already
establishing control over northern Persia (contrary to agreements
made at Tehran in 1943), he was pressing claims upon Turkey which
would have had the effect of placing Istanbul under Russian guns, and
there were rumors of Russian aspirations to a role in Lebanon. Eden
anticipated that Tangier would be added to the list of arenas for new
Soviet activity. The Soviet Union, despite its adhesion to the Atlantic
Charter, emerged from the war with massive territorial spoils and
conquests: the Baltic states, Karelia, Petsamo, much of Poland, Königs-
burg, Bessarabia, Bukovina, and Ruthenia in Europe; the Kuriles, Port
Arthur, Sakhalin, and a sphere of influence in Mongolia in the Far East.
Intense pressure was placed on Iran and Turkey and claims were
extended to the Mediterranean. As James Byrnes was to lament in
1947, "certainly the Soviet Union is not a dispossessed nation" (United
States, Department of State, 1947:131).

From the Soviet perspective, of course, Stalin made a number of
concessions for the sake of maintaining Allied unity. The Red Army
could have captured Berlin by itself in the late winter or early spring of
1945 but waited instead; Stalin agreed to include China as an equal
partner (hardly justified by that all-important consideration to Stalin,
its military strength and contribution to the anti-Nazi cause); and he
accepted the admission of France into the club of the policemen – not
without making the point, however, that if Great Britain was to gain for
France a privileged position and an obvious "faggot" vote (Churchill's
term), then why shouldn't the Soviet Union obtain equal status for its
new friend, Poland?

In fashioning the postwar order in Europe primarily through use of
the Red Army, Stalin placed the international organization enterprise
in a lower priority. He was not about to rely upon a general organization with multiple tasks as a main pillar of postwar Soviet security.
With the prompting of his Politburo colleagues, Stalin would go along
with the establishment of such an organization, but Russia's safety
would rely essentially upon a system of satellites and the permanent
weakening of Germany (Stettinius, 1950:273). By 1945, moreover, the
American conception of the United Nations had begun to diverge from
the organization that Roosevelt and Stalin had agreed in 1943 would
have as its main task the policing of the defeated powers.

The Soviet Union worked reasonably well with the British and Americans at Dumbarton Oaks, deferring on most issues to American plans and projects, but by the time of the San Francisco Conference it gave evidence of being increasingly concerned about changes in Allied priorities, and specifically about the problem of numbers. The Soviet Union had started 1943 as one of the Big Three in a focused anti-German coalition. By April 1945 it was only one of the Big Five, four of whom could be presumed to be anti-communist and anti-Russian, and probably both. Moreover, there was increasing emphasis in Washington on the economic and social aspects of international organization, a development which in Stalin's eyes was rendering his concept of a strong, unifunctional agency increasingly diluted. Stalin wanted the United Nations to police the defeated powers, and he grew irritated at the prolonged discussions of "an endless number of superfluous functions" (Campbell, 1973.37) and at the Allies' rejection of the concept of a United Nations air force. The number of UN tasks was unnecessarily escalating.

There was also the problem of the number of members in the organization. In a bid to obtain support for the new international organization from Latin America, Roosevelt proposed that Brazil should be added as a permanent member of the Security Council and suggested adding as members of the General Assembly a number of Latin countries that had not declared war on Germany. It was at this point that Stalin proposed that the Soviet Union should be represented in the General Assembly by its sixteen constituent republics. And so the American universalist, multi-functional organization that was emerging in Washington in late 1944 and early 1945 was increasingly inconsistent with the anti-German, unifunctional body dominated by the three policemen that Stalin had in mind. The Americans were beginning to look beyond the immediate problem of Germany, while Stalin kept his focus trained on it. Finally, the United Nations was beginning to look like an organization where the Soviet Union would reside as a minority of one. Both Great Britain and the United States had their "faggot" votes in the Security Council, and that Council would become concerned with a variety of international issues where even Brazil's concerns might take precedence over those of the Soviet Union.

The differing American and Soviet conceptions of the postwar international organization were symbolized in the struggles over the veto question. This issue was complicated and had a long history. The essential differences were these: the Americans and British wanted the veto to apply only to enforcement action taken under Chapter VII as

261

well as to substantive decisions taken under Chapter VI dealing with peaceful settlement. They argued that when a great power was a party to a dispute being dealt with under Chapter VI, it should not have a vote. The Soviet Union took the position that the only possible basis for quick decisions and effective action against an aggressor (meaning Germany) was great power unanimity. Therefore, all issues whether procedural or substantive, whether under Chapter VI or Chapter VII, must have the concurrence of the great powers. Under this formula any great power could prevent an item even being placed on the Security Council agenda. A compromise was fashioned at Yalta, but from the Soviet point of view, it lacked precision. At San Francisco, therefore, Molotov created one of the many crises of the conference by reintroducing the idea of the absolute veto. Many saw this as a deliberate attempt to wreck the conference, but given the Soviet Union's understanding of the essential tasks and functions of the organization, it should hardly have been surprising. Stalin and his colleagues simply could not make the intellectual leap from their exclusive concern with Soviet security to the broader problem of general international security, an intellectual feat that the Russians were unable to make until Mikhail Gorbachev assumed leadership of the country in 1985. Wilson's concepts, the concerns of Edward Grey in 1914, and the functions of peaceful settlement and judicial procedures were foreign or even threatening to Soviet thinkers. They could not understand domestic analogies deriving from American political and constitutional practices and how these might operate in a system of sovereign states and global class antagonisms. If the international organization could not help resolve the Soviet Union's immediate security problems, then it would probably be irrelevant and there should be no onus for the Soviet government to participate actively and constructively in it.

Averell Harriman, America's ambassador in wartime Moscow, sent the following cable to Washington in 1944 summarizing his interpretation of the Soviet approach to international organization. It was prescient and supports the analysis above:

> It would appear that [the Russians] look upon the international security organization as a method by which the Soviet Union can be protected against aggressor nations, but it seems doubtful whether they believe that it can be useful to them in settling disputes between them and other countries through mediatory or judicial processes. The court, they believe, is packed against them. They appear, therefore, to be insisting upon the right of unilateral action in settling disputes of this character. I feel that we are faced with a very funda-

> mental question of what the effect on the international security organization will be with most of the nations looking to it to develop mediatory or judicial procedures in the advancement of international relations, whereas the Soviet Union appears to view it from a much narrower perspective. (Russell, 1958:501)

To summarize, the leaders of the Big Three operated under fundamentally different conceptions of the postwar order. At one extreme we find the Americans, until late 1944, epitomized by the thinking of Hull and his State Department planners. They were globalists who expected to transform the nature of international politics through international institution-building, by creating a liberal trade and investment regime, and by applying the principle of self-determination on a worldwide basis. In this scheme, the security of each state in the system would be protected by the international trustees, the Big Four, who would act as disinterested policemen and judges of the community of nations. American security would be achieved through general international security. They identified the causes of war as a combination of economic underprivilege, cyclical depressions, and the machinations of totalitarian dictators. The conditions of peace were based on the American domestic analogy, the principles of federalism, and the New Deal.

Churchill thought in terms of a territorial and military balance of power. The looming might of the Soviet Union could be balanced by the resurrection of France, the maintenance of the British Empire, and an American postwar involvement in Europe. Postwar international politics would represent a continuation of past patterns rather than a break from them. An international organization could play a constructive role in helping to resolve conflicts between minor powers. Churchill was convinced that the great powers would have to play a strong and distinct role in international politics. They would listen to the concerns of the small and in some cases accommodate them, but the maintenance of peace would depend primarily upon the decisions of those who had the military means to make a significant difference. They would collaborate to guarantee against renewal of German aggression and police the peace more generally. In all cases responsibilities were to be consistent with power resources. Collaboration is nice, but there can be no firm basis for acting in concert unless there is a balance of power.

Stalin was the nationalist unilateral. Soviet security concerns were to take precedence over all other considerations. Allied unity was to be nurtured and maintained, but the Soviet Union would have to provide for its security primarily through territorial expansion. International

263

institutions are of value only to the extent that they could make a direct contribution to Soviet security concerns, defined primarily in terms of rendering and maintaining Germany a second- or third-rate power. In a world of potentially hostile states, the Soviet Union also had to make certain that any international organization would not be used against its interests: hence the strong commitment to the absolute veto. The international organization as it was developing in late 1944 and early 1945 looked in Moscow less like an organization of a community of nations than an instrument for an anti-Soviet coalition. Whatever American motives – and Stalin found it difficult to believe all of Roosevelt's proclamations of disinterest in war prizes – by 1945 the line-up in the United Nations was distinctly unsympathetic to Soviet interests. Soviet participation in the organization would thus be minimal, confined to the protection of its interests and those of its new clients.

The intellectual cleavages between these three visions of the postwar order were pronounced. Roosevelt had thought that at the Yalta Conference there had been a meeting of minds. On individual issues relating to the prosecution of the war, there was. But there was little philosophical discussion, no fundamental analysis of the postwar order, no exploration of alternatives, and certainly no detailed exposition of theories of international relations. The prime consideration at the wartime conferences was to maintain unity for the prosecution of the war and to develop some common understandings on the modalities of dealing with the vanquished. It is likely that if the personalities had dealt at length with their hopes and visions of the future they would have concluded that there was little prospect for extending wartime collaboration into peacetime. The theories of and prescriptions for peace were largely incompatible.

## CHANGING AMERICAN CONCEPTIONS OF INTERNATIONAL SECURITY

Throughout most of the war, American planners thought of international security in abstract terms. The four policemen would take care of the immediate problem of German or Japanese revitalization and aggression, but once these tasks had been handled and the defeated countries restored to the comity of nations, the universal organization would come into effect to handle other kinds of conflicts. The United States would act upon these in a relatively disinterested manner. Roosevelt and his colleagues did not raise the question of how the new organization could help resolve America's security problems because they did not identify any in concrete terms. American security could be achieved through a broader international security based on self-determination and global economic growth.

It was only towards the end of the war that some officials began to link the United Nations with the perceived emerging threat from the Soviet Union. And when they made the connection, they came to the conclusion, just like the Russians and the British, that the United States could not depend solely upon the new organization for solving its future security problems.

The Charter that emerged in June 1945 reflected the changing strategic outlook in Washington, one that played down general international security and emphasized America's unique problems. The attitudes of disinterested selflessness that imbued much of the early discussions on postwar security were being replaced by considerations and perspectives more familiar to the realist tradition in international relations: the center-point of analysis is the national interest defined in the context of a potentially hostile international environment. There is an identifiable opponent that threatens core values. Secretary of War Stimson and Navy Secretary Forrestal indulged in this type of analysis, as did leading military officials who were becoming increasingly prominent in policy-making in Washington.

By the time the San Francisco conference was in session – with American delegation head Stettinius anxious to bring the proceedings to a quick conclusion in an atmosphere of growing Soviet–American strains – President Truman had decided on a number of significant policy changes, including the termination of Lend-lease, hedging on a Soviet request for a postwar reconstruction loan (while granting a large loan to Great Britain at 2 percent interest), consideration of using the knowledge of the impending American atomic capability as leverage against the Russians, and pursuing the Polish question with great vigor. These policies were complemented by certain new positions the United States took on the Charter.

Original American proposals on international organization had included Security Council authority to recommend and enforce terms of settlement in a conflict judged to be a threat to the peace. This idea did not survive. By 1945, the Americans had begun to dismantle some of the authority of the Council. On this particular issue they successfully stood with the Russians against many delegations from smaller countries which, like Australia and Canada, championed a greater role for themselves and the Security Council. Instead of promoting the idea of a United Nations force in the tradition of Leon Bourgeois's ideas, the United States settled for national contingents to be made available to the Security Council – on a voluntary basis – and the wartime concepts

265

of United Nations bases and strong points were abandoned altogether. Stalin's project for a UN air force had been rejected by the United States long before the San Francisco meeting.

The United States and the Soviet Union also stood together against writing compulsory jurisdiction into the Statutes of the International Court of Justice. On the question of trusteeship territories the American delegation demanded that all security problems relating to them would have to be excluded from Trusteeship Council monitoring and investigation. This position was a response to the concern of the American military, who wanted to maintain maximum American control over the Japanese islands of the Pacific that were to be taken over by the United States.

Hull's ideas about disarmament as a necessary condition for peace were also jettisoned. One lesson of the 1930s – democracies would have to practice policies of deterrence rather than appeasement – was already conventional wisdom in Washington by the early 1940s, and Roosevelt's concept of the four policemen assumed a virtual monopoly of armaments maintained by the great powers. Early State Department drafts of the proposed Charter included elaborate provisions for disarmament, extending in effect Wilson's ideas on the subject. The Security Council would be given authority to "initiate, establish, and to adjust through periodic review, a system of regulation of armaments and armed forces upon the basis of [a] general agreement; to investigate and enforce . . . the observance of the general agreement; to include . . . the control of public and private manufacturing of and trade in arms" (Russell, 1958:267). None of this was consistent with the idea of the armed four policemen, but it hardly mattered: none of it went forward to San Francisco. The Charter makes some statements of hope on disarmament but leaves the whole problem to negotiations between the member states, with no particular role reserved for the Security Council.

The final step in the emergence of a national security rather than globalist perspective on the United Nations was the inclusion of Article 51. It was the outcome of a major crisis between the United States and the Latin American delegations. It also reflected the American Senate's concern for the sanctity of the Monroe Doctrine and for the emerging breakdown of Allied unity. By 1945 the United States wanted to make it explicit in the Charter (it had only been implied in earlier versions) that nothing in the document abrogated the right of self-defense, including collective self-defense. This provision paved the way for the construction of traditional alliances, the very thing Roosevelt had claimed would become obsolete and unnecessary once the world organization

266

was established. Neither the Soviet Union nor Great Britain objected to the resurrection of a traditional instrument of international politics.

Taken together, these late changes in American positions on the character of international organization represented significant deviations from Wilsonian principles. Most fundamentally, the Charter that emerged in June 1945 implied that the basic characteristics of international politics cannot be changed or transformed as long as the states system is organized around the principle of sovereignty. Mutual pledges and institutionalized procedures for handling international conflicts are not sufficient to bring about fundamental changes. Indeed, the Charter, except in a few highly circumscribed situations, is a monument to the principle of voluntarism. The United Nations was thus to become a part of the traditional means of conducting international relationships and not a means of transforming them.

## DEALING WITH ISSUES: PAST AND FUTURE IN INTERNATIONAL ORGANIZATION

The "problem" of international relations was not clearly defined by the wartime analysts and policy-makers. Wilson had articulated a clear set of conditions in the international system and in its constituent units which he associated with war. His British counterparts had concentrated on the problem of communication during crisis, and Clemenceau saw only an immediate problem, Germany, in a never-ending contest between nations. In the 1940s, the top policy-makers identified no single source of war or conflict. Hull and Roosevelt spoke of transforming international relations and they articulated a new theory about the economic and social conditions that bred insecurity and war. Churchill seems not to have thought deeply about these matters, and Stalin was armed with ideological assumptions about the inherent aggressiveness of capitalism (which he shelved in his wartime propaganda) but which appeared less significant than the overriding problem of ensuring against a renewal of German aggression.

In thinking about war and peace, then, there were few commonalities except a consensus regarding some of the lessons of the 1930s. The United Nations was created essentially to deal with those lessons, and in that sense it was a backward-looking organization. To the extent that the Charter endowed the organization with greater power than the League of Nations had possessed, it was because the League, with its recommendatory and unanimity principles, could not act in the event of aggression of the 1930s style. All the principals of the wartime coalition were aware of this problem and expressed a desire to overcome it. The Security Council was thus to be endowed with a capacity to identify quickly a threat to the peace or an act of aggression, to make rapid decisions, and to have the wherewithal to enforce those decisions. In pre-1945 versions of the Charter, the Council was to have deterrent as well as enforcement capabilities.

The model of international conflict implicit in the Charter is relatively simple: (1) a threat to the peace or an act of aggression is committed by states; (2) the threat and/or aggressor can be readily identified; and (3) the aggressor will normally act alone. These elements are similar to the image of war in the classical realist view of international relations. The drafters of the Charter did not contemplate murkier situations where, for example, non-state actors use force, where armies do not clearly breach recognized international borders, and where those who employ force have all sorts of ties to foreign sponsors and benefactors. The model of war incorporated in the Charter is, in brief, based on the practice of aggression in the 1930s. Other situations, such as the Nazi subversion of Czechoslovakia, were not included in the repertoire of United Nations competence. They might be handled under the procedures of conflict resolution in Chapter VI, but since this chapter rests on the principle of voluntarism – the organization can only recommend settlement procedures – the organization would be powerless to act against a party bent on conquest through subversion.

To add to the problem of a very narrow vision of the nature of aggression, the wartime leaders and planners did not develop a variety of scenarios that the new organization might confront. Roosevelt speculated about the activities of small states and believed that they could be coerced or deterred by the four policemen. On the question of great power aggression, however, the leaders worried mostly about a renewal of German military activity. Stalin, Roosevelt, and Churchill were attempting to prevent the recurrence of the present war; this was to be the supreme task of the United Nations. They agreed that for the organization to function properly, Allied unity would have to continue into the postwar period. But they did not take this analysis one step further: what would the organization do if one of the four policemen was the perpetrator of aggression? As in 1648, 1714, 1814–15, and 1919, the victors of war assume that they will remain the champions of peace. It was not, of course, a question that could be raised at the wartime meetings. There, the task was to cement unity, not to introduce embarrassing questions that could threaten that unity. Although they were certainly aware of the problem, it was not one that received collective analysis. Roosevelt and Stalin believed that wartime

Allied unity could result in about fifty years of peace, but this estimation may have resulted more from their evaluation of the consequences of Germany's military defeat and dismemberment than from
speculation about other sources of international conflict. In brief, the
Allied leaders' thoughts about the postwar world were Eurocentric,
backward-looking in defining the nature of threats, and focused on the
problem of German resurgence. They did not anticipate the kinds of
issues and behavior that were likely to arise elsewhere, involving
different states or actors, and different kinds of threats to peace. The
experience of the 1930s commanded their minds. In this sense they
were very much in the mold of the peacemakers following previous
great wars.

An important caveat has to be added. American planners were
concerned with two new problems: economic liberalization and colonialism. On these two issues, they were forward-looking, anticipating new difficulties and tasks rather than merely replaying the past.
We have already seen how Hull and his colleagues were committed to
the construction of a liberal economic order and how they had hypothesized on the basis of the depression experience that competitive
mercantilism, protectionism, and the search for autarky result both in
lower welfare and in armed conflict. Hull's emphasis on the necessity
of guaranteeing free access to sources of raw materials may have been
an acknowledgment of the economic pressures that had propelled
Japan to war in the 1930s. The liberal international economic order
envisioned in Washington during the war was not so much a search for
hegemony, much less a deliberate form of imperialism, as it was a
response to the perceived linkages between depression, trade restriction, and war. The United Nations and the organizations launched at
Bretton Woods in 1944 were to take upon themselves an array of social
and economic activities not just to expand American economic influence in the world, but more importantly, to build the bases of world
peace. The linkage between economics and politics was clear and
persistent in the thought of America's postwar planners. Indeed,
American articulation of a new and different set of international
problems was probably the greatest contribution to postwar order that
any of the wartime allies made.

Similarly, the United States, personified in Roosevelt's thought on
the matter, was the only power to give serious thought to the problem
of colonialism in the postwar world. The process of decolonization and
the task of creating new states has been the premier source of war and
violence in the postwar world (see next chapter). Roosevelt and his
colleagues could not have foreseen how bloody the globalization of the

269

states system would become, but at least they anticipated that here was a new issue that should command serious attention. The solution to the problem was not particularly far-seeing – the Trusteeship Council's mandate was rather limited and the Americans did not press the allies to decolonize – but it represented at least a step forward in the sense that both the British and the French more or less had to concede that the long-run purpose of colonialism was to foster the capacity for ultimate self-government and to advance the welfare of the colonial peoples. Roosevelt did not achieve nearly so much as he had hoped on this issue, but here again the exigencies of wartime alliance unity intruded.

Both the French and the British were committed to maintaining or reestablishing their colonial positions; even during the San Francisco conference the French fought their way back into Syria, much to the angered amazement of the independent Arab countries. The Charter of the United Nations was not drafted with these kinds of problems in mind. Wars of national liberation, guerrilla conflicts, and armed rebellion against colonial authority were not yet visible on the international horizon, and they remained a matter of vague conjecture among most of the postwar planners. Intellectually, the people who thought about the world after the defeat of Germany and Japan were predominantly Eurocentric. The major task of the United Nations was to avoid repeating the mistakes of 1919 and to prevent a recurrence of the economic and military events of the 1930s. Matters involving the colonial domains were at best peripheral. The new world that was to emerge from the ashes of German and Japanese defeat was still a world where security was defined in European (and partly Asian) terms. Hull and Roosevelt anticipated the globalization of international politics, with new types of issues and corresponding tasks, but they could not push beyond the problems that formed the intellectual universe of their wartime allies.

# 11 THE DIVERSIFICATION OF WARFARE: ISSUES AND ATTITUDES IN THE CONTEMPORARY INTERNATIONAL SYSTEM

The blessings of peace which mankind enjoys today do not come from the gods. They are the concrete result of the staunch resistance of the peace forces to attempts to unleash nuclear war, as a result of the growing power of the Soviet Union and other socialist countries.
                                                                    Mikhail Suslov, 1964

All wars that are progressive are just, and all wars that impede progress are unjust . . . Not only do we Communists not oppose just wars, we actively participate in them.          Mao Tse-tung, 1938

Bear in mind that we had . . . a monopoly on nuclear weapons for some years and never used them. And that is . . . widely known to the Soviets, that we would never launch a first strike . . . And all of their attacks, and all of their preparations – I should say, and all of their acquisitions in the military field in the last few years – have been offensive in character.          Caspar Weinberger, 1983

As the balance between costs, risks, and advantages has shifted with the development of weapons of mass destruction, the menu of policy alternatives to war has expanded. For most contemporary governments, the choice is no longer between diplomacy and war. Many other instruments of persuasion, leverage, and/or control exist. The techniques of subversion perfected by the Nazis in the interwar period and emulated subsequently by most of the great powers and some minor ones as well are available. So are propaganda, transfers of arms, military training, economic forms of coercion and reward, and many others. Most of them can be employed singly or in combination. The cast of characters that has employed subversion, economic coercion, limited forms of intervention, all techniques short of organized military campaigns, includes all the major powers as well as Iran, Syria, Iraq, Libya, India, Ghana, Somalia, Indonesia, Nicaragua, and many others.

The ways that force can be employed have also proliferated. In contrast to the eighteenth and nineteenth centuries, today the instruments of violence can be calibrated in a variety of ways to deter or threaten opponents. These can range at the low end of the spectrum from subtle but coercive military maneuvers and displays to more potent signaling devices such as warnings, alerts, call-ups, and demonstrations of force. Because of the low mobility and slow speed of land forces in previous eras, such tactics were seldom employed. The ladder of escalation then moves up to limited surgical strikes (such as the American bombing of Libya in 1986), through various forms of reprisals (Israeli strikes against P.L.O. bases in Lebanon following terrorist incidents), constrained interventions (the United States in Vietnam until 1965), limited but overt interventions (the United States and Grenada), to limited conventional wars, and so forth. A typical foreign policy problem facing many governments today is to find that mix of activities that will achieve or defend purposes or settle issues short of the overt and massive use of military power. It is when these alternatives fail that war in the classical sense often breaks out.

In the second half of the twentieth century, the forms of armed combat have diversified to the point where we can no longer speak of war as a single institution of the states system. Few formalities (declarations of war) are exchanged, the identity of parties employing force is not always easy to establish, many civil wars have become internationalized, and some military actions do not conform to the traditional idea of two or more organized armies fighting against each other. If war was once an institution in the sense that it had established norms, rules, etiquettes, and standardized strategies and tactics, that is no longer the case today. The uses of force for political purposes range from intifadas, terrorism, and guerrilla wars, through peacekeeping interventions, to conventional set warfare between organized armies.

Because of the great variations of force in contemporary international relationships, there is a significant problem in identifying cases of "war." The Correlates of War Project at the University of Michigan has identified 18 interstate wars and 12 "extra-systemic" wars in the period 1945–80 (Small and Singer, 1982:59–60), while Evan Luard (1988:61) states that there have been at least 127 "significant" wars since 1945. Others, such as a study prepared by the Canadian Department of National Defense's Operations Research and Analysis Establishment (1981), have even higher numbers.

As the forms of the use of force have proliferated, it becomes increasingly difficult to employ traditional, Eurocentric conceptions of war for research purposes. To limit the instances of the use of force in international relations solely to those situations where two distinct national armies engage each other with the objective of inflicting enough casualties and destruction of matériel to compel one party to surrender, with a minimum of 1,000 casualties, would be to overlook a great deal of state-organized violence in contemporary international relations. I will therefore include various wars of national liberation and armed interventions. Most interventions have had as their purpose something more akin to police functions: restoring or maintaining order in a client state, often as a means of shoring up a beleaguered ally. In fact the two types of phenomena, war and armed intervention, appear to be going in opposite directions: the incidence of classical interstate wars has declined dramatically, from 1.69 wars per nation in the 1816–97 period to 0.75 wars per nation in the 1898–1980 period (Small and Singer, 1982:129). Or, to make the periods more precise and of higher contrast, the number of classical wars begun, per state, was 0.70 in the relatively peaceful 1816–48 period, whereas for the postwar period until 1980, the figure had declined to 0.23 (Small and Singer, 1982:131). Meanwhile, the number of interventions where military activity was not directed against an opposing army has grown rapidly. There were eight such events in the 1815–1914 period, whereas for the 44-year period since 1945 there have already been ten clear cases.

The items in table 11.1 thus contain wars both in the sense that Small and Singer have employed and operationalized the term, and in the sense of the organized uses of force where neither the destruction of an opposing military force nor 1,000 battle casualties resulted. The reason for this choice, aside from the murky problems of definition, derives from the research purposes. We have not been concerned with measuring war in terms of its incidence, duration, costs, and the like. The problem for examination is the identification of the issues and stakes that were in contention prior to the use of force. It was the issues and stakes at risk that prompted the policy-makers to employ force; that 1,000 or more casualties did not ensue was more a consequence of the type of military operations that developed after the decision had been made than a result of careful calculations by the policy-makers. Aside from those classical wars that conform to the Small–Singer criteria, the rules for inclusion (but with some significant exceptions) derive from the following questions: (1) was at least one of the parties a recognized state in the international system (as indicated by membership in the United Nations)? (2) did one or more of the parties employ regular military units, as an exception to normal policy, in the territory of a separate political jurisdiction? That jurisdiction could be a colonial territory (we will overlook legal fictions; for example, Algeria as a *département* of France); and (3) did these regular troops maintain a

273

Table 11.1 *Wars and issues, 1945–89*

| Wars/major armed interventions | Issues for original combatants |
| --- | --- |
| 1. Indonesia (rebels)–Netherlands (1945–1949) | 1. national liberation/state creation (I.)<br>2. maintain integrity of empire (N.) |
| 2. Vietminh–France (Bao Dai) (1946–1954) | 1. national liberation/state creation (V.M.)<br>2. ideological liberation (V.M.)<br>3. maintain integrity of empire (F.) |
| 3. India–Pakistan (Pathans) (1947–1948) | 1. ethnic/religious unification (P.)<br>2. territory<br>3. national consolidation (I.) |
| 4. Jewish settlers–Great Britain (1946–1948) | 1. national liberation/state creation (J.)<br>2. maintain integrity of mandate (G.B.)<br>3. population protection/peacekeeping (G.B.)<br>4. strategic territory (G.B.) |
| 5. Malay Insurgency (1948–1960) | 1. national liberation/state creation (M.)<br>2. ideological liberation (M.)<br>3. ethnic unity (M.)<br>4. population protection/peacekeeping (G.B.) |
| 6. India–Hyderabad (1948) | 1. national consolidation (I.)<br>2. state survival (H.) |
| 7. Israel–Arab League (1948–1949) | 1. national liberation/state creation (I.)<br>2. nation survival (A.)<br>3. protect ethnic/religious confrères (A.) |
| 8. North Korea–South Korea (1950–1953) | 1. national unification (N.K.)<br>2. ideological liberation (N.K.)<br>3. state/regime survival (S.K.) |
| 9. U.S.A.–North Korea (1950–1953) | 1. meet treaty obligations (collective security) (U.S.)<br>2. defend/support ally (U.S.)<br>3. maintain balance of power (U.S.) |
| 10. People's Republic of China–U.S.A. (1950–1953) | 1. national security (C.)<br>2. defend/support ally (C.) |
| 11. China–Tibet (1950–1951) | 1. national consolidation (C.)<br>2. ideological liberation (C.)<br>3. state/regime survival (T.) |
| 12. Tunisia–France (1952–1956) | 1. national liberation/state creation (T.)<br>2. maintain integrity of state (F.) |

Table 11.1 *continued*

| Wars/major armed interventions | Issues for original combatants |
|---|---|
| 13. Morocco–France (1953–1956) | 1. national liberation/state creation (M.)<br>2. maintain integrity of state (F.) |
| 14. F.L.N.–France (1954–1962) | 1. national liberation/state creation (F.L.N.)<br>2. maintain integrity of state (F.) |
| 15. E.O.K.A.–Great Britain (1955–1960) | 1. national liberation/state creation (E.O.K.A.)<br>2. strategic territory (G.B.) |
| 16. U.S.S.R.–Hungary (1956) | 1. autonomy (H.)<br>2. national security (U.S.S.R.)<br>3. preserve alliance unity (U.S.S.R.)<br>4. government composition<br>5. protect ideological confrères (U.S.S.R.) |
| 17. Israel (France, Great Britain)–Egypt (1956) | 1. strategic territory (I., G.B.)<br>2. commerce/navigation<br>3. autonomy (E.)<br>4. enforce treaty terms (G.B.)<br>5. prevent regional hegemony (G.B.) |
| 18. Nicaragua–Honduras (1957) | 1. territory<br>2. enforce treaty obligations (arbitral award) (H.) |
| 19. U.S.A.–Lebanon (1958) | 1. defend/support ally (U.S.)<br>2. government composition |
| 20. North Vietnam (Viet Cong)–South Vietnam (1958–1975) | 1. national unification (N.V.N., V.C.)<br>2. ideological liberation (N.V.N., V.C.)<br>3. regime/state survival (S.V.N.) |
| 21. Katanga (Belgium)–Congo (U.N.) (1961) | 1. secession/state creation<br>2. protect nationals/commercial interests abroad (B.)<br>3. maintain integrity of state (C., U.N.) |
| 22. India–Portugal (Goa) (1961) | 1. national consolidation (I.)<br>2. colonialism (I.)<br>3. maintain integrity of empire (P.) |
| 23. U.S.A.–Cuba (1961) | 1. government composition (U.S.)<br>2. ideological liberation (U.S.)<br>3. regime survival (C.) |
| 24. Egypt–Yemen (1962- 1967) | 1. government composition<br>2. defend/support ally (E.) |
| 25. E.P.R.L.–Ethiopia (1962– ) | 1. secession/state creation (E.P.R.L.)<br>2. maintain integrity of state (E.)<br>3. strategic territory (E.) |
| 26. India–China (1962) | 1. territory (border dispute) |

Table 11.1 *continued*

| Wars/major armed interventions | Issues for original combatants |
|---|---|
| 27. Portuguese Guinea–Portugal (1962–1974) | 1. national liberation/state creation<br>2. maintain integrity of empire (P.) |
| 28. Indonesia–Malaysia (1963–1966) | 1. territory (West Irian)<br>2. colonialism (I.)<br>3. maintain integrity of state (M.) |
| 29. Mozambique (N.L.F.)–Portugal (1965–1975) | 1. national liberation/state creation (N.L.F.)<br>2. ideological liberation (N.L.F.)<br>3. maintain integrity of empire (P.) |
| 30. U.S.A.–Dominican Republic (1965) | 1. government composition<br>2. protect nationals/commercial interests abroad (U.S.)<br>3. population protection/peacekeeping (U.S.) |
| 31. India–Pakistan (1965) | 1. ethnic/religious unity (P.)<br>2. national consolidation (I.)<br>3. territory |
| 32. U.S.A.–Viet Cong (North Vietnam) (1965–1975) | 1. defend/support ally (U.S.)<br>2. meet treaty obligations (U.S.)<br>3. strategic territory (U.S.)<br>4. national unification (N.V.N.)<br>5. ideological liberation (V.C./N.V.N.) |
| 33. SWAPO–South Africa (1966–1969) | 1. national liberation/state creation (SWAPO)<br>2. strategic territory (S.A.)<br>3. commerce/resources (S.A.) |
| 34. Biafra–Nigeria (1967) | 1. secession/independence (B.)<br>2. ethnic/religious unification (B.)<br>3. maintain integrity of state (N.)<br>4. commerce/resources |
| 35. Israel–Egypt (1967) | 1. national survival (I.)<br>2. strategic territory<br>3. commerce/navigation<br>4. territory<br>5. liberate ethnic/religious confrères (E.) |
| 36. ZAPA, ZANU (Angola, Zambia, Tanzania)–Rhodesia (S. Africa) (1967–1980) | 1. government composition<br>2. majority rule principle<br>3. regime survival (R.) |
| 37. M.P.L.A. (Zaire, Zambia)–Portugal (1968–1974) | 1. national liberation/state creation (M.P.L.A.)<br>2. maintain integrity of empire (P.) |
| 38. U.S.S.R.–Czechoslovakia (1968) | 1. government composition<br>2. preserve alliance unity (U.S.S.R.)<br>3. protect ideological confrères (U.S.S.R.) |

Table 11.1 *continued*

| Wars/major armed interventions | Issues for original combatants |
|---|---|
| 39. El Salvador–Honduras (1969) | 1. territory (border dispute)<br>2. protect nationals abroad (El Sal.)<br>3. prevent population movement/refugees (H.)<br>4. enforce domestic legislation (H.) |
| 40. Mukti Bahini (India)–Pakistan (1971) | 1. secession/independence<br>2. protect ethnic confrères (I.)<br>3. territory (Kashmir)<br>4. prevent population movement/refugees (I.)<br>5. maintain integrity of state (P.) |
| 41. Egypt, Syria–Israel (1973) | 1. territory<br>2. strategic territory<br>3. national survival (I.) |
| 42. Turkish Cypriots (Turkey) E.O.K.A. (Cyprus) (1974) | 1. protect ethnic confrères (T.)<br>2. ethnic unification (E.O.K.A.)<br>3. government composition<br>4. autonomy (Tur. Cypriots) |
| 43. Polisario–Mauritania, Morocco (1974– ) | 1. national liberation/state creation (P.)<br>2. territory<br>3. commerce/resources (Ma., Mo)<br>4. ethnic/language unification (Ma.) |
| 44. Angola (Cuba)–UNITA (S. Africa) (1975– ) | 1. government composition<br>2. commerce/resources<br>3. defend/support ally (Cuba, S. Af.) |
| 45. East Timor (U.D.T., Upodeti, Fretilius)–Indonesia (1975) | 1. national liberation/state creation (T.)<br>2. national consolidation (I.)<br>3. government composition |
| 46. Syria–Lebanon (1976– ) | 1. government composition<br>2. strategic territory (S.)<br>3. protect religious confrères (S.)<br>4. protect population/peace-keeping (S.) |
| 47. Somalia–Ethiopia (1977–1978) | 1. ethnic unification (S.)<br>2. territory<br>3. protect integrity of state (E.)<br>4. strategic territory |
| 48. Vietnam–Kampuchea (1978–1979) | 1. territory (border dispute)<br>2. government composition (V.N.)<br>3. humanitarian aid (V.N.)<br>4. regime survival (K.)<br>5. maintain regional dominance (V.N.) |
| 49. Uganda–Tanzania (1978) | 1. territory (border dispute)<br>2. government composition (T.) |

Table 11.1 *continued*

| Wars/major armed interventions | Issues for original combatants |
|---|---|
| 50. Libya–Chad (France) (1978–1987) | 1. government composition<br>2. defend/support ally (F.)<br>3. commerce/resources (C., L.)<br>4. territory (C., L.) |
| 51. U.S.S.R.–Afghanistan (1979–1989) | 1. defend/protect ally (U.S.S.R.)<br>2. government composition<br>3. national security (protect borders) (U.S.S.R.)<br>4. autonomy/independence (rebels) |
| 52. China–Vietnam (1979) | 1. maintain regional dominance<br>2. territory (Spratly, Paracel) |
| 53. Iraq–Iran (1979–1989) | 1. strategic territory<br>2. territory |
| 54. South Yemen–North Yemen (1979) | 1. territory (border dispute)<br>2. national unification (S.Y.) |
| 55. Israel–P.L.O. (Lebanon) (1982) | 1. strategic territory (I.)<br>2. protect domestic population (I.)<br>3. national liberation/state creation (P.L.O.) |
| 56. Argentina–Great Britain (1982) | 1. territory<br>2. regime survival (A.)<br>3. protect nationals/commercial interests abroad (G.B.)<br>4. self-determination (G.B.)<br>5. colonialism (A.) |
| 57. U.S.A.–Grenada (1983) | 1. government composition (U.S.)<br>2. protect nationals/commercial interests abroad (U.S.)<br>3. regime survival (G.)<br>4. maintain regional dominance (U.S.) |
| 58. U.S.A.–Lebanon (1983) | 1. population protection/peacekeeping (U.S.)<br>2. support/defend ally (U.S.) |

physical presence of at least two weeks in that separate political jurisdiction (thus excluding phenomena such as the American bombing raid on Libya in 1986)?

Table 11.1 lists the 58 wars/interventions that meet the criteria. Twenty-two were wars in the classical form of two states employing established military force against each other. The remainder were wars of national liberation undertaken by irregular forces, various military interventions, usually to prop up or topple regimes, and several cases that might better be termed "peacekeeping," where the purpose was to maintain or restore order, to put an end to fighting, and/or to protect the citizens and economic interests of the intervening party. While these operations did not usually involve 1,000 or more battle casualties, they were undertaken by the regular military forces of one state in the territory of another political jurisdiction, and the decisions to employ those forces were made in the expectation that there would be fighting and casualties.

Some of the cases are no doubt marginal, and the reader may question some judgments. The Chinese invasion of Tibet in 1950, for example, was a war only if one assumes that Tibet was a sovereign state at that time. Otherwise it would be a civil war. Some cases may have been overlooked. But it is unlikely that the addition or deletion of a few cases would significantly alter the profile of issues that have generated international conflict and war in the period since 1945.

Table 11.2 lists the frequencies that the various issues appeared as sources of war and interventions. Several of the figures are notable. Government composition, which was a relatively minor issue in all of the previous periods, now ranks first. This reflects the cold war competition between the United States and the Soviet Union, where control over governments of client states, friends, and allies was more important as a means of conducting the competition against the opponent than control over territory or resources. The second significant figure is the number of wars whose essential purpose was to create states. We will return to this finding below. A third interesting figure is the number of occasions when the subject of contention was the continued existence of a state or regime (7 percent of all issues). The resulting wars were total in the sense that the purpose of armed combat was not just to defeat the enemy's military forces, but to eliminate the opponent as an international actor or a government. In the investigation that goes back to 1648, this is the third highest ranking that state/regime survival has achieved in any of the constituent periods. It was surpassed only in the immediate post-Westphalia period and during the 1930s.

A final observation is the number of separate issues that have generated international conflicts and wars in the postwar period. Twenty-four issues appear at least twice. In part this is an artifact of the investigator's judgment where, for example, a distinction is made between wars over territory and boundary disputes. This may be a quantitative rather than qualitative distinction. Wars over the exact location of boundaries involve territory, but there is a preexisting acknowledgment of and legitimacy for a territorial distribution of the past. The issue is to determine an exact location. In wars involving

279

Table 11.2 *Distribution of issues that generated wars, 1945–89*

| Issues | Frequency | % of all issues | Previous period % |
|---|---|---|---|
| Government composition | 16 | 9 | 5 |
| National liberation/state creation | 16 | 9 | 4 |
| Maintain integrity of state/empire | 16 | 9 | 9 |
| Territory | 14 | 8 | 14 |
| State/regime survival | 12 | 7 | 11 |
| Strategic territory | 12 | 7 | 9 |
| National unification/consolidation | 10 | 6 | — |
| Defend/support ally | 9 | 5 | 3 |
| Ideological liberation | 8 | 4 | 3 |
| Ethnic/religious unification | 7 | 4 | 5 |
| Commerce/resources | 5 | 3 | 6 |
| Protect nationals/commercial interests abroad | 5 | 3 | 5 |
| Protect ethnic/religious confrères abroad | 5 | 3 | 2 |
| Population protection/peacekeeping | 5 | 3 | — |
| Territory (boundary dispute) | 4 | 2 | — |
| Meet treaty obligations/enforce treaty terms | 4 | 2 | 9 |
| Autonomy | 4 | 2 | 2 |
| Secession/state creation | 4 | 2 | — |
| National security (border threat) | 3 | 2 | — |
| Colonialism | 3 | 2 | — |
| Maintain regional dominance | 3 | 2 | 2 |
| Prevent population movement/refugees | 3 | 2 | — |
| Protect ideological confrères | 2 | 1 | — |
| Preserve alliance unity | 2 | 1 | — |
| Commerce/navigation | 2 | 1 | — |
| Other | 7 | 4 | — |
| Total | 183 | 99 | |

territorial spoils, in contrast, the purpose is to alter fundamentally a preexisting and commonly acknowledged distribution. National unification/consolidation also needs explanation. National unification wars took place between units of a formerly unified political entity (e.g., Korea), whereas consolidation wars incorporated territories that had no previous, formal status as an integral part of a large entity (e.g., India and Goa). An alternative designation might be wars of reunification and wars of unification.

But even allowing for these rather fine distinctions, the number of issues in the list is unprecedentedly extensive, reflecting no doubt the increasing complexity of international relationships and stakes that involve important national values. We live in an age when economic resources, nationalism, religion, ideology, state creation, national security, ethnic affiliation, territory, spheres of influence (regional domination), and many other values coexist and frequently conflict. Those who have seen in growing global interdependence a stabilizing and pacifying factor for international relations have oversimplified the consequences of this trend. Whatever the special characteristics and consequences of increasing commercial and communications links between societies, they have not eliminated or muted the proliferation of stakes, issues, and passions for which men are willing to fight.

Table 11.3 displays the frequency that particular issues were contributing factors to wars and interventions, comparing these with the interwar period. Again, the themes of government composition and state creation emerge in positions much higher than in the previous period. Territory remains, however, a significant and continuing source of international conflict. Ideological liberation reaches a historically high figure, a source of 14 percent of the armed conflicts. Items such as protection of ideological confrères, secession, fighting colonialism or neo-colonialism, and preserving alliance unity are all new issues and stakes on the international agenda. Maintenance of state/nation/empire integrity appeared in previous periods, but except for 1919–41, at much lower levels. Its high ranking for the post-1945 period reflects the attempts of the colonial powers to hold on to their overseas territories or to disengage according to their own timetables and transition formulae rather than those of national liberation movements.

In order to highlight the major cleavages in the international system and to identify separate issues that converge on similar stakes, table 11.4 compresses several of the issues into three clusters or "mega-issues." The figures are the combined frequencies of the issues listed in table 11.3. Here we see unmistakably the two major dimensions of conflict in the postwar world: the cold war, and in the Third World, the search for statehood. The first deals with the deep ideological divisions that underlay the Soviet–American relationship and the attempt by the United States to form some sort of balance of power that would incorporate what for many years was termed the "free world" under effective American leadership and protection. The conflict in many cases was fought in terms of establishing and maintaining reliable and ideologically compatible allies and clients abroad. The composition of foreign governments was one of the major indices of the state of the balance. Almost one-half of the wars of the 1945–89 period had government composition and ideological liberation as critical issues and purposes underlying the conflict.

But even more significant has been the problem of decolonization and the birth of new states. Although this process has frequently

Table 11.3 *Issues that generated wars, 1945–89*

| Issues | Frequency | % of wars | Previous period % |
|---|---|---|---|
| Government composition | 16 | 28 | 17 |
| National liberation/state creation | 16 | 28 | 13 |
| Maintain integrity of state/empire | 16 | 28 | 30 |
| Territory | 14 | 24 | 47 |
| State/regime survival | 12 | 21 | 37 |
| Strategic territory | 12 | 21 | 30 |
| National unification/consolidation | 10 | 17 | — |
| Defend/support ally | 9 | 16 | 10 |
| Ideological liberation | 8 | 14 | 10 |
| Ethnic/religious unification/irredenta | 7 | 12 | 17 |
| Commerce/resources | 5 | 9 | 20 |
| Protect nationals/commercial interests abroad | 5 | 9 | 17 |
| Protect ethnic/religious confrères abroad | 5 | 9 | 7 |
| Population protection/peacekeeping | 5 | 9 | — |
| Territory (border dispute) | 4 | 7 | — |
| Meet treaty obligations/enforce treaty terms | 4 | 7 | 30 |
| Autonomy | 4 | 7 | 7 |
| Secession/state creation | 4 | 7 | — |
| National security/immediate threat | 3 | 5 | — |
| Colonialism | 3 | 5 | — |
| Maintain regional dominance | 3 | 5 | 7 |
| Prevent population movement/refugees | 3 | 5 | — |
| Protect ideological confrères | 2 | 3 | — |
| Preserve alliance unity | 2 | 3 | — |
| Commerce/navigation | 2 | 3 | — |
| Other | 7 | 12 | — |
| Total | 182 | | |

become entangled with cold war issues, the dynamics are not the same. State creation is a process that began as a serious source of international conflict in the early nineteenth century. It slowed down after the great wave of self-determination following the First World War, but spread to the colonies during and immediately after the Second World War. The combined issues of national liberation, national unification/consolidation, and secession – all designed to create and establish states – were major sources of war in 52 percent of the fifty-eight conflicts.

Finally, more than one-half of the conflicts had a territorial dimension: either gaining or maintaining control over strategically significant pieces of real estate (e.g., Great Britain attempted to maintain sovereignty over Cyprus in the 1950s primarily because of its military bases there), more general concerns over territory (e.g., Indonesia and West

Iran), or over the precise demarcation of boundaries (China and India). This aspect of international conflict remains fairly constant throughout all of the periods of this study, although there has been a decline in the incidence of wars that had non-strategic territorial spoils as a major source of conflict.

The figures in table 11.4 suggest that there are really two different international systems, connected in significant ways, yet distinct in the etiologies and profiles of their conflicts. The first is a "mature" system that is the progeny of the European states system of the seventeenth to twentieth centuries, albeit with two revolutionary departures, nuclear weapons, and Marxist-Leninist ideology. The identity of most of the players is well established and they constitute relatively well-integrated societies, where external threats are generally more significant than internal ones. Boundaries and state consolidation were achieved by 1919 or shortly after and threats of secession (with a few notable exceptions such as the Basques and the Baltic peoples) are dormant or have disappeared.

The other system is new. The players are not well established in the sense of having a long history of statehood, secure boundaries, an absence of secession movements, and generally impermeable societies and government structures. Regimes, some of dubious legitimacy and others highly penetrated by foreign agents, tend to face more internal threats in the form of attempted *coups d'état*, secession, ethnic, language, and religious violence, and subversion, than external threats. Many are only conditionally viable, existing on the sufferance of external patrons through military and economic assistance. The stakes of politics for them are primarily sovereignty-related: establishing some reasonably well-defined national identity, creating stable borders, controlling a permanent population, and in general trying to keep themselves together as something akin to a modern state. Their

Table 11.4 *Mega-issues and war, 1945–89*

| Issue | Frequency | % of wars |
|---|---|---|
| National liberation + national unification/consolidation + secession/state creation | 30 | 52 |
| Territory + strategic territory + boundary | 30 | 52 |
| Government composition + ideological liberation + protect ideological confrères | 26 | 45 |

fragility derives in part from the fact that their international status as states was created by other members of the international community, even though most of them had not and could not meet the traditional legal criteria of sovereignty and nationhood: a well-defined territory, control over a permanent population, capacity to enter into international agreements, and the like. In the European states system, members were sovereign in fact, prior to their entrance into the international club. Since 1945, the international community has created the new states, in many cases before those states existed in fact (Jackson, 1987). And to compound their problems, most of the new states are composed of two or more nations or other significant socio-political units. The states are often weak in various dimensions of social control, legitimacy, well-established constitutional procedures, and rules for succession of regimes and top political personnel. Not infrequently, the most organized and disciplined social units are the armed forces, themselves often the seekers of political power.

The security problems of the inhabitants of the two systems are thus quite distinct. For the old and established, it is to avoid nuclear war while maintaining a capacity to resist external coercion and intimidation. Security is needed to uphold a vision of the good life and to help those who share that vision. For the new, it is to survive both domestic and external assaults on statehood and regimes, while attempting to create integrated societies and provide some leadership in the area of economic development (K. J. Holsti, 1989).

## THE ISSUES

The category commerce/resources appears five times in the list of issues. This has reference to armed conflicts in which one or more of the combatants sought to gain control over or access to specific resources. There have been recent suggestions to the effect that in an interdependent world, economic issues for a variety of reasons are not likely to cause wars and other forms of armed conflict. We will return to this question in the next chapter in a discussion of issues of the future, but we should note here that whatever may be the case in the economic relations among the industrial countries, attempts to gain control over resources need not be peaceful ones – at least not in the Third World, and not when access to oil for the industrial countries may be threatened. The contest between Mauritania, Morocco, and the Polisario over western Sahara involves a resource dimension, the large phosphate deposits at BuCraa; and Libya's intervention in Chad has had a source located in the uranium deposits in the Aozou strip. Though not listed in table 11.1, Greece and Turkey went to the brink of war in 1986 regarding issues of territorial jurisdiction over the Aegean seabed and Turkish exploration for oil in disputed areas. A number of potentially-lethal disputes over resources were probably preempted by the new law of the sea, but when we consider that for some small, developing nations access to and control over resources is vital for national survival (e.g., fisheries for the Pacific Island states), it is not unlikely that force will become an occasional arbiter of conflicting claims and actions to secure those claims.

A new issue of interest arises from large population/refugee movements. Most of these have been the results of both international and civil wars (e.g., Pakistan in 1971); refugees stream to a neighboring country to escape the killing and destruction. In other cases, the population movement results from overcrowding and highly concentrated landholding patterns, depletion of resources, and conversion of land to low labor-intensive activities such as cattle-ranching (e.g., El Salvador). Refugees migrate searching for land, economic security, and employment without going through formal immigration and citizenship proceedings. The El Salvador–Honduras War of 1969 had such an etiology, and in several instances similar patterns developed in Africa but were handled without significant bloodshed.

The remainder of the issues should be reasonably clear and familiar. We turn, then, to a discussion of the "meaning" of war in the post-1945 period. Again, we see two distinct sets of attitudes, reflecting the two types of international systems that have emerged since the end of the last great world war.

## ATTITUDES TOWARD WAR

There has been no general war in more than forty-five years, and with the Korean case a marginal one, no direct war between the major powers in the same period. This fact is unprecedented in the history of the states system since the Treaties of Westphalia. Yet, the raw incidence of war has increased dramatically since 1945. The combination of the higher incidence of warfare with the lower incidence of inter-great power war would suggest that there are different logics at work in the different international systems. As we have seen, almost all war since 1945 has taken place in what we generally call the Third World. There are numerous explanations for this trend, but here we will concentrate only on the comparisons of attitudes. The argument is, briefly, that warfare in the Third World (including military activities of the great powers in these areas) has been generally perceived as relatively low in costs and risks, while the advantages or necessities have been perceived as significant. In contrast, the immense destructive power of nuclear weapons has fundamentally altered the relationship between costs, risks, and advantages in the relationships among the great powers in the European theatre. Different types and degrees of constraints and opportunities operate in the two systems.

### The United States: facing the nuclear dilemma

By late 1946 American policy-makers faced two interconnected problems: dealing with the Soviet Union and developing a rationale for nuclear weapons. The postwar world was not developing along the lines of any of the scenarios imagined during the war against Germany and Japan. Roosevelt's strategy of trying to integrate the Soviet Union into a stable postwar world order had largely failed by late 1945. Likewise, Truman's strategy of employing economic rewards and punishments also failed to bring about desired responses (Gaddis, 1982:20). The Soviet Union was rapidly becoming identified in Washington as the new enemy. War against the Soviet Union had to be contemplated even though America had demobilized with speed in 1945 and 1946.

The intellectual response to the development of the cold war was to abandon Roosevelt's and Hull's theories about the transformation of international politics and to adopt typical balance of power thinking. George Kennan wrote in the summer of 1947 that the idea of perpetual world peace in the Wilson–Roosevelt–Hull concepts of world politics was a "premature, unworkable and grandiose form of day dreaming" (Gaddis, 1982:29). President Truman and Secretary of State George Marshall adopted this point of view firmly by late 1947, and by 1950 in the famous National Security Council Memorandum 68, the balance was depicted in brittle, zero-sum terms: any Soviet gains would be a loss for the United States. The American national security problem was how to deal with an enemy who was characterized as fundamentally hostile, dedicated to world domination, and armed with a panoply of policy instruments ranging from subversion to the employment of a growing nuclear arsenal – and to do all of this without precipitating a nuclear war.

The second problem was how to make nuclear weapons relevant to the kinds of threats posed by the Soviet Union. When the terrible destructive powers of nuclear weapons had been demonstrated against Japan in 1945, different responses emerged in Washington. Two in particular stand out. In his influential book *The Absolute Weapon*

(1946:76), Bernard Brodie made the point that the chief purpose of military forces in the past had been to win wars. In the nuclear environment their sole purpose would be to avert wars. These weapons could be used only for deterrence. The second response, represented by people like Paul Nitze, was that nuclear weapons had not been decisive in terminating the war with Japan and that they must be regarded at least initially as traditional but enhanced instruments of warfare to compel an opponent to surrender (Talbott, 1988:33–39).

There were and continue to be many variations within the boundaries established by these two views, and some people have managed to occupy positions that incorporate both perspectives. Inconsistencies and waverings back and forth between deterrence and war-fighting strategies abound. In the postwar period, there has been no fixed American war doctrine for the primary reason (there are economic reasons as well) that there is no way to solve a fundamental intellectual problem that arises from the possession of nuclear weapons. That problem is how to reconcile the use of weapons of mass destruction with classical conceptions of war.

An actor cannot use such weapons in the Clausewitzian instrumental sense of war, which assumes that parties engaged in war maintain an essential political relationship, and that they will both survive as political entities whether they win or lose a battle or a war. To say that any political value is worth national self-immolation and probably the destruction of modern civilization makes no sense. Yet, to use the weapons, even if just for deterrence, *requires both sides to believe and to act as if they would be used*. Thus, we see the phenomenon of American policy-makers, like their Soviet counterparts, underlining their rational determination to protect vital interests through the use of nuclear weapons while almost in the same breath arguing that nuclear war would represent the height of human folly.

Postwar American defense policies have fluctuated with various emphases, but each has been an attempt to come to grips with this unsolvable dilemma. There have been at least four major responses to it, all variations on the two ideal types or themes of pure deterrence and war-fighting.

The first response was to jettison the concept of war in its instrumental sense and to claim, as Brodie suggested, that the sole aim of national security policy must be war avoidance. National security policy must thus "wage peace." The main threat to the nation is not the Soviet Union, but nuclear war and any conventional war that contains a serious risk of escalation to nuclear war. As early as December 1953 President Eisenhower in a United Nations speech told his audience that even though the United States maintained a significant superiority in nuclear weapons and delivery systems, any war involving these weapons would bring "fearful material damage," including the significant probability that such a war would result in the destruction of civilization and "the condemnation of mankind to begin all over again the age-old struggle upward from savagery" (Dinerstein, 1962:69). Eisenhower's successors were to make similar statements on a variety of occasions. John Kennedy wrote to Khrushchev in 1963 that "there appear to be no differences between your views and mine regarding the need for eliminating war in this nuclear age" (Gaddis, 1982:229), and Henry Kissinger stated in 1974 that the overriding objective of American foreign and defense policy was to prevent nuclear war (Gaddis, 1982:315). Defense allocations, arms control policies, targeting lists, and a plethora of other defense-related policies have been justified in terms of their ability to reduce the risks of war, to attain a rough balance of forces, to enhance "crisis stability" (e.g., to reduce the temptation to strike first or escalate), and/or to force the cold war into channels other than military competition.

One main means of achieving war avoidance was to make nuclear war certain under specific conditions: expand the horror, ensure a holocaust, and presumably the opponent will be driven to taking fewer risks. In the 1960s the emphasis on pure deterrence came to be known as "mutual assured destruction." The policy was to develop and position weapons in such a manner that neither side could launch a first strike without facing certain and devastating retaliation. Such a deployment would in fact deter not only the Soviet Union, but would also lead to self-deterrence (avoiding certain foreign policy actions for fear of provoking war; an example is the non-intervention of the United States in the Hungarian Revolution of 1956). The problem of establishing credibility of retaliation is solved, or at least so it was thought, by making the system as automatic as possible through declaratory policy and by rendering retaliatory weapons invulnerable. The purpose was to remove any ambiguity as to what an American response to a Soviet first strike would be. The problem with the approach was that the area of choice was not really reduced. The capacity to ride out a first strike did not necessarily mean that retaliation would be automatic if the aggressor had third, fourth, and $n$th strike possibilities. The only escape from this difficulty was to build a retaliatory force of immense proportions; but the opponent could respond merely by building up its third, fourth, and subsequent strike capacities. In short, there was no way to make retaliation certain and at the same time save anything of society in case of accidental or premeditated war.

A second response to the dilemma was to conceive of nuclear weapons as war-fighting instruments, should deterrence fail. During most of the Truman administrations, when the United States held either a monopoly of atomic bombs or a pronounced superiority (and when the creation of a large standing army was still considered to be both unpopular and too costly), American authorities emphasized the war-fighting capacities of these weapons. John Foster Dulles' strategy of "massive retaliation" underlined the utility of nuclear weapons as instruments of both deterrence and punishment. The purpose of his preferred strategy was to create the maximum ambiguity regarding possible American responses to Russian "aggression," thereby reducing the probabilities that the weapons would have to be used at all. Dulles' solution to the dilemma was of course no solution, since the threat to use nuclear weapons for low-level conflicts was inherently incredible, and once the Soviets developed the capacity to retaliate in kind, the policy made no sense at all. But the important point is that the Dulles doctrine blurred the distinction between nuclear and conventional weapons, looking upon the latter as means of waging a traditional Clausewitzian war.

In 1957, Henry Kissinger published his influential volume advocating the deployment and possible use of tactical nuclear weapons in Europe (*Nuclear Weapons and Foreign Policy*). The idea was to provide the United States with a range of weapons both to enhance deterrence and to avoid the situation where, should deterrence fail, there would be only the options of surrender or waging strategic war. These ideas were translated into the official NATO strategy of "flexible response" during the early years of the Kennedy administration. The policy of providing options provoked the opposition of "pure" deterrence theorists, including Charles de Gaulle, who insisted that only the certainty of massive nuclear reprisal would prevent the Russians from undertaking adventures in Europe and elsewhere. The problem with Kissinger's position was that the threshold between tactical and strategic nuclear weapons was blurred, not only in Washington but also in Moscow. Who would establish rules of warfare that precluded the escalation of a war fought with tactical nuclear weapons into an exchange of strategic weapons? It would require an act of great faith to assume that all the parties engaged in such a conflict would agree during time of war what, exactly, constituted tactical as opposed to strategic weapons. And the amount of destruction involved in either case would render the distinction academic. Kissinger's was a classic attempt to reconcile Clausewitzian conceptions of war with nuclear weapons.

The modern version of this attempt to impose traditional war-fighting concepts on to a nuclear environment was developed during the 1980s under the Reagan administration. The strategy of "escalation domination" was based on the assumption that if the United States maintained a clear superiority of nuclear weapons of all types it could deter the Soviet Union from escalating a war to the next higher level, or indeed, from jumping several rungs up the ladder. The vision of war in this strategy was incredibly optimistic and rationalistic. Under conditions of nuclear exchanges, the parties would signal and negotiate; they would pause for reflection between salvos; they would maintain full control over the use of violence on a massive scale; and eventually the opponent would see that the costs of continuing or escalating the war outweighed any conceivable advantages. Appended to this strategy and in contradiction to it was a targeting policy that emphasized "decapitation" strikes against the opponent's communications, command, and control facilities. These strikes were to eliminate the very people and control facilities that would have to be used to maintain a rational direction of the war. This strategy did not eliminate the deterrent function of weapons, but it was based on the argument that the best deterrent is one that is capable of being used for military victory. The foreknowledge of probable defeat in the field is supposed to deter the opponent. The strategies of "flexible response" and "escalation domination" are excellent examples of attempts to impose on nuclear war the traditional concepts of military coercion, victory, defeat, and bargaining.

A third response to cope with the insoluble problems represented by nuclear weapons was to concentrate instead on conventional capabilities. This was one of the strands of thinking in Washington during the Kennedy administration. The top priority of defense planning would be to decrease reliance upon nuclear weapons, at least in the non-European theatres of conflict. The reasons for this change of emphasis were partly the recognition of the costs of nuclear war, but also the observation that nuclear weapons had been irrelevant to the kinds of war that had occurred since 1945. Guerrilla and unconventional wars were to Washington the prime problems of the 1960s, and it was relatively easy to demonstrate that the possession of nuclear weapons provided no advantages or leverage to the United States when it confronted the likes of the Viet Cong. In a State Department analysis of February 1961, the nuclear dilemma was pushed to the side in the announcement that "we attach the greatest importance to raising the threshold beyond which the President might have to decide to initiate the use of nuclear weapons." And in an address to Congress during the same month, Kennedy announced – and thereby repudiated the Dulles perspective on strategy – that local wars and wars of national liberation "do not justify and must not lead to a general nuclear attack." The United States, he suggested, had to "increase [its] ability to confine our responses to non-nuclear weapons and to lessen the incentive for any limited aggression by making clear what our response will accomplish" (Gaddis, 1982:215). Kennedy appeared to be convinced that nuclear weapons, despite all their symbolic significance as indices of national power and status, were becoming increasingly irrelevant to the real challenges. Post-mortems on the Cuban missile crisis had suggested that the successful resolution of that dangerous episode had more to do with the significant asymmetries of conventional armed strength than they did with nuclear weapons. And until the late 1960s, there was great hope in Washington that the techniques of anti-insurgency warfare, combined with generous economic assistance and doses of American-style political reform, could take care of the new form of communist aggression.

The Kennedy administration did not of course ignore the problem of deterrence. The strategy of mutual assured destruction was perfected by Kennedy's Secretary of Defense, Robert McNamara, who above all wanted to impose some form of rationality in the whole messy area of nuclear weapons. His solution was automaticity and invulnerability of weapons. It did not resolve the nuclear dilemma, however. In addition to problems already mentioned, it would work only if the Russians agreed to play by the rules he developed. During the 1960s they had other strategies in mind.

The fourth response was to eliminate nuclear weapons altogether. This could be done through negotiated disarmament agreements, through the development of fool-proof anti-ballistic missiles systems such as those proposed in March 1983 by President Reagan in the Strategic Defense Initiative, or through some combination of both approaches. Scientific evidence in the 1980s did not provide much support for the idea of a space-based anti-missile system that could protect the United States against incoming missiles. There were numerous arguments against the scheme on the grounds that it would be highly destabilizing, that it was inefficient "on the margins" (Soviet offensive build-ups could simply overwhelm the system), and newer weapons systems such as cruise missiles would simply fly beneath the umbrella of the "star wars" gadgetry that was stationed in orbit. Research on the scheme continues, but the strategy of reducing nuclear stockpiles has appeared more feasible. In Reagan's thinking, then, the best solution to the insoluble problem posed by nuclear weapons was simply to get rid of them.

The portraits of these four responses are ideal types and are not mutually exclusive. American strategic policy has reflected them in various combinations and emphases. At no time has an administration failed to place a number of eggs in the deterrence basket, but no administration has relied exclusively on nuclear weapons. The United States has learned to live with the dilemma of the inherent lack of credibility of nuclear weapons, shifting back and forth between various assumed solutions to the insoluble problem. The twists and turns of policy have had their sources in economic constraints, the developments of new weapons technologies, alterations in the external environment, and many other factors.

Underlying all variations of the deterrence and war-fighting strategies was a consensus on the essential malevolence of the Soviet Union. The standard analytical device for inferring Soviet intentions was to estimate its capabilities. As the opening quotation to the chapter by Caspar Weinberger indicates, these capabilities were presumed to be configured for an attack. American deployments are characterized as solely defensive, Soviet interpretations to the contrary notwithstanding. Through the 1940s and 1950s most professional military thinkers and several presidents defined the primary threat to the United States as a surprise Soviet nuclear attack. This was Eisenhower's nightmare, and it resurfaced as the most serious presumed threat during the Reagan administration. This time it was dubbed the "window of vulnerability," the erosion of America's ability to retaliate with immense force against a Soviet first strike. But in all the debates about first and second strikes, vulnerabilities, "gaps," and the like, there was never a convincing evaluation of the probabilities that the Soviet Union would launch such a strike even in the most favorable circumstances. Soviet plans to unleash a nuclear war, given a reasonable opportunity of a successful first strike were simply assumed. None of the incessant strategic debates that continued since the late 1940s was based on an empirical validation of Soviet intentions, on authoritative analyses of the links between Soviet military doctrines and Marxism-Leninism, or on any other analysis that somehow sought to establish the "strike out of the blue" as a realistic scenario upon which to base a nation's defense policies. NSC–68 seems to have established once and for all that the goal of the Soviet Union was world conquest according to some master plan and that the Soviet Union would not flinch from furthering its goals by nuclear war, given a reasonable opportunity. The legacy of Pearl Harbor dominated American strategic thinking in many ways.

The second nightmare was a conventional attack against one or more of America's allies. NATO and a variety of bilateral and regional alliances was the response to this problem. In terms of strategy, nuclear weapons would be the means to compensate for the Soviet Union's vast manpower and other forms of superiority in the central sector. It was not until the Kennedy administration that concern with conventional wars in the Third World began to command significant attention. This was in part a response to the dilemmas posed by nuclear weapons, but also to the successful guerrilla campaigns waged by Fidel Castro and the Viet Cong, and to Khrushchev's and Mao Tse-tung's public and vigorous espousal of "wars of national liberation." In Washington, such wars were seen primarily through the lens of the East–West conflict. There would have to be American involvement in them through economic assistance, psychological warfare, counterinsurgency operations, and the like. The literature of the period, which generally reflected official thinking in Washington, assumed that these wars were necessarily against the interests of the United States and more or less inspired through Soviet and/or Chinese prompting.

During the latter years of the Reagan administration, there was a renewed interest in wars of the Third World. The difference from the Kennedy years was that officials in Washington began to see these wars as independent of the East–West conflict, that they might have essentially regional or local etiologies. But this did not diminish American interest and possible involvement in them. On the contrary, the Commission on Integrated Long-Term Strategy, which included such luminaries as Henry Kissinger, Fred Iklé, and Zbigniew Brzezinski, reported in January 1988 that although these conflicts may be less threatening than a direct Soviet–American confrontation, "they have had and will have an adverse cumulative effect on U.S. access to critical regions, on American credibility among allies and friends, and on American self-confidence." Because these types of challenges are multiplying, "in the coming decades the United States will need to be better prepared to deal with conflicts in the Third World" (quoted in Klare, 1989:31). Former Secretary of Defense Frank C. Carlucci underlined this concern when he wrote in 1988 that "ambiguous aggression in the form of low intensity conflict has become an increasing threat to our interests, as well as those of our allies and friends" (quoted in Klare, 1989:31). The point is reasonably explicit: regardless of whether or not a conflict in the Third World is linked to Soviet–American relations, the United States has a strong interest in and perhaps an

293

obligation to become involved, presumably on the side of the forces of "stability," whatever those might be. The globalist conception of American interests prevails and the presumption of military involvement has been articulated. The attitude toward the use of force turns largely upon the definition of interests; when these are threatened, and non-violent methods of defense or coercion fail, force should be the response. The attitude was expressed clearly in President Bush's decision to employ force to unseat General Noriega of Panama in December 1989.

However, American public opinion, still under the influence of the Vietnam tragedy, does not seem enthusiastic about American military adventurism. Vocal and effective opposition to the American assistance provided to the Contras in Nicaragua and considerable resistance to an overt American military role in El Salvador indicate that any administration would find it difficult to commit troops to a high-risk (meaning high casualties) military operation, given the contemporary distribution of attitudes toward the use of force in Congress and throughout the country.

Despite the proclivity of the United States to employ conventional force as an instrument of foreign policy in relatively low-risk situations, the underlying attitudes have been muted, cautious, and primarily pragmatic. As Barry Buzan (1988:39) has noted, the very concept of "national security" under which all American strategies have been formulated is essentially conservative. Preventive war, even when the United States enjoyed a nuclear monopoly, was never raised to a serious policy alternative. When employed, military forces have remained under a tight leash emanating from the White House. President Truman fired General MacArthur for challenging the official policy of not escalating the Korean War into China. During the Vietnam engagement, President Johnson's strategy was to employ force in a highly calibrated and controlled manner, as an instrument of coercion designed to fashion a diplomatic bargain, rather than to annihilate the enemy. And in numerous limited interventions American forces were rapidly withdrawn as soon as "stability" was restored. With only a few exceptions, there is little evidence that America's professional military leaders sought action unrestrained by prudence (Betts, 1977). On the contrary, some presidents have chosen to employ force against the advice of some or all of the Chiefs of Staff. There has been over the entire postwar period a pronounced concern with the problems of escalation. Only a few top policy-makers have sought to play down the consequences of nuclear war. None of this is to suggest that official Washington has regarded the use of force, in whatever form, as a type of deviant or exceptional behavior. But neither has it gloried in military accomplishment or swaggered in forms reminiscent of the Germans prior to the First World War. In most cases, the United States has sought to achieve its purposes through non-violent instruments, resorting to economic coercion, overthrow of reputedly non-compliant regimes through subversion (Guatemala and Chile), and providing military training and supplies to client regimes before committing American troops to combat. The United States has waged its version of the cold war and its defense of the "free world" (along with its own economic interests) without relying on extensive and highly destructive warfare. The Korean and Vietnamese exceptions support the generalization.

### The Soviet Union and war

In the early forms of Marxism, the proletarian revolution was to take place as the result of class contradictions within societies. War between states was not an important analytical problem for Marx and his followers, partly because the latter half of the nineteenth century was relatively peaceful in continental Europe (Engels, however, wrote a great deal on military matters, but primarily from a descriptive rather than theoretical point of view). Lenin presented an explanatory theory of war between capitalist societies, locating its source in the problem of surplus capital and the resulting "push" for colonies. In his theory, war was a distinct product of bourgeois society and in a universe of socialist states it would no longer be a problem since class contradictions and surplus capital would no longer exist. The debates on war around the turn of the century were, however, academic in so far as there was no socialist society that might prove or support alternative hypotheses about the social sources of international conflict.

Once in power, Lenin and his colleagues, Leon Trotsky in particular, had to come to grips politically rather than theoretically with the problem of war. The political collapse of much of eastern Europe as well as Germany in 1918–19 presented a revolutionary situation that could be exploited through a variety of means. But what of armed force? Lenin's general position was that revolution itself could not be achieved through conventional military operations, but if the Soviet Republic were to become involved in war, it should exploit the resulting turmoil for revolutionary purposes. A war would be good or bad according to whether or not it advanced the cause of the revolution.

In 1920 the opportunity became available. Poland had launched a war against the Ukraine, actually capturing and holding Kiev for a short period. In its counter-attack, the Soviet forces led by Generals Budenny and Tukhachevsky, swept through eastern Poland, the latter reaching the gates of Warsaw. All of this was ostensibly to assist Polish "patriots." A Soviet victory was commonly predicted by Western observers, and they expected that the revolutionary army would continue westward to the Oder River and possibly to Berlin. If victorious, the Soviet leadership probably would have erected socialist regimes in the wake of the Red Army. Polish resistance was effective, however, so the opportunity for extending socialism through war outside of the frontiers of the Soviet Republic never materialized (military force was used, of course, to reconsolidate Georgia and the Ukraine, both of which had a brief existence as independent states after the Bolshevik Revolution).

The pattern of "liberation" following upon the heels of the Red Army was repeated in 1939 when, shortly after the outbreak of war with Finland, the Soviet government created a Finnish "People's Government" headed by one of Stalin's main ideologists, Otto Kuusinen. Stalin immediately signed a treaty of alliance with this government, and had the Red Army succeeded in destroying its Finnish opponent in the Winter War, the Kuusinen government no doubt would have been installed as the official regime of Finland. And again in 1944 and 1945 the Red Army "liberated" most of eastern Europe and used a variety of means to ensure that regimes friendly to the Soviet Union were put in place. In all of these instances, the Soviet Union did not begin a war specifically to further the cause of the revolution, but it did exploit wars which had fundamentally different sources to extend both Soviet national and ideological interests. From the point of view of furthering the fortunes of socialism, war had paid rich dividends.

Yet, the war against Nazi Germany had also cost the Soviets unprecedented destruction of productive facilities and loss of life (although by most reckonings Stalin killed more Soviet comrades than the Nazis did). Another war, even were it to offer opportunities for the development of socialism abroad, could hardly have been welcome. Stalin maintained a traditional and pessimistic outlook on the possibilities for the future. His analysis of the condition of the world and the correlation of forces emphasized the inherently aggressive nature of imperialism. The capitalists, in his estimation, would attack rather than give way to socialism peacefully. In addition, there was Stalin's continued nightmare of a revitalized Germany and a war of revenge. He believed to the end of his life in the inevitability of war involving the Soviet Union (Dinerstein, 1962:66). His analyses suggested a country beleaguered by hostile forces. Yet, in 1951, according to Czech émigrés who had seen the relevant archives in Prague, when the United States was pushed back by Chinese forces in Korea, Stalin admonished his satellite leaders to emphasize the build-up of power potential so that in several years the socialist bloc could undertake the task of communizing Western Europe by military means (Baring, 1989:18).

By the time of his death in March 1953, the Soviet Union had the atomic bomb and was soon to have hydrogen weapons as well. What did this mean for Stalin's notion of the inevitability of war between the Soviet Union and imperialism, this doctrine that fundamentally altered Lenin's original concept of war inevitability? Given the destructive power of these weapons, what would be the importance of Stalin's "permanently operating factors" in Soviet military strategy? What would the superiority of socialism (which included industrial, population, geographic, and moral factors) mean in case of nuclear war?

Georgii Malenkov, Stalin's successor, suggested that in the new atomic era there could be peace. Capitalism does not inevitably breed war, either because it had changed its fundamental nature or because the costs of war had far outgrown any possible gains. The introduction of nuclear weapons, he and a few bold military writers suggested, might have fundamentally altered the calculus of gains and losses in decisions to employ military force. For expressing this revolutionary perspective on the problem of war, Malenkov was demoted and replaced by Nikita Khrushchev, who had rather different views (Dinerstein, 1962:67ff.).

Khrushchev grudgingly admitted that nuclear war would involve great costs and losses, but it did not change the traditional logic of war, where there are always winners and losers. Even in nuclear war, he argued, the Soviet Union would emerge victorious. What, exactly, victory meant was never publicized in detail, but it included as a minimum the survival of most of the Soviet population and industrial resources. Unlike Malenkov's implied notion that peace could be guaranteed by the goodwill of the imperialists or by the changing calculus of war decisions, Khrushchev argued that the imperialists might very well unleash a war and that no technological innovation had fundamentally altered the aggressive nature of capitalist societies. The task, then, was to prevent aggression through force deployments that emphasized a capacity to win any war. This was a strategy of deterrence by perfecting the art of winning a war.

At the Twentieth Party Congress in 1956, Khrushchev came close to admitting that nuclear weapons made war unthinkable. But he did not go so far as to admit that technological and scientific developments could change the atavistic drives of the imperialists. Rather, he chose

297

to argue that the likelihood of war had receded because of the growing strength of socialism. War was still a possibility, but it was not inevitable. If some degree of rationality is attributed even to the hottest heads in Washington and Bonn, the strength of the forces of socialism was forcing the imperialists to alter their own calculations of costs and benefits in launching war. Soviet vigilance and continued strengthening of the armed forces, particularly the rocket troops, could maintain this state of affairs.

But the changing correlation of forces did not solve all problems. Khrushchev recognized that there was more than one avenue to war. There was the problem of accidental nuclear war. It was becoming more acute with the accumulation of ever larger stockpiles of weapons and the development of dangerous new weapons systems (Dinerstein, 1962:84–85). There was also the difficult problem of local conflict escalation. A war anywhere in the world contained explosive potential, and both sides would have to learn to handle them with prudence. By 1958, the Soviet leader had confirmed that nuclear war would be a disaster – at least for others: "the employment of nuclear weapons will poison the atmosphere with radioactive fallout and this could lead to the annihilation of almost all life, especially in countries of small population and high population density. They all will be literally wiped off the face of the earth" (quoted in Dinerstein, 1962:79). Presumably since the Soviet Union was neither small nor typified by high population density, it could avoid this fate.

The most explicit statements of Soviet attitudes toward war were contained in the numerous speeches, diatribes, and notes exchanged between Moscow and Beijing during the height of their ideological estrangement in the late 1950s and the 1960s. One of the most elaborate speeches connecting the fortunes of socialism with the problem of war was presented by Mikhail Suslov in 1964 at a plenary session of the Central Committee. It is worth quoting at length because it shows how far Soviet attitudes have changed since the days of Stalin. Suslov's speech was aimed directly at the Chinese, but it has to be regarded as more than a mere propaganda statement. Suslov's views survived Brezhnev and in some respects remain operative in the thinking of Gorbachev and his colleagues.

The first point, from which all further analysis derived, was that nuclear war would be a disaster not just for small states, as Khrushchev suggested, but for the cause of socialism itself: "Without mincing words, one can say that if a world thermonuclear conflict breaks out it would be the greatest tragedy for humanity and would, of course, deal the cause of communism a heavy blow" (Suslov, 1964:23). But, to answer Chinese criticisms that in their fear of war the Russians were neglecting their revolutionary obligations, Suslov argued (resembling in some ways Malenkov's thoughts) that the cause of socialism is best advanced by peace and not by war or by the revolutionary opportunities war produces:

> The Marxist-Leninist parties see their consistent struggle for peace as fulfillment of their historical mission towards mankind, which is to prevent the extermination of peoples in the flames of thermonuclear war. Furthermore, they see it as a most important condition for the successful construction of socialism and communism and for the expansion of the revolutionary struggle of the proletariat of the capitalist countries and of the liberation movement of the peoples oppressed by imperialism. An all-round analysis of the balance of world forces enables the Communist and Workers' parties to draw the cardinal conclusion that world war can best be averted even before socialism triumphs . . . and to re-emphasize that the Leninist principle of peaceful coexistence of countries with different social systems is the unshakable basis for the foreign policies of the socialist countries (Suslov, 1964:20).

It is Soviet strength that in fact allows the revolutionary process to proceed apace:

> Under conditions where the might of the Soviet Union and the entire Socialist commonwealth holds the main forces of international reaction and aggression in check, the working masses and peoples of the colonial countries have the most favorable opportunity for waging a struggle against imperialism and internal reaction. People who have followed the development of international events in the post-war years could not fail to see that there is an extremely close link between the success of the revolutionary struggle in the capitalist countries, the victories of the national liberation movement and the growth of the might of the world socialist system (Suslov, 1964:13).

These, and subsequent comments by Brezhnev, suggest a profound alteration of Lenin's view that war offered distinct revolutionary opportunities; now the view was that socialism can progress only in conditions of peace, and war poses a distinct threat to all the gains of socialism. Revolution and war have become antinomies rather than partners. Although Suslov argued that peace and the progress of socialism are not only compatible but essentially connected, Gorbachev has appeared to put a higher priority on peace. At the 1985 Geneva Summit meeting he associated himself with a final communiqué that made the straightforward assertion that "a nuclear war cannot be won and must never be fought."

These attitudes were translated into official strategic doctrine in

299

various ways during the 1970s. Lectures at the Soviet General Staff Academy, for example, stated explicitly that the Soviet Union would not initiate war (Wardak, 1989:70). Those lectures consistently portrayed Soviet forces as responding to aggression by others. They also underlined the Clausewitzian notion that war is the continuation of (class) politics by other means (pp. 63–64), and thus implied that only the political leadership will decide on the circumstances when to use force. Nuclear war is not inevitable, but should be avoided if at all possible. The lectures also allowed that there could be no winners in a nuclear war (p. 72), but they did not resolve the inconsistency between war-winning strategies and the destructive consequences of nuclear war. Finally, in 1974, the Central Committee directed the military to adhere to a doctrine of no-first-use of nuclear weapons.

Despite Khrushchev's gamble in Cuba and his repeated threats to use force to resolve the Berlin issue, there is little in Soviet behavior to indicate an alarming willingness to take military risks or to suggest that even in the most favorable of circumstances the cause of socialism could be advanced by a nuclear strike against the United States or any other country. Studies that have compared various eras of Soviet foreign policy note no peculiar patterns of risk-taking (cf. Adomeit, 1982). Statements of policy regarding war as well as military actions indicate a relatively conservative and prudent set of attitudes toward the use of force. There have been exceptions such as the decision to intervene in Afghanistan, which apparently was taken by Brezhnev and just a few of his confidants, but the profile of the Soviet use of force since Stalin's death stands in contrast to the record of military aggression during the 1930s. There are of course the ritual recitations of the mighty strength of the Soviet military establishment and the unwavering commitment to deliver a devastating rebuff to any imperialist attack on the Soviet Union. The language may differ, but such messages are not significantly different from those issued periodically from the Pentagon.

This is not to suggest that Soviet rhetoric and action were always consistent. There were many discontinuities between professions of peaceful intent and the actual deployment of forces. The Soviet Union used these deployments as means of intimidation and providing an umbrella under which, as Suslov suggested, wars of national liberation could take place without the threat of imperialist intervention. Soviet build-ups in Europe could hardly invoke votes of thanks among the NATO countries, despite Brezhnev's pledges of restraint and goodwill.

Brezhnev's speech in Tula in January 1977 formally announced a doctrine of nuclear sufficiency. Nuclear superiority, he suggested, echoing Kissinger's 1974 words, was "pointless." It was madness to think of victory in nuclear war – a radical departure from Khrushchev's thoughts on these matters. And the Soviet Union needed only enough nuclear weapons to keep the United States in check (Talbott, 1988:172). But these words were belied by deployments in Europe. The Soviet Union began emplacing SS-20 missiles, and the modernization of conventional forces continued apace. This poor concordance between policy statements and some military dispositions helped to sustain the belief in Washington that the massive Soviet military capabilities signaled an intention to use war to advance Soviet interests. The constant theme of Western complaints about Soviet capabilities was that they were vastly out of proportion to the Soviet Union's "true" security needs. Although this complaint did not take into consideration the view from Moscow, which during most of the 1980s saw the country ringed by hostile states, including China, it has not been until Gorbachev's leadership that Soviet commentators have conceded that there might be some basis to Western fears.

### China and the use of force

A brief discussion of Chinese views on war during the 1960s and early 1970s is instructive not because those views easily predict to actual Chinese military behavior, but because they have had considerable influence among leaders of national liberation movements in the Third World. Part of the great ideological controversy between China and the Soviet Union derived from different perspectives on the role of force and violence in the revolutionary process and in international relations. The Chinese position as it was articulated in the 1950s and early 1960s derived to a large extent from Mao's experiences during the wars against Japan and Chiang Kai-shek. In his view, war and revolution are inseparable; a war against imperialism is and must be a revolutionary war. It has the twin purposes of crushing imperialism and laying the foundations for a socialist society. All revolutionary war is by definition just. Destruction and loss of life should never be factors in deciding against war. Given conditions in most of the Third World there is little chance of progressing to socialism without a people's war. Wars are not so much a matter of choice as of necessity.

Imperialism, in Mao's inimitable style, is inherently aggressive and rapacious. Like a tiger, it cannot abandon its carnivorous habits as a matter of choice (to which the Russians replied that tigers do not have nuclear teeth). Thus, imperialist aggression, oppression, and counter-revolution are inevitable and can be overcome only through the organized violence of people's war. True revolutionaries are not deterred by superior weapons capabilities, including nuclear weapons. The Chinese victory over Japan proved that revolutionary fervor combined with adept guerrilla tactics culminating in conventional war can overcome the greatest military inequalities.

Making a virtue out of necessity, Mao frequently belied the importance of nuclear weapons (while embarking on a crash program to obtain them himself) and, reminiscent of Stalin's "permanently operating factors" in warfare, suggested that "spiritual atomic bombs" – meaning socialist doctrine and high morale – could compensate for the imperialists' weapons of mass destruction. In a flippant comment to Nehru, Mao had mentioned – and was often reminded of it by the Russians – that one-half of China's and the world's population would survive a nuclear war and would be there to oversee the construction of a glorious world socialist society where there would be no further wars.

Such attitudes did not translate easily into actions. The Chinese were strong material and moral supporters of wars of national liberation, but Lin Piao (1964), in his lengthy essay on the virtues of such wars, went out of his way to underline that these wars must have strong indigenous roots, that the revolutionaries have to be self-reliant (e.g., don't expect too much aid from China), and that in any case, revolution cannot be exported. As for using the People's Liberation Army for purposes of exporting revolution, the Chinese never proposed it or acted in such a way as to suggest that a Chinese-sponsored war could begin a revolution abroad. There could be money, arms, training, propaganda, and other services for foreign revolutionaries, but not direct military intervention.

China's use of force has been limited, circumspect, calibrated to specific goals, and temporary (Tibetans might argue otherwise). There has been little in Chinese behavior, as distinct from revolutionary rhetoric, to suggest the militarization of foreign policy, a pronounced willingness to follow high-risk courses of action or to glorify war for its own sake. Military force has been used primarily for purposes of national consolidation (Tibet, Taiwan), for fending off a direct threat posed by the United States in North Korea, "punishing" its wayward neighbor, Vietnam, and forcing the border issue with India. But despite this conservative record, the Chinese theory of revolutionary warfare has had significant impact in other areas of the world.

## Attitudes toward war in the Third World

The defensive, cautious, and self-deterring attitudes found commonly in the United States and more recently in the Soviet Union are less visible in the Third World. The goals of national liberation and state creation have been fundamental and usually non-compromisable. The strategies of wars of national liberation, moreover, have been eminently successful. Dozens of leaders of these movements took their strategic and tactical cues from Mao Tse-tung as well as from the Vietminh and Viet Cong. In the 1960s, the theorists of revolutionary war became folk heroes, not only among the oppressed and marginalized in Central and Latin America, Southeast Asia, and Africa, but even among radicals in the industrial countries. Che Guevara, Fidel Castro, Vo Nguyen Giap, and others wrote extensively about guerrilla warfare, its philosophy, strategy, and tactics. All proved that the superior military forces of the imperial powers were ultimately no match for the higher sense of purpose and the nationalist/ethnic/religious élan of the revolutionaries. Of all the major wars of national liberation only two clearly failed (the Philippines and Malaya; ethnic secession rebellions in Burma also failed); most others succeeded or became dormant. In terms of probabilities, then, the calculation of costs, risks, and advantages lay clearly on the side of war – and the leaders did not have to worry about escalations resulting in possible nuclear war. In this area of the world, nuclear weapons were irrelevant.

The experience of warfare in the Third World has been substantially different from that of Europe. The Great War, as Michael Howard reminds us (Howard, cited in Cohen, 1986:168), "de-bellated" industrial civilization. Despite the glorification of militarism under the Nazis and Fascists, the general mood of vast publics in the industrial countries has been anti-war since 1918. Avoiding most of the fighting in the two great intra-European conflagrations, populations in the Third World have quite different historical memories. The Second World War, in fact, was a great fillip for the anti-colonial movement. Most of the wars of national liberation were relatively free of the scale of destruction found in Europe in the 1940s (Vietnam and Korea are exceptions) and they served as exemplars for others rather than as situations to be avoided at all costs. The profound commitment to nationalist, ethnic, and religious purposes combined with relatively low risks and costs has thus made war in parts of the Third World a winning proposition.

Revolutionary leaderships and some governments of Third World

303

countries have been able to exploit these attitudes to sustain wars with low probabilities of success and high casualty rates. The Iranian Revolutionary Guards suffered hundreds of thousands of casualties for limited gains; P.L.O. operatives have knowingly given up their lives on innumerable but hopeless suicide missions; and the capacity of the Viet Cong and their northern suppliers to absorb high casualty rates attests to the high motivation underpinning the use of force in the Third World.

One of the prominent attributes of warfare in the Third World, reflecting these distinct attitudes toward the use of force, has been the length of combat. The average length of the wars of national liberation/unification contained in table 11.1 was 7.6 years. In contrast, the average length of classical interstate wars in the eighteenth century was 3.7 years. The P.L.O. has been in a state of undeclared war against Israel since 1964; the Vietnamese fought for most of the period 1946–75 before winning; the Eritrean rebellion has gone on for more than thirty years; and the Polisario contest, although largely dormant today, has continued without resolution since the mid 1950s. The quick war of national liberation (Bangladesh, 1971) is the exception rather than the norm (K. J. Holsti, 1989).

Eliot Cohen (1986:170) has made the comparative point that current and recent wars between states in the Third World have been "the products of hatreds and clashes of interest as profound as those in nineteenth and early twentieth century Europe." The statement underlines earlier comments to the effect that in the contemporary world we really have two separate but overlapping international systems. The propensity to engage in warfare, whether of the limited insurgency or more conventional type, is related to attitudes, and these attitudes have been significantly different in parts of the Third World compared to those that have prevailed in most industrial countries since the Great War.

This is not to argue that war in the Third World has approached epidemic proportions. On the contrary, even though almost all war since 1945 has occurred in these areas, we must acknowledge that the number of states in the Third World system has grown to well over one hundred, and if we control for these numbers as well as for several chronic areas of armed conflict such as the Middle East, the rest of the area has become relatively war-free. There have been only limited clashes in Latin America since the 1940s, the entire South Pacific basin has been free of war, and Southeast Asia appears to be heading for a pattern of relatively peaceful relationships. Nevertheless, of the 58 cases of war listed in table 11.1, 56 (the exceptions are the Turkish invasion of Cyprus and the marginal case of the war between the Koreas) took place in areas constituent of the Third World. That is an incidence of more than one war per year, approximately forty times the incidence of war within the industrial world. There are numerous explanations for this fact, but the absence or irrelevance of nuclear weapons and the distinct attitudes toward the use of force provide an important part of the explanation. There have been numerous Soviet–American crises, any one of which would probably have led to war in earlier eras (cf. Gaddis, 1986:121). That they were contained or managed short of the use of force attests more to the significance of deterrence and self-deterrence than to superior statesmanship. But changed attitudes expressed in the fear of war are also significant. Western publics and leaders have learned profound lessons from the experience of the two world wars. These devastating wars have provided support for Kant's prediction that man would ultimately abandon war by learning through the crucible of its death and destruction. But in some areas of the Third World there have been few such experiences, and the structural problems of state weakness and ethnic/religious passions create high probabilities that wars of various kinds will continue to erupt there in the foreseeable future.

# 12 WAR: ISSUES, ATTITUDES, AND EXPLANATIONS

> You have no idea how much it contributes to the general politeness and pleasantness of diplomacy when you have a little quiet force in the background.                                    George Kennan, 1946

A profile of issues that have generated international conflict chronicles the values, stakes, and purposes for which people have been willing to use force in the states system. Those who made war decisions implicitly or explicitly calculated that the potential costs of men, matériel, property, and the possibility of humiliating defeats and terms of surrender did not outweigh the values and purposes that they sought or that were being challenged or threatened by opponents. A map of the issues that rose, declined, or persisted in the years that separate the Treaties of Westphalia from today also tells us something about the sociology of international relations. Many of the issues reflect critical processes of political, economic, and ideological transformation going on within states and societies. This mapping exercise will remain primarily descriptive, but there are some tantalizing opportunities for causal analyses that would seek to account for the rise and decline of various kinds of issues over time. Finally, the profiles offer some explanations for the successes and failures of the great historical peacemaking efforts. Those efforts have had mixed success. All sought to create some sort of international order and to settle authoritatively those issues that had generated the preceding war or wars. A key requirement, however, was not just to dispose of them, but also to anticipate the issues of the future and to establish means by which they could be handled short of war.

Tables 12.1 and 12.2 report the frequency of individual issues, identified as a percentage of all issues that appeared in a time period, and the frequency, represented as a percentage, that a particular issue contributed to the origin of wars in the period. The first measures the relative significance of an issue compared to all conflict-generating issues; the latter identifies the salience of a particular issue as a source of war. We

306

Table 12.1 *Frequency of conflict-producing issues, 1648–1989*
*(percent of total issues per period)*

| Issues | 1648–1714 | 1715–1814 | 1815–1914 | 1918–1941 | 1945–1989 |
|---|---|---|---|---|---|
| Territory | 24 | 26 | 14 | 14 | 8 |
| Strategic territory | 10 | 7 | 4 | 9 | 7 |
| Territory (boundary) | — | 1 | — | — | 3 |
| National liberation/state creation | 2 | 3 | 10 | 4 | 9 |
| National unification/consolidation | — | 1 | 9 | — | 6 |
| Secession/state creation | — | — | — | — | 2 |
| Empire creation | 0 | 4 | 3 | 6 | — |
| Commerce/navigation | 16 | 14 | 4 | — | 1 |
| Commerce/resources | 2 | — | — | 6 | 3 |
| Colonial competition | 4 | 4 | 1 | — | — |
| Protect nationals/commercial interests abroad | — | — | 1 | 5 | 3 |
| Protect religious confrères | 6 | 4 | 3 | — | — |
| Protect ethnic confrères | — | — | 5 | 2 | 3 |
| Ethnic/religious unification/irredenta | — | — | 2 | 5 | 4 |
| Defend/support ally | 2 | 4 | — | 3 | 5 |
| Ideological liberation | — | 1 | 3 | 3 | 4 |
| Government composition | — | 5 | 4 | 5 | 9 |
| Maintain integrity of state/empire | — | 3 | 18 | 9 | 9 |
| Enforce treaty terms | 6 | 3 | 1 | 9 | 2 |
| Maintain regional dominance | — | — | 3 | 2 | 2 |
| Dynastic/succession | 14 | 9 | 3 | — | — |
| State/regime survival | 10 | 7 | 2 | 11 | 7 |
| Autonomy | — | 1 | 2 | 2 | 2 |
| Balance of power | 4 | 1 | 1 | 1 | 1 |

must remember that most wars arose over multiple issues. The tables summarize the figures that appeared in the previous chapters. They include only issues that appeared in a minimum of two historical periods (the post-1945 period is the exception so that we can identify possible issues of the future) and that had a minimum frequency of 1 percent of all issues in those periods. The tables demonstrate the comparative importance and rise and decline of the various issues, but for purpose of analysis it will be helpful to transform the figures into graphic form and to combine some of the issues into a single issue cluster.

### TERRITORY

Figure 12.1 shows the profile of contests over territory, including boundary wars, since 1648. Quarrels involving control, access to, and/or ownership of physical space figured in about one-half of all wars between Westphalia and the outbreak of the First World War, but since Napoleon's defeat there has been a gradual decline in the prominence of this issue, both as a percentage of all conflict-producing issues and as a source of war. As a source of war the decline has been

307

Table 12.2 *Frequency of issues that generated wars, 1648–1989 (frequency of issue as percent of wars)*

| Issues | 1648–1714 | 1715–1814 | 1815–1914 | 1918–1941 | 1945–1989 |
|---|---|---|---|---|---|
| Territory | 55 | 67 | 42 | 47 | 24 |
| Strategic territory | 23 | 17 | 13 | 30 | 21 |
| Territory (boundary) | — | 1 | — | — | 7 |
| National liberation/state creation | 4 | 8 | 29 | 13 | 28 |
| Secession/state creation | — | — | — | — | 7 |
| National unification/consolidation | — | — | 26 | — | 17 |
| Empire creation | — | 11 | 10 | 20 | — |
| Commerce/navigation | 36 | 36 | 13 | — | 3 |
| Commerce/resources | 4 | — | — | 20 | 9 |
| Colonial competition | 9 | 11 | 3 | — | — |
| Protect nationals/commercial interests | — | — | 3 | 17 | 9 |
| Protect religious confrères | 14 | 11 | 10 | — | — |
| Protect ethnic confrères | — | — | 16 | 7 | 9 |
| Ethnic/religious unification/irredenta | — | — | 6 | 17 | 12 |
| Defend/support ally | 4 | 11 | — | 10 | 16 |
| Ideological liberation | — | 1 | 10 | 10 | 14 |
| Government composition | — | 14 | 13 | 17 | 28 |
| Maintain integrity of state/empire | — | 8 | 55 | 30 | 28 |
| Enforce treaty terms | 14 | 8 | 3 | 30 | 7 |
| Maintain regional dominance | — | — | 10 | 7 | 5 |
| Dynastic/succession | 31 | 22 | 10 | — | — |
| State/regime survival | 23 | 17 | 6 | 37 | 22 |
| Autonomy | — | — | 6 | 7 | 7 |
| Balance of power | 9 | 1 | 3 | 3 | — |

particularly notable since 1945. In this period it has attained a level (31 percent) less than one-half of what it had been in the eighteenth century and about 30 percent lower than it had been between Waterloo and the outbreak of the Second World War. As a percentage of all issues its decline (from 14 to 10 percent compared to the previous period) has been less pronounced. Nevertheless both measures are presently at historic lows.

This does not necessarily mean that policy-makers value territory less than they did in previous eras. Territory still evokes sentiments of national pride and prestige, and often symbolizes the spatial foundations of the national society. The passions engendered by the Rann of Kutch, uninhabited Himalayan plateaus, and small islands in the South Atlantic sustained wars involving thousands of casualties. There are some eighty contested boundaries and territorial claims currently on the international agenda, although most of them are dormant (Day, 1987). But there is less willingness to use force to solve these problems than there was previously. A possible explanation, aside from cost-benefit analysis, is that international constraints against resolving issues of this type by force have gathered strength. The Charter of the Organization of African Unity, for example, sanctifies colonial boundaries and discourages attempts to revise them. One

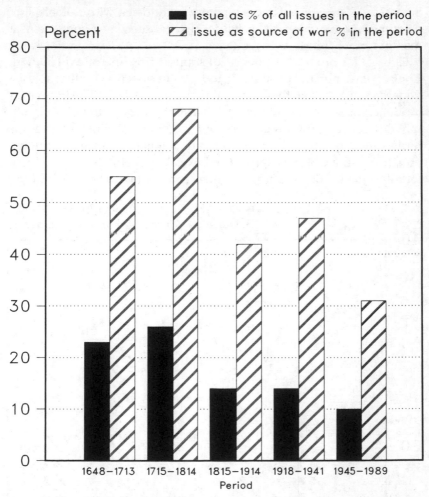

Figure 12.1   Territory and war

can also make the case that territory no longer exists as an index of power and serves less as a source of international prestige than it did in previous eras. In contemporary circumstances, technological/scientific and economic leadership may be more significant foundations of international status. Vast territorial expanse may actually constitute a source of weakness, particularly in developing nations. The state apparatus may find it difficult to maintain effective administrative and communications control over large areas, and extensive space may correlate with a higher distribution of distinct ethnic/language/religious groups upon the national territory. The possibility of secession then increases and potentially threatens an already weak political-

309

bureaucratic structure. Unless territory is endowed with notable strategic or economic value, today it is less likely to become a source of war than in former times.

Figure 12.2 provides evidence to support this line of explanation. Control or ownership of strategic territory has been a significant issue underlying wars in all the historical periods since 1648. The figures for incidence show no strong trends. As a source of war there are significant differences between periods, but no general decline as there was for territory in general. We are reminded almost daily about the importance of the Golan Heights, the Bekaa Valley, the Northern Territories off Japan, the Strait of Hormuz, and the like. The geo-strategic

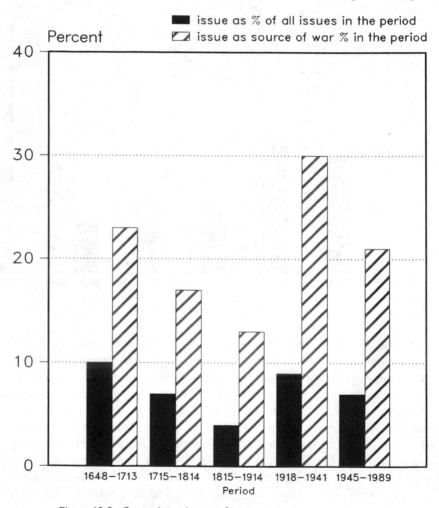

Figure 12.2   Strategic territory and war

310

outlook continues to influence policy-making, and most governments propose to "solve" their security problems by guaranteeing access to or seeking exclusive control over major routes of commerce or avenues of military threat.

## NATION-STATE CREATION AND WAR

When we aggregate three issues – national liberation/state creation, national unification/consolidation, and secession – we deal with similar values and stakes if not behaviors. They all identify efforts to create states and symbolize that long historical process that began in Europe in the fifteenth and sixteenth centuries and that has extended into the non-European parts of the world in the twentieth century. The locale and the modalities of state creation have changed significantly over time, but the ends have not altered. Modern man has chosen to underline human political fragmentation and to base community pol itical organization on other than imperial (hierarchical) or world communitarian principles. Statehood today is usually identified as the sole legitimate political manifestation of an ethnic/language/religious group's exclusiveness. It is the prime political expression of group identity in a pluralistic and fragmented world. The ideological underpinning of political exclusiveness is the doctrine of national self-determination. Not infrequently it is accorded greater priority than other political beliefs, including democracy, civil liberties, welfare, and socialism.

The search for statehood has commanded the international agenda since the late eighteenth century, and in two of the periods (1815–1914 and since 1945) it has been more often associated with war and armed intervention than any other issue. And while the importance of territory has been declining from its high levels of the seventeenth and eighteenth centuries, the search for statehood has been increasing, if not steadily. Figure 12.3 records the explosion of national independence movements of the nineteenth century, followed by the hiatus of the interwar period when the seeds of independence and self-government were being planted in what is today termed the Third World, and their germination in the post-1945 period. More than one-half (52 percent) of the wars of the post-1945 period were manifestations of the state-creation enterprise. In terms of the relative frequency of issues it ranks highest by a considerable margin.

### IDEOLOGY AND WAR

Men have frequently gone to war over ideas – an important fact neglected in most realist versions of international relations that depict international politics as a permanent search for power and security, where ideas serve only as fig leaves for the cruder concerns of power. But politics cannot be reduced to such simplicities. Political principles and ideological aspirations play a prominent role in shaping relations between nations. Empirical research has established that democracies do not war against each other, and the number of governments that have been overturned by the great powers primarily for reasons of ideological incompatibility is substantial. But the extent to

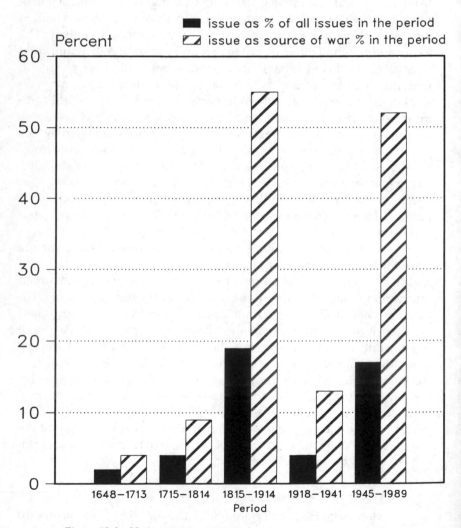

Figure 12.3   Nation-state creation and war

312

which ideas have animated international conflicts has varied throughout the history of interstate relations since 1648.

Westphalia put an end to Europe's most destructive and longest armed conflict (if measured in terms of direct and indirect casualties as a proportion of population, the Thirty Years War was the most destructive). While power and dynastic factors were involved, contests over religious and derivative civil principles drove the war from the beginning. They were sufficient conditions for bloodshed. The Treaties of Münster and Osnabrück effectively settled these issues, and the succeeding century and one-half was marked by conflicts over more concrete issues. The political principles and practices of dynasticism went largely unchallenged. Courts frequently dabbled in each others' intrigues and generously funded various factions abroad, but for the most part the alignments had little to do with political or constitutional principles. Uniformity of political beliefs, forms, and practices stretched from Lisbon to Moscow and Stockholm to Naples well into the late 1700s.

Only in the late eighteenth century did the consensus and uniformity begin to break down. Republicanism became infectious, spawning radical challenges to dynastic principles in the American colonies, Sweden, Holland, and Poland. These all occasioned wars and interventions before France's revolutionary regime formally took up the task of "liberating" Europe in the name of liberty, equality, and fraternity. Figure 12.4 chronicles the rise and accelerating importance of ideological and government composition issues throughout the period of this study.

They were and have remained a prominent source of international conflict since the settlements of 1814–15. The importance of these kinds of issues has been particularly notable in the post-1945 period where, combined, they have been involved in 42 percent of the wars. This constitutes the second-highest-ranking issue cluster after state creation. International politics has been increasingly revolving around ideas and the people who represent them in government rather than around concrete issues such as territory and commerce. The purpose of many of the great powers and some of the lesser ones as well have concentrated on controlling or influencing the government personnel of near and distant states, rather than occupying their territories. Conversely, they have also sought to undermine the authority of foreign regimes whose policies and political principles they found unpalatable. The ideological issue involves, for the most part, attempts to influence and control political change abroad. Force was frequently used where other methods failed (cf. Luard, 1988:2–3).

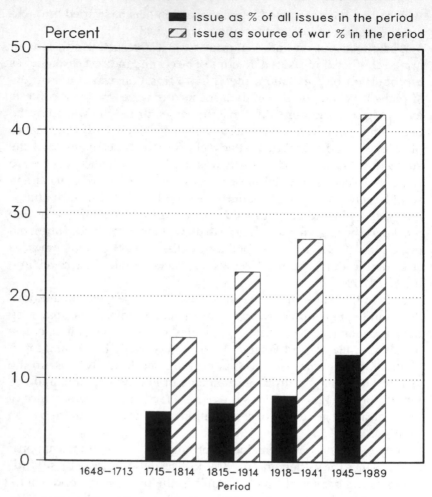

Figure 12.4   Ideology and war

## ECONOMICS AND WAR

There is archeological evidence that man's earliest collective armed combat was used to establish monopolies over trade routes, access to water, and exclusive use of grazing lands (Morley and Marwitt, 1975; Roper, 1975). Greek history is littered with wars the purpose of which was to establish trade monopolies and to control commercial waterways. After 1648, colonial activity, which hitherto had been sponsored, organized, and largely funded by private concerns, became increasingly state supported and protected. Competition for monopolies over trade and for exclusive and preferential access to

314

markets created serious diplomatic problems and frequent wars. Such activities were buttressed and justified by mercantilist theories that held that a state's power could be increased by ruining the foreign trade of its rivals. In the seventeenth century there were also few rules of navigation that commanded widespread observance. The limits of territorial jurisdiction and the rights of neutral shipping during wartime caused serious conflicts and were the issues around which several wars were fought.

One century later economic theorists and policy-makers increasingly recognized that commerce was not necessarily a zero-sum activity, and that war and trade did not mix well: the damage to commerce through armed combat was often greater than the expected spoils of military victory. Commerce and navigation became increasingly regulated by international legal norms and, as we have seen, disputes arising over these problems began to decline. Some thorny problems, such as rights of transit through the Turkish Straits, continued to play an important role in generating conflicts well into the twentieth century, but none was sufficient to lead to war. Colonial competition among the European governments and the United States over Africa, the Middle East, Persia, and China caused a number of dangerous crises (Fashoda, Algeciras), generally strained diplomatic relations between the powers, and served as sources of the Spanish–American and Russo-Japanese Wars. There were as well the numerous campaigns and skirmishes by the Europeans against indigenous populations, none of which, however, had an impact on security interdependence between the states of the central system.

The spread of economic imperialism as well as more benign forms of trade and commerce in the late nineteenth and early twentieth centuries created a set of interests that required protection from the home government. Governments frequently relied upon coercive means, including military interventions, to protect the lives, property, and investments of their citizens residing in non-European lands. In some cases, such as the Anglo-Chinese Opium Wars of the mid nineteenth century, force was used to promote what by any standards was illicit trade. Gunboat diplomacy was the term applied to "protection." Armed force was also employed in the nineteenth century to control piracy and to abolish the practice of slavery. While there is a relatively well-articulated legal regime that defines the rights and obligations of both host governments and citizens doing business abroad, some areas remain contested, and in conditions of turmoil, civil war, and rebellion the host government may not be able to provide protection. Foreign intervention is a frequent result. I have labeled the issue "protect nationals/commercial interests abroad."

315

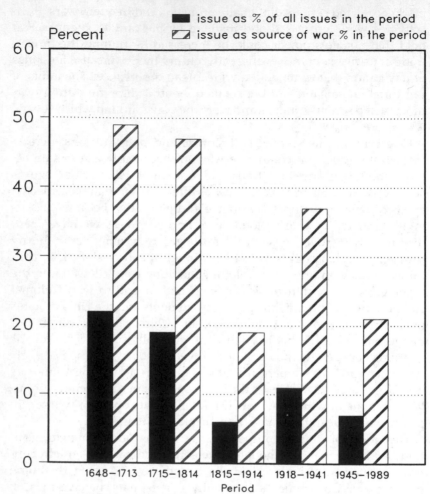

Figure 12.5   Economics and war

To examine the relative importance of the economic bases of war, we can aggregate the separate issues of commerce/navigation, commerce/resources, colonial competition, and protect nationals/commercial interests abroad into a single economic issue cluster. Figure 12.5 provides the profile of economic issues in generating international conflict since 1648.

There has been a general decline in the significance of economic issues as sources of international conflict. Between Westphalia and the Congress of Vienna they figured significantly in the etiology of wars. The nineteenth century, in contrast, saw the rapid diminution of armed contests over commercial and navigational issues. They revived during the 1930s thanks to Japanese and Italian imperialism, only to decline again after the Second World War. Contests over resources continue to appear and may become significant issues of the future. But on the whole, most problems of a commercial/navigational character have been regularized or controlled through well-articulated legal regimes. The few that remain (e.g., incompatible Canadian and American positions on the status of the Northwest Passage) are not likely to lead to military hostilities.

Access to resources and critical waterways during times of diplomatic tension may be more problematic, however. Local wars or domestic turmoil may disrupt critical traffic lanes, thus posing a threat to resource consumers. During the 1970s the United States issued several warnings that it would use force if necessary to maintain the vital oil shipping routes open in the Persian Gulf, and during the 1980s a NATO flotilla escorted Kuwaiti and other vessels through Gulf waters that had been mined by Iran. In the contemporary international environment it is difficult to envisage that conflicts surrounding economic and transportation issues would be sufficient to spark large-scale wars. But interventions may occur when the economic interests of the great powers in particular are threatened by turmoil, civil wars, and interstate wars in the Third World. In an environment of serious depression or severe resource shortage, moreover, this type of issue could emerge as a significant source of potentially lethal international conflict.

### HUMAN SYMPATHY: ETHNICITY, RELIGION, AND WAR

Men fight not only over ideas, territory, power, and welfare values. They also sympathize with those whom they consider their ethnic, religious, and ideological kin. When these kin are threatened, persecuted, or physically harmed, their benefactors abroad may come to their assistance – sometimes with armed force. This sympathy factor in international relations may also take the form of seeking to incorporate the kin into one's own nation through annexation or in response to an irredentist movement in a neighboring jurisdiction. All periods in this study have featured conflicts in which the sympathy factor played a prominent role.

Figure 12.6 represents the evidence of the continued importance of the use of force as a means of protecting kin abroad. It aggregates the separate issues of "protect religious confrères," "protect ethnic confrères," and "ethnic/religious unification/irredenta." The high frequency of wars in the nineteenth century in which these sorts of issues played a role is partly accounted for by the persecution of Orthodox

317

Christians and fellow Slavs in the Ottoman Empire and the frequent championing of their cause by Russia. There has been a decline of sympathy issues since the First World War, but they have been one source of conflict in more than one-fifth of the post-1945 wars. The Kashmir, Cyprus, and Palestinian problems have involved these types of issues; it is significant that each has remained intractable since inception many years ago. Sympathy may be harder to appease than concerns over power or territory.

## PREDATION AND SURVIVAL

The term "total war" has been used conventionally to describe

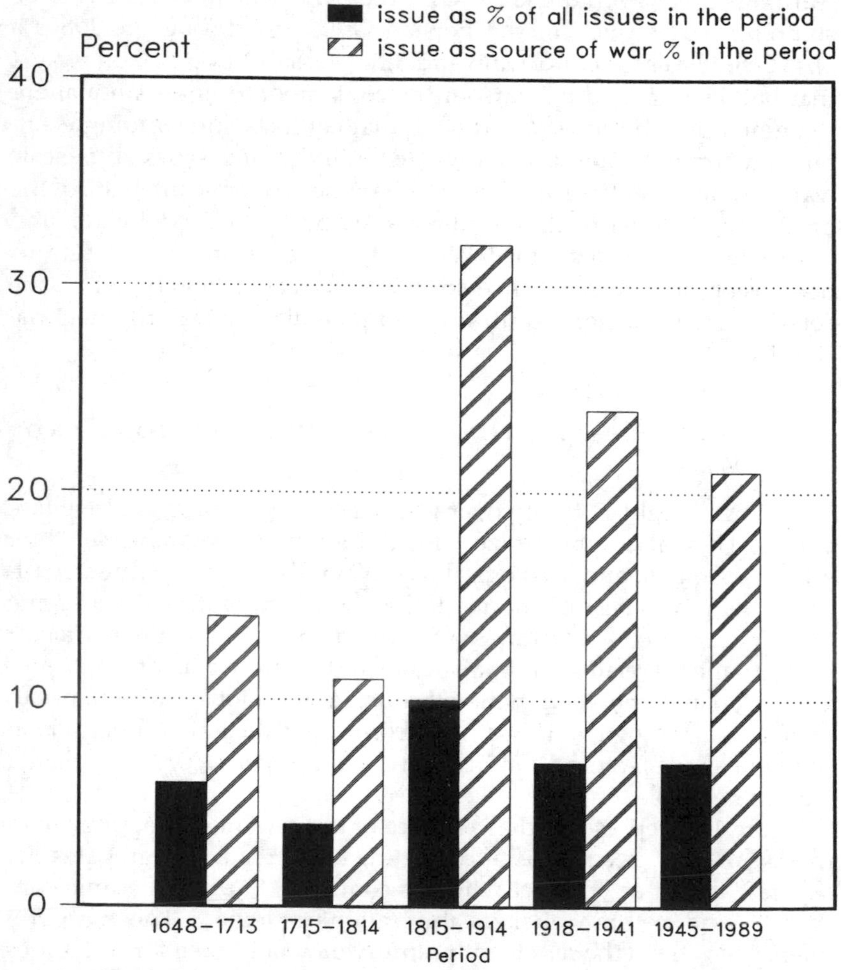

Figure 12.6  Human sympathy and war

318

levels of destruction, casualties, and the explosive power of modern weapons. But in many of our periods war has been total in another sense: one or more of the participants sought to eliminate another state or regime as an officially independent political entity. At its worst extreme there was the Nazi attempt to liquidate Poland as a state and to exterminate its population through executions, massacres, starvation, and slave labor. A somewhat more problematical example has been Israel. Each of its wars has been perceived as a contest for national survival, though it is not known exactly what would have happened to Israel as a state, to its government, and to its population had the Arabs achieved military victory in 1947–48, 1956, 1967, or 1973. We do know, however, what happened to the regimes of countries that were "liberated" by communist armies.

Figure 12.7 is a barometer of the amount of predation in the international system, where predation is defined as the attempt to destroy a regime or dismember, partition, or liquidate a sovereign state. The profile adds more support to the view of nineteenth-century Europe as relatively moderate in its international politics. Only 6 percent of the wars included regime/state survival as a stake or issue, while in the era of the Hitlerian, Italian, and Japanese onslaughts more than one-third (37 percent) of the wars had as one of their purposes the elimination of a government or the liquidation of a state. Since 1945 the figure has declined, but it still remains slightly above the historical average of 21 percent of all wars and substantially above the averages for the nineteenth century.

## REMAINING ISSUES

The remaining issues do not have high frequencies and/or have disappeared from the international agenda. Referring back to tables 12.1 and 12.2 we see that dynastic/succession issues went the way of the theory of divine right, and that empire-building enterprises, which revived briefly under the Germans, Italians, and Japanese in the 1930s, have become obsolete, in part because of the mystique of the self-determination doctrine and also because formal territorial control is no longer necessary to gain access to markets and sources of supply or to dominate lesser economies. The support of allies – the obligation to fulfill alliance commitments – is an issue throughout the post-Westphalian period, but as a proportion of all issues it has remained low since 1648. Few governments are willing to go to war solely to protect an ally. Usually other issues are involved simultaneously (e.g., Great Britain's decision to declare war on Germany in 1939). Nevertheless, governments have gone to war reasonably frequently to enforce

319

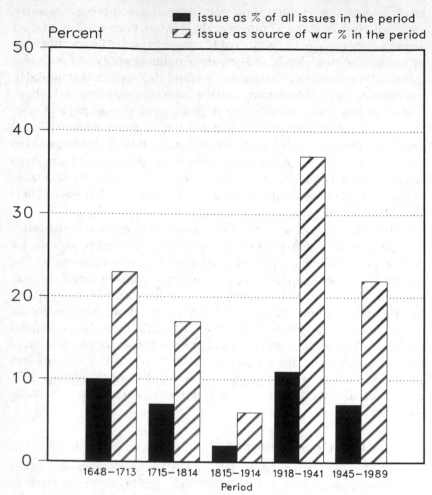

Figure 12.7   Predation and survival

other kinds of treaty obligations. In the interwar period, 9 percent of all issues involved attempts to enforce previous legal obligations; this meant that 30 percent of the wars and armed interventions had a treaty obligation at issue.

Maintenance of imperial or state integrity (usually offsetting a challenge of the "national liberation" variety) remains prominent across all periods, but was especially high in the nineteenth century when the Ottoman and Austro-Hungarian Empires were constantly beleaguered by the actions of disaffected ethnic and religious minorities.

The post-1945 period has seen the demise of overseas empires, sometimes dismantled voluntarily according to set schedules but at other times resulting only from protracted wars. The last remaining empire, the Soviet Union, faces serious challenges from the Baltic and other peoples.

Attempts to maintain regional dominance – America's activities in Central America are a contemporary example – cut across all periods, but there are no trends in this stake or issue. Perhaps most surprising is the low incidence of issues defined in balance of power terms. Policy-makers in the seventeenth, eighteenth, and nineteenth centuries were fully familiar with the concept and often employed it as a guide to diplomatic and military actions. But it would appear that it operated more in the genesis of alliances and in the decisions to join wars after conflicts had already arisen than as a conflict-producing issue itself. Concern for the balance of power was more a manifestation of conflict than a source of it. Statesmen launched wars for specific purposes, but those wars would escalate to greater participation by the powers if they made the calculation that a victory by the initiator would threaten the balance. The Crimean War and several others fit this pattern.

To summarize, we have chronicled the profiles of various issues and stakes that have figured in the etiology of armed conflict since 1648. One pattern that emerges from the figures is that relatively abstract issues – self-determination, principles of political philosophy and ideology, and sympathy for kin – have become increasingly important as sources of war while concrete issues such as territory and wealth have declined. One explanation for this pattern might lie in the ability of governments to create legal and other conflict-avoiding regimes for concrete-type issues, while for abstract issues regulation is difficult to develop. There can be compromises over territory, access to water-ways, rules of navigation, and the location of boundaries, for example, and many of these issues can be handled in such a fashion that both parties to a conflict can gain through compromise or regime construc-tion. In contrast, statehood has been viewed typically in zero-sum terms. Federal and other schemes that provide degrees of cultural, economic, and political autonomy may offer partial solutions, but the mystique of national self-determination defined in terms of indepen-dence and sovereignty remains vigorous; the aim of the group is not autonomy but sovereignty. Similarly, it has been difficult to compro-mise the great ideological issues of an era. Totalitarian ideologies by definition require total obedience at home and conformity abroad. At the foreign policy level the purpose of the revolutionary totalitarian state is to recreate the world or one of its regions in its own image. Ideological conformity is, however, incompatible with the social,

321

political, religious, and value fragmentation of mankind. It is therefore difficult to fashion compromises between fundamentally incompatible belief systems. Conflict and war historically have been seemingly inevitable results of the clash of two or more *Weltanschauungen*. Only through slow learning and increasing pragmatism, and after shouldering the heavy burdens of ideological purity above all other values, does reconciliation start to become a possibility. But ideological accommodation has been a slow process, often accompanied by considerable violence both domestically and internationally. It took great wars to resolve the religious issues of the sixteenth and seventeenth centuries, to replace the dynastic principles with republican principles in the late eighteenth and entire nineteenth centuries, and to defeat the most pernicious of all political doctrines, Nazism. The conflict between communism and liberalism has seen much bloodshed, but it has been muted under the threat of civilization-destroying war. The increasing pragmatism of contemporary communist leaders, notable particularly in their recent acknowledgments of the existence of an international society and the necessity of their states to live at peace within it, may mean that we will be spared the ordeal of another general war and that at least some of the issues emanating from communist ideology may be handled by means other than the use of force.

The search for nation-statehood has been a predominant goal of ethnic, social, language, and religious groups for more than two centuries. But it goes back much further. An extended debate among anthropologists, philosophers, and legal scholars in the late nineteenth and early twentieth centuries revolved around the proposition that historically the process of state creation and war correlate with each other (R. Holsti, 1913; Windsor, 1987: 175–91). Aside from ideological issues, the history of international relations since the late eighteenth century has been largely constituted of the state-creating and state consolidation urges. A significantly high proportion of the world's existing states came into being through war and violence. The United States was born through rebellion and achieved its present territorial dimensions largely through armed conquests at the expense of the Mexicans, Hawaiians, and Spanish. Germany, Italy, the Balkan countries, Israel, Algeria, Indonesia, and dozens of other states became members of the society of states only after prolonged armed conflicts. There is also evidence that states which come into being through revolution and violence are more likely to be involved in subsequent international conflict (Maoz, 1989). The birth of nations often starts with war, culminates with war, and helps produce post-independence armed conflicts.

A substantial amount of war since 1815 and even earlier has been associated with the transformation of the main principles of human political organization, the change from the loose, tribute-based multi-ethnic/ religious empire to the nation-state. We must not forget that the "powers" of the nineteenth century were structurally more dissimilar than similar. The Ottoman, Austrian, and Russian Empires were indeed "powers," but their constitutional formats represented an older type of political organization that was inconsistent with the exclusivist and communitarian sentiments implied in the doctrine of national self-determination. And the dissolution of those empires, culminating through and immediately after the First World War, could not take place for the most part through peaceful means. The retreat of overseas empire after the Second World War was somewhat more orderly, but wars of "national liberation" were necessary to prove conclusively that the days of formal empire had finally come to an end.

Despite all the rhetoric about global interdependence, the shrinking world, and the presumably unifying impact of technological innovations on social and economic life, a more primordial sentiment seeks to assert autonomy, separateness, uniqueness, cultural survival, and, ultimately, sovereignty (K. J. Holsti, 1985b:675–96). Since most of the states of the world are composed of multiple ethnic/language/religious groups, we could expect the future international agenda to be crowded with cases of civil wars, wars of secession, and the breakdown of multi-community states – all with the possibility of foreign intervention. That agenda is already well populated and growing annually: it includes the Tamils of Sri Lanka, the Karens and Shans of Burma, pro-independence movements in Kashmir and the Punjab, armed secessionist/autonomy struggles in Nagaland and the Sind, and in Africa, the Eritreans and southerners of the Sudan. Even industrial states are not immune from these urges, as the actions of the I.R.A., the Basques, some Corsicans and Quebecois, and most recently, the Baltic peoples, attest.

We are witnessing the creation of a genuinely global international system whose essential and primary units are states constructed upon distinct social communities. This system is still in the birth process and it is coming into existence, as it has in the past, largely through violent means. In the industrial world the process is largely completed, and it may not be accidental that the mutual relations of the states comprising it have become predictably peaceful. Borders are settled and legitimated, the societies are reasonably well integrated – though strong regional sentiments and secession movements still exist in some of them – and their political systems enjoy general legitimacy and the rules for changing parties and personnel are no longer contested. Constitutionalism has prevailed over other means of achieving power.

Little of this can be said of most of the newer nations. Their state apparatuses are in many cases weak, divided, and ineffective in meeting a host of grass-roots expectations and providing adequate services. The societies over which they have jurisdiction in varying degrees are fractured into more meaningful and effective political communities based on tribal, ethnic, religious, and other bases. State and nation do not coincide, thus inviting movements to make them consistent. Although colonial boundaries enjoy substantial legitimacy as the permanent demarcation lines of the new states, few would venture to predict that they are and will remain as stable as, for example, the boundaries separating Switzerland from France and Italy, or the United States from Canada.

The challenges of the future will thus arise in large part from the continuing process of state formation and consolidation. As in the past fifty years, most of the wars will revolve around these issues and will occur in the Third World. There will be many arms races, wars of national liberation, attempted secessions, and possible foreign interventions. Another possibility is that the destructiveness of modern conventional war will render the costs of achieving independence greater than the advantages.

Historically states could be created through contests of arms without unduly endangering the society that was to be integrated into a single and separate political order. The military technology and levels of force employed to unite Italy and Germany, for example, presented only low-level threats to most Germans and Italians. Under contemporary conditions of warfare, in contrast, the attempt to create a state through armed force may involve such high levels of destruction to the community that the resulting state will face potentially insurmountable problems of social, economic, and political reconstruction and survival. Vietnam has never fully recovered from its war of national liberation and unification; Mozambique barely exists as anything akin to a state; and Lebanon is mostly a legal fiction. As Philip Windsor (1987:186) has noted, under contemporary conditions of war the greatest threat to the state is war. This is the paradox: if wars create states, in today's conditions they may also destroy them.

## ISSUES OF THE FUTURE

We may encounter new types of issues that will generate serious international conflicts, even among the industrial countries.

324

Trade issues have become "high politics" among many governments and in an environment of serious economic recession or depression it is possible to imagine some governments resorting to coercive measures to protect various welfare values. These might involve demonstrations of force that could escalate to the point of large casualties. Environmental aggression causing substantial harm to adjacent countries offers possible scenarios, although the responses so far to disasters such as Chernobyl and major oil spills at sea that fouled foreign coast lines have been surprisingly muted and non-hostile.

In the list of wars and major interventions since 1945, we have already seen several cases where overpopulation, resource depletion, and pollution contributed to international conflicts, usually through the mass migrations that those conditions spawned. The situation in Central America may unfortunately be typical of many areas of the Third World. There, it is a combination of explosive birth rates, highly skewed land-ownership patterns, the alienation of prime agricultural land for export-oriented crops and meat production, deforestation by the marginalized in search of land for subsistence agriculture, and pollution. These patterns, along with highly stratified social structures, offer prime conditions for domestic revolutionary activity and ultimate external intervention and/or migration to neighboring countries that have similar problems and thus cannot accommodate large influxes of refugees. Other possibilities include the use of armed force by one government against drug producers in another jurisdiction, and armed operations against terrorist organizations. The point is not to predict exactly what will be the contentious issues of the future but to underline that as some issues decline others may rise to take their place; or the menu may just keep expanding.

## ATTITUDES AND WAR

It is not possible to draw accurate configurations of attitudes toward war, their change, and their impact on war–peace decisions. Precise measures do not yet exist. We can only hypothesize that the more decision-making elites regard war as an honorable, profitable, desirable, and/or prestige-generating activity, the more likely it is that when calculating costs, risks, and potential gains during a diplomatic conflict they will tend to minimize the former and maximize the latter. There are many intervening variables between attitudes and decisions/actions, but there are also likely to be correlations between them. Knowing Hitler's and Chamberlain's attitudes toward war – even if that is all we knew – we could predict with reasonable confi-

325

dence which would decide to take up the sword. Admittedly, these two figures represent extremes. For other policy-makers, the prediction would be more difficult to make.

If we look at the configuration of attitudes toward war historically and impressionalistically, there appears to be a slow decline in the appeal of bellicosity. Until the end of the Napoleonic Wars, few policy-makers saw war as an extraordinary problem of the international system, one that demanded severe reforms of international institutions, processes, and norms. Throughout the seventeenth and eighteenth centuries war served many functions and purposes: as avenues to personal glory, reputation, and prestige; as essential instruments in the state-building endeavor; as indices of national status and prestige; and as means of achieving and defending diplomatic and commercial objectives. Policy-makers certainly did not see war as unusual, as an indicator of national, court, or royal pathology, or as a form of deviant diplomatic behavior. On the contrary, many personal, court, and state interests could be served by the military enterprise. To the extent that the societies of the day valued heroic activity, war was the heroic undertaking par excellence.

The French Revolutionary and Napoleonic Wars brought some subtle changes to attitudes toward war among the decision-making elites. Those wars had been sufficiently destructive to bring home the point that war was indeed a problem of the system and that something should be done about it. Political elites no longer sought personal fame and reputation through military exploits (Napoleon was the last major ruler who fulfilled generalship and civic roles simultaneously), although valor on the battlefield was still sought by the professional military. National reputation and prestige began to be based on foundations other than military exploits and great victories: science, industry, the arts and letters, and education. The diplomatic memorandums of the period 1815 to approximately 1870 indicate that the policy-makers increasingly saw war as an exceptional activity, a sort of last resort after all other avenues of settling conflicts had failed. The norms of the Concert of Europe also suggested that war should not be undertaken without the consent of at least some of the other powers. In these and other ways, the contrasts between 1750 and 1850 are pronounced.

Chapter 7 chronicled the changes in attitudes toward war that took place in the latter decades of the nineteenth century and the fourteen years of the twentieth century prior to the Great War. Once again, war came to be seen by many in a positive light: as a means of social regeneration, as a necessary instrument in the eternal struggle between nations, as an indicator of national superiority in the struggle for the survival of the fittest, and as God's instrument for weeding out the weak from the strong. These views had little to do with the traditional instrumental view of war, and a lot to do with national jingoism, racial hatreds, and the seamier sides of nineteenth-century philosophy that equated peace with degeneracy. The portrait of attitudes toward war in this period, particularly in Russia, Austria-Hungary, Germany, and Italy, may not do justice to the variety of views that actually existed, but there were enough high-level policy-makers who shared them that we could predict that war would once again become a regular feature of the international politics of the period.

The First World War de-bellicized important segments of European publics and policy-making circles. But the great totalitarian movements of the interwar period once again raised war to a positive social good, a major means of proving the superiority of given races, nationalities, and ideologies. Hitler, Mussolini, and their emulators in many European countries resurrected the mystique of national glory through violence, and they attempted to reestablish the connection between civic and military leadership in the Napoleonic manner. The dictators' personal glory and prestige could be established and enhanced through the great victories of the nations' armed forces, the forces which they personally commanded. The relationship between their attitudes toward war and their decisions and actions was close, perhaps determining.

The Second World War and its conclusion with the atomic destruction of Hiroshima and Nagasaki proved to all but the most committed warriors that general war was no longer an option in the lives of modern states. Henceforth, the purpose of armed forces would be primarily to prevent war through deterrence rather than to fight. Most responsible policy-makers have publicly acknowledged that nuclear war would be an unprecedented disaster for all humanity. Attitudes have shifted dramatically to the point that in conflict situations, risks and costs have come to loom as critically important variables in decision-making. Concerns about escalation, loss of control, "events getting out of hand," and the like have assumed more prominence than in previous eras. Few states have renounced the potential use of force, but clearly today it is seen among millions as an exceptional, if not pathological, form of behavior. Buttressing these attitudes is the growing recognition that the use of force seldom achieves its purposes. For the most part, the great powers have all suffered humiliating losses when undertaking armed interventions against wars of national liberation and other forms of violence in the Third World.

In the Third World, however, apocalyptic visions of war are not

327

predominant. Those countries were mostly spared the ravages and destruction of this century's two great European wars, and many of them achieved their independence only through armed struggle. There may be some lessons learned from futile armed contests such as those between Iran and Iraq in the 1980s, but the historical experience of many Third World countries regarding war has been generally more favorable than the industrial countries' tragic and suicidal wars of this century. Religious fundamentalism may also shift views in favor of violence. Attitudes may of course change, and certainly there are many international norms that lend weight to the more pacific hopes and expectations of populations and policy-makers in the industrialized countries. There are no regimes today that have gone to war with the enthusiasm and frequency of, for example, Louis XIV. But when the security problems facing many of the newer countries are combined with generally less pacific attitudes toward war, we could anticipate that wars will persist in many of these areas of the world. There is still a long way to go before the entire planet becomes "de-bellicized."

## ISSUES, WAR, AND INTERNATIONAL THEORY

Recent debates about appropriate formats for studying international politics have underlined different visions of the essential actors, structures, and processes of the world. These visions have been accorded the unfortunate title of "paradigms," and there is considerable disagreement about the purposes for developing them. For some, they are analytical devices for ordering a field of inquiry and for organizing research programmes. For others, they represent preferred worlds or trends toward which the world is heading. In previous work I have labeled these visions according to the criteria of (1) the nature of the essential actors; (2) the normative problem that animates ethical and scientific concern; and (3) the images of the world/system/society of states (K. J. Holsti, 1985a:7–8). There are three resulting models of international politics: the realist school and its derivative neo-realist model, dependency theory, and world society models. I would modify this trinity for the purposes of this study by deleting the dependency model (because its normative focus is justice and equality, not peace and war) and adding a model developed in some detail at the turn of the century and during the First World War (Petersson, 1964) but popularized more recently in the work of Robert Keohane and Joseph Nye (1972) under the term "transnational relations." It can be called a pluralist model because it emphasizes the variety of actors involved in international politics and the mixture of processes that takes place between these actors.

The realist vision places power as a central concept in describing and explaining the behavior of states. Power is a tangible resource founded upon territory, industrial capacity, population, and the like. It is both a means and an end. To Hans Morgenthau (1948), for example, all state interests are defined in power terms, and the processes of international politics are depicted as a constant struggle for power. Morgenthau also discusses three "policies": imperialism, status quo, and balance of power. This is about as close as he comes to discussing issues.

This version of power politics has its roots not so much in the thought of Hobbes, Machiavelli, or Rousseau as in a group of German, French and Italian political analysts of the late nineteenth and early twentieth centuries. These analysts strongly reflected Darwinian, Hegelian, and Nietzschean power-through-struggle themes. Like Morgenthau and his successors, they depicted international politics as a struggle for power, a ceaseless search for safety and supremacy, where resources, population, and, above all, territory provide the wherewithal for success (Petersson, 1964:35–43). In their preference for establishing a world on hierarchical principles (one great power must dominate or be dominated by another) they differed from Morgenthau, who was a champion of balance and moderation. But the central organizing concepts and the vision of both the structures and processes of international politics are notably similar.

The neo-realist derivative is best exemplified in the structural analysis of Kenneth Waltz (1979). His parsimonious explanatory theory of international politics posits international structures as the main, though not sole, sources of the recurrent behavior of states. Structures, which are defined in terms of the organizing principles of the states system (anarchy), the positions of the main actors, and their relative capabilities, lead to recurring outcomes, of which war, balances of power, concerns for the relative rewards of cooperation, and the reproduction of statehood are the most significant. Structural characteristics also influence how the great powers will manage international affairs. Waltz observes that regardless of the intentions of policy-makers, these forms of behavior recur. Structures condition and determine regardless of the attributes of states, ideologies, the nature of processes between states, individual personalities, and all other phenomena located at the state or process levels. The main theme of structuralist analyses of international relations is that despite great differences between states, system outcomes are similar. Whereas theories of foreign policy emphasize differences between states as explanations of

329

war, structuralists adhere to the principle of similarity of units and similarity of behaviors.

Waltz has made a major contribution to the development of a parsimonious and rigorous theoretical statement about international politics. Yet, as he himself admits, he has not explained all. And the reader might well ask whether the things to be explained – the recurrent behaviors – are really what we want to know about international politics. Some critical questions are overlooked. Why, for example, do we see such great variations in the location and incidence of war? Why are some balances relatively stable (for most of the nineteenth century) while others change with unusual frequency (mid eighteenth century)? What are the limits of imitation? To speak of states today as "units," as if they are functionally the same despite their tremendous variations, may overlook some important discontinuities that have significant effects on behavior. For example, the security problematics of many of the newer states are vastly different from those of the more established members of the system. In the Third World, most wars occur because of domestic cleavages, not because of the security dilemma, arms races, or structural characteristics associated with Europe's diplomatic experience. It would be inappropriate to examine the etiology of war in the Third World using concepts and approaches that derive from and are germane only to the progeny of the European states system. If, as I have claimed, we really have two interlocking state systems, it would be misleading to analyze the dynamics of one with the concepts from the other. Waltz and his fellow structuralists' concept of the state is too undifferentiated. The vast differences between pre- and post-1945 states has to be acknowledged in any theory of international relations (K. J. Holsti, 1989).

This book started with the assumption that politics is purposeful activity. But the identification of purpose is an empirical problem and not one of *a priori* definition. I have demonstrated in the substantive chapters that in the international political arena man has multiple purposes. These purposes change over time and reflect fundamental social and ideological transformation taking place within societies and in international society. Governments are perennially concerned with questions of power and influence – the means of policy – but they are just as preoccupied with purposes. The range of goals is vast, running from the peaceful advancement and protection of welfare values to dreams of universal empire. They are animated by ideals and ideas, values and interests, and sentiments of kinship and sympathy. These are often more potent explanations of behavior than some ubiquitous struggle for power or structural conditions. Most wars, in fact, have

330

been struggles over values, beliefs, and sympathies, and not over power.

If all states are condemned to behave in a similar fashion because of structural factors (anarchy) or because of an eternal struggle for power, we would expect wars and balances to be relatively constant forms of behavior or outcomes between all pairs of states. These behavioral patterns no doubt recur, but the variations in recurrence are so great that they must command inquiry. No living Swede can recall his or her country being involved in a war (the last one was in 1809), while an Israeli of middle age can recall five wars and was probably an armed combatant in at least two of them. Venezuela has been officially (and in that case, only symbolically) at war only once; Russia has engaged in armed combat or armed intervention at least thirty-seven times since the early seventeenth century. Many neighbors have been at peace for a century or more (Canada and the United States, Chile and Bolivia, Spain and Portugal), while others have faced chronic tensions, disputes, and wars (Greece and Turkey, India and Pakistan). Between 1947 and the late 1960s, approximately, there was no balance of power – there was a preponderance of power, as there was in the 1920s and many other eras. Structural and power theories cannot account for these significant variations. The discussion of issues cannot account for them either, but at least it alerts us to the many different things governments quarrel about and how these change over time. A vision of a ubiquitous struggle for power or of a determining systemic structure explains recurrence without accounting for non-recurrence or the great deviations from an "average" pattern of recurrence. To argue that we have war because of systems structures is analogous to an argument that we have automobile accidents because we have highways. Can a comprehensive explanation of war avoid asking what men fight about, how issues rise and decline, and how man's concepts of and attitudes toward the social act of warfare arise and change?

Power is linked to purposes in the sense that it shapes, enhances, or constrains the definition and achievement of values and goals (it would be difficult to envisage the leaders of Vanuatu proclaiming a goal of universal hegemony); but it is seldom an end in itself. Just as the First World War cannot be treated as a typical war – as it often has been in the literature on war and crisis – so the search for power and security in Europe at the turn of the century cannot be taken as the model for all international relationships since 1648. If there is one significant recurrence in the world of diplomacy and war throughout our historical period since 1648, it is the search for statehood (one of Waltz' recurring outcomes), and not a struggle for power or a balance of power.

331

This study also underlines the continuing importance of the state and its agents on questions of war, peace, and order-building. A state-centric vision of the world is appropriate if not complete when examining these problems. Since 1648 it has been governments or those who aspire to become governments (national liberation movements, for example) that ultimately decide the great questions of war and peace, and it is largely governments that define the purposes that must be pursued or defended.

But non-state actors' roles in the etiology of war cannot be overlooked; indeed their importance may be increasing. Social groups and communities have frequently generated "sympathy" issues that have attracted foreign attention and occasional armed intervention. Early colonial wars were often rooted in the operations of private individuals and the chartered companies, irredenta movements usually developed at the grass-roots level, and, as in the case of the Kwantung army, foreign policy was occasionally driven by the activities of armies in the field. Yet, in our 177 wars and armed interventions, the majority were defined by the policy-makers in terms of state and/or dynastic interests.

To the extent that environmental issues, international drug trafficking, and large population migrations may become increasingly important issues on the international agenda, the transnational relations approach can help organize significant research programmes on future international conflict. In the new states of the world, moreover, transnational links between secessionist groups and external patrons who fund, train, and in other ways support them help to explain the transformation of local rebellions and civil wars into international conflicts and wars.

The evidence provided in the preceding chapters is not congenial to world society models, either as analytical devices or as relevant scenarios for the future. The major cleavages in the international system have been between those who sought to fashion the world on hierarchical principles and those who have championed ideological pluralism and the continued political fragmentation of mankind. The predominance of the values of autonomy, independence, and exclusiveness are pronounced throughout the three and one-half centuries covered here. That there are powerful homogenizing tendencies that bring people closer together – physically, culturally, and ideologically – cannot be denied. But there are also forces that drive them to assert their uniqueness and separateness. Whatever the long-run outcomes of these tendencies, the conditions for a relatively egalitarian and symmetrical world society do not exist today. A single world political

332

order, reflecting the emerging global economy, would be one of hegemony and subordination, no matter how benign it might look on the surface. We know upon whose societies a "world community" would be modeled. It would certainly not be Indonesia, India, or Tonga. It would not even be Japan. (Europeans and Americans have had no end of difficulties trying to understand the Japanese, particularly in their business practices and their penchant for hard work. The plethora of English-language books that try to explain Japanese society and business practices take the same approach: they basically criticize the Japanese for being *different*.) Lurking behind many of the models of world society is a hidden ethnocentrism. Everyone wants a world society (if it results in peace) so long as it reflects one's own society, language, economy, and political institutions (cf. Rummel, 1981). World society models may offer analytical possibilities for exploring new sorts of transnational processes, emerging social patterns, the impact of technological innovations, and other social phenomena that arise from scientific and economic trends, but questions of war and peace, which often revolve around issues of statehood (confirming the world's political fragmentation) are better explored through state-centric analytical devices.

The final theoretical question concerns the appropriateness of a Clausewitzian conception of war in a nuclear age. I have argued that we learn more about war when we conceive of it in political-instrumental terms as compared to conceptions based on deviant, pathological, or epidemiological analogies. It has become the conventional wisdom even in the Soviet Union that nuclear war can serve no rational purpose because it would destroy the state and society that weapons have traditionally been designed to protect. In the last chapter we explored the various intellectual means the Americans have developed to try to escape the dilemma – particularly the idea of "limited nuclear war." But society and the state cannot coexist with any nuclear war. The greatest threat to the security of the modern industrial state, then, is not a particular adversary but nuclear war and perhaps even some forms of conventional war. Thus technology has rendered Clausewitz irrelevant and possibly very dangerous.

But most states do not possess instruments of mass destruction, and those that do have not renounced the use of force in general. There have been too many wars – many for at least minimally justifiable reasons – in other areas of the world to suggest that the nuclear reality facing Washington, Moscow, London, Paris, and Beijing necessarily extends beyond the great power relationships. The costs of war and armaments may have risen substantially, but they have not yet fundamentally altered the decision calculus: war remains one of several techniques of advancing and protecting values, beliefs, and interests. This is not to say that it will always or even occasionally succeed – Saddam Hussein must have wondered many times why he started the war against Iran – but there is little evidence to suggest that the verbal and emotional commitment to peace so often expressed in the context of potential nuclear war finds strong echoes in thinking on the use of force in general. We have chronicled changing attitudes toward the use of force over the past three centuries. These have been significant in many ways, in some respects even revolutionary. In the industrial countries in particular, there is a strong presumption against the use of force. But that presumption has not yet taken on the character of a universal legal or moral imperative. For the foreseeable future the Clausewitzian model of war remains regrettably valid.

# 13 THE PEACEMAKERS: ISSUES AND INTERNATIONAL ORDER

> We are never completely contemporaneous with our present. History advances in disguise; it appears on stage wearing the mask of the preceding scene, and we tend to lose the meaning of the play. Each time the curtain rises, continuity has to be re-established. The blame ... is not history's but lies in our vision, encumbered with memory and images learned in the past. We see the past superimposed on the present, even when the present is a revolution.          Regis Debray

Some issues in international politics have been irreconcilable. They involve fundamentally incompatible positions on beliefs, essential values, and political purposes. Among the most important were conflicts over the structure and nature of the international system or society of states. The issues of religious conformity and tolerance, their expression in civil law and education, and conflicts over hierarchical versus pluralistic images of the appropriate political organization of Christendom combined to produce the Thirty Years War. Incompatible positions on hegemony versus pluralism, as maintained by the balance of power, were at the heart of the War of the Spanish Succession. The same issues were raised again during the French Revolution and Napoleon's reign.

, The bilateral conflict between Serbia and Austria-Hungary in 1914 did not touch upon the vital interests of Germany, France, and England. Although Europe was divided by two hostile alliance systems, no party sought hegemony in the way that the Hapsburg family complex, Louis XIV, or Napoleon had pursued it. The states system was not at issue in 1914, only the relative ranking of the powers and Germany's fear of encirclement. Despite this fear, numerous German statements indicated a commitment to predominance in Europe, if not hegemony.

The Second World War resurrected the old cluster of issues dividing those who sought to organize the European states system on hierarchical and monolithic lines, placing Germany in a position of undisputed

335

mastery over all others, and those who were committed to the perpetuation of the Westphalian system. In the Nazi New Order there would be no room for sovereign states. The states of Europe, after armed conquest or occupation, were to be organized upon various degrees of subordination and exploitation by the Third Reich. Some, like Poland, were to be eliminated.

In each of these cases the major issues between the protagonists were clear enough, although there was plenty of misperception, poor calculation (Chamberlain's view of Hitler), false hopes, and unjustified expectations. But on the eve of the great wars most of the participants understood that the threats were not directed against a single state but challenged the system of states in general. With hindsight it is difficult to see how political organizations committed to such fundamentally incompatible visions of domestic and international arrangements could have reconciled the issues through ordinary modes of conflict resolution. Wars may not have been inevitable, but most policymakers, given the purposes to which they were committed, could see few alternatives in 1618, 1700, the 1790s, and 1939.

The great wars led to great peacemaking efforts. The victors were committed to preventing a recurrence of the previous war, and they all attempted to create some sort of order which would enhance security for all and sustain the principles of political fragmentation and pluralism. These orders were constructed through territorial adjustments, the establishment of conflict-resolving procedures and institutions, various provisions for dealing with the vanquished, and the elaboration of legal principles and less formal norms for regulating the mutual transactions of the several states. The great peace conferences authoritatively resolved the issues that had led to war; they registered in legal terms, usually backed by the power of the victors, the outcomes of armed combat. They also debated and resolved many other kinds of issues that had disturbed bilateral and multilateral relationships in the previous period.

How are we to evaluate these great attempts to build international order? Each chapter dealing with the individual peacemaking efforts has offered some implicit and explicit judgments. But the analyses were neither comparative nor comprehensive.

### THE PREREQUISITES FOR PEACE

One way to proceed is to construct a hypothetical international order whose members share the following purposes: (1) maintenance of sovereign independence; (2) security; (3) economic and social welfare; and (4) autonomy, meaning the enhancement or maintenance of decision-making latitude and freedom on problems both of domestic and foreign policy. They are also committed to controlling, reducing, or eliminating war, but they would rather suffer uncertainty, insecurity, and some war than lose their independence. The first-order purpose of system members is thus to perpetuate anarchy or the principle of pluralism. The architects of the order assume that there will be *états de mauvaise foi*, some states that do not share the general principles underlying the order. Some states will have different priorities.

What would be needed to achieve or sustain these common purposes? The requirements listed below derive from no theory of peace (there is none that applies convincingly to the states system), or from any body of empirical knowledge. They are arbitrary judgments and do not purport to include all the sufficient conditions for a stable international order, where stable is defined as the avoidance of system-threatening wars, effective control over those who might seek to destroy the order, and significant reduction in the incidence of war. They are probably necessary conditions, however. The prerequisites are not exclusive; some of the categories may overlap at the fringes.

### A system of governance

Governance at the international level does not imply centralized legislative, administrative, and police powers. An international order need not be designed on the domestic analogy of nation-states. It does mean that some or all actors, or an agency acting on their behalf, must be able to make decisions on what constitutes tolerable foreign policy behavior, identify major transgressions of rules and norms, and be prepared to act jointly to enforce them. Governance need not include formal international organizations. It can be manifested in guarantee treaties, periodic summit meetings, and similar devices. In 1648, for example, Sweden and France were the guarantors of the peace and obtained the right to intervene in the affairs of the Holy Roman Empire to make certain that the terms of the settlements were observed.

### Legitimacy

A stable order cannot be founded upon injustice and repression. The peace settlement that establishes both the results of the war and the foundations for the postwar order should not create the breeding ground for a new war to overturn the results of the previous conflict. This can be avoided in part by assimilating the defeated actor(s) into the postwar order. Regimes "beyond the pale" – those that retain commitments to principles fundamentally incompatible with the four common purposes of states – would have to be altered or suppressed. There could have been no question of a negotiated peace with Hitler, for example.

Principles of justice (easier asserted than defined) have to be incorporated into the postwar settlement. These would include notions of self-determination, self-abnegation by the military victors by forgoing extensive territorial and other spoils; modest reparations, if any, based on some objective analysis of war responsibility, and the like.

### Assimilation

The purpose of assimilation is to demonstrate that the gains of living within the system even as a temporarily vanquished state outweigh the potential advantages of seeking to destroy or dominate it. Assimilation, as suggested, is closely connected to the legitimacy requirement. Both assimilation and legitimacy may be increased by knowledge of the recent historical record: most of the losers of the Second World War had impressive postwar recovery records and today are world leaders in economic achievement.

### A deterrent system

The victors should create a coalition, including the vanquished, that is committed to the settlement. That coalition should be large enough so that the defection of one great power (or perhaps more, depending upon the total number in the coalition) will not destroy the capacity of the remainder to enforce, by arms if necessary, the major terms of the settlement and the norms of the system, or to change them through peaceful processes.

### Conflict-resolving procedures and institutions

The system of governance should include procedures and institutions for identifying, monitoring, managing, and resolving major conflicts between members of the system. In some cases this might include the authority and capacity to impose settlement terms where continuation of a conflict poses a threat to the system as a whole. The norms of the system include the presumption that states in conflict would employ the various facilities; non-use would imply aggressive intent.

338

### Consensus on war

System members must recognize and acknowledge that war is the fundamental problem facing the community of states. Those who design the order should develop and foster strong norms against the use of force and carefully articulate those circumstances in which it might be justified. Such circumstances, aside from self-defense, would include the collective or delegated use of force for the welfare and benefit of the society of states.

### Procedures for peaceful change

Change is a constant of social, economic, and political life. No peace settlement can successfully hope to freeze a moment in history. What may seem just and practical shortly after the conclusion of a major war may be unjust and impractical twenty or thirty years later. The problem of peaceful change fostered through diplomatic and other procedures, a subject of great controversy and debate in the 1930s, has been all but forgotten in the post-Second World War era. The vocabulary of diplomacy has included terms such as a "lasting peace," "peace with justice," and "permanent peace," but few agreements have incorporated methods and procedures for reviewing settlement terms, for raising new grievances, in general for adjusting commitments and responsibilities to new social, economic, demographic, and diplomatic conditions. Peaceful change also requires the provision, bilaterally or multilaterally, of face-saving devices and means of persuading recalcitrant parties to acknowledge and adjust to the inevitable. The United Nations offered many useful services in the process of decolonization, but much bloodshed surrounding the state-creation process could have been avoided if some metropole governments had learned more rapidly that maintenance of overseas empire was no longer possible or acceptable. Peaceful change is one of the most difficult problems in international relations and requires much greater thought.

### Anticipation of future issues

Closely related to the problem of peaceful change is the peacemakers' ability to anticipate the kinds of issues that will generate international conflict in the future. The territorial settlements, institutions, and system norms should include provision for identifying, monitoring, and handling not just the problems that created the previous war but future conflicts as well.

339

## PEACEMAKING AND INTERNATIONAL ORDER: A COMPARISON

How well did the five great peacemaking efforts meet these criteria? Table 13.1 presents judgments based on the descriptive accounts in previous chapters. Several of the evaluations require elaboration and explanation.

The items with superscripts indicate that the settlement in question made provisions to meet the criterion but that in the period immediately following the settlement the provisions were not implemented. The Covenant of the League of Nations, for example, established a Council whose major power members would monitor both the war settlement and postwar international relations in general. The norms of the system were clearly spelled out in numerous articles in the document. But the United States failed to join the governance system, Germany was excluded for an indefinite period, and the Soviet Union neither sought nor was admitted to original membership. The remaining great powers were marginally sufficient to provide governance during the 1920s, but when Italy, Japan, and Germany defected from the postwar order and in fact sought to dismantle it, the governance system collapsed. The Treaties of Münster and Osnabrück contained conflict-resolving procedures, but they were never institutionalized or employed in relation to major postwar issues. The Charter of the United Nations provided for the establishment of a deterrent system in the form of a United Nations armed force that was to be organized under a blueprint developed by the Security Council's Military Staff Committee. By 1947, its work was undermined by the cold war. The question mark following the assimilation criterion for San Francisco raises the problem of how rapid the assimilation should be. France was

Table 13.1 *The prerequisites of peace: the major settlements compared*

| Prerequisite | Westphalia | Utrecht | Vienna | Paris | San Francisco |
|---|---|---|---|---|---|
| Governance | yes | yes | yes | no[a] | yes |
| Legitimacy | yes | no | yes | no | yes |
| Assimilation | yes | yes | yes | no | yes? |
| Deterrent | yes | no | yes | no | no[a] |
| Conflict resolution | no[a] | no | yes | yes | yes |
| War/problem | no | no | no | yes | yes |
| Peaceful change | no | no | no | yes | no |
| Future issues | no | no | no | no | no |
| Total | 4/8 | 2/8 | 5/8 | 3/8 | 5/8 |

[a] = designed but never implemented

reincorporated into the order by the time the diplomats met in Vienna in 1815; Germany entered the League of Nations in 1926, seven years after the Versailles Treaty was imposed on it. It took about as long to assimilate Japan and Germany (but not Italy) after the Second World War, but it could be argued that the blueprint for assimilation of Germany was already in place by the time of the Potsdam Conference in July 1945, and of Japan early after the installation of the Occupation. Hence the affirmative judgment.

If table 13.1 is read horizontally, several conclusions become apparent. First, all the great peacemaking conferences were concerned not only with settling the issues of the past war, but also with establishing some governance system. In most cases some or all of the victors were also the governors: Sweden and France in 1648, England and Holland in 1713–14, all the great powers at Vienna, and the victorious great powers in Paris and San Francisco. Vienna, however, was the only settlement where there was a universal great power commitment to the governance system. In all others, defeated great powers were not immediately made parties to the governance system, or the winning wartime coalition fell apart before the system became institutionalized and legitimized.

Second, those peace settlements that were not considered legitimate by the vanquished and other states were soon threatened or overthrown. Spain sought immediately to undo the Utrecht settlements and Hitler's long-range programme was devoted to a systematic dismantling of the key elements of the Treaty of Versailles. Japanese military leaders in the 1930s also rejected the Paris settlement and the order it brought into being.

Third, in all but the Paris settlements the vanquished were assimilated into the postwar order within a reasonable period of time. The exclusion of Germany in 1919 paid bitter dividends. There was considerable justification for the German view that Wilson had betrayed his own principles of a negotiated peace – a point that Hitler was to repeat frequently, the last time in a mocking speech in reply to Roosevelt's famous 1938 telegram asking the *Führer* not to attack a long list of countries the American president supplied.

Fourth, only two of the settlements provided deterrent systems, but both were fundamentally flawed. France was a guarantor of the Westphalia treaties, but those treaties made no provision against one of the guarantors becoming a major revisionist power. By the 1670s Sweden had no military capacity to enforce the treaties by itself. The Utrecht treaties provided mutual guarantees and the stationing of Dutch and British troops in key garrisons. But the commitments were never put into effect and it is doubtful that even if they had, they would have been sufficient to command respect and prevent the revisionist powers, particularly Spain, from seeking to undo the settlements. Wilson's deterrent of public opinion was built on hopes rather than on realities, but there is little evidence that most governments would have been prepared to construct a League of Nations armed force along the lines advocated by Leon Bourgeois. The "policemen" of the world organization launched in 1945 had intentions similar to those of Bourgeois, but because the two pillars of the system became embraced in the cold war they had no chance of implementation. The history of the great powers after 1945 underlined the importance of the question: who will police the policemen?

Fifth, four of the five settlements organized procedures for resolving future conflicts. Those of the Westphalia treaties were never implemented, and the loose system of consultation among the powers during the nineteenth century, while working very well for most of the period, lapsed into disuse or ineffectiveness by the late nineteenth century. The idea of formal organizations responsible for bringing disputing parties together did not develop until shortly before the Great War, and at that time the term "peaceful settlement of disputes" referred primarily to legal procedures. As the documents resulting from the Hague conferences in 1899 and 1907 showed, governments were not yet willing to allow third-party intervention in disputes involving vital national interests or national honor. Both the League and the United Nations made substantial strides in institutionalizing conflict-resolving procedures, and they were and have been used with sufficient frequency and general effectiveness to warrant optimism. However, those procedures were hedged with all sorts of constraints, including the principle of voluntarism, the requirement for unanimous voting in the League of Nations, the availability of the veto in Security Council deliberations, and the inability or unwillingness of the organizations to develop terms of settlement for specific conflicts. In practice, moreover, both organizations were reactive rather than proactive. They did not monitor situations well, and they rarely interjected themselves into a conflict until the fighting had already begun. Peacekeeping operations were improvised starting in 1956, but these were rarely predecessors for formal settlements. The conflicts became frozen instead of settled. In contrast to the United Nations, however, the League successfully employed plebiscites and legal procedures to settle a variety of conflicts before they reached the shooting stage (K. J. Holsti, 1988:116–19). But whatever the success rates of the various procedures used since the Congress of Vienna, the important point is

342

that the formal intervention of third parties into international disputes and conflicts has become an accepted norm of the system. There is a presumption against the use of force; this represents a radical change from the perspectives of the eighteenth and early nineteenth centuries.

Sixth, attitudes toward the use of force in international relations have changed perhaps more fundamentally than have institutions and procedures. The substantive chapters have sought to chronicle these changes. In the first three of the great settlements, war was not recognized as a problem requiring special attention. It was commonly viewed as an inherent right deriving from sovereignty, fully justified by *raison d'état*. Even into the latter part of the nineteenth century, war was celebrated in many circles as a positive virtue. It took the slaughter and destruction of the Great War to compel the diplomats to acknowledge that a main task of the society of states was to prevent all war. The theory of collective security could not develop until there was universal recognition that war was indeed the primary problem on the international agenda. The Paris and San Francisco conferences made the necessary declaratory statements on the issue and carefully specified under what conditions force could be used, but they did not create the mechanisms by which those norms could be enforced.

Seventh, none of the architects of peace really focused deeply on the problem of peaceful change. Most, in fact, wanted to prevent change (Westphalia, Utrecht, Vienna) or to ignore the problem (San Francisco). There was not even much consideration given to changes of specific terms contained in the settlements. Only the diplomats in Paris in 1919 seriously examined the problem. The Covenant of the League of Nations addressed the issue, but in legalistic terms (primarily as a problem of treaty revision). Wilson assumed that the constitution of the League would be amended and changed as conditions warranted. He saw the Covenant as the foundation of an order rather than as a final and fixed plan. But given certain constraints built into the Covenant and the onslaught on the norms of the Paris–Geneva system launched by the dictators, the organization had little opportunity to grow and develop.

The problem of peaceful change remains largely unexamined today, although there is periodic discussion of altering and improving conflict-resolving institutions and procedures. The question of changing the United Nations has been dealt with on an ad hoc basis: the Uniting for Peace Resolution of 1950 and the introduction of peacekeeping operations were probably the most important innovations. Given the impossibility of obtaining sufficient voting support for Charter amendments, however, it is unlikely that the United Nations will develop

343

significant new powers or resources. Recent changes in Soviet attitudes toward the United Nations may, however, offer possibilities. In a series of proposals beginning in 1987, Soviet leaders have urged the organization to expand its peacekeeping functions and to augment its roles and tasks in crisis management and the definition of terms of peaceful settlement. General Secretary Gorbachev proposed the creation of a United Nations war risk reduction center in which there would be direct communications links between the United Nations headquarters and the capitals of the permanent members of the Security Council and the chairman of the non-aligned group. Most importantly, the Russians have sought to expand the monitoring and proactive capacities of the organization. Soviet Foreign Minister Shevardnadze has proposed the creation of a multilateral verification center under the auspices of the Secretary-General. Its purpose would be to dispatch fact-finding missions to areas of international tension and conflict. The information could then be used to initiate consultations with the conflict parties and members of the Security Council. The Office of Research and the Collection of Information (ORCI) has already been established. It will provide the Secretary-General with early warning of serious developments that might require his attention and initiatives (von Riekhoff, 1989:6).

If implemented, these could be significant changes to the capacities of the organization. But the problem of social change and international conflict remains largely unexplored. There has been and remains a lack of empirical knowledge about the relationship so that proper diagnoses and evaluations of future trouble spots will be difficult to develop. Augmenting the research and proactive capacities of the United Nations and regional organizations should be helpful, but it will no doubt require much more than increasing the tasks and responsibilities of the international civil service to make effective contributions.

Finally, all the great peace settlements failed in one important respect. The architects of peace were backward-looking. Understandably, perhaps, they focused on resolving the issues that had been the source of the previous war and some lesser ones as well. They attempted to construct international orders that would prevent a recurrence of previous crises, but most were insufficiently farsighted to note important new issues already appearing on the diplomatic horizon. The peacemakers at Osnabrück and Münster did nothing about the emerging colonial conflicts or about the scramble for control of the open seas. They assumed that France would be a conservative champion of the new order rather than an aggressive and territorially expansionist power. They apparently did not think through what would be

344

the implications of sovereignty if there were no universal norms or institutions to monitor and control its worst consequences – predation against other sovereigns. The peacemakers at Utrecht – particularly the French and British – wanted to create a general order for western Europe, but they assumed that only Spain or the Holy Roman Empire could upset that order. The problem in international relations at the time was more fundamental. Most of the princes of Christendom were engaged in activities that were inconsistent with order. Utrecht defined a particular peace for a particular problem (French hegemony), but it ignored more important problems that were generic to the system. The architects of Paris and Vienna in 1814–15 were captivated by the twin problems of revolution and future French aggression. They ignored or wanted to suppress the rising forces of republicanism and nationalism. They were certainly not ignorant of them, but with the exception of the Tsar (when he was wearing his liberal hat) they saw them as forces subversive to their main enterprise, which was to construct a territorial balance of power. They approached the issues not as challenges but as mortal threats. It is only on issues such as slavery and navigation on the Rhine that the diplomats gathered in Vienna demonstrated significant foresight.

The peacemakers at Paris had learned important lessons during the Great War, the most important of which was that there must be no repetition of it. The protagonists all had different recipes for preventing another conflagration, most of them based on different diagnoses of the causes of the previous war. But they also learned that they could not carve up the world without taking into consideration the wishes, interests, and opinions of those who inhabited the various territories. Following Wilson's lead with different degrees of enthusiasm, they anticipated that an enduring settlement would have to be based on elements of justice (usually defined in terms of self-determination) as well as of power. They did anticipate that the principle of nationality would have to be reckoned with in future international relationships. There was also some constructive thinking – thanks in part to the activities of numerous public groups – on the question of colonies. The mandates system was based on the principle that the primary purpose of colonialism was to improve the lot of the people under colonial rule. Practice did not match the expectations, but at least there was a recognition that unless something positive were done, the colonies would emerge as a significant issue of the future. There were other areas of innovation (the I.L.O. and the like), but they dealt primarily with problems that were unlikely to breed armed conflicts between states. Not surprisingly, most of the intellectual energy at Paris, however,

345

was devoted to dealing with the German question and the structure of the new international organization. Looming issues such as world trade, the role and position of the new Bolshevik regime in the international system, and the rise of numerous anti-democratic movements in Europe were either ignored or defied solution. Wilson certainly cannot be accused of being backward-looking. However, his gaze toward the future was ethnocentric, heroically optimistic, and for the most part impractical. He sought and fought for a new system of international relationships (based, of course, on significant currents of opinion and thought in the United States and Britain) constructed with liberal and democratic principles. In that kind of world there would be no issues that would defy peaceful resolution. The edifice of the new world would have to be created so that any issues of the future could be handled through reason, persuasion, and the force of world public opinion rather than through armed combat. But on the plane of foresight, Wilson stood mostly alone. His colleagues for the most part sought only to prevent a recurrence of the past.

Those who planned for the peace during the struggle against the Axis ranged in their perspectives as broadly as did Clemenceau, Lloyd George, and Wilson. Stalin was undoubtedly the most backward-looking among the Big Three. His vision of the future was defined largely in terms of the past: the threat of German revival and revenge. Not an active participant in the international system prior to the war, Stalin gave little evidence of being interested in its problems except where they might impinge on Soviet security concerns or offer opportunities for revolutionary activity. Russian diplomats were uninterested in and did not participate vigorously in the numerous Allied discussions of world economic problems, colonialism, reconstruction in Europe, refugees, the Jewish problem, and the like.

The American planners, in contrast, were the most concerned with the future, defined in terms of new sets of problems and new opportunities. They accurately forecast that colonialism would emerge as a major source of international conflict unless it was addressed through commitments to de-colonization. Preoccupied with issues of more immediate moment and concerned about their postwar status as great powers, neither the British nor the French wanted to discuss these problems. Both Churchill and de Gaulle assumed that their countries would continue to meet their "responsibilities" as far as the colonies and mandates were concerned. The Americans also initiated discussions on world economics, trade, and finance. They were the first to make explicit theoretical linkages between economic conditions and war, and to underline the harmful consequences of the increasingly visible gap between the "have" and "have not" countries and colonies. The task was to put into place institutions and norms that could prevent a recurrence of the depression. And it was the Americans and British who abandoned – much to the consternation of the Russians – the idea of German dismemberment and substituted for it policies aimed at postwar assimilation. Despite the capacity to anticipate future issues, I have judged that in 1945 this criterion was not met adequately. The reader may disagree. The reasons for the judgment are that (1) despite all the growing evidence of the breakdown of the wartime coalition (for which American and British policies were in part responsible), the world organization was built on an assumption of continued solidarity; (2) despite American prescience on the issue of colonialism and state creation, it was not emphasized for fear of disrupting the coalition. The legacy of America's support of its allies' colonial policies continued into the 1960s; the war in Vietnam was one of them; and (3) population growth in what was to become known as the Third World was ignored although there was accumulating evidence that it would result in serious postwar dilemmas.

Given the press of events and the short time available for establishing the framework of peace (the Versailles Treaty, which sought to construct a new Europe had to be negotiated in less than six months. It is amazing that the 448 articles of that voluminous document, encompassing innumerable compromises between national positions, could have been negotiated in such a short time), it may be asking too much for wartime leaders to cast their minds more to the future. The immediate war settlements are difficult enough. But in so far as the peacemakers were involved not just in settling a past war but also in constructing the foundations of a new international order, foresight is mandatory. The peace system must not only resolve the old issues that gave rise to previous wars; it must anticipate new issues, new actors, and new problems, and it must design institutions, norms, and procedures that are appropriate to them.

If we look at the columns representing each of the great peace settlements, there is a relationship between the number of the criteria that were met and the subsequent history of war: the fewer the criteria fulfilled, the greater the number of immediate and subsequent wars involving central members of the new international order against each other. France and Spain remained critical enemies after Westphalia, and the peace did nothing to ameliorate the worsening conflicts between Holland and Great Britain. Within ten years of the settlement seven wars took place, although some of them involved parties (Russia) that were not part of the new order yet. Utrecht was similarly ineffective in maintaining peace in western Europe. Spain was at war twice within a decade after the settlements and the War of the Polish Succession (1733) involved six of the powers against each other. The Paris–Vienna settlement of 1814–15, in contrast, was followed by an extended era of intra-great power peace, disrupted only thirty-eight years later by the Crimean War. The record after 1919 and its various settlements is characterized by a number of forceful revisions of the resulting treaties, general turmoil, and within fifteen years, three great powers well launched on the road to serial aggressions and dedicated to the destruction of the order created by the architects of peace in Paris.

The organizers of the post-Second World War order were indifferent to or incapable of addressing effectively the problem of state creation, and the result was that the agenda of the new United Nations was soon filled with dozens of wars involving the quest for national liberation or national unification. There were, however, no intra-great power wars (China's intervention in the Korean War is a marginal exception), and that record has been maintained for a historically unprecedented period. The explanation for this fact does not lie so much in the wisdom of the peace planners in Moscow, London, and Washington, however, as it does in the spectre of nuclear war.

None of the great peacemaking exercises ended war; but some were more successful than others in constructing orders that helped to reduce the incidence of war or confined them to tolerable levels. The Paris–Vienna settlement stands out in particular. It may not be co-incidental that, along with San Francisco, this settlement met a greater number of the hypothesized requisites of a peaceful international order than the others.

### THE PEACEMAKERS: THEORIES OF PEACE

In this review of the major peace settlements, three common strategies for forging settlements and postwar orders emerge: (1) punishment and deterrence through domination; (2) balance of power; and (3) the transformation of the international system. Gustav Adolph (who was killed in battle before the peace negotiations began), the Prussians in 1813–15, Clemenceau, and Stalin represent the first category. All had a common diagnosis of the causes of war (the evil intentions of their adversaries), and they shared a common solution, which was permanently to weaken the aggressor and to keep it in a position of prolonged subordination through the overwhelming might of the victor(s). All assumed that the next war would come from the same sources as the last, and all entertained punitive and non-assimilative attitudes toward the defeated power(s). They were equally suspicious of attempts to build more general edifices of peace. Their vision of a postwar international order was hierarchical: the victors were entitled to extract from the vanquished whatever benefits they could obtain through their military forces, not only as recompense for the ills they had suffered prior to and during the war but also as means of maintaining the vanquished in a state of permanent weakness. The whole purpose of constructing any general international order was to prevent a recurrence of the previous war. None could imagine new issues and new actors. The prescription for peace flowed from the diagnosis: peace through the maintenance of overwhelming might by the victors.

Some elements from this category can be found in those peacemakers who emphasized the creation of a general international order based on principles of the balance of power. Castlereagh, for example, while a champion of assimilating France into the balance, also succeeded in constructing a territorial balance of power that was simultaneously a deterrent system against any renewal of French continental imperialism. Balance of power peacemakers like Richelieu, Mazarin, Stanhope, Castlereagh, Metternich, Lloyd George, and Churchill all thought of preventing the past war from recurring by constructing coalitions of those who were committed to the new order. Their central concept, then, was not so much balance as a preponderance of those who fashioned and were committed to the overall settlement conception. Where they differed fundamentally from the "peace through domination" group was in their desire to assimilate the vanquished and in their understanding of the changing complexion of international politics. Enmities do not last forever, new alignments and cleavages may emerge, old enemies may become new friends, and so the system has to be designed to be flexible, but always with the fundamental principle that those who are committed to the vision of a system of independent states must predominate over those who may have some other vision.

The "peace through balance" thinkers were generally pragmatic, understanding that conflict is an endemic part of all international relationships and that while war is an important problem and must be controlled and managed, a more significant problem is the maintenance of the system of independent states. It is not so much wars that are to be feared as the rise of those seeking hegemony and wishing to create empires in their own images. The problem, then, is systemic war, a particular type of cataclysmic confrontation between two funda-

349

mentally incompatible visions of how the world should be organized. Little wars cannot be prevented. The task is to keep them limited and to manage them so that they do not become a threat to the system. All of these problems can best be treated through directorates of the great powers that are committed to the system. And the best way of ensuring that the powers maintain that commitment is to design a rough and flexible balance of power with appropriate mechanisms for maintaining it.

The last category encompasses those who locate the sources of war (and not just the most recent war) in systemic characteristics and/or in certain types of socio-economic and political orders within its units. Aggression, expansion, competition, and war are the fundamental problems of international relations. In order to end these forms of behavior, the international system and/or its component units must be transformed. All of the traditional artifices such as balances of power, in their view, do not prevent wars. Therefore, revolutionary and all-encompassing strategies for building new orders must be pursued. The task of peacemaking is not to reconstruct a world on the ashes of the previous war but to start all over again with entirely new institutions and processes. Human institutions can resolve the problem of war; struggle, power contests, and violence are not an inevitable consequence of anarchy and of the states system. Tsar Alexander, Woodrow Wilson, Cordell Hull, and to a lesser extent Franklin Roosevelt epitomize this strand of thought. It is distinctly forward-looking and optimistic, and is not satisfied with just preventing the recurrence of the last war. New systems can be devised through human intelligence, negotiations, solemn pledges, and universal constitutions. One can create a peaceful world of states just as some countries have fashioned peaceful domestic orders. The domestic analogy – particularly the United States in 1919 and during the Second World War – commands the analysis of possible world futures. Not infrequently the ideas of perpetual peace are also rooted in conceptions of justice: not the situational justice of military victors, as the first group would have it, but a universal justice. They defined justice largely in classical liberal terms: self-determination, free trade, reciprocity, and democratic procedures for decision-making on international questions.

Another central point in the "peace through transformation" group of thinkers is that while it is utopian to believe that any peace system can eliminate international conflict, it is both realistic and possible to persuade the parties to conflicts to resolve them through means short of the use of force. War, as they saw it, is a deviant form of human behavior. It can therefore be eliminated. Conflict, however, is ubiqui-

350

tous. The task is to create those institutions and procedures – again using the domestic analogy – that can ensure their peaceful resolution.

But these theorists of peace failed to consider one major problem that was preeminent in the minds of those who promoted other strategies for peace: what can institutions, pledges, covenants, and universal principles of justice do in a system that contains one or more *états de mauvaise foi*, states that are committed to the destruction of the society of states, states that propound and extend by force political philosophies that are fundamentally incompatible with the four purposes that most states share? The Alexanders, Wilsons, and Hulls started with the assumption of a world community in which all members are committed to the system. Were such a community to exist, conflicts could be handled because the issues at stake would be relatively minor. But what if there is only a partial community? How can pledges and institutions deal with Napoleons and Hitlers?

The three strategies are of course ideal types. No one individual embraced all of the diagnoses, assumptions, and prescriptions they entailed, although Gustav Adolph, Wilson, and Stalin came close to embracing them exclusively. None of the great peace settlements reflected only a single approach. They were compromises fashioned through diplomacy and sometimes through the threat of force. We cannot therefore judge that one formula for peace is superior to another. Nevertheless, we could propose that those approaches that incorporate the eight prerequisites of peace are more likely to result in an enduring order and a lower incidence of system-threatening wars. The "peace through punishment and predominance" type is the most deficient because it cannot meet the criteria of legitimacy (justice) and assimilation, and would probably be deficient on the problems of peaceful change and concern with future issues. In its focus on preventing the wars of the past, its adherents were particularly blind to future problems. It is the most particularistic – concerned only with settling the outcome of the immediate war – and the most backward-looking.

The two other strategies can be consistent with most of the eight criteria, but each suffers the faults of the other's virtues. The "peace through transformation" ideal type is founded on overly-optimistic assumptions (e.g., it assumes a community of relatively benign states) and poor empirical analysis. Yet in its concern for justice it locates a fundamental source of international conflict and proposes to do something about it. Self-determination is an admirable principle entailing important liberal conceptions of justice. But its practical application may actually result in a greater incidence of conflict and war, because if it is applied as an essential principle for legitimating some new states, it has to be applied universally. In so doing it may conflict with other important foundations of statehood such as natural frontiers, effective government control, language/religious/ethnic contiguity, and the like. Self-determination also may be inconsistent with balancing principles, which require a limited number of viable and effective states to operate properly. Self-determination applied universally may result in the proliferation of conditionally viable and ineffective states, many of which will become the sources of future international conflict.

Balance of power prescriptions are in some ways admirable for their understanding of the dynamics of international politics, for acknowledging change, and for establishing the fundamental groundrules for perpetuation of a system of sovereign states. But in carving up territories and otherwise distributing populations and resources so as to contrive the balances, they overlook or are indifferent to modern ideas of justice. They are also based on a one-dimensional view of international politics, one that emphasizes power rather than issues and values as the mainsprings of foreign policy. Balance strategies remedy the weaknesses of the "peace through transformation approach," but they cannot be implemented without compromising important concepts of justice. The best avenues to peace, to the extent that they are human contrivances, thus remain a dilemma. We can argue that some may be better than others, but none is sufficient to guarantee the absence of war in the future.

Is there any message that derives from the analysis? Since in a nuclear environment we are not likely to have another general peace settlement, or if we do it will be beset with such unprecedented problems that no lessons from the past will be relevant, it could be argued that the study of how statesmen in the past have handled the issues that generated wars is only of archeological interest. This may well be the case, but many of the findings and generalizations in the study should be relevant to contemporary bilateral and multilateral regional peace efforts. In our academic fetish for studying the activities of the great powers we often lose sight of the diplomatic problems of lesser states. Some of them may face regional problems that are not structurally different from the wars of the European states system; they search for regional rather than universal peace (Westphalia and Utrecht were regional peace arrangements in the sense that they did not involve all the actors of the European states system). If there is to be a relatively enduring peace in post-Cold War Europe or the Middle East, for example, the eight criteria outlined above might well serve as guides to the policy-makers and negotiators. The same comment would apply to South Asia and to Southeast Asia. Given the great diversity of the world, of different societies and states, it is probably a chimera to think of universal peace. It may pay greater dividends to think in terms of the issues that generate conflict within regional settings.

This survey, I hope, has demonstrated the importance of addressing the problem of war from a Clausewitzian perspective. In assessing the question "what do men fight about?" we provide no causal explanations, nor can we shed light on the other significant question of why some conflicts end in war while others are either resolved or "frozen" so that the casualties cease piling up. But we can illuminate the kinds of issues that excite passions, how they arise and change over time, and how they are dealt with authoritatively in major peace settlements. To the extent that these peace settlements anticipate and devise means to cope with issues of the future, they can help mold reasonably stable and less war-prone international orders. Where they fail to do so, or where their recipes for dealing with the last war are seriously flawed, they help create the conditions for the wars of the future. Peace then becomes the father of war.

353

# REFERENCES

Adelman, Jonathon R. 1985. *Revolutions, Armies and War: A Political History.* Boulder, Colo.: Lynne Reinner.

Adomeit, Hannes. 1982. *Soviet Risk-taking and Crisis Behavior: A Theoretical and Empirical Analysis.* London: Allen & Unwin.

Albrecht-Carrie, René. 1968. *The Concert of Europe.* New York: Walker.

Bain, R. Nisbet. 1894. *Gustavus III and his Contemporaries.* 2 vols. London: Kegan Paul, Trench, Trubner.

Baker, Ray Stannard. 1923. *Woodrow Wilson and World Settlement.* 3 vols. New York: Doubleday, Page. Vol. III: *Original Documents of the Peace Conference.*

Bamba, Nobuya. 1972. *Japanese Diplomacy in a Dilemma: New Light on Japan's China Policy, 1924–1929.* Vancouver, B.C.: University of British Columbia Press.

Baring, Arnulf. 1989. "Transatlantic Relations: The View from Europe," *NATO Review* (February), 17–23.

Barnhart, Michael A. 1987. *Japan Prepares for Total War: The Search for Economic Security, 1919–1941.* Ithaca, New York: Cornell University Press.

Baynes, Norman H. 1942. *The Speeches of Adolf Hitler, April 1922–August 1939.* 2 vols. London: Oxford University Press.

Beales, Arthur C. F. 1931. *The History of Peace.* London: Bell.

Beer, Francis A. 1981. *Peace Against War: The Ecology of International Conflict.* San Francisco: W. H. Freeman.

Ben-Israel, Hedva. 1969. *English Historians on the French Revolution.* Cambridge: Cambridge University Press.

Best, Geoffrey. 1982. *War and Society in Revolutionary Europe, 1770–1870.* Suffolk: Richard Clay (The Chaucer Press) Ltd.

Betts, Richard K. 1977. *Soldiers, Statesmen, and Cold War Crises.* Cambridge, Mass.: Harvard University Press.

Blainey, Geoffrey. 1973. *The Causes of War.* New York: The Free Press.

Bond, Brian. 1983. *War and Society in Europe 1870–1970.* Leicester: Leicester University Press, and London, Fontana Paperbacks.

Bonsal, Stephen. 1944. *Unfinished Business.* New York: Doubleday.

Bourgeois, Emile. 1901. *Manuel historique de politique étrangère.* Vol. I. *Les Origines.* 3rd edn. Paris: Belin Frères.

   1909. *La Diplomatie secrète au XVIIIᵉ siècle.* 3 vols. Vol. I: *Le Secret du Régent;* Vol. II: *Le Secret des Farnèse;* Vol. III: *Le Secret de Dubois.* Paris: Armand Colin.

Bourgeois, Léon. 1910. *Pour la Société des Nations.* Paris: Bibliothèque Charpentier.

354

1919. *Le Pacte de 1919 et la Société des Nations*. Paris: Eugène Fasquelle.

Bouthoul, Gaston and René Carrère. 1976. *Le Défi de la guerre, 1749–1974*. Paris: Presses Universitaires de France.

Bozeman, Adda. 1984. "The International Order in a Multicultural World," in Hedley Bull and Adam Watson (eds.), *The Expansion of International Society*. Oxford: Clarendon Press, 387–486.

Braun, Rudolf. 1975. "Taxation, Sociopolitical Structure, and State-Building: Great Britain and Brandenburg–Prussia," in Charles Tilly (ed.), *The Formation of Nation States in Western Europe*. Princeton: Princeton University Press, 243–327.

Bridge, F. R. and Roger Bullen. 1980. *The Great Powers and the European States System 1815–1914*. London: Longman.

Brodie, Bernard. 1946. *The Absolute Weapon*. New York: Harcourt, Brace.

Broglie, Albert, duc de (ed.). 1891. *Memoirs of the Prince de Talleyrand*. 3 vols., trans. Angus Hall. New York: G. P. Putnam's Sons.

Bruun, Geoffrey. 1968. *Clemenceau*. Hamden, Conn.: Archon Books.

Bueno de Mesquita, Bruce. 1981a. "Risk, Power Distribution, and the Likelihood of War," *International Studies Quarterly*, 25 (December), 541–68.

1981b. *The War Trap*. New Haven: Yale University Press.

Bueno de Mesquita, Bruce and David Lalman. 1988. "Empirical Support for Systemic and Dyadic Explanations of International Conflict," *World Politics*, 41 (October), 1–20.

Buffinton, Arthur H. 1929. *The Second Hundred Years War 1689–1815*. New York: Henry Holt.

Bull, Hedley. 1984a. "The Emergence of Universal International Society," in Hedley Bull and Adam Watson (eds.), *The Expansion of International Society*. Oxford: Clarendon Press, 117–26.

1984b. "The Revolt Against the West," in Hedley Bull and Adam Watson (eds.), *The Expansion of International Society*. Oxford: Clarendon Press, 217–28.

Burkhardt, Carl J. 1971. *Richelieu and his Age*. Vol. III: *Power Politics and the Cardinal's Death*. Trans. Bernhard Hoy. London: Allen & Unwin.

Buzan, Barry. 1988. "People, States and Fear: The National Security Problem in the Third World," in Edward E. Azar and Chung-in Moon (eds.), *National Security in the Third World*. Aldershot, Hants.: Edward Elgar Publishing Ltd., 14–43.

Byrnes, James F. 1947. *Speaking Frankly*. New York: Harper and Brothers.

Campbell, Thomas M. 1973. *The Masquerade Peace: America's U.N. Policy, 1944–1945*. Tallahassee, Florida: Florida State University Press.

Canada, Department of National Defense. Operational Research and Analysis Establishment. Directorate of Strategic Analysis. 1981. *Major Armed Conflict: A Compendium of Interstate and Intrastate Conflict, 1730–1980*. Ed. A. D. Mitchell, D. A. Grant, and E. J. Emond. Ottawa, May.

Carroll, Berenice A. and Clinton F. Fink. 1975. "Theories of War Causation: A Matrix for Analysis," in Martin A. Nettleship et al. (eds.), *War, its Causes and Correlates*. The Hague: Mouton, 55–71.

Carver, Michael. 1986. "Conventional Warfare," in Peter Paret (ed.), *Makers of Modern Strategy*. Princeton: Princeton University Press, 779–814.

Cecil, Lord Robert. 1941. *A Great Experiment*. London: Jonathan Cape.

Chamberlain, Neville. 1939. *The Struggle for Peace*. London: Hutchinson.

Chance, J. F. 1909. "The Foreign Policy of George I, 1714–1721," in *The Cambridge Modern History*, Vol. VI. *The Eighteenth Century*. Cambridge: Cambridge University Press, 21–39.

Chevallaz, G. A. 1964. *The Congress of Vienna and Europe*. Oxford: Pergamon Press.

Choucri, Nazli and Robert C. North. 1974. *Nations in Conflict: National Growth and International Violence*. San Francisco: Freeman.

Church, William F. 1972. *Richelieu and Reason of State*. Princeton: Princeton University Press.

Clark, George N. 1934. *The Later Stuarts, 1660–1714*. Oxford: Clarendon Press.
1958. *War and Society in the Seventeenth Century*. Cambridge: Cambridge University Press.

Clausewitz, Carl von. 1984. *On War*. Ed. and trans. Michael Howard and Peter Paret. Princeton: Princeton University Press.

Clemenceau, Georges. 1930. *Grandeurs et misères d'une victoire*. Paris: Plon.

Clemens, Diane Shaver. 1970. *Yalta*. New York: Oxford University Press.

Cohen, Eliot A. 1986. "Distant Battles: Modern War in the Third World," *International Security*, 10 (Spring), 143–71.

Combes, François. 1854. *Histoire de la formation de l'équilibre européen par les Traités de Westphalie et des Pyrénées*. Paris: E. Dentu.
1884. *Histoire de la diplomatie Européene: Traités de Westphalie et des Pyrénées*. Paris: E. Dentu.

Commission des Archives Diplomatiques au Ministère des Affaires Étrangères. 1885. *Suède*, introduction et notes par A. Geoffroy. Paris: Broccard.
1922. *Recueil des Instructions données aux ambassadeurs et ministres de France*. Vol. XX: *Holland*, introduction et notes par Louis André et Emile Bourgeois. Paris: Broccard.

Conférence des Préliminaires de Paix, Commission de la Société des Nations. 1919a. *Etude bibliographique*, annex no. 20, March 21, 1919.
1919b. *Procès Verbaux*, February 3–April 11, 1919. Mimeo, 1919.

Corvisier, André. 1979. *La France de Louis XIV: Ordre intérieur et place en Europe*. Paris: Société de'Editions d'Enseignement Supérieur.

Cowie, Leonard W. 1963. *Eighteenth-Century Europe*. New York: Frederick Ungar.

Craig, Gordon A. and Alexander L. George. 1983. *Force and Statecraft: Diplomatic Problems of Our Time*. New York: Oxford University Press.

Crankshaw, Edward. 1963. *The New Cold War: Moscow v. Pekin*. Baltimore: Penguin.

Cronon, E. David (ed.). 1965. *The Political Thought of Woodrow Wilson*. Indianapolis: Bobbs-Merrill.

Davis, W. W., G. T. Duncan, and R. M. Siverson. 1978. "The Dynamics of Warfare: 1816–1965," *American Journal of Political Science*, 22: 772–92.

Day, Alan J. 1987. *Border and Territorial Disputes*. 2nd edn. London: Longman.

Debray, Regis. 1967. *Revolution in the Revolution? Armed Struggle and Political Struggle in Latin America*. New York and London: Monthly Review Press.

Deutsch, Karl W. and Dieter Senghaas. 1971. "A Framework for a Theory of War and Peace," in Albert Lepawsky et al. (eds.), *The Search for World Order: Studies by Students and Colleagues of Quincy Wright*. New York: Appleton-Century-Croft, 23–46.

Deutscher, Isaac. 1960. *Stalin: A Political Biography*. New York: Vintage Books.

Dickmann, Fritz et al. (eds.), 1962. *Acta Pacis Westphalicae: Instruktionen*. Vol. I: *Frankereich, Schweden, Kaiser*. Münster: Aschendorffische Verlagsbuchhandlung.

1963. "Rechtsgedanke und Machtpolitik bei Richelieu," *Historische Zeitschrift*, 195: 265–319.

Dinerstein, Herbert S. 1962. *War and the Soviet Union*. Rev. edn. New York: Frederick A. Praeger.

Donnadieu, Léonce. 1900. *La Théorie de l'équilibre*. Paris: Arthur Rousseau.

Doran, Charles. 1971. *The Politics of Assimilation: Hegemony and its Aftermath*. Baltimore: Johns Hopkins University Press.

1983. "War and Power Dynamics," *International Studies Quarterly*, 27 (December), 419–42.

Dore, Ronald. 1984. "Unity and Diversity in World Culture," in Hedley Bull and Adam Watson (eds.), *The Expansion of International Society*. Oxford: Clarendon Press, 407–24.

Dorn, Walter L. 1940. *Competition for Empire*. New York: Harper & Row.

Droz, Jacques. 1959. *Histoire diplomatique de 1648 à 1919*. Paris: Dalloz.

Dunn, David. 1974. "War and Social Change," in Fred S. Northedge (ed.), *The Use of Force in International Relations*. London: Faber, 220–47.

Dupuis, Charles. 1909. *Le Principe d'équilibre et le Concert Européen*. Paris: Librairie Académique.

Duvall, Raymond. 1976. "An Appraisal of the Methodological and Statistical Procedures of the Correlates of War Project," in Francis W. Hoole and Dina A. Zinnes (eds.), *Quantitative International Politics: An Appraisal*. New York: Frederick A. Praeger, 67–98.

Eagleton, Clyde. 1972. *Analysis of the Problem of War*. New York and London: Garland.

Earle, Edward M. 1986. "Smith, Hamilton, List," in Peter Paret (ed.), *Makers of Modern Strategy: From Machiavelli to the Nuclear Age*. Princeton: Princeton University Press, 217–61.

Eden, Anthony. 1965. *The Reckoning*. Boston: Houghton Mifflin.

Egerton, George. 1978. *Great Britain and the Creation of the League of Nations*. Chapel Hill, N.C.: University of North Carolina Press.

Farrar, L. L., Jr. 1978. *Divide and Conquer: German Efforts to Conclude a Separate Peace, 1914–1918*. East European Monograph No. 45, *East European Quarterly*.

Fenno, Richard F., Jr. (ed.) 1955. *The Yalta Conference*. Boston: D. C. Heath.

Finer, Samuel E. 1975. "State- and Nation-Building in Europe: The Role of the Military," in Charles Tilly (ed.), *The Formation of National States in Western Europe*. Princeton: Princeton University Press, 84–163.

Foley, Hamilton, comp. 1923. *Woodrow Wilson's Case for the League of Nations*. Port Washington, N.Y.: Kennicot Press.

Fuchser, Larry W. 1982. *Neville Chamberlain and Appeasement: A Study in the Politics of History*. New York: Norton.

Fugier, André. n.d. *La Révolution française et L'Empire Napoléonienne*. Paris: Librairie Hachette.

Gaddis, John Lewis. 1972. *The United States and the Origins of the Cold War, 1941–1947*. New York: Columbia University Press.

———. 1982. *Strategies of Containment: A Critical Appraisal of Postwar American National Security Policy*. New York: Oxford University Press.

———. 1986. "The Long Peace," *International Security*, 10 (Spring), 103–42.

Gallie, W. B. 1978. *Philosophers of Peace and War: Kant, Clausewitz, Engels and Tolstoy*. Cambridge: Cambridge University Press.

Geller, Daniel S. 1988. "Power System Membership and Patterns of War," *International Political Science Review*, 9 (October), 365–80.

George, Alexander and Richard Smoke. 1974. *Deterrence in American Foreign Policy: Theory and Practice*. New York: Columbia University Press.

Gershoy, Leo. 1944. *From Despotism to Revolution, 1763–1789*. New York and London: Harper and Brothers.

Gilbert, Martin. 1966. *The Roots of Appeasement*. New York: New American Library.

Gillard, David. 1984. "British and Russian Relations with Asian Governments in the Nineteenth Century," in Hedley Bull and Adam Watson (eds.), *The Expansion of International Society*. Oxford: Clarendon Press, 87–98.

Giraud, Charles. 1847. *Le Traité d'Utrecht*. Paris: Plon Frères.

Gochman, Charles. 1980. "Status, Capabilities, and Major Power Conflict," in J. David Singer (ed), *The Correlates of War*. New York: The Free Press, 83–124.

Gonda, Eugène. 1981. *La Conférence de Versailles: La Bataille perdue de Clemenceau*. Paris: L.P.F.

Gooch, G. P. 1947. *Frederick the Great: The Ruler, The Writer, The Man*. New York: Alfred A. Knopf.

Gooch, John. n.d. "Attitudes to War in Late Victorian and Edwardian England," in Brian Bond and Ian Roy (eds.), *War and Society: A Yearbook of Military History*. London: Croom Helm, 88–102.

Gottschalk, Louis and Donald Lach. 1973. *Toward the French Revolution*. New York: Charles Scribner's Sons.

Gross, Leo. 1948. "The Peace of Westphalia, 1648–1948," *The American Journal of International Law*, 42: 20–41.

Guerlac, Henry. 1986. "Vauban: The Impact of Science on War," in Peter Paret (ed.), *Makers of Modern Strategy*. Princeton: Princeton University Press, 64–90.

Gulick, Edward Vose. 1955. *Europe's Classical Balance of Power*. New York: Cornell University Press.

———. 1965. "The Final Coalition and the Congress of Vienna, 1813–15," in *The New Cambridge Modern History*, Vol. IX: *War and Peace in an Age of Upheaval*. Cambridge: Cambridge University Press, 639–67.

Hafner, D. L. 1980. "Castlereagh, the Balance of Power, and 'Non-Intervention,'" *Australian Journal of Politics and History*, 26: 71–84.

Hale, J. R. 1985. *War and Society in Renaissance Europe, 1450–1620*. New York: St. Martin's Press.

Halévy, Elie. 1924. *A History of the English People in 1815*. New York: Harcourt, Brace.

358

Harkavy, Robert E. and Stephanie G. Neumann. 1985. *The Lessons of Recent Wars in the Third World*. Vol. I. Lexington, Mass.: Lexington Books.

Hatton, Ragnhild M. 1963. "Scandinavia and the Baltic," in *The New Cambridge Modern History*, Vol. III: *The Old Regime 1713–63*. Cambridge: Cambridge University Press, 339–64.

1968. *Charles XII of Sweden*. London: Weidenfeld & Nicolson.

1976 (ed.). *Louis XIV and Europe*. London: Macmillan.

1980. "Nijmegen and the European Powers," in *The Peace of Nijmegen 1676–1679/La Paix de Nimègue*. Proceedings of the International Congress of the Tricentennial, September 14–16, 1978. Amsterdam: APA-Academic Publishers.

Hayes, Carlton J. H. 1924. *A Political and Social History of Modern Europe*, Vol. II. New York: Macmillan.

Hayes, Carlton J. H. and Charles Woolsey Cole. 1949. *History of Europe*, Vol. II. New York: Macmillan.

Hinsley, F. H. 1963. *Power and the Pursuit of Peace*. Cambridge: Cambridge University Press.

1966. "The Concert of Europe," in Laurence W. Martin (ed.), *Diplomacy in Modern European History*. New York: Macmillan, 43–57.

Hitler, Adolf. 1943. *Mein Kampf*. Trans. Ralph Manheim. Boston: Houghton Mifflin.

1962. *L'Expansion du III<sup>ème</sup> Reich* (Hitlers Zweites-Buch). Trans. Francis Brière. Paris: Librairie Plon.

Holbraad, Carsten. 1970. *The Concert of Europe*. London: Longman.

Holsti, Kalevi J. 1985a. *The Dividing Discipline: Hegemony and Diversity in International Theory*. London: Allen & Unwin.

1985b. "The Necrologists of International Relations," *Canadian Journal of Political Science*, 17 (December), 675–96.

1988. "Paths to Peace: Theories of Conflict Resolution and the Realities of International Politics," in Ramesh Thakur (ed.), *International Conflict Resolution*. Boulder, Colo. and Dunedin, New Zealand: Westview Press and University of Otago Press, 105–32.

1989 *The States System and War*. The Ford Foundation Lectures in International Relations Studies. Baroda/Vadodara: Department of Political Science, the Maharaja Sayajirao University of Baroda, India.

1990. "The Comparative Analysis of Foreign Policy: Some Notes on the Pitfalls and Paths to Theory," in David Wurfel and Bruce Burton (eds.), *Political Economy of Foreign Policy in Southeast Asia*. London and New York: Macmillan.

Holsti, Rudolf W. 1913. *The Relation of War to the Origin of the State*. Helsingfors: Uusi Kirjapaino.

Horn, D. 1963. "The Diplomatic Revolution," in *The New Cambridge Modern History*, Vol. VII: *The Old Regime 1713–63*. Cambridge: Cambridge University Press, 440–64.

House, Edward M. and Charles Seymour (eds.). 1921. *What Really Happened at Paris*. New York: Charles Scribner's Sons.

Howard, Michael. 1983. *The Causes of Wars and Other Essays*. London: Temple Smith.

1986. *War in European History*. Oxford: Oxford University Press.

Hull, Cordell. 1948. *The Memoirs of Cordell Hull*. 2 vols. New York: Macmillan.

Hyde, H. Montgomery. 1976. *Neville Chamberlain*. London: Weidenfeld & Nicolson.

Hyvärinen, Pekka. 1989. "Talvisota Stalinin Syyta," *Suomen Kuvalehti*, No. 6 (February 10), 42–44.

Iriye, Akira. 1981. *Power and Culture: The Japanese–American War, 1941–1945*. Cambridge, Mass.: Harvard University Press.

Jackel, Eberhard. 1972. *Hitler's Weltanschauung: A Blueprint for Power*. Trans. Herbert Arnold. Middletown, Conn.: Wesleyan University Press.

Jackson, Robert H. 1987. "Quasi-states, Dual Regimes, and Neo-classical Theory: International Jurisprudence and the Third World," *International Organization*, 41 (Autumn), 519–49.

Jakobson, Max. 1984. *Finland Survived: An Account of the Finnish–Soviet Winter War*. Helsinki: Otava.

Jane, L. Cecil. 1910. *From Metternich to Bismarck*. Oxford: Clarendon Press.

Jervis, Robert. 1976. *Perception and Misperception in International Politics*. Princeton: Princeton University Press.

Johnston, Whittle. 1982. "Reflections on Wilson and the Problems of World Peace," in Arthur S. Link (ed.), *Woodrow Wilson and a Revolutionary World, 1913–1921*, Chapel Hill, N.C.: The University of North Carolina Press, 190–231.

Kennedy, John F. 1940. *Why England Slept*. New York: Wilfred Funk.

Keohane, Robert O. and Joseph Nye. 1972 (eds.). *Transnational Relations and World Politics*. Cambridge, Mass.: Harvard University Press.

1977. *Power and Interdependence: World Politics in Transition*. Boston: Little, Brown.

Kim, Kyung-won. 1970. *Revolution and International System*. New York: New York University Press.

Kissinger, Henry A. 1957a. *Nuclear Weapons and American Foreign Policy*. New York: Council on Foreign Relations.

1957b. *A World Restored*. London: Weidenfeld & Nicolson.

Klare, Michael T. 1989. "The Development of Low-Intensity Conflict Doctrine," in Peter J. Schraeder (ed.), *Intervention in the 1980s: U.S. Foreign Policy in the Third World*. Boulder and London: Lynne Rienner Publishers, 31–44.

Koenigsberg, Richard A. 1975. *Hitler's Ideology: A Study in Psychoanalytic Sociology*. New York: The Library of Social Science.

Kuehl, Warren F. 1969. *Seeking World Order*. Nashville: Vanderbilt University Press.

Lebow, Richard N. 1981. *Between War and Peace*. Baltimore: Johns Hopkins University Press.

Legge, L. G. 1925 (ed.). *British Diplomatic Instructions: France, 1689–1721*. London: The Royal Historical Society.

Legrelle, A. 1900. *La Diplomatie française et la succession d'Espagne*, Vol. VI: *La Paix*. Braine-le-Comte: Zech et Fils.

Lenin, V. I. 1939. *Imperialism, the Highest Stage of Capitalism*. New York: International Publishers.

Levin, N. Gordon, Jr. 1968. *Woodrow Wilson and World Politics*. New York: Oxford University Press.

1972. *Woodrow Wilson and the Paris Peace Conference*. 2nd edn. Lexington, Mass.: D. C. Heath.

Levy, Jack S. 1981. "Alliance Formation and War Behavior: An Analysis of the Great Powers, 1495–1975," *Journal of Conflict Resolution*, 25 (December), 581–613.

    1982. "The Contagion of Great Power War Behavior," *American Journal of Political Science*, 26, 562–84.

    1983. *War in the Modern Great Power System, 1495–1975*. Lexington: University of Kentucky Press.

    1987. "Declining Power and the Preventive Motivation for War," *World Politics*, 40 (October ), 82–107.

Levy, Jack S. and T. Clifton Morgan. 1986. "The War-Weariness Hypothesis: An Empirical Test," in Margaret P. Karns (ed.), *Persistent Patterns and Emergent Structures in a Waning Century*. New York: Praeger, 126–48.

Lin Piao. 1964. *Long Live the Victory of the Peoples' War*. Peking: Foreign Languages Publishing House.

Lindsay, J. O. 1963. "International Relations," in *The New Cambridge Modern History*, Vol. VII: *The Old Regime 1713–63*. Cambridge: Cambridge University Press, 191–213.

Link, Arthur S. 1971. *The Higher Realism of Woodrow Wilson and Other Essays*. Nashville, Tenn.: Vanderbilt University Press.

    1982 (ed.). *Woodrow Wilson and a Revolutionary World, 1913–1921*. Chapel Hill, N.C.: The University of North Carolina Press, 1982.

Lockhart J. G. 1932. *The Peacemakers 1814–1815*. Freeport: Books for Libraries Press.

Louis XIV. 1970. *Mémoires for the Instruction of the Dauphin*. New York: Free Press.

Luard, Evan. 1986. *War in International Society: A Study in International Sociology*. London: Tauris.

    1988. *The Blunted Sword: The Erosion of Military Power in Modern World Politics*. London: Tauris.

McKay, Derek. 1977. *Prince Eugene of Savoy*. London: Thames & Hudson.

McKay, Derek and H. M. Scott. 1983. *The Rise of the Great Powers 1648–1815*. Longman.

Maland, David. 1980. *Europe at War: 1600–1650*. London: Macmillan.

Mandelbaum, Michael. 1979. *The Nuclear Question: The United States and Nuclear Weapons, 1946–1976*. Cambridge: Cambridge University Press.

Mansbach, Richard W. and John A. Vasquez. 1981. *In Search of Theory: A New Paradigm for Global Politics*. New York: Columbia University Press.

Mantoux, Paul. 1955. *Les Délibérations du Conseil des Quatres (24 mars–28 juin 1919). Notes de l'Officier Interprète, Paul Mantoux*, Vol. I. Paris: Editions du Centre National de la Recherche Scientifique.

Mao Tse-tung. 1961. *On Guerrilla Warfare*. Trans. Samuel B. Griffith. New York: Praeger.

    1969. *On Revolution and War*. Ed. M. Rejai. Garden City, New York: Doubleday.

Maoz, Zeev. 1982. *Paths to Conflict*. Boulder, Colo.: Westview Press.

    1989. "Joining the Club of Nations: Political Development and International Conflict," *International Studies Quarterly* (June), 199–231.

Marin, Louis. 1920. "Le Traité de Paris," *La France de Demain*, no. 215 (April).

Marriott, J. A. R. 1936. *Castlereagh*. London: Methuen.

Maser, Werner. 1970. *Hitler's Mein Kampf: An Analysis*. Trans. R. H. Barry. London: Faber & Faber.

Massie, Robert K. 1980. *Peter the Great*. New York: Alfred A. Knopf.

Mayer, Arno J. 1968. *Politics and the Diplomacy of Peace-Making: Containment and Counter-revolution at Versailles, 1918–1919*. London: Weidenfeld & Nicolson.

Medlicott, W. N. 1969. *Bismarck, Gladstone and the Concert of Europe*. New York: Greenwood Press Publishers.

Metzger, Hans. 1984. *Kolmannen Valtaknunnan Edustajana Talvisodan Suomessa*. Helsinki: Otava.

Miller, David H. 1921. "The Making of the League of Nations," in Edward M. House and William Seymour (eds.), *What Really Happened at Paris*. New York: C. Scribner's Sons, 398–424.

    1928. *The Drafting of the Covenant*. 3 vols. New York: G. P. Putnam's Sons 1948.

Morgenthau, Hans J. 1948. *Politics Among Nations: The Struggle for Power and Peace*. New York: Alfred A. Knopf.

Morley, Robert V. and John P. Marwitt. 1975. "Ecology, Economy, and Warfare in Lowland South America," in Martin Nettleship et al. (eds.), *War: Its Causes and Correlates*. The Hague: Mouton, 440–50.

Mowat, R. B. 1928. *A History of European Diplomacy, 1451–1789*. London: Edward Arnold.

    1930. *The Concert of Europe*. London: Macmillan.

Naff, Thomas. 1984. "The Ottoman Empire and the European States System," in Hedley Bull and Adam Watson (eds.), *The Expansion of International Society*. Oxford: Clarendon Press, 143–70.

Naroll, Raoul, V. L. Bullough, and Freda Naroll. 1974. *Military Deterrence in History: A Pilot Cross-Historical Survey*. Albany, N.Y.: State University of New York Press.

Nef, John U. 1952. *War and Human Progress*. Cambridge, Mass.: Harvard University Press.

    1963. *Western Civilization Since the Renaissance*. New York: Harper & Row Publishers.

Nère, Jacques. 1975. *The Foreign Policy of France from 1914 to 1945*. London: Routledge & Kegan Paul.

Nicholas, Herbert G. 1982. "Woodrow Wilson and Collective Security," in Arthur S. Link (ed.), *Woodrow Wilson and A Revolutionary World, 1913–1921*, Chapel Hill, N.C.: The University of North Carolina Press, 174–89.

Nicolson, Harold. 1946. *The Congress of Vienna*. London: Constable.

Nisbet, Robert. 1969. *Social Change and History*. New York: Oxford University Press.

Northedge, Fred S. (ed.). 1974. *The Use of Force in International Relations*. London: Faber & Faber.

Oakes, Augustus and R. B. Mowat. 1918. *The Great European Treaties of the Nineteenth Century*. Oxford: Clarendon Press.

Oka, Ushitake. 1983. *Konoe Fumimaro: A Political Biography*. Trans. Shumpei Okamoto and Patricia Murray. Tokyo: University of Tokyo Press.

Organski, A. F. K. 1968. *World Politics*. 2nd edn. New York: Alfred A. Knopf.

Ostrom, Charles W. Jr. and Francis W. Hoole. 1978. "Alliances and War Revisited: A Research Note," *International Studies Quarterly*, 2 (June), 215–36.

Paasivirta, Juhani. 1957. *Suomi Vuonna 1918*. Helsinki: Werner Söderström.

1961. *Ensimmäisen Maailman Sodan Voittajat ja Suomi*. Helsinki: Werner Söderström.

Pages, Georges. 1949. *Naissance du grand siècle de Henri IV à Louis XIV, 1598–1661*. Paris: Hachette.

1949. *La Guerre de Trente Ans, 1618–1648*. Paris: Editions Payot.

Palmer, R. R. 1986. "Frederick, Guibert, Bulow," in Peter Paret (ed.), *Makers of Modern Strategy*. Princeton: Princeton University Press, 91–119.

Paret, Peter. 1986. "Smith, Hamilton, List," in Edward Mead Earle (ed.), *Makers of Modern Strategy*. Princeton: Princeton University Press, 217–61.

Parker, Geoffrey. 1984. *The Thirty Years' War*. London: Routledge & Kegan Paul.

Pearton, Maurice. 1982. *The Knowledgeable State*. London: Burnett Books.

Peattie, Mark R. 1975. *Ishiwara Kanji and Japan's Confrontation with the West*. Princeton, N.J.: Princeton University Press.

Perré, Jean. 1948. *Les Mutations de la guerre moderne: des origines à 1792*. Paris: Payot.

1962. *Les Mutations de la guerre moderne: de 1792 à 1962*. Paris: Payot.

Petersson, Hans F. 1964. *Power and International Order*. Lund, Sweden: CWK Gleerup.

Petrie, Sir Charles. 1946. *Diplomatic History 1713–1933*. London: Hollis & Carter.

Phillips, Walter Alison. 1907. "The Congresses, 1815–22," in A. W. Ward (ed.), *The Cambridge Modern History*, Vol. X: *The Restoration*. Cambridge: Cambridge University Press, 1–39.

1920. *The Confederation of Europe*. London: Longmans, Green.

Piao, Lin. 1964. *Long Live the Victory of Peoples' War*. Peking: Foreign Languages Publishing House.

Pillorget, René. 1980. "La France et les Etats Allemands, 1678–1679," in *The Peace of Nijmegen, 1676–1679/La Paix de Nimègue*, Proceedings of the International Congress of the Tricentennial, September 14–16, 1978. Amsterdam: APA–Academic Publishers, 225–36.

Rabb, Theodore K. 1975. *The Struggle for Stability in Early Modern Europe*. New York: Oxford University Press.

Randle, Robert F. 1973. *The Origins of Peace: A Study of Peacemaking and the Structure of Peace*. New York: The Free Press.

Ransel, David L. 1975. *The Politics of Catherinian Russia*. New Haven: Yale University Press.

Ranum, Orest. 1975. *National Consciousness, History and Political Culture in Early Modern Europe*. Baltimore: Johns Hopkins University Press.

Ratinaud, Jean. 1958. *Clemenceau, ou la colère et la gloire*. Paris: Arthème Fayard.

Rauschning, Hermann. 1939. *Hitler Speaks: A Series of Conversations with Adolf Hitler on his Real Aims*. London: Thornton Butterworth.

Renouvin, Pierre. 1930. *Histoire diplomatique, 1815–1914*. Conférence de M. le professeur P. Renouvin, novembre 1928–juin 1929. Paris: Centre européen de la Dotation Carnegie.

1955. *Histoire des relations internationales*, Vol. VI: *Le XIXᵉ Siècle de 1871 à 1914: L'Apogée de l'Europe*. Paris: Hachette.

1969. *Le Traité de Versailles*. Paris: Flammarion.

Rice, Edward E. 1988. *Wars of the Third Kind: Conflict in Underdeveloped Countries*. Berkeley: University of California Press.

Richelieu, A. J. D., Cardinal de. 1947. *Testament politique*. Paris: L. André.

Riekhoff, Harald von. 1989. "Canadian Attitudes and Approaches to the United Nations Security Council," Background Paper, Canadian Institute for International Peace and Security, No. 26 (February).

Rietbergen, P. J. 1980. "Papal Diplomacy and Mediation," in *The Peace of Nijmegen, 1676–1679/La Paix de Nimègue*, Proceedings of the International Congress of the Tricentennial, September 14–16, 1978. Amsterdam: APA–Academic Publishers, 29–96.

Roberts, Michael. 1958. *Gustavus Adolphus: A History of Sweden 1611–1632*. 2 vols. London: Longmans, Green.

1967. *Essays in Swedish History*. London: Weidenfeld & Nicolson.

Roberts, Penfield. 1947. *The Quest for Security*. New York: Harper and Brothers.

Rokkan, Stein. 1975. "Dimensions of State Formation and Nation-Building: A Possible Paradigm for Research on Variations within Europe," in Charles Tilly (ed.), *The Formation of National States in Western Europe*. Princeton: Princeton University Press, 562–600.

Roper, Marilyn K. 1975. "Evidence of Warfare in the Near East from 10,000 to 4,300 B.C.," in Martin A. Nettleship, R. Dalegivens and Anderson Nettleship (eds.), *War: Its Causes and Correlates*. The Hague: Mouton, 299–344.

Ropp, Theodore. 1959. *War in the Modern World*. Durham: Duke University Press.

Rosecrance, Richard N. 1963. *Action and Reaction in World Politics*. Boston: Little, Brown.

Rosenau, James N. 1966. "Pre-theories and Theories of Foreign Policy," in R. Barry Farrell (ed.), *Approaches to Comparative and International Politics*. Evanston, Ill.: Northwestern University Press, 27–92.

Rudé, George. 1972. *Debate on Europe 1815–1850*. New York: Harper & Row.

Rummel, Rudolph. 1968. "The Relationship Between National Attributes and Foreign Conflict Behaviour," in J. David Singer (ed.), *Quantitative International Politics*. New York: The Free Press, 187–215.

1972. *The Dimensionality of Nations*. Beverly Hills, Calif.: Sage.

1976. *Understanding Conflict and War*, Vol. II. New York: John Wiley and Sons.

1981. *Understanding Conflict and War: The Just Peace*. Beverly Hills, Calif.: Sage.

1983. "Libertarianism and International Violence," *Journal of Conflict Resolution*, 27 (March), 27–72.

Russell, Ruth B. 1958. *A History of the United Nations Charter*. Washington, D.C.: The Brookings Institution.

Ruyssen, Theodore. 1958. *Les Sources doctrinales de l'internationalisme*. Paris: Presses Universitaires de France.

Rystad, Göran. 1980. "Sweden and the Nijmegen Peace Conference," in *The Peace of Nijmegen 1676–1679/La Paix de Nimègue*. Proceedings of the International Congress of the Tricentennial, September 14–16, 1978. Amsterdam: APA–Academic Publishers.

Sabrosky, Alan N. 1985 (ed.). *Polarity and War: The Changing Structure of International Conflict*. Boulder, Colo.: Westview Press.

Schenk, Hans G. 1947. *The Aftermath of the Napoleonic Wars*. London: Kegan Paul.

Schwabe, Klaus. 1985. *Woodrow Wilson, Revolutionary Germany, and Peacemaking, 1918–1919*. Chapel Hill, N.C.: University of North Carolina Press.

Shaw, Albert. 1924 (ed.). *The Messages and Papers of Woodrow Wilson*. 2 vols. New York: The Review of Reviews Corp.

Shirer, William L. 1960. *The Rise and Fall of the Third Reich*. New York: Simon & Schuster.

Singer, J. David. 1970. "From a Study of War to Peace Research: Some Criteria and Strategies," *Journal of Conflict Resolution*, 14, 533–42.

———— 1981. "Accounting for International War: The State of the Discipline," *Journal of Peace Research*, 18, 1–18.

Singer, J. David and Associates. 1979. *Explaining War*. Beverly Hills, Calif.: Sage.

Singer, J. David, Stuart Bremer, and John Stuckey. 1972. "Capability Distribution, Uncertainty, and Major Power War, 1820–1965," in Bruce Russett (ed), *Peace, War, and Numbers*. Beverly Hills, Calif.: Sage, 19–48.

Siverson, Randolph M. and Harvey Starr. 1990. "Opportunity, Willingness and the Diffusion of War, 1816–1965," *American Political Science Review* (March).

Small, Melvin and J. David Singer. 1982. *Resort to Arms: International and Civil Wars 1816–1980*. Beverly Hills, Calif.: Sage.

Smith, Denis. 1988. *Diplomacy of Fear: Canada and the Cold War, 1941–1948*. Toronto: University of Toronto Press.

Snyder, Jack. 1978. "Rationality at the Brink: The Role of Cognitive Processes in Failures of Deterrence," *World Politics*, 30: 345–65.

Stettinius, Edward R. 1950. *Roosevelt and the Russians: The Yalta Conference*. London: Jonathan Cape.

Suslov, Mikhail. 1964. *Struggle of the CPSU for the Unity of the World Communist Movement*. Speech to the Central Committee of the CPSU, February 14, 1964. Press Office of the U.S.S.R. Embassy in Canada.

Symcox, Geoffrey. 1974 (ed.). *War, Diplomacy and Imperialism 1618–1763*. New York: Walker.

Talbott, Strobe. 1988. *The Master of the Game: Paul Nitze and the Nuclear Peace*. New York: Alfred A. Knopf.

Tanter, Raymond. 1966. "Dimensions of Conflict Behavior Within and Between Nations," *Journal of Conflict Resolution*, 10: 41–64.

Tardieu, André. 1921. *La Paix*. Paris: Payot.

Taylor, A. J. P. 1954. *The Struggle for Mastery in Europe, 1848–1918*. Oxford: Clarendon Press.

Temperley, Harold W. 1920 (ed.). *A History of the Peace Conference of Paris*. 3 vols. London: Henry Fraude and Hodder & Stoughton.

Temperley, Harold W. and Lillian M. Penson. 1938. *Foundations of British Foreign Policy: Documents, Old and New*. Cambridge: Cambridge University Press.

Tillman, Seth B. 1961. *Anglo-American Relations at the Paris Peace Conference of 1919*. Princeton: Princeton University Press.

Treasure, Geoffrey. 1985. *The Making of Modern Europe 1648–1780*. London: Methuen.

Tuchman, Barbara W. 1984. *The March of Folly: From Troy to Vietnam*. New York: Ballantine.

Turretini, Robert. 1949. *La Signification des Traités de Westphalie dans le domaine du droit des gens*. Geneva: Imprimerie genevoise.

United States, Department of State 1947. *Making the Peace Treaties 1941–1947*. Washington, D.C.: United States Government Printing Office. Department of State Publication No. 2774.

   1950. *Postwar Foreign Policy Preparation, 1939–1945*. Washington, D.C.: United States Government Printing Office. Department of State Publication No. 3580.

   1955. *Foreign Relations of the United States: The Conference at Malta and Yalta*. Washington, D.C.: United States Government Printing Office. Department of State Publication No. 6199.

Vasquez, John A. 1987. "The Steps to War: Toward a Scientific Explanation of Correlates of War Findings," *World Politics*, 40 (October), 108–45.

Vast, Henri. 1899. *Les Grands Traités du règne de Louis XIV*, Vol. III. Paris: Picard.

Vaughan, C. E. 1915. *The Political Writings of J. J. Rousseau*. Cambridge.

Vo, Nguyen Giap. 1970a. *Guerre de Libération*. Paris: Editions Sociales.

   1970b. *The Military Art of People's War: Selected Writings of General Vo Nguyen Giap*. Ed. Russell Stetler. New York and London: Monthly Review Press.

Wallace, Michael. 1972. "Status, Formal Organization, and Arms Levels as Factors Leading to the Onset of War, 1820–1964," in Bruce Russet (ed.), *Peace, War, and Numbers*. Beverly Hills, Calif.: Sage, 49–69.

   1973. *War and Rank Among Nations*. Lexington, Mass.: D. C. Heath.

   1979. "Arms Races and Escalation: Some New Evidence," *Journal of Conflict Resolution*, 23 (March), 3–16.

Waltz, Kenneth N. 1957. *Man, the State, and War*. New York: Columbia University Press.

   1979. *Theory of International Politics*. Reading, Mass.: Addison-Wesley.

Walworth, Arthur. 1977. *America's Moment, 1918: American Diplomacy at the End of World War I*. New York: Norton.

   1986. *Wilson and His Peacemakers: American Diplomacy at the Paris Peace Conference, 1919*. New York: Norton.

Ward, A. W. 1906. "The Peace of Westphalia," in *The Cambridge Modern History*, Vol. IV: *The Thirty Years' War*. Cambridge: Cambridge University Press, 395–433.

   1908. "The Peace of Utrecht and the Supplementary Pacifications," in *The Cambridge Modern History*, Vol. V: *The Age of Louis XIV*. Cambridge: Cambridge University Press, 437–59.

Wardak, Chulam Dastgagir (comp.) and Graham Hall Turbiville, Jr. (ed.). 1989. *The Voroshilov Lectures: Materials from the Soviet General Staff Academy*, Vol. I: *Issues of Soviet Military Strategy*. Washington, D.C.: National Defense University Press.

Watson, Adam. 1984. "Russia and the European States System," in Hedley

Bull and Adam Watson (eds.), *The Expansion of International Society*. Oxford: Clarendon Press, 61–74.

Webster, Charles K. 1922. "The Pacification of Europe, 1813–1815," in A. W. Ward and G. P. Gooch (eds.), *The Cambridge History of British Foreign Policy 1783–1919*, Vol. I: *1783–1815*. Cambridge: Cambridge University Press, 392–521.

1934. *The Congress of Vienna*. London: Bell.

1961. *The Art and Practice of Diplomacy*. London: Chatto & Windus.

Weede, Erich. 1984. "Democracy and War Involvement," *Journal of Conflict Resolution*, 28 (December), 562–84.

Wheeler-Bennett, John W. 1964. *The Nemesis of Power: The German Army in Politics 1918–1945*. 2nd edn. London: Macmillan.

Wilkenfeld, Jonathan. 1969. "Domestic and Foreign Conflict Behavior of Nations," *Journal of Peace Research*, 6: 148–56.

Wilkinson, David. 1980. *Deadly Quarrels: Lewis F. Richardson and the Statistical Study of War*. Berkeley: University of California Press.

Wilmot, Chester. 1952. *The Struggle for Europe*. New York: Harper and Brothers.

Wilson, Charles. 1957. *Profit and Power: A Study of England and the Dutch Wars*. London: Longmans, Green.

Wimer, Kurt. 1982. "Woodrow Wilson and World Order," in Arthur S. Link (ed.), *Woodrow Wilson and a Revolutionary World, 1913–1921*, Chapel Hill, N.C.: The University of North Carolina Press, 46–73.

Windsor, Philip. 1987. "War and the State," *The L.S.E. Quarterly*, 1 (June), 175–91.

Wolf, John B. 1951. *The Emergence of the Great Powers, 1685–1715*. New York: Harper and Brothers.

1968. *Louis XIV*. New York: Norton.

1972. *Early Modern Europe*. Glenville, Ill.: Scott Foresman.

Wright, Quincy. 1942. *A Study of War*. 2 vols. Chicago: University of Chicago Press.

1955. *The Study of International Relations*. New York: Appleton-Century-Crofts.

1961. *The Role of International Law in the Elimination of War*. Manchester: Manchester University Press.

Zeller, Gaston. 1953, 1955. *Les Temps modernes*, Vol. II: *De Christophe Colombe à Cromwell*; Vol. III: *De Louis XIV à 1789*. Paris: Hachette.

# ADDITIONAL DATA SOURCES

*Africa South of the Sahara: 1980–1981.* 1980. 10th edn. London: Europa.

*Annual Review of the United Nations.* New York: United Nations Association.

Barraclough, Geoffrey. 1978. (ed.). *The Times Atlas of World History.* London: Times Books.

Boulding, Elise et al. 1979 (eds.). *Bibliography on World Conflict and Peace.* Boulder: Westview.

Cannon, Terrence, 1983. *Revolutionary Cuba.* Havana: José Marti Publishing House of Foreign Languages.

Carr, E. H. 1947. *International Relations between the Two World Wars, 1919–1939.* London: Macmillan Press.

Carter, Jimmy. 1985. *The Book of Abraham.* Boston: Houghton Mifflin.

Castro, Fidel. 1983. *A Pyrrhic Military Victory and a Profound Moral Defeat.* La Habana: Editora Politica.

Chen, King C. 1987. *China's War with Vietnam, 1979: Issues, Decisions, and Implications.* Stanford: Hoover Institution Press.

Chew, Allen F. 1971. *The White Death: The Epic of the Soviet–Finnish Winter War.* Lansing, Mich.: Michigan State University Press.

Coox, Alvin D. 1977. *The Anatomy of a Small War: The Soviet–Japanese Struggle for Changkufeng/Khasan, 1938.* Westport, Conn.: Greenwood Press.

Crouch, Harold. 1978. *The Army and Politics in Indonesia.* Ithaca: Cornell University Press.

Daniel, Clifton. 1987 (ed.). *Chronicles of the Twentieth Century.* Mount Kisco, New York: Chronicle Publications.

Derry, T. K. 1979. *A History of Scandinavia.* London: Allen & Unwin.

Dmytryshyn, Basil. 1977. *A History of Russia.* Englewood Cliffs, N.J.: Prentice-Hall.

Elliott, David W. P. 1981. *The Third Indochina Conflict.* Boulder: Westview Press.

Encyclopedia Britannica. *Book of the Year.*

Evron, Yair, 1987. *War and Intervention in Lebanon.* London: Croom Helm.

Fletcher, Arnold. 1965. *Afghanistan, Highway of Conquest.* Ithaca, New York: Cornell University Press.

Franck, Thomas M. 1985. *Nation Against Nation.* London: Oxford University Press.

Freedman, Lawrence. 1985. *Atlas of Global Strategy.* Oxford: Equinox.

Garner, William R. 1966. *The Chaco Dispute: A Study of Prestige Diplomacy.* Washington, D.C.: Public Affairs Press.

Gathorne-Hardy, G. M. 1950. *A Short History of International Affairs 1920–1939.* London: Oxford University Press.

368

Gose, Stephen D. 1987. "Armed Conflicts in 1986: the Iraq–Iran War," in *SIPRI Yearbook 1987: World Armaments and Disarmament*. New York: Oxford University Press, 297–310.

Grenville, J. A. S. 1980. *A World History of the Twentieth Century*, Vol. I: *1900–1945: Western Dominance*. Sussex: Harvester.

Hargreaves-Mawdsley, W. N. 1979. *Eighteenth-Century Spain 1700–1788*. London: Macmillan Press.

Harvey, A. D. 1978. *Britain in the Early Nineteenth Century*. London: Batsford.

Hasan, K. Sarwar. n.d. (ed.). *Documents on the Foreign Relations of Pakistan: China, India and Pakistan*. Karachi: Pakistan Institute of International Affairs.

Hata, Ikuhiko. 1976. "The Japanese–Soviet Confrontation 1935–1938," in James William Morley (ed.), *Deterrent Diplomacy: Japan, Germany and the U.S.S.R. 1935–1940*. New York: Columbia University Press, 113–78.

*Issues Before the General Assembly of the United Nations*. Lexington, Mass.: Lexington Books. Annual.

Jeffrey, Robin. 1981. *Asia: The Winning of Independence*. London: Macmillan Press.

*Keesings Contemporary Archives*. Bath: Keesings Publications. Annual.

Keylor, William R. 1964. *The Twentieth Century World: An International History*. New York: Oxford University Press.

Koch, Hannsjoachim W. 1978. *A History of Prussia*. London: Longman.

Kohn, George C. 1986. (ed.). *Dictionary of Wars*. New York: Facts on File.

Kossmann, Ernst H. 1978. *The Low Countries 1780–1940*. Oxford: Clarendon Press.

Koumoulides, John T. 1986. (ed.). *Cyprus in Transition*. London: Trigraph.

Kratochwil, Friedrich, Paul Rohrlich, and Harpreet Mahajan. *Peace and Disputed Sovereignty*. 1985. Lanham: University Press of America.

Launay, Jacques de. 1965. *Major Controversies of Contemporary History*. Trans. J. J. Buckingham. London: Pergamon Press.

League of Nations. *Monthly Summary*. Geneva.

Leurdijk J. H. 1986. *Intervention in International Politics*. Leeuwarden, Netherlands: Eisma BV.

Lewis, William H. 1985. "Ethiopia–Somalia, 1977–1978," in Robert E. Harkavy and Stephanie G. Neuman (eds.), *The Lessons of Recent Wars in the Third World*. Lexington, Mass.: Lexington Books, 103–15.

Lloyd, Alan. 1968. *The Spanish Centuries*. New York: Doubleday.

Longrigg, Stephen Hemsley. 1958. *Syria and Lebanon under French Mandate*. London: Oxford University Press.

Lowenthal, Abraham F. 1987. *Partners in Conflict: The United States in Latin America*. London: Johns Hopkins University Press.

Macauley, Neill. 1967. *The Sandino Affair*. Chicago: Quadrangle Books.

Marriott, J. A. R. and Charles Grant Robertson. 1915. *The Evolution of Prussia*. Clarendon Press.

May, Ernest R. 1964. "Between World Wars," in Vincent J. Esposito (ed.), *A Concise History of World War II*. New York: Praeger, 3–34.

Miliukov, Paul, Charles Seignobos and L. Eisenmann, 1968. *The Successors of Peter the Great: from Catherine I to the Reign of Nicholas I*. New York: Funk and Wagnalls.

369

Natkiel, Richard and John Pimlott. 1988. (eds.). *Atlas of Warfare*. Greenwich, Conn.: Bison Books.

Northedge, F. S. 1986. *The League of Nations, its Life and Times 1920–1946*. Leicester: Leicester University Press.

Nyangoni, Wellington. 1985. *Africa in the United Nations System*. London and Toronto: Associated University Press.

Panteli, Stavros. 1984. *A New History of Cyprus*. London and The Hague: East–West Publications.

Parry, J. H. 1962. "Rivalries in America," in *The New Cambridge Modern History*, Vol. VII: *The Old Regime 1713–63*. Cambridge: Cambridge University Press, 514–28.

Pillar, Paul R. 1983. *Negotiating Peace*. Princeton, N.J.: Princeton University Press.

Riasanovsky, Nicholas V. 1963. *A History of Russia*. New York: Oxford University Press.

Rodes, John E. 1964. *Germany: A History*. New York: Holt, Rinehart & Winston.

Salvatorelli, Luigi. 1940. *A Concise History of Italy*. New York: Oxford University Press.

Scalapino, Robert A. et al. 1986 (eds.). *Internal and External Security Issues in Asia*. Berkeley: Institute of East Asia Studies.

Soward, F. H. 1944. *Twenty Five Troubled Years 1918–1943*. London: Oxford University Press.

Stoessinger, John G. 1982. *Why Nations Go to War*. 3rd edn. New York: St. Martin's Press.

*Survey of International Affairs*. London: Royal Institute of International Affairs. Annual.

Thompson, Sir Robert. 1981. (ed.). *War in Peace: Conventional and Guerrilla Warfare Since 1945*. London: Orbis.

Thompson, Vincent Bakpetu. 1969. *African Unity: The Evolution of Pan-Africanism*. London: Longmans, Green.

Vagts, Alfred. 1959. *A History of Militarism*. Rev. edn. New York: Meridian.

Werner, Manfred W. 1967. *Modern Yemen 1918–1966*. Baltimore: Johns Hopkins University Press.

Zacher, Mark W. 1979. *International Conflicts and Collective Security, 1946–77*. New York: Praeger.

# INDEX

DATE D

APR 7 - 1995

APR - 3 1997

MAR 5

APR 14 19

NOV 3 0

MAR 3 19

MAR 3

JUN 1 8

AUG

MAR

Broda